Business, Human Rights and Sustainable Development

International Studies in Human Rights

VOLUME 146

The titles published in this series are listed at *brill.com/ishr*

Business, Human Rights and Sustainable Development

Edited by

Md Jahid Hossain Bhuiyan and M Rafiqul Islam

BRILL | NIJHOFF

LEIDEN | BOSTON

Library of Congress Cataloging-in-Publication Data

Names: Bhuiyan, Md Jahid Hossain, editor. | Islam, M. Rafiqul, editor.
Title: Business, human rights and sustainable development / edited by Md Jahid Hossain Bhuiyan and M Rafiqul Islam.
Identifiers: LCCN 2024059562 (print) | LCCN 2024059563 (ebook) | ISBN 9789004530935 (hardback) | ISBN 9789004530942 (ebook)
Subjects: LCSH: Sustainable development–Law and legislation. | Law and economic development–International cooperation. | Social responsibility of business–Law and legislation. | Human rights–Economic aspects.
Classification: LCC K3830 .B87 2025 (print) | LCC K3830 (ebook) | DDC 338.9/27–dc23/eng/20241223
LC record available at https://lccn.loc.gov/2024059562
LC ebook record available at https://lccn.loc.gov/2024059563

Typeface for the Latin, Greek, and Cyrillic scripts: "Brill". See and download: brill.com/brill-typeface.

ISSN 0924-4751
ISBN 978-90-04-53093-5 (hardback)
ISBN 978-90-04-53094-2 (e-book)
DOI 10.1163/9789004530942

This book is printed on acid-free paper and produced in a sustainable manner.

Contents

PART 2
Interaction of Human Rights with Trade, Investment, and Finance

PART 3
Business and Human Rights: Challenges for Implementation

Acknowledgments

We thank all at Martinus Nijhoff (Brill) for their helpful and professional handling of the production of this book, in particular Lindy Melman, Bea Timmer, Lauren Danahy, and Akiko Hakuno.

Jahid Bhuiyan would like to thank Max Planck Institute for Comparative Public Law and International Law (MPIL), Germany and Alexander von Humboldt Foundation for their support during his research stay in MPIL. He made substantial progress of the book while he was a Humboldt Research Fellow at MPIL.

Figures and Tables

Figures

Tables

Acronyms and Abbreviations

AB	Appellate Body
ABC	Anticorruption and bribery
ACHPR	African Commission on Human Rights
AFD	Agence Française de Développement
AI	Artificial Intelligence
AMSA	Australia Modern Slavery Act
APIS	Application Programming Interfaces
ARSIWA	Articles of State Responsibility for Internationally Wrongful Acts
ATCA	Alien Tort Claims Act
BHP	Broken Hill Proprietary Company
BHR	Business and human rights
BII	British International Investment
BUILD	Better Utilization of Investments Leading to Development
CAO	Compliance Advisor Ombudsman
CARE	Collective Benefit, Authority to Control, Responsibility and Ethics
CBAMS	Carbon border adjustment measures
CBD	Convention on Biological Diversity
CBP	Customs and Border Protection
CEPI	Coalition for Epidemic Preparedness Innovations
CH	Cultural heritage
CHRB	Corporate Human Rights Benchmark
COP	Conference of the Parties
COVAX	COVID Vaccines Global Access
CRC	Committee on Children's Rights
CS	Citizen science
CSDDD	Corporate Sustainable Due Diligence
CSR	Corporate social responsibility
CSRD	Corporate Sustainability Reporting Directive
DAC	Development Assistance Committee
DFC	Development Finance Corporation
DFIS	Development finance institutions
DSA	Digital Services Act
DSB	Dispute Settlement Body
ECHR	European Convention on Human Rights
EDFI	European Development Finance Institutions
EIAS	Environmental Impact Assessments
ESCR	Economic, social and cultural rights

ESG	Environmental, social, and governance
ESIAS	Environmental and Social Impact Assessments
EU	European Union
EUCFR	EU Charter for Fundamental Rights
EW	Electronics Watch
FAIR	Fair Recruitment Initiative
FAIR	Findable, Accessible, Interoperable, Reusable principle
FCDO	Foreign, Commonwealth & Development Office
FCPA	Foreign Corrupt Practices Act
FCTC	Framework Convention on Tobacco Control
FDI	Foreign Direct Investment
FFATA	Federal Funding Accountability and Transparency Act
FinCEN	Financial Crimes Enforcement Network
FMO	Nederlandse Financierings-Maatschappij voor Ontwikkelingslanden N.V.
FPIC	Free, prior and informed consent
GATT	General Agreement on Tariffs and Trade
GCM	Global Coal Management Resources
GDPR	General Data Protection Regulation
GDPS	Gross Domestic Products
GHG	Greenhouse gas
GIDA	Global Indigenous Data Alliance Promoting Indigenous Control of Indigenous Data
GLAM	Galleries, Library, Museum and Archives
GNP	Gross National Product
GPOG	General Principles and Operational Guidelines for Fair Recruitment
GRI	Global Reporting Initiative
HRC	Human Rights Council
HRDD	Human rights due diligence
HRIAS	Human Rights Impact Assessments
HRL	Human rights law
IACHR	Inter-American Court of Human Rights
IAMS	Independent Accountability Mechanisms
IAP	International Accountability Project
ICC	International Criminal Court
ICESCR	International Covenant on Economic, Social and Cultural Rights
ICHR	International Council on Human Rights
ICM	Independent Complaints Mechanism
ICTS	Information and communication technologies
IEL	International economic law
IEP	Independent Expert Panel

IFC	International Finance Corporation
IFIs	International financial institutions
IHL	International humanitarian law
IHRB	Institute for Human Rights and Business
ILC	International Law Commission
ILO	International Labor Organization
IMF	International Monetary Fund
INC	Intergovernmental negotiating committee
IoT	Internet of Things
IPCC	Intergovernmental Panel on Climate Change
IPRs	Intellectual property rights
IRA	Inflation Reduction Act
IUU	Illegal, unreported, and unregulated
KCM	Konkola Copper Mines plc
KTC	KnowTheChain
LLC	Limited liability companies
MARPOL	International Convention for the Prevention of Pollution from Ships
MDBs	Multilateral Development Banks
MDGs	Millennium Development Goals
MiB	Mapped in Bangladesh
MIC	Methyl isocyanate
ML	Machine Learning
MNCs	Multinational corporations
MNE	Multinational Enterprise
MNEs	Multinational Enterprises
MSA	Modern Slavery Act
NAP	National Action Plan
NFRD	Non-Financial Reporting Directive
NGOs	Non-government organisations
NSGMs	Non-judicial grievance mechanisms
ODA	Official Development Assistance
OECD	Organisation for Economic Co-operation and Development
OGMs	Operational-Level Grievance Mechanisms
OPIC	Overseas Private Investment Corporation
OSH	Open Supply Hub
OWS	Operation Warp Speed
PLC	Public Limited Companies
POPs	Persistent Organic Pollutants
PPPs	Public-Private Partnerships

PROPARCO	Société de Promotion et de Participation pour la Coopération Economique
PS	Performance Standards
PVC	Polyvinyl Chloride
RDS	Royal Dutch Shell
RICO	Racketeer Influenced and Corrupt Organisation
RMG	Readymade Garment
RSC	RMG Sustainability Council
SDA	Agenda for Sustainable Development
SDGS	Sustainable Development Goals
SERAC	Social and Economic Rights Action Center & The Center for Economic and Social Rights
SOE	State-Owned Enterprises
SPF	Sustainability Performance Framework
SR	Special Rapporteur
TEU	Treaty of European Union
TNCS	Transnational Corporations
TOC	Theory of Change
TPP	Tobacco Plain-Packaging
TSCA	Transparency in Supply Chains Act
TJ	Transitional justice
TJCA	Transitional Justice and Corporate Accountability
UCC	Union Carbide Corporation
UCIL	Union Carbide India Limited
UDHR	Universal Declaration of Human Rights
UFLPA	Uyghur Forced Labor Prevention Act
UNFCCC	UN Framework Convention on Climate Change
UNGC	United Nations Global Compact
UNGPS	United Nations Guiding Principles for Business and Human Rights
UI	User Interface
UN	United Nations
UNCAC	United Nations Convention against Corruption
UNCLOS	UN Convention on the Law of the Sea
UNDP	United Nations Development Programme
UNDRIP	UN Declaration on the Rights of Indigenous Peoples
UNEA	UN Environmental Assembly
UNEP	UN Environmental Programme
UNGA	United Nations General Assembly
UNGPS	United Nations Guiding Principles on Business and Human Rights
UNICOR	Federal Prison Industries, Inc.

UNSC	UN Security Council
UNWGBHR	UN Working Group on Business and Human Rights
USMT	US Military Tribunal in Germany
VCLT	Vienna Convention on the Law of Treaties
WG	Working Group
WHO	World Health Organisation
WROs	Withhold Release Orders
WTO	World Trade Organization
XPCC	Xinjiang Production and Construction Corps

Notes on Editors

Md Jahid Hossain Bhuiyan
is Professor at the Department of Law, Independent University, Bangladesh and an External Fellow at the TC Beirne School of Law, The University of Queensland, Australia. He was a Humboldt research fellow at the Max Planck Institute for Comparative Public Law and International Law (MPIL), Germany. He was a visiting scholar at the University of Oxford, UK; Cardiff University, UK; Emory University, US; and University of British Columbia, Canada. He holds a Ph.D. in law from the University of Queensland, Australia and an LLM from Vrije Universiteit Brussel, Belgium. He has co-edited *Human Rights and International Criminal Law* (Brill | Nijhoff, 2022), *Revisiting the Geneva Conventions: 1949–2019* (Brill | Nijhoff, 2020), *Law and Religion in the Liberal State* (Hart Publishing, 2020), *International Natural Resources Law, Investment and Sustainability* (Routledge, 2017), *International Trade Law and the WTO* (Federation Press, 2013), *An Introduction to International Refugee Law* (Brill | Nijhoff, 2013), *Globalization, International Law, and Human Rights* (Oxford University Press, 2012), *Routledge Handbook of International Environmental Law* (Routledge, 2012), *An Introduction to International Human Rights Law* (Brill | Nijhoff, 2010), and *International Humanitarian Law – An Anthology* (LexisNexis Butterworths, 2009) amongst other scholarly books.

M Rafiqul Islam
is currently Emeritus Professor of Law at Macquarie University, Sydney, Australia. He obtained Ph.D. and LLM from Monash University Australia; LLB, BA (Honours, Economics), and MA (Economics) from Rajshahi University, Bangladesh. Professor Islam has been an active legal academic and researcher and has published extensively in his areas of teaching and research interest, mostly in public international law. He has well over hundred publications including *International Trade Law of the WTO* (Oxford University Press, 2006); *An Introduction to International Refugee Law* (Brill | Nijhoff,, Leiden/Boston, 2013, co-ed); *International Law: Current Concepts and Future Directions* (LexisNexis Australia, 2014), *National Trials of International Crimes in Bangladesh: Transitional Justice as Reflected in Judgments* (Brill | Nijhoff, Leiden/Boston, 2019), *The Constitutional Law of Bangladesh: Progression and Transformation at its 50th Anniversary* (Springer, 2023, co-ed). He was awarded the "Outstanding Teacher Award" by Macquarie University in 2000 for his

contributions to teaching and higher degree research supervision and administration. Professor Islam is also the recipient of the Macquarie University Arts Faculty Best Higher Degree Research Supervisor Award in 2013 and the Vice Chancellor's special award 'in appreciation of [his] service, loyalty and commitments to the University' in 2016.

Notes on Contributors

Rosa Maria Ballardini

is Professor of IP law and Vice Dean (research) at the University of Lapland, Faculty of Law. Rosa's research interests focus on the interface between law (with focus on IP law), technology and sustainability. She has led several multidisciplinary research projects and written extensively especially in the fields of patent and copyright law, open innovation and open source, as well as IP strategies and management in various technological contexts (e.g. software, 3D printing, Artificial Intelligence, industrial internet and polymer-related technologies). Her research approach is multidisciplinary, combining law, technology, business and policy via using different types of methodologies (e.g. traditional legal research methods, empirical methods and design thinking in legal studies).

Md Jahid Hossain Bhuiyan

Ph.D. in Law, University of Queensland, Australia, is Professor at the Department of Law, Independent University, Bangladesh. He was a Humboldt research fellow at the Max Planck Institute for Comparative Public Law and International Law (MPIL). His primary research areas are public international law, and law and religion. He is co-editor of *Human Rights and International Criminal Law* (Brill, 2022), *Revisiting the Geneva Conventions: 1949– 2019* (Brill, 2020), and *Law and Religion in the Liberal State* (Hart Publishing, 2020).

Jernej Letnar Černič

is Full Professor of Constitutional and Human Rights Law at the Faculty of National and European Studies at the New University, Ljubljana, Slovenia. He has. recently published two scientific monographs: "Slovenia at the Crossroads: The Genesis of Human Rights Protection in the Slovenian Society", (Kranj: New University, Faculty of National and European Studies, 2018) and "Corporate Accountability under Socio-economic Rights", (Oxon/New York: Routledge, 2019). His work has been cited in reports by the United Nations, the European Parliament and the Council of Europe, in decisions of the Slovenian Constitutional Court and in academic studies all over the world.

Isabel Ebert

is Senior Research Fellow at the Institute for Business Ethics, University of St. Gallen, and serves as a Strategic Adviser to the United Nations Office of the

High Commissioner for Human Rights B-Tech Project, focusing on Business & Human Rights in the technology sector.

Paolo Galizzi

is Clinical Professor of Law and Director of the Sustainable Development Legal Initiative (SDLI) and the Corporate and Social Responsibility Program at the Leitner Center for International Law and Justice at Fordham Law School. After graduating in 1993 *summa cum laude* at the University of Milan, he obtained LLM in Public International Law from the School of Oriental and African Studies, University of London and doctoral degree from the University of Milan. Prof. Galizzi has edited volumes on customary law in Africa and international environmental law; he contributed to chapters in academic volumes and has written numerous articles.

Dino Girardi

is a Ph.D. Candidate at the University of Lapland, Faculty of Law, where he carries out research in the field of Legal Informatics. Currently, his primarily interest is on Open Data and the digitisation of cultural heritage, particularly in relation with issues concerning Indigenous people and minorities. The focus of his research covers legal, ethical and technological issues.

David Hess

is Professor of Law and Ethics at the Ross School of Business at the University of Michigan. He has a Ph.D. in Management from The Wharton School of the University of Pennsylvania, and a JD from the University of Iowa College of Law. Professor Hess is currently the Business Law, Public Policy and Business Ethics section editor for the *Journal of Business Ethics*. He served as the Reporter for the American Bar Association's Criminal Justice Standards on corporate monitors. He is currently co-President of the Global Business and Human Rights Scholars Association.

M Rafiqul Islam

is Emeritus Professor of Law at Macquarie University, Australia. He obtained Ph.D. and LLM from Monash University Australia; LLB, BA (Honours, Economics), and MA (Economics) from Rajshahi University, Bangladesh. His extensive publications include monographs, edited books, book chapters, and refereed journal articles. *National Trials of International Crimes in Bangladesh: Transitional Justice as Reflected in Judgments* (Brill, Leyden/ Boston, 2019) is his recent book. He was awarded the Macquarie University "Outstanding Teacher Award" in 2000, Macquarie University Best Research

Supervisor Award in 2013 and Vice Chancellor's special award for his 'service, loyalty and commitments to the University' in 2016.

Victoria Kongats

BA, JD, LLM. is a graduate of Dalhousie University (Schulich School of Law) with a research focus in public interest law. Her LLM thesis (2022) explored the way that the Canadian Constitution could be used as a tool to increase safety standards for consumer products, specifically medical devices. She has also been a Research Assistant with the Marine & Environmental Law Institute (Schulich School of Law). While at the Institute she assisted in the development of training materials on a human rights based-approach to the regulation of plastics for a project funded by the United Nations Environment Programme.

Lisa J Laplante

is Professor of Law at New England Law| Boston where she also directs the Center for International Law and Policy (CILP). As a human rights practitioner and scholar, her work appears in top publications, including *Law and Social Inquiry*, *Harvard International Law Journal*, and *Michigan Journal of International Law*. In recognition of this work, she became a member of the Institute for Advanced Studies at Princeton in 2008 and is frequently invited to present at international forums as well as participate in UN expert meetings. She is a certified mediator through the Harvard Mediation Program. In 2016, she founded the Operational-level Grievance Mechanisms Research Project.

Jindan-Karena Mann

is a Ph.D. researcher and part of the Rethinking SLIC project on secondary liability for international crimes. Her research centers on how tort law applies to human rights harms arising out of business conduct. In particular, her research examines how transnational corporations may be liable when they contribute to or facilitate grave human rights violations committed by their business partners and subsidiaries in a common supply chain.

Olga Martin-Ortega

is Professor of International Law at the School of Law, University of Greenwich, where she leads the Business, Human Rights and the Environment Research Group (BHRE). She is currently Senior Advisor on Remedy in Global Supply Chains for Electronics Watch, member of the Board of Trustees of the Corporate Justice Coalition, UK and member of the Board of Directors of the London Universities Purchasing Consortium. She was a member of the

Board of Trustees of Electronics Watch for ten years. In 2023 she acted as Head of Natural Resources and Just Transition at the Business and Human Rights Resource Centre. Her research focuses on business, human rights and the environment, public procurement and human rights and remedy in global supply chains. She has also undertaken extensive research in the areas of post-conflict reconstruction, transitional justice and international criminal law.

Peter Muchlinski
is Emeritus Professor of International Commercial Law at the School of Law, Gender and Media, the School of Oriental and African Studies, University of London. He is the author of *Multinational Enterprises and the Law* (Oxford University Press, 3rd ed, 2021) and *Advanced Introduction to Business and Human Rights* (Cheltenham, Edward Elgar, 2022). He specialises in the regulation of multinational enterprises, international investment law and business and human rights. He has worked as a legal consultant for UNCTAD and is a door tenant at Brick Court Chambers, London. He was until recently a member of the Editorial Board of the Business and Human Rights Journal.

Ernst-Ulrich Petersmann
worked as legal counsel in German Ministry of Economic Affairs, GATT and the WTO, and taught international and European law at the Universities of St. Gallen, Fribourg, Geneva, and the European University Institute at Florence, where he served as head of the Law Department. He taught at the Hague and Xiamen Academies of International Law, the EUI Academy of European Law, and at numerous Universities in Germany, Switzerland, Italy, Spain, the US, Latin-America, South-Africa, China, India and Singapore. His publications include more than 35 books and 380 contributions to books and academic journals.

Nelson Camilo Sanchez
is Associate Professor of Law at the University of Virginia School of Law, where directs the International Human Rights Law Clinic and co-directs the Center for Comparative and International Law. Professor Sanchez holds an LLB and Ph.D. in Law from the National University of Colombia and an LLM from Harvard Law School. His research and scholarly work revolve around the complexities of transitional justice processes, exploring the ways in which societies reckon with human rights violations and navigate the path towards reconciliation and accountability.

Sara L Seck
is Associate Professor and the Yogis & Keddy Chair in Human Rights Law at the Schulich School of Law and Marine & Environmental Law Institute, Dalhousie University, Canada. Recent publications include as co-editor of the *Cambridge Handbook on Environmental Justice and Sustainable Development* (2021), and co-editor of the *Research Handbook on Climate Change Law and Loss and Damage* (2021). An expert on business, human rights and the environment, in 2022 she undertook the development and delivery of training materials on a human rights-based approach to the plastics value chain for the UN Environment Programme and partners in South-East Asia.

Mariam Shakil
is a Ph.D. candidate in the Organisation Studies and Cultural Theory (DOK) programme within the School of Humanities and Social Sciences at the University of St. Gallen. She received a bachelor's degree in law LLB (Hons) from Anglia Ruskin University, Cambridge (UK) and a master's degree in international law from the University of St. Gallen (HSG). She currently also works as a research associate at the Institute for Business Ethics at the HSG. Her academic interests surround critical assessment of human rights violations stemming from technology business practices, and in particular in the healthcare sector.

Robert Stumberg
is Professor of Law at Georgetown University, where he directs the Harrison Institute for Public Law. The Institute is a teaching and service program that works with public officials and coalitions in community development, health and food, climate and trade, and human rights for workers. His current research centers on standards to support food workers through institutional purchasing. He has worked with the Sweatfree Purchasing Consortium, Electronics Watch, and the International Corporate Accountability Roundtable (ICAR). BA, Macalester College; JD, Georgetown University; LLM Georgetown University.

Iiris Tuominen
is a Ph.D. Candidate at the University of Lapland, Faculty of Law. Her research interests include legal theory and legal philosophy but also more practical issues such as research ethics. She has previously worked with ethical and legal issues related to improving digital access to Sámi cultural heritage materials. Currently, in addition to her dissertation, she is working with the themes of cultural heritage, intellectual property rights and Indigenous rights and ethics. Within these subject areas, she is affiliated with several research projects.

Gamze Erdem Türkelli
is Associate Research Professor at the Law and Development Research Group, University of Antwerp. Her work is situated at the intersection of international law, human rights law and sustainable development. She leads the European Research Council (ERC) funded GENESIS project on multistakeholder partnerships and human rights, is a member of the IEL Collective, the Law and Development Research Network and the New Frontiers in Development Finance (NeFDeF) project. She is the author of *Children's Rights and Business: Governing Obligations and Responsibility* (Cambridge University Press, 2020), co-author of *Advanced Introduction to Children's Rights* (Edward Elgar, 2022) and of *Children's Rights: A Commentary on the Convention on the Rights of the Child and its Protocols* (Edward Elgar, 2019) and co-editor of the *Routledge Handbook on Extraterritorial Human Rights Obligations* (Routledge, 2022) and of the *Encyclopaedia of Law and Development* (Edward Elgar, 2019).

Florian Wettstein
is Chair and Professor of Business Ethics and Director of the Institute for Business Ethics at University of St. Gallen in Switzerland. Florian has published widely on topics at the intersection of corporate responsibility, business ethics and human rights. He is the author of *Multinational Corporations and Global Justice: Human Rights Obligations of a Quasi-Governmental Institution* (Stanford University Press, 2009) and the textbook, *Business and Human Rights: Ethical, Legal, and Managerial Perspectives* (Cambridge University Press, 2022). Florian is editor-in-chief of the Business and Human Rights Journal (BHRJ) and president of the International Society for Business, Economics and Ethics (ISBEE).

Stefan Zagelmeyer
is Reader in Comparative and International Business at Alliance Manchester Business School, Manchester, UK. He has held appointments at Manchester School of Management (UK), Université Paris II Panthéon-Assas (France), Turku School of Economics (Finland), University of Twente (The Netherlands) and the University of Stellenbosch (South Africa). He is author of numerous publications in academic and practitioner-oriented journals. His research contributions fall into the four areas of international business strategy, comparative business and management, international human resource management, and business and human rights.

Khorsed Zaman
is a lecturer at the Thomas More Law School, Australian Catholic University. He holds LLB Honours from Rajshahi University, Bangladesh; LLM in

International and Business Law from Yokohama National University, Japan; and Ph.D. in International Trade Law from Macquarie University, Australia. He served as a Lecturer at Macquarie University and University of Technology Sydney. Dr. Zaman's research expertise is mainly in the areas of International Economic Law, World Trade Organisation (WTO) Law, International Trade and Investment Law, and Intellectual Property Law. He regularly publishes in these areas of law in high impact-factor national and international law journals.

PART 1

Socially Responsible Corporate Conducts

CHAPTER 1

Business, Human Rights, and Sustainable Development: An Introduction

Md Jahid Hosain Bhuiyan and M Rafiqul Islam

1 Introductory Background

From the industrial revolution onwards, businesses have developed into ever bigger enterprises.[1] The production of goods by mechanised systems incorporating modern technologies ranging from steam-powered engines to sophisticated and rapidly developing industrial and commercial techniques became faster and more easily scaled up due to larger mass production systems. The organisation of enterprises also became more efficient, with their access to markets expanding from local and national populations to multinational corporations (MNCs) with revenues rivalling, and frequently exceeding, the gross domestic products of entire countries. Economies of scale meant larger businesses could produce goods more efficiently and at lower cost, further driving the increases in size of many corporations. Globally operating MNCs now dominate certain economic sectors and exploit the near-instant communication of the information needed to operate the entire production and marketing process. With increased scales of production and penetration into wider markets, the structure of large organisations is such that human elements in the process, labourers, and administrative workers, have become increasingly distant from the owners and high-level executives of the organisations within which they work. In effect, bureaucracy has erected a virtual wall between ordinary employees and individual citizens, and those responsible for their working conditions (in the case of employees) or environmental living conditions (in the case of affected but unaffiliated citizens).

In many ways large corporations function like states, but with even greater impacts on social and environmental conditions as their operations are not confined to a single country or as constrained by state laws. Large private corporations are less easily regulated than the public bodies of state governance;

1 *See* Gregory Clark, "The Industrial Revolution," in *Handbook of Economic Growth*, eds. Philippe Aghion and Steven N. Durlauf, vol. 2, (Amsterdam: Elsevier, 2014), 217–262.

 | DOI:10.1163/9789004530942_002

consequently, the conditions and rights of workers at the lower end of business hierarchies are more easily exploited in the interests of company profits. The singularly grossest global violation of human rights in relatively recent history was the slave trade, where forced labourers were denied even the most basic of human rights and treated as sub-human. This wide-scale institutionalised inhumanity was only abolished in the UK in 1838 – four years after the 1833 Slavery Abolition Act. Since the end of the Second World War and the dismantling of colonialism – essentially the multinational exploitation of labour and resources – corporations have increased in size and expanded their reach, but more recently there has been an increasing demand for businesses of all sizes to adhere to the human rights framework initiated by the 1948 Universal Declaration of Human Rights (UDHR).[2]

Since the UDHR, human rights have extended as normative social changes in the treatment of individuals evolved. However, the responsibility to promote, protect, and respond to human rights violations has remained largely with states rather than individuals or private organisations – a structure sometimes referred to as verticality. Human rights as enshrined in state laws were documented within constitutions and principally directed at protecting citizens from state actions – not private conducts or contracts between non-state entities. The US Civil Rights Act of 1875 and the thirteenth and fourteenth amendments to the US Constitution were largely a product of the American Civil War and the abolishment of slavery. Although the thirteenth amendment applied, in certain instances, to private parties, it did so only in respect of rights associated with citizenship, not to what we might term *social rights*. This historical background to human rights provisions is important because the constitutions of many modern states were modelled on that of the US. Accordingly, human rights protection was primarily about protecting the freedom and rights of citizens from state actions, as the state was the sole body imbued with the authority to exert legal force. This became known as the *State Action Doctrine* and was applied to numerous civil rights cases in the US after the Bill of Rights.[3] The US Supreme Court judgements in these cases overwhelmingly asserted that violations of the provisions in the Bill of Rights could only be addressed if those violations involved state actions or were linked directly to the exercise of sovereign power.

2 United Nations Human Rights Office of the High Commissioner, *The Corporate Responsibility to Respect Human Rights* (New York and Geneva: United Nations, 2012).

3 *See* Hala Ayoub, "The State Action Doctrine in State and Federal Courts," *Florida State University Law Review* 11, issue 4 (1984): 893–920; Wilson R. Huhn, "The State Action Doctrine and the Principle of Democratic Choice," *Hofsta Law Review* 34 (2016): 1379–1458.

However, there has recently been a marked increase in demands for businesses to operate responsibly, both to their employees and to the environment or social conditions their operations impact. The "Guiding Principles on Business and Human Rights: Implementing the United Nations (UN) "Protect, Respect and Remedy" Framework", initiated after the 2005 appointment of John Ruggie as the UN Special Representative on Business and Human Rights, was endorsed by the UN Human Rights Council in 2011. This was a significant achievement as the UN's first attempt, in the 1990s, at extending the human rights obligations of states to businesses in the proposal, 'Norms on Transnational Corporations and Other Business Enterprises', was never acted upon due to hostile reception by the international business community.[4]

The idea of corporate social responsibility (CSR) is also a relatively recent development in industry and, as one measure of company performance, becomes a factor in the competitive process between businesses that work to advance social welfare and sustainable practices.[5] Public pressure to force multinationals to operate responsibly and provide acceptable working conditions has resulted in the adoption of global codes of conduct by some of these organisations, triggering others to do the same for fear of reputational damage. Thus, the significance of human rights in some aspects of business operations is increasing. This is particularly evident regarding the environmental impact of production methods in sectors like energy and agriculture, as enterprises within such sectors have the greatest direct environmental impact. Indeed, the world's largest oil exporter, Saudi Arabia, was ranked high in the 2022 Green Future Index Report of countries' renewable energy production, advancing 10 places to the 51st spot.[6]

Furthermore, global public awareness of the importance of sustainable production methods has grown substantially as the impacts of global warming have become ever more apparent. The environmental impact of businesses directly affects fundamental rights like access to drinking water and other basic human needs. Thus, the actions of businesses can have both immediate and long-term impacts on the capacity of individuals to exercise their human rights, leading many environmentally and socially responsible companies to create effective communication channels between their policy makers and the

4 *See* Surya Deva and David Bilchitz, eds., *Human Rights Obligations of Business: Beyond the Corporate Responsibility to Respect?* (Cambridge: Cambridge University Press, 2013).

5 Risa Bhinekawati, *Corporate Social Responsibility and Sustainable Development: Social Capital and Corporate Development in Developing Economics* (Oxon: Routledge, 2017).

6 https://www.technologyreview.com/2022/03/24/1048253/the-green-future-index-2022/ (accessed 5 January 2024).

people affected by their activities. Nonetheless, national governments remain the primary bodies responsible for ensuring international human rights standards are adhered to, although the public perception that corporations should enforce such standards is growing.

While CSR can improve businesses' environmental and social practices, it remains only one measure of their performance and thus does not protect human rights directly but rather through effects on their reputation. Moreover, companies attempt to improve their public perception by drawing attention only to those aspects of their pro-environmental and pro-social operations that can easily be seen as linked to the company. However, the impacts of large MNCs can extremely wide, extending through subsidiaries, long supply chains, and subcontractors whose names are unrelated to the parent company, and often in different countries. Thus, while the impact of a company is far-reaching and can affect all aspects of the human rights of people in the vicinity of their operations, international awareness of any human rights violations is often hidden by the scale and complexity of corporate structures. The potential for corporations and businesses to affect human rights is further increased by the privatisation of health- and welfare-related services once provided by states. This state of affair sets the context for this book, which examines in detail the relations between corporations and human rights, and the responsibilities and obligations of multinational and transnational business organisations to promote human rights and maintain internationally accepted codes of conduct in their operations.

1.1 *The Focus and Features of the Book*

The focus of the book is on both the direct and indirect effects of corporations on human rights. Included within this remit are sustainable practices and development initiatives. For companies to achieve and maintain sustainable practices, they must satisfy both the long-term and current interests of stakeholders, which include the environment and consequent living conditions of future generations. Human rights cannot be abstracted away from corporate activities that affect the environment directly and people only indirectly, for these rights refer intrinsically to freedoms and conditions grounded in both the social and physical contexts that people inhabit. Companies must therefore prioritise the development of their operations in a manner that not only employs sustainable production methods but also produces environmentally friendly sustainable goods and services. As the UN Sustainable Development Goals Report 2023 emphasises, human rights are being threatened by both the direct physical environmental impacts of human activity and the less visible dominant corporate structures that control access to services – particularly to finance. The report makes for uncomfortable reading, with many targets for 2030 showing very slow progress and nearly a third (30%) either halting or back-tracking. The 30% includes goals on climate, poverty, and hunger, which inevitably affect the weakest developing countries and the most vulnerable global populations.

Large corporations have enormous power to protect human rights and advance sustainability, but equally to damage or impede both. Therefore, a framework for protecting human rights must be developed that involves corporations and effectively transfers to them state-like legal obligations to protect those rights. This need is too great to rely solely on market forces – the operative mechanism most natural to business entities. Furthermore, the onus of responsibility is on corporations based in high income countries, as their material per-capita impact is ten times that of poorer, developing countries.[7] Equally important, whilst the trickledown benefits of business profits tend to be channelled to their host countries, their adverse socioenvironmental impacts affect all countries, especially developing countries with industries and economies based on heavily natural raw materials. The most threatening impact to human living conditions, and which therefore relates to most fundamental human rights, comes from corporate activities that induce global warming. The United Nations Intergovernmental Panel on Climate Change (IPCC) said that the greenhouse gas emissions need to be cut by 43% by 2030 in order to meet the 2015 UN Paris Agreement goal of limiting temperature rises to 1.5% degrees Celsius by 2100.[8] These sustainability and environmental protection targets and initiatives initially seem distant from the realm of human rights. However, their significance to those affected is as great as those more well-established gross human rights violations, such as torture, military aggression, and genocide.

In legal human rights terms, this aspect reflects what Jean Thomas refers to as a major departure from the verticality of the established human rights framework, in that this framework originated when states were in unique positions of power relative to citizens.[9] All non-state actors were treated in law as equals, as states had a monopoly of legal coercion. Transferring legal rights obligations to the relations between private parties, such as companies and

7 https://www.un.org/sustainabledevelopment/sustainable-consumption-production/ (accessed January 12, 2024).

8 United Nations Climate Change, "Climate Plans Remain Insufficient: More Ambitious Action Needed Now," October 26, 2022, https://unfccc.int/news/climate-plans-remain-insufficient-more-ambitious-action-needed-now (accessed January 12, 2024).

9 Jean Thomas, *Public Rights, Private Relations* (Oxford: Oxford University Press, 2015).

citizens, is technically difficult as such horizontal application can engender an exponential and unmanageable proliferation of obligations and duties, unlike the well-defined framework of states as duty-bearers and citizens as rights-bearers. However, Thomas' suggestion is not to transplant the rights framework of public law rights to all private parties, but to explicate the principal relation that underlies the original rights framework between state and citizen. That relation, she contends, is 'interpersonal dependency' in which one party has greater vulnerability.[10] Such a relational principle could be used to specify particular parties and thereby avoid the unmanageable proliferation of rights and duties. This principle could then be used to develop a framework for protecting human rights in the context of large corporations and their impact on vulnerable populations.

1.2 *Moving Forward: The Need for Radical Change*

The Sustainable Development Goals (SDGs) do not simply reaffirm the importance of corporate social and environmental responsibility; they represent the need for a radical change in our ideas regarding the global role that business plays. This is due to the fact that many businesses no longer exist as isolated actors in market economies, but as fundamental operators affecting all aspects of human life at all scales. The UN Guiding Principles on Business and Human Rights enshrines this radical re-thinking of the nature of businesses and their relation to, and responsibility for, the welfare of all humanity and the world we inhabit. The SDGs are not on course to be met by 2030 – some have even moved backwards, and businesses and states must realise that SDGs are not achievable without the cooperation and coordination of all stakeholders. Protecting human rights and rapidly increasing sustainability in business operations, across all stages of the value chain, is not an optional marketing addition that a business employs to promote its appeal to an ethically aware customer base – it is also now necessary for their success.

The above requirement applies to businesses of all sizes and includes the protection and promotion of human rights at every level. Businesses have as much power, and some corporations considerably more, than state governments to protect and enhance human rights. Such power should come with the obligation to use it to promote and protect human rights and the socioenvironmental conditions those rights depend on. Human rights and sustainability are mutually dependent and businesses which do not adequately address them could fail, even in the short-term. Developing countries' markets as well

10 Ibid, 196.

as their input of labour and resources can only be sustained if their populations' human rights are protected and enhanced. The global middle class is growing rapidly, and customer preferences are quickly shifting towards sustainable, ethically manufactured products and business practices, demonstrating that businesses not only have an obligation to protect human rights and the environment, but that it is in their (business) best interests to do so. As the UN stated in 2017, '[s]imply put, a development path in which human rights are not respected and protected cannot be sustainable, and would render the notion of sustainable development meaningless'.[11]

1.3 *Structure of the Book: Summaries of Chapters*

This edited book covers some of the daunting challenges facing corporate role in protecting human rights and achieving sustainable development in the contemporary context. Its authorship includes renowned scholars, academics, and researchers from all over the world who have provided their collective cutting-edge views, careful analyses, critical voices, and palatable positive solutions to propel this corporate role from strength to strength in the 21st century and beyond. The summaries of their valuable contributions are provided below.

Apart from this introductory Chapter 1, the book is structured in three distinct yet interrelated parts. Part 1 contains chapters dealing with socially responsible corporate conducts. In Chapter 2, Stefan Zagelmeyer examines for the interaction between business, human rights, and the UN SDGs. The global discourse over sustainable development, business, and human rights has recently converged with the UN Guiding Principles on Business and Human Rights 2011, which is now widely regarded as a potential tool to support business organisations in contributing to achieving the SDGs. Against the background of the conceptual convergence of debates over their nexus among public policymakers and academics, this chapter traces the extent to which this convergence is also reflected in corporate practice. The chapter first introduces the debate on the linkage of sustainable development with business and human rights, focusing particularly on the role of business and human rights governance for business organisations. Drawing on corporate reports published by multinational corporations (MNCs) listed in the DAX 40, the chapter articulates and analyses the extent to which corporate activities designed

---

11 Office of the UN High Commissioner for Human Rights, Working Group on Business and Human Rights, "Key Recommendations for Connecting the Business and Human Rights Agenda to the 2030 SGDs," Preamble, para 1, https://www.ohchr.org/en/special-procedures/wg-business/key-recommendations-connecting-business-and-human-rights-agenda-2030-sustainable-development-goals (accessed January 5, 2024).

to achieve the SDGs are linked to the UN Guiding Principles. An overview of developments since 2010 is supplemented by the analysis and discussion of a selection of critical cases. The chapter concludes with an outlook on the role of business and human rights in the context of corporate social responsibility and sustainability.

Chapter 3 critically examines business, socio-economic rights, and global inequalities. Business and human rights have witnessed seminal developments since the UN Human Rights Council adopted the UN Guiding Principles. In recent years, several countries in the Global North have introduced binding national standards in the different sub-areas of business and human rights. However, little attention has been afforded to the obligations and responsibility of businesses to respect and protect human rights. Traditionally, states carry the primary responsibility to guarantee socio-economic rights, but they have played only a minor role in global and most domestic economies. With increasing globalisation, privately-owned businesses have influenced the enjoyment of socio-economic rights by individuals. Resultantly, they have propelled negative and positive impacts on individuals' enjoyment of socio-economic rights. In this chapter, Jernej Letnar Černič explores the normative basis and standards for business obligations, responsibilities, and accountability for socio-economic rights and argues that recognising corporate accountability for socio-economic rights is indispensable for achieving that every individual develops self-realisation and human development capabilities.

Sara L. Seck and Victoria Kongats in Chapter 4 identify the negative impacts of business-induced plastic pollution on human rights. The current fossil-fuel-based plastics life cycle negatively impacts human rights at every stage, from extraction and production to transportation, use, waste management and disposal. Humanity urgently needs to move towards circularity in the plastics value chain, and to eliminate or at least minimise the interconnected human rights and environmental harms of the current plastics model. Integrating a human rights-based approach into the transition to plastics circularity in the value chain requires an understanding of the different dimensions of an environmental human rights-based approach. It also requires an understanding of business responsibilities for human rights, as established in the UN Guiding Principles and embedded in related guidance on risk-based due diligence, such as the Organisation for Economic Co-operation and Development (OECD) Guidelines for Multinational Enterprises and related initiatives. This chapter analyses how business and human rights guidance tools can guide business enterprises in making the responsible transition towards circularity in the plastics value chain in order to better protect people and the planet from the ongoing plastic pollution crisis.

In Chapter 5, Peter Muchlinski applies the UN Guiding Principles in conflict areas with reference to corporate responsibilities, responses and non-responses in the context of the Ukraine War. The UN Guiding Principles are particularly interested in corporate human rights abuses in conflict affected areas. One of the most detailed Guiding Principles is Principle 7 – 'supporting business respect for human rights in conflict affected areas'. Though aimed at states as part of their duty to prevent corporate human rights abuses, the Principle also assumes corporate responsibilities. This chapter examines the parameters of corporate responsibility for human rights impacts in conflict areas. Most accounts of these responsibilities focus on small scale asymmetric conflicts and civil war. Few discuss these responsibilities in relation to traditional international wars between state armed forces. This chapter focuses on the Ukraine War and develops an analysis of corporate human rights based on the resulting human rights demands on corporate actors. It examines the interaction between the laws of war, humanitarian law, sustainable development principles, and business responsibilities for human rights infringements during the conflict. Post-conflict reconstruction is also discussed. The chapter concludes with an analysis of what remains to be done to improve corporate accountability for human rights compliance in conflict areas.

Paolo Galizzi scrutinises corporate responsibility to redress human rights violations related to the environment in Chapter 6. Over the years, corporations have grown exponentially in role and size. Corporations provide ample evidence of their power over the global economy, often driving political agendas, creating economic opportunities, fuelling economic and technological development, and exerting pervasive impacts on societies. Corporations are also responsible for the increasingly worrying environmental problems of unfettered economic growth. The footprint of corporate actions and their impact can be seen and measured for all the environmental problems the world is facing from the loss of biodiversity to waste generation, to climate change, to environmental justice, just to name a few. The international regulation of corporations and their general and specific impact on the environment has arguably been lacklustre. In recent years, however, rules have been emerging laying out corporate human rights obligations. The UN Guiding Principles is the most important soft law instruments in this area. Notable decisions within human rights bodies at the global, regional and national level are crystallising a set of corporate legal obligations. This chapter scrutinises this emerging human rights framework and its application to environmental violations to show how business and human rights norms regulate the environmental aspects of corporate activities. It studies selected cases to highlight environmental violations that harm human rights and how corporations could form part of sustainable solutions to myriad environmental problems.

Part 2 deals with chapters pertaining to the interaction of human rights with trade, investment, and finance. In Chapter 7, Ernst Ulrich Petersmann traces the inseparable linkage between the world trading system, human rights, and sustainable development. In the International Monetary Fund (IMF), the World Bank, General Agreement on Tariffs and Trade (GATT), and the World Trade Organization (WTO), international economic law tends to be justified on the grounds of state consent and welfare economics (efficiency). The UN Sustainable Development Agenda, by contrast, emphasises the importance of human rights, democratic governance, and rule of law for realising the agreed SDGs, including the protection of human rights for all. Can SDGs be achieved if the Bretton Woods and WTO institutions rarely refer to human rights, and many UN member states oppose transforming the UN Guiding Principles into new treaty rights and obligations of states, corporate actors, and victims of human rights abuses? This chapter explains how embedding European economic integration law into multilevel legal, democratic, and judicial protection of human and constitutional rights has strengthened the legitimacy of economic law in terms of human rights and sustainable development. It also shows how WTO and European dispute settlement jurisprudence has avoided conflicts, albeit through diverse legal methodologies, between economic law and human rights law. Yet, authoritarian state-capitalism, business-driven neo-liberalism and geopolitical conflicts increasingly disrupt post-1945 world order treaties militating against legal protection of the SDGs.

In Chapter 8, Md Jahid Hossain Bhuiyan highlights the potential of businesses to promote human rights and shift to a sustainable and just economy. FDI has enhanced citizens' welfare; however, it has also been linked to human rights violations. Everyone in the society has the responsibility to protect human rights. However, MNCs have a unique status in society that entails a greater responsibility to establish a just and sustainable world in which the human rights of all citizens are protected. It is also in the economic interest of large global enterprises to adopt policies promoting human rights and sustainability, as the public awareness of human rights violations by large corporations has increased. This puts pressure on investors to ensure adherence to globally acceptable human rights standards. States also need to encourage the development of a stable socio-political environment that benefits businesses and attracts FDI from MNCs. Globalisation has highlighted that to achieve sustainability, human rights should be protected at all levels in different economic sectors. Failing to protect human rights is not only unethical but also self-destructive for all parties involved in FDI relationships. The Guiding Principles is a significant achievement as it is the first corporate responsibility initiative approved by the UN. These principles create a guideline for corporations to operate in a manner that improves human welfare while decreasing suffering. The guidelines set a standard for business activity, using which states can evaluate corporate activities. Respecting human rights creates a favourable environment for human capital development, which attracts skilled workers and reduces risks for foreign investors. Corporations that respect human rights can decrease commercial risks, enhance their international reputation, and thus, would be preferred by global investors.

In Chapter 9 on national development finance institutions (DFIs), business and extraterritorial human rights obligations, Gamze Erdem Turkelli examines how DFIs operate to foster private sector growth in developing countries by using public funds from so-called 'donor' countries. Backed by public architectures in wealthy countries, DFIs are central to the 'private turn' in development financing, particularly by pushing for public-private partnerships, which increased since the SDG framework was adopted in 2015. Furthermore, DFIs play interlocution and intermediation roles and allow private actors such as corporations to infuse into national international development governance frameworks. When contextualised in the developments of international law around business and human rights, DFIs present dual challenges. First, DFIs may be fully or partially state-owned and working within policy frameworks determined by their countries of origin, engendering questions around the extraterritorial human rights obligations of their countries of origin in relation to business conduct, which are invariably the home countries of many MNCs. Secondly, DFIs are often established as private sector companies in their countries of origin, meaning that international and national business and human rights norms may be directly applicable to them. This chapter tackles these dual challenges and addresses the questions of accountability to human rights holders when DFIs finance private sector companies in developing countries by inspecting the current situation regarding the extraterritorial obligations of their countries of origin and the human rights duties of DFIs.

Part 3 includes chapters that explain the challenges facing human rights implementation in business. In this context, Olga Martin-Ortega examines human rights violations in global corporate supply chains in Chapter 10. Human and labour rights violations are not merely incidents in global supply chains. The complex structures through which the global production of goods is organised seek to minimise costs through highly fragmented and geographically dispersed networks. Goods production in global supply chains minimises not just labour costs, but also legal responsibility for most of the corporate actors involved. Global supply chains are characterised by their transnational dimension and complexity, and by the asymmetric power relations between brands and suppliers, contractor and subcontractors, and ultimately corporate actors and workers. Workers at the lower tiers of the chain become vulnerable to abuse from the moment they are recruited to how they are paid and made to work and when they are dismissed. This chapter analyses two systemic issues which lead to human rights violations in the supply chain: unfair labour recruitment and low wages. It argues that the failure to acknowledge these systemic abuses prevents them from being addressed and leads to further violations. It considers the deficiencies of current models of human rights due diligence in addressing them by focusing on the severity of risks whilst ignoring the role of purchasing practices in perpetuating abusive dynamics.

Robert Stumberg explains transparency theories of change in Chapter 11. According to the UN Guiding Principles, businesses need to 'know and show' that they exercise due diligence to protect human rights. Yet most institutional purchasers – like governments, universities, hospitals, and schools – are blind to abuses in their own supply chains. Why? The popular theory is that reputation risk in consumer markets motivates global brands to respect human rights. But institutional suppliers are often smaller companies with little exposure to broad consumer markets. Moreover, the meaning of transparency is vague and hotly contested, even in laws that call for it. Suppliers claim to be transparent when in fact they do not reveal their actual supply chain. Academic research confirms that transparency is commonly used to game the system for private gain and frustrate policy goals. Confronted with these challenges, transparency remains the key to accountable supply chains, both public and private. But the key must be shaped to work for public and institutional purchasers. This chapter shapes that key by applying the lessons from transparency critics to answer basic questions of transparency design: Why disclose? Disclose what? Disclose where? And how to compare?

In Chapter 12, Nelson Camilo Sanchez highlights the interface between the transitional justice and business and human rights fields that attracted increasing scholarly attention to the role of corporations during political transition and comments upon transitional responses to corporate abuses of human rights. For several decades, accountability efforts for gross human rights violations have documented the complicity of economic actors in the context of mass violence. However, until recently, the academic fields of Business & Human Rights and Transitional Justice began to systematically explore shared interests and connections. This chapter explores the progression of corporate responsibility in the context of transitional justice and analyses how this academic approach has contributed to achieving accountability for corporate abuses in the context of political transition. Underscoring the significance of interdisciplinary cooperation, the author calls upon peacebuilding, sustainability studies, and corporate accountability scholars to expand the ambit of their research. The goal should be to develop a comprehensive understanding and generate all-encompassing solutions to address the complex issues inherent in transitional justice and corporate accountability, and thus provide greater justice for the victims of corporate abuses of human and labour rights in political transition.

In Chapter 13, Lisa Laplante analyses the role of operational level grievance mechanisms in ensuring corporate accountability for human rights violations and affording the victim's redress. Although discussions on corporate accountability often focus on judicial mechanisms, the UN Guiding Principles strongly emphasise non-judicial mechanisms as valid means for remediating human rights harms resulting from corporate activities. This chapter shares empirical data that tracks the development of operational-level grievance mechanisms, a novel approach introduced through the UN Guiding Principles that is increasingly recommended or required by due diligence laws, industry associations, voluntary certification programs and other compliance-oriented initiatives. Increasingly, companies implement these purely private redress mechanisms comply with the UN Guiding Principles and assure they offer full justice for the victims of human rights violations. But this compliance occurs without government oversight and in a non-transparent manner to avoid public interest and scrutiny. Critically analysing this development, the chapter concludes with guidance on how operational-level grievance mechanisms may better serve stakeholders whilst assuring corporations fulfil their responsibility to respect human rights. It recommends including in the compliance process community engagement in minimising conflict and maximising sustainable development.

Jindan-Karena Mann critically examines the scope of the corporate duty of care in the context of business and human rights under tort law in Chapter 14. She addresses the tort liability of transnational companies when human rights violations are committed by their subsidiaries or contracting partners along a common supply chain. Concerns of temporal, geographic, and causal remoteness between the defendant and plaintiff in such cases has long been considered a barrier to establishing corporate liability. However, recent cases from the UK suggest that parent companies may owe a duty of care towards the victims of their subsidiaries when they avail themselves of the opportunity to take over, intervene in, control, supervise, or advise operations that result in human rights infringements. Although these developments provide a promising remedy for business-related human rights violations, accountability gaps remain. This chapter considers two such gaps: first, that the UK precedents might create a perverse incentive for parent companies to avoid overseeing and supporting their subsidiaries to uphold human rights in their bid in order to escape liability; and second, it remains unclear whether MNCs owe a duty of care to their non-subsidiary business partners who operate along a common supply chain. The chapter explores how these accountability gaps can be closed, focusing particularly on the role of mandatory human rights due diligence obligations.

Chapter 15 critically examines international vaccines trade by pharmaceutical corporations during the COVID-19 pandemic. Khorsed Zaman and M Rafiqul Islam explain how the lopsided global distribution of COVID-19 vaccines under the stringent patent protection laws of the WTO undermined corporate obligations towards protecting human rights in developing and the least developed countries. The unprecedented COVID-19 pandemic has inflicted devastating impacts on human lives and health, worsened inequalities, and curtailed human rights worldwide. Repeated appeals by the UN and third world countries for equitable distribution of COVID vaccines went unheeded. Big pharmaceutical manufacturers and wealthier countries failed to fulfil global imperative to save human lives. Instead, they monopolised their technology under the protection of intellectual property rights (IPRs), charged exorbitant prices for COVID vaccines, and prioritised supplies to the rich over the poor. Hoarding of vaccines by rich countries delayed and reduced the supply to poor countries, exposing those most in need to life-threatening vulnerability. This global public health crisis has serious human rights implications, bringing together the IPRs and international human rights obligations of the COVID vaccine producers and wealthier countries. This chapter examines international patent protection law as applied to COVID vaccines to demonstrate (a) its marginalising effect on the right to life, health, and access to lifesaving COVID vaccines particularly in the third world; and (b) how the stringent application of patent rights and IPRs protection mechanisms ignored the international human rights obligations of big pharma and wealthy countries exacerbating the pandemic.

In Chapter 16, Rosa Ballardini, Iiris Tuominen and Dino Girardi reconcile intellectual property rights, human rights, and indigenous worldviews through proactive approaches and engagement in the context of digital Indigenous Cultural Heritage. Cultural heritage is an important element of identity for both Indigenous communities and individuals. The UNESCO Convention for the Safeguarding of the Intangible Cultural Heritage defines 'cultural heritage' as a legacy inherited from the past and bestowed for the future, but also as a process elaborated in present day communities. The need to protect, provide access to, and manage indigenous cultural heritage through legal or other means has been growing in momentum due to multiple developments. First, although Indigenous peoples have long expressed concern over the lack of respect for their own ethics and human rights in governing their culture, recent awareness of this matter worldwide has proliferated. Second, technological developments such as digitalisation, comprising Artificial Intelligence applications have greatly enhanced possibilities for protecting, accessing, further developing, and exploiting cultural heritage. In the context of digitalisation of Indigenous cultural heritage, an ethically fundamental challenge is how to examine the distortions and biases caused to Indigenous peoples by using new technologies. Because the existing legal framework for protecting and managing Indigenous cultural heritage is dominated by Western legal views, it is a daunting task to design proper laws and policies, share knowledge, and raise awareness amongst the stakeholders, for solutions that respect indigenous 'cultural sensibilities', which are intrinsic elements of the heritage of a culture.

In Chapter 17, Mariam Shakil, Isabel Ebert and Florian Wettstein investigate the relationship between business and human rights in promoting a system in the data economy respecting human right. Vast troves of data are increasingly being utilised in finding innovative solutions for myriad social, economic, and environmental issues. Such data is accumulated from a wide array of sources, such as the Internet of Things, social media, and mobile apps. Whilst the connection and organisation of data from such sources promises to facilitate better services and products for citizens and consumers, generate better business insights and help develop untapped markets, there are significant risks associated with how, why, and by whom this information is being handled, monetised, monitored, and governed. Potential adverse impacts stretch from privacy concerns to data discrimination seen, for example, in automated decision making. Acknowledging the key role of the private sector in shaping the future data economy, the authors propose a Business and Human Rights lens to reflect on and outline the contours of a rights-respecting ecosystem in the data economy. Specifically, they articulate the role of the private sector in constructing such an ecosystem and by what means the state must uphold adequate governance structures that provide for the rights-respecting conduct of technology companies.

David Hess in Chapter 18 explores the possible alignment corporate initiatives and efforts to combat corruption and respect human rights in conducting business activities. Corruption and human rights abuses are strongly linked. Corruption impacts economic and social rights, such as the rights to food, work, health, education, and non-discrimination as well as civil and political rights, including the rights to a fair trial and to participate in the political system. Although this link is widely recognised by the global community, it has yet to receive sufficient attention in business and human rights nexus. This chapter elucidates this link by (a) describing the development of a global anticorruption norm over the last 25 years; (b) using modern slavery in supply chains as examples to illustrate the connection between corruption and business and human rights; (c) exploring how corruption can be a cause of human rights violations that businesses must address in their operations and supply chains, as well as a barrier to reducing negative human rights impacts and the benefits in doing so; (d) explaining how businesses' initiatives and efforts to combat corruption and respect human rights should be integrated and pursued, and the role of states in bringing corruption and business and human rights together; and (e) emphasing that a business and human rights perspective should shape a new corporate responsibility to combat corruption.

In concluding, this edited book has purported to highlight the key challenges and opportunities facing efforts to align business, human rights, and sustainable development. Its reformist goal is to identify and pursue a 'new path to the waterfall', where the three core issues – business, human rights, and sustainable development – can be transitioned onto a radical new trajectory which recognises their mutually supportive role propelled by respect, responsibility, and protection for both the human and natural resources of the world.

Bibliography

Book

Bhinekawati, Risa. *Corporate Social Responsibility and Sustainable Development: Social Capital and Corporate Development in Developing Economics*. Oxon: Routledge, 2017.

Clark, Gregory. "The Industrial Revolution." In *Handbook of Economic Growth*, edited by Philippe Aghion and Steven N. Durlauf, 217–262. Vol. 2. Amsterdam: Elsevier, 2014.

Thomas, Jean. *Public Rights, Private Relations*. Oxford: Oxford University Press, 2015.

United Nations Human Rights Office of the High Commissioner. *The Corporate Responsibility to Respect Human Rights*. New York and Geneva: United Nations, 2012.

Book Chapter

Deva, Surya, and David Bilchitz, eds. *Human Rights Obligations of Business: Beyond the Corporate Responsibility to Respect?* Cambridge: Cambridge University Press, 2013.

Journal Article

Ayoub, Hala. "The State Action Doctrine in State and Federal Courts." *Florida State University Law Review* 11, issue 4 (1984): 893–920.

Huhn, Wilson R. "The State Action Doctrine and the Principle of Democratic Choice." *Hofsta Law Review* 34 (2016): 1379–1458.

Website

https://www.technologyreview.com/2022/03/24/1048253/the-green-future-index-2022/ (accessed 5 January 2024).

https://www.un.org/sustainabledevelopment/sustainable-consumption-production/ (accessed January 12, 2024).

Office of the UN High Commissioner for Human Rights, Working Group on Business and Human Rights. "Key Recommendations for Connecting the Business and Human Rights Agenda to the 2030 SGDs." https://www.ohchr.org/en/special-procedures/wg-business/key-recommendations-connecting-business-and-human-rights-agenda-2030-sustainable-development-goals (accessed January 5, 2024).

United Nations Climate Change. "Climate Plans Remain Insufficient: More Ambitious Action Needed Now." October 26. 2022, https://unfccc.int/news/climate-plans-remain-insufficient-more-ambitious-action-needed-now (accessed January 12, 2024).

CHAPTER 2

Corporate Commitment to Human Rights and Sustainable Development

Stefan Zagelmeyer

1 Introduction

For several decades, the global human development agenda and the international human rights agenda have been heading in the same direction, sharing similar assumptions and ideas about the links between human development and human rights. Yet, in the early 2000s, it was observed that 'neither the human rights nor development communities has embraced this linkage with enthusiasm or conviction'.[1] Since then, discussions on both sustainable development and business and human rights have started to converge, with recent work emphasising the potential role of business and human rights governance in line with the United Nations Guiding Principles for Business and Human Rights (UNGPs) in order to achieve the Sustainable Development Goals (SDGs).[2]

Against the background of the gradual convergence of the two agendas and debates among public policymakers and academics, this chapter explores the extent to which signs of convergence can also be observed at the corporate level. Further, this chapter analyses and elaborates on the incidence and extent of corporate commitment to human rights and the SDGs, as measured through word frequency analysis and text-mining methods, drawing on annual reports and sustainability reports published in 2010 and 2020 of multinational corporations listed in the DAX-40 stock market index. This chapter also seeks to analyse the extent to which corporate disclosure on sustainable development and human rights is connected. More specifically, it analyses whether patterns of corporate commitment to human rights and the SDG have developed jointly

1 Philip Alston, "Ships passing in the night: The current state of the human rights and development debate seen through the lens of the Millennium Development Goals," *Human Rights Quarterly* 27, no. 3 (Aug 2005): 755.

2 Stefan Zagelmeyer and Rudolf R. Sinkovics, "MNEs, human rights and the SDGs – the moderating role of business and human rights governance," *Transnational Corporations* 26, no. 3 (2019): 33.

 | DOI:10.1163/9789004530942_003

in the same direction, potentially reinforcing each other, or whether both human rights and SDG reporting have developed in a substitutive way, with one replacing the other in corporate disclosure information.

The chapter first outlines the discussion on the link between business, sustainable development, and human rights. It then uses quantitative word frequency analysis and text-mining methods to map and analyse corporate reporting activities on the SDGs and on human rights. The last section discusses the implications of the findings for the debate on the role of business with respect to the potential links between sustainable development and human rights and proposes potentially fruitful avenues for future research.

2 Business, Human Rights and Sustainable Development

2.1 *Millennium Goals and Sustainable Development Goals*

Since the publication of the Brundtland Report,[3] there has been growing interest in the link between international business activities and sustainable development.[4] International development policy entered a new stage when the UN Millennium Declaration set out a strategic vision to work towards the achievement of eight goals until 2015.[5] The Millennium Development Goals (MDGs) aimed at supporting human capabilities and development by emphasising human capital, infrastructure, and human rights.

In 2015 the UN General Assembly adopted Agenda 2030, which encompasses 17 goals, known as the SDGs.[6] Building on the MDGs, they provide orientation for global development efforts for the period 2016–2030.[7] The SDGs aim at

3 World Commission On Environment and Development, *Our common future* (Oxford: Oxford University Press, 1987).

4 Klaus E. Meyer, "Perspectives on multinational enterprises in emerging economies," *Journal of International Business Studies* 35, no. 4 (2004): 273.

5 United Nations, Resolution adopted by the General Assembly [without reference to a Main Committee (A/55/L.2)] – 55/2 (2000).

6 United Nations, Resolution adopted by the General Assembly on September 25, 2015 [without reference to a Main Committee (A/70/L.1)] 70/1. Transforming our world: the 2030 Agenda for Sustainable Development., (2015); United Nations, Transforming our world: The 2030 agenda for sustainable development. United Nations Development Group (2015).

7 Thomas Pogge and Mitu Sengupta, "Assessing the sustainable development goals from a human rights perspective," *Journal of International and Comparative Social Policy* 32, no. 2 (2016): 84.

> "[B]ringing together Governments, the private sector, civil society, the United Nations system and other actors" to mobilise "all available resources", explicitly mentioning micro-enterprises, cooperatives and multinationals "as drivers of productivity, inclusive economic growth and job creation."[8]

In contrast to the MDGs, the SDG agenda is more comprehensive, emphasising the environmental dimension, and more universal in focus, addressing all countries' sustainability needs instead of focusing only on developing countries. In the development of both the MDGs and SDGs, the human rights-related capabilities approach to development has featured prominently.[9]

2.2 *Business and Human Rights*

While the International Bill of Human Rights, with the Universal Declaration of Human Rights adopted by the UN General Assembly in 1948 at its core, focuses on the responsibility of the state to prevent and remedy human rights abuses, the role of business in human rights has been scrutinised since the 1970s. The UN Commission on Transnational Corporations was created in 1973 to develop a code of conduct for transnational corporations; however, by 1994 it had been dissolved without completing its mission.[10]

The UN Working Group on Transnational Corporations was established in 1998 with the mandate to develop universal standards for the human rights obligations of transnational corporations to strengthen corporate accountability.[11] The 2003 draft document of the 'Norms of the Responsibilities of Transnational Corporations and Other Business Enterprises with Regard to Human Rights' stipulates that states as primary duty-holders are required to protect people from human rights harm caused by business activities, with transnational companies being assigned specific responsibilities under

8 United Nations, Short Transforming our world: The 2030 agenda for sustainable development. United Nations Development Group.

9 Amartya Sen, "Development as a Capability Expansion," in *Readings in Human Development*, ed. S. Fukuda-Parr (Oxford: Oxford University Press, 2003): 54; Amartya Sen, "Human rights and capabilities," *Journal of Human Development* 6, no. 2 (2005): 151.

10 Karl. P. Sauvant, "The Negotiations of the United Nations Code of Conduct on Transnational Corporations: Experience and Lessons Learned," *The Journal of World Investment & Trade* 16, no. 1 (2015): 19.

11 David Weissbrodt, "Corporate Human Rights Responsibilities," *Zeitschrift für Wirtschafts- und Unternehmensethik* 6, no. 3 (2005): 286.

international human rights law. In 2005, however, the draft norms were rejected by the UN Commission on Human Rights.[12]

The UNGPs, endorsed by the UN Human Rights Council in 2011, create a polycentric governance system by establishing a set of global standards that cover all business organisations and all human rights in all UN member states.[13] The first pillar, 'state duty to protect human rights', confirms the role of the state as the primary duty-bearer to protect human rights and its responsibility to prevent, investigate, punish, and redress human rights abuses by companies. The second pillar, 'corporate responsibility to respect', includes the expectation that companies explicitly express their commitment to human rights by declaring their policy commitment to respect human rights, as well as by conducting human rights risk analysis and due diligence. The third pillar, 'access to remedy', requires the state and companies to establish governance structures that allow victims of human rights abuses to access effective remedy.[14] Since 2014, the period of principled pragmatism connected to the UNGPs has been followed by discussion and subsequent negotiations of a business and human rights treaty at the UN level.[15]

---

12 Juli Campagna, "United Nations norms on the responsibilities of transnational corporations and other business enterprises with regard to human rights: The international community asserts binding law on global rule makers," *Marshall Law Review* 37 (2004): 1208; Patricia Feeney, "Business and human rights: The struggle for accountability in the UN and the future direction of the advocacy agenda," *Sur – International Journal on Human Rights* 6, no. 11 (2009): 165.

13 John Gerard Ruggie, *Just Business: Multinational Corporations and Human Rights* (New York: W. W. Norton & Company, 2013), xlii.

14 Ruggie, ibid; Larry Cata Backer, "On the evolution of the United Nations 'Protect-Respect-Remedy Project': The state, the corporation and human rights in a global governance context," *Santa Clara Journal of International Law* 9, no. 2 (2011): 38; Human Rights Council, Promotion and protection of all human rights, civil, political, economic, social and cultural rights, including the right to development: Protect, respect and remedy – A framework for business and human rights (2008);, Report of the Special Representative of the Secretary-General on the Issue of Human Rights and Transnational Corporations and other Business Enterprises, John Ruggie. UN Human Rights Council, A/HRC/8/5 (April 7, 2008).

15 Ruggie, *Just Business*; Surya Deva and David Bilchitz, *Building a treaty on business and human rights – Context and contours* (Cambridge: Cambridge University Press, 2017); Lee McConnell, "Assessing the feasibility of a business and human rights treaty," *International and Comparative Law Quarterly* 66, no. 1 (2016): 143.

2.3 *Business, Human Rights and the Sustainable Development Goals*

Reflecting on debate about the role of business in international development debate, human rights appear to have been largely ignored until recently.[16] This position is mirrored by the marginal role human rights have played in the international development literature and in the international business literature.[17] Still in early 2000s, it was claimed that the human rights debate and the development debate had largely developed in parallel.[18] More recently, research identified trends of convergence between the two debates.[19] Figure 2.1 provides an overview of the most important international initiatives with respect to (i) the sustainable development debate; and (ii) the business and human rights debate.

Although the debate on international development was traditionally not organised around the human rights approach to development, the Millennium Declaration placed human rights at the centre of international development,[20] explicitly suggesting implementing the MDG in a human rights-sensitive manner.[21]

As the SDGs are widely considered an extension of the MDG, one might assume that the role of human rights has become even more prominent. In fact, the 2030 Agenda was designed with an explicit commitment to human rights, as indicated in the preamble; several references to international human rights treaties and instruments; and the explicit aim to 'seek to realise the human rights of all'.[22] An analysis by the Danish Institute for Human Rights

---

16 Shift, Business, human rights and the sustainable development goals – Forging a coherent vision and strategy 2016, Business & Sustainable Development Commission, London.

17 Hans-Otto Sano, "Development and human rights: The necessary, but partial integration of human rights and development," *Human Rights Quarterly* 22, no. 3 (2000): 751; Florian Wettstein et al., "International business and human rights: A research agenda," *Journal of World Business* 54, no. 1 (2019): 54.

18 Alston (n 1), "Ships passing in the night."

19 Paul Gready and Jonathan Ensor, "What do Human Rights Mean in Development?," in *The Palgrave handbook of international development*, ed. Jean Grugel and Daniel Hammett (London: Palgrave Macmillan, 2016), 453.

20 Siobhan McInerney-Lankford and Hans-Otto Sano, *Human Rights Indicators in Development* (Washington: The World Bank, 2010); United Nations Development Group, Mainstreaming Human Rights In Development (2013).

21 Shyama Kuruvilla et al., "The Millennium Development Goals and Human Rights: Realizing Shared Commitments," *Human Rights Quarterly* 34, no. 1 (2012): 176; OHCHR, Human rights and the Millennium Development Goals in practice: A review of country strategies and reporting, (New York and Geneva: UN, 2010); OHCHR, Claiming the Millennium Development Goals: A human rights approach, (New York and Geneva: UN, 2008).

22 United Nations, Short Transforming our world: The 2030 agenda for sustainable development. United Nations Development Group.

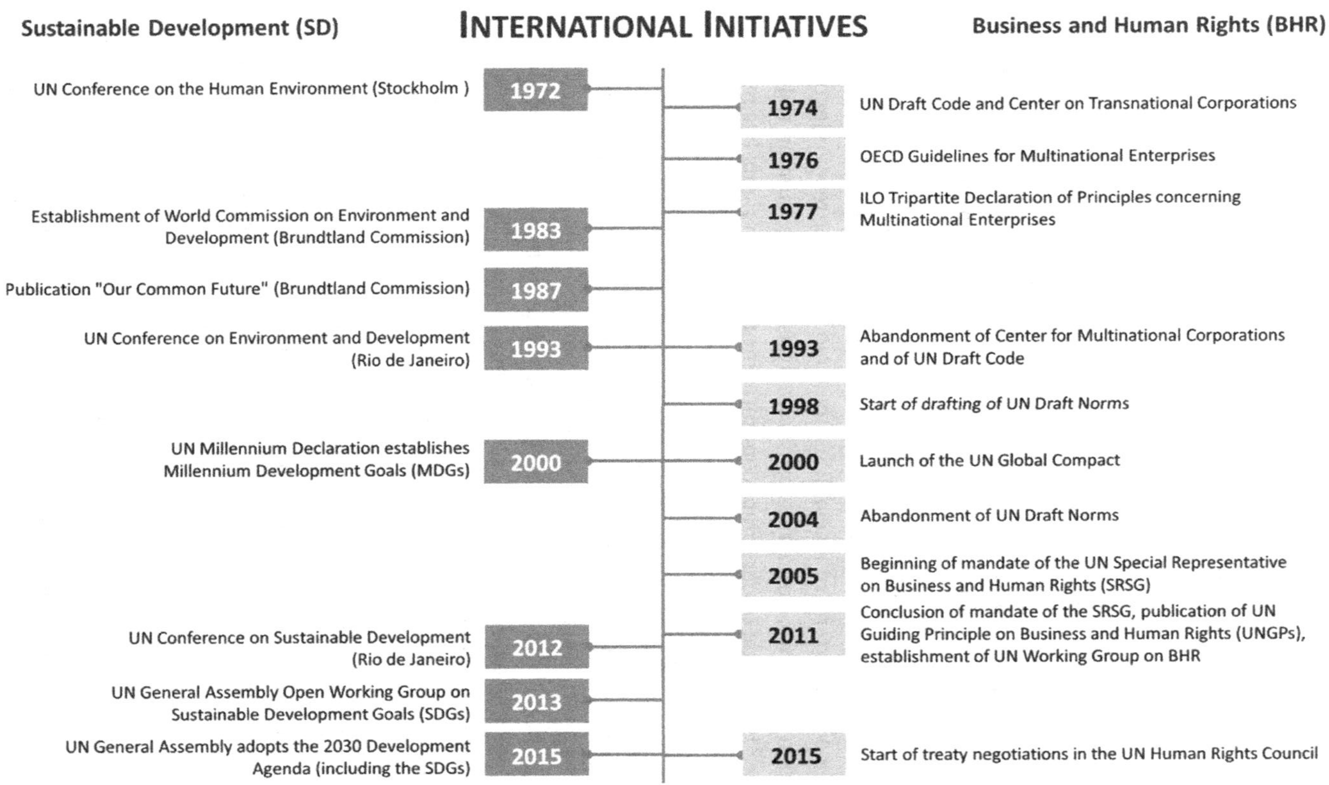

FIGURE 2.1 Timeline of initiatives on sustainable development and business and human rights[a]
Zagelmeyer and Sinkovics (2019), "MNEs, human rights and the SDGs" 7

shows that of the 169 SDG targets, 156 are linked to international human rights and labour standards.[23]

3 Corporate Reporting on Human Rights and Sustainable Development

3.1 *Background*

In the context of the sustainability agenda and the business and human rights agenda, both the SDGs and UNGPs encourage corporations to commit to sustainable development and human rights respectively. SDG target 12.6 explicitly encourages the adoption of sustainable practices and engagement in sustainability reporting and the second pillar of the UNGPs includes the expectation that companies explicitly declare their commitment to respect human rights, which can, for example, be accomplished by corporate human rights reporting. While extensive research has covered the other recommendations included in pillar two, human rights risk analysis as well as human rights due diligence,[24] the issue of corporate commitment to human rights has received scant attention.

This chapter addresses this gap and focuses on corporate commitment to human rights and sustainable development through analysing corporate disclosure information in the form of annual reports and sustainability reports. It provides a short overview of the topic of corporate reporting and introduces a framework for exploring and analysing corporate sustainability and human rights reporting, which informs the subsequent empirical analysis of sustainability and human rights -related reporting in the annual reports and the sustainability reports of German DAX-40 listed companies.

3.2 *Corporate Reporting*

Corporate reporting involves the disclosure of financial and non-financial information and can take many forms: financial reporting, corporate governance reporting, corporate social responsibility reporting, sustainability

---

23 The Danish Institute for Human Rights, Responsible business conduct as a cornerstone of the 2030 Agenda – A look at the implications, The Danish Institute for Human Rights, Copenhagen (2019).

24 Surya Deva, "Mandatory human rights due diligence laws in Europe: A mirage for rightsholders?," *Leiden Journal of International Law* 36, no. 2 (2023): 1; Lise Smit et al., "Human rights due diligence in global supply chains: evidence of corporate practices to inform a legal standard," *International Journal of Human Rights* 25, no. 6 (2020): 945.

reporting and human rights reporting.[25] While financial reporting may be a regulatory requirement, voluntary non-financial reporting has increasingly become common practice, especially by larger corporations, responding to the expectations and 'demands of various stakeholder groups – investors, employees, consumers, communities, and regulators'.[26] Non-financial reporting usually addresses broad topics related to environmental, social, and governance (ESG) concerns, and frequently involves sustainability reporting[27] and, more recently, also human rights reporting.[28]

Most companies, especially those listed on the stock-market, publish annual reports that provide a general view of company data, and may include information on management, strategy, the financial situation, and environmental and/or social issues. Other types of reports, such as sustainability reports, CSR reports or human rights reports, take a more focused approach, but frequently vary in terms of format, structure, content, and publication frequency. Over the years, sustainability reports and CSR reports – companies usually choose either label – have become established as a second pillar of corporate reporting, with many companies publishing a sustainability report or CSR report on an annual basis. More recently, some companies have moved towards integrated reporting, ie, to include non-financial information in their annual reports.[29]

3.3 *Analytical Framework*

The literature on non-financial and/or social reporting is dominated by three approaches, namely legitimacy theory, stakeholder theory, and signalling theory. 'Legitimacy is a generalised perception or assumption that the actions of an entity are desirable, proper or appropriate with in some socially constructed

25 Giovanna Michelon, Grzegorz Trojanowski, and Ruth Sealy, "Narrative Reporting: State of the Art and Future Challenges," *Accounting in Europe* 19, no. 1 (2022), https://doi.org/10.1080/17449480.2021.1900582.

26 Victoria Shoaf, Eva K. Jermakowicz, and Barry Jay Epstein, "Toward Sustainability and Integrated Reporting," *Review of Business* 38, no. 1 (Jan 2018): 1.

27 Ibid. "

28 Stefan Zagelmeyer, "Human Rights Reporting of BRIC and Non-BRIC MNEs: An Exploratory Comparative Analysis," in *The Changing Strategies of International Business*, ed. A. Chidlow et al. (Cham: Palgrave Macmillan, 2019), 157.

29 Janine Maniora, "Is Integrated Reporting Really the Superior Mechanism for the Integration of Ethics into the Core Business Model? An Empirical Analysis," *Journal of Business Ethics* 140, no. 4 (Feb 2017): 755; Patrick Velte, "Archival research on integrated reporting: a systematic review of main drivers and the impact of integrated reporting on firm value," *Journal of Management and Governance* 26, no. 3 (2021): 997.

system of norms, values, believes and definitions'.[30] The legitimacy theory argues that in order to obtain a 'social licence to operate',[31] corporations need to comply with values and norms that prevail in a particular institutional setting,[32] which is a necessary resource and prerequisite for the corporation's existence and success. Non-financial reporting, including sustainability reporting and human rights reporting, seeks to influence the perception of the corporation by its stakeholders by signalling how it meets the expectations, demands and requirements for being considered legitimate.

The stakeholder approach argues that the corporation is not only acting in the interests of the owners and investors, but that it must 'balance a multiplicity of stakeholder interests that can affect or be affected by the firm's actions'.[33] This is a political process in which different stakeholders urge the corporation to act in ways that are conducive to their interests and expectations. Following the instrumental approach to the stakeholder theory, one may distinguish stakeholders who are internal or external to the organisation. Internal stakeholders include, among others, the owners of the company, the workforce, or different actors from within the company, such as works councils. External stakeholders include actors in the external environment of business organisations, such as NGOs, government, consumers, or suppliers.

With respect to communicating corporate commitment to human rights, a third approach is particularly relevant. Based on the assumption of information asymmetries in the relationship of two parties, which may involve a market relationship or another type of cooperation, the signalling theory suggests that the informational situation and credibility can be improved by one party sending signals (ie, relevant information) to the other party, improving decision-making and cooperation between the two parties and avoiding

30 Andreas Tan, Desmiyawati Benni, and Warda Liani, "Determinants of corporate social responsibility disclosure and investor reaction," Article, *International Journal of Economics and Financial Issues* 6, no. 4 (2016): 12.

31 Craig Deegan, "The legitimising effect of social and environmental disclosures – a theoretical foundation," *Accounting, Auditing & Accountability Journal* 15, no. 3 (2002): 290; Craig Deegan, "Organizational legitimacy as a motive for sustainability reporting," in *Sustainability Accounting and Accountability*, ed. Unerman, Jeffrey, Jan Bebbington, and Brendan O'Dwyer (Abington: Routledge, 2014), 248.

32 Rüdiger Hahn and Michael Kühnen, "Determinants of sustainability reporting: A review of results, trends, theory, and opportunities in an expanding field of research," Review, *Journal of Cleaner Production* 59 (2013), 5.

33 Linda Thorne, Lois S. Mahoney, and Giacomo Manetti, "Motivations for issuing standalone CSR reports: a survey of Canadian firms," *Accounting, Auditing & Accountability Journal* 27, no. 4 (2014): 689.

adverse selection when it comes to choice of cooperation partners.[34] As far as social reporting and human rights reporting is concerned, this perspective suggests that companies signal their behavioural values and other information they consider relevant to the respective stakeholders to improve their reputation and gain approval and thus legitimacy. While some corporations may use several reporting channels and a higher intensity of reporting to signal their human rights commitment to different stakeholders, other companies try to hide or selectively disclose information.[35]

4 Methods, Data, and Analysis

4.1 *Research Objectives and Dataset*

Corporate disclosure information is assumed to indicate the commitment of business organisations to goals that align with the expectations of specific stakeholders. Specifically, we assume that corporate disclosure information with respect to sustainable development and human rights serves the purpose of signalling commitment to the respective stakeholders.

Against this background, the empirical part of this section will analyse the extent to which multinational companies engage in disclosing information related to the sustainable development goals and human rights. As argued above, corporate disclosure serves the purpose of signalling information to and meeting the expectations and requirements of relevant stakeholders, the ultimate goal being to obtain and/or keep the social licence to operate in a particular institutional setting. While this may require a specific configuration of reporting activities, potentially involving multi-channel reporting, one may assume that the decisions on the channel-configuration and the information included in corporate disclosure is based on a cost benefit analysis and serves a strategic business purpose.

The subsequent empirical analysis seeks to map the extent to which corporate disclosure information refers to the sustainable development agenda and the international human rights agenda, and changes thereof over time, drawing on the annual reports and sustainability reports of German corporations

34 Michael Spence, *Market Signaling: Informational Transfer in Hiring and Related Screening Processes.* (Cambridge, MA: Harvard University Press, 1974); Will Drover, Matthew S. Wood, and Andrew C. Corbett, "Toward a Cognitive View of Signalling Theory: Individual Attention and Signal Set Interpretation," *Journal of Management Studies* 55, no. 2 (2018): 209.

35 Hahn and Kühnen (n 33), "Determinants of sustainability reporting."

listed in the DAX 40 stock market index in 2021. Beyond describing (i) the incidence and development of reporting on sustainability-related and human rights-related issues, the empirical analysis also seeks to (ii) analyse the relationship between SDG reporting and human rights reporting. Following claims that the sustainability development agenda and the human rights agenda develop in parallel without much interaction,[36] the empirical analysis investigates whether corporate disclosure activities in relation to sustainable development and human rights are evolving independently of each other, reinforcing each other, or are involved in a substitutive relationship.

The dataset includes two types of corporate disclosure documents, annual reports and sustainability reports, for 2010 and 2020, published by companies included in the DAX 40 stock market index of 2021. The year 2010 was chosen because it represents the year before the UNGPs were agreed, so that the two data points allow for a before and after comparison. In addition, with respect to sustainability, the MDGs would be in their tenth year.

Reports were collected from different sources, including the EIKON Refinitiv database and corporate websites. The documents, usually in PDF format, were first downloaded and then transformed into (1) readable PDF files and then (2) RTF document files, using OCR software. This was necessary because, first, a considerable proportion of the downloaded files were image-only PDFs, while others were print- or read-protected, and still others included scrambled text; and second, the software packages used for text analysis required PDF format and RTF format for different types of analyses.

Table 2.1 provides an overview of all reports included in the dataset. All companies included in the dataset published an annual report in the year 2020. Seven of the companies did not exist in 2010, and thus did not publish an annual report. Sustainability reports have become very popular among corporations. However, there is considerable variation with respect to title, format, content, and detail. Most companies publish this type of report as a sustainability report, or a CSR report, but some use alternative titles such as 'citizenship report' or 'social performance report'.

As social reporting can take many forms, from full-text reports of several hundred pages to presentation-style or handout-style documents, each of the potential documents included in the analysis was checked for information on management structures, strategy, and policies and practices concerning sustainability and/or corporate social responsibility. Presentation-style and handout-style documents were not included in the analysis. Eighteen of the

36 Alston (n 1), "Ships passing in the night."

TABLE 2.1 Corporate reports of DAX 40 corporations (2010 and 2020)

	Annual reports		Sustainability reports	
	2010	**2020**	**2010**	**2020**
Adidas	x	x	x	
Airbus	x	x		
Allianz	x	x	x	x
BASF	x	x		
Bayer	x	x	x	x
BMW	x	x	x	
Beiersdorf	x	x	x	x
Brenntag	x	x		x
Continental	x	x		x
Covestro		x		x
Daimler	x	x	x	x
Delivery Hero		x		
Deutsche Bank	x	x		
Deutsche Boerse	x	x	x	
Deutsche Post	x	x	x	
Deutsche Telekom	x	x	x	x
Deutsche Wohnen	x	x		x
E.ON	x	x	x	x
Fresenius Medical Care	x	x		
Fresenius	x	x		
Heidelberg Cement	x	x		x
HelloFresh		x		x
Henkel	x	x	x	x
Infineon	x	x		x
Linde	x	x	x	x
Merck	x	x		x
MTU	x	x		x

TABLE 2.1 Corporate reports of DAX 40 corporations (2010 and 2020) (*cont.*)

	Annual reports		**Sustainability reports**	
Muenchener Rueck	x	x		x
Puma	x	x		
Qiagen	x	x	x	
RWE	x	x	x	x
SAP	x	x	x	
Sartorius	x	x		
Siemens	x	x	x	x
Siemens Energy		x		x
Siemens Health		x		
Symrise	x	x	x	x
Volkswagen	x	x	x	x
Vonovia		x		x
Zalando		x		x
number of reports	*33*	*40*	*18*	*25*

corporations published a sustainability report in 2010, increasing to 25 corporations in 2020. Seven of the 33 corporations that existed in both years did not publish any sustainability report at all, while six of these corporations published a sustainability report only in 2010.

4.2 *Overview of the Structure of the Empirical Analysis*

The empirical analysis involved both word frequency analysis as well as text-mining processes, using the Provalis WordStat software. The following section provides an introduction to and overview of the different steps of the analysis.

4.2.1 Word Frequency Analysis

With respect to the sustainable development goals, word count analysis included searching for the following keywords and phrases: 'millennium development goal', 'millennium development goals', 'MDG', 'MDGs', 'sustainable development goal', 'sustainable development goals', 'SDG' and 'SDGs'. The obtained word frequency data for the different search terms were then added to yield the total number of count data for the word frequency variable 'MDG'/ 'SDG'. For human rights, the search terms included 'human right' and 'human rights', and the word frequency data for the search terms were then added to generate the word frequency variable 'Human Rights'.

Word frequency data measuring the total number of keywords occurring in a text is a useful first step in text analysis, showing whether and how frequently specific terms or phrases are used in the analysed text. The next step in the analysis was then to measure the relative importance of a particular concept of phrase by calculating the frequency in relation to the total number of words in the text. For this purpose, we identified and used the total number of words included in the respective document, as calculated by Microsoft Word. As some of the analysed documents included several hundred thousand words, the following sections report the relative frequency scores per 10,000 words of the document.

4.2.2 Text-Mining Analysis

To analyse aspects related to human rights, an existing and validated multidimensional dictionary for the analysis of corporate social responsibility was used.[37] This dictionary covers four dimensions, namely employees, human rights, social and community, and environment. The human rights dimension, which was used for the purpose of this analysis, includes 297 key terms or phrases.

To measure aspects related to the sustainable development goals in text documents, the University of Auckland has developed a mapping tool, which allows scholars to analyse text data with respect to the SDGs 1 to 16, i.e., all SDGs except for SDG 17 (partnerships). This mapping tool includes a total of over 2300 keywords, which were transformed into a WordStat-compatible dictionary to measure the extent to which the text documents cover SDG-related terms and topics.

4.2.3 Structure of the Analysis

The analysis proceeded in four stages. Stage I included the separate word frequency analysis of the annual reports and the sustainability reports for 2010 and 2020 with respect to both SDG and human rights keywords. For those companies which published annual reports in 2010 and 2020, word frequency differences between both data points were calculated. This information was

37 Nadra Pencle and Irina Mălăescu, "What's in the Words? Development and Validation of a Multidimensional Dictionary for CSR and Application Using Prospectuses," *Journal of Emerging Technologies in Accounting* 13, no. 2 (2016): 109.

used to identify increases, decreases, or no change with respect to word frequency. Finally, this stage involved aggregating word frequency data by adding the work frequency scores for both annual reviews and sustainability reviews for 2010 and 2020 respectively.

Stage II involves the calculation of a relative word frequency score that measures the relative word count frequency of the respective SDG or human rights keywords per 10,000 words of the respective document. This provides information on the relative importance of the keywords in relation to the length of the document. As a standard measure applied to all documents, this variable also allows us to compare the relative importance of keywords across companies and across time. Then, the differences between both data points in 2010 and 2020 were calculated for each corporation to capture whether the relative frequency of the keywords had increased, decreased, or remained constant. Similar to stage I, the data was aggregated by adding up the scores for annual reports and sustainability reports.

Stage III involves the text-mining analysis in WordStat, drawing on the two dictionaries for SDG and CSR/human rights. The analysis yielded separate word frequency scores for SDG and human rights, and for both types of reports published in 2010 and 2020. Similar to stages I and II, calculating the difference of work frequency scores between two years allows for comparisons over time and the identification of changes. Finally, the data was then aggregated for both types of reports.

And stage IV used the word frequency scores generated during stage III and related these values to the total length (in words) of the respective document, generating a word frequency score per 10,000 words of each document, and for the summative score for both documents.

5 Empirical Findings

5.1 *Word Frequency Analysis*

5.1.1 Stage I: Total Number of Keywords

The following sections reports on the most important findings of the stage I analysis, covering (i) the annual reports, (ii) the sustainability reports, and (iii) the aggregate word frequency analysis for both reports together.

Let us first look at the analysis of the annual report. In 2010, Siemens AG was the only corporations to include a reference (and only one) to the MDGs/SDGs. By 2020, 24 of the 40 corporations in the dataset included between one and 58 references to the MDGs/SDGs in their annual reports. Of the 33 companies that published annual reports in both years, 2010 and 2020, 20 companies had moved from zero references to include information on the SDGs, and one corporation (Siemens AG) stopped referring to the SDG explicitly.

Six of the 18 reports in 2010 refer explicitly to the MDG/SDG. By 2020, 24 of the 25 sustainability reports referred to the MDGs/SDGs, with all 12 companies with sustainability reports in 2010 and 2020 increasing the frequency of using the MDGs/SDGs in their reports. As far as the aggregate word frequency analysis for both types of reports combined is concerned, in 2010 six of the 33 corporations in the sample included references to the MDGs/SDGs, increasing to 36 of the 40 corporations in 2020, with overall 31 corporations of 33 with reports in both years increasing the number of references to the MDGs/SDGs.

Turning to human rights, 15 of the 33 annual reports published in 2010 included one or more references to human rights, increasing to 35 out of 40 in 2020. For all 33 corporations with annual reports in 2010 and 2020, 29 corporations increased the number of references to human rights, while three corporations decreased the number of references to human rights. Of these three, Henkel AG and RWE AG stopped referring to human rights altogether.

Looking at sustainability reports published in 2010, 16 of the 18 corporations included in the sample for 2010 refer to human rights. This number increases to 25 out of 26 in 2020. Of all companies with sustainability reports in 2010 and 2020, 11 of the 13 corporations increase the number of references, while two corporations decreased the number of references to human rights, with Deutsche Post dropping their references to human rights. As far as the aggregate analysis for both types of reports together is concerned, 22 of the 33 corporations included references to human rights in 2010, increasing to 39 out of 40 in 2020. For companies with reports in both years, 30 of the 33 corporations increase the number of references to human rights, with three corporations (Adidas, Deutsche Bank, Deutsche Post) decreasing the total number of references to human rights.

5.1.2 Stage II: Relative Proportion of Keywords

While the total number of words gives the first indication of whether corporate disclosure information covers particular concepts, it is an imperfect measure as it does not take into consideration the specific format and length of the respective documents. For example, the length of the annual report documents in the sample ranges from 19,950 words (Deutsche Wohnen, 2010) to 282,488 words (Deutsche Bank, 2020). The respective figures for sustainability reports are 7,573 (Covestro, 2020) to 124,601 (Deutsche Telekom, 2010).

To improve the comparability between documents of the same category, Table 2.2 below includes information on the total number of keywords in relation to the length of the document, measured by keywords per 10,000 words

TABLE 2.2 Scores of the word frequency analysis (per 10,000 words)

	Annual reports				Sustainability reports				Annual & sustainability reports			
	MDG/ SDG		Human rights		MDG/SDG		Human rights		MDG/SDG		Human rights	
	2010	**2020**	**2010**	**2020**	**2010**	**2020**	**2010**	**2020**	**2010**	**2020**	**2010**	**2020**
Adidas	0,0	0,4	0,3	1,2	0,0		3,2		0,0	0,4	3,4	1,2
Airbus	0,0	1,7	0,5	8,5					0,0	1,7	0,5	8,5
Allianz	0,0	0,0	0,0	1,7	0,0	6,7	1,2	11,1	0,0	6,7	1,2	12,8
BASF	0,0	2,5	0,5	4,2					0,0	2,5	0,5	4,2
Bayer	0,0	0,5	0,0	1,8	0,6	2,4	4,6	12,9	0,6	2,9	4,6	14,7
BMW	0,0	0,6	0,2	3,1	0,3		3,3		0,3	0,6	3,5	3,1
Beiersdorf	0,0	1,3	0,0	1,9	0,0	19,1	11,6	2,2	0,0	20,4	11,6	4,1
Brenntag	0,0	0,0	0,0	0,4		3,9		10,0	0,0	3,9	0,0	10,4
Continental	0,0	0,0	0,0	0,5		1,4		3,4	0,0	1,4	0,0	4,0
Covestro		3,9		4,0		25,1		18,5		29,0		22,5
Daimler	0,0	0,3	0,3	3,1	0,0	2,4	4,7	17,3	0,0	2,8	4,9	20,5
Delivery Hero		0,4		0,7						0,4		0,7
Deutsche Bank	0,0	0,0	0,0	0,1					0,0	0,0	0,0	0,1
Deutsche Boerse	0,0	2,6	0,0	0,2	0,0		3,5		0,0	2,6	3,5	0,2
Deutsche Post	0,0	0,5	0,0	0,9	0,2		3,6		0,2	0,5	3,6	0,9
Deutsche Telekom	0,0	3,0	0,1	1,9	0,0	8,4	1,5	14,9	0,0	11,4	1,6	16,8
Deutsche Wohnen	0,0	0,0	0,0	1,9		2,9		4,6	0,0	2,9	0,0	6,5
E.ON	0,0	0,2	0,0	2,3	0,3	2,7	9,5	8,7	0,3	2,9	9,5	11,0
Fresenius Med Care	0,0	0,0	0,1	2,2					0,0	0,0	0,1	2,2
Fresenius	0,0	0,4	0,0	7,2					0,0	0,4	0,0	7,2
Heidelberg Cement	0,0	0,0	0,0	1,9		0,5		8,6	0,0	0,5	0,0	10,5
HelloFresh		0,0		0,0		6,2		0,7		6,2		0,7

TABLE 2.2 Scores of the word frequency analysis (per 10,000 words) (*cont.*)

			Annual reports		Sustainability reports				Annual & sustainability reports			
Henkel	0,0	0,0	0,1	0,0	1,3	5,4	2,2	6,1	1,3	5,4	2,3	6,1
Infineon	0,0	0,0	0,2	0,1		4,2		16,2	0,0	4,2	0,2	16,3
Linde	0,0	0,0	0,0	0,1	0,0	4,3	1,3	14,9	0,0	4,3	1,3	15,0
Merck	0,0	1,1	0,1	0,1		2,7		15,2	0,0	3,8	0,1	15,3
MTU	0,0	0,0	0,0	2,4		25,7		17,8	0,0	25,7	0,0	20,2
Muenchener Rueck	0,0	0,0	0,0	0,4		2,0		9,1	0,0	2,0	0,0	9,5
Puma	0,0	1,5	0,7	2,3					0,0	1,5	0,7	2,3
Qiagen	0,0	0,1	0,0	1,2	0,0		0,0		0,0	0,1	0,0	1,2
RWE	0,0	3,9	0,1	0,0	0,0	3,2	3,7	7,0	0,0	7,1	3,8	7,0
SAP	0,0	0,7	0,1	3,5	0,0		6,3		0,0	0,7	6,4	3,5
Sartorius	0,0	0,0	0,0	2,3					0,0	0,0	0,0	2,3
Siemens	0,1	0,0	0,1	0,1	0,2	13,9	2,0	21,1	0,3	13,9	2,0	21,1
Siemens Energy		0,1		0,1		21,4		18,0		21,5		18,1
Siemens Health		0,0		0,0						0,0		0,0
Symrise	0,0	7,0	0,0	0,8	0,0	5,4	0,0	13,4	0,0	12,4	0,0	14,2
Volkswagen	0,0	0,1	0,1	1,1	0,0	2,2	3,3	13,8	0,0	2,3	3,3	14,9
Vonovia		1,0		1,3		3,0		6,1		4,0		7,4
Zalando		0,0		0,0		0,0		11,6		0,0		11,6
number of reports	*33*	*40*	*33*	*40*	*18*	*25*	*18*	*25*	*33*	*40*	*33*	*40*

in the document. To illustrate the point, even though Covestro's sustainability report for 2020 is relatively short in terms of word count (7,573), the values for the relative keyword score (keywords per 10,000 words) are relatively high with, 3.9 for SDGs and 4.0 for human rights, while the respective score for the 2020 annual report of Deutsche Bank (length: 282,488 words) is much lower at 0.0 for SDGs and 0.1 for human rights. Yet, this type of analysis is limited in that it measures the relative quantity of keywords and does not allow for any more sophisticated interpretation of the content of the report.

Without going into every detail, the analysis of annual reports with respect to the relative frequency of keywords related to the SDGs and human rights in annual reports and sustainability reports for both years of observation is relatively consistent with the analysis of the absolute frequency of keywords reported in the previous section.

Yet, the analysis of the development of the relative keyword quantity provides for some more nuanced findings with respect to changes of overall reporting (annual reports and sustainability reports combined) on human rights. In contrast to the total word count analysis, which yields that 30 of the 33 companies in the sample operating in 2010 and 2020 have increased the use of the term 'human rights', with three companies reducing the use of the keyword of human rights, this trend is more pronounced when looking at the changes with respect to relative quantity of keywords in corporate disclosure; while none of the corporations had reduced the relative quantity of SDG-related keywords, six corporations which reduced the relative quantity of human rights-related keywords between 2010 and 2020.

5.2 *Text-Mining Analysis*

5.2.1 Stage III: Total Number of Keywords

In contrast to word frequency analysis, which accounts for the occurrence of specific keywords in a particular document, text-mining analysis is more sophisticated in that it seeks to capture the extent to which particular topics, measured through a set of related words of a (ideally validated) topic-related dictionary, are covered in the content of a particular document. Even though text-mining analysis includes different analytical methods and tools,[38] the reported analysis has taken the relatively simple approach of using existing dictionaries to map the incidence and change of SDGs and human rights reporting in annual reports and sustainability reports in 2010 and 2020.

In contrast to the keyword search reported above, which searched for a small number of keywords directly mapping the MDGs/SDGs and human rights, using dictionaries with several hundred of words to search for topical themes yields far higher numbers of 'hits' in the respective documents, without searching for specific keywords such as MDGs or SDGs, or phrases such as 'sustainable development goals' and 'human rights'. Thus, the findings reported in the subsequent sections cannot be directly compared to the word frequency analysis. In addition, as the dictionaries for SDGs and human rights

38 Charu C. Aggarwal and Cheng Xiang Zhai, *An Introduction to Text Mining* (Los Angeles: Sage, 2018); Ted Kwartler, *Text mining in practice with R* (Hoboken: Wiley, 2017).

were designed separately, it is difficult to directly compare the results for SDG and human rights and should be interpreted separately. However, since this chapter covers development from 2010 to 2020, the findings should give a good indication of the changes in SDG and human rights coverage over time. Similar to the structure of the report on word frequency analysis, the following sections will outline the most important observations of text-mining analysis, starting with the analysis of annual reports, followed by sustainability reports and the analysis for both types of reports combined.

Overall, in both 2010 and 2020, all annual reports and sustainability reports in the sample, and thus also both reports combined, covered material related to the SDGs and human rights, as specified by the respective dictionaries. Although this finding does not seem spectacular, it is noteworthy that apparently even annual reports of all companies cover topical themes that seem to relate to the SDG and human rights, opening opportunities for much more comprehensive and detailed research. Instead of reporting on descriptive information on specific companies or elaborating on the summary statistics for cross-sectional data, which, for example, would show significant variation in coverage across companies, the following paragraphs will focus on the changes between 2010 and 2020. With respect to SDG coverage in annual reports, the reported count values have increased for 31 of the 33 companies, while the respective value decreased for two (Linde AG and Siemens). Focusing on human rights, 28 corporations increased human rights reporting, with fewer mentions by five companies.

Focusing on sustainability reports, SDG reporting intensity increased for 11 of the 12 companies for which sustainability reports existed in 2010 and 2020, while it decreased for two companies for Deutsche Telekom. With respect to human rights reporting, the picture is quite similar, with an additional company, Beiersdorf, decreasing human rights reporting. As far as the analysis of both annual reports and sustainability reports combined is concerned, 30 (3) of the 33 companies increased (decreased) SDG reporting, while 28 (5) corporations increased (decreased) human rights reporting.

5.2.2 Stage IV: Relative Proportion of Keywords

Similar to word frequency analysis, focusing on count data in text-mining allows for the identification of the presence of particular topical themes in documents. However, given the variation in terms of format, structure and length, relative count data (i.e., words or phrases per 10,000 words in the document) provides information on the relative quantitative importance of different topical themes across corporations in the respective document or set of documents, and changes thereof over time. Table 2.3 provides an overview

TABLE 2.3 Score of the text-mining analysis (per 10,000 words)

	Annual reports				Sustainability reports				Annual & sustainability reports			
	MDG/SDG		Human rights		MDG/SDG		Human rights		MDG/SDG		Human rights	
	2010	2020	2010	2020	2010	2020	2010	2020	2010	2020	2010	2020
Adidas	23,3	39,3	192,4	212,4	961,4		3724,2		984,7	39,3	3916,5	212,4
Airbus	35,1	59,5	170,7	306,7					35,1	59,5	170,7	306,7
Allianz	14,4	43,8	191,1	185,0	1277,0	1963,0	3588,2	3685,9	1291,5	2006,8	3779,3	3870,9
BASF	55,2	85,0	245,6	296,9					55,2	85,0	245,6	296,9
Bayer	35,5	66,2	121,3	227,7	1087,2	1942,5	2666,8	3771,9	1122,7	2008,6	2788,0	3999,6
BMW	19,9	54,6	210,0	200,5	1046,1		2845,6		1066,0	54,6	3055,6	200,5
Beiersdorf	17,4	76,5	222,2	189,7	1001,5	1922,1	4011,5	3057,9	1018,9	1998,7	4233,8	3247,6
Brenntag	13,7	32,9	191,6	163,9		1128,2		3109,4	13,7	1161,2	191,6	3273,3
Continental	17,1	31,3	194,8	188,6		688,0		2727,0	17,1	719,3	194,8	2915,6
Covestro		103,2		233,9		2178,8		2852,2		2282,0		3086,1
Daimler	19,2	37,7	235,6	280,7	841,9	1168,2	2870,8	2843,7	861,1	1205,9	3106,4	3124,4
Delivery Hero		35,0		153,5						35,0		153,5
Deutsche Bank	12,4	27,6	204,2	448,7					12,4	27,6	204,2	448,7
Deutsche Boerse	12,4	26,1	194,3	180,3	658,4		3261,2		670,7	26,1	3455,6	180,3
Deutsche Post	10,8	42,0	134,2	152,7	1103,1		3883,3		1113,9	42,0	4017,5	152,7

TABLE 2.3 Score of the text-mining analysis (per 10,000 words) (*cont.*)

	Annual reports				Sustainability reports				Annual & sustainability reports			
Deutsche Telekom	14,0	28,5	187,2	291,7	809,0	1223,9	3101,9	3061,1	823,0	1252,5	3289,1	3352,8
Deutsche Wohnen	20,6	45,7	215,0	139,3		1703,2		2884,3	20,6	1748,9	215,0	3023,6
E.ON	32,1	43,2	167,0	189,9	1019,3	1147,8	3693,7	2706,6	1051,5	1191,0	3860,7	2896,5
Fresenius Med Care	42,5	71,2	258,1	339,8					42,5	71,2	258,1	339,8
Fresenius	60,5	104,0	248,1	431,6					60,5	104,0	248,1	431,6
Heidelberg Cement	28,7	46,9	186,4	182,8		1514,3		2953,7	28,7	1561,2	186,4	3136,4
HelloFresh		25,2		68,1		2336,4		3415,3		2361,6		3483,4
Henkel	19,2	54,4	215,4	237,9	906,5	1583,5	3564,4	3707,6	925,7	1638,0	3779,7	3945,4
Infineon	29,4	32,9	178,1	146,9		1630,0		3422,3	29,4	1663,0	178,1	3569,2
Linde	30,8	19,7	181,8	99,1	1211,8	1644,6	4659,3	4724,7	1242,5	1664,4	4841,1	4823,8
Merck	47,6	56,1	214,8	296,7		1372,8		3796,2	47,6	1428,9	214,8	4092,9
MTU	18,0	39,7	217,6	177,1		1647,6		3977,3	18,0	1687,3	217,6	4154,4
Muenchener Rueck	19,9	40,5	179,3	187,0		1635,8		3115,4	19,9	1676,3	179,3	3302,4
Puma	58,0	82,4	249,0	175,3					58,0	82,4	249,0	175,3
Qiagen	35,2	45,9	214,1	180,3	1252,4		3980,1		1287,6	45,9	4194,1	180,3
RWE	38,6	57,2	143,8	114,2	1057,6	1413,9	2269,1	3115,4	1096,2	1471,1	2412,8	3229,6
SAP	25,6	73,3	220,1	352,2	1129,2		3683,5		1154,8	73,3	3903,5	352,2
Sartorius	27,8	49,2	181,3	133,4					27,8	49,2	181,3	133,4
Siemens	36,3	27,9	225,0	76,2	1360,3	1517,3	2154,0	3529,8	1396,6	1545,2	2379,0	3605,9
Siemens Energy		58,9		137,3		1831,7		2993,8		1890,6		3131,0

TABLE 2.3 Score of the text-mining analysis (per 10,000 words) (*cont.*)

	Annual reports				**Sustainability reports**				**Annual & sustainability reports**			
Siemens Health		32,0		148,6						32,0		148,6
Symrise	33,3	104,6	229,1	54,1	590,6	1540,1	3195,3	3825,9	623,9	1644,8	3424,4	3880,1
Volkswagen	20,1	46,0	181,8	228,6	774,4	1475,9	2268,9	2661,0	794,5	1521,9	2450,7	2889,6
Vonovia		52,6		189,1		1566,5		3137,9		1619,1		3326,9
Zalando		25,2		116,6		1655,6		2644,7		1680,8		2761,3
number of reports	*33*	*40*	*33*	*40*	*18*	*25*	*18*	*25*	*33*	*40*	*33*	*40*

of the text-mining analysis, reporting on the overall frequency of words per 10,000 words in the document from the SDG and human rights dictionaries in annual reports and sustainability reports.

With respect to SDG reporting, the analysis of annual reports and sustainability reports separately show similar characteristics, as compared to the analysis in the previous section. However, there are noticeable differences concerning human rights reporting as well as concerning changes in terms of the combined coverage by annual or sustainability reports. As far as human rights reporting in annual reports, sustainability reports and the combination of the two reports are concerned, all companies in the respective samples cover aspects related to human rights. However, when looking at changes over time, there are noticeable differences in terms of the majority of companies (17 out of 33) reducing the quantity of human rights-related material in annual reports between 2010 and 2022. When analysing sustainability reports, however, two-thirds of companies (8 out of 12) increased the relative quantity of human rights reporting, while the remainder reduced the relative quantity of human rights-related reporting.

Finally, when analysing the relative quantity of SDGs-related and human rights-related reporting for the combined set of documents (annual reports and sustainability reports together), SDG-related reporting was reduced at 6 out of 33 companies, while human rights-related reporting decreased at 11 out of 33 corporations.

6 Discussion and Conclusions

This chapter analysed corporate disclosure information published in annual reports and sustainability reports of multinational corporations listed in the DAX 40 stock market index published in 2010 and 2020. The aim here was to capture the commitment of business organisation to the SDGs and to human rights, assuming this type of disclosure information is intended to signal commitment to specific stakeholder expectations. The findings provide a complex account of corporate reporting on the SDGs and human rights. Even though word frequency analysis and text-mining analysis do not allow for interpretation with respect to the content of corporate policies and practices, the analysis yields some interesting observations.

The first two stages of the analysis provided a descriptive overview of the quantitative use, both in absolute and relative terms, of keywords in both types of corporate reports at two points in time. The analysis shows the increasing, at least quantitative, importance of the SDGs in corporate reporting during the observation period. While only 1 company out of 33 referred to the MDGs/SDGs in 2010, this number increased to 24 out of 40 in 2020, with only one ceasing to report on MDGs/SDGs. Looking at annual reports and sustainability reports combined, the respective increase was from 6 out of 33 in 2010 to 36 out of 40 in 2020, representing a triumphant advance of sustainable development reporting in corporate reporting.

There has also been an increase in corporate reports referring to human rights, but the development is slightly different, starting from a higher level, and with a sizeable proportion of corporations reducing the number of mentions of human rights in their corporate reports during the observation period. In 2010, 15 out of 33 corporations already referred to human rights in their annual reports, increasing to 35 out of 40 by 2020. When looking at the analysis for both types of reports combined, in 2020, 39 out of the 40 corporations in the sample referred to human rights in either of the two reports, but six companies reduced the overall quantity of the use of the concept of human rights in their reporting.

There are various implications of these findings, which should be addressed and explored in future research. First, there seems to be considerable variation across companies with respect to cross-sectional data for both 2010 and 2020. Can this variation be explained by the usual control variables, such as company size or industry affiliation? Or are there other factors involved, such as company-specific events, NGO pressure, media reports, changes in corporate strategy, management composition, or formal and informal institutions? At a more general level, replicating the analysis with companies from other countries and covering different time periods may yield interesting insights on whether the findings are generalisable.

Second, looking at changes over time, additional information on company-specific trajectories would be useful in identifying industry-specific or company-specific factors. Adding additional data points for the years between 2010 and 2020 could result in a more nuanced and detailed picture of change processes. Does the sustainability and/or human rights-related intensity of corporate reporting change for all companies at the same time, or are there industry-or company-specific trajectories? What explains cross-company variation over time? While the reporting intensity seems to generally increase with respect to SDG reporting, there are several companies reducing human rights reporting, both in absolute and relative terms. How can this be explained?

Third, the findings show that purely quantitative keyword frequency count-based analysis of corporate disclosure information should be treated with caution, especially analysis that focuses exclusively on total count data, as it does not consider the characteristics of the analysed documents. In the reported analysis, moving from total count data to relative count data provided a more nuanced and differentiated picture of the reporting structures. Compared to the overall picture based on total count data that SDG-related and human rights-related reporting is on the increase, the relative count data show that a small but noticeable number of additional companies were reducing the quantity of human rights-related keywords between 2010 and 2020. This requires further investigation.

Fourth, moving from keyword search and word frequency analysis to text-mining methods confirms and reinforces the previous observation, especially with respect to relative reporting intensity concerning SDG-related and human rights-related issues over time. It is noteworthy that, already in 2010, without explicitly and expressively reporting on the SDGs and human rights, SDG-related and human rights-related topics were covered in all annual reports and all sustainability reports. However, when looking at the relative importance of SDG-related and human rights-related reporting over time, it is intriguing to see that the majority of companies in the dataset has reduced the relative quantity of human rights-related keywords (per 10,000 words) in annual reports, and that a sizeable number of companies reduced the relative quantity of SDG-related and human rights-related reporting between 2010 and 2020 when considering both the annual report and the sustainability report together.

From the business ethics, responsible business and business and human rights perspectives, the findings in this chapter raises several questions to be addressed in future research. Do these changes follow a linear trend? What are the drivers of the respective developments? How are these changes reflected in the qualitative content of the respective report, and of policies and practices? Or could it be that the general perception of the increasing importance of the SDGs and human rights in corporate disclosure information is just related to an as-many-boxes-as-you-can-tick exercise of including buzzwords in the respective reports, without corporations engaging substantively with the SDGs and human rights?

Bibliography

Books

Aggarwal, Charu C., and Cheng Xiang Zhai. *An Introduction to Text Mining*. Los Angeles: Sage, 2018.

Deva, Surya, and David Bilchitz. *Building a Treaty on Business and Human Rights – Context and Contours*. Cambridge: Cambridge University Press, 2017.

Kwartler, Ted. *Text Mining in Practice with R*. Hoboken: Wiley, 2017.

McInerney-Lankford, Siobhan, and Hans-Otto Sano. Human Rights Indicators in Development. Washington: The World Bank, 2010.

Ruggie, John Gerard. *Just Business: Multinational Corporations and Human Rights.* New York: W. W. Norton & Company, 2013.

Spence, M. *Market Signalling: Informational Transfer in Hiring and Related Screening Processes.* Cambridge, MA: Harvard University Press, 1974.

World Commission On Environment and Development. *Our Common Future.* Oxford: Oxford University Press, 1987.

Chapters in Edited Books

Deegan, Craig. "Organizational Legitimacy as a Motive for Sustainability Reporting." In *Sustainability Accounting and Accountability*, edited by Unerman, Jeffrey, Jan Bebbington and Brendan O'Dwyer, 248–72. Abington: Routledge, 2014.

Gready, Paul, and Jonathan Ensor. "What Do Human Rights Mean In development?" In *The Palgrave Handbook of International Development*, edited by Jean Grugel and Daniel Hammett, 453–70. London: Palgrave Macmillan, 2016.

Sen, Amartya. "Development as a Capability Expansion." In *Readings in Human Development*, edited by S. Fukuda-Parr, 41–58. Oxford: Oxford University Press, 2003.

Articles

Alston, Philip "Ships Passing in the Night: The Current State of the Human Rights and Development Debate Seen through the Lens of the Millennium Development Goals." *Human Rights Quarterly* 27, no. 3 (Aug 2005): 755–829.

Backer, Larry Cata. "On the Evolution of the United Nations "Protect-Respect-Remedy Project": The State, the Corporation and Human Rights in a Global Governance Context." *Santa Clara Journal of International Law* 9, no. 2 (2011): 37–80.

Campagna, Juli. "United Nations Norms on the Responsibilities of Transnational Corporations and Other Business Enterprises with Regard to Human Rights: The International Community Asserts Binding Law on Global Rule Makers." *Marshall Law Review* 37 (2004): 1205–52.

Deegan, Craig. "The Legitimising Effect of Social and Environmental Disclosures – a Theoretical Foundation." *Accounting, Auditing & Accountability Journal* 15, no. 3 (2002): 282–311.

Deva, Surya. "Mandatory Human Rights Due Diligence Laws in Europe: A Mirage for Rightsholders?". *Leiden Journal of International Law* 36, no. 2 (2023): 1–26.

Drover, Will, Matthew S. Wood, and Andrew C. Corbett. "Toward a Cognitive View of Signalling Theory: Individual Attention and Signal Set Interpretation." *Journal of Management Studies* 55, no. 2 (2018): 209–31.

Feeney, Patricia. "Business and Human Rights: The Struggle for Accountability in the Un and the Future Direction of the Advocacy Agenda." *Sur – International Journal on Human Rights* 6, no. 11 (2009): 174–91.

Hahn, R., and M. Kühnen. "Determinants of Sustainability Reporting: A Review of Results, Trends, Theory, and Opportunities in an Expanding Field of Research." *Review. Journal of Cleaner Production* 59 (2013): 5–21.

Kuruvilla, Shyama, et al. "The Millennium Development Goals and Human Rights: Realizing Shared Commitments." *Human Rights Quarterly* 34, no. 1 (Feb 2012): 141–77.

Maniora, J. "Is Integrated Reporting Really the Superior Mechanism for the Integration of Ethics into the Core Business Model? An Empirical Analysis." *Journal of Business Ethics* 140, no. 4 (Feb 2017): 755–86.

McConnell, Lee. "Assessing the Feasibility of a Business and Human Rights Treaty." *International and Comparative Law Quarterly* 66, no. 01 (2016): 143–80.

Meyer, Klaus E. "Perspectives on Multinational Enterprises in Emerging Economies." *Journal of International Business Studies* 35, no. 4 (2004): 259–76.

Michelon, Giovanna, Grzegorz Trojanowski, and Ruth Sealy. "Narrative Reporting: State of the Art and Future Challenges." *Accounting in Europe* 19, no. 1 (2022): 7–47.

Pencle, Nadra, and Irina Mălăescu. "What's in the Words? Development and Validation of a Multidimensional Dictionary for CSR and Application Using Prospectuses." *Journal of Emerging Technologies in Accounting* 13, no. 2 (2016): 109–27.

Pogge, Thomas, and Mitu Sengupta. "Assessing the Sustainable Development Goals from a Human Rights Perspective." *Article. Journal of International and Comparative Social Policy* 32, no. 2 (2016): 83–97.

Sano, Hans-Otto. "Development and Human Rights: The Necessary, but Partial Integration of Human Rights and Development." *Human Rights Quarterly* 22, no. 3 (2000): 734–52.

Sauvant, Karl P. "The Negotiations of the United Nations Code of Conduct on Transnational Corporations: Experience and Lessons Learned." *The Journal of World Investment & Trade* 16, no. 1 (2015): 11–87.

Sen, Armatya. "Human Rights and Capabilities." *Journal of Human Development* 6, no. 2 (2005): 151–66.

Shoaf, Victoria, Eva K. Jermakowicz, and Barry Jay Epstein. "Toward Sustainability and Integrated Reporting." *Review of Business* 38, no. 1 (Jan 2018): 1–15.

Smit, Lise, Gabrielle Holly, Robert McCorquodale, and Stuart Neely. "Human Rights Due Diligence in Global Supply Chains: Evidence of Corporate Practices to Inform a Legal Standard." *International Journal of Human Rights* 25, no. 6 (2020): 945–073.

Tan, Andreas, Desmiyawati Benni, and Warda Liani. "Determinants of Corporate Social Responsibility Disclosure and Investor Reaction." *International Journal of Economics and Financial Issues* 6, no. 4 (2016): 11–17.

Thorne, Linda, Lois S. Mahoney, and Giacomo Manetti. "Motivations for Issuing Standalone CSR Reports: A Survey of Canadian Firms." *Accounting, Auditing & Accountability Journal* 27, no. 4 (2014): 686–714.

Velte, Patrick. "Archival Research on Integrated Reporting: A Systematic Review of Main Drivers and the Impact of Integrated Reporting on Firm Value." *Journal of Management and Governance* 26, no. 3 (2021): 997–1061.

Weissbrodt, David. "Corporate Human Rights Responsibilities." *Zeitschrift für Wirtschafts- und Unternehmensethik* 6, no. 3 (2005): 279–97.

Wettstein, Florian, Elisa Giuliani, Grazia D. Santangelo, and Günter K. Stahl. "International Business and Human Rights: A Research Agenda." *Journal of World Business* 54, no. 1 (Jan 2019): 54–65.

Zagelmeyer, Stefan. "Human Rights Reporting of Bric and Non-Bric Mnes: An Exploratory Comparative Analysis." In *The Changing Strategies of International Business*, edited by A. Chidlow, P. Ghauri, T. Buckley, E.C. Gardner, A. Qamar and E. Pickerimg, 157–74. Cham: Palgrave Macmillan, 2019.

Zagelmeyer, Stefan, and Rudolf R. Sinkovics. "MMEs, Human Rights and the SDGs – the Moderating Role of Business and Human Rights Governance." *Transnational Corporations* 26, no. 3 (2019): 1–30.

Official Documents

Human Rights Council. "Promotion and Protection of All Human Rights, Civil, Political, Economic, Social and Cultural Rights, Including the Right to Development: Protect, Respect and Remedy – a Framework for Business and Human Rights 2008." Report of the Special Representative of the Secretary-General on the Issue of Human Rights and Transnational Corporations and other Business Enterprises, John Ruggie. UN Human Rights Council, A/HRC/8/5. 7 April 2008.

OHCHR. *Claiming the Millennium Development Goals: A Human Rights Approach.* New York and Geneva: UN, 2008.

OHCHR. *Human Rights and the Millennium Development Goals in Practice: A Review of Country Strategies and Reporting.* New York and Geneva: UN, 2010.

United Nations. Resolution Adopted by the General Assembly [without Reference to a Main Committee (a/55/L.2)] – 55/2., 2000.

United Nations. Resolution Adopted by the General Assembly on 25 September 2015 [without Reference to a Main Committee (a/70/L.1)] 70/1. Transforming Our World: The 2030 Agenda for Sustainable Development., 2015.

United Nations. Transforming Our World: The 2030 Agenda for Sustainable Development. United Nations Development Group., 2015.

United Nations Development Group. Mainstreaming Human Rights in Development 2013.

Miscellaneous

Shift. Business, Human Rights and the Sustainable Development Goals – Forging a Coherent Vision and Strategy 2016. Business & Sustainable Development Commission, London.

The Danish Institute for Human Rights. Responsible Business Conduct as a Cornerstone of the 2030 Agenda – a Look at the Implications. 2019. The Danish Institute for Human Rights, Copenhagen.

CHAPTER 3

Business, Socio-economic Rights, Responsibilities, and Global Inequalities

Jernej Letnar Černič

1 Introduction*

Amulsar mine is one of the most controversial if not most controversial, gold mining projects in Armenia, about 170km southwest of Yerevan. It has been under scrutiny for many years, with successive Armenian governments backed this project. Following the Velvet Revolution in 2018, there emerged a growing sentiment that the project should be abolished. The mine directly affects the environment and the health and socio-economic livelihoods of the local population.[1] It affects several socio-economic rights, ranging from the right to food to the right to water of local people.[2] In 2023, the Armenian government accepted investment by the Eurasian Development Fund.[3] Furthermore, it also affects civil and political rights as many individuals, including young students who have protested against that mine, have faced compensation claims before the Armenian courts aimed at stifling dissent and instilling a sense of fear to intimidate potential future claims.[4]

---

* This chapter was written under the auspices of the Jean Monnet Module on EU Human Rights and Business Law, co-financed by the European Commission (holder: prof. Dr. Jernej Letnar Černič), Faculty of Government and European Studies, New University, 1 October 2022 – 30 September 2025.

1 Bankwatch, "Amulsar gold mine," Armenia, accessed July 10, 2023, https://bankwatch.org/project/amulsar-gold-mine-armenia.

2 Lama Almoayed, ""Water is our gold": Lesson from a community struggle in Armenia," June 5, 2023, accessed July 10, 2023, https://www.accountabilityconsole.com/newsletter/articles/water-is-our-gold-lessons-from-a-community-struggle-in-armenia/.

3 Euroasian Development Fund, "The Government of Armenia, the EDB and Lydian Armenia to restart the Amulsar gold mine project," February 22, 2023, accessed July 10, 2023, https://eabr.org/en/press/news/the-government-of-armenia-the-edb-and-lydian-armenia-to-restart-the-amulsar-gold-mine-project/.

4 David Hoffman, Fidanka Bacheva-McGrath, "SLAPPd: the Armenian activists fighting a mining multinational's lawsuits," Bankwatch Network, June 22, 2020, accessed July 10, 2023, https://bankwatch.org/blog/slappd-the-armenian-activists-fighting-a-mining-multinational-s-lawsuits.

 | DOI:10.1163/9789004530942_004

Business and human rights is an area that does not require avoiding investing in non-democratic countries. Nonetheless, when corporations invest, they must conduct due diligence and ensure the preservation of individual human rights and respect for the environment throughout their supply chains. In situations where businesses operate within a low-regulatory frameworks, they should identify human rights and environmental risks, manage them and take measures to minimise them. Business operations go hand in hand with ensuring dignified socio-economic environments for employees, their families, and society. Corporations should be able to perform stable economic activities in dignified socio-economic environments. Their obligation to ensure respect for socio-economic is more outstanding in the case of fully or partially state-owned enterprises.[5] In an illustrative case, the European Court of Human Rights ruled in 2019 that Armenia had violated the right to property under the European Convention on the Protection of Human Rights and Fundamental Freedoms by nationalisation of private land in the Shnogh and Teghout villages in order to facilitate another mining project by Armenian Copper Corporation.[6] The Court noted in *Osmanyan and Amiraghyan v. Armenia* that 'the margin of appreciation available to the legislature in implementing social and economic policies should be a wide one, will respect the legislature's judgment as to what is "in the public interest" unless that judgment is manifestly without reasonable foundation'.[7] It further observed 'that in consequence of the expropriation the applicants had lost their main source of income, ... The courts decided that, despite the circumstances, the applicants should be provided with compensation which was determined in relation to the prices of real estate situated in the area subject to expropriation.'[8] It added that 'they did not address the issue of whether the compensation granted would cover the applicants' actual loss involved in the deprivation of means of subsistence or was at least sufficient for them to acquire equivalent land within the area in which they lived.'[9] Therefore, it found that 'the applicants had to bear an excessive individual burden.'[10]

5 See, for instance, Judith Schönsteiner, "Inter-American Elements for a Systemic Approach to State-Owned Enterprises' Human Rights Obligations," *Business and Human Rights Journal* 7, no. 3 (2022): 397–417.

6 Kristine Aghalaryan, "European Court Rules Against Armenia in Six Cases Linked to Teghout Mine," Hetq, 14 February 2019, accessed July 10, 2023, https://hetq.am/en/article/100901.

7 ECtHR, Osmanyan and Amiraghyan v. Armenia, no. 71306/11, October 16, 2018, para. 66.

8 Ibid, para. 70.

9 Ibid.

10 Ibid, para. 71.

In the past few decades, business and human rights have witnessed seminal developments, particularly the wit adoption of the United Nations Guiding Principles on Business and Human Rights (hereinafter UNGPs on Business and Human Rights) by the United Nations Human Rights Council in 2011. In recent years, several countries in the Global North have introduced binding national standards in different business and human rights subareas. However, little attention has been paid to the obligations and responsibility of businesses in respecting and protecting socio-economic rights.[11] Traditionally, states bear the primary responsibility of guaranteeing socio-economic rights, but they have assumed a peripheral role in global and domestic economies. The rise of globalisation has strongly affected the influence of privately owned businesses on the enjoyment of individuals' socio-economic rights, resulting in both negative and positive impacts extending to both wealth and income inequality.[12] Litwin argues that 'The impact of business on economic inequality is increasingly on the agenda of businesses and civil society. These impacts are structurally implicated with a number of adverse human rights impacts,'.[13] Inequality, in turn, affects how societies function, from protecting human dignity to economic growth.[14] Tackling inequality is not the sole obligations of states but

11 See, for instance, Larry Catá Backer, "Realizing Socio-Economic Rights under Emerging Global Regulatory Frameworks: the Potential Impact of Privatization and the Role of Companies in China and India," *The George Washington International Law Review* 45, no. 4 (2023): 615–680. See also Gamze Erdem Türkelli, *Children's rights and business: governing obligations and responsibility* (Cambridge, UK/NY: Cambridge University Press, 2020).

12 Leigh A Payne, Gabriel Pereira and Laura Bernal-Bermúdez, *Transitional Justice and Corporate Accountability from Below: Deploying Archimedes' Lever* (Cambridge: Cambridge University Press, 2020); Georges Enderle, *Corporate Responsibility for Wealth Creation and Human Rights* (Cambridge: Cambridge University Press, 2021); Nicholas Bloom, "Corporations in the Age of Inequality Inequality isn't just about individuals – it's risen between companies, too," March 21, 2017, *Harvard Business Review*, accessed July 10, 2023, https://hbr.org/2017/03/corporations-in-the-age-of-inequality; Thomas Piketty, *Capital in the Twenty-First Century* (Massachusetts: Harvard University Press, 2014); Todd Cort, Stephen Park, and Decio Nascimento, "Business Risks Stemming from Socio-Economic Inequality," The CLS Blue Lion Sky Blog, Columbia Law School's Blog on Corporations and the Capital Markets, April 15, 2022, https://clsbluesky.law.columbia.edu/2022/04/15/business-risks-stemming-for-socio-economic-inequality/, accessed July 10, 2023.

13 Daniel Litwin, "Business Impacts on Economic Inequality: An Agenda for Defining Related Human Rights Impacts and Economic Inequality Due Diligence," *Business and Human Rights Journal* 8, no. 1 (2023): 90–96, 96. See also EU Platform on Sustainable Finance, 'Final Report on Social Taxonomy' (February 2022), 24; Casey O'Connor-Willis, "Making ESG Work: How Investors can Help Improve Low-Wage Labor and Ease Income Inequality," (2021).

14 Ines A, Gisselquist, Rachel M and Tarp, Finn, "On the Impact of Inequality on Growth, Human Development and Governance," *International Studies Review* 24 (2022): 1.

demands their active participation.[15] Accordingly, this chapter explores the normative basis and standards for business obligations, responsibilities, and accountability for socio-economic rights. It argues that recognising corporate accountability for socio-economic rights is indispensable for fostering individual self-realisation and human development capabilities.[16]

The body of literature addressing business, responsibilities, and socio-economic rights remains scarce, with only a few monographs[17] and articles published in recent years.[18] Therefore, a research gap still exists regarding corporate accountability and obligations concerning socio-economic rights. This chapter argues that business actors have been one the most significant drivers of inequality, and they, therefore, carry obligations and responsibilities to ensure socio-economic rights. While states bear the primary obligation to respect, protect and fulfil socio-economic rights, corporations carry complementary commitments in this regard. Their obligations and accountability also depend on the extent to which the state is absent or cannot provide at least a minimum level of socio-economic rights.[19] Corporations are burdened with both negative and positive obligations to ensure socio-economic rights. ttis chapter employs conventional legal research methods, including analytical, legal, historical, and comparative legal methods. This chapter is further divided into four sections. Section 2 deals with state regulation and socio-economic rights. Section 3 discusses the UNGPs on Business and Human Rights as the central pillar of corporate obligations concerning socio-economic rights. Section 4 discusses corporate obligations to protect socio-economic rights by discussing

15 Ibid.

16 Amartya Sen, *Development as Freedom* (Oxford: Oxford University Press, 1999); Martha C. Nussbaum, *Creating Capabilities* (Cambridge, MA, and London: The Belknap Press of Harvard University Press, 2011).

17 Gillian MacNaughton, "Emerging Human Rights Norms and Standards on Vertical Inequalities," In *Human Rights and Economic Inequalities*, eds. Gillian MacNaughton, Diane Frey, and Catherine Porter (Cambridge: Cambridge University Press, 2021), 33–62; Jernej Letnar Černič, *Corporate accountability under socio-economic rights, (Transnational Law and Governance)*. (Oxon; New York: Routledge, cop. 2018); Laura Garcia Martin, *Transitional Justice, Corporate Accountability and Socio-Economic Rights* (Abingdon, Oxon; New York, NY: Routledge, 2020); Judith Schrempf-Stirling, Harry J Van Buren, "Business and Human Rights Scholarship in Social Issues in Management: An Analytical Review," *Business and Human Rights Journal* 5, no. 1 (2020): 28–55.

18 Florian Wettstein, Elisa Giuliani, Grazia D. Santangelo, Günter K. Stahl, "International business and human rights: A research agenda," *Journal of World Business* 54, no. 1 (2019): 54 – 65.

19 Elisa Giuliani, Chiara Macchi, "Multinational Corporations' Economic and Human Rights Impacts on Developing Countries: A Review and Research Agenda," *Cambridge Journal of Economics* 38, no. 2 (2014): 479–517.

their source, nature, and scope. Finally, section 5 explores access to remedies for business-related abuses of socio-economic rights. This chapter argues that corporations must respect, protect, and fulfil socio-economic rights.

2 State Regulation and Socio-economic Rights

The essence of a market economy has been to promote free enterprise initiatives, investment, job creation, and economic growth. In contrast, human rights and socio-economic considerations have taken a back seat.[20] The challenge lies in balancing the right to entrepreneurial freedom with the imperative of safeguarding public interest in the form of protection of human rights and the environment?[21] As such, most constitutions premise free entrepreneurial initiative as one of the fundamental principles, if not a constitutional right. However, such a right is not absolute. State authorities should only interfere in implementing this free entrepreneurial initiative only if there is a justified public benefit to ensure equal capabilities for everyone.[22] But what precisely constitutes public benefit? Public interest benefits the protection of health of people's, preserving nature, protecting consumers, protecting the rights of workers, especially those belonging to vulnerable groups of disabled people, preventing corruption, and reducing the risks of human rights abuses.[23] The state can interfere with a free business initiative in these exceptions by employing a strict proportionality test. As such, it is necessary to find when the state can determine that this intervention is justified.[24] The line between free entrepreneurial initiative, on the one hand, and public benefit is always fluid and depends on the socio-economic economic conditions. The state must first ensure that this public benefit is secured in the operations of state-owned enterprises, as their obligation is broader.

---

20 Surya Deva, *Regulating Corporate Human Rights Violations: Humanizing Business* (London: Routledge, 2012); Peter Edward, Andy Sumner, *The End of Poverty: Inequality and Growth in Global Perspective* (Cham: Palgrave Pivot. 2019).

21 Jernej Letnar Černič, Nicolas Carrillo-Santarelli (eds). *The Future of Business and Human Rights: Theoretical and Practical Considerations for a UN Treaty* (Cambridge; Antwerp; Portland: Intersentia. cop. 2018).

22 Amartya Sen, "From Income Inequality to Economic Inequality," *Southern Economic Journal* 64 (1997): 383.

23 Sheldon Leader, "Human Rights, Risks and New Strategies for Global Investment," *Journal of International Economic Law* 9, no. 3 (2006): 657.

24 Surya Deva, ed., *Socio-economic rights in emerging free markets: comparative insights from India and China* (Abingdon, Oxon: New York, NY: Routledge, 2016).

The European Commission in 2024 adopted on Corporate Sustainability Due Diligence Directive requiring mandatory due diligence of supply chains regarding human rights, environmental protection, and anti-corruption in companies with more than 1000 employees.[25] Such due diligence obligations already exist concerning imports of conflict-affected minerals.[26] The business sector is highly averse to additional regulation, whereas some countries and civil society strongly advocate for such additional regulation and concern for the public good in supply chains. How to find the right measure? It imposes additional costs on entrepreneurs and requires them to undertake additional effort on them with all the daily obligations and challenges that entrepreneurs have. On the other hand, they are expected to protect the values that underpin socio-economic and other rights. The framework of the European Union obliges corporations that do business in markets outside the European Union to respect socio-economic rights and introduce socio-economic rights due diligence in the supply chains. Additionally, the largest corporations in the EU are obliged to conduct mandatory non-financial reporting, which has been compulsory for some time in the European Union.[27] Therefore, corporations are expected to voluntarily formulate environmental protection, human rights, and anti-corruption policies and include them in their supply chains.

25 European Commission, Directive (EU) 2024/1760 of the European Parliament and of the Council of 13 June 2024 on corporate sustainability due diligence and amending Directive (EU) 2019/1937 and Regulation (EU) 2023/2859 (Text with EEA relevance), PE/9/2024/REV/1, OJ L, 2024/1760, 5.7.2024. For a detailed account, see Jernej Letnar Černič, "The Human Rights Due Diligence Standard-Setting in the European Union: Bridging the Gap Between Ambition and Reality," *Global Business Law Review of the Cleveland-Marshall College of Law of Cleveland State University* 10 (2022): 1.

26 Regulation (EU) 2017/821 of the European Parliament and of the Council of 17 May 2017 laying down supply chain due diligence obligations for Union importers of tin, tantalum and tungsten, their ores, and gold originating from conflict-affected and high-risk areas, OJ L 130, 19.5.2017, 1–20.

27 Directive (EU) 2022/2464 of the European Parliament and of the Council of December 14, 2022 amending Regulation (EU) No 537/2014, Directive 2004/109/EC, Directive 2006/43/EC and Directive 2013/34/EU, as regards corporate sustainability reporting (Text with EEA relevance), PE/35/2022/REV/1, OJ L 322, 16.12.2022, 15–80.

3 The United Nations Guiding Principles on Business and Human Rights as the Central Pillar of Corporate Obligations Concerning Socio-economic Rights

In the sphere of business and socio-economic rights, fundamental questions arise: Who are the actors violating socio-economic rights in the business environment? Who are the actors responsible for the commission of violations? The field of business and human rights aims for companies to not only to make a profit to generate added value for stakeholders, but also to comply with social and environmental considerations. The business and human rights field has progressed steadily in the last two decades, catalysed by the adoption of the United Nations Guiding Principles on Business Human Rights in 2011 by the United Nations Human Rights Council, the leading human rights body of the General Assembly.[28] The United Nations Human Rights Council adopted those principles without any objections. UNGPS obligate states to protect human rights against adverse business conduct on their territory.[29] States bear primary responsibilities to protect human rights and should lead by example. Such expectations are even more apparent concerning state-owned enterprises, for example, in the cases of a corporate state mining corporation. In the cases before the European Court of Human Rights, states should ensure that businesses do not violate local populations' rights and create examples for privately owned corporations. State obligations to protect human rights represent a primary pillar under UNGPS on Business and Human Rights. These state obligations, both in domestic and international law, encompass the obligation to respect, protect and fulfil socio-economic rights.[30]

The UNGPS on Business and Human Rights provide in the second pillar that businesses respect human rights, including socio-economic ones. The corporate responsibility to protect is based on social expectations for businesses to do good, even though normative sources provide for direct human rights

28 UNHRC, The Guiding Principles on Business and Human Rights: Implementing the United Nations 'Protect, Respect and Remedy' Framework, UN Doc. A/HRC/17/31, March 21, 2011.

29 Larry Cata Backer, "From Institutional Misalignments to Socially Sustainable Governance: The Guiding Principles for the Implementation of the United Nations Protect, Respect and Remedy and the Construction of Inter-Systemic Global Governance," Pacific McGeorge Global Business & Development Law Journal 25, no. 1 (2012):: 69–172.

30 UN, CESCR, "General Comment No. 9: The Domestic Application of the Covenant," UN Doc. E/C.12/1998/24, December 3, 1998; UN, CESCR, 'General Comment No. 24 (2017) on State Obligations Under the International Covenant on Economic, Social and Cultural Rights in the Context of Business Activities', UN Doc. E/C.12/GC/24, August 10, 2017.

obligations of corporations.[31] Nonetheless, the UNGPs on business and human rights do not differentiate between small and large companies. Equally, they do not differ between different categories of human rights and fundamental freedoms. Every company must ensure respect for human rights through its global supply chains. Smaller companies would incur many costs for respecting and protecting human rights. As such, corporations have negative and positive socio-economic rights obligations under the UNGPs on Business and Human Rights.

There exists a growing consensus that extraterritorial obligations are the norm. Companies based in Italy, Germany, and France have accessorial obligations to conduct socio-economic due diligence throughout their supply chain. What is due diligence? Due diligence is a process by which companies must ensure that their supply chains comply with human rights and the environment. For example, for EU companies, there exist obligations even now that EU companies must report on the respect for human rights and the environment when they extract conflict diamonds. The EU regulation on due diligence in supply chains on conflict minerals, which imposes obligations on EU importers, requests that they identify risks in their supply chains first.[32] After placing them in the management plans, they must manage the risks and then take measures to remedy potential abuses in their global supply chains.

The novel EU Corporate Sustainability Due Diligence Directive imposes due diligence obligations on companies larger than 1000 employees. Moreover, those obligations will apply within the EU and when EU companies do business in third countries. Also, when the EU company does business with a non-EU company, and that company then resells the products to the Russian Federation products on the sanctions list, then the EU company would be in breach of its due diligence obligations.[33] Many small and medium-sized companies have done business since the start of aggression in Ukraine, through

31 John G. Ruggie, "Business and Human Rights: The Evolving Agenda," *American Journal of International Law* 101 (2004): 41; John G. Ruggie, Protect, Respect, and Remedy: A Framework for Business and Human Rights: Report of the Special Representative of the Secretary-General on the Issue of Human Rights and Transnational Corporations and Other Business Enterprises, A/HRC/8/5, 2008.

32 Regulation (EU) 2017/821 of the European Parliament and of the Council of May 17, 2017 laying down supply chain due diligence obligations for Union importers of tin, tantalum and tungsten, their ores, and gold originating from conflict-affected and high-risk areas, OJ L 130, 19.5.2017, 1–20.

33 See, for example, Jernej Letnar Černič, "The Reformed EU Human Rights Sanctions Regime: A Step Forward or an Empty Threat?," *Business and Human Rights Journal* 6, no. 3 (2021): 559–566.

parallel product reselling through, for example, Central-Asian countries, then they sell the products to the Russian Federation.[34] As such, an EU company would have to ensure that its business partners will not resell the products sold to Central Asian countries to the Russian Federation. Otherwise, that company would breach EU directives and be sanctioned by a competent authority. What is essential is the supervision, measuring, and managing of business and human rights in global supply chains.

The third pillar under UNGPs requires states and corporations to establish adequate access to remedy. States and companies must provide a remedy for business-related human rights violations.[35] In an introductory case chapter from Armenia, domestic courts could not protect the socio-economic, civil, and political rights of rights-holders from the mining project, which ended at the European Court of Human Rights. Furthermore, the victim's rights holders went to the European Court of Human Rights against the state for failing to fulfil its positive obligations concerning business and socio-economic rights under the UNGPs. The UNGPs encourage states to establish quasi-judicial and non-judicial business and human rights remedies in national human rights institutions and other public bodies. Several enterprises have established internal remedial procedures for employees and external stakeholders to enforce alleged business-related socio-economic rights abuses. The UNGPs on business and human rights have established a platform for state and corporate socio-economic obligations as part of broader obligations towards society.[36]

4 Corporate Obligations Concerning Socio-economic Rights: From Sources to Their Nature and Scope

What are the legal obligations of corporations towards social and economic human rights? Who is duty-holders of obligations under socio-economic rights? Where can victims of social and economic rights violations enforce duty-holders accountability? Socio-economic rights protect basic human

34 Barbara Moens, Leonie Kijewski, Suzanne Lynch, 'EU targets Central Asia in the drive to stop sanctioned goods reaching Russia' Politico, 8 May 2023, accessed July10. 2023, https: //www.politico.eu/article/eu-aims-central-asia-sanction-circumvention-russia-war/.

35 See, for example, United Nations High Commissioner for Human Rights, "Improving accountability and access to remedy for victims of business-related human rights abuse," United Nations General Assembly, A/HRC/32/19, May 10, 2016.

36 John Ruggie, Caroline Rees, Rachel Davis, "Years After: From UN Guiding Principles to Multi-Fiduciary Obligations," *Business and Human Rights Journal* 6, no. 2 (2021): 179–97.

needs to realise and perfect their personal and family goals. Socio-economic rights require states and corporations to, at minimum, provide for basic equality levels between societal actors. They, among others, include the right to education, food, health, housing, and water. States have been the primary duty-holders of the obligation to protect human rights. However, growing local and global income and wealth inequalities have shown that private actors should and shall have obligations to respect, protect and fulfil human rights.[37] In recent decades, corporations have seized considerable powers, in some cases more extensive than states, and have increasingly come to the fore of global public debates. In addition, states and businesses carry obligations to respect and protect socio-economic rights from education, food, health care, and housing to water.

This chapter argues that corporations have obligations in the field of social-economic rights. They depend on available financial resources. They usually create state obligations of conduct to realise them progressively over a long period.[38] If the state or a corporation lacks many resources, realising the right to food, water, education, social care, and housing will be more challenging.[39] Then the next challenge that arises is how to enforce them. Generally, many of these rights have a very programmatic and general legal nature.[40] They are rarely successfully enforced against states or corporations in domestic courts.[41] Nonetheless, there are some exceptions. Some of the highest national courts, such as the Constitutional courts in Colombia, South Africa, and Slovenia, have previously reinforced socio-economical rights against state and public institutions and private bodies. Traditionally, states must guarantee the minimum reasonable core of social and economic rights.[42] However, it is necessary to connect state obligations to the business world of companies. It is submitted that even commercial companies must ensure social and economic rights at

---

37 Asbjørn Eide, "Realisation of Social and Economic Rights and the Minimum Threshold Approach," 10(2) *Human Rights Law Journal* 10, no. 2 (1989): 37.

38 Surya Deva, ed., *Socio-economic rights in emerging free markets: comparative insights from India and China* (Abingdon, Oxon: New York, NY: Routledge, 2016).

39 Janice R. Bellace and Beryl ter Haar, eds., *Research Handbook on Labour, Business and Human Rights Law*, (Cheltenham: Edward Elgar Publishing, 2019).

40 Christina Binder, Jane A. Hofbauer, Flávia Piovesan and Amaya Úbeda de Torres, eds., *Research handbook on international law and social rights* (Cheltenham, UK: Edward Elgar Publishing Limited, 2020).

41 Marius Pieterse, *Rights-based litigation, urban governance and social justice in South Africa: the right to Joburg* (Abingdon, Oxon: Routledge, 2017).

42 Asbjørn Eide (n 37), "Realisation of Social and Economic Rights and the Minimum Threshold Approach".

this narrower part of their business operations. As such, the obligations are broader and more direct if companies play an essential role in realising the economic and social rights of their employees and society; for example, if they are obliged to ensure health and safety at work, they are also obliged to provide the minimum core of their obligations.[43] Business practice shows that some corporations recognise socio-economic rights, such as the right to water.[44]

The backbones of equal opportunities and capabilities are the right to food, nutrition, education, primary health, and decent housing for their employees and the wider community. If an individual has access to this essential public good, she can realise herself in other areas of family, private, and professional lives. These obligations are more reinforced in states of the Global South, where the state is absent and does not have a welfare state as broad states in the Global North.[45] More and more companies can become providers of socio-economic rights even in connection with environmental pollution and when their products harm consumers. The main challenge is how individuals and victims of business-related socio-economic rights violations can enforce state and corporate accountability before judicial or quasi-judicial authorities. Domestic and international jurisprudence illustrate that socio-economic have been increasingly ascribed to corporations.[46] Domestic and constitutional frameworks already provide for corporate obligations under socio-economic

---

43 See, for instance, Jernej Letnar Černič (n 17); Rashmi Venkatesan, "The [UN] Framework on Business and Human Rights: A Workers' Rights Critique," *Journal of Business Ethics* 157, no. 3 (2017): 635 – 652; Florian Wettstein, Elisa Giuliani, Grazia D. Santangelo, Günter K. Stahl, "International business and human rights: A research agenda," *Journal of World Business* 54, no. 1 (2019): 54 – 65; Kishanthi Parella, "Hard and Soft Law Preferences in Business and Human Rights," American Journal of International Law 114 (2020): 168–173; Jernej Letnar Černič, "Corporate Human Rights Obligations under Socio-economic Rights," *Philosophy of law and general theory of law* 1 (2021): 64–102, Yaroslav Mudryi National Law University; Laura Garcia Martin, Transitional Justice, *Corporate Accountability and Socio-Economic Rights* (Routledge, Abingdon, Oxon; New York, NY: Routledge, 2020); Jernej Letnar Černič (N 25).

44 Shannon Marcoux, "Coca-Cola's Cape Town Crisis: Examining Companies' Water Rights Obligations in a Changing Climate," *Business and Human Rights Journal* 7, no. 2 (2022): 298–302.

45 Shelley Marshall, Kate Taylor, Tim Connor, Fiona Haine, "Sara Tödt, Will Business, and Human Rights regulation help Rajasthan's bonded labourers who mine sandstone?," *Journal of Industrial Relations* 64, no. 2 (2021): 248 – 271.

46 Malcolm Langford, "Domestic Adjudication and Economic, Social and Cultural Rights: A Socio-Legal Review," 6(11) *Sur International Journal of Human Rights* 91 (2009); Michael D. Goldhaber, "Corporate Human Rights Litigation in Non-US Courts: A Comparative Scorecard," *UC Irvine Law Review* 3, no. 1 (2013): 127 .

rights.[47] Regional and international legal systems complement the existing obligations under socio-economic rights.[48]

Nevertheless, it is controversial to argue that businesses have obligations concerning economic and social human rights and responsibilities to compact global inequality. Several initiatives have been developed to reform the domestic and international order, especially of business and civil and political rights, in recent years. This chapter argues that it is necessary to transfer socio-economic obligations, which most of us associate with the state apparatus, to ensure the welfare state, and social, economic, and human rights, to business actors, which have so far generated positive and negative impacts on socio-economic rights. It established that corporations carry obligations concerning the right to food, water, education, health, and decent housing. The normative regulation of these obligations and responsibilities needs to be further improved and strengthened so that the victims can assert the duties of these corporate companies towards socio-economic rights, maybe in the sense of adopting the United Nations Treaty on Business and Human Rights.

As for the nature of obligations, there is often a question in business and human rights whether companies have obligations only negative obligations, or whether they also have positive obligations.[49] There is a growing consensus that companies and states are obligated to protect socio-economic rights.[50]

---

47 Marina Prieto-Carrón, "Bringing Resistance to the Conceptual Center: Threats to Social Reproduction and Feminist Activism in Nicaraguan Commodity Chains," in *Gendered Commodity Chains: Seeing Women's Work and Households in Global Production*, ed. Wilma A Dunaway (Stanford: Stanford University Press, 2013), 225–238.; Jernej Letnar Černič (n 17), Chapters 5–6.

48 Jernej Letnar Černič (n 17), Chapters 5–6.

49 Jernej Letnar Černič, "Corporate Human Rights Obligations under Socio-economic Rights," *Philosophy of law and general theory of law* 1 (2021): 64–102, Yaroslav Mudryi National Law University; Leigh A. Payne, Laura Bernal-Bermúdez and Gabriel Pereira,.*Economic actors and the limits of transitional justice: truth and justice for business complicity in human rights violations* (Oxford: Published for The British Academy by Oxford University Press, 2022); Nerea Belmonte Aliaga, "The Right to Housing and the Spanish Banking Sector: Implementing the UN Guiding Principles on Business and Human Rights," (Barcelona: Huygens Editorial, 2014), pp. 473–492. In: España y la implementación de los Principios Rectores de las Naciones Unidas sobre Empresas y Derechos Humanos: oportunidades y desafíos = Spain and the implementation of the United Nations Guiding Principles on Business and Human Rights: challenges and opportunities.

50 See, for instance, Mohammed M M Chowdhury, Nazamul Hoque, and Jonayed Kabir, "Work-Life Balance of Female Garment Workers in Bangladesh: An Imperial Investigation," *Global Journal of Management and Business Research* 15, no. 7 (2015):18; Fiona H McKay and Hayley J McKenzie, "Life Outside the Garment Factories: The Lived Experiences of Cambodian Women Garment Factory Workers," *International Journal of Migration, Health and Social Care* 16, no. 4 (2020): 415.

Negative obligations only require businesses not to harm individuals' enjoyment of socio-economic rights.[51] Their business operations should uphold access to water, food, housing, health care, and education. However, corporations should not only not interfere with state provision of socio-economic rights. In their companies, they should take active measures to ensure at least socio-economic rights. Businesses carry positive obligations to ensure socio-economic rights beyond their business operation, particularly in countries where states do not have sufficient resources to provide for socio-economic rights. They must protect to ensure socio-economic tights in their global supply chain. As such, corporations must exercise socio-economic due diligence. Companies are expected to prevent business-related human rights abuses and their adverse socio-economic impacts.[52] They must conduct due diligence in their process. Positive obligations to control the supply chain are procedural obligations. It is not an obligation of result. They must show that they must manage human rights and environmental risks in their supply chains. For companies is not acceptable is that they do not need to supervise and manage their supply chains. Since 2011, many countries have adopted mandatory diligence concerning the disclosure and management of corporations' global supply chains.

There is a growing trend for Global North countries to adopt due diligence rules which require companies to respect human rights and supervise them in the supply chain, including socio-economic rights. For instance, the German Act on Corporate Due Diligence in Supply Chains has established obligations to identify human rights risks in the global supply chains of the largest companies, measure and manage them and respond to alleged business-related violations.[53] The Act refers under human rights obligations of corporations to several socio-economic rights such as health and safety,[54] the prohibition of withholding an adequate living wage,[55] the right to water,[56] and other socio-economic rights included in the International Covenant on Economic, Social,

51 Chiara Macchi, "Right to Water and the Threat of Business: Corporate Accountability and the State's Duty to Protect," 2017, *Nordic journal of human rights*. Marius Pieterse, *Rights-based litigation, urban governance and social justice in South Africa: the right to Joburg* (Abingdon, Oxon: Routledge, 2017).

52 Ramona Vijeyarasa, and Mark Liu. "Fast Fashion for 2030: Using the Pattern of the Sustainable Development Goals (SDGs) to Cut a More Gender-Just Fashion Sector," *Business and Human Rights Journal* 7, no. 1 (2022): 45–66.

53 Act on Corporate Due Diligence in Supply Chains, Bundestag, July 16, 2021.

54 Ibid., Section 2 (2) (5).

55 Ibid., Section 2 (2) (7).

56 Ibid., Section 2 (2) (9) (b).

and Cultural Rights and other conventions.[57] Corporations also carry obligations under the German Act to fulfil socio-economic rights to complement state responsibilities. Different jurisdictions have also adopted mandatory disclosure and reporting laws, requiring the largest corporations to report social and human rights risks in their business activity. For example, the Australian Modern Slavery Bill,[58] California Transparency in Supply Chains Act,[59] and UK Modern Slavery Act,[60] French Duty of Vigilance Law,[61] and the German Act on Corporate Due Diligence in Supply Chains, Bundestag, 16 July 2021.[62] The updated EU Corporate Sustainability Reporting Directive started to apply in early 2023, imposing businesses to report on non-financial indicators of their business operations.[63] Lastly, the proposal is now under discussion in the European Parliament on the Corporate Sustainability Due Diligence Directive. In contrast, the Council of the EU and the European Parliament have already adopted their positions.[64]

Overall, a plethora of law sources exist attesting to corporate human rights obligations in different legal regimes. Domestic legal systems provide for foundations of corporate obligations under socio-economic rights. Regional and international human rights regimes complement them. Internal company and sector-based human rights due diligence processes and policies reinforce state-based legal regimes. The recognition of corporate responsibilities is increasingly a lesser problem than their enforcement, which will be harder to crack given the layers of corporate legal personality and extraterritorial issues.

57 Ibid., Section 2 (1) and Annex, para. 11.

58 Modern Slavery Act 2018 (No. 153, 2018), Australia, October 12, 2018.

59 The California Transparency in Supply Chains Act of 2010 (SB 657).

60 Modern Slavery Act 2015, UK Public General Acts2015 c. 30.

61 Loi 2017–399 du 27 Mars 2017 relative au devoir de vigilance des sociétés mères et des entreprises donneuses d'ordre, Official Gazette of the Republic of France, March 27, 2017, article L. 225-102-4.

62 Act on Corporate Due Diligence in Supply Chains, Bundestag, July 16, 2021.

63 Directive (EU) 2022/2464 of the European Parliament and of the Council of December 14, 2022 amending Regulation (EU) No 537/2014, Directive 2004/109/EC, Directive 2006/43/EC and Directive 2013/34/EU, as regards corporate sustainability reporting (Text with EEA relevance), PE/35/2022/REV/1, OJ L 322, 16.12.2022, 15–80.

64 European Commission, Proposal for a Directive the European Parliament and of the Council on Corporate Sustainability Due Diligence and amending Directive (EU) 2019/1937, COM/2022/71 final.

5 Access to Remedy for Business-Related Abuses of Socio-economic Rights

Access to remedy for business-related abuses of socio-economic rights is essential for normative recognition of corporate obligations under socio-economic rights.[65] The UNGPs on Business and Human Rights place a burden on states to ensure efficient access to fair, impartial, and independent justice. Difficulties enforcing corporate accountability for social and economic rights violations are not new.[66] After the toxic disaster in Bhopal in India in the early 1980s, where a chemical spill occurred, killing and affecting the lives of over 50,000 people, little has been engineered to ensure corporate accountability for infringing socio-economic rights.[67] Baxi noted concerning the 2023 Indian Supreme Court decision[68] to dismiss the petition that 'The Court may have been haunted by the spectre of the 1989 Bhopal settlement order. Our Constitution insists not just on closure, but on just closure.'[69] Challenges to ensure water, food, and decent housing for everyone in Bhopal remain. What actions can confirm that corporations respect social and economic rights in countries with weaker regulatory frameworks? How can international legal systems be improved to provide judicial protection in case of business-related socio-economic rights abuse? Could the International Convention on Business and Human Rights within the framework of the United Nations be a likely panacea?[70]

65 Jernej Letnar Černič (n 17), Chapter 7.

66 Malcolm Langford, "Domestic Adjudication and Economic, Social and Cultural Rights: A Socio-Legal Review," 6(11) *Sur International Journal of Human Rights* 6, no. 11 (2009): 91.

67 Upendra Baxi, "Human Rights Responsibility of Multinational Corporations, Political Ecology of Injustice: Learning from Bhopal Thirty Plus?," *Business and Human Rights Journal* 1, no. 1 (2016): 21–40.

68 Indian Supreme Court, Union of India & Ors. V. M/S. Union Carbide Corporation & Ors Curative Pet (C) No. 345–347 of 2010 in RP No.229/1989 & 623-624/1989 in CA No.3187-3188/1988 and SLP (C) No.13080/1988, March 14, 2023.

69 Upendra Baxi, "Upendra Baxi on SC ruling on Bhopal Gas tragedy curative petition: Where did the constitutional sympathy for the victims vanish?," *The Indian Express*, March 22, 2023, accessed July 10, 2023, https://indianexpress.com/article/opinion/columns/upendra-baxi-on-sc-ruling-on-bhopal-gas-tragedy-curative-petition-where-did-the-constitutional-sympathy-for-the-victims-vanish-8511141/.

70 Jernej Letnar Černič and Nicolas Carrillo-Santarelli, eds., *The Future of Business and Human Rights: Theoretical and Practical Considerations for a UN Treaty* (Cambridge; Antwerp; Portland: Intersentia. cop. 2018).

of these obligations within the corporate sphere. Moreover, several state and non-state mechanisms have reinforced state and corporate accountability for business-related socio-economic rights abuses. Corporations are increasingly challenged to provide access to water, food, dignity, shelter, accommodation, and health care in these countries of the Global North and South.

Nevertheless, there may be some instances in which state authorities cannot fulfil their obligations. Even in the absence of a rule of law environment, major multinationals carry an obligation to guarantee a minimum of these essential socio-economic rights. This chapter contends that corporations are obliged to respect the right to water, food and accommodation, health care, and education on a narrow scope, particularly in contexts where states do not guarantee these rights, or where there is no rule of law. Moreover, our claim is substantiated through various legal sources of law in different domestic and regional legal orders and international law. Nonetheless, to improve both domestic and international legal systems, adopting even more transparent state and corporate human rights obligations and ensuring judicial protection in case of alleged violations of socio-economic rights, is indispensable.

Bibliography

Books

Bellace, Janice R., and Beryl ter Haar, eds. *Research Handbook on Labour, Business and Human Rights Law*. Cheltenham: Edward Elgar Publishing, 2019.

Binder, Christina, Jane A. Hofbauer, Flávia Piovesan, and Amaya Úbeda de Torres, eds. *Research Handbook on International Law and Social Rights*. Cheltenham, UK: Edward Elgar Publishing Limited, 2020.

Deva, Surya, ed. *Socio-economic Rights in Emerging Free Markets: Comparative Insights from India and China*. Abingdon, Oxon: Routledge, 2016.

Deva, Surya. *Regulating Corporate Human Rights Violations: Humanizing Business*. London: Routledge, 2012.

Edward, Peter, and Andy Sumner. *The End of Poverty: Inequality and Growth in Global Perspective*. Cham: Palgrave Pivot, 2019.

Enderle, Georges. *Corporate Responsibility for Wealth Creation and Human Rights*. Cambridge: Cambridge University Press, 2021.

Letnar Černič, Jernej ed. *The Future of Business and Human Rights: Theoretical and Practical Considerations for a UN Treaty*. Cambridge; Antwerp; Portland: Intersentia, 2020.

Letnar Černič, Jernej. *Corporate Accountability under Socio-economic Rights. Transnational Law and Governance*. Oxon; New York: Routledge, 2018.

Letnar Černič, Jernej. and Nicolas Carrillo-Santarelli, eds. *The Future of Business and Human Rights: Theoretical and Practical Considerations for a UN Treaty*. Cambridge; Antwerp; Portland: Intersentia, 2018.

Martin, Laura Garcia. *Transitional Justice, Corporate Accountability and Socio-Economic Rights*. Abingdon, Oxon: Routledge, 2020.

Nussbaum, Martha C. *Creating Capabilities*. Cambridge, MA, and London: The Belknap Press of Harvard University Press, 2011.

Payne, Leigh A., Gabriel Pereira, and Laura Bernal-Bermúdez. *Transitional Justice and Corporate Accountability from Below: Deploying Archimedes' Lever*. Cambridge: Cambridge University Press, 2020.

Payne, Leigh A., Laura Bernal-Bermúdez, and Gabriel Pereira. *Economic Actors and the Limits of Transitional Justice: Truth and Justice for Business Complicity in Human Rights Violations*. Oxford: Published for The British Academy by Oxford University Press, 2022.

Pieterse, Marius. *Rights-based Litigation, Urban Governance and Social Justice in South Africa: The Right to Joburg*. Abingdon, Oxon: Routledge, 2017.

Piketty, Thomas. *Capital in the Twenty-First Century*. Massachusetts: Harvard University Press, 2014.

Sen, Amartya. *Development as Freedom*. Oxford: Oxford University Press, 1999.

Türkelli, Gamze Erdem. *Children's Rights and Business: Governing Obligations and Responsibility*. Cambridge, United Kingdom; New York, NY, USA: Cambridge University Press.

Book Chapters

Aliaga Belmonte, Nerea. "The Right to Housing and the Spanish Banking Sector: Implementing the UN Guiding Principles on Business and Human Rights." In *España y la implementación de los Principios Rectores de las Naciones Unidas sobre Empresas y Derechos Humanos: oportunidades y desafíos = Spain and the implementation of the United Nations Guiding Principles on Business and Human Rights: challenges and opportunities*, 473–492. Barcelona: Huygens Editorial, 2014.

MacNaughton, Gillian. "Emerging Human Rights Norms and Standards on Vertical Inequalities." In *Human Rights and Economic Inequalities*, edited by Gillian MacNaughton, Diane Frey, and Catherine Porter, 33–62. Cambridge: Cambridge University Press, 2021.

Prieto-Carrón, Marina. "Bringing Resistance to the Conceptual Center: Threats to Social Reproduction and Feminist Activism in Nicaraguan Commodity Chains." In *Gendered Commodity Chains: Seeing Women's Work and Households in Global Production*, edited by Wilma A. Dunaway, 225–238. Stanford: Stanford University Press, 2013.

Journal Articles

Baxi, Upendra. “Human Rights Responsibility of Multinational Corporations, Political Ecology of Injustice: Learning from Bhopal Thirty Plus?.” *Business and Human Rights Journal* 1, no. 1 (2016): 21–40.

Buhmann, Karin. “Analyzing OECD National Contact Point Statements for Guidance on Human Rights Due Diligence: Method, Findings and Outlook.” *Nordic Journal of Human Rights* 36, no 4 (2018): 390–410.

Catá Backer, Larry. “From Institutional Misalignments to Socially Sustainable Governance: The Guiding Principles for the Implementation of the United Nations Protect, Respect and Remedy and the Construction of Inter-Systemic Global Governance.” *Pacific McGeorge Global Business & Development Law Journal* 25, no. 1 (2012): 69–172.

Catá Backer, Larry. “Realizing Socio-Economic Rights under Emerging Global Regulatory Frameworks: the Potential Impact of Privatization and the Role of Companies in China and India’.” *The George Washington international law review* 45, no. 4 (2013): 615–680.

Chowdhury, Mohammed M, Hoque, Nazamul, Kabir, Jonayed. “Work-Life Balance of Female Garment Workers in Bangladesh: An Imperial Investigation.” *Global Journal of Management and Business Research* 15, no. 7 (2015): 19–25.

Eide, Asbjørn. “Realisation of Social and Economic Rights and the Minimum Threshold Approach.” *Human Rights Law Journal* 10, no. 2 (1989): 36–51.

Gisselquist, Ines A, M Rachel, Tarp, Finn. “On the Impact of Inequality on Growth, Human Development and Governance.” *International Studies Review* 24 (2022): 1–28.

Giuliani, Elisa, Macchi, Chiara. “Multinational Corporations’ Economic and Human Rights Impacts on Developing Countries: A Review and Research Agenda.” *Cambridge Journal of Economics* 38, no. 2 (2014): 479–517.

Goldhaber, Michael D. “Corporate Human Rights Litigation in Non-US Courts: A Comparative Scorecard.” *UC Irvine Law Review* 3, no. 1 (2013): 127–149.

Langford, Malcolm. “Domestic Adjudication and Economic, Social and Cultural Rights: A Socio-Legal Review.” 6(11) *Sur International Journal of Human Rights* 6, no. 11 (2009): 91–121.

Leader, Sheldon. “Human Rights, Risks and New Strategies for Global Investment.” *Journal of International Economic Law* 9, no. 3 (2006): 657–705.

Letnar Černič, Jernej. “Corporate Human Rights Obligations under Socio-economic Rights.” *Philosophy of Law and General Theory of Law* no. 1 (2021): 64 – 102.

Letnar Černič, Jernej. “The Reformed EU Human Rights Sanctions Regime: A Step Forward or an Empty Threat?.” *Business and Human Rights Journal* 6, no. 3 (2021): 559–566.

Letnar Černič, Jernej. "The Divergent Practices of NCPs under OECD Guidelines for Multinational Enterprises: Time for a More Uniform Approach?." *International Labour Rights Case Law* 7, no. 1 (2021): 11–16.

Letnar Černič, Jernej. "The Human Rights Due Diligence Standard-Setting in the European Union: Bridging the Gap Between Ambition and Reality." *Global Business Law Review of the Cleveland-Marshall College of Law of Cleveland State University* 10 (2022): 1–23.

Litwin, Daniel. "Business Impacts on Economic Inequality: An Agenda for Defining Related Human Rights Impacts and Economic Inequality Due Diligence." *Business and Human Rights Journal* 8, no. 1 (2023): 90–96.

Macchi, Chiara. "Right to Water and the Threat of Business: Corporate Accountability and the State's Duty to Protect." *Nordic journal of human rights* (2017): 186–202.

Marcoux, Shannon. "Coca-Cola's Cape Town Crisis: Examining Companies' Water Rights Obligations in a Changing Climate." *Business and Human Rights Journal* 7, no. 2 (2022): 298–302.

Marshall, Shelley, Taylor, Kate, Connor, Tim, Haine, Fiona, Tödt, Sara. "Will Business, and Human Rights regulation help Rajasthan's bonded labourers who mine sandstone?." *Journal of Industrial Relations* 64, no. 2 (2021): 248–271.

McKay, Fiona H, McKenzie, Hayley J. "Life Outside the Garment Factories: The Lived Experiences of Cambodian Women Garment Factory Workers." *International Journal of Migration, Health and Social Care* 16, no. 4 (2020): 415–427.

Parella, Kishanthi. "Hard and Soft Law Preferences in Business and Human Rights." *American Journal of International Law* 114 (2020): 168–173.

Ruggie, John G. "Business and Human Rights: The Evolving Agenda." *American Journal of International Law* 101 (2007): 819–840.

Ruggie, John, Caroline Rees, Rachel Davis. "Years After: From UN Guiding Principles to Multi-Fiduciary Obligations." *Business and Human Rights Journal* 6, no. 2 (2021): 179–97.

Schönsteiner, Judith. "Inter-American Elements for a Systemic Approach to State-Owned Enterprises' Human Rights Obligations." *Business and Human Rights Journal* 7, no. 3 (2022): 397–417.

Schrempf-Stirling, Judith, Van Buren, Harry J. "Business and Human Rights Scholarship in Social Issues in Management: An Analytical Review." *Business and Human Rights Journal* 5, no. 1 (2020): 28–55.

Sen, Amartya. "From Income Inequality to Economic Inequality." *Southern Economic Journal* 64 (1997): 383–401.

Venkatesan, Rashmi. "The [UN] Framework on Business and Human Rights: A Workers' Rights Critique." *Journal of Business Ethics* 157, no. 3 (2017): 635–652.

Vijeyarasa, Ramona, Liu, Mark. "Fast Fashion for 2030: Using the Pattern of the Sustainable Development Goals (SDGs) to Cut a More Gender-Just Fashion Sector." *Business and Human Rights Journal* 7, no. 1 (2022): 45–66.

Wettstein, Florian, Giuliani, Elisa, Santangelo Grazia D., K. Stahl Günter. "International business and human rights: A research agenda." *Journal of World Business* 54, no. 1 (2019): 54–65.

Cases

Akpan v *Royal Dutch Shell Plc*, Case no. C/09/337005/HA ZA 09-1580 (District Court of The Hague), 3 January 30, 2014.

Anvil Mining Ltd v *Association Canadienne contre l'Impunité*, QCCA 117 (Québec Court of Appeal) Canada, January 20, 2012.

Araya v *Nevsun Resources Ltd.*, 2016 BCSC 1856 (Superior Court of British Columbia, Canada), October 6, 2016; Association France-Palestine Solidarité v Société Alstom *Transport SA* (Case No. 11/05331), Versailles Court of Appeal, March 22, 2013.

Bowoto et al. v *Chevron Co. et al.*, June 5, 2007, Case 3:99-cv-02506-SI, Document 1628, June 5, 2007 (States District Court, N.D. California).

CAO, Complaint concerning IFC investment in Dragon Capital Group and VEIL (Project no. 10740 and 20926), February 10, 2014.

Choc v *Hudbay Minerals*, 2013 ONSC 1414 (Superior Court of Justice Ontario, Canada), July 22, 2003.

Consejo de Defensa del Estado demanda a tres mineras por daño ambiental en Salar de Atacama, Primer Tribunal Ambiental, Peru, April 8, 2022, D-15-2022.

ECtHR, *Osmanyan and Amiraghyan* v. *Armenia*, no. 71306/11, October 16, 2018.

Indian Supreme Court, *Union of India & Ors.* v *M/S. Union Carbide Corporation & Ors Curative PET* (C) No. 345–347 of 2010 in RP No.229/1989 & 623–624/1989 in CA No.3187–3188/1988 and SLP (C) No.13080/1988, March 14, 2023.

Mazibuko and Others v *City of Johannesburg and Others*, CCT 39/09 (Constitutional Court of South Africa), October 8, 2009.

Documents

Act on Corporate Due Diligence in Supply Chains, Bundestag, July 16, 2021.

Act on Corporate Due Diligence in Supply Chains, Bundestag, July 16, 2021.

Directive (EU) 2022/2464 of the European Parliament and of the Council of December 14, 2022 amending Regulation (EU) No 537/2014, Directive 2004/109/EC, Directive 2006/43/EC and Directive 2013/34/EU, as regards corporate sustainability reporting (Text with EEA relevance), PE/35/2022/REV/1, OJ L 322, 16.12.2022, 15–80.

European Commission, Directive (EU) 2024/1760 of the European Parliament and of the Council of 13 June 2024 on corporate sustainability due diligence and amending

Directive (EU) 2019/1937 and Regulation (EU) 2023/2859 (Text with EEA relevance), PE/9/2024/REV/1, OJ L, 2024/1760, 5.7.2024.

Loi 2017–399 du 27 Mars 2017 relative au devoir de vigilance des sociétés mères et des entreprises donneuses d'ordre, Official Gazette of the Republic of France, March 27, 2017, article L. 225-102-4.

Modern Slavery Act 2015, UK Public General Acts, 2015 .

Modern Slavery Act 2018 (No. 153, 2018), Australia, October 12, 2018.

OECD, Guidelines for Multinational Enterprises on Responsible Business Conduct, Paris: OECD, 2023.

OECD, Stocktaking Report on the OECD Guidelines for Multinational Enterprises, Paris: OECD, 2022.

Regulation (EU) 2017/821 of the European Parliament and of the Council of May 17, 2017 laying down supply chain due diligence obligations for Union importers of tin, tantalum and tungsten, their ores, and gold originating from conflict-affected and high-risk areas, OJ L 130, 19.5.2017, 1–20.

The California Transparency in Supply Chains Act of 2010 (SB 657).

UN, CESCR, 'General Comment No. 9: The Domestic Application of the Covenant', UN Doc. E/C.12/1998/24, December 3, 1998; UN, CESCR, 'General Comment No. 24 (2017) on State Obligations Under the International Covenant on Economic, Social and Cultural Rights in the Context of Business Activities', UN Doc. E/C.12/GC/24, August 10, 2017.

UNHRC, The Guiding Principles on Business and Human Rights: Implementing the United Nations 'Protect, Respect and Remedy' Framework, UN Doc. A/HRC/17/31, March 21, 2011.

Internet Sources

Aghalaryan, Kristine "European Court Rules Against Armenia in Six Cases Linked to Teghout Mine," Hetq, February 14, 2019. Accessed July 10, 2023, https://hetq.am/en/article/100901.

Barbara Moens, Leonie Kijewski, Suzanne Lynch, "EU targets Central Asia in the drive to stop sanctioned goods reaching Russia", Politico, May 8, 2023. Accessed July 10, 2023, https://www.politico.eu/article/eu-aims-central-asia-sanction-circumvention-russia-war/.

Cort, Todd, Stephen Park, and Decio Nascimento, "Business Risks Stemming from Socio-Economic Inequality", The CLS Blue Lion Sky Blog, Columbia Law School's Blog on Corporations and the Capital Markets, April 15, 2022. Accessed July 10, 2023, https://clsbluesky.law.columbia.edu/2022/04/15/business-risks-stemming-for-socio-economic-inequality/.

David Hoffman, Fidanka Bacheva-McGrath, "SLAPPd: the Armenian activists fighting a mining multinational's lawsuits", Bankwatch Network, June 22, 2020. Accessed

July 10, 2023, https://bankwatch.org/blog/slappd-the-armenian-activists-fighting-a-mining-multinational-s-lawsuits.

Euroasian Development Fund, "The Government of Armenia, the EDB and Lydian Armenia to restart the Amulsar gold mine project." February 22, 2023. Accessed July 10, 2023, https://eabr.org/en/press/news/the-government-of-armenia-the-edb-and-lydian-armenia-to-restart-the-amulsar-gold-mine-project/.

Lama Almoayed. ""Water is our gold": Lesson from a community struggle in Armenia." 5 June 2023. Accessed July 10, 2023, https://www.accountabilityconsole.com/newsletter/articles/water-is-our-gold-lessons-from-a-community-struggle-in-armenia/.

Nicholas Bloom, "Corporations in the Age of Inequality Inequality isn't just about individuals – it's risen between companies, too," Harvard Business Review, March 21, 2017. Accessed July 10, 2023, https://hbr.org/2017/03/corporations-in-the-age-of-inequality.

Upendra Baxi, "Upendra Baxi on SC ruling on Bhopal Gas tragedy curative petition: Where did the constitutional sympathy for the victims vanish?" The Indian Express, March 22, 2023. March 21, 2017, https://indianexpress.com/article/opinion/columns/upendra-baxi-on-sc-ruling-on-bhopal-gas-tragedy-curative-petition-where-did-the-constitutional-sympathy-for-the-victims-vanish-8511141/.

Bankwatch. "Amulsar gold mine." Armenia. Accessed 10 July 2023, https://bankwatch.org/project/amulsar-gold-mine-armenia.

Reports

EU Platform on Sustainable Finance, "Final Report on Social Taxonomy" (February 2022), 24; Casey O'Connor-Willis, "Making ESG Work: How Investors can Help Improve Low-Wage Labor and Ease Income Inequality" (2021).

Ruggie, John G. Protect, Respect, and Remedy: A Framework for Business and Human Rights: Report of the Special Representative of the Secretary-General on the Issue of Human Rights and Transnational Corporations and Other Business Enterprises, A/HRC/8/5, 2008.

United Nations High Commissioner for Human Rights, "Improving accountability and access to remedy for victims of business-related human rights abuse." United Nations General Assembly, A/HRC/32/19, May 10, 2016.

CHAPTER 4

Business, Human Rights and Plastic Pollution

Sara L Seck and Victoria Kongats

1 Introduction

Plastics are ubiquitous and highly diverse products that provide various public benefits across many industries. However, the latest plastics science according to the United Nations Environment Programme (UNEP) confirms that 'plastic pollution in all forms causes lethal and sublethal effects in marine, freshwater and terrestrial environments' with implications for human rights.[1] The packaging industry represents the most prevalent application of plastic in terms of total tons used, followed by uses in building and construction, transportation, electrical and electronics, and clothing and textiles.[2] One key characteristic of plastic concerns its short-term intended use. Data from UNEP suggests that 'half of all plastic produced is designed for single-use purposes.'[3] Moreover, the Organisation for Economic Co-operation and Development (OECD) stated that two-thirds of most plastic waste has a maximum lifespan of less than five-years.[4] Based on the prevalence of its short-term intended use, plastics are considered to have introduced an 'era of disposability'[5] and are described as 'everywhere we look.'[6] Increasingly, this includes the natural environment where '[e]ven pristine environments such as the Arctic and remote mountain

1 United Nations Environment Programme (UNEP), "Plastics Science" UN Doc. UNEP/PP/INC.1/7, Annex, "Plastic Pollution Science," September 13, 2022, 3, https://wedocs.unep.org/bitstream/handle/20.500.11822/40831/K2221533%20-%20%20UNEP-PP-INC.1-7%20-%20AMENDED%20ADVANCE%20-%2014.10.2022.pdf.

2 Organisation for Economic Co-operation and Development (OECD), "Plastics use by application-projections," *OECD.Stat*, accessed May 5, 2022, https://stats.oecd.org/Index.aspx?DataSetCode=PLASTIC_USE_V2_3.

3 UNEP, "Our planet is choking on plastic" *UNEP*, accessed January 27, 2023, https://www.unep.org/interactives/beat-plastic-pollution/.

4 OECD, "Plastic pollution is growing relentlessly as waste management and recycling fall short, says OECD," *OECD*, February 2, 2022, https://www.oecd.org/environment/plastic-pollution-is-growing-relentlessly-as-waste-management-and-recycling-fall-short.htm.

5 National Academies of Sciences, Engineering, and Medicine (NASEM), *Reckoning with the U.S. Role in Global Ocean Plastic Waste*, Washington, DC: The National Academies Press, 2022, 1, https://doi.org/10.17226/26132.

6 Ibid, *vii.*

 | DOI:10.1163/9789004530942_005

areas have been found to be contaminated with plastics.'[7] In 2022, microplastics were discovered in human blood[8] and placenta.[9]

In addition to problems posed by the magnitude of plastic waste, plastic is considered to have adverse human rights impacts across all stages of its life cycle. These impacts occur during the extraction of raw materials for plastic, predominantly from fossil fuels, and upon plastic manufacturing, transportation, use, and end-disposal.[10] For example, plastics are linked with alterations to global carbon cycling and contribute to climate change throughout their life cycle, accounting for 3.4 percent of global greenhouse gas (GHG) emissions in 2019.[11]

These adverse impacts that occur throughout the life cycle are, furthermore, inequitably distributed in a geographic, social, and ecological manner.[12] Concerns regarding the harms to human health and the environment have spurred a rapidly developing field of research and litigation. Notably, the majority of the approximately 5,000 papers on plastics' harms have been published since about 2017.[13] In particular, microplastics research expanded from approximately 2,500 papers in 2021 to 4,500 in 2022.[14] By mid-2022, it was observed that the frequency of litigation related to plastic pollution has rapidly increased and diversified in the variety of plaintiffs and the types of claims

---

7 Eleonora Mavroeidi, Maarten Dubois, Elena Buzzi and Daniel Ostalé Valriberas, *Global Plastics Outlook: Policy Scenarios to 2060*, OECD, 2022, 5.1, https://www.oecd-ilibrary.org/sites/aa1edf33-en/1/2/2/index.html?itemId= /content/publication /aa1edf33 -en&_csp_= ca738cf5d4f327be3b6fec4af9ce5d12&itemIGO=oecd&itemContentType =book (citations omitted).

8 Heather A. Leslie et al., "Discovery and quantification of plastic particle pollution in human blood," Environment International 163, 107199 (May 2022): 1, https://doi.org/10.1016/j.envint.2022.107199.

9 Antonio Ragusa et al., "Plasticenta: First evidence of microplastics in human placenta," *Environment International* 146, 106274 (January 2021): 1, https://doi.org/10.1016/j.envint.2020.106274.

10 United Nations General Assembly (UNGA), *Report of the Special Rapporteur on the implications for human rights of the environmentally sound management and disposal of hazardous substances and wastes, Marcos Orellana: The stages of the plastics cycle and their impacts on human rights*, United Nations General Assembly, 76th session, UN Doc A/76/207, July 2021, https://digitallibrary.un.org/record/3936771?ln=en (Marcos Orellana, *Report of the Special Rapporteur*).

11 UNEP, "Plastics Science" (n 1), 3.

12 NASEM, *Reckoning* (n 5), 43.

13 Andreas Merkl and Dom Charles, *The Price of Plastic Pollution: Social Costs and Corporate Liabilities*, Minderoo Foundation, October 2022, 19, https://cdn.minderoo.org/content/uploads/2022/10/14130457/The-Price-of-Plastic-Pollution.pdf.

14 Ibid, 22.

advanced by plaintiffs.[15] In 2022, there has been a trend towards analysing this litigation to identify themes and predict liabilities.[16]

The convergence of science, litigation, and human rights-related policies pertaining to the plastics burden highlights the urgent need to prevent adverse impacts on environmental human rights across the plastics life cycle. There is a growing need for this industry to internalise its externalities by applying responsible business conduct guidance tools throughout its supply chains. These guidance tools include the 2011 *United Nations Guiding Principles on Business and Human Rights*,[17] and risk-based due diligence frameworks, such as the OECD *Guidelines for Multinational Enterprises*.[18]

This chapter describes a broad approach to address the burden of plastic waste and it draws on our previous work, which involved developing training materials for a UNEP-funded project on a human rights-based approach to plastic pollution in South-East Asia.[19] The first part describes a life cycle and environmental human rights-based approach as a means to help business enterprises understand the impacts of their activities and their obligations at each stage of the life cycle. The second part introduces two significant factors that are contributing to the circular economy transition: the evolution of international environmental law leading to the emergence of a global plastics treaty, and the growing field of plastics liability. The third part explores key business and human rights (BHR) guidance tools that businesses may adopt to prevent human rights impacts throughout the entire plastics life cycle.

---

15 Connor Fraser, "Plastics in the Courtroom: The Evolution of Plastics Litigation," *State Energy & Environmental Impact Center* (*blog*), New York University School of Law, July 15, 2022, https://stateimpactcenter.org/insights/plastics-in-the-courtroom-the-evolution-of-plastics-litigation.

16 See ibid; Rosa Pritchard and Alice Merry, *Plastics on trial: a briefing series on evolving liability risks related to plastics*, ClientEarth, September 2022, https://www.clientearth.org/latest/documents/plastics-on-trial-1-greenwashing/.

17 United Nations, *United Nations Guiding Principles on Business and Human Rights*, UN Doc. A/HRC/17/31, Annex, https://www.ohchr.org/sites/default/files/documents/publications/guidingprinciplesbusinesshr_en.pdf, (*UNGPs*).

18 OECD, *OECD Guidelines for Multinational Enterprises* (Paris: OECD Publishing, 2011), http://dx.doi.org/10.1787/9789264115415-en (*MNE Guidelines*).

19 See Sara L. Seck, *Business, Human Rights and the Environment in South-East Asia: Overcoming the Plastics Challenge,* Policy Training Resource, *UNEP*, September 30, 2022, 33–37, https://wedocs.unep.org/handle/20.500.11822/41852 (UNEP, *BHRE Plastics*).

2 A Life Cycle and Environmental Human Rights-Based Approach to the Plastics Burden

2.1 *Introduction*

In July 2021, Marcos Orellana, the Special Rapporteur on toxics and human rights (SR Toxics) released a report on adverse human rights impacts at each stage of the linear plastics life cycle.[20] Under a social-based life cycle lens, a product's adverse impacts such as those that impact human rights, are explored at each life cycle stage (also referred to as 'value chain'). The analysis begins by describing impacts that arise on the extraction of raw earth materials and ends with impacts that arise on the product's return to the earth (from 'cradle-to-grave').[21] Intermediate stages include production, transportation, use, waste management and disposal.[22] The approach of the SR Toxics is consistent with the work of UNEP, which has described the core problem at the heart of the plastics crisis as the 'resource-inefficient, linear, take-make-waste plastic economy.'[23] A shift to circular economy is therefore essential, recognising that for some plastic uses circularity may be impossible. Scientific studies have demonstrated that 'most plastic pollution could be prevented' through a 'comprehensive circular economy approach' that would also reduce GHG emissions from plastics by 25 percent.[24] Attention to human rights impacts at each stage of the linear life cycle could help to drive the transition to circularity.

As the plastics challenge is an intersecting environmental and human rights problem, it is helpful to frame it with reference to the right to a clean, healthy and sustainable environment, recognised in a July 2022 resolution of the United Nations General Assembly (UNGA).[25] The recognition of this right follows the adoption of a similar resolution by the UN Human Rights Council in 2021,

20 Marcos Orellana, *Report of the Special Rapporteur*; see also United Nations General Assembly, *Mandate of the Special Rapporteur on the implications for human rights of the environmentally sound management and disposal of hazardous substances and wastes*, UN Doc. A/HRC/RES/45/17, October 09, 2020, https://documents-dds-ny.un.org/doc/UNDOC/GEN/G20/259/12/PDF/G2025912.pdf?OpenElement (emphasising the need to adopt life cycle approaches).

21 Marcos Orellana, *Report of the Special Rapporteur*; see also Jeroen B. Guinée et al., "Life Cycle Assessments: Past, Present, and Future," *Environmental Science & Technology* 45, no. 1 (2011): 90–96, https://doi.org/10.1021/es101316v.

22 Ibid.

23 UNEP (n 1).

24 Ibid.

25 United Nations General Assembly, "The human right to a clean, healthy and sustainable environment" UN Doc. A/RES/76/300, resolution adopted by the General Assembly on July 28, 2022, https://digitallibrary.un.org/record/3983329?ln=en.

and builds upon numerous reports prepared over the last ten years by successive UN Special Rapporteurs on human rights and the environment.[26] These include the 2018 *Framework Principles on Human Rights and the Environment*,[27] which are specifically referenced in the UNGA resolution. Related reports by successive SR Toxics' mandate holders also inform an environmental human rights approach to plastics, including not only the 2021 report focused specifically on plastics, but also earlier work, notably the 2019 *Principles on human rights and the protection of workers from exposure to toxic substances*.[28]

A broad overview of environmental human rights serves as a reference to assess adverse impacts on these rights at each stage of the plastics life cycle. Environmental human rights may be divided into substantive, procedural, and equitable elements. The substantive elements include the right to: clean air, clean water, a safe climate, healthy ecosystems and biodiversity, healthy and sustainable food, and non-toxic places to live, work and play.[29] The procedural elements include the right to: prevention, prior assessment and precaution of harm; access to information; freedom of expression and association; public participation in environmental decision-making (and free, prior and informed consent for Indigenous peoples), and; accountability and access to justice and remedies.[30] Procedural rights also account for the need for a safe space for environmental human rights defenders to exercise their rights.[31]

Each of these substantive and procedural rights are further interdependent. For instance, without a clean, healthy and sustainable environment it is impossible to enjoy a vast range of human rights; while, concurrently, procedural

26 See Office of the United Nations High Commissioner for Human Rights (OHCHR), Special Rapporteur on Human Rights and the Environment, accessed March 29, 2023, https://www.ohchr.org/en/special-procedures/sr-environment; see also OHCHR, *Right to a healthy environment: good practices: Report of the Special Rapporteur on the issue of human rights obligations relating to the enjoyment of a safe, clean, healthy and sustainable environment*, UN Doc. A/HRC/43/53, December 30, 2019.

27 OHCHR, *Report of the Special Rapporteur on the issue of human rights obligations relating to the enjoyment of a safe, clean, healthy and sustainable environment*, "Framework Principles on Human Rights and the Environment UN Doc. A/HRC/37/59, January 24, 2018, 3, (*Framework Principles*).

28 OHCHR, *Principles on human rights and the protection of workers from exposure to toxic substances*, Special Rapporteur on Toxic Substances and Human Rights, UN Doc. A/HRC/42/41, 2019; see also OHCHR, *Right to Science in the Context of Toxic Substances*, Special Rapporteur on Toxic Substances and Human Rights, UN Doc. A/HRC/48/61, 2021.

29 See OHCHR, Special Rapporteur on Human Rights and the Environment; see also UNEP, *BHRE Plastics* (n 19), 33–37.

30 See Marcos Orellana, *Report of the Special Rapporteur*, 18/24–21/24; UNEP, *BHRE Plastics*, 37–43.

31 UNEP, *BHRE Plastics* (n 19), 41; OHCHR, "Framework Principles" (n 27), Principle 4.

rights must be exercised in order to ensure the maintenance of environmental human rights. Finally, equity and non-discrimination are also a focus point in each substantive and procedural element, as persons and groups in vulnerable situations are disproportionately exposed to adverse impacts across the plastics life cycle. These individuals often lack tools and opportunities to protect themselves from exposure to human rights harms. Some have been rendered vulnerable due to historic issues of discrimination, including gender discrimination and colonial practices, such as the undermining of Indigenous peoples' rights of self-determination. Therefore, when assessing adverse impacts on these rights across the plastics life cycle, attention is given to determine if vulnerable or marginalised groups are disproportionately impacted.[32] Individuals and groups specifically impacted by the plastics burden include: children and future generations; women and persons of diverse genders; Indigenous, tribal or traditional peoples and coastal communities; ethnic, racial or other minorities and persons living in poverty; and formal and informal workers.[33] Many of these individuals also experience overlapping ('intersecting') vulnerabilities and disadvantages that gives rise to unique identities or intensified human rights-associated burdens.[34]

The substantive, procedural and equity elements of an environmental human rights-based approach to the plastics burden places positive and negative obligations on states and businesses. These obligations must be secured at each stage of the plastics life cycle. Differentiating how substantive, procedural and equity elements may be impacted at each stage helps to account for impacts on stage-specific stakeholders that may be obscured under a non-life cycle lens.[35] The life cycle lens offers a way to systematically describe adverse

32 Ibid, UNEP, *BHRE Plastics*, 43–54.

33 Marcos Orellana, *Report of the Special Rapporteur*, 9/24–13/24. For example, the disproportionate impacts of plastic pollution on women and girls arising at the intersection of social, biological and economic inequalities combined with underrepresentation in political decision-making points to the need for the collection of disaggregated data on gender and plastics, and to ensure that law and policy responses enable meaningful participation and leadership roles that are also attentive to gender.

34 See Kimberlé W. Crenshaw, "Demarginalizing the Intersection of Race and Sex: A Black Feminist Critique of Antidiscrimination Doctrine, Feminist Theory and Antiracist Politics," *University of Chicago Legal Forum* 1, no. 8 (1989), https://scholarship.law.columbia.edu/faculty_scholarship/3007/

35 UNEP, *Guidelines for Social Life Cycle Assessment of Products*, UNEP, 2009, 5, https://wedocs.unep.org/bitstream/handle/20.500.11822/7912/-Guidelines%20for%20Social%20Life%20Cycle%20Assessment%20of%20Products-20094102.pdf?sequence=3&amp%3BisAllowed=.

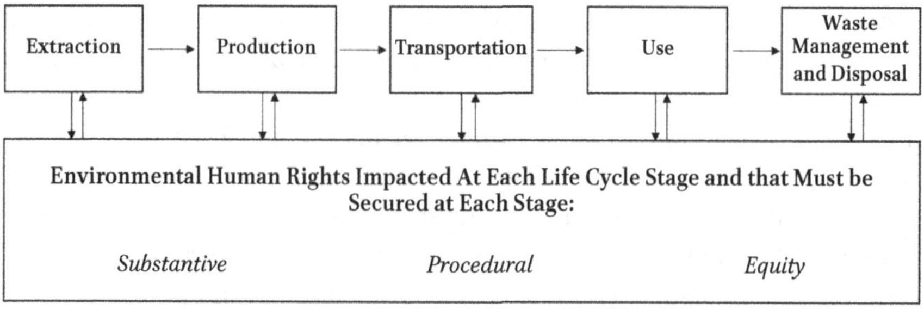

FIGURE 4.1 A life cycle and environmental human rights-based approach to plastic pollution

impacts on environmental human rights and as a lens to understand how these rights can be secured at each life cycle stage, as described in Figure 4.1.

The following sections will discuss various types of adverse human rights impacts experienced by diverse groups at each stage of the plastics life cycle.[36] The aim is to demonstrate the value of life cycle thinking towards securing environmental human rights and the complexities of rights-infringements encountered through a life cycle lens.

2.2 *Extraction*

Synthetic plastics are categorised as fossil fuel-based or bio-based.[37] Fossil fuel-based plastics comprise the vast majority of plastics (99%) and are made from virgin crude oil (petroleum) or natural gas, which is plastics' primary feedstock (i.e., hydrocarbons).[38] Fossil fuel exploration and extraction causes 'deforestation, ecosystem fragmentation and chemical contamination of land and water with production waters, drilling fluids and by-products.'[39] Hydraulic fracking is also increasingly used as a method to extract trapped oil and gas specifically for plastic production.[40] Fracking, which releases carcinogens into the air and wastewater, is associated with 'increased risk of asthma, childhood cancers, and adverse birth outcomes, including preterm delivery, low birth weight, and

36 See further UNEP, *BHRE Plastics* (n 19).

37 NASEM (n 5).

38 NASEM (n 5).

39 Marcos Orellana (n 33), *Report of the Special Rapporteur*, 5/24.

40 Robert W. Adler et al., "Plastics and the Limits of U.S. Environmental Law," *Harvard Environmental Law Review* 47, no. 1 (Spring 2023): 1–62, 6 (n 32), https://dc.law.utah.edu/cgi/viewcontent.cgi?article=1351&context=scholarship.

congenital defects.'[41] Businesses have an obligation to take a precautionary approach and protect vulnerable populations at the extraction stage.

2.3 *Production*

At the production stage, toxic chemicals are added to refined crude oil (petroleum) to add properties such as colour, flexibility, clarity, softness, and durability. Over 10,000 registered chemicals are added to plastics and only a subset of these chemicals have been studied.[42] Of this group, 1,254 have been deemed chemicals of 'high concern.'[43] Polyvinyl chloride (PVC or vinyl) and polystyrene (known as styrofoam), for example, contain 'a myriad of harmful additives,' and are known to have carcinogenic properties.[44]

Two highly prevalent and well-studied chemical groups, phthalates and bisphenols, are known endocrine (hormone) disruptors. Broadly, chemicals that disrupt the endocrine system have been associated with intersex variations, which are increasingly prevalent in the US population, particularly if a fetus is exposed to these chemicals in utero during critical developmental phases.[45] Phthalates are often added to increase the durability of plastics, yet are linked to a wide range of diseases including breast cancer, type II diabetes, asthma and fertility issues, while biosphenol A is linked to cancer, and liver and cardiovascular disease.[46] Businesses have an obligation to conduct prior assessment of each toxic substance prior to adding them to products, to take a precautionary approach and avoid substances that create a risk of harm, so as to protect workers, communities and the environment. Businesses also have an obligation to provide the public with access to information about toxic substances used in plastics.

41 See Florencia Pascual, "Fracking and Childhood Leukemia: New Evidence Supports Greater Residential Setbacks," *Environmental Health Perspectives* 130, no. 9 (September 2022), https://doi.org/10.1289/EHP11982.

42 Merkl and Charles (n 13), *The Price of Plastic Pollution*, 20.

43 Merkl and Charles (n 13), *The Price of Plastic Pollution*, 20.

44 Rosa Pritchard and Alice Merry, *Plastics on trial: a briefing series on evolving liability risks related to plastics: Brief 2: Hazardous chemicals*, ClientEarth, September 2022, 10, https://www.clientearth.org/latest/documents/plastics-on-trial-2-hazardous-chemicals/.

45 Alisa L. Rich et al., "The Increasing Prevalence in Intersex Variation from Toxicological Dysregulation in Fetal Reproductive Tissue Differentiation and Development by Endocrine-Disrupting Chemicals," *Environmental Health Insights* 10, (September 2016), doi: 10.4137/EHI.S39825.

46 Marcos Orellana (n 33), *Report of the Special Rapporteur*, 5/24.

2.4 *Transportation*

Before certain types of plastics are molded, they exist as pre-production plastic pellets. In May 2021, the cargo ship MV X-Press that was transporting these pellets ignited 10 miles off the coast of Sri Lanka, which released 175 billion pellets into the Indian Ocean and polluted the coastal environment.[47] The MV X-Press disaster is not isolated. Approximately 10 trillion pellets are spilled into the environment and remain unrecovered each year,[48] which has prompted calls for stronger regulatory controls to improve pellet handling.[49]

The transportation stage is also one that relates to various life cycle stages. Transporting toxic chemicals, for example, to produce plastics is another key issue associated with plastics. In February 2023, for example, a train carrying polyvinyl chloride used to make plastic known as PVC, among other chemicals, derailed. These chemicals needed to be burned to prevent an explosion, which contaminated the surrounding environment and raised numerous health concerns.[50]

2.5 *Usage*

Many chemicals used in the production of plastics leach from plastics during their use because the chemicals are not bound to the underlying polymer structure.[51] As consumers are in contact with plastic products and packaging on a daily basis, they are routinely exposed to toxic compounds whether absorbed through the skin, or ingested as microplastics or toxic compounds in water, the food chain or food packaging.[52] Women may be disproportionately impacted by plastics at the use stage of the life cycle due to their exposure to endocrine disrupters.[53] Road wear of tires is also increasingly recognised as a major

47 Marcos Orellana (n 33), *Report of the Special Rapporteur*, 6/24.

48 As You Sow, "Record-Setting 81% of DuPont Shareholders Approve Proposal Calling for Plastic Pellet Pollution Reporting," *As You Sow*, May 3, 2021, https://www.asyousow.org/press-releases/2021/5/3/dupont-shareholders-approve-plastic-pellet-pollution-reporting.

49 Therese M. Karlsson et al., "The Unaccountability Case of Plastic Pellet Pollution," *Marine Pollution Bulletin* 129, no. 1 (April 2018), https://doi.org/10.1016/j.marpolbul.2018.01.041.

50 Raymond Zhong and Catrin Einhorn, "Health and Environmental Fears Remain After Ohio Derailment and Inferno," *New York Times*, February 14, 2023, https://www.nytimes.com/2023/02/14/climate/ohio-train-derailment-chemical-spill-health.html.

51 See Robert W. Adler et al. (n 40), "Plastics and the Limits," 16, citing John N. Hahladakis et al., "An Overview of Chemical Additives Present in Plastics: Migration, Release, Fate and Environmental Impact During Their Use, Disposal and Recycling," *Hazardous Materials* 344, (February 2018), https://doi.org/10.1016/j.jhazmat.2017.10.014.

52 Marcos Orellana (n 33), *Report of the Special Rapporteur*, 6/24.

53 Marcos Orellana (n 33), *Report of the Special Rapporteur*, 11/24, 8/24.

environmental pollutant with approximately 6 million tons of microplastic tire particles shed in the environment each year.[54] When economic growth increases transportation needs that are not met by public transit, microplastic leakage from tires and brake abrasion increasingly pollutes the air and terrestrial and aquatic environments.[55]

2.6 *Waste Management and Disposal*

In terms of global statistics, most plastic waste is either landfilled (49%), mismanaged or uncollected (22%), incinerated (19%), or recycled (9%).[56] The following differentiates various human rights impacts across each of these different disposal or waste management stages.

2.6.1 Recycling

Recycling of plastics is a small portion of plastic waste management practice. Only 9% of world plastic has been recycled[57] and various OECD countries' recycling rates fall below this average. For example, the United States' recycling rate is approximately 4% and in Canada it is averaged to be 6% (in contrast, the OECD's European Union countries average 14%).[58] Consequently, recycling has been described as 'more of a mirage, an optical illusion that perpetuates the severe human rights impacts of plastics.'[59] Many people in western countries believe their plastic waste is shipped and consequently recycled in emerging economies.[60] However, recycling facilities within these economies are insufficient for this waste,[61] and furthermore, the magnitude of plastic production and resulting waste would overwhelm 'even the most well-developed recycling systems.'[62] In April 2022, California's Attorney General, Rob Bonta, opened an investigation to determine if the plastic industry's alleged historic

---

54 Government of Canada, "Plastics Challenge: Mitigating the Release of Microplastics from Tire Wear," *Innovation, Science and Economic Development Canada*, date modified, August 31, 2022, https://ised-isde.canada.ca/site/innovative-solutions-canada/en/plastics-challenge-mitigating-release-microplastics-tire-wear.

55 Eleonora Mavroeidi et al. (n 7), "Global Plastics Outlook," s. 5.4.

56 Ibid.

57 Ibid.

58 Ibid.

59 Marcos Orellana (n 33), *Report of the Special Rapporteur*, 6/24.

60 Ibid, 7/24.

61 Ibid.

62 Rosa Pritchard and Alice Merry, *Plastics on trial: a briefing series on evolving liability risks related to plastics: Brief 4: Waste disposal & recycling,* Client Earth, September 2022, 5, https://www.clientearth.org/media/durfpjzw/plastics-on-trial-4-waste.pdf.

and current initiates to deceive the public into believing that plastic recycling is a viable waste management strategy is a violation under California law.[63]

Despite the low prevalence of recycling in the waste management of plastic, adverse health impacts, human trafficking, child labour and forced labour occur within the plastic recycling sector. The Global Initiative Against Transnational Organized Crime has stated that Biffa Waste Management Service, a UK-based corporation that recycles plastic, was accused of human trafficking and modern slavery in its UK plant.[64] Human Rights Watch has also reported that human trafficking and child labour occurs "throughout Turkey's plastic recycling industry," which handles a large portion of Europe's waste.[65] In the US, several private corporations as well as the Federal Prison Industries (a federally-owned corporation known as UNICOR) that produce or assemble plastic, or recycle e-waste (eg printers and computers), use civilly or criminally incarcerated workers as a cheap labour source where workers are often compensated in cents or uncompensated.[66] Within UNICOR, prisoners have been exposed to toxic fine dust from plastic sanding (brominated flame retardants, including polybrominated diphenyl ethers) that can bioaccumulate in the human body,[67] and have further been subjected to poor occupational safety protections in the management of hazardous waste.[68] Further, incarcerated workers are 'disproportionately made up of people who are Black.'[69] Businesses have an obligation to provide all workers, and especially vulnerable workers, such as racialised groups, with high standards of occupational safety and fair compensation whether or not they are officially recognised as employees.

---

63 State of California, Department of Justice, "Attorney General Bonta Announces Investigation into Fossil Fuel and Petrochemical Industries for Role in Causing Global Plastics Pollution Crisis," *Rob Bonta Attorney General*, April 28, 2022, https://oag.ca.gov/news/press-releases/attorney-general-bonta-announces-investigation-fossil-fuel-and-petrochemical.

64 Virginia Comoli, *Plastic for Profit: Tracing Illicit Plastic Waste Flows, Supply Chains and Actors*, Global Initiative Against Transnational Organized Crime, November 2021, 16, https://globalinitiative.net/wp-content/uploads/2021/10/GITOC-Plastic-for-Profit.pdf.

65 Human Rights Watch, "'It's as If They're Poisoning Us' The Health Impacts of Plastic Recycling in Turkey," September 2022, https://www.hrw.org/report/2022/09/21/its-if-theyre-poisoning-us/health-impacts-plastic-recycling-turkey.

66 American Civil Liberties Union (ACLU) and the University of Chicago Law School Global Human Rights Clinic (UCLSGHRC), *Captive Labor: Exploitation of Incarcerated Workers*, ACLU and GHRC Research Report, 2022, https://aboutblaw.com/3Xl.

67 United States of America, Office of the Inspector General (OIG), *A Review of Federal Prison Industries' Electronic-Waste Recycling Program*, United States Department of Justice, October 2010, 129, https://oig.justice.gov/reports/BOP/o1010.pdf.

68 ACLU and UCLSGHRC, *Captive Labour*, 14; see also Ibid.

69 Ibid, ACLU and UCLSGHRC, *Captive Labour*, 8.

2.6.2 Landfilled, Mismanaged/Uncollected or Incinerated

As described above, most plastic is landfilled, mismanaged, burned in an open or closed environment, or incinerated.[70] Each of these practices releases toxic chemicals into the air and environment. For example, plastics' lightweight characteristic, whether packaging or as degraded microplastics, is susceptible to drifting (mismanagement) causing it to be transported to remote locations through wind, air, rivers, and oceans.[71] While incineration at certain temperatures may be perceived as eliminating toxic chemicals, it has been suggested that 'incineration does not eliminate plastic polymers; significant amounts of microplastics and heavy metals have been detected in residual incineration ash that may enter the environment.'[72] Businesses have an obligation to assess the risks created, adopt a precautionary approach, and provide access to accurate information about incineration to advance procedural environmental human rights at the incineration stage.

Mismanaged and uncollected waste has also resulted in an economy of informal waste pickers, many of whom are women and children with intersecting vulnerabilities (being urban poor or from rural communities). In contrast, men are more likely to be employed in formal waste management.[73] Due to the informal nature of their work, informal waste pickers do not benefit from occupational protections, such as health and safety equipment or clothing.[74] They are also more likely to be exploited through low compensation and are at increased risk of gender-based violence because of the intersection of their unsecure employment and gender.[75]

Plastic crediting businesses have also emerged to control mismanaged and uncollected waste. This business model is substantially similar to the carbon credit business model that permits corporations to claim they 'offset' their carbon footprint or are plastic 'net zero' or 'plastic neutral.'[76] In the case of plastics, a business can purchase credits as a means to state they have 'offset' their plastic footprint. Plastic credits as a business model have been 'highly

---

70 OECD (n 4), "Plastic pollution is growing."

71 See e.g., Steve Allen et al., "Atmospheric transport and deposition of microplastics in a remote mountain catchment" *Nature Geoscience* 12, no. 5 (April 2019), doi: 10.1038/s41561-019-0335-5.

72 Robert W. Adler et al. (n 40), "Plastics and the Limits," 11.

73 May Thazin Aung et al., *Marine Plastic Litter in East Asian Seas: Gender, Human Rights and Economic Dimensions*, United Nations Environment Programme, 2019, 22, https://www.sea-circular.org/wp-content/uploads/2019/11/SEI_SEA-circular-1.pdf.

74 Ibid, 22.

75 Ibid.

76 Pritchard and Merry (n 62), *Brief 4: Waste*, 7.

criticized for their reliance on informal waste workers,' and because it is difficult to confirm the amount of waste diverted or where it ends-up.[77] Under a life cycle environmental human rights-based approach, a person has a right to access meaningful remedies. Plastic credits do not appear to be a meaningful remedy to address plastics' adverse impacts across the life cycle. Further, there have been "recent legal actions challenging corporate 'net zero' and 'climate neutrality' claims and commitments based on carbon offsetting schemes,"[78] which suggests that corporations engaging in plastic crediting/offsetting may also be at risk of liability.[79]

First Nations (Indigenous) communities in Canada may also use dumping and burning to manage their waste, particularly if located in remote geographic areas where they are unable to partner with local municipalities.[80] Elders (Indigenous knowledge holders) have stated that the increase in waste, and thus of dumping and burning on or off-reserve, is partially a result of 'the increased availability of over-packaged commercial commodities within these communities.'[81] Businesses have an obligation to ensure that packaging does not pollute the ecology of First Nations' communities or undermine their cultural rights.[82]

3 Initiatives to Address Plastic Pollution

3.1 *Introduction*

Laws and policies that govern plastic, directly or indirectly, have been described as 'fragmented solutions that fall short of resolving the global plastics problem.'[83] However, the increased attention on the plastic pollution problem is creating pressure driving the emergence of new legal instruments and understandings of legal responsibility and liability. The first pressure discussed is the development of a multilateral global plastics treaty. The second pressure relates to an anticipated rise in plastics-related liabilities.

77 Ibid.

78 Ibid.

79 Ibid.

80 Rebecca Zagozewski et al., "Perspectives on Past and Present Waste Disposal Practices: A Community-Based Participatory Research Project in Three Saskatchewan First Nations Communities," *Environmental Health Insights* 5, (January – December 2011), https://doi.org/10.4137/EHI.S6974.

81 Ibid.

82 See further Max Liborion, *Pollution Is Colonialism* (Durham: Duke University Press, 2021).

83 Marcos Orellana (n 33), *Report of the Special Rapporteur*, 22/24.

3.2 *Multilateral Environmental Agreements and the Global Plastics Treaty*

A diverse set of international treaties touch upon different aspects of the plastics crisis, although to date they form a patchwork rather than a comprehensive approach. For example, the 2019 amendments to the *Basel Convention on the Control of Transboundary Movements of Hazardous Wastes*,[84] together with the ban amendment in force in 2019, tackle the problem of exports of plastic waste from developed to developing states, but do not address transboundary movements of plastics destined for recycling that are 'almost free from contamination.'[85] The *Stockholm Convention on Persistent Organic Pollutants* (POPs)[86] also plays a crucial role as several additives in plastics or generated from plastic incineration are POPs listed for elimination.[87] The MARPOL Convention (International Convention for the Prevention of Pollution from Ships)[88] prohibits the discharge of any plastics into the sea under Annex V, while the reduction of inadvertent spillage of plastic pellets in maritime transport is a subject of study by the International Maritime Organisation[89] together with the need to ensure adequate facilities at ports that receive plastic waste.

Due to the patchwork of existing treaties' solutions, the UN Environmental Assembly (UNEA) has adopted several resolutions aimed at tackling the plastics crisis, with an initial focus on marine litter and microplastics. Resolution 5.2 of the 2022 UNEA created an intergovernmental negotiating committee (INC) tasked with developing an internationally binding instrument to tackle plastic pollution, through a life cycle approach, including in the marine environment, with a complete text to be available in 2024.[90] The first INC session[91]

---

84 United Nations, *Basel Convention on the Control of Transboundary Movements of Hazardous Wastes*, 1673 UNTS 126, March 22, 1989, entered into force May 5, 1992.

85 Marcos Orellana (n 33), *Report of the Special Rapporteur*, 14/24.

86 United Nations, *Stockholm Convention on Persistent Organic Pollutants*, 2256 UNTS 119, 22 May 2001, entered into force May 17, 2004.

87 Marcos Orellana (n 33), *Report of the Special Rapporteur*, 15/24.

88 United Nations, *International Convention for the Prevention of Pollution from Ships*, 1340 UNTS 61, 2 November 1973, entered into force October 2, 1983 (MARPOL).

89 International Maritime Organization, "Sub-Committee on Pollution Prevention and Response (PPR 9)," Meeting Summary, 2022, https://www.imo.org/en/MediaCentre/MeetingSummaries/Pages/PPR-9th-session.aspx.

90 UNEP, "Resolution 14: End Plastic Pollution: Towards an Internationally Legally Binding Instrument" UNEP/EA.5/Res.14, 2022, https://wedocs.unep.org/bitstream/handle/20.500.11822/39764/END%20PLASTIC%20POLLUTION%20-%20TOWARDS%20AN%20INTERNATIONAL%20LEGALLY%20BINDING%20INSTRUMENT%20-%20English.pdf?sequence=1&isAllowed=y.

91 UNEP, "First session of Intergovernmental Negotiating Committee to develop an international legally binding instrument on plastic pollution,…," *UNEP* (Conference: November

was held in November/December 2022 in Uruguay, while the second session of the INC[92] was held in Paris in May/June 2023. Submissions to the second INC from member states and diverse stakeholders were posted on the UNEP website[93] which, together with the views expressed by members at the first INC, informed the drafting of a document outlining potential options for the structure of the treaty, including its objective, core obligations, control measures and implementation. Among key questions is whether an approach based on voluntary national action plans mirroring the Paris Agreement will prevail despite criticisms.[94] Following further negotiating sessions in Nairobi (2023) and Ottawa (2024), the final negotiating session will be held in Busan in late 2024.

3.3 *A Rise in Harm-Based Plastics Liabilities*

Liability against the plastics industry is a growing trend that has the potential to put pressure on key stakeholders to adopt circular economy principles. Between 2022–2030, corporate liabilities facing the plastics industry is expected to exceed US $20 billion in the United States alone and will likely arise against chemical manufacturers and primary polymer producers.[95] This estimate is considered substantially lower than the true social burdens posed by the plastics industry.[96] Impediments to a more 'equitable' corporate liability include the general infancy of plastics litigation and issues in attributing fault, i.e., legal causation and legal burdens of proof.[97] As it relates to legal causation, it is predicted that courts may expand legal standards of 'conventional causational theory, and increasingly accomodat[e] theories of complex and shared causation of harm.'[98]

28–December 02, 2022), https://www.unep.org/events/conference/inter-governmental-negotiating-committee-meeting-inc-1.

92 UNEP, "Second session of Intergovernmental Negotiating Committee to develop an international legally binding instrument on plastic pollution,…," *UNEP* (Conference: May 29–June 02, 2023), https://www.unep.org/events/conference/second-session-intergovernmental-negotiating-committee-develop-international.

93 Ibid.

94 See John Geddie and Valerie Volcovici, "Exclusive: U.S. seeks allies as split emerges over global plastics pollution treaty," *Reuters*, September 27, 2022, https://www.reuters.com/world/exclusive-us-seeks-allies-split-emerges-over-global-plastics-pollution-treaty-2022-09-27/.

95 Merkl and Charles (n 13), *The Price of Plastic*, 11.

96 Ibid.

97 Ibid, 11 and 16.

98 Ibid, 16.

Plastics litigation has and is expected to continue to gather around four themes: greenwashing; hazardous chemicals; release of plastics in the environment; and, waste disposal and recycling.[99] It is also expected that efforts to make the plastics industry more transparent, as led by the Minderoo Foundation, will increase litigation risks for plastic-related entities.[100] One key initiative of the Minderoo Foundation is to increase transparency in terms of 'how plastics are funded, produced, consumed, and disposed of.'[101] These types of transparency initiatives create liability risks by identifying major contributors to plastic pollution including plastic producers and, less directly, their financiers.[102] These less direct actors in plastic pollution may become relevant parties if courts are willing to apply 'complex and shared causation of harm' theories as the Minderoo Foundation suggests may happen.[103]

Given the predicted momentum of liability, business enterprises should familiarise themselves with BHR frameworks to reduce risks of liability and as duty bearers with a responsibility to respect environmental human rights. The following section will set out key provisions within BHR frameworks as they may apply to the plastics industry.

4 Applying Business and Human Rights (BHR) Guidance to the Plastics Burden

The three pillars of the 2011 *United Nations Guiding Principles on Business and Human Rights* (UNGPs)[104] are all relevant to addressing the plastics challenge through a human rights lens. Unlike many BHR issues, however, the plastics challenge necessitates integration of BHR into tools that are designed to address the transition away from the 'resource-inefficient, linear, take-make-waste plastic economy'[105] and towards a circular economy.[106] Many initiatives are emerging to guide businesses in the transition to circularity including

99 See Pritchard and Merry (n 16, n 44, n 62, n 100), *Plastics on trial: a briefing series.*

100 See Rosa Pritchard and Alice Merry, *Plastics on trial: a briefing series on evolving liability risks related to plastics: Brief 3: In the environment,* ClientEarth, September 2022, 7, https://www.clientearth.org/media/vrsfilit/plastics-on-trial-3-environment.pdf.

101 Minderoo Foundation, "No Plastic Waste: What We Do," accessed February 27, 2023, https://www.minderoo.org/no-plastic-waste/.

102 Pritchard and Merry (n 100), *Brief 3: In the environment,* 7.

103 Merkl and Charles (n 13), *The Price of Plastic,* 16.

104 United Nations (n 17), *UNGPs.*

105 UNEP (n 1), "Plastics Science," 3.

106 See further UNEP, *BHRE Plastics* and accompanying training materials (n 19).

specifically in relation to plastics,[107] however few of these tend to integrate attention to human rights.

The below discussion will briefly explore how BHR frameworks can provide guidance to business enterprises to ensure that their actions to address plastics both contribute to circularity and respect human rights. Considered here are initiatives of the UN Global Compact, the UN Working Group on Business and Human Rights, and OECD Responsible Business Conduct.

4.1 *United Nations Global Compact and Sustainable Oceans Principles*

The United Nations Global Compact's (UNGC) *Ten Principles*[108] move tentatively towards integration of human rights and circularity. Principles 1 and 2 focus on human rights, while Principles 7, 8 and 9 address the environment, including the adoption of a precautionary approach, the promotion of environmental responsibility, and the 'development and diffusion' of technologies that are environmentally friendly. However, the UNGC treats human rights and the environment as well as labour and anti-corruption as separate rather than interdependent challenges in contrast to a true environmental human rights approach.

The UNGC's *Sustainable Oceans Principles*[109] takes small steps towards integration of relevance to plastics. For example, Principle 1 calls upon businesses to assess the impact of their operations on ocean health, while Principle 3 requires businesses to '[t]ake action to prevent pollution affecting the ocean, reduce greenhouse gas emissions in their operations to prevent ocean warming and acidification, and work towards a circular economy.'[110] Principle 7 requires businesses to 'Respect human-, labour-, and indigenous peoples' rights in the company's ocean related activities, including exercise appropriate due diligence in their supply-chain, consult and engage with relevant stakeholders and communities in a timely, transparent and inclusive manner, and address identified impacts.'[111] Sector-specific practical guidance is being developed to

107 Sarah J. Morath, *Our Plastic Problem and How to Solve It* (Cambridge: Cambridge University Press, 2022): 138–139 (discussing the ISO Responsible Plastic Management Standard), 190 (discussing the MacArthur Foundations' three circular economy principles) and 193 (discussing extended producer responsibility schemes).

108 United Nations Global Compact, *The Ten Principles of the UN Global Compact*, https://unglobalcompact.org/what-is-gc/mission/principles.

109 United Nations Global Compact, *The Sustainable Ocean Principles: a principles-based approach to sustainable ocean business*, https://unglobalcompact.org/take-action/ocean/communication/sustainable-ocean-principles.

110 United Nations Global Compact, *Sustainable Ocean Principles*, Principles 1–9, https://d306pr3pise04h.cloudfront.net/docs/publications%2FSustainable+Ocean+Principles.pdf.

111 Ibid.

supplement the *Sustainable Oceans Principles*, with seaweed industry guidance specifically identifying seaweed's potential in the development of alternatives to plastic packaging.[112]

4.2 *UN Guiding Principles*

A business and human rights-based approach following the UNGPs necessarily requires attention to the duties of states to protect human rights (pillar 1), the responsibilities of businesses as duty bearers to respect human rights (pillar 2), and the vital importance of access to remedy (pillar 3). While the UNGPs themselves make no explicit reference to environmental human rights, the UNGA resolution on the right to a clean, healthy, and sustainable environment specifically takes note of the UNGPs, in keeping with the approach of multiple reports by special rapporteurs that inform the content of the right.[113]

The expectations of business enterprises under the UNGPs are well known and described in Principle 15 as requiring the adoption of a policy commitment to respect human rights (elaborated in Principle 16), a human rights due diligence process (elaborated in Principles 17–21) designed to 'identify, prevent, mitigate and account for how [the business] address(es) their impacts on human rights'[114] and '[p]rocesses to enable the remediation of any adverse human rights impacts' that the business causes or to which it contributes[115] (elaborated in Principle 22). Principle 13 of the UNGPs clarifies that the responsibility of business enterprises across the value chain differs depending on whether it is the business' own activities that have caused or contributed to the adverse impacts on human rights (in which case the business has a responsibility to address the resulting impacts), or whether the impacts arise from business relationships directly linked to business 'operations, products or services,' even in the absence of contribution (in which case the business has a responsibility to 'seek to prevent or mitigate' the impacts).[116] Responsibility based on contribution to harm from the UNGPs is gaining legal traction in courts,[117] and

112 United Nations Global Compact, *Practical Guidance for the UN Global Compact Sustainable Ocean Principles*, 8, https://ungc-communications-assets.s3.amazonaws.com/docs/publications/UN%20Global-Compact-Sustainable-Ocean-Principles-Seaweed.pdf.

113 United Nations General Assembly (UNGA), "The human right to a clean, healthy and sustainable environment," 2; see generally Sara L. Seck "Teaching Note: Human Rights and the Environment" in *Teaching Business and Human Rights*, ed. Anthony Ewing (Massachusetts: Edward Elgar Publishing, 2023), 265–279.

114 United Nations, *UNGPs* (n 17), Principle 15(b).

115 Ibid, Principle 15 (c).

116 Ibid, Principle 13.

117 See e.g., *Milliuedefensie et al. v. Royal Dutch Shell, plc*, ECLI:NL: RBDHA:2021:5339, https://climatecasechart.com/wp-content/uploads/non-us-case-documents/2021/20210526_8918_judgment-1.pdf; Commission on Human Rights of the Philippines, *National Inquiry*

so it is to be anticipated that it will also influence plastics-related litigation that also draws upon ideas of extended producer responsibility.[118]

The UN Working Group on Business and Human Rights has produced many reports that clarify aspects of the business responsibility under the UNGPs, many of which have relevance to an environmental human rights approach to plastics. For example, the 2019 *Gender lens* report[119] addresses the responsibilities of all businesses toward informal economy workers,[120] of particular importance to informal plastics waste workers who in many countries are predominantly women. The need to gather gender-disaggregated data and to consider intersectional dimensions is also identified, along with the importance of meaningful engagement with grassroots organisations, women human rights defenders and experts.[121]

A 2021 UN Working Group report provides guidance for businesses on ensuring respect for human rights defenders by engaging with them and safeguarding their rights—an essential component of a procedural environmental human rights approach.[122] The report calls for a cultural shift so that businesses and states see human rights defenders as 'essential allies in protecting people and the planet' rather than as enemies.[123] Accordingly, when businesses conduct human rights due diligence, environmental human rights defenders and community leaders should be seen as expert resources—of importance to each stage of the plastics life cycle.[124]

Another issue that the Working Group has addressed is the need for states to ensure policy coherence across government practices, including in the

---

on Climate Change Report, 2022, https://www.ciel.org/wp-content/uploads/2023/02/CHRP-NICC-Report-2022.pdf.

118 On extended producer responsibility, see UNEP, *BHRE Plastics* (n 19), 92–94.

119 OHCHR, *Gender dimensions of the Guiding Principles on Business and Human Rights*, Report of the Working Group on Business and Human Rights, UN Doc A/HRC/41/43, May 23, 2019, https://www.ohchr.org/sites/default/files/Documents/Issues/Business/Gender_Booklet_Final.pdf.

120 Ibid, Principle 14.

121 Ibid, Principle 18.

122 OHCHR, *The Guiding Principles on Business and Human Rights: guidance on ensuring respect for human rights defenders*, UN Doc A/HRC/47/39/Add.2, June 22, 2021, https://documents-dds-ny.un.org/doc/UNDOC/GEN/G21/161/49/PDF/G2116149.pdf?OpenElement.

123 Ibid, para 33.

124 Ibid, (workers, whether formal or informal, may also act as human rights defenders when engaged in whistle blowing, see UNEP, *BHRE Plastics* (n 19), 92).

development of National Action Plans on BHR that should explicitly link seemingly different agendas in support of the SDGs.[125] As states develop action plans on plastics and action plans on business and human rights, an ideal opportunity exists to align these agendas.[126]

4.3 *OECD Responsible Business Conduct*

The OECD's work on Responsible Business Conduct provides increasingly pertinent guidance for businesses serious about tackling the plastics crisis through both a circular economy and human rights lens.[127] The OECD *Guidelines for Multinational Enterprises* (*MNE Guidelines*)[128] integrate the due diligence approach of the UNGPs but apply more expansively. The *MNE Guidelines* went through a 'targeted update'[129] following the release of a Stocktaking Report released in May 2022.[130] The updated *MNE Guidelines* provide even deeper engagement with the human rights and circular economy relationship as well as biodiversity loss and climate change,[131] and many important insights may be drawn from the chapters together with the 2018 *OECD Due Diligence Guidance on Responsible Business Conduct* that elaborates upon the OECD's risk-based approach to due diligence.[132] In addition, sector-specific tools may provide

125 UNGA, *Report of the Working Group on the issue of human rights and transnational corporations and other business enterprises,* UN Doc. A/74/198, July 19, 2019, paras 7–8, https://documents-dds-ny.un.org/doc/UNDOC/GEN/N19/224/00/PDF/N1922400.pdf?OpenElement (the report highlights the need to strengthen holistic environmental assessment laws, ensure environmental and health and safety laws are enforced, and protect environmental human rights defenders, see paras 34–37, and 57).

126 UNEP, *BHRE Plastics* (n 19), 67–68.

127 See generally OECD, *Responsible Business Conduct: OECD Guidelines for Multinational Enterprises,* accessed March 29, 2023, https://mneguidelines.oecd.org/ (*MNE Guidelines*).

128 OECD, *MNE Guidelines* (n 18).

129 OECD, "Targeted update of the OECD Guidelines for Multinational Enterprises," *OECD*, accessed March 29, 2023, https://mneguidelines.oecd.org/public-consultation-targeted-update-of-the-oecd-guidelines-for-multinational-enterprises.htm.

130 OECD, "Stocktaking exercise on the OECD Guidelines for Multinational Enterprises," *OECD*, accessed March 29, 2023, https://mneguidelines.oecd.org/stocktaking-exercise-on-the-oecd-guidelines-for-multinational-enterprises.htm.

131 The extent to which existing guidelines can be used to address the circularity challenge is discussed in, OECD, *The role of OECD instruments on responsible business conduct in progressing environmental objectives, OECD*, 2021, http://mneguidelines.oecd.org/The-role-of-OECD-instruments-on-responsible-business-conduct-in-progressing-environmental-objectives.pdf.

132 See OECD, *OECD Due Diligence Guidance for Responsible Business Conduct,* (Paris: OECD Publishing, 2018), https://mneguidelines.oecd.org/OECD-Due-Diligence-Guidance-for-Responsible-Business-Conduct.pdf; see analysis in UNEP, *BHRE Plastics* (n 19), 82–83.

additional insights such as the 2016 *OECD-FAO Guidance for Responsible Agricultural Supply Chains*,[133] and the 2018 *OECD Due Diligence Guidance for Responsible Supply Chains in the Garment and Footwear Sector*.[134] The interpretive work of OECD National Contact Points also plays a role in supplementing these tools.[135]

For example, the chapter on disclosure in the OECD *MNE Guidelines* supports the need for businesses to gather information on human rights impacts at each stage of the plastics life cycle, as well as to the accessible disclosure of this information to those at risk of environmental harm so that they may exercise their procedural rights.[136] The employment and industrial relations chapter clarifies the role of businesses in supporting the exercise of rights by both formal and informal workers so as to reduce exposure to toxic substances through global supply chains at each stage of the plastics life cycle.[137] The environment chapter provides comprehensive support for the exercise of environmental human rights by communities and workers through supply chain relationships as well as emphasising the importance of avoiding impacts through responsible product design.[138] The consumer-interests chapter draws attention to the role of businesses in respecting the rights of consumers to access relevant environmental information, and to consumer education in support of safe and sustainable consumption, with attention to equity and vulnerability.[139] Additional chapters provide guidance on combatting bribery, a particular challenge at the importation and incineration stage of the plastics cycle,[140] and science and technology, highlighting the important role of business enterprises in the development of innovative, equitable and sustainable solutions to the long-term challenges of the plastics crisis.

---

133 OECD/Food and Agriculture Organization of the United Nations (OECD-FAO), *OECD-FAO Guidance for Responsible Agricultural Supply Chains*, (Paris: OECD Publishing, 2016), http://dx.doi.org/10.1787/9789264251052-en.

134 OECD, *OECD Due Diligence Guidance for Responsible Supply Chains in the Garment and Footwear Sector*, (Paris: OECD Publishing, 2018), http://dx.doi.org/10.1787/9789264290587-en; see analysis in UNEP, *BHRE Plastics* (n 19), 83–84.

135 OECD, "What are National Contact Points For RBC?," accessed March 29, 2023, https://mneguidelines.oecd.org/ncps/ (among proposals in the targeted update are changes designed to strengthen the effectiveness of NCPs).

136 UNEP, *BHRE Plastics* (n 19), 77–78.

137 Ibid, 78–79.

138 Ibid, 79–80.

139 Ibid, 80–81.

140 Ibid, 80.

5 Conclusion

This chapter described the adverse impacts on environmental human rights associated with plastics as a common commodity and as a pollutant that is liable to become 'a geographic indicator of the Anthropocene era.'[141] As this chapter explored, various types of substantive and procedural environmental human rights are impacted at each stage of the plastics life cycle with disproportionate impacts on equity-seeking groups. However, there is also an opportunity to secure these rights systematically at each stage. To this extent, existing BHR frameworks offer guidance on responsible business conduct to help secure these rights, reduce risks of liability and to help achieve the right to a clean, healthy, and sustainable environment that many human rights ultimately depend on for their implementation.

Bibliography

Books

Liborion, Max. *Pollution Is Colonialism.* Durham: Duke University Press, 2021.

Morath, Sarah J. *Our Plastic Problem and How to Solve It.* Cambridge: Cambridge University Press, 2022.

Chapters in Edited Books

Seck, Sara L. "Teaching Note: Human Rights and the Environment." In *Teaching Business and Human Rights*, edited by Anthony Ewing, 265–279. Massachusetts: Edward Elgar Publishing, 2023.

Articles

Adler, Robert W. and Carina E. Wells. "Plastics and the Limits of U.S. Environmental Law." *Harvard Environmental Law Review* 47, no. 1 (Spring 2023): 1–62.

Allen, Steve, Deonie Allen, Vernon R. Phoenix, Gaël Le Roux, Pilar Durántez Jiménez, Anaëlle Simonneau, Stéphane Binet and Didier Galop. "Atmospheric transport and deposition of microplastics in a remote mountain catchment." *Nature Geoscience* 12, no. 5 (April 2019): 339–344.

141 UNEP, "Our planet is drowning in plastic pollution," *UNEP*, May 18, 2018, https://www.unep.org/news-and-stories/story/our-planet-drowning-plastic-pollution.

Crenshaw, Kimberlé W.. "Demarginalizing the Intersection of Race and Sex: A Black Feminist Critique of Antidiscrimination Doctrine, Feminist Theory and Antiracist Politics." *University of Chicago Legal Forum* 1, no.8 (1989): 139–167.

Guinée, Jeroen B., Reinout Heijungs, Gjalt Huppes, Alessandra Zamagni, Paolo Masoni, Roberto Buonamici, Tomas Ekvall, and Tomas Rydberg. "Life Cycle Assessments: Past, Present, and Future." *Environmental Science & Technology* 45, no. 1 (2011): 90–96.

Hahladakis, John N., Costas A. Velis, Roland Weber, Eleni Iacovidou, and Phil Purnell. "An Overview of Chemical Additives Present in Plastics: Migration, Release, Fate and Environmental Impact During Their Use, Disposal and Recycling." *Hazardous Materials* 344, (February 2018): 179–199.

Karlsson, Therese M., Lars Arneborg, Göran Broström, Bethanie Carney Almroth, Lena Gipperth, and Martin Hassellöv. "The Unaccountability Case of Plastic Pellet Pollution." *Marine Pollution Bulletin* 129, no. 1 (April 2018): 52–60.

Leslie, Heather A., Martin J.M. van Velzen, Sicco H. Brandsma, A. Dick Vethaak, Juan J. Garcia-Vallejo, and Marja H. Lamoree. "Discovery and quantification of plastic particle pollution in human blood." Environment International 163, 107199 (May 2022): 1–8.

Pascual, Florencia. "Fracking and Childhood Leukemia: New Evidence Supports Greater Residential Setbacks." *Environmental Health Perspectives* 130, no. 9 (September 2022): 094002-1–094002-2. https://doi.org/10.1289/EHP11982.

Ragusa, Antonio, Alessandro Svelato, Criselda Santacroce, Piera Catalano, Valentina Notarstefano, Oliana Carnevali, Fabrizio Papa et al. "Plasticenta: First evidence of microplastics in human placenta." *Environment International* 146, 106274 (January 2021): 1–8. https://doi.org/10.1016/j.envint.2020.106274.

Rich, Alisa L., Laura M Phipps, Sweta Tiwari, Hemanth Rudraraju, and Philip O. Dokpesi. "The Increasing Prevalence in Intersex Variation from Toxicological Dysregulation in Fetal Reproductive Tissue Differentiation and Development by Endocrine-Disrupting Chemicals." *Environmental Health Insights* 10, (September 2016): 163–171.

Zagozewski, Rebecca, Ian Judd-Henrey, Suzie Nilson and Lalita Bharadwaj. "Perspectives on Past and Present Waste Disposal Practices: A Community-Based Participatory Research Project in Three Saskatchewan First Nations Communities." *Environmental Health Insights* 5, (January–December 2011): 9–20. https://doi.org/10.4137/EHI.S6974.

Online/Internet Sources

American Civil Liberties Union (ACLU) and the University of Chicago Law School Global Human Rights Clinic (UCLSGHRC). *Captive Labor: Exploitation of Incarcerated Workers*. ACLU and GHRC Research Report (2022). https://aboutblaw.com/3Xl.

As You Sow. "Record-Setting 81% of DuPont Shareholders Approve Proposal Calling for Plastic Pellet Pollution Reporting." *As You Sow*, May 3, 2021. https://www.asyousow.org/press-releases/2021/5/3/dupont-shareholders-approve-plastic-pellet-pollution-reporting.

Aung, May Thazin, Andreea Raluca Torre, Cannelle Guegeun-Teil, Bernadette P. Resurrección, Natalie Harms, and Jerker Tamelander. *Marine Plastic Litter in East Asian Seas: Gender, Human Rights and Economic Dimensions*. United Nations Environment Programme, 2019. https://www.sea-circular.org/wp-content/uploads/2019/11/SEI_SEA-circular-1.pdf.

Comoli, Virginia. *Plastic for Profit: Tracing Illicit Plastic Waste Flows, Supply Chains and Actors*. Global Initiative Against Transnational Organized Crime (November 2021) https://globalinitiative.net/wp-content/uploads/2021/10/GITOC-Plastic-for-Profit.pdf.

Fraser, Connor. "Plastics in the Courtroom: The Evolution of Plastics Litigation." *State Energy & Environmental Impact Center* (*blog*), New York University School of Law, July 15, 2022. https://stateimpactcenter.org/insights/plastics-in-the-courtroom-the-evolution-of-plastics-litigation.

Geddie, John and Valerie Volcovici, "Exclusive: U.S. seeks allies as split emerges over global plastics pollution treaty." *Reuters*, September 27, 2022. https://www.reuters.com/world/exclusive-us-seeks-allies-split-emerges-over-global-plastics-pollution-treaty-2022-09-27/.

International Maritime Organization. "Sub-Committee on Pollution Prevention and Response (PPR 9)," Meeting Summary. 2022. https://www.imo.org/en/MediaCentre/MeetingSummaries/Pages/PPR-9th-session.aspx.

Mavroeidi, Eleonora, Maarten Dubois, Elena Buzzi and Daniel Ostalé Valriberas. *Global Plastics Outlook: Policy Scenarios to 2060*. OECD, 2022. https://www.oecd-ilibrary.org/sites/aa1edf33-en/1/2/2/index.html?itemId= /content/publication /aa1edf33-en&_csp_=ca738cf5d4f327be3b6fec4af9ce5d12&itemIGO=oecd&itemContentType=book.

Merkl, Andreas and Dom Charles. *The Price of Plastic Pollution: Social Costs and Corporate Liabilities*, Minderoo Foundation, October 2022: 19. https://cdn.minderoo.org/content/uploads/2022/10/14130457/The-Price-of-Plastic-Pollution.pdf.

Minderoo Foundation. "No Plastic Waste: What We Do." Accessed February 27, 2023. https://www.minderoo.org/no-plastic-waste/.

Organization for Economic Co-operation and Development. "Plastic pollution is growing relentlessly as waste management and recycling fall short, says OECD." *OECD*, February 2, 2022. https://www.oecd.org/environment/plastic-pollution-is-growing-relentlessly-as-waste-management-and-recycling-fall-short.htm.

Organization for Economic Co-operation and Development. "Plastics use by application-projections." *OECD.Stat*, May 5, 2022. https://stats.oecd.org/Index.aspx-?DataSetCode=PLASTIC_USE_V2_3.

Organization for Economic Co-operation and Development. "Stocktaking exercise on the OECD Guidelines for Multinational Enterprises." *OECD*, accessed March 29, 2023. https://mneguidelines.oecd.org/stocktaking-exercise-on-the-oecd-guidelines-for-multinational-enterprises.htm.

Organization for Economic Co-operation and Development. "Targeted update of the OECD Guidelines for Multinational Enterprises." *OECD*. Accessed March 29, 2023. https://mneguidelines.oecd.org/public-consultation-targeted-update-of-the-oecd-guidelines-for-multinational-enterprises.htm.

Organization for Economic Co-operation and Development. "The role of OECD instruments on responsible business conduct in progressing environmental objectives." *OECD*, 2021. http://mneguidelines.oecd.org/The-role-of-OECD-instruments-on-responsible-business-conduct-in-progressing-environmental-objectives.pdf.

Organization for Economic Co-operation and Development. "What are National Contact Points for RBC?." *OECD*, accessed March 29, 2023, https://mneguidelines.oecd.org/ncps/.

Office of the United Nations High Commissioner for Human Rights. *Special Rapporteur on Human Rights and the Environment*. https://www.ohchr.org/en/special-procedures/sr-environment.

Pritchard, Rosa and Alice Merry. *Plastics on trial: a briefing series on evolving liability risks related to plastics*. ClientEarth, September 2022. https://www.clientearth.org/latest/documents/plastics-on-trial-1-greenwashing/.

Pritchard, Rosa and Alice Merry. *Plastics on trial: a briefing series on evolving liability risks related to plastics: Brief 2: Hazardous chemicals*. ClientEarth, September 2022. https://www.clientearth.org/latest/documents/plastics-on-trial-2-hazardous-chemicals/.

Pritchard, Rosa and Alice Merry. *Plastics on trial: a briefing series on evolving liability risks related to plastics: Brief 3: In the environment*. ClientEarth, September 2022. https://www.clientearth.org/media/vrsfilit/plastics-on-trial-3-environment.pdf.

Pritchard, Rosa and Alice Merry. *Plastics on trial: a briefing series on evolving liability risks related to plastics: Brief 4: Waste disposal & recycling*. Client Earth, September 2022. https://www.clientearth.org/media/durfpjzw/plastics-on-trial-4-waste.pdf.

Seck, Sara L. *Business, Human Rights and the Environment in South-East Asia: Overcoming the Plastics Challenge*, Policy Training Resource. *United Nations Environment Programme*, September 30, 2022. https://wedocs.unep.org/handle/20.500.11822/41852.

Shennum, Krista. "'It's As If They're Poisoning Us' The Health Impacts of Plastic Recycling in Turkey." *Human Rights Watch*, September 2022. https://www.hrw.org/report/2022/09/21/its-if-theyre-poisoning-us/health-impacts-plastic-recycling-turkey.

State of California, Department of Justice. "Attorney General Bonta Announces Investigation into Fossil Fuel and Petrochemical Industries for Role in Causing Global Plastics Pollution Crisis." *Rob Bonta Attorney General*, April 28, 2022. https://oag.ca.gov/news/press-releases/attorney-general-bonta-announces-investigation-fossil-fuel-and-petrochemical.

United Nations Environment Programme. "First session of Intergovernmental Negotiating Committee to develop an international legally binding instrument on plastic pollution,…." *UNEP* (Conference: November 28–December 02, 2022). https://www.unep.org/events/conference/inter-governmental-negotiating-committee-meeting-inc-1.

United Nations Environment Programme. "Our planet is choking on plastic." *UNEP*, accessed January 27, 2022, https://www.unep.org/interactives/beat-plastic-pollution/.

United Nations Environment Programme. "Our planet is drowning in plastic pollution." *UNEP*, May 18, 2018, https://www.unep.org/news-and-stories/story/our-planet-drowning-plastic-pollution.

United Nations Environment Programme. "Second session of Intergovernmental Negotiating Committee to develop an international legally binding instrument on plastic pollution,…." *UNEP* (Conference: May 29–June 02, 2023). https://www.unep.org/events/conference/second-session-intergovernmental-negotiating-committee-develop-international.

Zhong, Raymond and Catrin Einhorn. "Health and Environmental Fears Remain After Ohio Derailment and Inferno." *New York Times*, February 14, 2023. https://www.nytimes.com/2023/02/14/climate/ohio-train-derailment-chemical-spill-health.html.

Official Documents

Commission on Human Rights of the Philippines. *National Inquiry on Climate Change Report*, 2022, https://www.ciel.org/wp-content/uploads/2023/02/CHRP-NICC-Report-2022.pdf.

Government of Canada. "Plastics Challenge: Mitigating the Release of Microplastics from Tire Wear." *Innovation, Science and Economic Development Canada*. Date modified: August 31, 2022. https://ised-isde.canada.ca/site/innovative-solutions-canada/en/plastics-challenge-mitigating-release-microplastics-tire-wear.

National Academies of Sciences, Engineering, and Medicine. *Reckoning with the U.S. Role in Global Ocean Plastic Waste*. Washington, DC: The National Academies Press, 2022. https://doi.org/10.17226/26132.

Office of the United Nations High Commissioner for Human Rights. *Gender dimensions of the Guiding Principles on Business and Human Rights*. Report of the Working Group on Business and Human Rights, UN Doc A/HRC/41/43, May 23, 2019. https://www.ohchr.org/sites/default/files/Documents/Issues/Business/Gender_Booklet_Final.pdf.

Office of the United Nations High Commissioner for Human Rights. *Principles on human rights and the protection of workers from exposure to toxic substances*. Special Rapporteur on Toxic Substances and Human Rights. UN Doc. A/HRC/42/41, 2019.

Office of the United Nations High Commissioner for Human Rights. *Report of the Special Rapporteur on the issue of human rights obligations relating to the enjoyment of a safe, clean, healthy and sustainable environment*. "Framework Principles on Human Rights and the Environment." UN Doc. A/HRC/37/59, January 24, 2018.

Office of the United Nations High Commissioner for Human Rights. *Right to a healthy environment: good practices: Report of the Special Rapporteur on the issue of human rights obligations relating to the enjoyment of a safe, clean, healthy and sustainable environment*. UN Doc. A/HRC/43/53, December 30, 2019.

Office of the United Nations High Commissioner for Human Rights. *Right to Science in the Context of Toxic Substances*. Special Rapporteur on Toxic Substances and Human Rights. UN Doc. A/HRC/48/61, 2021.

Office of the United Nations High Commissioner for Human Rights. *The Guiding Principles on Business and Human Rights: guidance on ensuring respect for human rights defenders*. UN Doc A/HRC/47/39/Add.2, June 22, 2021. https://documents-dds-ny.un.org/doc/UNDOC/GEN/G21/161/49/PDF/G2116149.pdf?OpenElement.

Organization for Economic Co-operation and Development. *OECD Due Diligence Guidance for Responsible Business Conduct*. Paris: OECD Publishing, 2018. https://mneguidelines.oecd.org/OECD-Due-Diligence-Guidance-for-Responsible-Business-Conduct.pdf.

Organization for Economic Co-operation and Development. *OECD Due Diligence Guidance for Responsible Supply Chains in the Garment and Footwear Sector*. Paris: OECD Publishing, 2018. http://dx.doi.org/10.1787/9789264290587-en.

Organization for Economic Co-operation and Development. *OECD Guidelines for Multinational Enterprises*. Paris: OECD Publishing, 2011. http://dx.doi.org/10.1787/9789264115415-en.

Organization for Economic Co-operation and Development. *Responsible Business Conduct: OECD Guidelines for Multinational Enterprises*. Accessed: March 29, 2023. https://mneguidelines.oecd.org/.

Organization for Economic Co-operation and Development and Food and Agriculture Organization of the United Nations. *OECD-FAO Guidance for Responsible Agricultural Supply Chains*, Paris: OECD Publishing, 2016. http://dx.doi.org/10.1787/9789264251052-en.

United Nations. *Basel Convention on the Control of Transboundary Movements of Hazardous Wastes*. 1673 UNTS 126, March 22, 1989, entered into force May 5, 1992.

United Nations. *International Convention for the Prevention of Pollution from Ships*. 1340 UNTS 61, November 2, 1973, entered into force October 2, 1983.

United Nations. *Stockholm Convention on Persistent Organic Pollutants*. 2256 UNTS 119, 22 May 2001, entered into force May 17, 2004.

United Nations. *United Nations Guiding Principles on Business and Human Rights*. UN Doc. A/HRC/17/31 (Annex). https://www.ohchr.org/sites/default/files/documents/publications/guidingprinciplesbusinesshr_en.pdf.

United Nations Environment Programme. *Guidelines for Social Life Cycle Assessment of Products*. UNEP, 2009. https://wedocs.unep.org/bitstream/handle/20.500.11822/7912/-Guidelines%20for%20Social %20Life%20Cycle %20Assessment%20of%20Products-20094102.pdf?sequence=3&amp%3BisAllowed=.

United Nations Environment Programme. "Plastics Science." UN Doc. UNEP/PP/INC.1/7, Annex, "Plastic Pollution Science," 3, September 13, 2022. https://wedocs.unep.org/bitstream/handle/20.500.11822/40831/K2221533%20-%20%20UNEP-PP-INC.1-7%20-%20AMENDED%20ADVANCE%20-%2014.10.2022.pdf.

United Nations Environment Programme. "Resolution 14: End Plastic Pollution: Towards an Internationally Legally Binding Instrument." UNEP/EA.5/Res.14, 2022, https://wedocs.unep.org/bitstream/handle/20.500.11822/39764/END%20PLASTIC%20POLLUTION%20-%20TOWARDS%20AN%20INTERNATIONAL%20LEGALLY%20BINDING%20INSTRUMENT%20-%20English.pdf?sequence=1&isAllowed=y.

United Nations General Assembly, *Report of the Special Rapporteur on the implications for human rights of the environmentally sound management and disposal of hazardous substances and wastes, Marcos Orellana: The stages of the plastics cycle and their impacts on human rights*. United Nations General Assembly, 76th session, UN Doc A/76/207, July 2021. https://digitallibrary.un.org/record/3936771?ln=en.

United Nations General Assembly. *Mandate of the Special Rapporteur on the implications for human rights of the environmentally sound management and disposal of hazardous substances and wastes*. UN Doc. A/HRC/RES/45/17, October 09, 2020. https://documents-dds-ny.un.org/doc/UNDOC/GEN/G20/259/12/PDF/G2025912.pdf?OpenElement.

United Nations General Assembly. *Report of the Working Group on the issue of human rights and transnational corporations and other business enterprises*. UN Doc. A/74/198, July 19, 2019. https://documents-dds-ny.un.org/doc/UNDOC/GEN/N19/224/00/PDF/N1922400.pdf?OpenElement.

United Nations General Assembly. "The human right to a clean, healthy and sustainable environment." UN Doc. A/RES/76/300, resolution adopted by the General Assembly on July 28, 2022. https://digitallibrary.un.org/record/3983329?ln=en.

United Nations Global Compact. *Practical Guidance for the UN Global Compact Sustainable Ocean Principles.* https://ungc-communications-assets.s3.amazonaws.com/docs/publications/UN%20Global-Compact-Sustainable-Ocean-Principles-Seaweed.pdf.

United Nations Global Compact. *Sustainable Ocean Principles.* https://d306pr3pise04h.cloudfront.net/docs/publications%2FSustainable+Ocean+Principles.pdf.

United Nations Global Compact. *The Sustainable Ocean Principles: a principles-based approach to sustainable ocean business.* https://unglobalcompact.org/take-action/ocean/communication/sustainable-ocean-principles.

United Nations Global Compact. *The Ten Principles of the UN Global Compact.* https://unglobalcompact.org/what-is-gc/mission/principles.

United States of America, Office of the Inspector General (OIG). *A Review of Federal Prison Industries' Electronic-Waste Recycling Program.* United States Department of Justice, October 2010. https://oig.justice.gov/reports/BOP/o1010.pdf.

Cases

Milliuedefensie et al. v. Royal Dutch Shell, plc, ECLI:NL: RBDHA:2021:5339, https://climatecasechart.com/wp-content/uploads/non-us-case-documents/2021/20210526_8918_judgment-1.pdf.

CHAPTER 5

The Application of the UN Guiding Principles on Business and Human Rights in Conflict Areas: Corporate Responsibilities, Responses, and Non-responses in the Context of the Ukraine War

Peter Muchlinski

1 Introduction

This chapter considers business responsibilities for human rights arising from the Ukraine War. The role of business enterprises in armed conflict has a long history.[1] Armed conflict requires the active participation of economic actors, whether as producers and suppliers of arms and other goods or services essential to the conduct of war, or as providers of logistical support, finance, raw materials, utilities and, crucially for modern warfare, information technology. Increasingly, armed conflict is being commercialised with the involvement of private security firms as military actors and advisers alongside formal state militaries.[2] Equally, post-conflict reconstruction offers huge business opportunities, although space limitation prevents an examination of this issue here.[3] All these activities expose businesses to the risk of direct violations of human rights through their own actions or by participating in violations primarily caused by other actors such as military forces, their governments or other business partners. Recognising this risk, the UN Guiding Principles on Business and Human Rights (UNGPs) require businesses to undertake heightened human rights due diligence (HRDD) assessments to avoid, or at least to mitigate, any adverse human rights impacts arising from operations linked to armed conflict.

The current phase of the Ukraine War began on 24 February 2022 when Russian forces entered Northern, Eastern and Southern Ukraine aiming to

1 Mark B. Taylor *War Economies and International Law: Regulating the Economic Activities of Violent Conflict* (Cambridge:, Cambridge University Press, 2021), 1.

2 On which see generally Naomi Klein *The Shock Doctrine* (London: Penguin Books, 2007).

3 See e.g. Klein *The Shock Doctrine* especially Part 6 covering the reconstruction of Iraq after the 2003 invasion.

 | DOI:10.1163/9789004530942_006

overthrow the government of President Volodymyr Oleksandrovych Zelenskyy and control the whole country. The conflict originated in 2014 when Russian forces invaded Eastern Ukraine, occupied the Donetsk and Luhansk regions and annexed Crimea into the Russian Federation.[4] Russian President Vladimir Putin justifies the current escalation as a response to the alleged strategic threat that Ukraine, apparently encouraged by NATO, poses for the occupied regions of Eastern Ukraine and Crimea. President Putin alleges that ethnic Russians living in those regions have been subjected to 'genocide' at the hands of Ukrainian forces, entitling Russia to intervene in accordance with the right to self-defence under Article 51 of Chapter VII of the UN Charter.[5]

This has no legal foundation for the simple reason that, by attacking Ukraine, Russia has violated a core principle of the UN Charter. By Article 2(4) of the Charter

> All Members shall refrain in their international relations from the threat or use of force against the territorial integrity or political independence of any state, or in any other manner inconsistent with the Purposes of the United Nations.[6]

The escalation of the war in 2022 caused widespread, though not universal, condemnation.[7] The UN Security Council has been unable to act due to Russia's veto as a Permanent Member.[8] However, the UN General Assembly passed a resolution on March 2, 2022, condemning Russia's actions by a vote of

---

4 For a summary of the main phases of the war up to November 2022 see Center for Preventive Action "Conflict in Ukraine", updated November 8, 2022, (accessed June 22, 2023) https://www.cfr.org/global-conflict-tracker/conflict/conflict-ukraine.

5 See President Vladimir Putin "Address by the President of the Russian Federation," (February 21, 2022 The Kremlin, Moscow), (accessed June 22, 2023) http://en.kremlin.ru/events/president/news/67828; Andrew Osborn and Polina Nikolskaya "Russia's Putin authorises 'special military operation' against Ukraine," *Reuters*, February 24, 2022, (accessed June 22, 2023) https://www.reuters.com/world/europe/russias-putin-authorises-military-operations-donbass-domestic-media-2022-02-24/.

6 United Nations Charter, (accessed June 22, 2023) https://www.un.org/en/about-us/un-charter/full-text.

7 For a detailed analysis of state responses see Kristen E. Eichensehr, ed., "Contemporary Practice of the United States Relating to International Law," *American Journal of International Law* 116, no 3 (July 2022) 605–14, doi:10.1017/ajil.2022.27.

8 An attempted Security Council resolution condemning the Russian action was voted upon with eleven countries in favour, India, China, and the UAE abstaining and Russia exercising its veto: ibid at 610.

141 in favour and five votes against, with thirty-five abstentions.[9] On balance, it is reasonable to consider that the majority of states see the Ukraine War as an illegal war of aggression.[10]

This contribution explores the nature of the corporate responsibility to respect human rights in the context of the Ukraine War. This is a 'classic war' where the armed forces of sovereign states engage in warfare. In this context, apart from human rights law, international humanitarian law (IHL) also becomes a source of obligations for businesses operating in the course of the conflict. Businesses and their managers risk violating IHL when operating directly within the war zone or occupied territories. As will be discussed in section 3, IHL applies both to states and individuals and can include corporations.

In response to Russia's aggression, national sanctions were instituted by the US, UK, the EU, and other states, which required their corporations to cease trading with and/or divest from Russia.[11] Sanctions have a strong impact on how the corporate responsibility to respect human rights is carried out. Even if a business is not subject to sanctions, continued trade with and/or investment in Russia and its occupied territories during the conflict creates a heightened risk of committing human rights violations, or aiding and abetting such violations, through the provision of finance, investment and/or goods and services to the Russian war effort.

Equally, firms trading with, or investing in Ukraine should consider the risk of participation in human rights abuses. This concerns, in particular, the interaction of Ukrainian state powers with the human rights of Ukrainian citizens.

---

9 Russia, Belarus, North Korea, Syria, and Eritrea voted against the resolution. General Assembly Resolution Demands End to Russian Offensive in Ukraine, UN NEWS, March 2, 2022, (accessed June 22, 2023) https://news.un.org/en/story/2022/03/1113152; UNGA Resolution, A/RES/ES-11/1, adopted March 2, 2022, (accessed June 22, 2023) https://digitallibrary.un.org/record/3965290?ln=en#record-files-collapse-header.

10 See for an academic perspective Michael N. Schmitt "Russia's 'Special Military Operation' and the (Claimed) Right of Self-Defence" *Articles of War*, February 28, 2022, (accessed June 22, 2023) https://lieber.westpoint.edu/russia-special-military-operation-claimed-right-self-defense/; Adil Ahmad Haque, "An Unlawful War," (Symposium on Ukraine and the International Order). *American Journal of International Law* 116 (2022): 115; Yarik Kryvoi et al "Russia's Invasion of Ukraine and International Law: Questions and Answers," *British Institute of International and Comparative Law*, March 17, 2022, (accessed June 22, 2023) https://www.biicl.org/blog/34/russias-invasion-of-ukraine-and-international-law-questions-and-answers.

11 See e.g. for UK sanctions UK Government Statutory Guidance "Russia sanctions: guidance", updated 21 June, 2023, (accessed June 22, 2023) https://www.gov.uk/government/publications/russia-sanctions-guidance/russia-sanctions-guidance; Kristen E. Eichensehr, ed., "United States and Allies Target Russia and Belarus with Sanctions and Other Economic Measures," *American Journal of International Law* 116, no 3 (July, 2022) 614–31.

Firms operating in Ukraine may be required to act in a manner that restricts citizens freedoms in the name of national security. A specific focus for this discussion concerns the passing of new laws in July 2022 which legalised zero-hours contracts and exempted 70% of the Ukrainian workforce from workplace protections.[12]

The chapter is divided as follows: Section 2 examines how HRDD should adapt to establish core corporate human rights responsibilities in time of conflict. Section 3 considers the impact of IHL on HRDD. Section 4 then examines business dealings with Russia in light of heightened HRDD, while Section 5 discusses the role of business in Ukraine as a promoter of human rights for Ukrainian citizens. The chapter ends with section 6 which briefly considers the broader implications of the Ukraine War on the development of business and human rights.

2 The UNGPs and Corporate Responsibilities to Respect Human Rights in Conflict Affected Areas

Principle 7 of the UNGPs, entitled 'Supporting business respect for human rights in conflict affected areas' outlines home state duties under the first pillar of the UNGPs, the state duty to protect against business infringements of human rights.[13] There is no corresponding principle outlining 'business respect for human rights in conflict affected areas' under the second pillar of the UNGPs, the corporate responsibility to respect human rights. Instead, the UNGPs rely on the idea of 'heightened human rights due diligence' in such areas.[14] Conflict affected areas create acute risks of human rights violations and so businesses operating in such areas must carry out HRDD with a heightened awareness of those risks.[15]

12 See Thomas Rowley and Serhiy Guz, "Ukraine uses Russian invasion to pass laws wrecking workers' rights," *Open Democracy*, July 20, 2022, (accessed June 22, 2023) https://www.opendemocracy.net/en/odr/ukraine-draft-law-5371-workers-rights-war-russia/.

13 UNGPs Principle 7, (accessed June 22, 2023) https://www.ohchr.org/sites/default/files/documents/publications/guidingprinciplesbusinesshr_en.pdf.

14 See United Nations Development Programme (UNDP), *Heightened Human Rights Due Diligence for Business in Conflict-Affected Contexts: A Guide*, New York, June 16, 2022, (accessed June 22, 2023) https://www.undp.org/publications/heightened-human-rights-due-diligence-business-conflict-affected-contexts-guide.

15 See Report of the UN Working Group on Business and Human Rights "Business, human rights and conflict-affected regions: towards heightened action," UN Doc A/75/212, July 21, 2020 para. 13, (accessed June 22, 2023) https://www.ohchr.org/en/calls-for-input/report-business-human-rights-and-conflict-affected-regions-towards-heightened .

Principle 7 proposes several graded steps states should take to ensure that business enterprises are not involved in human rights abuses. These include:

(a) Engaging at the earliest stage possible with business enterprises to help them identify, prevent and mitigate the human rights-related risks of their activities and business relationships;
(b) Providing adequate assistance to business enterprises to assess and address the heightened risks of abuses, paying special attention to both gender-based and sexual violence;
(c) Denying access to public support and services for a business enterprise that is involved with gross human rights abuses and refuses to cooperate in addressing the situation;
(d) Ensuring that their current policies, legislation, regulations and enforcement measures are effective in addressing the risk of business involvement in gross human rights abuses.[16]

Key here is early intervention by the home state of the business before serious abuses arise.[17] In the case of investment by multinational enterprises (MNEs), the host state in which the conflict arises is often unable to protect human rights adequately as it may have lost effective control over a part or the whole of its territory. In such cases, the home state must be proactive in helping MNEs to identify, prevent and mitigate risks, provide assistance and punish those firms that do not cooperate and/or are involved in gross human rights abuses.[18]

As already noted, businesses should adapt HRDD to the realities of heightened human rights risks in conflict affected areas. The United Nations Development Programme (UNDP) has offered guidance in its publication *Heightened Human Rights Due Diligence for Business in Conflict-Affected Contexts: A Guide* (the UNDP Guide).[19] The key message is that any business which operates in a conflict affected area,[20] must be aware of the high risk

16 UNGPs (n 13), Principle 7.

17 UNGPs Commentary to Principle 7, (accessed June 22, 2023). https://www.ohchr.org/sites/default/files/documents/publications/guidingprinciplesbusinesshr_en.pdf.

18 See Report of the Special Representative of the Secretary-General on the issue of human rights and transnational corporations and other business enterprises, John Ruggie "Business and human rights in conflict-affected regions: challenges and options towards State responses," UN Doc. A/HRC/17/32, May 27, 2011 para. 6, (accessed June 22, 2023) https://digitallibrary.un.org/record/706417?ln=zh_CN.

19 UNDP Guide (n 14).

20 This is a broad term covering, "any geographical areas, regions or countries that experience various levels of armed conflict or widespread violence including inter-state or civil

of being implicated directly or indirectly in gross abuses of human rights and that its presence is not 'neutral' or without impact, even if the business takes no sides, as its presence involves it in the conflict's dynamics.[21] Accordingly,

> Business needs to identify and assess not only actual or potential adverse human rights impacts, but also actual or potential adverse impacts on conflict that the company may cause or contribute to through its own activities, or that may be directly linked to its operations, products or services.[22]

In addition, as the Commentary to UNGP Principle 12 notes, 'in situations of armed conflict enterprises should respect the standards of international humanitarian law'.[23] The impact of business obligations under IHL for heightened HRDD will be discussed in the next section.

The process of heightened HRDD involves the same steps as HRDD in non-conflict situations but at an increased level of complexity proportionate to the higher human rights risks.[24] There are four core components.

First, the business must identify and assess actual or potential adverse conflict and human rights impacts caused or contributed to through its own activities, or through its business relationships.

Second, it must act on the findings of the initial identification or assessment. If the assessment is made at the pre-investment stage, the business should not get involved at all. If it has already invested and is contributing, or at risk of contributing to, the impact it should take steps to cease or prevent its contribution and mitigate any remaining impact. This raises the key question of how war affects what impacts are impermissible, requiring action by the business. On this the UNGPs are silent, a consequence of not containing a specific principle covering corporate responsibilities in conflict affected areas. That, coupled with the voluntary nature of HRDD under the UNGPs, leaves considerable discretion to the business in how it responds, leaving open the risk that it will do little or nothing to avoid or mitigate adverse human rights impacts where this conflicts with commercial interests.

---

war, armed insurrections, violent extremism or other forms of organized violence." It also covers post-conflict settings. UNDP Guide, 9.

21 UNDP Guide (n 14), 10.

22 Ibid.

23 UNGPs Commentary to Principle 12, (accessed June 22, 2023) https://www.ohchr.org/sites/default/files/documents/publications/guidingprinciplesbusinesshr_en.pdf.

24 UNDP Guide (n 14), 14, on which this paragraph draws.

In cases of human rights impacts arising out of its business relationships, the business should, 'take steps to gain and use leverage to prevent and mitigate the impact, to the greatest extent possible'.[25] Leverage refers to the capacity of the business to affect the behaviour of its business partners by means of the commercial and other influence it may have over them.[26] According to the UNDP Guide,

> In the context of heightened human rights due diligence, leverage is about changing the thinking and behaviour of key people within a supplier, contractor, business partner, customer, client or most likely within governments, opposition parties, armed groups where that organization's actions are increasing the likelihood of conflict or the risk to human rights.[27]

Third, the business must track the effectiveness of the measures taken and processes adopted to address adverse conflict and human rights risks or impacts to understand if they are working.

Fourth, the business must communicate on how risks or impacts are being addressed and show all affected stakeholders that there are adequate policies and processes in place to implement effective respect for human rights.

Businesses implicated in the Ukraine War have a responsibility to undertake heightened HRDD as they operate in an 'armed conflict' under international law involving a 'resort to armed force between States'.[28] This raises the question of where the business must operate to be in the area of armed conflict. The UNDP Guide is clear that,

> [I]n 'classical wars', i.e. when one state is at war against another, business needs to exercise heightened human rights due diligence with regard

25 Ibid.

26 See further Peter T. Muchlinski, *Advanced Introduction to Business and Human Rights* (Cheltenham: Edward Elgar Publishers, 2022), 104–6.

27 UNDP Guide (n 14), 34.

28 International Criminal Tribunal for the former Yugoslavia (ICTY), *The Prosecutor v. Dusko Tadic*, Decision on the Defence Motion for Interlocutory Appeal on Jurisdiction, IT-94-1-A, October 2, 1995, para. 70, (accessed June 22, 2023) https://www.icty.org/x/cases/tadic/acdec/en/51002.htm. See too International Committee of the Red Cross (ICRC) "How is the Term 'Armed Conflict' Defined in International Humanitarian Law?" Opinion Paper, 2024, (accessed October 23, 2024) https://www.icrc.org/sites/default/files/document_new/file_list/armed_conflict_defined_in_ihl.pdf

> to its activities, products and services in BOTH states (emphasis in the original).[29]

In performing HRDD the UNDP Guide advises businesses to ask three key questions:

> Is there an actual or potential adverse impact on human rights or the conflict connected either to the company's activities (actions or omissions), products or services in any of the state parties to the conflict?
>
> If so, do the company's activities in any of the state parties to the conflict increase the risk of that impact?
>
> If so, would the company's activities in any of the state parties to the conflict in and of themselves be sufficient to result in that impact?[30]

The UNDP Guide covers only the belligerent states. Are economic operations occurring away from Russia or Ukraine, but which have an impact on the conduct of the war within these states, subject to HRDD as well? This is important because war economies are inherently transnational in nature.[31] Both the Russian and Ukrainian economies are highly integrated into global markets as shown by the impact of the war on gas and other fossil fuel supplies from Russia, the amount of Russian finance located in overseas financial centres, or the supply of grain and other agricultural commodities from Ukraine.[32]

Wider transnational transactions and investments that might impact the Ukraine War should be included in any corporate HRDD process. For example, where an MNE sells goods to an intermediary in full knowledge that the latter will sell these on to a Russian associate involved in commercial activities connected to the war then heightened HRDD would direct it to include this transaction in its assessment even though it has not taken place in Russia. If such a transaction is caught by sanctions this in itself should act as a warning 'red light' to the MNE of the need for heightened HRDD. As the UNDP Guide notes, 'the imposition of sanctions may be a useful indicator, but not a substitute, for a business to exercise heightened due diligence'.[33]

29 UNDP Guide (n 14), 28.

30 Ibid.

31 See Taylor (n 1), 12–14 on which this paragraph draws.

32 See generally Center for Preventive Action (n 4); David Sheppard, Emiko Terazono, George Steer and Kate Dugiud, "Traders ride Ukraine war rollercoaster one year on from Putin's invasion," *Financial Times* (February 25, 2023), 17.

33 UNDP Guide (n 14), 10.

In the context of sanctions, transnational business transactions can be structured to pass from illegal to lawful especially where they cross legal jurisdictions, thereby opening a space for their 'legalisation'.[34] Whether to include or exclude such a transaction in the heightened HRDD assessment is left to the subjective judgment of a business that may profit from such a transformation. It is likely to exclude it on the basis of its 'legality' and thus avoid effective HRDD. This issue needs to be more fully addressed by focusing on impacts and not on the legal form of the transaction. Future developments in HRDD, such as mandatory HRDD laws, should provide for this situation.[35]

A further element is the occupation of the Eastern regions of Ukraine and the annexation of Crimea. Occupied territories form part of the area of armed conflict under international law. There is no doubt that Russia is in 'effective control' of these territories for the purposes of international law meaning that IHL applies to these territories.[36] Accordingly, businesses operating within these territories must also undertake heightened HRDD in accordance with the standards discussed in the next section.

The illegal nature of the Ukraine War increases the risk of gross violations of human rights being perpetrated by business.[37] The UNGPs warn of the need for greater vigilance on the part of businesses that operate in conflict situations where the risk of complicity in gross human rights abuses committed by belligerent forces is heightened. This requires a business to avoid exacerbating a situation which could lead to corporate and/or individual liability under IHL through effective heightened HRDD, to which the next sections turn.[38]

34 See Taylor (n 1), 13–14.

35 See e.g. International Peace Information Service "Joint statement on conflict and due diligence legislation," (October 14, 2022) (accessed June 22, 2023) https://ipisresearch.be/joint-statement-on-conflict-due-diligence-legislation/.

36 See ICRC, "Occupation and international humanitarian law: questions and answers," August 4, 2004, (accessed June 22, 2023) https://www.icrc.org/en/article/occupation-international-humanitarian-law-questions

37 UNDP Guide (n 14), 28.

38 UNGPs Commentary to Principle 23 (n 17) states: "In all contexts, business enterprises should: (a) Comply with all applicable laws and respect internationally recognized human rights, wherever they operate; (b) Seek ways to honour the principles of internationally recognized human rights when faced with conflicting requirements; (c) Treat the risk of causing or contributing to gross human rights abuses as a legal compliance issue wherever they operate."

3 Norms of International Humanitarian Law and Heightened HRDD

While both human rights law and IHL protect basic human rights the former applies in all situations while IHL applies only to armed conflict. Equally, some human rights provisions may be derogated from by states in cases of national emergency threatening the life of the nation, which includes war. This power excludes nonderogable human rights which constitute, under the European Convention on Human Rights, the right to life,[39] freedom from torture, inhuman or degrading treatment, freedom from slavery or servitude, and no punishment without law.[40] The list of nonderogable rights is wider under the UN Covenant on Civil and Political Rights.[41] The derogation must be strictly necessary to meet the exigencies of the situation and must respect all applicable rules of IHL. The impact of Ukraine's derogation from the ECHR on heightened HRDD will be discussed in section 5.

IHL has primarily focused on the regulation of state conduct in armed conflict and, more recently, on the conduct of irregular forces.[42] IHL also applies to non-state actors including businesses. There is now greater awareness of the

39 The European Convention on Human Rights (ECHR) art15(2) permits derogation from this right only "in respect of deaths resulting from lawful acts of war" connoting the norms of the laws of war which regulate the lawful taking of life in war, (accessed June 22, 2023) https://www.echr.coe.int/documents/convention_eng.pdf . See too UNDP Guide (n 14) 13.

40 ECHR art.15. The ECHR entered force in Ukraine on 11 September 1997. The ECHR entered force in the Russian Federation on May 5, 1998 and was formally denounced on March 16, 2022 the denunciation entering force on September 16, 2022, (accessed June 22, 2023) https://www.coe.int/en/web/conventions/full-list?module=signatures-by-treaty&treatynum=005 . See too Council of Europe "Russia ceases to be party to the European Convention on Human Rights" September 16, 2022, (accessed June 22, 2023) https://www.coe.int/en/web/portal/-/russia-ceases-to-be-party-to-the-european-convention-on-human-rights#:~:text=Russia%20ceases%20to%20be%20party%20to%20the%20European%20Convention%20on%20Human%20Rights,-Deutsch%20English%20espa%C3%B1ol&text=Six%20months%20after%20its%20exclusion,Rights%20on%2016%20September%202022.

41 In addition to the rights listed in the ECHR the UN Covenant adds: article 11 (prohibition of imprisonment because of inability to fulfil a contractual obligation), article 16 (the recognition of everyone as a person before the law), and article 18 (freedom of thought, conscience and religion): see further UN Human Rights Committee "General comment no. 29 states of emergency (article 4)", UN Doc.CCPR/C/21/Rev.1/Add.11, August 31, 2001, (accessed June 22, 2023) https://digitallibrary.un.org/record/451555?ln=en . The Russian Federation remains a party to the CCPR as does Ukraine both having ratified the Covenant in 1973, (accessed June 22, 2023) https://tbinternet.ohchr.org/_layouts/15/TreatyBodyExternal/Treaty.aspx?Treaty=CCPR&Lang=en.

42 See for a detailed analysis Taylor (n 1).

nexus between commercial conduct and armed conflict.[43] In particular, the involvement of business actors and business managers in investments made in conflict affected areas, or the conduct of transactions that promote the interests of conflict participants in that they are 'closely linked' to the conflict,[44] has produced numerous examples of exposure to liability for violations of IHL discussed further below.

Additionally, a significant number of states have passed laws incorporating the Statute of the International Criminal Court (ICC) and other recognised sources of international criminal law into their domestic law. Liability for international crimes arising under IHL might extend to business entities through the application of pre-existing national corporate criminal liability and accomplice liability laws.[45] The latter risk arises where a business or individual aids and abets the commission of state crimes under IHL or other areas of international criminal law.[46]

The turn towards increased business liability under national laws has also been recognised at the international level. The International Law Commission (ILC) issued *Draft Articles on Prevention and Punishment of Crimes Against Humanity* in 2019.[47] By Article 6(8) thereof:

> Subject to the provisions of its national law, each State shall take measures, where appropriate, to establish the liability of legal persons for the offences referred to in this draft article. Subject to the legal principles of the State, such liability of legal persons may be criminal, civil or administrative.[48]

---

43 See Taylor ibid and see further the special issue of the International Review of the Red Cross "Business, Violence and Conflict" No.887, September 2012, (accessed June 22, 2023) https://international-review.icrc.org/reviews/irrc-no-887-business-violence-and-conflict.

44 Australian Red Cross and RMIT University *Doing Responsible Business in Armed Conflict* (2020), 7, (accessed June 22, 2023) https://www.redcross.org.au/ihl/business-and-ihl/.

45 See Taylor (n 1), 251–2; Anita Ramasastry, Robert C. Thompson, and Mark B. Taylor, "Translating Unocal: The Expanding Web of Liability for Business Entities Implicated in International Crimes," *George Washington International Law Review* 40 (2009): 841–902; James G. Stewart, "The Turn to Corporate Criminal Liability for International Crimes: Transcending the Alien Tort Statute," *New York University Journal of International Law and Politics* 47, no. 1 (Fall 2014): 121–206.

46 See Australian Red Cross and RMIT University (n 44), 17.

47 International Law Commission (ILC) *Draft articles on Prevention and Punishment of Crimes Against Humanity 2019* (A/74/10), (accessed June 22, 2023) https://legal.un.org/ilc/texts/instruments/english/draft_articles/7_7_2019.pdf.

48 For detailed analysis see ibid, Article 6 Commentary paras. 41–51, (accessed June 22, 2023) https://legal.un.org/ilc/texts/instruments/english/commentaries/7_7_2019.pdf.

The ILC included this provision to reflect the capacity of legal persons to be involved in, 'acts committed as part of a widespread or systematic attack directed against a civilian population'.[49] According to the ILC, the language used, 'has been widely accepted by states in the context of other crimes and that contains considerable flexibility for States in the implementation of their obligation'.[50] Though not a binding instrument, the ILC Draft Articles represent a serious indicator of international consensus on the content of international law.

Of equal importance are the recently adopted ILC *Draft Principles on Protection of the Environment in Relation to Armed Conflicts* of 2022.[51] Principle 10 introduces a requirement of corporate due diligence, 'with respect to the protection of the environment, including in relation to human health, when acting in an area affected by an armed conflict. Such measures include those aimed at ensuring that natural resources are purchased or otherwise obtained in an environmentally sustainable manner'. Principle 11 requires that,

> States should take appropriate measures aimed at ensuring that business enterprises operating in or from their territories, or territories under their jurisdiction, can be held liable for harm caused by them to the environment, including in relation to human health, in an area affected by an armed conflict. Such measures should, as appropriate, include those aimed at ensuring that a business enterprise can be held liable to the extent that such harm is caused by its subsidiary acting under its *de facto* control. To this end, as appropriate, States should provide adequate and effective procedures and remedies, in particular for the victims of such harm.

As with the *Draft Articles on Prevention and Punishment of Crimes Against Humanity* there is stress on the need for national measures to hold businesses to account for environmental harm in times of conflict and, significantly, that

49 Ibid para. 47.

50 ibid. John Ruggie advocated a treaty covering corporate involvement in "gross human rights violations" on the basis that, "the underlying prohibitions already enjoy widespread consensus among states." see Third United Nations Forum on Business and Human Rights Closing Plenary Remarks John G. Ruggie Former UN Special Representative for Business and Human Rights Geneva, December 3, 2014, (accessed June 22, 2023) https://www.ohchr.org/Documents/Issues/Business/ForumSession3/Submissions/JohnRuggie_SR_SG_BHR.pdf.

51 (accessed 22 June 2023) https://legal.un.org/ilc/texts/instruments/english/draft_articles/8_7_2022.pdf.

liability should extend to the parent within the regulating jurisdiction for harm arising out of the activities of its subsidiary, introducing an element of extraterritorial application where the subsidiary operates overseas.

The main war crimes that businesses should be aware of are listed in numerous international conventions, the most significant being the four Geneva Conventions of 1949 and their Additional Protocols of 1977.[52] Their basis lies in respect for private property and human dignity in conflict.[53] From these core principles IHL has developed detailed rules that apply to the conduct of the conflict itself, the conduct of the occupying power in territory seized by armed conflict, the financing of conflict, controls over arms trade, and the mobilisation and recruitment of military personnel and labour.[54]

Businesses and their managers can act illegally in any of these situations. The most notorious examples arose out of the trials of German industrialists before the US Military Tribunal in Germany (USMT).[55] It established that active and willing participation in the use of forced labour could constitute a violation of IHL.[56] In addition, although the corporations were not indicted, the interaction between the corporation and its executives was a system which enabled mass violations of human rights. For example, in the case against twenty-three employees of I. G. Farben, the USMT held that 'the defendants individually and collectively used the Farben organization as an instrument and through which they committed the crimes enumerated in the indictment'.[57] Furthermore, I. G. Farben and Krupp, through their executives, had violated the prohibition against seizure of private property in occupied lands under the Hague Rules when these corporations acquired confiscated factories in a number of Nazi-occupied countries.[58] Other situations giving rise to liability risks include: violations of human rights by private security contractors

---

52 See ICRC "The Geneva Conventions and Their Commentaries," (accessed June 22, 2023) https://www.icrc.org/en/law-and-policy/geneva-conventions-and-their-commentaries

53 See for a detailed analysis Australian Red Cross and RMIT University (n 44), 14–15.

54 See ibid, 18–23.

55 See further Doreen Lustig *Veiled Power: International Law and the Private Corporation, 1886–1981*. (Oxford: Oxford University Press, 2020), chs 4–5, who criticises the legal and political reasoning that led to the exclusion of indictments against corporations.

56 See further Antia Ramasastry "Corporate complicity: From Nuremberg to Rangoon – an examination of forced labor cases and their impact on the liability of multinational corporations," *Berkeley Journal of International Law* 20, no 1 (2002) 91.

57 *See U.S. v. Krauch, et. al, The I.G. Farben Case,* VIII Trials of War Criminals Before the Nuremberg Military Tribunals, iii-iv at 1108 (1952).

58 See Ramasastry (n 56), 107–11.

employed by a business in a conflict affected area;[59] trading in illegally pillaged goods or commodities;[60] illegal arms sales to combatants;[61] and contributing to environmental degradation in a conflict affected area.[62]

The conduct of heightened HRDD in relation to potential breaches of IHL requires additional steps.[63] As conflict is already underway in Ukraine, and extensive sanctions exist to stop trade and investment with Russia, these are clear 'red flags' to business that heightened HRDD must apply and include considering the risk of direct or complicit violations of IHL.[64] HRDD must be continuous as the conflict situation is malleable and changing. In addition, businesses must understand the nature and causes of the conflict, identify their impact on the conflict and act upon those findings by identifying business responsibility. Furthermore, businesses must understand the particular impacts both of the conflict and of business activities on specific groups in conflict and post-conflict situations. Moreover, according to the UNDP Guide, 'because the impact of conflict is usually more severe for more people, business should prioritize salient conflict issues which are not necessarily identified as salient in terms of human rights, and then salient human rights issues which are considered unlikely to cause or exacerbate conflict'.[65]

Once heightened HRDD has been undertaken the business response can be divided into two categories. First, exit from the area of conflict and/or from the belligerent states. Here the impact of sanctions will be important in dictating the legality or otherwise of continued business presence, but it is not the only

59 See Stuart Wallace, "Private Security Companies and Human Rights: Are Non-Judicial Remedies Effective?" *Boston University International Law Journal* 35, no.1, (Spring 2017): 69. See too in relation to corporate responsibility for the conduct of security personnel hired to protect corporate assets, *The Voluntary Principles on Security and Human Rights* (2000), (accessed June 22, 2023) https://www.voluntaryprinciples.org/the-principles/; ICRC, "The Montreux Document on Private Military and Security Companies," (Geneva, August 2009), (accessed June 22, 2023) https://shop.icrc.org/the-montreux-document-on-private-military-and-security-companies-pdf-en.html

60 See *Argor-Heraeus SA Case* summarised in ICRC "How Does Law Protect in War?" (accessed June 22, 2023) https://casebook.icrc.org/case-study/switzerland-gold-looting-case .

61 See further Christian Schliemann and Linde Bryk *Arms Trade and Corporate Responsibility: Liability, Litigation and Legislative Reform* (Berlin: Friedrich-Ebert-Stiftung, November 2019), (accessed June 22, 2023) https://library.fes.de/pdf-files/iez/15850.pdf .

62 See the ILC (n 51).

63 See UNDP Guide (n 14), 20–31 on which this paragraph draws.

64 On HRDD "red flags" in conflict affected areas see further International Alert and FAFO "Red Flags: Liability Risks for Companies Operating in High-Risk Zones" (2008), (accessed June 22, 2023) https://www.international-alert.org/publications/red-flags-liability-risks-companies-high-risk-zones/.

65 UNDP Guide (n 14), 30–1.

consideration. Sanctions may not offer clear guidance as to when a business should exit or stay nor do they always resolve real dilemmas such as whether a business providing essential services should comply with sanctions regardless of consequential human rights impacts. Nor does the existence of sanctions absolve the business from making an informed decision based on heightened HRDD. Secondly, a business many take actions short of exit. The question of exit arises mainly in relation to Russia and the Ukrainian occupied territories. Actions short of exit are more likely in relation to independent Ukraine where commercial relations are not prevented by sanctions and so commercial activity remains possible. The next two sections will now consider each situation in turn.

4 The Human Rights Responsibilities of Businesses Investing in and/or Trading with Russia: The Issue of Exit

Sanctions were adopted by the US, EU, UK and other states immediately after the annexation of Crimea in 2014.[66] These included bans on trade, investment and financial relations with Russia that contributed to the destabilisation of Ukraine. Trade with, and investment in, Crimea were prohibited. In response to the current phase of the war further and wider sanctions were adopted.[67] These targeted key Russian financial, natural resources, technology and transport companies, and key Russian individuals, but also non-Russian firms doing business with Russia. For example, both the UK and US prohibited investment in Russia by UK and US businesses and persons. On 6 April 2022 the UK Government announced an outright ban on all new UK investment in Russia.[68] On the same day the US imposed a blanket prohibition on 'new investment in the Russian Federation by a United States person, wherever located'.[69] The order also prohibited the supply from the US or by US persons

66 See Claire Mills, "Russian Sanctions Prior to the Invasion of Ukraine," (15 May, 2023), 9–10, (accessed June 22, 2023) https://researchbriefings.files.parliament.uk/documents/CBP-9797/CBP-9797.pdf; see on current UK sanctions Claire Mills "Sanctions Against Russia," (23 May, 2023) (accessed June 22, 2023) https://researchbriefings.files.parliament.uk/documents/CBP-9481/CBP-9481.pdf.

67 See Eichensehr (n 11), 614–631.

68 UK Government, "UK imposes sweeping new sanctions to starve Putin's war machine," *Press release*, April 6, 2022, (accessed June 22, 2023) https://www.gov.uk/government/news/uk-imposes-sweeping-new-sanctions-to-starve-putins-war-machine.

69 Exec. Order No. 14,071, 87 Fed. Reg. 20,999, 20,999 (April 6, 2022), (accessed June 22, 2023) https://home.treasury.gov/system/files/126/14071.pdf.

to anyone in Russia 'of any category of services' determined by the Treasury Secretary, 'in consultation with the Secretary of State' and 'any approval, financing, facilitation, or guarantee by a United States person, wherever located, of a transaction by a foreign person where the transaction by that foreign person would be prohibited by this section if performed by a United States person or within the United States'.[70] In response, Russia has undertaken retaliatory measures including: prohibitions against sales of foreign held securities, curbs on debt repayments, and the reclassification of states imposing sanctions as 'unfriendly' permitting the exercise of powers restricting investors from those states in their commercial dealings with Russian residents and allowing for patent confiscation.[71]

Unsurprisingly, these extensive rules, and the increasing difficulties of doing business in wartime Russia, have led to numerous UK, US and other firms from sanctioning home states to exit.[72] Several firms have also left due to reputational concerns.[73] Additionally, some firms may decide to leave due to pressure from investors though, to date, this has not had a significant impact.[74]

Business exit in a non-conflict situation is a 'last resort' after attempts at preventing or mitigating severe impacts have failed, or where such impacts

70 ibid.

71 See OECD (2022), "International investment implications of Russia's war against Ukraine," (OECD Publishing, Paris, 2022), 11–12, (accessed June 22, 2023) https://doi.org/10.1787/a24af3d7-en. Evgeniya Rakhmanina "Leaving Russia: the price of exit and other regulatory hurdles," *Linklaters Foreign Investment Links* (January 16, 2023), (accessed June 22, 2023) https://www.linklaters.com/en/insights/blogs/foreigninvestmentlinks/2023/january/leaving-russia-the-price-of-exit-and-other-regulatory-hurdles. For English translations of the applicable laws see William E. Butler "Russian Economic Sanctions," *International Legal Materials* 62, no. 3 (2023): 528–47.

72 See "Companies Are Getting Out of Russia, Sometimes at a Cost" *New York Times* (October 14, 2022), (accessed June 22, 2023) https://www.nytimes.com/article/russia-invasion-companies.html. For a detailed database of corporate responses see Business and Human Rights Resource Centre "Russian Military Aggression in Ukraine," (accessed June 22, 2023) https://www.business-humanrights.org/en/big-issues/russian-invasion-of-ukraine/ and for a list of firms leaving or staying see Yale School of Management, Chief Executive Leadership Institute "Over 1,000 Companies Have Curtailed Operations in Russia – But Some Remain," (accessed June 22, 2023) https://som.yale.edu/story/2022/over-1000-companies-have-curtailed-operations-russia-some-remain.

73 See *New York Times* "Companies Are getting out of Russia," Eichensehr (n 11) 624–5.

74 See Rebecca DeWinter-Schmitt, Samuel Jones, and Richard Stazinski. "Missing in Action? Investor Responses to the War in Ukraine," *Business and Human Rights Journal* 7, no. 3 (2022): 487–93.

are irremediable and there is no reasonable prospect of change.[75] In a conflict situation, the UNDP Guide stresses that, 'the overarching element is to consider whether exiting could exacerbate tensions within a conflict-affected setting and whether the adverse impacts of the decision to exit or suspend the operations outweigh the benefits.'[76]

Exit in the context of armed conflict is a difficult decision often requiring a balancing of harms. For example, should US owned social media platforms deprive Russian citizens of access to alternative information about the war by denying them access to virtual private network and encrypted communications apps?[77] In the course of HRDD the platform has to consider whether exit would cause more human rights harm than staying. In such cases the business may enjoy an exemption from exit requirements as is the case with internet access for Russian citizens under US and UK sanctions.[78]

Equally, if a business providing essential services such as water, food, electricity, healthcare, or telecommunications decides to exit, who, if anyone, will then provide the service and might valuable assets fall into the hands of a party to the conflict or a connected crony business?[79] In such cases, the business must consider all relevant factors before a decision to stay on is taken. In particular, it must assess its power and independence to act regardless of any pressure imposed by the Russian authorities. Assisting the Russian war effort through the continued payment of taxes and compliance with wartime obligations, such as assistance with war related production and facilitating the conscription of workers, is likely to lead to complicity in human rights infringements and so leads inexorably to the conclusion that exit is the only viable response.[80]

---

75 OECD *Due Diligence Guidance for Responsible Business Conduct* (OECD, Paris, 2018), 31 (accessed June 22, 2023) https://mneguidelines.oecd.org/OECD-Due-Diligence-Guidance-for-Responsible-Business-Conduct.pdf

76 UNDP Guide (n 14), 35.

77 Eichensehr (n 11) 625.

78 See Peter Micek "When sanctions undermine human rights online," *Access Now* (18 January 2023) (accessed June 22, 2023) https://www.accessnow.org/sanctions-undermining-human-rights/.

79 See Irene Pietropaoli and Daniel Aguirre "Responsible Exit from Russia: Business and Human Rights in a Global Governance Gap," *BIICL Blog*, March 22, 2022,(accessed June 22, 2023) https://www.biicl.org/blog/36/part-2-responsible-exit-from-russia-business-and-human-rights-in-a-global-governance-gap.

80 See further Tara Van Ho "Not all parties are equal: understanding the responsibility for reparations in conflict-affected areas," *Opinion* (Business and Human Rights Resource Centre, 20 February 2023) (accessed June 22, 2023) https://www.business-humanrights.org/en/blog/not-all-parties-are-equal-understanding-the-responsibility-for-reparations-in-conflict-affected-areas/; B4Ukraine "Russia's "Partial Mobilization" Order: A New

Nonetheless many Western firms subject to sanctions remain active in Russia.[81]

In addition, should firms from states that have not passed sanctions continue to operate in Russia, or the occupied regions of Ukraine? For example, no Chinese firms have left to date, though some have ceased to trade with Russia.[82] Since the war started, Indian firms have sought new business opportunities in Russia.[83] While legally free to do so, Indian firms can also suffer reputational risk. For example, the Indian software giant Infosys agreed to pull out of Russia in April 2022 for reputational reasons when Akshata Murty, the daughter of Infosys' founder and wife of then UK Chancellor and former Prime Minister, Rishi Sunak, was accused of capitalising off Russia through her 0.91% shareholding in Infosys while the UK government called for companies to divest from the country.[84] However, as of November 2022, Infosys though having reduced its commercial ties was still active in Russia.[85]

Where a business concludes on the basis of heightened HRDD that it must exit, both short and long term impacts on the people affected, including business partners and communities, should be considered.[86] This involves a range of questions focused on: the effects on the workforce concerning their continued income, help in mitigating the effects loss of employment and ensuring the safety of remaining staff who cannot be evacuated; effects on the local community including broader economic and social effects; effects on suppliers

Red Line in Complicity & Material Risk for Companies Operating in Russia," *Issue Brief* (7 November 2022) (accessed June 22, 2023) https://b4ukraine.org/whats-new/russias-partial-mobilization.

81 See further B4Ukraine "What's New?" examining French, Swiss, German and US firms that remain operating in Russia, (accessed June 22, 2023) https://b4ukraine.org/whats-new. See too Kyiv School of Economics "SelfSanctions/Leave Russia" (accessed June 22 2023) https://kse.ua/selfsanctions-kse-institute/.

82 See B4Ukraine "No Chinese Company Has Ever Legally Left Russia After Invasion of Ukraine," (December 27, 2022), (accessed June 22, 2023) https://b4ukraine.org/learn/stats/no-chinese-company-has-ever-legally-left-russia.

83 See Kripa Jayaram "Sanctions-Ravaged Russia Offers Opportunities for Indian Firms," *Bloomberg UK* (June 30, 2022), (accessed June 22, 2023) https://www.bloomberg.com/news/articles/2022-06-30/sanctions-ravaged-russia-offers-opportunities-for-indian-firms?leadSource=uverify%20wall.

84 ibid.

85 Daniel Boffey and Andrew Roth, "Infosys still operating from Russia eight months after saying it was pulling out," *The Guardian* (November 4, 2022), (accessed June 22, 2023) https://www.theguardian.com/world/2022/nov/04/infosys-still-operating-russia-rishi-sunak-akshata-murty.

86 UNDP Guide (n 14) 35–6 on which this paragraph draws.

and their business; and where there is a transfer of the business to local owners, assessing the human rights capacities of the buyer including the possibility of a contractual commitment by the buyer to put in place specific human rights-related policies and procedures that facilitate responsible and sustainable operation.

Such a commitment by a future Russian acquirer is rather unlikely. The Russian government has adopted laws enabling it to nationalise the assets of foreign firms seeking to divest from Russia as a result of sanctions. Should the remaining firms be forced to sell, it is highly doubtful that any human rights related commitments would follow.[87] Even where exit may involve sale to a Russian business, the prospects for ensuring respect for human rights may be rather slim. A recent survey of 100 largest firms listed on the Moscow Stock Exchange shows that while some firms are experimenting with non-financial reporting most do not undertake HRDD, there is no institutional or social pressure to promote human rights responsibilities for business and that the conceptualisation of human rights is linked to the degree to which the company is internationalised which, given the growing isolation of Russian firms due to the war, is likely to retard commitments to human rights.[88] In addition, Russian firms have mostly remained silent on human rights violations by Russia in Ukraine.[89]

5 The Human Rights Responsibilities of Businesses in Ukraine

Ukraine has not so far prioritised business and human rights as a policy objective.[90] However the need to establish business responsibilities for human rights

87 On May 23, 2024, Russian President Vladimir Putin signed a decree allowing Russia to seize the assets of U.S. companies and nationals as compensation for Russian assets confiscated in application of U.S. sanctions: President Putin Signs Decree Further Threatening Foreign-Owned Property in Russia: Investment Treaties May Provide a Remedy for Foreign Investors (May 28, 2024), *Covington Alert* at https://www.cov.com/en/news-and-insights/insights/2024/05/president-putin-signs-decree-further-threatening-foreign-owned-property-in-russia-investment-treaties-may-provide-a-remedy-for-foreign-investors#layout=card&numberOfResults=12 (accessed 23 October 2024).

88 See Michael Rogerson "Business and Human Rights in Russia: Emerging or Merging?" *Business and Human Rights Journal* First View Articles (January 19, 2023), 1–26, doi:10.1017/bhj.2022.29.

89 Ibid, 22–3.

90 See Kharkiv International Legal Forum "Business and Human Rights in Central and Eastern Europe: Kharkiv Forum's Summary," (September 23–25, 2020), (accessed June 22, 2023) https://www.osce.org/project-coordinator-in-ukraine/482918.

exists and the conflict makes this more urgent.[91] In particular, a war economy requires restrictions on certain rights and freedoms as part of the war effort while the imposition of martial law also impacts on the normal enjoyment of basic rights.

On February 28, 2022, the Ukrainian authorities derogated from the European Convention on Human Rights (ECHR) in accordance with Article 15 of the Convention referring to martial law and to the armed conflict.[92] Ukraine must apply its derogations proportionately, it cannot infringe nonderogable rights,[93] and it remains subject to claims under the ECHR.[94] Equally, acts of aggression likely to lead to breaches of IHL committed on Ukrainian soil by Russian forces may be subject to subsequent claims under the ECHR as they would have been committed on the territory of a signatory state, bearing in mind that Russia too remained a party to the ECHR until it denounced the Convention on 16 September 2022.[95]

---

91 See Olena Uvarova "Ukrainian companies and human rights during the war" Opinion, Business and Human Rights Resource Centre (April 4, 2022), (accessed June 22, 2023) https://www.business-humanrights.org/en/blog/ukrainian-companies-and-human-rights-during-the-war/ . See too Business and Human Rights in Ukraine (accessed June 22, 2023) http://bhr.in.ua/category/our-projects/ . For a detailed assessment of the business and human rights situation in Ukraine carried out prior to the war see UNDP *Business and Human Rights in Ukraine: Accelerating Sustainable and Equitable Development through Implementation of the UN Guiding Principles on Business and Human Rights* (Kiyv, 2022), (accessed June 22, 2023) https://www.undp.org/ukraine/publications/business-and-human-rights-ukraine-accelerating-sustainable-and-equitable-development-through-implementation-un-guiding.

92 See Kanstantsin Dzehtsiarou and Vassilis P. Tzevelekos, "A Thorny Road to Democracy, Human Rights and the Rule of Law: Ukraine and the European Court of Human Rights," *European Convention on Human Rights Law Review* 3, no.4 (2022): 427, 428. The Ukrainian authorities derogated from a number of ECHR provisions, including Articles 4(3) (forced labour), 8 (right to private and family life), 9 (freedom of religion), 10 (freedom of expression), 11 (freedom of assembly and association), and 14 (prohibition of discrimination).4 Later, the Ukrainian authorities also derogated from Articles 5 (right to liberty and security), 6 (right to a fair trial), and 13 (right to an effective remedy).

93 See text above n 39–41.

94 Ibid.

95 European Court of Human Rights "The European Court grants urgent interim measures in application concerning Russian military operations on Ukrainian territory" *Press Release* (ECHR 068 (2022) 01.03.2022), (accessed June 22, 2023) https://hudoc.echr.coe.int/eng-press?i=003-7272764-9905947. On March 4, the President of the Court issued the same interim measures for the protection of civilians who had submitted claims to the European Commission on Human Rights: "Decision of the Court on requests for interim measures in individual applications concerning Russian military operations on Ukrainian territory" *Press release* (ECHR 073 (2022) 04.03.2022), (accessed June 22, 2023) https://hudoc.echr.coe.int/eng-press?i=003-7277548-9913621.

Derogation is not a green light for businesses to disregard human rights in the course of their Ukrainian operations. Businesses must be conscious of how their decisions impact on employees, business partners and local communities. In this regard, several firms have ensured that their employees were evacuated from active war zones, provided financial support for employee relocation both internally and abroad, the continued payment of full salaries and allowing flexible working.[96] These practices have been carried out mainly by subsidiaries of foreign multinationals and larger Ukrainian firms. Smaller local businesses have tended to prioritise financial survival at the expense of employee welfare.[97]

The Ukrainian government, as an adherent to the UNGPs, is also subject to a state duty to protect against business infringements of human rights.[98] This duty will be subject to the right of derogation in the case of derogable human rights. A particular example is the adoption in July 2022 of restrictive labour reforms in accordance with the requirements of martial law.[99] By article 2 of this law, constitutional rights to work, freedom from forced labour, the right to safe and healthy working conditions, the prohibition on employment of women and minors in work hazardous to health, the right against illegal dismissal, the right to timely payment of wages and the right to strike have been suspended for the duration of martial law. Employers are also given wide ranging rights over their workers and the working week is stipulated at 60 hours.[100] Individual businesses may conclude that they can offer better terms and conditions for their employees based on their HRDD. However, the absence of state backing for such responses enhances the risk of abuses taking place.

In order to reduce such risks, Ukrainian business, civil society groups and the state should engage in a multi-stakeholder process ensuring that businesses hear the concerns of the most impacted groups.[101] Equally, as already noted, firms could take the initiative and act to improve workplace and other local conditions especially as business responsibilities to respect human rights are not subject to determination by the Ukrainian state but are rooted in international standards. The main issue here is whether that would disadvantage

96 Uvarova (n 91).

97 Ibid.

98 Ibid.

99 Law on the organization of labour relations under martial law (19 July 2022, with changes introduced in accordance with Law No. 2352-IX dated July 1, 2022) (accessed June 22, 2023) https://zakon.rada.gov.ua/laws/show/2136-20#Text

100 Ibid articles 3–6.

101 UNDP Guide (n 14), 41. See also Uvarova (n 91).

the human rights compliant business should the majority of businesses take advantage of the deregulated environment. The Ukrainian authorities may also be unsupportive, seeing such activity as creating division among employers at a time when unity is required. However, given that Ukraine's war aims include retaining independence and gaining acceptance into the mainstream of democratic European states through eventual membership of the EU, which lists among its accession criteria, 'stable institutions guaranteeing democracy, the rule of law, human rights and respect for and protection of minorities', a movement towards serious recognition of the need to promote human rights observance by businesses may be in the state's wider interests and long-term objectives.[102] It remains to be seen if the Ukrainian authorities will take this route or use the war to make the restrictions on basic rights a permanent feature of the local political and social landscape.

A final question arises out of the continued operation of Ukrainian enterprises in the Russian occupied territories. Unlike MNEs caught up in the occupation domestic firms are unlikely to be able to exit. Accordingly, does their continued presence require special consideration by the Ukrainian government? It would appear harsh to sanction these businesses for remaining given the coercive conditions under which they are most likely operating. However, they should still undertake heightened HRDD so as to mitigate so far as possible the adverse human rights and IHL impact their operations might have. This requires further research and analysis that is beyond this chapter.

6 Concluding Remarks

The Ukraine War has become a laboratory for business and human rights in the context of a 'classic war' between the armed forces of two sovereign states. In this it differs from the more common situations of armed conflict that raise business and human rights issues, namely, civil wars and asymmetrical wars involving irregular forces such as terrorist or organised crime groups.

In such conflicts the line between civilian and military activities is more blurred than in a 'classic war', making it more likely that a business will stay

102 See EU "Conditions for Membership", (accessed June 22, 2023) https://neighbourhood-enlargement.ec.europa.eu/enlargement-policy/conditions-membership_en . Ukraine applied for EU membership on February 28, 2022 see EU Commission "Support for Ukraine: Application for Membership," (accessed June 22, 2023) https://neighbourhood-enlargement.ec.europa.eu/european-neighbourhood-policy/countries-region/ukraine_en.

in order to protect its investment and returns while seeking to avoid and/or minimise any adverse human rights impacts. In relation to Russia, even in the absence of sanctions, a strong case exists for exit. The sheer magnitude of the risks of gross violations of human rights committed by Russia on Ukrainian soil, and towards dissenters and others adversely affected by the war in Russia, should prompt a look at exit.[103]

A further distinctive feature of the 'classic war' scenario is that business becomes embroiled in the risk of committing, or being complicit in, breaches of IHL. IHL creates, as shown above, the real risk of direct legal liability for such breaches. Heightened HRDD must therefore extend consideration beyond simply human rights risks and towards IHL risks. Again, these point strongly towards exit from business dealings with Russia.

A third important feature is that heightened HRDD should be undertaken not only for business with, or in, Russia and the occupied territories it controls, but also in independent Ukraine. The war entitles the government to derogate from certain human rights, as Ukraine has done, but does not excuse businesses operating in Ukraine from undertaking heightened HRDD, quite the opposite. In times of war the state may be tempted to acquire extensive executive powers and curtail workers and citizens' rights beyond what the strict exigencies of war may require. Businesses should examine through heightened HRDD whether they can protect the rights of their workers and the communities in which they work through the kinds of responses outlined in the previous section. Equally, the Ukrainian state should conclude that, as its war aims include defending the evolving independent democracy of Ukraine and the pursuit of EU membership, entering into dialogue with business and other stakeholders on how best to mitigate the impacts of martial law and other restrictions on the rights of workers and citizens seems a clear example of best practice. Through such multi-stakeholder co-operation much could be achieved for the future of business and human rights in Ukraine. It would also set the tone for business and state responsibilities to respect human rights in the post-conflict reconstruction of Ukraine, should the latter prevail.

103 See OHCHR *Situation of human rights in Ukraine in the context of the armed attack by the Russian Federation, 24 February–15 May 2022* (June 29, 2022) (accessed June 22, 2023) https://www.ohchr.org/en/documents/country-reports/situation-human-rights-ukraine-context-armed-attack-russian-federation . On human rights risks to Russian dissenters see Rafael Behr "Putin's holy war is terrorising Ukraine – and Russian dissenters. All they ask is that we don't forget them" *The Guardian* (10 March 2023) (accessed June 22, 2023) https://www.theguardian.com/commentisfree/2023/mar/10/russians-putins-holy-war-loyalty-fear.

Acknowledgement

My thanks to Professors Olena Uvarova and David Blichitz for their very helpful comments on an earlier draft.

Bibliography

Books

Klein, Naomi. *The Shock Doctrine* London. London: Penguin Books, 2007.

Lustig, Doreen. *Veiled Power: International Law and the Private Corporation, 1886–1981.* England: Oxford University Press, 2020.

Muchlinski Peter T. *Advanced Introduction to Business and Human Rights* Cheltenham: Edward Elgar Publishers, 2022.

Taylor, Mark B. *War Economies and International Law: Regulating the Economic Activities of Violent Conflict.* Cambridge: Cambridge University Press, 2021.

Articles

Butler, William E. "Russian Economic Sanctions." *International Legal Materials* 62, no. 3 (2023): 528–47.

DeWinter-Schmitt, Rebecca, Samuel Jones, and Richard Stazinski. "Missing in Action? Investor Responses to the War in Ukraine." *Business and Human Rights Journal* 7, no. 3 (2022): 487–93.

Dzehtsiarou, Kanstantsin and Tzevelekos, Vassilis P. "A Thorny Road to Democracy, Human Rights and the Rule of Law: Ukraine and the European Court of Human Rights". *European Convention on Human Rights Law Review* 3, no.4 (2022): 427, 428.

Eichensehr, Kristen E. "Contemporary Practice of the United States Relating to International Law". *American Journal of International Law* 116, no 3 (July 2022) 605–14.

Eichensehr, Kristen E. "United States and Allies Target Russia and Belarus with Sanctions and Other Economic Measures". *American Journal of International Law* 116, no 3 (July 2022) 614–31.

Haque, Adil Ahmad. "An Unlawful War" Symposium on Ukraine and the International Order. *American Journal of International Law* 116 (2022): 115.

Ramasastry, Antia. "Corporate complicity: From Nuremberg to Rangoon – an examination of forced labor cases and their impact on the liability of multinational corporations". *Berkeley Journal of International Law* 20, no 1 (2002): 91.

Ramasastry, Anita, Thompson, Robert C, and Taylor, Mark B. "Translating Unocal: The Expanding Web of Liability for Business Entities Implicated in International Crimes". *George Washington International Law Review* 40 (2009): 841–902.

Stewart, James G. "The Turn to Corporate Criminal Liability for International Crimes: Transcending the Alien Tort Statute," *New York University Journal of International Law and Politics* 47, no. 1 (Fall 2014): 121–206.

Wallace, Stuart. "Private Security Companies and Human Rights: Are Non-Judicial Remedies Effective?". *Boston University International Law Journal* 35, no.1, (Spring 2017): 69.

Internet Sources

Aguirre, Daniel and Pietropaoli, Irene. "Responsible Exit from Russia: Business and Human Rights in a Global Governance Gap". *BIICL Blog*, March 22, 2022. https://www.biicl.org/blog/36/part-2-responsible-exit-from-russia-business-and-human-rights-in-a-global-governance-gap.

Australian Red Cross and RMIT University. *Doing Responsible Business in Armed Conflict*. (2020), https://www.redcross.org.au/ihl/business-and-ihl/.

B4Ukraine. "No Chinese Company Has Ever Legally Left Russia After Invasion of Ukraine". (December 27, 2022), https://b4ukraine.org/learn/stats/no-chinese-company-has-ever-legally-left-russia.

B4Ukraine. "Russia's "Partial Mobilization" Order: A New Red Line in Complicity & Material Risk for Companies Operating in Russia." *Issue Brief*, November 7, 2022. https://b4ukraine.org/whats-new/russias-partial-mobilization.

B4Ukraine. "What's New?" (no date). https://b4ukraine.org/whats-new.

Behr, Rafael. "Putin's holy war is terrorising Ukraine – and Russian dissenters. All they ask is that we don't forget them". *The Guardian*, March 10, 2023,. https://www.theguardian.com/commentisfree/2023/mar/10/russians-putins-holy-war-loyalty-fear.

Boffey, Daniel and Roth, Andrew. "Infosys still operating from Russia eight months after saying it was pulling out". *The Guardian*, November 4, 2022. https://www.theguardian.com/world/2022/nov/04/infosys-still-operating-russia-rishi-sunak-akshata-murty.

Business and Human Rights Resource Centre. "Russian Military Aggression in Ukraine". (no date). https://www.business-humanrights.org/en/big-issues/russian-invasion-of-ukraine/.

Business and Human Rights Resource Centre. "Business and Human Rights in Ukraine" (no date). http://bhr.in.ua/category/our-projects/.

Center for Preventive Action. "Conflict in Ukraine". November 8, 2022, https://www.cfr.org/global-conflict-tracker/conflict/conflict-ukraine.

Council of Europe. *The European Convention on Human Rights*. https://www.echr.coe.int/documents/convention_eng.pdf.

Council of Europe. "Russia ceases to be party to the European Convention on Human Rights". September 16, 2022, https://www.coe.int/en/web/portal/-/russia-ceases-to-be-party-to-the-european-convention-on-human-rights#:~:text=Russia%20ceases%20to%20be%20party%20to%20the%20European%20Convention%20on%20Human%20Rights,-Deutsch%20English%20espa%C3%B1ol&text=Six%20months%20after%20its%20exclusion,Rights%20on%2016%20September%202022.

European Court of Human Rights. "Decision of the Court on requests for interim measures in individual applications concerning Russian military operations on Ukrainian territory". *Press release*, ECHR 073 (2022) 04.03.2022, https://hudoc.echr.coe.int/eng-press?i=003-7277548-9913621.

European Court of Human Rights. "The European Court grants urgent interim measures in application concerning Russian military operations on Ukrainian territory". *Press Release*, ECHR 068 (2022) (01.03.2022), https://hudoc.echr.coe.int/eng-press?i=003-7272764-9905947.

European Union. "Conditions for Membership" (no date). https://neighbourhood-enlargement.ec.europa.eu/enlargement-policy/conditions-membership_en.

European Union Commission. "Ukraine: Application for Membership". February 28, 2022,. https://neighbourhood-enlargement.ec.europa.eu/european-neighbourhood-policy/countries-region/ukraine_en.

International Alert and FAFO. "Red Flags: Liability Risks for Companies Operating in High-Risk Zones". (2008), https://www.international-alert.org/publications/red-flags-liability-risks-companies-high-risk-zones/.

International Criminal Tribunal for the former Yugoslavia. *The Prosecutor v. Dusko Tadic*. Decision on the Defence Motion for Interlocutory Appeal on Jurisdiction, IT-94-1-A, October 2, 1995, https://www.icty.org/x/cases/tadic/acdec/en/51002.htm.

International Committee of the Red Cross. "Business, Violence and Conflict". *International Review of the Red Cross* No.887, September 2012, https://international-review.icrc.org/reviews/irrc-no-887-business-violence-and-conflict.

International Committee of the Red Cross. "The Montreux Document on Private Military and Security Companies". Geneva, August 2009, https://shop.icrc.org/the-montreux-document-on-private-military-and-security-companies-pdf-en.html.

International Committee of the Red Cross. "How is the Term 'Armed Conflict' Defined in International Humanitarian Law?". Opinion Paper, March 2024, https://www.icrc.org/sites/default/files/document_new/file_list/armed_conflict_defined_in_ihl.pdf

International Committee of the Red Cross. "Occupation and international humanitarian law: questions and answers". August 4, 2004. https://www.icrc.org/en/article/occupation-international-humanitarian-law-questions.

International Committee of the Red Cross. “The Geneva Conventions and Their Commentaries”. (no date) https://www.icrc.org/en/law-and-policy/geneva-conventions-and-their-commentaries.

International Committee of the Red Cross. *“How Does Law Protect in War?”* (no date). https://casebook.icrc.org/case-study/switzerland-gold-looting-case.

International Law Commission. *Draft Principles on Protection of the Environment in Relation to Armed Conflicts*. 2022, (A/77/10), https://legal.un.org/ilc/texts/instruments/english/draft_articles/8_7_2022.pdf.

International Law Commission. *Draft articles on Prevention and Punishment of Crimes Against Humanity* 2019. (A/74/10), https://legal.un.org/ilc/texts/instruments/english/draft_articles/7_7_2019.pdf.

International Peace Information Service. “Joint statement on conflict and due diligence legislation”. October 14, 2022, https://ipisresearch.be/joint-statement-on-conflict-due-diligence-legislation/.

Jayaram, Kripa. “Sanctions-Ravaged Russia Offers Opportunities for Indian Firms”. *Bloomberg* UK. June 30, 2022, https://www.bloomberg.com/news/articles/2022-06-30/sanctions-ravaged-russia-offers-opportunities-for-indian-firms?leadSource=uverify%20wall.

Kharkiv International Legal Forum. “Business and Human Rights in Central and Eastern Europe: Kharkiv Forum’s Summary”. September 23–25, 2020, https://www.osce.org/project-coordinator-in-ukraine/482918.

Kryvoi, Yarik et al. “Russia’s Invasion of Ukraine and International Law: Questions and Answers”. British Institute of International and Comparative Law, March 17, 2022. Accessed June 22, 2023, https://www.biicl.org/blog/34/russias-invasion-of-ukraine-and-international-law-questions-and-answers.

Kyiv School of Economics. “SelfSanctions/Leave Russia”. (no date) https://kse.ua/selfsanctions-kse-institute/.

Micek, Peter. “When sanctions undermine human rights online”. *Access Now*, January 18, 2023, https://www.accessnow.org/sanctions-undermining-human-rights/.

Mills, Claire. “Russian Sanctions Prior to the Invasion of Ukraine”. United Kingdom Parliament Research Briefings, May 15, 2023, https://researchbriefings.files.parliament.uk/documents/CBP-9797/CBP-9797.pdf.

Mills, Claire. “Sanctions Against Russia”. United Kingdom Parliament Research Briefings, May 23, 2023, https://researchbriefings.files.parliament.uk/documents/CBP-9481/CBP-9481.pdf.

New York Times. “Companies Are Getting Out of Russia, Sometimes at a Cost”. (October 14, 2022), https://www.nytimes.com/article/russia-invasion-companies.html.

Nuremberg Military Tribunal. *U.S. v. Krauch, et. Al, The I.G. Farben Case*. VIII Trials of War Criminals Before the Nuremberg Military Tribunals, iii-iv (1952).

Office of the High Commissioner for Human Rights. *Situation of human rights in Ukraine in the context of the armed attack by the Russian Federation, 24 February – 15 May 2022*. June 29, 2022, https://www.ohchr.org/en/documents/country-reports/situation-human-rights-ukraine-context-armed-attack-russian-federation.

Organisation for Economic Cooperation and Development, (OECD). "International investment implications of Russia's war against Ukraine". Paris: OECD Publishing, 2022, https://doi.org/10.1787/a24af3d7-en.

OECD. *Due Diligence Guidance for Responsible Business Conduct*. Paris, 2018, https://mneguidelines.oecd.org/OECD-Due-Diligence-Guidance-for-Responsible-Business-Conduct.pdf

Osborn, Andrew and Nikolskaya, Polina. "Russia's Putin authorises 'special military operation' against Ukraine". *Reuters*, February 24, 2022, June 22, 2023, https://www.reuters.com/world/europe/russias-putin-authorises-military-operations-donbass-domestic-media-2022-02-24/.

Putin, Vladimir. "Address by the President of the Russian Federation". The Kremlin, Moscow, February 21, 2022, http://en.kremlin.ru/events/president/news/67828.

Rakhmanina, Evgeniya. "Leaving Russia: the price of exit and other regulatory hurdles". *Linklaters Foreign Investment Links*. January 16, 2023, https://www.linklaters.com/en/insights/blogs/foreigninvestmentlinks/2023/january/leaving-russia-the-price-of-exit-and-other-regulatory-hurdles.

Reuters. "Russia not interested in nationalising foreign enterprises, says minister". July 15, 2022, https://www.reuters.com/world/europe/russia-not-interested-nationalising-foreign-firms-minister-2022-07-15/.

Rogerson, Michael. "Business and Human Rights in Russia: Emerging or Merging?". Business and Human Rights Journal First View Articles. January 19, 2023, 1–26 doi:10.1017/bhj.2022.29.

Rowley, Thomas and Guz Serhiy. "Ukraine uses Russian invasion to pass laws wrecking workers' rights". *Open Democracy*, July 20, 2022, https://www.opendemocracy.net/en/odr/ukraine-draft-law-5371-workers-rights-war-russia/.

Ruggie, John. "Business and human rights in conflict-affected regions: challenges and options towards State responses". Report of the Special Representative of the Secretary-General on the issue of human rights and transnational corporations and other business enterprises, UN Doc. A/HRC/17/32, May 27, 2011 https://digitallibrary.un.org/record/706417?ln=zh_CN.

Schmitt, Michael N. "Russia's 'Special Military Operation' and the (Claimed) Right of Self-Defence". *Articles of War*, February 28, 2022, https://lieber.westpoint.edu/russia-special-military-operation-claimed-right-self-defense/.

Schliemann, Christian and Bryk, Linde. *Arms Trade and Corporate Responsibility: Liability, Litigation and Legislative Reform*. Berlin: Friedrich-Ebert-Stiftung, November 2019, https://library.fes.de/pdf-files/iez/15850.pdf.

Ukrainian Parliament (Verkhovna Rada). "Law on the organization of labour relations under martial law". July 19, 2022, with changes introduced in accordance with Law No. 2352-IX dated July 1, 2022, https://zakon.rada.gov.ua/laws/show/2136-20#Text

United Kingdom Government Statutory Guidance. "Russia sanctions: guidance". June 21, 2023, https://www.gov.uk/government/publications/russia-sanctions-guidance/russia-sanctions-guidance.

United Kingdom Government. "UK imposes sweeping new sanctions to starve Putin's war machine". *Press release*, April 6, 2022, https://www.gov.uk/government/news/uk-imposes-sweeping-new-sanctions-to-starve-putins-war-machine.

United Nations. *General Assembly Resolution* A/RES/ES-11/1, adopted March 2, 2022, https://digitallibrary.un.org/record/3965290?ln=en#record-files-collapse-header.

United Nations. *Guiding Principles on Business and Human Rights*. New York and Geneva: United Nations, 2011. https://www.ohchr.org/sites/default/files/documents/publications/guidingprinciplesbusinesshr_en.pdf.

United Nations. "Third Forum on Business and Human Rights Closing Plenary Remarks John G. Ruggie Former UN Special Representative for Business and Human Rights". Geneva, December 3, 2014. https://www.ohchr.org/Documents/Issues/Business/ForumSession3/Submissions/JohnRuggie_SR_SG_BHR.pdf.

United Nations Development Programme (UNDP). *Heightened Human Rights Due Diligence for Business in Conflict-Affected Contexts: A Guide*. New York, June 16, 2022. https://www.undp.org/publications/heightened-human-rights-due-diligence-business-conflict-affected-contexts-guide.

UNDP. *Business and Human Rights in Ukraine: Accelerating Sustainable and Equitable Development through Implementation of the UN Guiding Principles on Business and Human Rights*. (Kiyv, 2022), https://www.undp.org/ukraine/publications/business-and-human-rights-ukraine-accelerating-sustainable-and-equitable-development-through-implementation-un-guiding.

United Nations Human Rights Committee. "General comment no. 29 states of emergency (article 4)". UN Doc.CCPR/C/21/Rev.1/Add.11, August 31, 2001, June 22, 2023, https://digitallibrary.un.org/record/451555?ln=en.

United Nations Working Group on Business and Human Rights. "Business, human rights and conflict-affected regions: towards heightened action". UN Doc A/75/212, July 21, 2020 https://www.ohchr.org/en/calls-for-input/report-business-human-rights-and-conflict-affected-regions-towards-heightened.

United States Government Executive Order No. 14,071, 87 Fed. Reg. 20,999, 20,999, April 6, 2022, https://home.treasury.gov/system/files/126/14071.pdf.

Uvarova, Olena. "Ukrainian companies and human rights during the war". Opinion Business and Human Rights Resource Centre. April 4, 2022, https://www.business-humanrights.org/en/blog/ukrainian-companies-and-human-rights-during-the-war/.

Van Ho, Tara. "Not all parties are equal: understanding the responsibility for reparations in conflict-affected areas". *Opinion* (Business and Human Rights Resource Centre, February 20, 2023). https://www.business-humanrights.org/en/blog/not-all-parties-are-equal-understanding-the-responsibility-for-reparations-in-conflict-affected-areas/.

Voluntary Principles on Security and Human Rights (2000), https://www.voluntaryprinciples.org/the-principles/.

Yale School of Management, Chief Executive Leadership Institute. "Over 1,000 Companies Have Curtailed Operations in Russia – But Some Remain". https://som.yale.edu/story/2022/over-1000-companies-have-curtailed-operations-russia-some-remain.

CHAPTER 6

Corporate Responsibility to Redress Human Rights Violations Related to the Environment: The Long Road towards Ever-Growing Call for Legal Regulation and Accountability

Paolo Galizzi

1 Introduction

Over the years, the role and size of corporations has grown exponentially. At the beginning of April 2023, Apple, for example, the largest corporation in the world by market capital valued at U$ 2.6 trillion, generated yearly revenues of over U$ 380 billion.[1] Saudi Arabian Oil Co., the largest oil producing company in the world, generated revenues in the region of U$600 billion annually and was valued at U$1.92 trillion.[2] These are just two of the largest corporations globally measured in capitalisation. Countless other examples could be given as evidence of the power of corporations, who often overshadow the traditional role played by (several) States in the international community. From Google to Facebook, from Amazon to Walmart to Tesla, to mention some other globally known household names, corporations dominate the global economy, often drive political agendas, create economic opportunities, contribute to economic and technological development, and have pervasive impacts on society. At the same time though, corporations are often responsible for the increasingly worrying environmental and social problems caused by unfettered economic growth and power. The footprint of corporate actions and their impact can be seen and measured on all the environmental problems the world is facing, from the loss of biodiversity to waste generation, to climate change, to environmental justice, just to name a few.

1 "Apple Reports Fourth Quarter Results", Apple Newsroom, accessed May 23, 2023, https://www.apple.com/newsroom/2022/10/apple-reports-fourth-quarter-results/.
2 "Saudi Aramco (2222.SR) – Market Capitalization," CompaniesMarketCap.com – companies ranked by market capitalization, accessed July 17, 2023, https://companiesmarketcap.com/saudi-aramco/marketcap/.

 | DOI:10.1163/9789004530942_007

International law has been slow in regulating multinational corporations largely due to outdated doctrinal debates on legal subjectivity in international law. Legally binding international regulation of corporations and their impact in general, and more specifically on the environment, are in fact arguably almost entirely lacking. In the late 1970s though, several soft rules have emerged, for example, within the Organization for Economic Cooperation and Development (OECD) and the International Labor Organization (ILO) to address the conduct of multinationals on the global stage. Within the United Nations regulations of corporations was also pursued with various degrees of success. More recently, soft rules have also been adopted over the past decade laying out the human rights obligations applicable to businesses: the United Nations Guiding Principles on Business and Human Rights (UNGP) are undoubtedly the most important soft law instrument in this area. Landmark decisions within human rights bodies at the global and regional level and other international bodies as well as at the national level have also contributed to the creation of an ever-evolving set of legal obligations for corporations at the intersection of business, human rights, and the environment.

This chapter focuses on the emerging human rights framework for corporations and analyse its application to environmental violations caused by corporate actors. It examines how business and human rights norms regulate the environmental aspects of corporate activities. The chapter starts with an overview of the key rules that have emerged on the regulation of business and human rights to make an argument on the link between human rights and environmental protection. It then examines selected case studies to highlight how environmental violations causing human rights harms have been addressed by courts. It concludes with a discussion on how a business and human rights framework could help corporations be part of a sustainable solutions to many of the environmental problems challenging the Planet rather than continuing to be an obstacle in urgently addressing the environmental crisis Earth is facing.

2 Human Rights, the Environment and Corporations: The Emerging Regulatory Framework at the International Level

Historically, international laws that regulate businesses – and thus corporations – have been lacking due to the traditional view that only States and international organisations hold legal personality under the international legal system.[3]

Over the years though, such orthodox view on the entities having legal personality under international law has been challenged and many scholars now believe that corporations do have, at least, some limited legal personality and therefore obligations under international law.[4]

In the past decade, the debate on the legal obligations of corporations in international law has been further heavily influenced by the evolving legal regulations addressing the relationship between business and international human rights norms.[5] Traditional scholars also believed that human rights obligations are exclusively directed to States.[6] However, with increasing globalisation and the rising influence of transnational corporations, the international community arguably has entered a new era with serious attempts to govern businesses and the undeniable human rights impacts of their activities.[7]

The history of international efforts to address corporate human rights harms can be traced back to several key moments and developments over the past few decades.[8] It took the late 20th century before specific attention was paid to the responsibility of corporations within an international legal framework. In 1976 and 1977, OECD[9] and ILO[10] released soft law

3 For an overview of corporations in international law, see Jennifer Zerk, *Multinationals and Corporate Social Responsibility: Limitations and Opportunities in International Law* (Cambridge: Cambridge University Press, 2006).

4 Paolo Galizzi, "From Ignorance, to Indifference, to Limited Familiarity: An Analysis of the Relationship Between International Environmental Law & Multinational Corporations," *Fordham Law Legal Studies Research Paper* No. 2779332 (2014): 102–147, https://ssrn.com/abstract=2779332.

5 Alan S Gutterman, "Evolving Relationship of Business and Human Rights," *Business Law Today*, February 2, 2021, <https://businesslawtoday.org/2021/02/evolving-relationship-business-human-rights/>.

6 *See ibid.*

7 *See* Surya Deva, and David Birchall, "From 'Business or Human Rights' to 'Business and Human Rights': What Next?," in *Research Handbook on Human Rights and Business*, eds. Surya Deva (Cheltenham, UK: Edward Elgar Publishing, 2020), 1–21.

8 This chapter only mention some of the most salient and selected efforts to regulate corporations at the international level. For a more detailed history of the evolving international legal landscape on business and human rights, see Michael A Santoro, "Business and human rights in historical perspective," *Journal of Human Rights* 14, no. 2 (2015): 155–161.

9 See "OECD Guidelines for Mulatinational Enterprises" firstly adopted in 1976, Organization for Economic Cooperation and Development', www.oecd.org, accessed July 14, 2023.

10 See "Tripartite Declaration of Principles concerning Multinational Enterprises and Social Policy," International Labour Organization, accessed July 14, 2023, https://www.ilo.org/wcmsp5/groups/public/@ed_emp/@emp_ent/documents/publication/wcms_101234.pdf.

norms[11] to guide the responsibilities of transnational corporations.[12] Although these instruments lacked specific references to human rights harms by corporations, they set the stage for further regulatory actions.

Another attempt to define business responsibilities under international law[13] was the UN Draft Code of Conduct on Transnational Corporations, a document never formally adopted.[14]

For the purposes of this chapter though, while there are several non-binding instruments addressing the nexus between businesses and human rights,[15] the next section only briefly examines the guidance and recommendations proposed to businesses by the UNGPs, as the specific leading legal instrument for our purposes.[16]

---

11 The ILO Tripartite Declaration of Principles concerning Multinational Enterprises and Social Policy (MNE Declaration). The Declaration sets out a series of principles and guidelines for multinational enterprises with regard to employment, training, working conditions, and industrial relations. It also encourages dialogue and cooperation between multinational enterprises and workers' organisations and provides a framework for governments to regulate the activities of multinational enterprises in their jurisdictions.

12 *See* Deva, "From 'Business or Human Rights' to 'Business and Human Rights': What Next?" 1–21; *see also* Raymond Markey, and Katherine Ravenwood, "The Impact of MNEs and FDI on Aspects of Working Conditions as Contained in the ILO 1977 Tripartite Declaration of Principles Concerning Multinational Enterprises and Social Policy," *New Zealand Journal of Employment Relations* 35, no. 3 (2010): 27–38; *See* Samuel Sarpong and Ishaque Kwabena Otoo, "Survey on the Implementation of the Mne Declaration in Ghana," *International Labour Organization*, June 1, 2009.

13 While the Draft Code was never adopted by the General Assembly, it helped to raise awareness about the importance of corporate social responsibility and the need for greater regulation of transnational corporations. It also later inspired the development of other international initiatives aimed at promoting corporate social responsibility, in particular the UN Guiding Principles on Business and Human Rights.

14 UN Code of Conduct of Transnational Corporations, ILM 23 (1984): 626; *See also* Axel Marx and Jan Wouters, "Global Governance and Business Responsibility: The UN Draft Code of Conduct on Transnational Corporations Revisited," *Journal of Business Ethic* 87, no. 3 (2009): 385–404; https://doi.org/10.1007/s10551-008-9965-7.

15 These instrument include the UN Guiding Principles on Business and Human Rights (UNGPs); Guiding principles on business and human rights: Implementing the United Nations "Protect, Respect and Remedy" Framework; OECD Guidelines for Multinational Enterprises, OECD Guidelines for Multinational Enterprises; International Labor Organization Tripartite Declaration of Principles Concerning Multinational Enterprises and Social Policy; and Tripartite declaration of principles concerning multinational enterprises and social policy.

16 For a more detailed discussion of the use of existing international human rights instruments, both at the global and regional level, to hold corporate actors accountable for their human rights abuses see: Florian Wettstein, *Business and Human Rights: Ethical, Legal, and Managerial Perspectives* (Cambridge: Cambridge UP, 2022).; Peter Muchlinski, *Advanced introduction to business and human rights* (London: Edward Elgar Publishing,

3 The United Nations Guiding Principles on Business and Human Rights: The Protect, Respect and Remedy Framework

Several high-profile cases involving human rights abuses by corporations, such as the Union Carbide's pesticide plant exploding in India and the protests against Shell's oils operations resulting in the hanging of Ken Saro-Wiwa in Nigeria by the military,[17] raised increased awareness of the need for international measures to hold corporations accountable for their human rights and environmental impacts. Following major corporate environmental disasters and tragedies,[18] corporations suffering huge reputational damage from shaming by international non-government organisations (NGOs) and public opinion, initially responded by adopting various initiatives of self-regulation.[19] However, these attempts to self-regulate were viewed both with suspicion and as insufficient as businesses faced little to no accountability, as their self-regulatory initiatives were legally non-binding. Civil society therefore lobbied for the adoption of stronger enforcement and accountability mechanisms for corporations, calling for a 'global legal framework of legal accountability'.[20]

A landmark progression towards the development of such framework was the adoption in 2003, within the UN Sub-Commission on the Promotion and Protection of Human Rights, of the *Norms on the Responsibilities of Transnational Corporations and Other Business Enterprises with Regard to Human Rights*.[21] The non-legally binding norms provide guidance on the obligations of corporations to respect human rights[22] and they have been cited

---

2022); Dorothée Baumann-Pauly and Justine Nolan, *Business and human rights: from principles to practice* (Oxon: Routledge, 2016).

17 John Sherman III, "Beyond CSR: The Story of the UN Guiding Principles on Business and Human Rights," *Corporate Responsibility Initiative Working Paper* No. 71, (2020).

18 *See* Valeria Cavotta, Guido Palazzo, and Antonino Vaccaro, "Mobilizing after corporate environmental irresponsibility in a community of place: A framing microprocess perspective," *Journal of Business Ethics* (2021): 1–15; Edward Broughton, "The Bhopal disaster and its aftermath: a review," *Environmental Health* 4.1 (2005): 1–6; *See* Alessia MM Giurdanella, "International Environmental History and Law," *Journal of Management Policy and Practice, no.* 23.3 (2022): 43–120; *See* Mandavilli, Apoorva, "The World's worst industrial disaster is still unfolding," *The Atlantic*, July 10, 2018 https://www.theatlantic.com/science/archive/2018/07/the-worlds-worst-industrial-disaster-is-still-unfolding/560726/.

19 Sherman, "Beyond," 71.

20 Ibid, 6.

21 See David Weissbordt and Muria Kruger, "Norms on the Responsibility of Transnational Corporations and Other Business Enterprises with Regard to Human Rights," *The American Journal of International Law*, Vol 97, No. 4 (Oct. 2003): 91 – 92.

22 Weissbordt, "Norms," 91–92.

in national and international legal cases as evidence of emerging customary international law in this area and have played an important role in the future developments in the field.[23]

Indeed these efforts to regulate corporate impact on human rights culminated in the appointment in 2005 by then UN Secretary-General Kofi Annan of Professor John Ruggie as the Special Representative on Business and Human Rights to develop a human rights framework to govern businesses.[24] John Ruggie successfully concluded his mandate (2005 – 2011)[25] with the adoption of the United Nations Guiding Principles on Business and Human Rights (UNGP) hailed as 'the first globally accepted standards" to address the relationship between human rights and business as an "authoritative point of reference' and the main guiding instrument in this field.[26]

In 2008, John Ruggie, the Special Representative of the UN Secretary-General, proposed a 'conceptual and policy framework' to address the relationship between business and human rights.[27] The UNGP are the result of 6 years of research and extensive multi-stakeholder consultations around the world on the issue of human rights and transnational corporations and other business enterprises.[28] This Framework articulated businesses' responsibility to respect human rights, which was said to be grounded in widely shared expectations of appropriate business conduct.[29] The 2011 UNGP[30] were an attempt

23 See Doe v. Unocal Corporation 395 F.3d 932 (9th Cir. 2002): In this 2005 case, Burmese citizens sued Unocal (now part of Chevron) for complicity in human rights abuses by the Burmese military during the construction of a gas pipeline. The U.S. Court of Appeals for the Ninth Circuit cited the Norms as evidence that corporations have a responsibility to respect human rights under customary international law.; See also Wiwa v. Royal Dutch Petroleum Co 226 F.3d 88.: In this 2009 case, Nigerian citizens sued Royal Dutch Shell for its alleged involvement in human rights abuses against the Ogoni people in Nigeria, including the execution of environmental activist Ken Saro-Wiwa. The U.S. Court of Appeals for the Second Circuit cited the Norms as evidence that corporations can be held liable for human rights abuses under customary international law.

24 Sherman, "Beyond," 71.

25 Sherman, "Beyond," 71.

26 Beata Faracik, "Implementation of the UN Guiding Principles on Business and Human Rights," *European Parliament's online database,* (2017), doi:10.2861/527765.

27 "Protect, Respect and Remedy: A Framework for Business and Human Rights, Report to the UN Human Rights Council," *United Nations,* accessed August 20, 2023, www.reports-andmaterials.org/Ruggie-report-7-Apr-2008.pdf.

28 Sherman, "Beyond," 71.

29 Ibid., para. 54. On the logic of appropriateness, as opposed to the logic of consequences, see John Gerard Ruggie, *Just business: Multinational corporations and human rights* (ww Norton & Company, 2013).

30 "Guiding Principles on Business and Human Rights: Implementing the United Nations 'Protect, Respect and Remedy' Framework (Guiding Principles)," United Nations

'to provide concrete and practical recommendations for ... implementation [of the Framework]'.[31] The Guiding Principles were endorsed by the UN Human Rights Council[32] and have since been incorporated in a range of international regulatory instruments addressing corporate responsibility for human rights violations[33] making them the most authoritative global reference point on business and human rights.[34]

The Guiding Principles rest on three interdependent and mutually supporting pillars:[35]

1. The state duty to *protect* against human rights abuses by third parties, including business, through appropriate policies, regulation and adjudication;

Human Rights, accessed August 20, 2023, www.ohchr. org/Documents/Publications/GuidingPrinciplesBusinessHR_EN.pdf; "The Corporate Responsibility to Respect Human Rights: An Interpretive Guide," UN Office of the High Commissioner for Human Rights, accessed August 20, 2023, http://www.ohchr.org/Documents/Publications/HR.PUB.12.2_En.pdf).

31 Report to the UN Human Rights Council on 'Guiding Principles on Business and Human Rights: Implementing the United Nations "Protect, Respect and Remedy" Framework' (Report on Guiding Principles), UN Doc. A/HRC/17/31, 21 March 2011, para. 9.

32 UN Human Rights Council Resolution 17/4, UN Doc. A/HRC/RES/17/4, 16 June 2011.

33 "Guidelines for Multinational Enterprises," *Organisation for Economic Co-operation and Development* (OECD), accessed August 20, 2023, http://oecd.org/daf/inv/mne/48004323.pdf; "Sustainability Performance Standards," *International Finance Corporation*, accessed August 20, 2023. www.ifc.org/wps/wcm/connect/7540778049a792dcb87efaa8c6a8312a/SP_English_2012.pdf?MOD=AJPERES; "Equator Principles on Project Finance Requirements," *Equator Principles*, accessed August 20, 2023. www.equator-principles.com/index.php/ep3, which all now incorporate human rights due diligence requirements based on the Guiding Principles, supra note 3.

34 See UN Doc. A/HRC/17/31, Guiding Principles on Business and Human Rights: Implementing the United Nations 'Protect, Respect and Remedy' Framework, 21 March 2011, unanimously endorsed by the United Nations Human Rights Council on 16 June 2011. The Council also created a new expert Working Group on business and human rights to take forward the dissemination and implementation of the Guiding Principles.

35 The Guiding Principles, published in 2011, build upon the topics introduced in the UN Framework by elaborating "the implications of existing standards and practices for states and businesses." Thirty-one Guiding Principles, organized as "foundational" and "operational" principles for each of the three pillars, are accompanied by commentaries clarifying the meaning and implications of each Principle. More detailed interpretation of each Principle, approved by the Special Representative, was subsequently published by the UN Office of the High Commissioner for Human Rights. A detailed analysis of the UNGP is beyond the scope of chis chapter. There is a vast literature on the UNGP and for a more in depth examination see, inter alia, ...

2. The corporate responsibility to *respect* human rights, with the explicit obligation to avoid infringing on the rights of others and to address adverse impacts with which businesses are involved; and
3. The need for greater access by victims to effective *remedy*, both judicial and non-judicial.[36]

The UNGP's first pillar simply reiterates the customary law obligation of States to ensure the protection of fundamental human rights within their territory or jurisdiction from all violations, expressly including abuses committed by business enterprises.[37]

The most groundbreaking legal development under the UNGP is the recognition of 'the corporate responsibility to respect human rights' in pillar 2.[38] Under Principle 11:

> Business enterprises should respect human rights. This means that they should avoid infringing on the human rights of others and should address adverse human rights impacts with which they are involved.[39]

Principle 12 specifies that, 'at a minimum', the human rights businesses must respect are those 'expressed in the International Bill of Human Rights and the principles of fundamental rights set out in the International Labour Organization's Declaration on Fundamental Principles and Rights at Work'.[40]

---

36 UN Guiding Principles, para. 6.

37 UNGP Principle 1; See Anthony P. Ewing, "Teaching Note: Introducing the UN Guiding Principles on Business and Human Rights," in *Teaching Business and Human Rights Handbook* (Teaching Business and Human Rights Forum, 2016), https://teachbhr.org/resources/teaching-bhr-handbook/teaching-notes/introducing-the-un-guiding-principles-on-business-and-human-rights-2/.

38 "Guiding Principles on Business and Human Rights, principle 11, U.N. Doc. HR/PUB/11/04 (2011)," United Nations Human Rights, Office of the High Commissioner, accessed August 20, 2023. https://www.ohchr.org/sites/default/files/documents/publications/guidingprinciplesbusinesshr_en.pdf; *See* Claire Methven O'Brien and Sumithra Dhanarajan, "The corporate responsibility to respect human rights: a status review," *Accounting, Auditing and Accountability Journal* 29.4 (2016): 542–567; *See* Giulia Botta and Claire Methven O'Brien, "The Corporate Responsibility to Respect Human Rights: An Updated Status Review," in Responsabilidade Social Corporativa e Governança Socioambiental: Greenwashing e Direitos Humanos [Corporate Social Responsibility and Social and Environmental Governance: Greenwashing and Human Rights](Rio de Janeiro, Lumen Iuris, (2022).

39 UNGP Principle 11.

40 UNGP Principle 12.

Under pillar 2, business entities are called upon to develop a regulatory framework that operationalises their commitment to respect human rights.[41] The obligation to respect human rights requires that businesses avoid and mitigate operations that cause or could cause adverse human rights impacts and to implement policies that consider their size, operations, and structure.[42] This duty also encompasses omissions and business relationships.[43]

The operational principles of Part 2 of the UNGP detail steps companies should take to ensure compliance with their obligation to 'respect' human rights: adopting a human rights policy that is embedded throughout the enterprise;[44] conducting human rights with due diligence to 'identify, prevent, mitigate and account for how they address their adverse human rights impact' and it should be 'ongoing' to reflect and respond to changes in the businesses' operations and related human rights risks.[45] Lastly, businesses are to ensure remedies to adverse impacts they are linked to.[46]

Pillar 3,[47] 'remedy' under the Principles Framework, requires that when there are human rights abuses, States are to ensure that harmed individuals and communities have access to a remedy – whether through the court system or a non-judicial process. Companies themselves are also expected to create and be part of grievance mechanisms.[48] States are encouraged to consider non-state grievance mechanisms administered either by businesses, industry associations, or multi-stakeholder groups[49] that are legitimate, accessible, predictable, equitable, transparent, rights-compatible,[50] and most importantly, culturally appropriate.[51]

Since their adoption the UNGP have gained extensive support from States, businesses, trade unions, NGOs, investors, and other stakeholders. Virtually all large enterprises now have policies addressing human rights, sustainability, and the broader human rights impacts of their operations. This trend has expanded to cover enterprises in all sectors and increasingly all sizes.[52] Thus,

41 UNGP Principles 11 to 24.
42 UNGP Principles 13–14.
43 UNGP Principle 13 & Commentary.
44 UNGP Principle 16.
45 UNGP Principle 17.
46 See id; *See also* UNGP Principle 22 & Commentary.
47 UNGP Principles 25 – 31.
48 See ibid.
49 UNGP Principle 28.
50 UNGP Principle 31.
51 UNGP Principle 28, Commentary.
52 *See* "Human rights principles." *The Coca-Cola Company.* (n.d.), accessed April 25, 2023, https://www.coca-colacompany.com/policies-and-practices/human-rights-principles;

the adoption of the UNGPs has 'normalize[d]' the understanding that businesses should respect human rights and has resulted in many publicly committing to the principles,[53] such as Apple, Chevron, Exxon Mobil, Facebook, Google, Microsoft, Nestle, and Target to name a few.[54] As mentioned, not only have the UNGP been endorsed by the UN Human Rights Council, but there are several examples of their enduring influence and a further convergence of standards around the Guiding Principles at the global level. For example, the OECD, in revising its Guidelines for Multinational Enterprises in 2011, added a new human rights chapter that closely mirrors the Guiding Principles.[55] The recent International Organization for Standardization ISO 26000 Guidance on Corporate Social Responsibility standard also reflects the Guiding Principles in its human rights provisions.[56] The International Finance Corporation (IFC) has incorporated the corporate responsibility to respect human rights in its revised Sustainability Framework and Performance Standards,[57] which have in turn been picked up and applied by the private 'Equator Principles' banks and the OECD 'Common Approaches' for Export Credit Agency.[58] Finally, the European Commission has issued a new communication on corporate social

---

See Blanton, J. (2023, April 5). "Northrop Grumman Human Rights Policy." *Northrop Grumman*. Accessed April 25, 2023, https://www.northropgrumman.com/corporate-responsibility/northrop-grumman-human-rights-policy/; *See* "Chevron's human rights policy," *Chevron*, accessed April 25, 2023, https://www.chevron.com/sustainability/social/human-rights; *See* "Meta Corporate Human Rights Policy. (n.d.)," *Meta*, accessed April 25, 2023, https://about.fb.com/wp-content/uploads/2021/03/Facebooks-Corporate-Human-Rights-Policy.pdf.

53 Arvind Ganesan, "Why Laws Are Needed to Avoid Corporate Rights Abuses," *HUM. RTS. WATCH*, accessed August 20, 2023, https://www.hrw.org/news/2021/07/01/why-laws-are-needed-avoid-corporate-rights-abuses.

54 "Companies," *UN GUIDING PRINCIPLES REPORTING FRAMEWORK*, https://www.ungpreporting.org/database-analysis/explore-disclosures/companies-page/.

55 See "OECD Guidelines for Multinational Enterprises," *OCED*, accessed August 20, 2023, https://www.oecd.org/corporate/mne/.

56 See "ISO 26000 Guidance on Social Responsibility," *International Organization for Standardization*, Accessed August 20, 2023, www.iso.org/iso/iso_catalogue/management_standards/iso26000.

57 See Elisa Morgera, "Significant trends in corporate environmental accountability: the new performance standards of the international finance corporation," *Colorado Journal of International Environmental Law and Policy 18* (2007): 151; See Steven Herz, et al, "The International Finance Corporation's Performance Standards and the Equator Principles: Respecting Human Rights and Remedying Violations?" *Center for International Environmental Law, Oxfam Australia, World Resources Institute*, August (2008).

58 See "Performance Standards on Environmental and Social Sustainability," *International Finance Corporation*, accessed August 20, 2023, https://www.ifc.org/content/dam/ifc/doc/2010/2012-ifc-performance-standards-en.pdf.

responsibility that calls on all companies operating in the EU to respect human rights in line with the UN Guiding Principles.[59]

Furthermore, the UN Global Compact Human Rights Principles also reflect the UNGP; the UNGP received affirmation from G7 Summit Leaders within the supply chains context and have been referenced in the 2030 Agenda for Sustainable Development.[60] Support has also been apparent at the regional level as the EU, the Council of Europe and the Organization of American States have all adopted measures in support of the UNGPs.[61] Guidance documents from 'international and national bar associations and legal societies' have reflected the UNGPs.[62] Several provisions from the UNGPs have also been incorporated in domestic legislation in a few countries. For example, France and Germany have enacted laws that require the identification and prevention of 'human rights violations and environmental damage', permitting victims to sue or imposing fines,[63] and the EU recently adopted a proposal that requires companies to respect human rights.[64] Further, court decisions have increasingly been referring to the UNGP in holding companies accountable for their activities harming human rights.[65]

To sum up, the UNGP have now become the minimum legal standards when addressing the relationship between business and human rights. Although they represent soft rules at this stage, it is undeniable that they influence the daily operations of corporate activities[66] and are now the fundamental framework

---

59 See "A Renewed EU strategy 2011–14 for Corporate Social Responsibility," European Commission, accessed August 20, 2023, http://ec.europa.eu/enterprise/policies/sustainable-business/corporate-socialresponsibility/index_en.htm.

60 "Directorate-General For External Policies, Implementation of the UN Guiding Principles on Business and Human Rights 14, 16," European Parliament, accessed August 20, 2023, https://www.europarl.europa.eu/RegData/etudes/STUD/2017/578031/EXPO_STU(2017)578031_EN.pdf.

61 See ibid, 15.

62 John F. Sherman III, ABA, "A Lawyer's Guide to Key Businesses and Human Rights Documents," accessed August 20, 2023, https://www.americanbar.org/groups/human_rights/business-human-rights-initiative/key-business-and-human-rights-documents/.

63 Arvind Ganesan, "Why Laws Are Needed to Avoid Corporate Rights Abuses".

64 *See* "Just and Sustainable Economy: Commission Lays Down Rules for Companies to Respect Human Rights and Environmental in Global Value Chains," *European Commission*, accessed August 20, 2023, https://ec.europa.eu/commission/presscorner/detail/en/ip_22_1145.

65 European Parliament, "Directorate-General".

66 Michelle Langlois, "Reporting Trends & Insights: Are Companies Making the Commitment to Respect Human Rights?," *UN Guiding Principles Reporting Framework*, https://www.ungpreporting.org/reporting-insights-trends-are-companies-making-the-commitment-to-respect-human-rights/. Note that while this report took place 5 years after the U.N. endorsed the UNGPs, many of the issues reported in this article still stand true today.

for any discussion on this topic. Their implementation in the corporate world varies greatly[67] and there is a growing momentum for the adoption of binding norms to ensure enforceable rules and not just voluntary standards.[68]

4 The UNGP and the Corporate Environmental Harm: A Missing Link?

The UNGP did not address specifically the relationship between business, human rights, and the environment, although harm to the environment is inextricably linked to the violations of several human rights and therefore the UNGP implicitly also regulate the conduct of corporations when their activities harm the environment.[69]

There is indeed widespread recognition that human rights are intrinsically linked to the environment.[70] The 1972 UN Conference on the Environment in Stockholm, for example, marked the first time that issues related to the environment were 'at the forefront of international concerns' and started discussions from countries about how economic growth is linked to environmental harm.[71] Various resolutions pertaining to human rights and the environment have been adopted by the Human Rights Council from 2012 to present, when a Special Rapporteur on human rights and the environment was established.[72] At the domestic level, countless state constitutions have increasingly grown to reflect the right to a healthy environment.[73] As of 2020, the Human Rights

67 James Gomme, "10 Years of the UN Guiding Principles on Business & Human Rights," *WBCSD,* June 16, 2021, https://www.wbcsd.org/Overview/News-Insights/WBCSD-insights/10-years-of-the-UN-Guiding-Principles-on-Business-Human-Rights; For more information on human rights benchmarks across various sectors, see "CORPORATE HUMAN RIGHTS BENCHMARK," World Benchmarking Alliance, accessed August 20, 2023, https://assets.worldbenchmarkingalliance.org/app/uploads/2020/11/WBA-2020-CHRB-Key-Findings-Report.pdf.

68 Arvind Ganesan, "Why Laws Are Needed to Avoid Corporate Rights Abuses."

69 See below.

70 See Sheila Foster and Paolo Galizzi, "Human Rights and Climate Change: Building Synergies for a Common Future," in *Climate Change Law*, eds. Daniel Farber and Marjan Peeter (Cheltenham: Edward Elgar Publishing, 2016).

71 "The Right to a Healthy Environment: 6 Things You Need to Know," *United Nations News*, Oct. 15, 2021, https://news.un.org/en/story/2021/10/1103082.

72 "About the Mandate," *United Nations Office of the High Commissioner*, accessed August 20, 2023, https://www.ohchr.org/en/special-procedures/sr-environment/about-mandate.

73 *See* "About Human Rights and the Environment," *United Nations Office of the High Commissioner*, accessed August 20, 2023, https://www.ohchr.org/en/special-procedures/sr-environment/about-human-rights-and-environment.

Council reported that over 150 States 'have explicitly recognized the right to a healthy environment' in various forms such as through national legislations or constitutions, and in regional agreements.[74] The African Charter on Human and Peoples' Rights,[75] the San Salvador Protocol to the American Convention on Human Rights,[76] the Escazu Agreement,[77] the Arab Charter on Human Rights,[78] and the ASEAN Declaration on Human Rights[79] each include a right to a healthy environment. Other human rights frameworks, such as the Convention on the Rights of the Child[80] refer to environmental issues as they relate to the framework's focus, in this case children's rights.[81] The lack of an express reference to the environment has not prevented regional human right bodies to recognise the existence of human rights violations caused by environmental harms.[82]

Indeed, a 'healthy and sustainable environment is integral to the full enjoyment of a wide range of human rights', which includes the 'rights to life, health, food, water and sanitation'.[83] The right to environment completes the other rights guaranteed to each human being. The requirement of a healthy and

74 "Good practices on the right to a healthy environment," United Nations Human Rights Office of the High Commissioner, accessed August 20, 2023, https://www.ohchr.org/en/special-procedures/sr-environment/good-practices-right-healthy-environment.

75 "African Charter on Human and People's Rights," *Organisation of African Unity*, accessed August 20, 2023, https://au.int/sites/default/files/treaties/36390-treaty-0011_-_african_charter_on_human_and_peoples_rights_e.pdf.

76 Organization of American States, American Convention on Human Rights, Nov. 22, 1969, O.A.S.T.S. No. 36, 1144 U.N.T.S. 123 (entered into force July 18, 1978).

77 "Regional Agreement on Access to Information, Public Participation and Justice in Environmental Matters in Latin America and the Caribbean". *CEPAL*, accessed August 20, 2023, https://www.cepal.org/en/escazuagreement.

78 "Arab Charter on Human Rights," *League of Arab States*, accessed August 20, 2023, https://digitallibrary.un.org/record/551368?ln=en.

79 "ASEAN Human Rights Declaration," *Association of Southeast Asians Nations*, accessed August 20, 2023, https://asean.org/asean-human-rights-declaration/.

80 United Nations (2020). "Chapter IV. Human Rights. 11) Convention on the Rights of the Child" in: United Nations Treaty Collection. Depositary. Status of Treaties. Archived 8 September 2020 at the Wayback Machine. Retrieved 04-02-2022.

81 Dinah Shelton, "Human Rights, Health & Environmental Protection: Linkages in Law & Practice," *Health and Human Rights Working Paper Series* No 1. (2007), World Health Organization.

82 See Birgit Peters, "The European Court of Human Rights and the Environment," in *International Courts and Tribunals and the Protection of the Environment*, eds. Mead/Samsson/Sobenes, (The Hague: Asser Press, 2020).

83 "About Human Rights and the Environment," *United Nations Office of the High Commissioner*, accessed August 20, 2023, https://www.ohchr.org/en/special-procedures/sr-environment/about-human-rights-and-environment.

balanced environment and of the environmentally sound management of the natural resource is a condition for the implementation of other fundamental rights.[84] These are rights that are reflected in the 17 Sustainable Development Goals adopted by all UN members in 2015 as part of the 2030 Agenda for Sustainable Development.[85] Some of these goals aim for no poverty, zero hunger, gender equality, clean water and sanitation, sustainable cities and communities, and climate action.[86] These goals are interrelated. This was recognised by the member states as goals like ending deprivations, such as poverty, 'must go hand-in-hand' with plans to improve health and education and combating climate change while preserving 'our oceans and forests'.[87] These goals also recognise a key fact that there must be a global partnership which cuts across not only nations but also other sectors of society, including businesses. Businesses are indeed and undeniably key actors in sustainable development. Businesses have 'a considerable environmental, economic, and societal footprint' and by conducting business responsibly and promoting positive impacts, businesses can be a key force in achieving many of the sustainable development goals.[88] As such, businesses' duty to respect human rights includes helping to create and maintain a healthy and sustainable environment.

Recently, there has been ample support for the identification of an environmental right that may be safeguarded by the current human rights framework, either as a separate right or one that is inherent in other rights. As a result, the Human Rights Council has declared the 'right to a decent environment as a human right' in 2021.[89] By passing this resolution, the Council has recognised that the right to a healthy and sustainable environment is a 'universal right'.[90] This shared relationship between environmental pollution and human rights

84 Lawrence Atsegbua, Vincent Akpotaire, Folarin Dimowo. *Environmental Law in Nigeria: Theory and Practice*. (Lagos: Ababa Press, 2004), 131.

85 "The 17 Goals," *United Nations Department of Economicsand Social Affairs*, accessed August 20, 2023, https://sdgs.un.org/goals.

86 See ibid.

87 See ibid.

88 "The SGD Partnership Guidebook: A Practical Guide to Building High Impact Multi-Stakeholder Partnerships for the Sustainable Development Goals," *United Nations, The Partnering Initiatives*, accessed August 20, 2023, https://sdgs.un.org/sites/default/files/2022-02/SDG%20Partnership%20Guidebook%201.11.pdf.

89 John F. Sherman III, "The United Nations Guiding Principles on Business and Human Rights (UNGPs): Implications for Corporate Legal Practice, in A Lawyer's Guide to Key Businesses and Human Rights Documents," ABA, accessed August 20, 2023, https://www.americanbar.org/groups/human_rights/business-human-rights-initiative/key-business-and-human-rights-documents/.

90 *United Nations News, "The Right to a Healthy Environment".*

violations is also evidenced in the 2022 General Assembly Resolution A/RES/76/300 or A/76/L.75 which 'recognizes the right to a clean, healthy and sustainable environment as a human right'. The UNGA resolution 'notes that the right to a clean, healthy and sustainable environment is related to other rights and existing international law; and affirms that the promotion of the human right to a clean, healthy and sustainable environment requires the full implementation of the multilateral environmental agreements under the principles of international environmental law. It calls upon states, international organisations, business enterprises, and other relevant stakeholders to adopt policies, to enhance international cooperation, strengthen capacity-building and continue to share good practices to scale up efforts to ensure a clean, healthy, and sustainable environment for all.

As mentioned above relating to the UNGP, the fundamental set of principles setting norms for business on human rights norms, just like many traditional human rights treaties, do not directly refer to the environment, but as argued in this chapter, they nonetheless implicitly apply to the environmental activities of corporations and their impacts on human rights.

After the adoption of the UNGP there has been a growing support for the drafting of a legally binding instrument to regulate business and their human rights impacts. Of particular significance for the purposes of this chapter is the fact that the most recent text of the Third Draft Legally Binding Instrument to Regulate, in International Human Rights Law, the Activities of Transnational Corporations and Other Business Enterprises[91] specifically includes references and regulates environmental harm caused by corporate activities. For example, the Preamble of the Third Draft refers to the 2030 Agenda for Sustainable Development[92] and to the 'capacity of businesses to foster sustainable development through an increased productivity, inclusive of economic growth and job creation that respect internationally recognized human rights, labour rights, health and safety standards an, the environment and climate…'.[93]

The Draft furthermore defines human rights abuse to include 'any direct or indirect harm in the context of business activities, through acts or omissions,

---

91 Text of the third revised draft legally binding instrument with textual proposals submitted by States during the seventh and the eighth sessions of the open-ended intergovernmental working group on transnational corporations and other business enterprises with respect to human right available at "Open-ended intergovernmental working group on transnational corporations and other business enterprises with respect to human rights," United Nations Human Rights Council, accessed August 20, 2023, https://www.ohchr.org/en/hr-bodies/hrc/wg-trans-corp/igwg-on-tnc.

92 PP 3.

93 PP 10.

against any person or group of persons, that impedes the full enjoyment of internationally recognized human rights and fundamental freedoms, including the right to a safe, clean, healthy and sustainable environment'.[94] Article 4 of the Third Draft, Rights of Victims, specifies that victims shall be guaranteed fair access to justice and remedies including 'environmental remediation, and ecological restoration'.[95] The obligation to ensure human rights due diligence under the Third Draft now specifically includes the obligation for enterprises to undertake and publish regular 'environmental and climate change impact assessments throughout their operations'.[96]

Other provisions in the Third Draft further reflect the clear intent on the negotiating parties to recognise the link between human rights, the environment, and climate and business enterprises. It remains to be seen whether the Third Draft will remain in its current form as negotiations on the Legally Binding Instrument are ongoing. Currently, there are States attempting to strengthen the recognition of environment and climate in the text, whilst others are arguably attempting to weaken such provisions.[97]

Although it is hard to predict the outcome of the ongoing negotiations within the Open-Ended Working Group on Transnational Corporations and Other Business Enterprises with Respect to Human Rights,[98] it is safe to predict that the recognition of the nexus environment, climate, human rights and business is here to stay.

To sum up, existing business and human rights norms such as the Guiding Principles require corporations to respect human rights in their operations. Under pillar 2 of the UNGP, businesses have a responsibility to respect all internationally recognized human rights. With the current widespread recognition of a right to environment, a duty to take measures to protect or refrain from conducts causing environmental harm can be inferred from such existing business and human rights norms. Thus, corporate responsibility to respect human

94 Article 1.2 Third Draft.

95 Article 4.2(c) Third Draft.

96 Article 6.4(a) Third Draft.

97 See "Text of the third revised draft legally binding instrument with textual proposals submitted by States during the seventh and the eighth sessions of the open-ended intergovernmental working group on transnational corporations and other business enterprises with respect to human right," *United Nations*, accessed August 20, 2023, https://documents-dds-ny.un.org/doc/UNDOC/GEN/G23/008/93/PDF/G2300893.pdf?OpenElement.

98 For up-to-date information on the activities and progress of the Open-ended working group see "Open-ended intergovernmental working group on transnational corporations and other business enterprises with respect to human rights," *United Nations*, accessed August 20, 2023, https://www.ohchr.org/en/hr-bodies/hrc/wg-trans-corp/igwg-on-tnc.

rights, requires businesses to respect human rights, including environmental rights, throughout their operations and value chains.[99] This would include conducting due diligence to identify, prevent, mitigate, and account for their environmental impacts, and ensuring that their business relationships do not contribute to human rights abuses. Businesses must also engage with stakeholders, including affected communities and civil society organisations, to understand their environmental impacts and seek their input on mitigating them.[100]

Also, corporations must ensure that there is effective and ready access to remedies for victims of human rights abuses, including those related to the environment. Businesses must establish grievance mechanisms that are accessible, predictable, equitable, and transparent.[101]

5 Human Rights, the Environment, Enterprises in the Courts: Litigating to Save the Planet

This chapter briefly highlights selected cases as examples of the growing judicial trend at every level to apply international human rights instruments and the UNGP in particular to address environmental violations by corporations. With the increasing degradation of the environment coupled with the growth of corporations and their role, courts have increasingly been called upon to address disputes involving human rights, the environment and enterprises. Indeed, there are now so many cases that specialised databases have emerged to follow the growing case load in this field.[102] Litigation involving

---

99 UNGP Principle 16; See Weissbordt, "Norms," 91–92; Olivier De Schutter, "Towards a new treaty on business and human rights," *Business and Human Rights Journal* 1.1 (2016): 41–67.

100 UNGP Principle 18; See Uwem E. Ite, "Multinationals and corporate social responsibility in developing countries: a case study of Nigeria," *Corporate Social Responsibility and Environmental Management* 11.1 (2004): 1–11; Heledd Jenkins and Natalia Yakovleva, "Corporate social responsibility in the mining industry: Exploring trends in social and environmental disclosure," *Journal of cleaner production* 14.3–4 (2006): 271–284.

101 UNGP Principle 31; See James Harrison and Mark Wielga, "Grievance Mechanisms in Multi-Stakeholder Initiatives: Providing Effective Remedy for Human Rights Violations?," *Business and Human Rights Journal* (2023): 1–23; Mark Wielga and James Harrison, "Assessing the effectiveness of non-state-based grievance mechanisms in providing access to remedy for rightsholders: A case study of the Roundtable on Sustainable Palm Oil," *Business and Human Rights Journal* 6.1 (2021): 67–92.

102 For example, see "Lawsuit Database," *The Business and Human Rights Resource Centre*, accessed August 20, 2023, https://www.business-humanrights.org/en/from-us/lawsuits-database/.

corporations and the environment are taking place at the domestic, regional, and global level all over the world. Litigation focuses on all aspects of environmental harm and a large number of groundbreaking decisions involve the issue of climate change for example[103] on what has been called 'a rights-turn' in climate litigation.[104] The year 2021 was hailed as a 'landmark' for corporate human rights litigation at the UN Forum on Business and Human Rights where 'delegates discussed how environmental damage is being viewed as a human right violation in a growing number of cases around the world – and that the UN Guiding Principles may increasingly be criteria for court judgments'.[105]

Litigants have used all legal tools and fora at their disposal to fight corporate environmental harm. Human rights and the UNGP are just one additional legal tool that could become extremely effective in holding corporations accountable.

As stated, it is impossible to cover even the majority let alone all cases on corporations, their environmental impact, and human rights and that would be beyond the scope of this chapter.[106] The cases briefly examined below are simply designed to highlight a few decisions as evidence of the growing role of courts in holding corporations accountable through a business, human rights, and environment framework. These cases are selected for their impact on climate litigation and reference to the international human rights framework and UNGP. In some instances, the cases have been brought directly against corporations before national courts, whilst in other litigation indirectly involved corporate activities before international human rights bodies, where States are called into account for their failures to rein in activities of corporations.

Arguably, one of the most important decisions that marked a turning point in climate litigation and the application of the international human rights framework to prevent environmental and climate harm was *Urgenda Foundation v. the State of Netherlands*.[107]

Urgenda Foundation and a group of 900 Dutch citizens sued the Dutch government to compel the State to reduce greenhouse gas emissions – primarily CO_2 – more aggressively. The Hague District Court determined the

103 See Climate Change Litigation Databases at http://climatecasechart.com/.

104 Joana Setzer and Catherine Higham, "Global Trends in Climate Litigation: 2021 Snaptshot, Policy Report," July 2021 https://www.lse.ac.uk/granthaminstitute/wp-content/uploads/2021/07/Global-trends-in-climate-change-litigation_2021-snapshot.pdf.

105 Richar Howitt, "2021 a Landmark for Corporate Human Rights Litigation," https://sustainablebrands.com/read/walking-the-talk/2021-a-landmark-for-corporate-human-rights-litigation, Accessed April 22 2023.

106 Please see the databases mentioned above for a comprehensive list of such cases.

107 [2015] HAZA C/09/00456689 (24 June 2015).

Dutch government must reduce greenhouse gas emissions by at least 25 percent (compared to 1990) by 2020 to fulfill its duty of care to protect Dutch citizens against the imminent danger caused by climate change. The State appealed the District Court's decision. In the landmark decision, the Supreme Court held that the State has a duty of care to protect its citizens from climate change in accordance with its obligations under the European Convention for the Protection of Human Rights and Fundamental Freedoms (ECHR).[108] The court explained that the rights under the ECHR impose a positive obligation on the state to protect its citizens from 'all activities – public and non-public, which could endanger the rights protected in these articles'.[109] Climate change, according to the court, is a real and imminent threat and requires the State to take precautionary measures to prevent infringement of rights as far as possible.[110]

A further example and one of the most significant cases to emerge in the past year is the decision by the Hague District Court in the *Milieudefensie et al. v. Royal Dutch Shell plc.* In 2019, Royal Dutch Shell (RDS) was sued by the environmental group Milieudefensie/Friends due to the company violating its duty of care obligations under both Dutch law and human rights obligations for its climate change contributions.[111] The plaintiffs requested a declaratory judgement that (1) if RDS 'does not reduce the combined volume of all CO_2 emissions associated with its business activities and fossil products' then the company is acting unlawfully towards the claimants; and (2) that RDS accordingly lower its CO_2 emissions.[112] While Shell agreed that its emissions should be reduced, it argued that its obligations were individual and under its group-wide policies.[113]

108 Ibid, para 42.

109 Ibid, para 43.

110 Ibid.

111 *Milieudefensie et al. v. Royal Dutch Shell plc.*, ClimateCaseChart, http://climatecasechart.com/non-us-case/milieudefensie-et-al-v-royal-dutch-shell-plc/ (last visited Mar. 25, 2023); *see also* Miliudefensie, How We Deated Shell: Milieudefensie et al. v Royal Dutch Shell PLC – A Peek Behind the Scenes 5 (2021), https://foei.org/wp-content/uploads/2021/11/How-we-defeated-Shell.pdf.

112 Juliette Luycks & Anne Hendrikx, *Climate Change Actions Against Corporations: Milieudefensie et al. v. Royal Dutch Shell plc*, CLIFFORD CHANCE (Jan. 13, 2021), https://www.cliffordchance.com/insights/resources/blogs/business-and-human-rights-insights/2021/01/climate-change-actions-against-corporations-milieudefensie-et-al-v-royal-dutch-shell-plc.html.

113 Maurits Dolmans & Michael J. Preston, *Dutch Court Orders Shell to Reduce Emissions in First Climate Change Ruling Against Company*, Cleary Gottlieb (June 30, 2021), https://www.clearygottlieb.com/news-and-insights/publication-listing/dutch-court-orders-shell-to-reduce-emissions-in-first-climate-change-ruling-against-company.

In 2021, 'in a groundbreaking judgement', the Hague District Court affirmed an 'unwritten duty of care in Dutch tort law' and ordered RDS to 'reduce its worldwide CO_2 emissions by 45% by 2030) despite RDS not yet being in violation.[114] The court found RDS's climate policies to be 'insufficient' and thus there is a 'danger of "imminent breach".'[115] This is the first time that a court has imposed on a company an obligation 'to do its share to prevent dangerous climate change'.[116] Although the plaintiffs could not directly 'invoke human rights against Shell', the court relied on human rights obligations in its interpretation of the standard of care,[117] drawing on the UN Human Rights Committee, ECHR, and soft law, focusing on the UNGP.[118] Furthermore, this ruling encompassed the 'entire Shell group'.[119] Shell appealed the decision, and the case is currently pending.

A further example of a major judicial contribution to the recognition of corporate climate responsibility was the case of *Asghar Leghari vs. Federation of Pakistan*[120] decided in 2015. The plaintiff filed a public interest action challenging the Federal Government of Pakistan and Regional Government of Punjab for their inaction, delay, and lack of seriousness in addressing climate change. The government passed the National Climate Change Policy 2012[121] and the Framework for Implementation of Climate Change Policy (2014–2030).[122] However, the plaintiff argued that the government's lack of implementation violated his article 9 constitutional right to life and article 14 right to a healthy and clean environment and to human dignity since climate change presents serious threats to water, food, and energy security in Pakistan. The court

114 Ibid.

115 Ibid.

116 Ibid.

117 Ibid.

118 *Id.*; *Milieudefensie v. Shell – A Landmark Court Decision for Energy and Energy Intensive Companies*, SHERMAN & STERLING (June 1, 2021), https://www.shearman.com/en/perspectives/2021/06/milieudefensie-v-shell--landmark-court-decision-for-energy-companies.

119 Miliudefensie, How We Defeated Shell: Milieudefensie et al. v Royal Dutch Shell PLC – A Peek Behind the Scenes 6 (2021), https://foei.org/wp-content/uploads/2021/11/How-we-defeated-Shell.pdf.

120 W.P. No. 25501/2015, https://sys.lhc.gov.pk/appjudgments/2018LHC132.pdf.

121 "National Climate Change Policy," *Government of Pakistan Ministry of Climate Change*, accessed August 20, 2023, http://www.gcisc.org.pk/National_Climate_Change_Policy_2012.pdf.

122 "Framework for implementation of Climate Change Policy (2013)," Government of Pakistan Climate Change Division, accessed August 20, 2023, http://www.gcisc.org.pk/Framework%20for%20Implementation%20of%20CC%20Policy.pdf.

found that the defendants took no measures to implement their policies.[123] The court ordered twenty ministries, departments, and authorities to name climate change focal points to work with the Ministry of Climate Change to implement the Framework and assist the court in the instant petition. Those institutions were to create a list of achievable adaptation points. Further, the court ordered the government to create a Climate Change Commission consisting of the aforementioned focal points, NGO representatives, and technical experts, among others.[124]

The court also found that the State's delay and lethargy in implementing the Framework offends the fundamental rights of citizens that need to be safeguarded.[125] Within the Pakistani legal and constitutional context, the court found climate change to be a 'clarion call for the protection of fundamental rights of the citizens of Pakistan, in particular, the vulnerable and weak segments of society who are unable to approach the Court'.[126] Furthermore, the court recognised climate change as a global problem, whereby Pakistan is a victim due to its relatively low-level contribution to global warming but required immediate remediate adaptation measures to cope with disruptive climatic patterns.[127]

As mentioned, interesting decisions on climate, human rights, and corporate responsibility have been issued within the context of human rights bodies, where actions were taken against States for failure to regulate corporate activities in violations of fundamental human rights.

Earlier on, of particular interest and an example of a regional human right body issuing an important decision involving corporations and their role in the climate crisis was the 2002 African Commission on Human Rights (ACHPR) decision in the *Social and Economic Rights Action Center and the Center for Economic and Social Rights v. Nigeria*.[128]

In this case, two non-governmental organisations (the Social and Economic Rights Action Center and the Center for Economic and Social Rights) brought a suit against the Nigerian government on behalf of the Ogoni people of Nigeria. The Ogoni people had been protesting the environmental damage caused by oil extraction in their region, which was carried out by the Nigerian government

---

123 Asghar Leghari v Pakistan, W.P. No. 25501/2015, https://sys.lhc.gov.pk/appjudgments/2018LHC132.pdf.

124 See Ibid.

125 See Ibid.

126 See Ibid.

127 See Ibid.

128 African Commission on Human and People's Rights, Communication No. 155/96 (2002).

in partnership with multinational oil companies. The protests were met with violent repression by the Nigerian military, resulting in the deaths of several Ogoni leaders, including environmental activist Ken Saro-Wiwa.[129] The Ogoni people alleged that Royal Dutch Shell, a multinational oil company, caused the environmental harm in their community.

The ACHPR relied on various international human rights instruments and principles in its decision, including the African Charter on Human and Peoples' Rights,[130] the Universal Declaration of Human Rights[131] and the Rio Declaration on Environment and Development.[132] The ACHPR found Nigeria responsible for violating the Ogoni people's rights to life, health, and a healthy environment and their right to participate in decisions affecting their environment.[133] The Commission also found that Nigeria had violated the African Charter on Human and Peoples' Rights by failing to conduct a proper investigation into the deaths of the Ogoni leaders and by denying the Ogoni people an effective remedy for the violations of their rights.[134]

Within the Inter-American system, a case referencing international human rights framework and the UNGP to protect the environment was the *Inter-American Court of Human Rights 2017 Advisory Opinion requested by Colombia.*[135] On March 14, 2016, the Republic of Colombia presented a request for an advisory opinion under the American Convention concerning State obligations in relation to the environment in the context of the protection and guarantee of the rights to life and to personal integrity.[136] The court was asked to determine how the Convention should be interpreted when there is a danger that the construction and operation of major new infrastructure projects may have severe effects on the marine environment in the Wider Caribbean Region and, consequently, on the human habitat that is essential for the full enjoyment and exercise of the rights of the inhabitants of the coasts and/or islands of a State

129 "Investigate shell for complicity in murder, rape and torture." *Amnesty International.* Accessed August 20, 2023 from https://www.amnesty.org/en/latest/press-release/2017/11/investigate-shell-for-complicity-in-murder-rape-and-torture/.

130 African Union. *African Charter on Human and Peoples' Rights.* African Union, 1981.

131 UNDHR, Generally Assembly Resolution 217 A (III) of 10 December 1948.

132 UN Doc. A/CONF.151/26 (vol. I), *International Legal Materials* 31 (1992): 874.

133 African Commission on Human and People's Rights, Communication No. 155/96 (2002).

134 See Ibid.

135 "Advisory Opinion OC-23/17 of November 15, 2017 Requested by the Republic of Colombia: The Environment and Human Rights," *Inter-American Court of Human Rights* (IACrtHR), accessed August 20, 2023, https://www.refworld.org/cases,IACRTHR,5e67c7744.html .

136 Ibid.

Party to the Convention, in light of the environmental standards recognised in international customary law and the treaties applicable among the respective States.[137]

In addressing these issues, not only did the court refer to documents of the Organization of American States and review its own jurisprudence, but also looked to decisions and other statements or reports by other human rights bodies such as the European Court of Human Rights, the African Commission on Human and Peoples Rights, and experts such as the UN Special Rapporteur on human rights and the environment and the UNGP. On the UNGP, the court stated that States have an obligation to supervise and monitor activities within their jurisdiction that may cause significant damage to the environment. Accordingly, the court reiterated that states must develop and implement adequate independent monitoring and accountability mechanisms.[138] These mechanisms must not only include preventive measures, but also appropriate measures to investigate, punish and redress possible abuse through effective policies, regulations, and adjudication.[139]

Another decision within the Inter-American system to recognise corporate climate obligations could be found in the Inter-American Court of Human Rights (IACHR) 2015 *Kaliña and Lokono Peoples v. Suriname*.[140] In this case, the Kaliña and Lokono peoples claimed that the government of Suriname had granted mining concessions on their ancestral lands without their prior consultation or consent and that this had caused significant environmental damage to their lands and waters, affecting their livelihoods and cultural traditions. The IACHR ruled in favor of the Kaliña and Lokono peoples, finding that the government of Suriname had violated their rights under the American Convention on Human Rights.[141] The court ordered the government of Suriname to take measures to restore and protect the lands and waters of the Kaliña and Lokono peoples and to ensure their effective participation in decision-making processes related to the management of their ancestral lands.[142]

In arriving at its decision, the court noted that the mining activities that resulted in the adverse impact on the environment and, consequently, on the

137 Ibid.

138 Ibid, para 304.

139 Ibid, para 305.

140 "Case of the Kaliña and Lokono Peoples v. Suriname, Merits, Reparations and Costs," *Inter-Am. Ct. H.R.*, accessed August 20, 2023, http://www.corteidh.or.cr/docs/casos/articulos/seriec_309_ing.pdf.

141 See Ibid.

142 See Ibid.

rights of the indigenous peoples, were carried out by private agents; first by Suralco alone, and then by the joint venture, BHP Billiton-Suralco.[143] However, under the UNGP businesses must respect and protect human rights, as well as prevent, mitigate, and accept responsibility for the adverse human rights impacts directly linked to their activities.[144] Also, states have an obligation to protect against human rights abuse within their territory and/or jurisdiction by third parties, including business enterprises.[145] This requires taking appropriate steps to prevent, investigate, punish, and redress such abuse through effective policies, legislation, regulations, and adjudication.

Within the European system, another potentially major judicial contribution to the recognition of corporate climate responsibility is the ECHR case of *The People vs. Artic Oil*.[146] In this case, Greenpeace and Nature and Youth (Young Friends of the Earth Norway) sued the government of Norway, the world's 7th largest exporter of CO_2, for granting ten new licenses for oil exploration in the Barents Sea.[147] The granted permits pave the way for new oil discovery and extraction even though the already discovered petroleum resources resulted in global warming beyond 1.5 degrees.[148]

The petitioners argued that the granting of new oil permits is in violation of article 112 of the Norwegian constitution.[149] The article declares that citizens have the right to '[a]An environment that secures good health, and to nature where diversity and productive capacity are conserved',[150] and that the state must take measures to ensure these rights. The article also states that natural resources should be managed with a long term and all-round considerations which secure this right also for future generations. The plaintiffs lost the first local lawsuit in November 2017, when the court there did not find a violation

143 See Ibid.

144 See United Nations. (2011). Guiding principles on business and human rights: implementing the united nations "protect respect and remedy" framework. United Nations Office of the High Commissioner for Human Rights.

145 See Ibid.

146 Frances Schwartzkopff, "European Rights Court Takes Up Norway Arctic Drilling Case," *Bloomberg News*, January 3, 2022, https://www.bloomberg.com/news/articles/2022-01-03/european-human-rights-court-takes-up-norway-arctic-drilling-case.

147 "Media Brief: People vs. Arctic Oil," Greenpeace Norge, accessed August 20, 2023, https://www.greenpeace.org/norway/nyheter/klimaendringer/media-brief-the-people-vs-arctic-oil/

148 Ibid.

149 "The Constitution, as laid down on 17 May 1814 by the Constituent Assembly at Eidsvoll and subsequently amended, most recently in May 2018," Stortinget, accessed August 20, 2023, https://www.stortinget.no/globalassets/pdf/english/constitutionenglish.pdf.

150 Ibid, 27.

of article 112. However, the judge concluded that the article is indeed a rights provision, and that climate is included in the provision.[151] The petitioners lost the appeal in November 2019 on similar grounds but also the court concluded that Norway has a responsibility for emissions from the oil that it exports to other countries.[152]

After these rounds in local court, the petitioners filed an application before the ECHR arguing that Norway is responsible for violating article 2 and article 8 of the European Convention on Human Rights (ECHR).[153] The case is currently pending before the Grand Chamber due to its potential revolutionary impact should the court recognise that granting new oil explorations permit violate fundamental human rights and establishing a de facto ban on new explorations within the Council of Europe countries.

The cases briefly examined above are just a very limited sample of the cases decided and currently pending before domestic and international bodies. Corporations can expect litigation to grow,[154] with the associated reputational

151 "Greenpeace Norway vs. Government of Norway," InforMEA, accessed August 20, 2023, https://www.informea.org/en/court-decision/greenpeace-norway-vs-government-norway.

152 Ibid.

153 "People vs. Arctic Oil – Summary of the case," Greenpeace Norge, accessed August 20, 2023, https://www.greenpeace.org/norway/nyheter/klimaendringer/people-vs-arctic-oil-summary-of-the-case/#:~:text=The%20Court%20judges%20that%20Norwegian,the%20licences%20to%20be%20invalid.

154 A potentially important case involving corporations and their role in the climate crisis is the 2020 case of *FoE Australia and Others v ANZ Bank Group Limited.* On January 30, 2020, Friends of the Earth and three individuals submitted a "specific instance" complaint to the Australian National Contact Point for the OECD Guidelines for Multinational Enterprises regarding the activities of ANZ bank. The complaint alleged that ANZ had failed to adhere to the OECD Guidelines through its lack of climate-related disclosure and due diligence, inadequate environmental policies and management, particularly as it relates to the Paris Agreement, and disregard for consumer interests. The authors of the complaint wanted, among other things, wanted ANZ to commit to greenhouse gas emission targets that are in line with the Paris Agreement. On November 24, 2020, the NCP, in their initial assessment stated that "Issues of climate change, fossil fuels (and associated GHG) are sufficiently material to responsible business conduct understood by the OECD Guidelines." This case will clearly have a huge impact on how companies address their climate change obligations under the OCED, a "soft law" instrument that has been often ignored in the past. Another potentially important case involving corporations and their role in the climate crisis is the communications issued by the UN Special Procedures on human rights and hazardous wastes and human rights and the environment against Bosnia Herzegovina (BiH) and China for approving the construction or extension of several coal-fired power plants in BiH. The coal-fired power plants at issue were Chinese-State Owned Enterprises with finance from the China Development Bank. Many people complained that the plants lead to water and air pollution, and negative effects on climate change.

and economic damage involved. A human rights approach to addressing their environmental responsibility would prevent and at a minimum mitigate such risks.

6 Conclusion

The perilous state of the environment is undeniable. There is hardly a day that goes by without another authoritative warning on the state of our Planet. Climate change is now a climate crisis. The loss of biodiversity has now reached extinction like proportion. Pollution of the ocean and water scarcity are threatening the survival of species and creating conflicts around the world. Corporations are contributing to these trends whilst also suffering the consequences of an ecologically unstable and unsustainable Planet. Businesses though could and should be part of the solution to create a transition to a green economy as called upon by the Sustainable Development Goals. Rules, including international law, can help this transition and certainly the business, human rights and environment framework discussed in this chapter can and should be a key regulatory toolkit to guide corporate actions toward a sustainable path. A human rights policy spelling out specifically goals to avoid and address environmentally related harms, coupled with human/environmental rights impact assessments to carry out due diligence in assessing risks involved in all corporate activities and lastly effective remedies to provide relief when

The communication raised concerns about both BiH and China's failure to meet "international human rights obligations for human and environmental rights." Alleged violations of human rights related to pollution, waste, and effects on climate change resulting from the operation of several Chinese-supported coal-fired plants operating or planned to operate in the Federation of Bosnia and Herzegovina were discussed in the communications. The Special Rapporteurs relied on International Human Rights legal instruments including the Universal Declaration of Human Rights, the International Covenants on Economic Social and Cultural Rights, and Civil and Political Rights, the Convention on Rights of the Child, the UNECE Aarhus Convention, the UN Framework Principles on Human Rights and Environment, and the UN Guiding Principles on Business and Human Rights in their communication. The communication especially used HRC General Comment No. 36 on the right to life with dignity to environmental degradation, pollution, and climate change (paras. 26, 62) and the importance of protecting underlying environmental determinants of health under Article 14 ICESCR and 24 CRC, and related general comments. On May 27, 2021, China responded and denied the human rights violations in respect to the power plants. They stated that they require all foreign projects to be carried out in compliance with local laws. Additionally, the Tuzla plant was intended to meet environmental requirements under EU carbon emissions standards.

things go wrong, should be embraced by businesses, and indeed legally required.

Responsible businesses must lead the way to 'respect' human rights and the environment. These obligations are now simply a soft law requirement under international law but are increasingly being translated into legally binding rules within regional and domestic legal systems. They ought to be legally binding requirements at the international level too. Furthermore, courts are stepping up to ensure corporations are held accountable for their environmental damaging activities and their consequences on the enjoyment of human rights, including on the right to a healthy environment where specifically recognised. The environmental crisis facing the Planet requires creative mindset and innovative legal solutions. International law should provide corporations with the legal framework to be at the forefront of the solution alongside states, civil society, international organisations and all other stakeholders. Human rights and the environment demand no less.

Bibliography

Website Content

Amnesty International. "Investigate shell for complicity in murder, rape and torture." Accessed August 20, 2023.https://www.amnesty.org/en/latest/press-release/2017/11/investigate-shell-for-complicity-in-murder-rape-and-torture/.

Apple Newsroom. "Apple Reports Fourth Quarter Results." Accessed May 23, 2023. https://www.apple.com/newsroom/2022/10/apple-reports-fourth-quarter-results/.

Association of Southeast Asians Nations. "ASEAN Human Rights Declaration," Accessed August 20, 2023. https://asean.org/asean-human-rights-declaration/.

CEPAL. "Regional Agreement on Access to Information, Public Participation and Justice in Environmental Matters in Latin America and the Caribbean." Accessed August 20, 2023. https://www.cepal.org/en/escazuagreement.

Chevron. "Chevron's human rights policy." Accessed April 25, 2023. https://www.chevron.com/sustainability/social/human-rights.

Climate Change Actions Against Corporations: milieudefensie et al. v. Royal Dutch Shell plc. CLIFFORD CHANCE (January 13, 2021), https://www.cliffordchance.com/insights/resources/blogs/business-and-human-rights-insights/2021/01/climate-change-actions-against-corporations-milieudefensie-et-al-v-royal-dutch-shell-plc.html.

CompaniesMarketCap.com. "Saudi Aramco (2222.SR) – Market Capitalization." Companies ranked by market capitalization. Accessed July 17, 2023. https://companiesmarketcap.com/saudi-aramco/marketcap/.

European Commission. "A Renewed EU strategy 2011–14 for Corporate Social Responsibility." Accessed August 20, 2023. http://ec.europa.eu/enterprise/policies/sustainable-business/corporate-socialresponsibility/index_en.htm.

European Commission. "Just and Sustainable Economy: Commission Lays Down Rules for Companies to Respect Human Rights and Environmental in Global Value Chains." Accessed August 20, 2023. https://ec.europa.eu/commission/presscorner/detail/en/ip_22_1145.

European Parliament. "Directorate-General For External Policies, Implementation of the UN Guiding Principles on Business and Human Rights 14, 16." Accessed August 20, 2023. https://www.europarl.europa.eu/RegData/etudes/STUD/2017/578031/EXPO_STU(2017)578031_EN.pdf.

Equator Principles. "Equator Principles on Project Finance Requirements." Accessed August 20, 2023. www.equator-principles.com/index.php/ep3.

Government of Pakistan Climate Change Division. "Framework for implementation of Climate Change Policy (2013)." Accessed August 20, 2023. http://www.gcisc.org.pk/Framework%20for%20Implementation%20of%20CC%20Policy.pdf.

Government of Pakistan Ministry of Climate Change. "National Climate Change Policy." Accessed August 20, 2023. http://www.gcisc.org.pk/National_Climate_Change_Policy_2012.pdf.

Greenpeace Norge. "People vs. Arctic Oil – Summary of the case" Accessed August 20, 2023. https://www.greenpeace.org/norway/nyheter/klimaendringer/people-vs-arctic-oil-summary-of-the-case/#:~:text=The%20Court%20judges%20that%20Norwegian,the%20licences%20to%20be%20invalid.

Greenpeace Norge. "Media Brief: People vs. Arctic Oil." Accessed August 20, 2023. https://www.greenpeace.org/norway/nyheter/klimaendringer/media-brief-the-people-vs-arctic-oil/.

InforMEA. "Greenpeace Norway vs. Government of Norway." Accessed August 20, 2023. https://www.informea.org/en/court-decision/greenpeace-norway-vs-government-norway.

International Finance Corporation. "Performance Standards on Environmental and Social Sustainability." Accessed August 20, 2023. https://www.ifc.org/content/dam/ifc/doc/2010/2012-ifc-performance-standards-en.pdf.

International Finance Corporation. "Sustainability Performance Standards". Accessed August 20, 2023. www.ifc.org/wps/wcm/connect/7540778049a792dcb87efaa8c6a8312a/SP_English_2012.pdf?MOD=AJPERES.

International Labour Organization. "Tripartite Declaration of Principles Concerning Multinational Enterprises and Social Policy." Accessed July 14, 2023. https://www.ilo.org/wcmsp5/groups/public/@ed_emp/@emp_ent/documents/publication/wcms_101234.pdf.

International Organization for Standardization. "ISO 26000 Guidance on Social Responsibility." Accessed August 20, 2023. www.iso.org/iso/iso_catalogue/management_standards/iso26000.

Inter-American Court of Human Rights (IACrtHR). "Advisory Opinion OC-23/17 of November 15, 2017. Requested by the Republic of Colombia: The Environment and Human Rights." Accessed August 20, 2023. https://www.refworld.org/cases,IACRTHR,5e67c7744.html.

Inter-Am. Ct. H.R. "Case of the Kaliña and Lokono Peoples v. Suriname, Merits, Reparations and Costs." Accessed August 20, 2023. http://www.corteidh.or.cr/docs/casos/articulos/seriec_309_ing.pdf.

League of Arab States. "Arab Charter on Human Rights." Accessed August 20, 2023. https://digitallibrary.un.org/record/551368?ln=en.

Meta. "Meta Corporate Human Rights Policy. (n.d.)." Accessed April 25, 2023. https://about.fb.com/wp-content/uploads/2021/03/Facebooks-Corporate-Human-Rights-Policy.pdf.

Northrop Grumman. "Northrop Grumman Human Rights Policy." Accessed April 25, 2023. https://www.northropgrumman.com/corporate-responsibility/northrop-grumman-human-rights-policy/.

OECD. "OECD Guidelines for Multinational Enterprises." Accessed August 20, 2023. https://www.oecd.org/corporate/mne/.

Organisation for Economic Co-operation and Development (OECD). "Guidelines for Multinational Enterprises." Accessed August 20, 2023. http://oecd.org/daf/inv/mne/48004323.pdf;.

Organisation of African Unity. "African Charter on Human and People's Rights." Accessed August 20, 2023. https://au.int/sites/default/files/treaties/36390-treaty-0011_-_african_charter_on_human_and_peoples_rights_e.pdf.

Stortinget. "The Constitution, as laid down on 17 May 1814 by the Constituent Assembly at Eidsvoll and subsequently amended, most recently in May 2018." Accessed August 20, 2023. https://www.stortinget.no/globalassets/pdf/english/constitutionenglish.pdf.

The Business and Human Rights Resource Centre. "Lawsuit Database." Accessed August 20, 2023. https://www.business-humanrights.org/en/from-us/lawsuits-database/.

The Coca-Cola Company. "Human rights principles." Accessed April 25, 2023. https://www.coca-colacompany.com/policies-and-practices/human-rights-principles.

UN Guiding Principles Reporting Framework. "Companies." Accessed August 20, 2023. https://www.ungpreporting.org/database-analysis/explore-disclosures/companies-page/.

UN Office of the High Commissioner for Human Rights. "The Corporate Responsibility to Respect Human Rights: An Interpretive Guide." Accessed August 20, 2023. http://www.ohchr.org/Documents/Publications/HR.PUB.12.2_En.pdf.

United Nations Human Rights Office of the High Commissioner. "Good practices on the right to a healthy environment." Accessed August 20, 2023. https://www.ohchr.org/en/special-procedures/sr-environment/good-practices-right-healthy-environment.

UNITED NATIONS DEP'T OF ECON. & SOC/ AFFS. "The 17 Goals." Accessed August 20, 2023. https://sdgs.un.org/goals.

United Nations. "Protect, Respect and Remedy: A Framework for Business and Human Rights, Report to the UN Human Rights Council." Accessed August 20, 2023. www.reports-andmaterials.org/Ruggie-report-7-Apr-2008.pdf.

United Nations Human Rights. "Guiding Principles on Business and Human Rights: Implementing the United Nations 'Protect, Respect and Remedy' Framework (Guiding Principles)." Accessed August 20, 2023. www.ohchr. org/Documents/Publications/GuidingPrinciplesBusinessHR_EN.pdf.

United Nations, The Partnering Initiates. "The SGD Partnership Guidebook: A Practical Guide to Building High Impact Multi-Stakeholder Partnerships for the Sustainable Development Goals." Accessed August 20, 2023. https://sdgs.un.org/sites/default/files/2022-02/SDG%20Partnership%20Guidebook%201.11.pdf.

United Nations News. "The Right to a Healthy Environment: 6 Things You Need to Know." Accessed Oct. 15, 2021. https://news.un.org/en/story/2021/10/1103082.

United Nations Office of the High Commissioner. "About the Mandate." Accessed August 20, 2023. https://www.ohchr.org/en/special-procedures/sr-environment/about-mandate.

United Nations Office of the High Commissioner. "About Human Rights and the Environment." Accessed August 20, 2023. https://www.ohchr.org/en/special-procedures/sr-environment/about-human-rights-and-environment.

Books

Baumann-Pauly, Dorothée and Justine Nolan. *Business and human rights: from principles to practice*. Routledge, 2016.

Lawrence Atsegbua. Vincent Akpotaire, Folarin Dimowo. *Environmental Law in Nigeria: Theory and Practice*. Lagos: Ababa Press, 2004.

Muchlinski, Peter. *Advanced introduction to business and human rights*. London: Edward Elgar Publishing, 2022.

Peters, Birgit. "The European Court of Human Rights and the Environment." In *International Courts and Tribunals and the Protection of the Environment*, Mead/Samsson/Sobenes (eds), Asser Press, 2020.

Ruggie, John Gerard. *Just business: Multinational corporations and human rights*. WW Norton & Company, 2013.

Wettstein, Florian. *Business and Human Rights: Ethical, Legal, and Managerial Perspectives*. Cambridge: Cambridge UP, 2022.

Zerk, Jennifer. *Multinationals and Corporate Social Responsibility: Limitations and Opportunities in International Law.* Cambridge University Press, 2006.

Book Chapters

Botta, Giulia and Claire Methven O'Brien. "The Corporate Responsibility to Respect Human Rights: An Updated Status Review." In Responsabilidade Social Corporativa e Governança Socioambiental: Greenwashing e Direitos Humanos (Corporate Social Responsibility and Social and Environmental Governance: Greenwashing and Human Rights, (Rio de Janeiro, Lumen Iuris, 2022.

Deva, Surya and David Birchall. "From 'Business or Human Rights' to 'Business and Human Rights': What Next?" In *Research Handbook on Human Rights and Business,* by Surya Deva, 1–21. Cheltenham, UK: Edward Elgar Publishing, 2020.

Ewing, Anthony P. "Teaching Note: Introducing the UN Guiding Principles on Business and Human Rights." In *Teaching Business and Human Rights Handbook.* Teaching Business and Human Rights Forum, 2016, https://teachbhr.org/resources/teaching-bhr-handbook/teaching-notes/introducing-the-un-guiding-principles-on-business-and-human-rights-2/.

Foster, Sheila and Paolo Galizzi. "Human Rights and Climate Change: Building Synergies for a Common Future." In *Climate Change Law,* Daniel Farber & Marjan Peeter (eds), Edward Elgar Publishing, 2016.

Journal Articles

Broughton, Edward. "The Bhopal disaster and its aftermath: a review." *Environmental Health* 4.1 (2005): 1–6.

Cavotta, Valeria, Guido Palazzo, and Antonino Vaccaro. "Mobilizing after corporate environmental irresponsibility in a community of place: A framing microprocess perspective." *Journal of Business Ethics* (2021): 1–15.

Faracik, Beata. "Implementation of the UN Guiding Principles on Business and Human Rights." *European Parliament's online database,* (2017). doi:10.2861/527765.

Galizzi, Paolo. "From Ignorance, to Indifference, to Limited Familiarity: An Analysis of the Relationship Between International Environmental Law & Multinational Corporations." *Fordham Law Legal Studies Research Paper* No. 2779332 (2014): 102–147. https://ssrn.com/abstract=2779332.

Giurdanella, Alessia MM. "International Environmental History and Law." *Journal of Management Policy and Practice, no.* 23.3 2022.

Harrison, James and Mark Wielga. "Grievance Mechanisms in Multi-Stakeholder Initiatives: Providing Effective Remedy for Human Rights Violations?" *Business and Human Rights Journal* (2023): 1–23.

Herz, Steven, et al, "The International Finance Corporation's Performance Standards and the Equator Principles: Respecting Human Rights and Remedying Violations?"

Center for International Environmental Law, Oxfam Australia, World Resources Institute, August (2008).

Ite, Uwem E. "Multinationals and corporate social responsibility in developing countries: a case study of Nigeria," *Corporate Social Responsibility and Environmental Management* 11.1 (2004).

Jenkins, Heledd and Natalia Yakovleva, "Corporate social responsibility in the mining industry: Exploring trends in social and environmental disclosure," *Journal of cleaner production* 14.3–4 (2006): 271–284.

Santoro, Michael A. "Business and human rights in historical perspective." *Journal of Human Rights* 14, no. 2 (2015): 155–161.

Sarpong, Samuel and Ishaque Kwabena Otoo. "Survey on the Implementation of the Mne Declaration in Ghana." *International Labour Organization*, June 1, 2009.

Schutter, Olivier De. "Towards a new treaty on business and human rights," *Business and Human Rights Journal* 1.1 (2016): 41–67.

Shelton, Dinah. "Human Rights, Health & Environmental Protection: Linkages in Law & Practice." *Health and Human Rights Working Paper Series* No 1. (2007) World Health Organization.

Sherman III, John. "Beyond CSR: The Story of the UN Guiding Principles on Business and Human Rights." *Corporate Responsibility Initiative Working Paper* No. 71, (2020).

Markey, Raymond and Katherine Ravenwood. "The Impact of MNEs and FDI on Aspects of Working Conditions as Contained in the ILO 1977 Tripartite Declaration of Principles Concerning Multinational Enterprises and Social Policy." *New Zealand Journal of Employment Relations* 35, no. 3 (2010): 27–38.

Marx, Axel and Jan Wouters, "Global Governance and Business Responsibility: The UN Draft Code of Conduct on Transnational Corporations Revisited." *Journal of Business Ethic* 87, no. 3 (2009): 385–404.

Morgera, Elisa, "Significant trends in corporate environmental accountability: the new performance standards of the international finance corporation." *Colo. J. Int'l Envtl. L. & Pol'y 18* (2007): 151.

O'Brien, Claire Methven and Sumithra Dhanarajan. "The corporate responsibility to respect human rights: a status review." *Accounting, Auditing and Accountability Journal* 29.4 (2016): 542–567.

Weissbordt, David and Muria Kruger. "Norms on the Responsibility of Transnational Corporations and Other Business Enterprises with Regard to Human Rights." *The American Journal of International Law*, Vol 97, No. 4 (Oct. 2003): 91–92.

Wielga, Mark and James Harrison. "Assessing the effectiveness of non-state-based grievance mechanisms in providing access to remedy for rightsholders: A case study of the Roundtable on Sustainable Palm Oil." *Business and Human Rights Journal* 6.1 (2021): 67–92.

News or Magazine Articles

Dolmans, Maurits & Michael J. Preston, *Dutch Court Orders Shell to Reduce Emissions in First Climate Change Ruling Against Company*, CLEARY GOTTLIEB (June 30, 2021), https://www.clearygottlieb.com/news-and-insights/publication-listing/dutch-court-orders-shell-to-reduce-emissions-in-first-climate-change-ruling-against-company.

Ganesan, Arvind. "Why Laws Are Needed to Avoid Corporate Rights Abuses," *HUM. RTS. WATCH*. July 1, 2021. https://www.hrw.org/news/2021/07/01/why-laws-are-needed-avoid-corporate-rights-abuses.

Gomme, James. "10 Years of the UN Guiding Principles on Business & Human Rights," *WBCSD*, June 16, 2021. https://www.wbcsd.org/Overview/News-Insights/WBCSD-insights/10-years-of-the-UN-Guiding-Principles-on-Business-Human-Rights.

Gutterman, Alan S. "Evolving Relationship of Business and Human Rights." *Business Law Today*, February 2, 2021. https://businesslawtoday.org/2021/02/evolving-relationship-business-human-rights/.

Howitt, Richar, "2021 a Landmark for Corporate Human Rights Litigation," https://sustainablebrands.com/read/walking-the-talk/2021-a-landmark-for-corporate-human-rights-litigation, Accessed April 22 2023.

Langlois, Michelle. "Reporting Trends & Insights: Are Companies Making the Commitment to Respect Human Rights?," *UN GUIDING PRINCIPLES REPORTING FRAMEWORK*. https://www.ungpreporting.org/reporting-insights-trends-are-companies-making-the-commitment-to-respect-human-rights/.

Luycks, Juliette & Anne Hendrikx, *Climate Change Actions Against Corporations: milieudefensie et al. v. Royal Dutch Shell plc*, CLIFFORD CHANCE (Jan. 13, 2021), https://www.cliffordchance.com/insights/resources/blogs/business-and-human-rights-insights/2021/01/climate-change-actions-against-corporations-milieudefensie-et-al-v-royal-dutch-shell-plc.html.

Mandavilli, Apoorva. "The World's worst industrial disaster is still unfolding." *The Atlantic*, July 10, 2018. https://www.theatlantic.com/science/archive/2018/07/the-worlds-worst-industrial-disaster-is-still-unfolding/560726/.

Schwartzkopff, Frances. "European Rights Court Takes Up Norway Arctic Drilling Case." *Bloomberg News*, January 3, 2022. https://www.bloomberg.com/news/articles/2022-01-03/european-human-rights-court-takes-up-norway-arctic-drilling-case.

Sherman III, John F. "The United Nations Guiding Principles on Business and Human Rights (UNGPs): Implications for Corporate Legal Practice, in A LAWYER'S GUIDE TO KEY BUSINESSES AND HUMAN RIGHTS DOCUMENTS," *ABA*. Accessed August 20, 2023, https://www.americanbar.org/groups/human_rights/business-human-rights-initiative/key-business-and-human-rights-documents/.

Setzer, Joana and Catherine Higham, "Global Trends in Climate Litigation: 2021 Snaptshot, Policy Report," July 2021 https://www.lse.ac.uk/granthaminstitute/wp-content/uploads/2021/07/Global-trends-in-climate-change-litigation_2021-snapshot.pdf.

Other

"Guiding Principles on Business and Human Rights, principle 11, U.N. Doc. HR/PUB/11/04 (2011)," United Nations Human Rights, Office of the High Commissioner, accessed August 20, 2023. https://www.ohchr.org/sites/default/files/documents/publications/guidingprinciplesbusinesshr_en.pdf.

UN Code of Conduct of Transnational Corporations. International Legal Materials 23 (1984): 626.

United Nations (2020). "Chapter IV. Human Rights. 11) Convention on the Rights of the Child" in: United Nations Treaty Collection. Depositary. Status of Treaties. Archived 8 September 2020 at the Wayback Machine. Retrieved 04-02-2022.

Organization of American States, American Convention on Human Rights, Nov. 22, 1969, O.A.S.T.S. No. 36, 1144 U.N.T.S. 123 (entered into force July 18, 1978).

PART 2

Interaction of Human Rights with Trade, Investment, and Finance

CHAPTER 7

The World Trading System, Human Rights and Sustainable Development

Ernst Ulrich Petersmann

1 Introduction: Economic Law, Democratic Constitutionalism and Human Rights

Legal civilisation refers to citizens (*cives*) and to the legal protection of their rights as recognised in ancient Greek and Italian city republics around the Mediterranean since the 5th century BC. It responds to the 'paradox of liberty' as explained by Plato in his book, *The Laws*: Freedoms risk destroying themselves by abuses of public and private power unless equal freedoms are protected by laws and institutions. The Roman *jus gentium* prompted some European jurisdictions to protect trading rights and judicial remedies long before the 'democratic revolutions' proclaiming human rights since the 18th century. Following World Wars I and II, European democracies embedded their social, economic, democratic and legal orders into multilevel democratic constitutionalism, national and European human rights law (HRL), such as the EU Charter for Fundamental Rights (EUCFR) and the European Convention of Human Rights (ECHR), in addition to UN HRL. These measures also implement the ordo-liberal insight that 'competitive social market economies' (Treaty of European Union (TEU) Article 3) need to legally restrain market failures, governance failures and constitutional failures in order to avoid social and economic crises (as experienced during the 1920/30s) that undermine democracies and the rule-of-law.[1]

---

1 Cf, Ernst-Ulrich Petersmann, "German and European Ordo-Liberalism and Constitutionalism in the Post-War Development of International Economic Law," in *The European International Law Tradition*, ed. Peter Hilpold (Heidelberg: Springer, 2020), 305–332. European ordo-liberalism rejects *laissez-faire* liberalism and Anglo-Saxon, business-driven neo-liberalism; it emphasizes the need for limiting market-, governance-and constitutional-failures through multilevel legal restraints ('economic constitutionalism') and 'constitutional economics' protecting individual and democratic autonomy (eg voluntary informed consent), non-discriminatory competition and 'social market economies' beyond national frontiers; cf Ernst-Ulrich Petersmann, "Neoliberalism, Ordoliberalism and the Future of Economic Governance," *Journal of International Economic Law* 26, no. 4 (2023): 836 -42;

 | DOI:10.1163/9789004530942_008

In authoritarian countries (like China and Russia) and neo-liberal countries (like Australia and the US), the absence of robust national and regional human rights legislation hinders the institutionalisation of protections for economic, social, and democratic rights. This deficiency diminishes the ability of citizens to seek remedies within the multilevel governance framework for public goods. The Preamble and Articles 1 of the UN Charter and of the Universal Declaration of Human Rights (UDHR) oblige all UN member states to 'recognition of the inherent dignity and of the equal and inalienable rights of all members of the human family (as) the foundation of freedom, justice and peace in the world' (Preamble UDHR). The national, regional and UN human rights obligations incorporated into positive law since WW II also led to general international law obligations to respect, protect, and fulfil human rights and interpret treaties 'in conformity with the principles of justice of international law', including 'human rights and fundamental freedoms for all' (as recalled in the Preamble of the Vienna Convention on the Law of Treaties (VCLT)). Yet, the continuing suppression of human and democratic rights by authoritarian governments demonstrates how – notwithstanding the universal recognition that 'all human beings are born free and equal in dignity and rights' (UDHR Article 1) – HRL suffers from 'implementation deficits' in many states.

National and regional constitutional law systems incorporate and protect human rights in diverse ways. For instance, the 2009 EUCFR goes far beyond the UN HRL by protecting civil, political, economic, and social rights, as well as providing judicial remedies. This extended protection applies not only within the common market of the 27 EU member states, but also beyond it. By contrast, many Anglo-Saxon jurisdictions prioritise civil and political over economic and social rights without participating in regional human rights conventions and human rights courts, based on process-based conceptions of representative democracy, constitutional nationalism, and discretionary foreign policy powers.[2] Many authoritarian states adopted 'fake constitutions' that neither constrain power monopolies (such as China's communist party or

Thomas Biebricher, Peter Nedergaard and Werner Bonefeld (eds), *The Oxford Handbook of Ordoliberalism* (Oxford: Oxford University Press, 2022).

2 Martin Loughlin, *Against Constitutionalism* (Cambridge, MA: Harvard University Press, 2022), claims that elected representatives of the people, rather than citizens and courts of justice invoking human and constitutional rights for social change, should define the nation's political identity and make its most important policy decisions (pp. 124–35). The focus in US courts on 'negative freedoms' from coercion by government – and on judicial deference to 'political questions' to be decided by the US Congress – impedes judicial recognition of 'positive constitutional rights' (eg to health and environmental protection) if they have not been recognised in legislation.

the oligarchic rulers in the Kremlin) nor protect human and democratic rights and independent, judicial remedies. The synergies between multilevel human, constitutional, economic, and social rights in European common market law have no equivalent outside Europe.[3]

The universal recognition of 'inalienable' human rights requires justifying and protecting the 'basic structures' of law – including international economic law (IEL) – by democratic constitutionalism and agreed principles of justice such as human rights, rather than only by government powers and utility maximisation. The starting point for regulating 'business and human rights' (BHR) must be HRL rather than only corporate rights and duties. The added value of human rights for trade and corporate regulation should be to 'humanise' and 'constitutionalise' IEL and transnational corporations, for instance in cases of insufficient protection of human rights in trade, investment, and business law. Promoting synergies between the UN's SDGs and human rights requires interpreting the SDGs of both UN law and World Trade Organization (WTO) law in mutually consistent ways (sections 2–3). Even though some WTO members invoke human rights also in WTO legal practices, WTO law and jurisprudence avoid references to human rights (section 3). As more authoritarian countries suppress human and democratic rights and the WTO dispute settlement system remains disrupted by US power politics, it becomes increasingly necessary to establish plurilateral WTO agreements among 'like-minded democracies' making market access and trade regulation conditional on respect for human rights and the SDGs. Without reforms of WTO dispute settlement practices, investor-state arbitration and stronger judicial remedies, the WTO legal system and the UN Guidelines on BHR cannot effectively protect the SDGs (section 4).

3 For a discussion from comparative constitutional law perspectives see: Meinhard Hilf and Ernst-Ulrich Petersmann (eds.), *National Constitutions and International Economic Law* (Deventer: Kluwer 1993); Ernst-Ulrich Petersmann, "Taking Human Dignity, Poverty and Empowerment of Individuals More Seriously: Rejoinder to Alston," *European Journal of International Law* 13 (2002): 845–851. The 'Alston/Petersmann controversy' over diverse Anglo-Saxon and European conceptions of human rights was discussed in: Thomas Cottier, Joost Pauwleyn and Elisabeth Burgi (eds), *Human Rights and International Trade* (Oxford: Oxford University Press, 2005); Frederick M. Abbott, Christine Breining-Kaufmann and Thomas Cottier (eds), *International Trade and Human Rights* (Ann Arbor: Michigan University Press, 2006).

2 Need for Inclusive UN and WTO 'Sustainable Development' Agendas

All UN member states adopted national Constitutions (written or unwritten) constituting, regulating, and justifying national governance of PGs that are not provided for in private markets. They also joined multilateral treaties of a higher legal rank for protecting transnational PGs like human rights and rule-of-law. At the 70th anniversary of the UN in 2015, a summit meeting adopted the '2030 Agenda for Sustainable Development' (SDA) aimed at 'Transforming our World' in order to 'realize the human rights of all', 'to end poverty and hunger everywhere', and to implement 17 agreed SDGs over the next 15 years with 'the participation of all countries, all stakeholders and all people'.[4] The Resolution explicitly recognised (para. 9) that 'democracy, good governance and the rule of law … are essential for sustainable development'. Yet, the 'constitutional principles' underlying UN HRL and the SDA are neither effectively implemented in the legislative, administrative, and judicial practices inside and among authoritarian states nor in UN law, which lacks effective democratic and judicial remedies. The current economic, environmental, food and migration crises, global health pandemics, Russia's unprovoked military aggression and war crimes in Ukraine confirm the constitutional insight (eg of Kantian legal theory) that national Constitutions and 'horizontal international law' cannot protect citizens against external human disasters unless abuses of public and private power are legally limited also in external relations for the benefit of all citizens.

The UN and WTO governance crises can be explained in terms of 'constitutional failures' (eg to protect human rights, rule of law, and the SDGs), related 'governance failures' (including public and private abuses of power) and 'market failures' (like unnecessary poverty, hunger, environmental pollution). Disregard for human and democratic rights is the main reason for unprovoked wars of aggression and related war crimes (as currently in Ukraine) and for 'constitutional implementation deficits' in UN and WTO legal practices ushering in governance failures to prevent unnecessary poverty (SDG1) and protect food security (SDG2), public health (SDG3) and public education for all (SDG4), gender equality (SDG5), access to water and sanitation for all (SDG6),

---

4 *Transforming Our World: The 2030 Agenda for Sustainable Development* (New York: UN 2015); the citations are from the Preamble of the Declaration (UN General Assembly Resolution A/RES/70/1 adopted 25 September 2015).

and many other SDGs like protection of the environment (SDGs 13–15) and 'access to justice' (SDG16).[5]

2.1 *The UN Human Rights Approach to Realising the SDGs: Implementation Deficits*

Human rights law and ordo-liberal constitutionalism perceive individual and democratic autonomy and voluntary, informed consent as main sources of human values and as necessary constitutional safeguards against abuses of public and private power by means of rules of a higher legal rank, 'institutional checks and balances', and legal protection of individual preferences (eg by means of human and fundamental rights). Constitutional economics – rather than calculating efficiency only by way of output-oriented cost-benefit analyses – derives values from reasonable, informed consent of individuals to mutually beneficial rules; it searches for inclusive, reasonable agreements protecting individual and democratic preferences, limiting special interests, and constraining government powers to discriminate (eg in response to rent-seeking pressures). Protection of equal basic freedoms as 'first principle of justice', of 'human capacities', equal opportunities and satisfaction of basic human needs, 'consumer sovereignty' and 'citizen sovereignty' constitute core values of constitutional economics aimed at protecting consumers and citizens in both economic and political markets.[6] The 'social contract ideal' of citizens making reasonably informed 'constitutional choices' remains, however, confronted with the reality that economic actors and political regulators have only limited knowledge of the complex interactions among private and public, national, transnational and international legal, economic, political and social rules and institutions.

Hence, the legal protection of open markets as decentralised information-, coordination- and sanctioning mechanisms, and freedoms of information, expression and action remain of constitutional importance for exercising human rights. The UN institutions and SDA recommend 'constitutional governance models' (including protection of human rights, democracy, separation

---

5 On the importance of democratically inclusive 'good governance' and of 'inclusive institutions' for promoting sustainable development in its economic, social, environmental and legal dimensions see: Stefan Dercon, *Gambling on Development: Why Some Countries Win and Others Lose* (London: Hurst, 2022).

6 On constitutional economics see: Stefan Voigt, *Constitutional Economics: A Primer* (Cambridge: Cambridge University Press, 2020); Ernst-Ulrich Petersmann, *Transforming World Trade and Investment Law for Sustainable Development* (Oxford: Oxford University Press, 2022), chapter 4.

of powers, checks and balances, judicial remedies, rule-of-law) also for transnational, multilevel governance of the SDGs.[7] Yet, constitutional reforms of UN and WTO law remained limited to a few policy areas like compulsory adjudication in WTO law, investment law and in the UN Convention on the Law of the Sea (UNCLOS). Without effective judicial remedies, UN HRL often cannot be enforced. Also, the UN Security Council continues being blocked by abuses of veto-powers. Only in exceptional situations did the UN Security Council (SC) assert 'legislative powers', for example to establish international criminal courts and respond to international health pandemics by adopting UN SC Resolutions 2532 and 2565 (2020) acknowledging that 'the unprecedented extent of the COVID-19 pandemic is likely to endanger the maintenance of international peace and security'[8] and calling 'upon all parties to armed conflicts to engage immediately in a durable humanitarian pause' to provide humanitarian assistance to the world's most vulnerable in conflict zones.[9]

Similar UN Security Council responses to environmental crises remain unlikely, notwithstanding the universal recognition of the need for decarbonising economies and for protecting the potentially millions of climate refugees against the risks of climate change and rising sea levels. Human rights, democratic governance, rule-of-law and 'corporate social responsibilities' (CSR) remain insufficiently protected also in the legal practices of the more than 10'000 transnational corporations participating in the 'UN Global Compact' on BHR and in the implementation of the UN Guiding Principles for 'protecting, respecting and remedying' human rights in business activities. The ordoliberal EU law (like the corporate sustainability due diligence directive, the forced labour regulation) prescribes national and EU stakeholder obligations specifying CSR duties for environmental, social and governance (ESG) reporting and adjustment measures; Anglo-Saxon neo-liberal interest group politics often contests such 'ESG regulation' as undue interference into 'free markets' and 'shareholder responsibilities' of companies.

2.2 *Lack of an Inclusive WTO 'Sustainable Development Agenda'*

The SDA explicitly acknowledges (eg in paras 17.10–12) that realising most SDGs – like ending poverty for everybody, securing access to food, water and

7 Cf Giuliana Ziccardi Capaldo, "Global Constitutionalism and Global Governance: Towards a UN-Driven Global Constitutional Governance Model," in *Globalization and its Impact on the Future of Human Rights and International Criminal Justice*, ed. M. Cherif Bassiouni (Oxford: Oxford University Press, 2015), 629–662.

8 SC Res. 2532 (July 1, 2020) pmbl. para 11; SC Res. 2565 (Feb. 26, 2021) pmbl. 17.

9 SC Res. 2532 para 2.

medicines, and de-carbonizing economies – requires a 'rules-based, open, non-discriminatory and equitable multilateral trading system under the WTO'. The International Monetary Fund (IMF), the World Bank and the General Agreement on Tariffs and Trade (GATT 1947) prioritized *welfare economics* (aimed at promoting efficient allocation of scarce resources through market competition and trade within a given set of national constitutional rules) and *institutional economics* (promoting efficiency-enhancing, institutional reforms like contract law, property rights, judicial remedies, and rule-of-law). The IMF principles (like monetary stability, convertibility of currencies, freedom of current payments, balance-of-payments assistance) and GATT principles (like transparent policy-making, non-discriminatory tariffs, prohibition of discriminatory non-tariff barriers, optional safeguard measures, judicial remedies protecting transnational rule-of-law) also applied 'constitutional economics' in the sense of rules of a higher legal rank prescribing use of efficient monetary and trade policy instruments. Yet, the lack of effective UN, GATT and WTO competition rules, environmental and social rules revealed business-driven, neoliberal biases for avoiding effective, legal limitations on 'market failures' (like anti-competitive abuses of market power, pollution of the environment, social inequalities) and 'governance failures' (like 'regulatory capture' of trade remedy rules and of intellectual property rights generating 'protection rents').

The Bretton Woods and GATT/WTO institutions prioritised macroeconomic, quantitative cost-benefit analyses (like 'Kaldor-Hicks efficiencies') rather than protecting human capabilities through human rights, which were perceived as domestic policy issues on which member countries disagreed. For instance:

- China has ratified the International Covenant on Economic, Social and Cultural Rights (ICESCR) but not the UN Covenant on Civil and Political Rights (ICCPR) in order to shield its communist party's political monopoly;
- the USA has ratified the ICCPR but not the ICESCR in view of US political preferences for business-driven, neo-liberalism and prioritisation of civil and political over economic, social and cultural rights;
- most European countries have ratified both the ICCPR and the ICESCR; in contrast to the rejection by China and the USA of individual UN complaint mechanisms and of regional human rights conventions and human rights courts, they protect civil, political, economic, social and cultural rights also through individual UN complaint procedures and regional HRL like the ECHR and the EUCFR with individual access to national and European courts;

– authoritarian states (like Russia) do not effectively implement human rights conventions; their oligarchic rulers suppress human rights (eg of political dissidents, freedom of information) and democratic self-determination.

The references of the UN SDA to human rights, democratic governance and rule-of-law reflect the UN legal objectives of citizen-driven, rules-based order protecting human and democratic autonomy. The WTO Agreement – even though committed to 'sustainable development' (Preamble) – lacks adequate rules for realising the universally agreed 17 SDGs. The 'systemic interpretation' requirements codified in the VCLT (eg the Preamble and Article 31) require interpreting the shared 'sustainable development' obligations in UN and WTO law in mutually consistent ways enabling every member state to respect, protect and fulfil his human rights obligations and the universally agreed SDGs not only as PGs, but also – depending on the diverse domestic constitutional systems – as human and constitutional rights of citizens (eg of access to food, medicines, public education, justice and gender equality). Yet, human rights are neither mentioned nor protected in WTO law.

3 Avoidance of Human Rights Discourse in WTO Governance and Jurisprudence

The 2030 SDA emphasises the need for a 'global partnership' with 'the participation of all countries, all stakeholders and all people' based on 'universal respect for human rights and human dignity, the rule of law, justice, equality and non-discrimination'.[10] The Agenda's explicit commitment to 'the rule of law at the national and international levels' and ensuring 'equal access to justice for all'[11] repeats earlier UN commitments to 'rule of law at national and international levels' as 'a principle of governance in which all persons, institutions and entities, including the State itself, are accountable to laws that are publicly promulgated, equally enforced and independently adjudicated, and which are consistent with internationally recognised human rights'.[12] At the

10 *Transforming Our World* (n 4), eg paras. 3–9.

11 *Transforming Our World* (n 4), at preamble and paras 8, 9 and 'goal 16'.

12 Cf Report of the Secretary-General, Delivering Justice: programme of action to strengthen the rule-of-law at the national and international levels, A/66/49 of 16 March 2012, para. 2; Ernst-Ulrich Petersmann, "The UN Sustainable Development Agenda and Rule of Law: Global Governance Failures Require Democratic and Judicial Restraints," *Max Planck Yearbook of United Nations Law* 25 (2022): 457–497.

worldwide level of governance, it is only since the 1990s that the compulsory WTO dispute settlement system – and the worldwide web of now more than 3,200 bilateral and multilateral investment agreements – provided for multilevel, judicial remedies promoting 'rule of law at national and international levels' through comprehensive jurisprudence.

3.1 *The GATT/WTO Dispute Settlement System*

The 316 dispute settlement proceedings under GATT 1947 and the 1979 Tokyo Round Agreements,[13] and the more than 630 formal dispute settlement proceedings under the WTO Agreement (1996–2024), protected – for the first time in world history – transnational rule-of-law in trade relations among now 166 WTO members.[14] The jurisprudence approved by GATT/WTO members clarified the rights and duties under international trade law with due regard to general international law and free trade agreements (FTAs) concluded among GATT/WTO members (often providing for additional judicial remedies). Up to 2020, more than 85% of the more than 500 GATT/WTO dispute settlement findings were approved and implemented, making the GATT/WTO dispute settlement system the most frequently used, worldwide dispute settlement system in the history of international law. GATT Article X:3 and equivalent provisions in GATT/WTO agreements on specific trade subjects (like anti-dumping duties, subsidies, technical barriers to trade, services trade, intellectual property rights) and on the accession of specific countries (like China) provide for access also to domestic legal or judicial remedies. Most GATT/WTO members did not allow citizens to 'directly invoke' and enforce GATT/WTO obligations in domestic jurisdictions. Yet, many GATT/WTO disputes were preceded or followed by domestic court proceedings (eg challenging illegal trade remedies). The global 'interpretive community' of trade lawyers, academics and judges scrutinising and developing GATT/WTO jurisprudence strengthened a 'trade law culture' promoting 'public reason' (eg in the sense of shared systems of public justification of multilevel trade rules and of their decentralised enforcement), providing 'security and predictability to the multilateral trading system' (DSU Article 3) and reducing transaction costs in the global division of labour.

'Diplomatic conceptions' reducing rule-of-law among states to the availability and relative effectiveness of international dispute settlement procedures are criticised by citizen-oriented conceptions of 'interactional law' exploring

---

13 Cf the list and analyses of cases in: *GATT Disputes 1948–1995*, 2 vols. (WTO Geneva 2018).

14 Cf Gabrielle Marceau (ed), *A History of Law and Lawyers in the GATT/WTO. The Development of the Rule of Law in the Multilateral Trading System* (Cambridge: Cambridge University Press, 2015).

whether international law rules are supported by citizens in a common practice of legality (eg rooted in Fuller's eight criteria of legality) in day-to-day decision-making.[15] As the WTO Agreement has been approved in 165 WTO member states and by the EU and continues to promote their economic welfare through rules-based, market-driven division of labour, it can assert 'input'- and 'output-legitimacy'. The economic, social and 'sustainable development' objectives of the WTO, the WTO legal rules and judicial remedies, and each WTO member's legal obligations to 'ensure the conformity of its laws, regulations and administrative procedures with its obligations under the annexed Agreements' (Article XVI.4 of the WTO Agreement) created a global trading, legal and compulsory dispute settlement system enabling member states to enhance peaceful legal, economic and political cooperation as never before in human history. In DSU Article 3.2, WTO members recognise that the dispute settlement system 'serves to preserve the rights and obligations of Members under the covered Agreements, and to clarify the existing provisions of those agreements in accordance with customary rules of interpretation of public international law'. The codification of these customary rules in VCLT Articles 31–33 prescribes interpretation of treaties based not only on their text, context, object and purpose; interpretation must also take into account, *inter alia*, 'any relevant rules of international law applicable in the relations between the parties' (Article 31.3.c), including also 'principles of justice' and 'human rights and fundamental freedoms for all', as recalled in the Preamble of the VCLT.

3.2 *Protection of Human Rights Values in WTO Jurisprudence*

The SDGs and the UN resolutions on rule-of-law emphasise the need for respecting human rights. Yet, human rights are nowhere mentioned in WTO law; they are hardly ever invoked and discussed in WTO bodies, or referred to in WTO dispute settlement reports, in view of the long-standing domination of the GATT/WTO trading system by Anglo-Saxon neo-liberalism, the deliberate separation of GATT and the WTO from the 'UN system', and the diversity of views among WTO members on the relationships of their respective human rights obligations and WTO law. Also the reports by the UN High Commissioner for Human Rights and by the International Labor Organization on the labour law and human rights dimensions of the WTO agreements (eg on trade in agricultural products, services and trade-related intellectual property rights) were

15 On constitutional conceptions of rule-of-law see the comparative law contributions to: Hilf/Petersmann (note 3).

hardly discussed in WTO institutions.[16] The design, interpretation and application of many GATT/WTO rules (eg on dumping and countervailing duties, safeguards, subsides, intellectual property rights) are dominated by neo-liberal, business-driven power politics; less-developed countries (like India and South Africa) occasionally invoked human rights (eg on access to food, medicines and public health protection) for justifying their interpretations of GATT/WTO rules (e.g. for granting 'waivers' from trade-related intellectual property rules, for the 'Kimberley Process' of controlling 'conflict diamonds', for reconciling interpretation of patent- and copyrights with human rights to health protection, for protecting food security through governmental subsidies and public stockholding).[17]

Yet, unlike 'social clauses' and 'human rights clauses' in FTAs, there is no consensus on including similar clauses into WTO agreements, for example following the example of some developed countries making market access conditional on respect for labour rights and human rights in the production of traded goods and services. As WTO law does not provide for individual access to WTO dispute settlement bodies, WTO complainants and defendants hardly ever invoke human rights in WTO dispute settlement proceedings. Such intergovernmental procedures justify the judicial WTO practice of focusing on the '*objective PGs values*' underlying human rights (like public health protection underlying the human right to health) rather than on *individual* human rights. GATT/WTO jurisprudence suggests that judicial protection of *human rights values* in WTO dispute settlement proceedings may be as effective as if the judges had referred to *individual human rights* in interpreting and 'balancing' state-centered WTO rights, obligations, and exceptions.

The WTO objectives and WTO 'general exceptions' protect human rights values like 'public morals', 'public order', 'human, animal or plant life of health', 'protection of national treasures of artistic, historic or archaeological value', 'conservation of exhaustible natural resources', protection of the environment, 'essential security interests', 'raising standards of living' and 'sustainable

16 Cf Ernst-Ulrich Petersmann, "The Human Rights Approach to International Trade Advocated by the UN High Commissioner for Human Rights and by the ILO: Is it Relevant for WTO Law and Policy?" in *Reforming the World Trading System: Legitimacy, Efficiency and Democratic Governance*, Ernst-Ulrich Petersmann (ed), (Oxford: Oxford University Press, 2005), 357–380.

17 On the indirect support of such human rights arguments by UN bodies see: Matias E. Margulis, *Shadow Negotiations. How UN Organizations Shape the Rules of World Trade for Food Security* (Stanford: Stanford University Press, 2023).

development'. WTO jurisprudence has interpreted these WTO provisions broadly. For instance:

- The 2018 WTO panel and 2020 Appellate Body (AB) reports on complaints by tobacco exporting countries against Australia's legislation on tobacco plain-packaging (TPP) confirmed that these health regulations restricting intellectual property rights and sales of tobacco products were consistent with WTO law (eg on technical barriers to trade and intellectual property rights). The reports refrained from referring to human rights, which had neither been invoked by the complainants nor by the defendant. But the interpretation of WTO rules in conformity with the 2001 WTO Declaration on the 'TRIPS Agreement and Public Health' and the 2003 WHO Framework Convention on Tobacco Control (FCTC) avoided conflicts with health rights, thereby illustrating the importance of 'systemic treaty interpretation' for maintaining the consistency of WTO rights and obligations with other international treaty commitments.[18]
- The 2014 WTO panel and appellate reports on EU import restrictions on seals products acknowledged, *inter alia*, that the EU exceptions for products from indigenous people in Greenland were justifiable under the 'public morals' exception in GATT Article XX(a) provided they did not discriminate against seal products imported from Canada and Norway.[19]
- The 2011 panel and 2012 appellate reports on US restrictions on tuna based on the 'Dolphin Protection Consumer Information Act' confirmed that US 'dolphin-safe' labelling measures could be consistent with WTO law provided they were applied in non-discriminatory ways.[20]
- The 2007 WTO panel and appellate reports on Brazil's import restrictions on retreaded tyres implied that the restrictions could be justified as being necessary for health protection reasons if applied in non-discriminatory ways.[21]

18 Cf Ernst-Ulrich Petersmann, "How to Reconcile Human Rights, Trade Law, Intellectual Property, Investment and Health Law? WTO Dispute Settlement Panel Upholds Australia's Plain Packaging Regulations of Tobacco Products," *The Global Community Yearbook of International Law and Jurisprudence* (2018): 69–102. The AB reports confirming the panel findings were published on 9 June 2020: WT/DS435/AB/R and WT/DS441/AB/R.

19 Cf. WT/DS400,401/R/AB adopted on 18 June 2014.

20 Cf. WT/DS/381/R/AB adopted 13 June 2012.

21 Cf. WT/DS/332/R/AB adopted on 12 December 2007.

- The 2004 panel and 2005 appellate reports on US restrictions of cross-border gambling and betting services implied that such restrictions can be justified as being necessary for protecting 'public morals' (Article XIV(a) GATS) if applied in non-discriminatory ways.[22]
- The 2003 panel and 2004 appellate reports on EC tariff preferences for combatting drug production and trafficking in less-developed countries implied that such preferences can be consistent with WTO law if applied in non-discriminatory ways.[23]
- The 2001 appellate report on EC import restrictions on asbestos confirmed the justifiability of these health protection measures; as health risks can affect the competitive relationship of asbestos and substitute products, non-discriminatory health protection measures may neither violate GATT Article III nor need justification under GATT law.[24]
- The 1998 and 2001 appellate reports on US import restrictions on shrimps confirmed that non-discriminatory animal protection conditioning imports of shrimp on the use of certain fishing nets protecting turtles is justifiable under GATT Article XX(g).[25]

All these WTO dispute settlement findings affected the regulation of business activities with potentially harmful or discriminatory economic, health or environmental effects. The findings influenced also global application of WTO rules beyond the specific disputes. They confirm the sovereign rights under WTO law to adopt *non-discriminatory* regulations protecting non-economic PGs like 'public morals' (including also human rights), public health and the environment. There is no evidence, so far, that any of the more than 500 GATT/WTO dispute settlement findings since 1948 has violated human rights.

3.3 *'Systemic WTO Interpretation' Limits 'Legal Fragmentation'*

The Covid-19 health pandemic is a reminder of the close interrelationships between economic and health systems. During the 20th century, tobacco consumption killed more than 100 million people, ie, more than World Wars I and II and the holocaust together. Yet, it was only in 2003 that the FCTC – the first multilateral treaty negotiated under Article 19 of the WHO Constitution – was signed and subsequently accepted by more than 180 countries. The co-existence of 15 separate UN Specialized Agencies (like the WHO) with functionally

22 Cf. WT/DS/285/R/AB adopted on 20 April 2005.
23 Cf. WT/DS246/R/AB adopted on 20 April 2004.
24 Cf. WT/DS135/R/AB adopted on 5 April 2001.
25 Cf. WT/DS58/R/AB adopted on 6 November 1998 and 21 November 2001 (Article 21.5 DSU).

separate mandates and legal systems responds to the fact that, in a world composed of more than 200 states, the 'sovereign equality of states' (UN Charter Article 2) makes legal and institutional 'fragmentation' inevitable: different states and governments have different priorities as to which bilateral and multilateral treaties each of the 193 UN member states is willing to conclude, subject to which judicial remedies, and how to implement treaty obligations inside diverse national legal and political systems. The WTO jurisprudence on health protection measures confirms that the customary rules of treaty interpretation – and judicial mandates of administering justice – offer dispute settlement bodies sufficient legal flexibility for interpreting fragmented treaty rights and obligations of WTO members in mutually coherent ways.

The WTO complaints initiated in 2012 by Ukraine, Honduras, and the Dominican Republic, and in 2014 by Cuba and Indonesia, challenged the consistency with WTO law of Australia's TPP measures. Yet, the complaints and defences also involved HRL, intellectual property law, investment law, health law and Australia's constitutional law and adjudication. As tobacco use is classified as a global epidemic responsible for the deaths of nearly 6,000,000 people annually, including 600,000 non-smokers exposed to second-hand smoke, the WTO disputes affected people and health regulations all over the world. After separate complaints by tobacco industries in the national courts of Australia[26] and in investor-state arbitration (under an investment treaty between Hong Kong and Australia) had already been rejected, two of the four separate yet largely identical WTO panel findings were adopted by the Dispute Settlement Body (DSB) in August 2018.[27]

The two other WTO panel reports were appealed; both appeals were rejected in two WTO AB reports adopted in June 2020.[28] The four Panel and two AB reports dismissed all claims of violations of GATT and WTO rules (notably under the TBT and TRIPS Agreements); as neither the complainants nor defendant had referred to human rights (eg to health protection), the judicial balancing of economic rights (e.g. market access rights and intellectual property rights protected by WTO law) and public health protection focused

26 For an overview of tobacco litigation in national, European and investment courts see Ernst-Ulrich Petersmann, *Multilevel Constitutionalism for Multilevel Governance of Public Goods* (Oxford: Hart 2017), 241ff, 256ff.

27 WT/DS435/R, WT/DS441/R, WT/DS458/R, WT/DS467/R of 28 June 2018 on Australia – Certain Measures Concerning Trademarks, Geographical Indications and other Plain Packaging Requirements Applicable to Tobacco Products and Packaging. For detailed legal analyses see Petersmann (n 16).

28 The AB reports confirming the panel findings were published on 9 June 2020 (WT/DS435/AB/R and WT/DS441/AB/R) and adopted on 29 June 2020.

on *governmental rights to protect public health* rather than on corresponding *human rights*. The dozens of separately negotiated agreements included into the WTO Agreement and WTO treaty practices (like the 2001 WTO Declaration on the TRIPS Agreement and Public Health) were construed by the WTO dispute settlement bodies as a mutually coherent legal system. Multilateral treaties on tobacco control negotiated in the WHO, WIPO conventions and related treaty practices were duly taken into account in the legal findings on the consistency of Australia's TPP regulations with WTO law. The 'systemic interpretations' of WTO rules in conformity with HRL and health law set an example for future WTO disputes relating, for example, to the consistency of environmental measures under the dozens of UN environmental agreements with relevant WTO legal obligations.

4 Need for Plurilateral Reforms of Human Rights Law and WTO Law

Russia's wars of aggression and war crimes, China's threats of war in order to suppress democratic rights in Taiwan, the US disruption of the WTO dispute settlement system by illegal 'blocking' of the appointment of AB members, the trade sanctions by democracies against China, Russia and other authoritarian countries, and the increasing 'weaponisation' of economic interdependence (eg by Russia's suspension of oil, gas and food exports) illustrate the new realities of multi-polar power politics undermining UN and WTO law, protection of human rights and the SDGs. Similar to the cooperation among authoritarian countries (like China, Iran, North Korea, Russia and other, formerly Soviet republics in Asia), the 're-globalisation' of supply chains and plurilateral 'climate mitigation clubs' (eg for supporting decarbonisation of economies) prioritise 'like-minded countries' sharing similar policy values and national interests (eg in maintaining 'democratic peace'). Due to their business-driven, neo-liberal constitutional traditions, many Anglo-Saxon democracies (like the US) do not share Europe's multilevel human rights constitutionalism and multilevel judicial protection of civil, political, economic, and social rights of EU citizens. Authoritarian disregard for human rights and for non-discriminatory market competition, neo-liberal disregard for Europe's 'competitive social market economy' (TEU Art 3) embedded into multilevel human rights protection, and the continuing US disruption of independent WTO adjudication are likely to further weaken the protection of human rights in world trade.

4.1 *Promoting Mutually Supportive UN and WTO 'Sustainable Development Strategies'*

The 12th WTO Ministerial Conference in June 2022 succeeded in concluding additional multilateral trade agreements, *inter alia*, on fisheries subsidies, food security, the 'WTO Response to the Covid-19 Pandemic and Preparedness for Future Pandemics', and a 'Ministerial Decision on the TRIPS Agreement' authorising limitations of intellectual property rights for the production and supply of Covid 19-vaccines.[29] This 'Geneva package' illustrated that the geopolitical rivalries do not prevent consensus-based WTO reforms aimed at protecting global PGs like public health, food security and protection of the environment. The 2021 'Glasgow climate pact' of the 26th Conference of the Parties (COP 26) of the UN Framework Convention on Climate Change (UNFCCC), the 2022 COP 27 'Sharm el-Sheikh Agreements', and the ongoing WTO negotiations on clarifying the WTO 'sustainable development agenda' suggest that future synergies between UN law and WTO law could be strengthened especially in the common pursuit of SDGs like climate change mitigation. The EU's 'climate law' adopted in June 2021 provides for complementing the EU carbon emissions trading system by carbon border adjustment measures (CBAMs) aimed at preventing 'carbon leakage' and distortions of international competition in countries with more ambitious climate change policies. Climate litigation increasingly acknowledges invocation by private and public complainants of greenhouse gas (GHG) reduction obligations of governments as recognised in EU law and UN law.[30]

Rights to the protection of the environment are recognised in the laws of now more than 150 states, regional treaties, and by the UN Human Rights Council (HRC).[31] In national and European environmental litigation, courts holding governments legally accountable for climate mitigation measures increasingly refer to human rights and constitutional principles. For example, the ruling of the Dutch Supreme Court on December 20, 2019 in *State of the Netherlands v Urgenda* confirmed that ECHR Articles 2 (right to life) and 8 (right to private and family life) entail legal duties of the Dutch government to reduce GHG emissions by at least 25% (compared to 1990 levels) by the end of 2020. The judgment clarified that human rights and related constitutional and environmental law guarantees (like the 1998 Aarhus Convention on access to justice in environmental matters) may be invoked by citizens to enforce

29 Cf WTO document WT/MIN(22) 24 of 17 June 2022.

30 Cf Petersmann (n 6), chapter 9.

31 See Resolution 48/13 adopted by the HRC on 8 October 2021, recognizing that having a clean, healthy and sustainable environment is a human right.

positive obligations to take appropriate measures mitigating climate change.[32] The ruling of the District Court of The Hague on May 26, 2021 in *Milieudefensie v Royal Dutch Shell* was the first judgment in which a multinational corporation was held responsible for its contribution to climate change based on national and international law.[33] The case was brought as a public interest class action by a Dutch NGO; it does not focus on compensation for past damages but on corporate obligations to reduce emissions and invest more in cleaner fuels to protect the common interest of current and future generations in preventing dangerous climate change.

Similar litigation against energy companies focusing on corporate responsibilities for climate change is pending in many countries. Even though the judgment is based on corporate duties of care under Dutch tort law, the Court's references to international law and to the shared responsibilities of corporate actors may influence the reasoning in future judgments by other courts. The Court found that the total CO_2 emissions of the Shell group exceeded the emissions of many states, including the Netherlands. The group's global CO_2 emissions contributed to global warming and climate change in the Netherlands; they entailed significant risks for residents of that country. The court agreed with the complainants that Shell had an obligation to reduce CO_2 emissions of the Shell group's entire energy portfolio, holding that:

- Shell is obliged to reduce the CO_2 emissions of the Shell group's activities by net 45 per cent by the end of 2030 relative to 2019 through the Shell group's corporate policy;
- the policy, policy intentions, and ambitions of the Shell group imply an imminent violation of this obligation;
- the Court, therefore, allowed the claimed order for compliance with this legal obligation.

The judgment took into account human rights and the Paris Agreement in its interpretation of the unwritten standard of care. The Court also referred to the UN Guiding Principles on Business and Human Rights (UNGP), which it found to constitute an authoritative, internationally endorsed soft law instrument setting out the responsibilities of states and businesses in relation to

32 *Supreme Court, State of the Netherlands v Stichting Urgenda* (2019, ECLI:NL:HR:2019:2007, Urgenda v NL, 2019). For comparative overviews of climate litigation see: Francesco Sindico and Moise Mbengue, *Comparative Climate Change Litigation: Beyond the Usual Suspects* (Cham: Springer Publishing, 2021).

33 *The Hague District Court, Milieudefensie et al. v. Shell* (2021, ECLI:NL: RBDHA:2021:5339).

human rights; the UNGP 'are suitable as a guideline in the interpretation of the unwritten standard of care'. According to the Court, the responsibility to respect human rights encompasses the company's entire value chain' including the end-users of the products produced and traded by the Shell group. The Court concluded that the human rights standards, the UNGP, and the Paris agreement all support the conclusion that Shell should be ordered to reduce the CO_2 emissions of the Shell group's activities by net 45 per cent at the end of 2030 relative to 2019 through the group's corporate policy. In the USA, by contrast, similar constitutional and human rights tend to be denied by US courts, for instance on grounds of judicial deference towards 'political questions' left open in the US Constitution and not (yet) decided by the US Congress, which remains reluctant to enact legislation recognising new human, constitutional or environmental rights and prescribing climate change mitigation based on the 'polluter pays principle' (aimed at protecting all citizens against environmental harms) rather than on macro-economic 'Kaldor-Hicks-efficiencies' (justifying also polluting industries).

4.2 *Climate Protection through 'Plurilateral Climate Clubs'?*

The US Inflation Reduction Act (IRA) adopted in August 2022 uses discriminatory tax credits, domestic content requirements and trade discrimination for promoting de-carbonisation of the US economy, thereby further undermining WTO law and increasing trade conflicts, for instance between the use of first-best, non-discriminatory tariffs in the EU's CBAM and the use of second-best, discriminatory trade policy instruments in the US IRA. To minimise the coercive effects of GHG-related tariffs imposed unilaterally and respect the environmental law principles in the 2015 Paris Agreement (like NDCs, 'common but differentiated responsibilities' of less-developed countries), the G7 countries recommended in June 2022 to embed CBAM's into broader 'carbon clubs' based upon mutual recognition of GHG reduction commitments among members and external CBAMs vis-à-vis third countries.[34] The theory behind 'climate protection clubs',[35] like constitutional and 'club theories' more generally, explains why socially harmful 'free-riding' can be reduced by making membership and rights conditional on mutually agreed cooperation and corresponding duties. For instance, CBAMs can be made more effective and more

34 On the 'Group of 7' proposal of June 2022 see: https://www.g7germany.de/resource/blob/974430/2057926/2a7cd9f10213a481924492942dd660a1/2022-06-28-g7-climate-club-data.pdf?download=1.

35 Cf William Nordhaus, "Climate Clubs: Overcoming Free-riding in International Climate Policy," *American Economic Review* 105 (2015): 1339–1370.

acceptable by making market access conditional on, *inter alia*, GHG reduction commitments, carbon tariffs, agreed 'green product and production standards', procedures for calculating 'embedded carbon' in products and equivalence of diverse GHG reduction policies, reductions of fossil fuel subsidies, agreed rules for renewable fuel subsidies, and elimination of tariffs on environmental goods and services, with due respect for the WTO principles of special and differential treatment of less-developed countries and the environmental law principle of 'common but differentiated responsibilities'.

Just as the multilaterally agreed trade restrictions in the UN Convention on Trade in Endangered Species and in the Montreal Protocol on Transboundary Movement of Hazardous Wastes were never challenged in WTO dispute settlement proceedings, multilaterally agreed GHG reduction clubs, 'environmental goods agreements', newly agreed subsidy rules and fossil fuel disciplines should set incentives for voluntary global cooperation and for 'critical mass membership' promoting non-discriminatory treatment without free-riding. Consensus on a 'package deal' and 'grand bargain' might require a broader 'WTO sustainability agenda' on how to promote the broader policy objectives of a 'circular economy' (eg reducing waste and plastic pollution by re-cycling), sustainable agriculture (eg addressing bio-diversity, water and food security issues), greening of transport services, the 'blue economy' (like over-fishing, ocean pollution) and a 'just transition' assisting less-developed countries through financial assistance.

The diversity of governmental and private company pledges of GHG reductions also calls for setting civil society incentives for active participation in decentralised monitoring of market failures (like pollution harms) and governance failures (like non-implementation of GHG pledges). This can be promoted by enhancing synergies between human and legal rights to protection of the environment and stronger democratic and judicial remedies. As prices of internationally traded goods often do not reflect their environmental and social costs, the UN and WTO sustainable development goals must factor in the pollution costs and 'planetary boundaries' in order to promote social welfare, just as neo-liberal 'shareholder conceptions' of company goals must be replaced by more inclusive 'stakeholder conceptions' and 'social corporate responsibilities'. This requires not only stronger reporting requirements of companies on their ESG performance. Also, constitutional democracies can remain effective only to the extent that the social and constitutional contracts among citizens are dynamically implemented through citizen-driven use of human and constitutional rights and their protection by democratic legislation, administration and adjudication empowering citizens and protecting rule-of-law.

4.3 *Lessons from European Integration Law?*

Is it realistic to expect UN and WTO law to limit human rights abuses in transnational business practices without stronger legal protection of individual rights and judicial remedies in domestic and regional legal systems (eg in authoritarian states like China and Russia)? Worldwide economic organisations often avoid interpreting IEL in conformity with UN HRL, for instance in view of the absence of human rights safeguards in worldwide economic agreements and the diverse ratification and implementation of UN human rights conventions inside UN member states. Proposals (eg by lawyers from countries without comprehensive national and regional human rights remedies) to interpret IEL in conformity with recommendations of UN human rights bodies are widely disregarded in worldwide, regional and national economic law practices.[36] European democracies, by contrast, tend to limit abuses of public and private powers (eg of transnational corporations) in IEL through 'bottom-up legal approaches' embedding economic markets into democratic constitutionalism and strengthening rights and judicial remedies of citizens and legal 'corporate accountabilities' in national and regional jurisdictions.[37] National and regional HRL and multilevel constitutionalism can protect human rights, democratic self-determination and legal remedies more effectively than international UN law.

Europe's multilevel constitutionalism has no equivalent outside Europe. The transformation of *national* into *transnational 'aggregate PGs'* (like the SDGs) leads to increasing participation of non-governmental organisations in transnational governance of PGs (like climate change mitigation, food, health and cyber security, disaster relief), often driven by civil society struggles for transforming the UN into more inclusive, participatory forms of governance. In a globalised 'world on fire', reasonable citizens must assume also cosmopolitan – rather than only national – responsibilities. The ordo-liberal objectives of promoting general consumer welfare, citizen welfare and global PGs like the SDGs call for stronger democratic, legal and judicial remedies inside and among states; the global governance crises confirm that neglect for human rights in UN and WTO practices undermines effective protection of PGs (like public health, indigenous peoples' rights, public morality, public order) and of agreed 'constitutional principles of justice' (like transparent policymaking, non-discrimination, proportionality and subsidiarity of governmental restrictions of individual freedoms).

---

36 Cf note 3.

37 Cf Petersmann (n 6) chapt 4.

Just as European integration law has successfully evolved by transforming governance crises into citizen-driven constitutional reforms, also UN and WTO governance of the SDGs – and stronger protection of human rights in transnational business – depend on civil society struggles for defending human rights through legal restraints on abuses of public and private power. UN HRL and IEL alone can contribute to peace, rule-of law and social justice only if the cosmopolitan rights of 'citizens of the world' (eg as codified in UN HRL) are protected in the domestic legal systems of UN member states. The effectiveness of UN HRL – including its subsidiarity principles and respect for democratic diversity and 'constitutional pluralism'- and of IEL depends on decentralised legislative, administrative, and judicial enforcement that must remain justified and accountable vis-à-vis citizens 'bottom up' through democratic constitutionalism (eg protecting also reasonable disagreements on social order and diverse justifications of IEL). Unless constitutional democracies struggle for plurilateral reforms of UN and WTO law and resist the international power politics by authoritarian rulers, the transformation of the UN SDA into a legally and institutionally secured *eunomia* protecting human rights in the world trading system will remain a *utopia*.[38] The Chinese and Russian pledges, in February 2022, for an 'unlimited partnership' risk further undermining the Kantian and UN ideals of '*perpetual peace*' based on national, international, and cosmopolitan freedoms and rule-of-law, especially if China should support wars of aggression by supplying arms and use military force against other WTO members like Taiwan.

Bibliography

Books

Dercon, Stefan. *Gambling on Development: Why Some Countries Win and Others Lose.* London: Hurst, 2022.

Loughlin, Martin. *Against Constitutionalism.* (Cambridge, MA: Harvard University Press, 2022).

Margulis, Matius E. *Shadow Negotiations. How UN Organizations Shape the Rules of World Trade for Food Security.* Stanford: Stanford University Press, 2023.

38 Cf Ernst-Ulrich Petersmann, "Self-Constitution of Mankind without Constitutional Constructivism?" *EJIL Talk* of 4 January 2022; *idem*, 'Constitutional Constructivism' for a Common Law of Humanity? Multilevel Constitutionalism as a 'Gentle Civilizer of Nations' *MPIL Research Paper Series* No. 2017–24.

Petersmann, Ernst-Ulrich. *Multilevel Constitutionalism for Multilevel Governance of Public Goods*. Oxford: Hart 2017.

Petersmann, Ernst-Ulrich. *Transforming World Trade and Investment Law for Sustainable Development*. Oxford: Oxford University Press, 2022.

Sindico, Francesco, and Moise Mbengue. *Comparative Climate Change Litigation: Beyond the Usual Suspects*. Cham: Springer Publishing, 2021.

Voigt, Stefan. *Constitutional Economics: A Primer*. Cambridge: Cambridge University Press, 2020.

Edited Books

Abbott, Frederick M., Christine Breining-Kaufmann C., and Thomas Cottier (eds). *International Trade and Human Rights*. Ann Arbor: Michigan University Press, 2006.

Biebricher, Thomas, Peter Nedergaard, and Werner Bonefeld (eds). *The Oxford Handbook of Ordoliberalism*. Oxford: Oxford University Press, 2022.

Cottier, Thomas, Joost Pauwleyn, and Elisabeth Burgi (eds). *Human Rights and International Trade*. Oxford: Oxford University Press, 2005.

Hilf, Meinhard, and Ernst-Ulrich Petersmann (eds.). *National Constitutions and International Economic Law*. Deventer: Kluwer, 1993.

Marceau, Gabrielle (ed.). *A History of Law and Lawyers in the GATT/WTO. The Development of the Rule of Law in the Multilateral Trading System*. Cambridge: Cambridge University Press, 2015.

Chapter in Edited Books

Petersmann, Ernst-Ulrich. "German and European Ordo-Liberalism and Constitutionalism in the Post-War Development of International Economic Law." In *The European International Law Tradition*, edited by Peter Hilpold, 305–32. Heidelberg: Springer, 2020.

Petersmann, Ernst-Ulrich. "The Human Rights Approach to International Trade Advocated by the UN High Commissioner for Human Rights and by the ILO: Is it Relevant for WTO Law and Policy?" In *Reforming the World Trading System: Legitimacy, Efficiency and Democratic Governance*, edited by Ernst-Ulrich Petersmann, 357–80. Oxford: Oxford University Press, 2005.

Ziccardi, Capaldo G. "Global Constitutionalism and Global Governance: Towards a UN-Driven Global Constitutional Governance Model." In *Globalization and its Impact on the Future of Human Rights and International Criminal Justice*, edited by M. Cherif Bassiouni, 629–62. Oxford: Oxford University Press, 2015.

Articles

Nordhaus, William. "Climate Clubs: Overcoming Free-riding in International Climate Policy." *American Economic Review* 105 (2015): 1339–70.

Petersmann, Ernst-Ulrich. "'Constitutional Constructivism' for a Common Law of Humanity? Multilevel Constitutionalism as a 'Gentle Civilizer of Nations'." *MPIL Research Paper Series* No. 2017–24.
Petersmann, Ernst-Ulrich. "How to Reconcile Human Rights, Trade Law, Intellectual Property, Investment and Health Law? WTO Dispute Settlement Panel Upholds Australia's Plain Packaging Regulations of Tobacco Products." *The Global Community Yearbook of International Law and Jurisprudence* 2018: 69–102.
Petersmann, Ernst-Ulrich. "Taking Human Dignity, Poverty and Empowerment of Individuals More Seriously: Rejoinder to Alston." *European Journal of International Law* 13 (2002): 845–51.
Petersmann, Ernst-Ulrich. "Self-Constitution of Mankind without Constitutional Constructivism?" *European Journal of International Law Talk* of January 4, 2022.
Petersmann, Ernst-Ulrich. "The UN Sustainable Development Agenda and Rule of Law: Global Governance Failures Require Democratic and Judicial Restraints." *Max Planck Yearbook of United Nations Law* 25 (2022): 457–97.
Petersmann, Ernst-Ulrich. "Neoliberalism, Ordoliberalism and the Future of Economic Governance." *Journal of International Economic Law* 26, no. 4 (2023): 836–42.

CHAPTER 8

Foreign Direct Investment and Responsibility of Multinational Corporations for Human Rights Violations

Md Jahid Hossain Bhuiyan

1 Introduction

Foreign Direct Investment (FDI) 'is a category of cross-border investment in which an investor resident in one economy establishes a lasting interest in and a significant degree of influence over an enterprise resident in another economy.' The ownership of a 10 percent or more benchmark is considered sufficient for the foreign direct investor to exert a significant influence on the host country.

Host countries typically desire direct investment inflows from a foreign economy because of the short- and long-term advantages it brings, including improved foreign exchange reserves, capital growth, and access to new international markets. These relationships also benefit the host country's information and knowledge base through the transfer of expertise and industrial technology, increased potential for innovation, labour skills, and institutional management practices, all of which can increase economic efficiency. The stimulation of economic growth by FDI and the concomitant improvements in living standards may also have positive knock-on effects on the approval ratings of the host country's government. The net result of the potential FDI, namely that it brings economic benefits to the host country, is therefore particularly attractive for developing countries, which often make the encouragement of such investment a key component of overall development strategy.

Securing economic growth and development by attracting the FDI of Multinational Corporations (MNCs), however, should only play a role in sustainable development if both parties in the investment relationship adhere to human rights norms. Globalisation has made it increasingly apparent that protecting human rights at every level of every sector involved in economic activity is central to sustainability. Not only is it unethical for any party involved in an investment relationship to fail to protect human rights, but also ultimately self-defeating. The reasons why human rights are central to sustainability, and why organisations like the United Nations (UN), and indeed many countries

 | DOI:10.1163/9789004530942_009

(Denmark being a good example) advocate a human rights-based approach to sustainable development is because the failure to protect such rights will have serious long-term repercussions on everyone. Even if one accepts Milton Friedman's doctrine that the only responsibility of a business is to maximise profits for shareholders, the need for rights protection by business policymakers remains, for those profits will be threatened, particularly in the short term. Global growth has also involved huge increases in awareness around the world, dramatically increasing the power of investors to punish both countries and companies that commit or allow human rights violations and unsustainable practices. In other words, countries wanting to attract foreign investment, and companies wanting to invest in those countries, are now more than ever exposed to reputational risk.

Human rights violations in the business community have been a significant public concern for many years. These types of abuses can take the form of forced and child labour, lack of respect for workers' rights, such as the freedom of association and right to form a union, collective bargaining and inadequate health and safety provisions in the workplace. Such abuses can also include appropriation of land, such as that belonging to indigenous peoples, violence committed by private security personnel, and environmental contamination and degradation, for example, pollution of water sources, among others. It is also inevitable that all these abuses will ultimately affect those responsible for committing them. Nonetheless, as Garriga observes, the reputational effect of human rights violations is complex and often counter-intuitive as countries with the worst human rights records appear to gain most from rights treaty ratifications. That is, countries having very little real intention to fulfil human rights obligations may use ratification of such treaties as a 'reputational umbrella' underneath which to hide their actual rights abuses.

It is worth reminding that since the 1948 Universal Declaration of Human Rights (UDHR), the legal and normative corpus relating to human rights has developed considerably through the adoption of many human rights instruments, including the 1966 International Covenant on Civil and Political Rights (ICCPR) and the 1966 International Covenant on Economic, Social and Cultural Rights (ICESCR). The provisions in these instruments obligate countries to ensure human rights in all aspects of state activity, including business and labour practices, as well as the physical and sociopolitical environment. However, in recent years the situation has become increasingly fraught and complex. MNCs exert enormous global power through the sheer scale of their operations. Some have budgets greater than the Gross Domestic Products (GDPs) of smaller countries, making them the most influential actors in the global economic system and allowing them to shape its governing rules. The economic might of MNCs has the potential to bring substantial benefits to the countries they invest in, including reductions in poverty, and progress towards sustainable practices, efficient production methods, and modern technologies. Their operations may also demand the host country to enforce more rigorously the rule of law and human rights.

However, their vast power to promote sustainability and human rights also means that these powerful corporation can seriously undermine both goals. This negative impact can occur directly and indirectly through their operations in the supply chain including subsidiaries, contractors, and resource extractors. Furthermore, by definition, the operations and influence of MNCs extends across multiple jurisdictions, whereas human rights law has developed assuming single states as individual entities bound by treaties and conventions – indeed, at the time of the 1948 UDHR, MNCs were non-existent. For the same reason, and as alluded to above, MNCs cannot be considered to have the same duties as states, as they typically do not perform public functions or have a public purpose. MNCs are not 'subjects' or 'persons' in public international law. This makes the legal enforcement of their compliance with human rights norms extremely complex and difficult, raising concerns about their ability to evade jurisdiction and violate human rights and sustainability with impunity. This chapter examines examples of MNCs' human rights violations occuring as a result of their FDI activities and influence. This is followed by an analysis of MNCs' responsibilities regarding human rights protection in their FDI activity.

2 Instances of Human Rights Violations by MNCs Involved in FDI Arrangements

There has been significant debate regarding how FDI influences human rights, and it has become a polarising topic with some advocating for human rights and others supporting the free market. Human rights abuses should be unacceptable to both these camps; not restricted to rights advocates. FDI arrangements, especially in the primary industries like mining or timber extraction, have often been associated with serious human rights neglect or direct violations, as well as environmental destruction. The mutual antagonism between rights activists and MNCs involved in FDI is wholly justified when those MNCs exploit foreign countries' lax enforcement human rights protection. In primary industries, just the physical environmental effects of MNC malpractice can have an enormous effect on local people's human rights and overall quality of life – pollution of water, air, and land, as well as the complete loss of land.

Furthermore, FDI arrangements where the chief component of an MNC's operations is human labour, often has involved the deliberate choice of a country for its poor enforcement of the human rights to a liveable wage and safe working environment. Seeking the cheapest labour of the same quality for production is not anything more than sound business practice. When it becomes more than that, ethically, is when that choice of a labour force is done in full knowledge of inhumane working conditions. It is inevitably the poor and who are most vulnerable to exploitation as they have the greatest need for income and very little bargaining power or means to take legal action for human rights violations by foreign MNCs or their own governments. Thus, those living in extreme poverty in developing countries are particularly vulnerable to being used as inexpensive labour by international corporations, and multinational/transnational corporations that operate in their home countries frequently take advantage of such groups. Furthermore, developing countries may have weak institutional structures that are unable to enforce regulations or the treaty obligations they have agreed to abide by. They may also deliberately not enforce international labour law to attract much needed FDI from MNCs. Several multinational companies worldwide are known for violating human rights. The nature of violation of human rights by these corporations are given below.

2.1 *Nestle*

In the 1970s, Nestle, a major MNC, launched an infant formula specifically aimed at 'developing countries'. This was the first time Nestle faced accusations of violating human rights. In these countries, the infant formula was advertised as a supplementary food that was to be given in addition to breast milk. Because of the compelling advertisements developed by Nestle, mothers thought that they needed to give the formula to their children. Nestle also failed to advice/notify consumers through appropriate labelling that its baby formula is not a substitute for breast feeding. The issue, however, was that in African countries, the key markets of Nestle, the clean water that was required for mixing the formula was lacking. Since the mothers in these countries were not well-educated, they mixed the formula with unclean water, which created serious health problems for the babies who drank the formula, with a few deaths also reported. According to some reports, the company was aware of the lack of literacy and inadequate clean water in African countries. However, it did not take any suitable measures as it did not want to lose its market share and profits. Thus, Nestle violated the right to life, particularly healthy life.

2.2 *Texaco*

MNCs in Ecuador also committed human rights violations. In 1967, Texaco, a US oil company, discovered oil in the Oriente region in Ecuador. Its extraction created substantial pollution, causing significant damage to the environment and human rights violations. The oil waste was disposed of in earthen pits; practices that were unacceptable in developed countries. Consequently, the company was involved in what led to the 'Amazon Chernobyl'. Oriente's citizens have been striving for decades to seek compensation for the widespread oil pollution and significant contamination caused by Texaco, in addition to appalling human rights violations.

On behalf of the region's 30,000 citizens, 76 Oriente residents filed a class action lawsuit against Texaco in the New York federal court in 1993. This followed the 1789 Alien Tort Claims Act (ATCA), which gives foreign nationals the right to file a lawsuit in US courts for offences violating the 'law of nations or a treaty of the United States'. Texaco argued that because almost all evidence was in Ecuador, the US was an inconvenient jurisdiction; hence the case should be dismissed. After years of legal battles, and Texaco's acquisition of Texaco in 2001, an appellate court dismissed the case in 2002, requiring Chevron to adhere to the verdict of Ecuador's judiciary.

The plaintiffs refiled the case in Ecuador in 2003. In February 2011, the Ecuador court passed a USD 8.6 billion judgment against Chevron. However, two weeks before the unparalleled judgment, Chevron filed a lawsuit under the 1970 Racketeer Influenced and Corrupt Organisation (RICO) Act against all plaintiffs and their lawyers in the New York federal court. The lawsuit contended that the proceedings were initiated to extract money from Chevron.

The New York judge forbade the plaintiffs from enforcing any verdict against Chevron in any court worldwide, even before the RICO case hearing. However, following an appeal that he exceeded his authority, the judgement was reversed. He later asserted in 2014 that the Ecuador court passed its judgment fraudulently. He instructed the plaintiffs' lawyers to hand over the money received through enforcement in other countries to Chevron, while forbidding the enforcement of Ecuador's judgment in the US. No compensation for the damage caused by Chevron to their environment has been received by the victims of the pollution in Ecuador, even after several years of litigation against the human rights violators. Nevertheless, the case illustrates that TNCs can be held liable in their home countries for their social and environmental actions in developing countries.

2.3 *Barrick Gold*

Allegations of human rights violations were also made against companies in the mining sector. Private security personnel of Barrick Gold, a Canadian company and the world's biggest gold producer, employed at gold mines in Papua New Guinea, were accused by the Human Rights Watch in February 2011 of being involved in ruthless gang rapes. Human Rights Watch, in its report titled 'Gold's Costly Dividend: Human Rights Impacts of Papua New Guinea's Porgera Gold Mine', recognised that the company was unsuccessful in determining the risk of human rights abuses and making appropriate responses when these risks occurred. Canada's failure to oversee company activities in foreign countries is also highlighted in the report, particularly in extraction activities. In addition, the report calls on Barrick Gold and other firms to exhibit increased transparency and corporate social responsibility when dealing with significant environmental and health issues. The Papua New Guinea government declared during the COVID-19 pandemic in April 2020 that the Porgera mining lease managed by Barrick Gold and a Chinese joint venture partner Zijin Mining would not be extended. Around 10% of the country's overall exports are composed of the mine's output. Local communities have made complaints regarding human rights and environmental violations at the mine, with the government also being dissatisfied with the mine operators due to their lack of compensation. According to Barrick, if the lease was terminated, it would lead to nationalisation. The local community members would claim that they did not receive adequate human rights due process from the lease operators before its termination.

2.4 *Bhopal Gas Leak*

In the 1970s, the Indian government introduced policies encouraging foreign companies to invest in local industry. To manufacture Sevin, a commonly used pesticide, Union Carbide Corporation (UCC) was tasked with developing a plant. The Indian government wanted local stakeholders to have a major percentage of the investment, while it held a 22% share in Union Carbide India Limited (UCIL), the company's subsidiary. Due to its central location and access to transport facilities, the plant was constructed in Bhopal. Located in the light industrial and commercial use zone, the plant was initially approved to produce pesticides from limited amounts of component chemicals. However, competitive pressures meant UCIL started implementing backward integration, producing raw materials and intermediate products to make the final product in the same facility. This process was more complex and hazardous.

The demand for pesticides decreased in 1984; consequently, the plant was operating at 25% of capacity. In the 1980s, the subcontinent suffered crop failures and famine. Because of declining profitability, local managers were instructed in July 1984 to sell the plant. Although the facility kept running, the local government did not impose stringent industrial safety and pollution control regulations because of the adverse economic effects of losing such a significant employer.

On 2 December 1984, at 11:00 pm, the plant operator noticed a minor leakage of methyl isocyanate (MIC) gas and increased pressure in the storage tank. Three weeks earlier, the vent-gas scrubber, a safety device that neutralised toxic discharge from the MIC system, was turned off. One ton of water used to clean internal pipes became mixed with forty tons of MIC due to a damaged valve. The pressure and heat increased due to the rigorous exothermic reaction. Subsequently, a safety valve burst, releasing MIC gas into the air at around 1.00 AM on 3 December.

The leak substantially impacted human rights of the local population, and within three days, almost 7,000 to 10,000 people had died and over 570,000 people were exposed to destructive levels of toxic gas. The leak also had a long-term inter-generational effect, causing ongoing health issues. It also exacerbated existing poverty and marginalisation. In 1989, the Supreme Court of India accepted a compensation package agreed by the Government of India and UCC. However, this package was viewed as inadequate because the affected communities were not involved in its negotiation, and health and environmental effects were not appropriately measured. UCC refused to come to India to face criminal charges of 'culpable homicide not amounting to murder'. Although the Dow Chemical Company bought UCC in 2001, it cannot force UCC to face these charges. The Bhopal courts have summoned Dow six times to appear and explain UCC's absence. Each has been completely ignored.

2.5 *Phulbari Coal Project*

In 1994, the Bangladesh government awarded an Australian mining firm, Broken Hill Proprietary Company (BHP), an exploration license for the Phulbari open-pit coal mine project. BHP discovered coal whilst drilling in the region from 1994 to 1997. In 1998, BHP handed over its exploration license to Asia Energy, a wholly owned subsidiary of London-based Global Coal Management Resources (GCM). The Bangladesh Department of Environment granted the project environmental clearance on 11 September 2005, but the government had not yet provided final approval.

The impact on local populations has meant that approximately 50,000 people may have been displaced and resettled, while 220,000 may have been gradually displaced. Analysing the company's draft resettlement plan, the International Accountability Project (IAP) deduced that the number of individuals projected to be displaced was highly understated. Around 50,000 indigenous people may also be evicted. Moreover, almost 4,900 hectares of the country's most fertile agricultural land in the Dinajpur district, Bangladesh's rice bowl, faces destruction. The project has also been criticised for the environmental effects impacting public health.

On 26 August 2006, 50,000 people, including local farmers, day labourers, and aboriginal community members, marched against the Phulbari coal project. Bangladesh Rifles, the paramilitary organisation, killed three protestors and wounded at least a hundred.

In February 2011, nearly 2,000 protestors blocked a highway to compel the government to cancel its agreement with Asia Energy. The protests continued till May 2011, receiving support from 80 international organisations and London Mining Network and UN independent human rights specialists, who asked the government not to commence open-pit mining operations.

On 6 February 2014, Prime Minister Sheikh Hasina declared that coal extraction would be left to "future technology since the foremost priority is to protect the food and land of the farmers". After nearly eight years of protests, the people of Phulbari had finally prevented open-pit coal mining in the region.

The struggle, however, is far from over. Climate, anti-coal, and human rights activists in London joined protestors in Bangladesh in December 2016 outside the annual general shareholders meeting of GCM Resources, demanding the company be shut down. The company continues to violate the human rights of indigenous peoples, local businessmen, and farmers in Phulbari. Although the government subsequently withdrew its mining licence, GCM Resources continues to sell shares in London to raise funds for the Phulbari project. GlobalData monitors over 170,000 power plants worldwide and they report that the project is now at the permitting stage.

3 The Responsibility of MNCs for Human Rights in Their FDI Operations

When businesses abuse and ignore human rights in their operational activities, this can be highly detrimental for their workers, customers, and the community as a whole. Instances in which significant human rights violations occur include when businesses do not pay their workers in a timely manner or deaths potentially resulting from the lack of compliance with appropriate safety standards. However, MNCs and other large businesses may see the state as having the sole responsibility to maintain its citizens' human rights and use the fact that international rights law has typically been concerned with the state-citizen relationship, to their advantage. MNCs have now become so large and powerful that it is essential that human rights are now integrated into their daily operations, culture, and organisational policies. Moreover, it is possible to achieve this without significant costs being incurred or major obstacles being encountered. The assumption that protecting human rights and achieving good business performance are mutually exclusive is no longer tenable.

The Special Representative of the Secretary-General for Business and Human Rights, John Ruggie, formulated the Guiding Principles on Business and Human Rights: Implementing the United Nations "Protect, Respect and Remedy" Framework (UNGPs), which were published by the UN in 2011. The guidelines set out the respective duties and responsibilities of governments and businesses to respect, protect and, if necessary, remedy abuses of human rights. However, as the title of the framework makes clear, these are not legally enforceable duties and responsibilities, but recommended standards that (it is hoped) both governments and economic enterprises including corporations will adopt voluntarily, the implication being that it is in their interests to do so. The UNGPs are universal in that they apply to all sovereign states and all economic institutions. They were framed in recognition of states' duty to protect the rights, freedoms, welfares of their citizens and the responsibility that business enterprises have, as key societal actors, to ensure that their business activity is conducted in compliance with all applicable laws and also respects human rights. A final point of recognition in the guidelines is that such rights and obligations must have the backing of an effective mechanism for remedial action in the event of violations.

The traditional idea is that only states are accountable for violations of human rights. States are the bearers of duties to protect the rights and freedoms of their citizens. A further character of human rights is that they are largely framed as rights of individuals, not of groups, and were designed to confer protection to individuals from government actions. As the representative of the public will, in democracies it is governments that are the rights observers of the human rights of its population (the rights holders).

Globalisation has had tremendous ramifications for human rights and the legal frameworks designed to protect them. The governments of states are in a much weaker position to ensure the human rights of its citizens in the wake of giant MNCs whose operations are often distributed across a network of different states, each with its own, often significantly different, legal framework. The weak ability and frequently weak willingness to protect human rights when confronted by corporate power makes it all the more important that pressure be put on governments to fulfil that duty of protection. Of course, the economic benefits that MNCs and TNCs bring to countries also place their governments in weak positions as rights protectors – to some extent they have their hands tied by the threat of losing the much-needed FDI whose economic benefits help ensure their public support. There is also, however, the fact that the operations of MNCs and TNCs play out in a globalised arena where the dominant ideology is of the free market, in which business entities compete on (supposedly) equal terms according to a minimalist set of rules. The free-market ideology pushes for deregularisation on the grounds that the freer market operations are, the better the equilibration of supply and demand, the more accurate the price mechanism, and so forth under Adam Smith's 'imperceptible' guidance.

The pressure to have less regulation in international trade makes human rights more vulnerable to abuses by large MNCs and TNCs. Corporations whose operations encompass many countries will naturally distribute those operations in a way that maximises profits. This also means they may exploit the lax human rights protection or sustainability policies of some countries, and typically it is in developing countries where the safeguarding structures for human rights are at their most vulnerable. Developing countries' weak institutional frameworks and legal systems, or corruption and political instability, contribute to these vulnerabilities. Thus, while large corporations may not alone be directly responsible for human rights abuses in countries with corrupt or volatile political systems/institutions, many people question the ethics of their operating in such countries, or worse, of their taking advantage of and being complicit in a country's inadequate protection of workers' rights to acceptable working conditions and/or, for instance, the protection of children from being exploited as cheap labour.

Corporate complicity in human rights violations can occur in several ways and Florian Wettstein defines four types: direct, indirect, beneficial, and silent complicity. Direct complicity takes place when a corporation may assist the perpetrator of a rights abuse financially (when the corporation is knowingly funding a violation of human rights), logistically (granting use of corporation facilities/infrastructure that a perpetrator can use for abusive practices, e.g., confinement and torture of protestors, dissidents, union members), and politically (by aiding in the manipulation of elections etc., or by supplying armaments or military technology, including digital technology for 'monitoring' the activities of citizens). Indirect complicity refers to corporations effectively supporting (financially or otherwise) a corrupt regime. It might occur, for example, when corporations help construct and/or maintain a rights-abusive regime's commercial infrastructure.

To hold a corporation accountable for complicity, it does not have to be involved directly or indirectly in a specific wrongdoing; it may be enough that the corporation consciously benefits from the violations of human rights done by a third party. Hence, the difference between a legal and moral issue emerges. Though making a legal argument for beneficial complicity may be difficult if the corporation does not make some real contribution to the abuses of human rights, it is definitely a sufficient basis on which to attribute moral blame. Silent complicity refers to corporations knowingly ignoring or 'turning a blind eye to' rights violations so they can continue their operations, and thus is a moral omission – doing nothing despite knowing about the rights violations of a regime, and taking no actions to protect or support the victims, or not criticising, or in other ways influencing, the regime to stop committing such violations. It is, therefore, the corporate equivalent of Edmund Burke's oft quoted "The only thing necessary for the triumph of evil is for good men to do nothing". In this sense, a corporation's inaction, its failure to speak out, is effectively acquiescence in, if not actually moral support for, a regime's ill doings. Such acts of omission by corporations can be seen to legitimise the perpetrators of human rights violations.

These different ways in which corporations may affect the human rights of citizens resident in the countries where they operate makes it important to establish the obligations they must support the protection of these rights.

3.1 *The Theoretical Grounds for Corporate Human Rights Obligations*

It is no longer possible for MNCs to purely focus on making profits, as advocated by economists such as Milton Friedman, who claimed that corporations are ultimately responsible for generating profits only. They have a responsibility to ensure shareholders' financial interests are prioritised for the benefit of all stakeholders, including their workers, indigenous communities, customers, and all those impacted by their business operations. The idea of the state as sole responsibility conception of human rights protection is an outdated model, one that is inadequate at addressing the power structures of a globalised world. Large corporations are now the most significant economic actors worldwide and thus exert the greatest impact on the social and physical environment. The people MNCs affect are not neatly contained within delineated state boundaries. Rather, they are widely dispersed across the globe through their cross-border operations.

With such power comes an equally great responsibility to respect human rights. The subsequent sections (3.1.1–3.1.3) explore the bounded freedom of MNCs from a theoretical stance. This includes the theoretical grounds for human rights obligations for corporations, including those based on utilitarian and deontological ethical principles, as well as those based on social contract theory.

3.1.1 The Utilitarian Perspective in Relation to Human Rights Obligations for Corporations

3.1.1.1 *The Concept of Utilitarian*

Utilitarianism, a species of consequentialism, saw relatively recent formulations in the Enlightenment philosophers Jeremy Bentham and John Stuart Mill, who proposed that actions are deemed good or bad in virtue of their effects on people's happiness and unhappiness. Thus, action X is considered morally good if it has an overall positive effect on the total level of happiness in a population, society, or other such relevant community, and where the total level of happiness is nothing more than some quantitative calculation of good effects minus bad effects.

While any precise calculation of utility may be impossible to achieve, and valuations of different goods and different sufferings equally impossible to make, the general idea that the welfare of all humanity is what should count in judgements of action or policies is hard to criticise.

3.1.1.2 *Utilitarian Grounds for Human Rights Obligations for Corporations*

Large corporations effectively run modern societies and their economies. Utilitarianism provides a useful framework with which to address the issue of corporate social and environmental responsibility as it frames responsibility in terms that make sense for entities that have as much influence on human happiness (or the lack of it) as they do on financial indicators like GDP. From a utilitarian perspective, the question large corporations should ask themselves, and that governance structures should ask of them, is what contribution to human happiness/welfare do they make to the societies in which they operate? That MNCs have such wide-ranging impacts effectively makes the entire society, even the entire global population when considering the largest corporations, stakeholders. Furthermore, it is no longer feasible to distinguish effects on the physical environment from effects on the social environment. Global warming, droughts, flooding, pollution, deforestation, and myriad other negative physical environmental effects of human activity have concomitant social, psychological, and political impacts that directly relate to human happiness and suffering.

The enormous power wielded by large corporations can be used to benefit humankind as much as diminish it, which, from a utilitarian perspective, implies that power confers on them the responsibility to act in a way that maximises human wellbeing and minimises human suffering. There is, however, an important difference between the utilitarian consequentialist approach to the moral worth of actions and the philosophy underlying the free market and classical economic liberalism. Classical liberalism as, espoused, for instance, by F. A. Hayek, has a fundamentally different and non-consequentialist conception of the moral status of actions of economic entities. The liberal view argues that only individual rules governing economic activity should be considered when determining whether the system is fair or just; the outcome cannot be planned for or judged as either just or unjust. This perspective emphasises the importance of adherence to established rules and processes over the consideration of outcomes. However, as with the UDHR, these ideas were formed before globalisation and before MNCs had emerged as dominant economic entities. In many ways, they are not applicable to the modern world, where economic activity exerts such a dramatic impact and cannot be ignored when determining the moral status of economic actors' actions.

In contrast, the utilitarian consequentialist approach to corporate responsibility suggests that the moral worth of actions should be judged by their outcomes, specifically in terms of their impact on human happiness and welfare. Such a position is posited by David Birchall in his analysis of corporate power and its impact on human rights. He argues that corporate power makes it necessary for corporations to assume consequentialist responsibilities. Their far reaching power has the potential to directly impact and affect three areas upon which those rights depend: materialities (i.e., the physical resources without which an individual's rights cannot be realised, such as water, food, shelter etc.), knowledge (including knowledge about the rights people are entitled to), and institutions. If businesses are not responsible for their effects on these areas as well as on individuals, they become unaccountable. Embracing a consequentialist approach to corporate responsibility enables a comprehensive undertaking of their operational impacts on human rights and facilitates the establishment of corrective measures to address rights violations. Birchall argues this approach is necessary because MNCs frequently evade their true responsibilities by skillfully framing their actions to comply with national or international human rights law without violating. While these actions may be legally non-violative, they can nonetheless drastically affect individuals' abilities to realise their rights.

In non-legal language, MNCs adhere to the letter of the law but not to its spirit, exploiting technicalities to avoid accountability. These ostensibly non-violative actions, while compliant with legal norms, can profoundly affect human rights by their consequences on the environment (e.g., effects on food and water quality and supply), information accuracy and availability regarding production methods and environmental impacts etc, and subtle yet pervasive influence institutions of governance. An example of this is lobbying, through which large corporations, like Big Pharma corporations in the US, wield enormous influence over government policies, often leading to widespread suffering (e.g., the artificially high costs of some medicines, or the over-prescription of addictive drugs). The silent obfuscation of information about corporate consequentialist effects results in many victims being unable to realise their fundamental rights and to seek redress or compensation because the loss of their 'effective' rights has been brought about through the cumulative effects of corporate actions, each of which is, in isolation, legitimate. This lack of consequentialist accountability for powerful corporate entities frequently undermines human rights, particularly socio-economic rights, while legal recourse is seldom appalling living conditions, hunger, and other consequences of poverty.

This discussion illustrates the need for a shift in how corporate responsibilities are viewed and managed in the modern, globalised world. This underscores the centrality of the utilitarian perspective in understanding the relationship between corporate responsibility and human rights.

3.1.2 Deontology

3.1.2.1 *The Concept of Deontology*

Deontology, derives from the Greek 'deon,' meaning duty or what is right, and 'logos' meaning science, is a branch of ethics that ascribe 'rightness' or 'wrongness' to an action based on the action itself, rather than its consequences. Deontological theories necessitates the existence of principles for determining what is a right or wrong action, leading philosophers in this realm to engage in intellectual acrobatics to justify their particular idea of what is, intrinsically, right or wrong. The best known candidate for this is Kant's notion of the "categorical imperative", advocating for the performance of acts which are not self-contradictory and accepted as universal duties for all to follow. However, it falls short in scenarios like that of a homicidal individual seeking their own demise, while it fails to provide a coherent moral guidelines. Deontological ethics, due to their reliance absolutist conception of good and evil, often exhibit rigidity, sometimes deeming an act as wrong when common sense or utilitarian principles suggest otherwise. Historically, deontological ethics derived moral status of an act was from sources like religion, either via doctrine, divine revelation, or an appeal to conscience, where having such a conscience was attributed to God. More modern iterations of the deontological approach would appeal to customary moral norms, although this replaces the absolutist stance with a democratic notion of intrinsic moral value.

Deontological theories are, therefore, the opposite of utilitarian ones as the act itself is the bearer of moral status, not its consequences. For instance, murder is always wrong, even it means saving innumerable lives. The deontological position does, however, highlight some of the shortcomings of consequentialism, particularly the impossibility of fully predicting the consequences of an action, thus complicating the calculation of moral status. The utilitarian would simply reply that you can, nonetheless, establish a reasonable idea of those consequences, and use past instances of similar acts to form an approximation. The latter rejoinder could also be used in utilitarian accounts that take sufficiently sophisticated approaches to estimating consequences, in which the effect of committing an act normatively considered intrinsically evil, actually has substantial psychological consequences both for individuals and communities.

Universal obligations, based on the well-known form of deontology advanced in Kant's idea of perfect obligation, can be considered deontological. Laws, which form the basis of legal systems, cannot rely solely on predicting the future consequences of an action. Instead, they must define certain actions as intrinsically impermissible or subject to specific constraints, as the legal system operates after actions are taken.

3.1.2.2 *Deontological Grounds for Human Rights Obligations for Corporations*

In the context of business/economic human rights, deontological approaches often inform codes of conduct, such as those in multi-stakeholder initiatives where businesses are bound to act in the value chain according to a set of rules that prohibit certain practices such as child labour or setting minimum wage standards or scheduled breaks during working hours.

The UNGPs also distinguish between perfect duties from imperfect duties, and their corollaries, perfect and imperfect rights. Perfect rights are those that cannot be violated under any circumstances and always necessitate redress, whereas imperfect rights are those which should not be violated except when doing so prevents the violation of other rights. The UNGPs implicitly contrast the obligations of states and businesses as if the former had the perfect duty to protect human rights and the latter the imperfect duty, or responsibility, to respect them. Wielding the power to enforce the law, states are obligated to ensure their legal systems can effectively protect human rights. This is part of the ratification process of treaties and conventions, where a state that agrees in principle to the provisions of a treaty or convention is given time to put into effect the necessary laws to realise those provisions for their citizens. However, business responsibilities with regard to human rights are often more voluntary, much like the notion of 'best practice', and usually only 'required' to take reasonable steps towards human rights protection.

The question of whether corporations possess moral agency at all is one that arises frequently in debates concerning businesses and human rights.

Because human rights have typically been considered individual rights, it can be argued that it is only the (or some of the) individuals who own or part-own a business can be accountable for human rights violations.

Michael Phillips argues that before one can understand whether a corporation has moral agency, one must first understand what exactly a corporation is. He highlights three conceptions of corporations: concession theory, aggregate theory, and real entity theory. The legal definition of a corporation comes from concession theory, in which it is defined as a purely legal entity. As John Marshall explained in 1819, a corporation derives all attributes from the law as it is the law to which it owes its existence.

The aggregate theory presents a more practical conception on corporations, viewing them as the sum of their constituent human parts. While shareholders often receive considerable attention, aggregate theory recognises all individuals within the corporation, especially those in positions of corporate power (directors, board members etc.) as they make decisions on behalf of shareholders. However, the substantial power wielded by large corporations is often instrumentalised through non-human structures and financial arrangements, contracts, and such like; hence, aggregate theories of the firm incorporate those elements into the definition of a corporation. Despite this, accountability for misconduct typically falls on the individuals that collectively comprise a corporation, as they are ultimately assumed under the theory to be responsible for corporate misconduct.

The question of the moral agency of a corporation is pivotal in human rights discourse, because when the rights of an individual are violated, a moral agent must be responsible for that violation. The real entity theory considers corporations to be more than merely artificial creations of a legal system and to have the same or greater autonomy than the sum of individual constituents. However, there is little agreement amongst theorists concerning whether and to what extent corporations have moral agency, with some, such as Peter French, considering them equivalent to human beings and having corresponding moral agency. Others, like Tom Donaldson, attribute responsibilities to corporations while reserving actual rights solely for their human constituents. He endeavours to understand what confers moral agency upon an entity. He does not believe that a corporation's status as a legal person automatically means it is a moral person, given their inherent differences from individuals. Nonetheless, he argues that corporations, under certain circumstances, can be regarded as moral agents and sets out two criteria for such an ascription. First, they should be capable of making decisions based on moral reasonings. Second, their decisions should have the capacity to control their actions, including the ability to modify actions that directly change their own structure.

The first condition is equivalent in human beings to the notion of free will, suggesting they are not deterministic systems driven by solely physical laws (i.e. automata). Thus, even though they are not persons, corporations can and do make decisions for reasons that they can choose, and hence, they have the capacity to choose moral ones. The second condition is essential for corporations to maintain their ability to make decisions according to moral reasons and to alter their decision-making structure if necessary. Corporations that meet the condition two cannot therefore be considered incapable of moral agency due to structural restraints, contrary to Werhane's view. Importantly, one of the criticisms Donaldson levels at structural restraint arguments against moral agency is that they assume all corporations are the same and that they lack the power to change their decision-making process to enable moral decision making. He questions the validity of such a claim and concludes that corporations do have, or at least can be changed to have, moral agency.

To ascribe obligations to corporations is to simultaneously ascribe them corresponding rights. This is the basis for the notion of corporate rights, but these, as David Ozar points out, are conventional rights and cannot be considered moral rights. Consequently, the UNGPs are somewhat ambivalent about a corporation's moral agency, sometimes framing corporations as having responsibilities and obligations, with language includes terms like 'ought' and 'should'; at other times, emphasising they are only 'expected' to act in a human right respecting way – a social expectation. The debate reflects differing views on where accountability for corporate misconduct should be placed, and underscores in the challenge of understanding emergent properties in complex systems, analogous to ongoing philosophical debates about artificial intelligence and consciousness. The question is whether a corporation has a separate and unique autonomy; that it has the ability to act by itself. In contrast to French, Werhane argues that they only have what she terms 'secondary' moral agency and cannot act independent of their human members. Nonetheless, she considers them to have sufficient autonomy to have obligations and therefore rights, but these are not equivalent to human inalienable rights.

Differing views also arise between ontological individualists and ontological collectivists. The former regard corporations mere aggregates of individual members, viewing the corporation as an abstract noun referring to a common property of that collection of individuals. Collectivists, conversely, believe there is a distinct entity that emerges from the collection of individuals that can only be understood at that level. Collectivists argue that corporations have an identity as a whole, one that can be said to have intentionality. Furthermore, from the collectivist perspective, the corporation has a will that is not reducible to individual members.

In response to the collectivist assertion that corporations have a separate will that is distinct from any or all the individuals who comprise it, Werhane argues that corporations are eliminable entities, whereas human beings are not. Consequently, any autonomy we ascribe to corporations is vicarious and depends crucially on their constituent members. The corporation cannot act without that action being causally linked to the individual actions of its constituents. Werhane contends that this secondary nature of Werhane's ascription of corporate agency justifies ascribing responsibility to corporations, which cannot necessarily be apportioned to a particular quantitative distribution of individual responsibilities among its constituents. Thus, corporations function as secondary actors, dependent on constituents' actions, and secondary moral agents, contingent on the moral decisions made by constituents. Werhane uses the idea of secondary moral agency as the ground for the UNGPs' assertion that corporations have a responsibility to respect human rights and to minimise the detrimental impact of their activities on such rights. Despite their moral force, she argues, these responsibilities, although their scope is global, are nonetheless voluntary, making the reciprocal rights of corporations similarly less extensive than human rights.

3.1.3 Social Contract Theory

3.1.3.1 *The Concept of Social Contract Theory*

The social contract theory concerns the basis of human societies, positing that peaceful coexistence hinges on mutual cooperation among members of a society. Within this framework, every member of society enters into an implicit contract with others, making belonging to a society a form of rational self-interest in which individuals agree to behave according to a code of conduct in exchange for reciprocal treatment. Social contract theory aims to account for the duties citizens have to respect the rights of others and obey governance structures by seeing this as a voluntary agreement between citizen and state. Individuals forfeit their absolute freedom in exchange for the protection of their partial or qualified freedoms when they agree to be bound by the rules of society. The roots of social contract theory traces back to ancient Greece, notably evidenced in Plato's Crito, where Socrates elucidates the concept by willingly accepting his fate in adherence to Athenian law, underscoring the reciprocal obligations inherent in the social contract.

3.1.3.2 *Social Contract Grounds for Human Rights Obligations for Corporations*

As noted earlier, some modern MNCs have greater financial power than many small states, which has led some political theorists like Thomas Donaldson to apply social contract theory to the relationship between the state, its citizens, and corporations, and derive the latter's moral obligations to society from this relationship. Given their substantial societal influence and wide-ranging social and environmental impacts, corporations are deemed to have a responsibility to society because, at least implicitly, members of society have agreed to let them conduct their operations in exchange for the economic benefits they bring. Donaldson views the relationship between corporations and societies as a form of social contract, which forms the basis for their moral obligations. In terms of the social contract, he grounds corporations' moral status on their being productive organisations that serve the welfare of the society.

The UNGPs similarly refer to corporations as 'specialized organs of society with specialized functions which are required to comply with all applicable laws and to respect human rights' (emphasis added). The societal benefits derived from corporations stem from their specialisation, enabling them to produce better goods at more affordable prices than individuals alone. However, the justification for corporations' existence under this social contract framework hinges on their continued benefit to society, necessitating an evaluation of both their contributions and detriments, including their impact on human rights and the environment. In response to critics of such an account, who might agree with Milton Friedman's claim that the only social responsibility corporations have is to their stockholders and to maximise profits, Donaldson responds by arguing that even if the social contract is not itself a right, it may override certain rights.

Donaldson acknowledges that rights are seldom absolute and often conflict, and the right of corporate managers to enter voluntary agreements with stockholders (to maximise profits) does not override employees' rights to safe working conditions. He further contends that nor does the social contract not being a right prevent the benefit of the society from trumping individual rights to property if those properties present a hazard to the public or are essential to connect an isolated community. Similarly, as Miguel Juan Tobaoda Calatayud, Jesus Campo Candelas and Patricia Perez Fernandez argue, one would be hard-pressed to demand that a corporation always respect rights such as free speech within its premises, may not always be feasible or applicable to the same extant as that of a nation-state. Thus, there are no absolutes in these discussions, nor any definitive principle that can determine the rights and obligations of corporations and their stakeholders. Like the evolution of most laws, those governing corporations will change as social norms and understanding changes –slowly.

3.2 *International Soft Law Framework for Multinational Corporations (MNCs)*

As remarked upon earlier, many violations of human rights occurred because of the liberalisation of international trade rules coupled with the growth of developing countries' FDI and the growing power and influence of MNCs. Such violations led to several frameworks being proposed by international organisations, such as the OECD, the UN, and even the World Bank, in order to establish guidelines, principles, and codes of conduct that incorporated MNCs' and TNCs' responsibilities towards human rights. As a developing corpus of quasi-legal instruments and best practice guidelines it became known as the international 'soft-law' framework. Soft-laws are non-binding international guidelines. The publication in 1976 of the OECD Guidelines for Multinational Enterprises represented the first concerted effort to establish a coherent and applicable set of guidelines relating to large corporations. Revised in 2000, these guidelines are still considered the standard reference and most widely used instrument for understanding MNCs' human rights and socioenvironmental obligations. The guidelines refer to MNCs human rights obligations throughout the document, including, inter alia, the right of workers to a safe environment and to form and join trade unions. They also state that MNCs should respect the rights of everyone affected by their operations in a manner consistent with the host county's international obligations.

A notable advance of the soft-law framework, particularly with regard to labour rights, was made by the International Labour Organization (ILO) in their Tripartite Declaration of Principles concerning Multinational Enterprises and Social Policy (MNE Declaration) as well as the Core Conventions. Article 8 of the Tripartite declaration asserts that corporations be required to respect the UDHR and the corresponding international covenants. Similar proclamations for corporations to respect human rights were made by the UN in the Code of Conduct on Transnational Corporations. The first Draft Code of Conduct was issued in 1978 and successive drafts were produced in 1983, 1988 and 1990. The Draft Code of Conduct was never implemented. The reasons for the failure of the UN's code of conduct for TNCs was partly because of opposition from Western state governments and businesses themselves. These failed attempts at regulating TNCs' operations led the UN to form a working group to address the growing incidence of human rights violations.

An alternative approach to the soft-law framework, also proposed by the UN, was the Global Compact Principles, 2005 which corporations could sign up to voluntarily. The Compact comprised ten principles, the first two of which stated that corporations should respect internationally agreed human rights and ensure they are not complicit in their violation, while the other eight principles relate to labour rights. To date, several thousand TNCs have agreed to and signed the compact, including those with high international profiles.

The first attempt to draft a common global framework for understanding the responsibilities of business enterprises with regard to human rights happened in 2003 with the UN's publication of Norms on the Responsibilities of Transnational Corporations and Other Business Enterprises with regard to Human Rights. The Norms first emphasise that states have the primary responsibility for human rights, but that TNCs, MNCs, and other business enterprises also have human rights obligations within their spheres of activity and influence. The human rights obligations for which transitional corporations have direct responsibility are then delineated, including equal opportunity and non-discriminatory treatment, security of persons, workers' rights, the prohibition of corruption, and obligations with regard to environmental protection. There is also a general obligation on TNCs to respect and contribute to the realisation of civil, cultural, economic, political, and social rights, with several of these rights given particular importance. The Norms then set out how they should be implemented, which includes TNCs having the responsibility to disseminate the information, create internal rules that comply with the Norms, the application of the Norms in contracts with third parties, provisions for monitoring the Norms and for requesting states to establish legal and administrative frameworks to ensure the Norms are implemented, and a requirement that TNCs and other business enterprises shall provide prompt, effective, and adequate compensation to those affected by violations of the Norms.

The 2003 Norms on the Responsibilities of Transnational Corporations and Other Business Enterprises with Regard to Human Rights set forth the legal responsibilities TNCs should have to respect human rights in all areas their activity has affected or influenced, only to have it rejected by the UN Commission on Human Rights. It was these setbacks that led the UN to ask John Ruggie to remedy the flaws in earlier attempts to formulate an applicable set of norms to impose on corporations in respect of human rights, and which finally resulted in the UNGPs, 2011, which contain three chapters, or pillars: protect, respect and remedy. Each defines concrete, actionable steps for governments and companies to meet their respective duties and responsibilities to prevent human rights abuses in company operations and provide remedies if such abuses take place.

3.2.1 The State Duty to Protect

Under international law, states have the duty to protect their citizens against human rights abuses regardless of who perpetrates them – that is a key component of the social contract and in most countries is written into their constitutions. The UNGPs remind the reader of the state's obligations to prevent, investigate, punish, and redress human rights abuses that occur due to corporate activity. They also set clear expectations that resident companies respect human rights in every country and context in which they operate.

3.2.2 The Corporate Responsibility to Respect

The UNGPs clearly state that businesses have the responsibility to prevent, mitigate and, where appropriate, remedy human rights abuses to which they contribute. This responsibility extends to all subsidiaries, partners, and suppliers, as well as any other party involved in a business's operations. The rights that business enterprises have a responsibility to respect are those declared in the International Bill of Human Rights and the International Labour Organization Declaration on Fundamental Principles and Rights at Work. The UNGPs do not differentiate business's responsibilities towards human rights based on the size of their operations – they apply to all businesses of any size, sector, and location.

Businesses are also required to be structured so that they have the capacity to meet their human rights responsibilities. This means they must have the necessary policies and processes in place, which requires that three conditions are met. First, companies must institute a policy commitment to meet the responsibility to respect human rights. Second, they must undertake ongoing human rights due diligence to identify, prevent, mitigate, and account for their human rights impacts. Finally, they must have processes in place to enable redress for any detrimental human rights effects they contribute to or cause.

Being duly diligent of their impact on human rights requires businesses to identify and address any negative impact its operations, operational networks, and products/services have on those rights. It also requires businesses to assess their internal procedures and engage with any groups affected by their business activity.

The UNGPs warn corporations that failure to respect human rights could lead to court appearances and reminds them that is in their self-interest to respect human rights so as not to harm their international reputation.

The UNGPs views corporations as specialised organs of societies as noted earlier. It is on this that their corporate responsibility to protect human rights is based – they have the licence to operate within society only on the condition that they bring benefits to that society, that is the social contract they have entered into. Any evaluation of the benefits they bring as specialised organs of society necessarily includes taking into account any negative impacts.

3.2.3 Access to Remedy

The state's duty to protect human rights include ensuring that any individual or group who considers that their rights have been violated has access to remedial procedures so that negative impacts by companies can be compensated.

The UNGPs are, as their name suggest, merely guidelines and they are not binding as part of international law. The primary shortcoming of the UNGPs is its lack of binding force, specifically with regard to the second foundational pillar pertaining to business organisations' obligation to respect human rights. In the absence of a formal legal framework that obliges business organisations to meet their human rights commitments, such organisations will always have a certain degree of freedom to violate human rights. Nevertheless, the guidelines constitute the authoritative international statement thus far established with regard to the duties of business organisations to respect human rights. This represents a significant step towards codifying the responsibilities non-state actors have to respect human rights and to have available a set of international norms that can be said to represent customary international law, which still remains ill-defined. Many of the past's legal distinctions (e.g., between a natural and legal entity) that have been used by large enterprises to evade prosecution, are, at least in public opinion, no longer satisfactory. Similarly, the distinction between a positive action that causes a direct human rights violation, and the lack of action that characterises complicity, is also no longer an acceptable difference in responsibility.

4 Conclusion

Businesses have enormous potential to promote human rights and transition the global economy to one that is sustainable as well as just. While FDI has brought significant improvements in the welfare of the citizens in the countries where they operate, it has also been associated with human rights abuses. Though the responsibility to protect human rights is shared by all actors in society and applies to all aspects of people's lives. MNCs have a particular responsibility on account of their special status in society and the scale of their operations, putting them in a position to be the key actors in achieving a more just and sustainable world in which the human rights of all citizens, in all countries, are protected and promoted. More than ever, it is also in all large global enterprises' purely economic interests to adhere to business policies that promote human rights and sustainability, as with the widening of access to information has come an increased public awareness of human rights violations by large corporations. Consequently, those corporations are more exposed to pressure from investors to maintain internationally acceptable human rights standards. Additionally, it is also in the interests of host states to foster a sociopolitical environment of stability as such stability is conducive to business success.

Businesses, therefore, have an essential role in enabling people to realise their human rights, as highlighted by the UNGPs, which represent the very first corporate responsibility initiative endorsed by the UN and thus a remarkable achievement. There is now a documented and internationally accepted framework that outlines the responsibilities corporations must conduct their operations in a way that maximises human welfare and minimises human suffering, offering a standard against which business activity can be judged and monitored by states. Corporations can no longer afford to ignore the normative standards the guidelines set out in this framework. In countries where human rights are respected, an environment is established suitable for human capital development, thus creating a highly-skilled workforce that corporations can employ to their advantage. Furthermore, when respect for human rights is established as a cultural norm, corporations seeking to engage in foreign investment experience less risk, as corporations that demonstrate respect for human rights in their operations can address business risks, benefit from increased risk in the international community, and are evaluated more favourably by global investors.

Bibliography

Book

Bentham, Jeremy. An Introduction to the Principles of Morals and Legislation (1789), edited by J Burns and H L A Hart. Oxford: Oxford University Press, 1996.

Bentham, Jeremy. Bentham: A Fragment on Government (1776), edited by Ross Harrison. Cambridge: Cambridge University Press, 1988.

Bromwich, David. The Intellectual Life of Edmund Burke: From the Sublime and Beautiful to American Independence. Cambridge, Massachusetts: The Belnap Press of Harvard University Press, 2014.

Choudhury, Barnali, and Martin Petrin. Corporate Duties to the Public. Cambridge: Cambridge University Press, 2019.

Donaldson, Thomas. Corporations and Morality. New Jersey: Prentice-Hall, Inc, 1982.

Edoho, Felix Moses. Corporate Environmental Accountability in Nigeria: A Global, National and Regional Study in the Age of Globalization. Oxon: Routledge, 2024.

French, Peter. Collective and corporate responsibility. New York: Columbia University, 1984.

Friedman, Milton. Capitalism and Freedom. 14th ed. Chicago: The Chicago University Press, 1962.

Gregor, Mary, and Jens Timmermann, eds. Immanuel Kant: Groundwork of the Metaphysics of Morals. Cambridge: Cambridge University Press, 2012.

Kamtekar, Rachana, ed. et al. Plato's Euthyphro, Apology, and Crito. Lanham, Maryland: Rowman & Littlefield Publishing, Inc, 2005.

Khanna, S.S. Business Ethics and Corporate Governance (Principles and Practices). New Delhi: S Chand and Company Limited, 2014.

List, Christian, and Philip Pettit. Group agency: the possibility, design and status of corporate agents. Oxford: Oxford University Press, 2011.

Loh, Christine. How COVID-19 Took Over the World: Lessons for the Future. Hong Kong: Hong Kong University Press, 2023.

Mendes, Errol P. Global Governance, Human Rights and International Law: Combating the Tragic Flaw. 2nd ed. Oxon: Routledge, 2023.

Mill, John Stuart. Utilitarianism, edited by Roger Crisp. Oxford: Oxford University Press, 1998.

Book Chapter

Cragg, Wesley. "Human Rights, Globalization, and the Modern Corporation." In Human Rights and the Moral Responsibilities of Corporate and Public-Sector Organizations, edited by Tom Campbell and Seamus Miller. Dordrecht: Kluwer, 2004.

Harrison, James. "Human rights and transnational corporations: establishing meaningful international obligations." In International Economic Law, Globalization and Developing Countries, edited by Julio Faundez and Celine Tan, 205–233. Cheltenham: Edward Elgar, 2010.

Hayek, F. A. "The Principles of a Liberal Social Order." In Studies in Philosophy, Politics and Economics, edited by F. A. Hayek, 160–177. Oxon: Routledge, 1967.

Kaptein, Muel, and Mihaela Constantinescu. "Corporations as Moral Entities." In Encyclopedia of Business and Professional Ethics, edited by Deborah C Poff and Alex C. Michalos, 1–4. Springer International Publishing, 2017.

Schutter, Olivier De. "The Challenge for imposing Human Rights Norms on Corporate Actors." In Transnational Corporations and Human Rights, edited by Olivier De Schutter, 1–40. Oxford: Hart Publishing, 2006.

Thiel, Karsten M. "Kant's Categorical Imperative and the Moral Worth of Increasing Profits." In Handbook of the Philosophical Foundations of Business Ethics, edited by Christoph Luetge, 339–354. Dordrecht: Springer, 2013.

Journal Article

Arnold, Denis G. "Transnational corporations and the duty to respect basic human rights." Business Ethics Quarterly 20, Issue 3 (2010): 371–399.

Birchall, David. "The Consequentialism of the UN Guiding Principles and Human Rights: Towards the Fulfilment of 'Do No Harm'." Electronic Journal Ethics and Organization Studies 24, no. 1 (2019): 28–39.

Bishop, John Douglas. "The Limits of Corporate Human Rights Obligations and the Rights of For-Profit Corporations." Business Ethics Quarterly 22, no. 1 (January 2012): 119–144.

Blanton, Shannon Lindsey. "A Sectoral Analysis of Human Rights and FDI: Does Industry Type Matter?." International Studies Quarterly 53 (2009): 469–493.

Buhmann, Karin. "Regulating Corporate Social and Human Rights Responsibilities at the UN Plane: Institutionalising New Forms of Law and Law-Making Approaches?." Nordic Journal of International Law 78, no. 1 (2009): 1–52.

Calatayud, Miguel Juan Taboada, Jesus Campo Candelas, and Patricia Perez Fernandez. "The accountability of multinational corporations for Human Rights' violations." Cuadernos constitucionales de la Catedra Fadrique Furio Ceriol 64–65 (2008): 171–186.

French, Peter A. "The Corporation as a Moral Person." American Philosophical Quarterly 16, no. 3 (July 1979): 207–215.

Garriga, Ana Carolina. "Human Rights Regimes, Reputation, and Foreign Direct Investment." International Studies Quarterly 60, no. 1 (March 2016): 160–172.

Gustafson, Andrew. "In Defence of a Utilitarian Business Ethics," Business and Society Review 118, no, 2 (2013): 325–360.

Korner, Anita, and Ronald Deutsch. "Deontology and Utilitarianism in Real Life: A Set of Moral Dilemmas Based on Historic Events." Personality and Social Psychology Bulletin 49, no. 10 (2023): 1511–1528.

Mallampally, Padma, and Karl Sauvant. "Foreign Direct Investment in Developing Countries." Finance and Development 36, no. 1 (1999): 34–37.

Otteson, James. The Essential Adam Smith. https://www.sipotra.it/wp-content/uploads/2019/03/The-Essential-Adam-Smith.pdf (accessed April 23, 2024).

Ozar, David T. "Do Corporations Have Moral Rights?." Journal of Business Ethics 4, no. 4 (August 1985): 277–281.

Phillips, Michael J. "Corporate Moral Personhood and Three Conceptions of the Corporation." Business Ethics Quarterly 2, issue 4 (October 1992): 435–459.

Sheffer, Megan Wells. "Bilateral Investment Treaties: A Friend or Foe to Human Rights?." Denver Journal of International Law & Policy 39, no. 3 (2011): 483–521.

Velasquez, Manuel. "Debunking corporate moral responsibility." Business Ethics Quarterly 13, no. 4 (October 2003): 531–562.

Werhane, Patricia H. "Corporate Moral Agency and the Responsibility to Respect Human Rights in the UN Guiding Principles: Do Corporations Have Moral Rights." Business and Human Rights Journal 1 (2015): 5–20.

Wettstein, Florian. "The Duty to Protect: Corporate Complicity, Political Responsibility, and Human Rights Advocacy." Journal of Business Ethics 96, no. 1 (September 2010): 33–47.

Case

Trustees of Dartmouth College v Woodward, 17 US (4 Wheat.) 518, 636 (1819).

Newspaper

Friedman, Milton. "A Friedman doctrine – The Social Responsibility of Business Is to Increase Its Profits." The New York Times, September 13, 1970.

Passow, Judah, and Tim Edwards. "The long, dark shadow of Bhopal: still waiting for justice, four decades on." The Guardians (UK), June 14, 2023. https://www.theguardian.com/global-development/2023/jun/14/bhopal-toxic-gas-leak-chemical-environmental-disaster-waiting-for-justice-union-carbide-dow (accessed April 14, 2024).

Website

Amnesty International. "The Bhopal tragedy: 30 years of injustice for victims and survivors Amnesty International written statement to the 25th session of the UN Human Rights Council (3–28 March 2018)." February 17, 2014. https://www.refworld.org/pdfid/530353204.pdf (accessed January 9, 2024).

Broughton, Edward. "The Bhopal disaster and its aftermath: a review." Environ Health (2005). https://www.ncbi.nlm.nih.gov/pmc/articles/PMC1142333/ (accessed January 9, 2024).

Castilho International Legal Corporation. "Multinational Companies' Responsibility in Human Rights." May 15, 2023. https://www.castilholegalcorp.com/en/publications/multinational-companies039-responsibility-in-human-rights/306/ (accessed March 26, 2024).

Goquingco, Anthony Raymond A. "UN Guiding Principles on Business and Human Rights." In Encyclopedia of Sustainable Management, edited by S.O. Idowu et al, 1–6. Springer Nature Switzerland AG, 2003. https://www.feu.edu.ph/wp-content/uploads/2023/07/UN-Guiding-Principles-on-Business-and-Human-Rights.pdf (accessed April 14, 2024).

https://conciseencyclopedia.org/entries/ethical-theory-utilitarianism/#:~:text=In%20business%20contexts%2C%20utilitarianism%20implies,harm%20to%20anyone%20at%20all. (accessed March 22, 2024).

https://ejatlas.org/print/protest-against-open-pit-coal-mine-project-in-phulbari-region (accessed January 12, 2024).

https://media.business-humanrights.org/media/documents/files/media/documents/ruggie/foley-hoag-briefing-guiding-principles-may-2011.pdf (accessed April 14, 2024).

https://www.europarl.europa.eu/RegData/etudes/BRIE/2018/620229/EPRS_BRI(2018)620229_EN.pdf (accessed April 14, 2024).

https://www.globaldata.com/store/report/phulbari-coal-fired-power-plant-ii-profile-snapshot/ (accessed April 19, 2024).

https://www.undp.org/rolhr/blog/why-should-businesses-respect-human-rights (April 14, 2024).

Human Rights Council. "Guiding Principles on Business and Human Rights: Implementing the United Nations "Protect, Respect and Remedy" Framework." A/HRC.17/31, March 21, 2011.

Human Rights Council. "Protect, Respect and Remedy: a Framework for Business and Human Rights." Report of the Special Representative of the Secretary-General on the issue of human rights and transnational corporations and other business enterprises, John Ruggie 16, UN Doc. A/HRC/8/5 (April 7, 2008) (prepared by John Ruggie).

Human Rights Watch. "Gold's Costly Dividend: Human Rights Impacts of Papua New Guinea's Porgera Gold Mine." February 1, 2011. https://www.hrw.org/report/2011/02/01/golds-costly-dividend/human-rights-impacts-papua-new-guineas-porgera-gold-mine (accessed April 20, 2024).

Ministry of Foreign Affairs of Denmark, "A Human Rights Based Approach to Denmark's Development Cooperation: Guidance and Inspiration for Policy Dialogue and Programming." https://amg.um.dk/library/hrba-guidance-and-screening-note (accessed May 6, 2024).

Organisation for Economic Co-operation and Development (OECD). Glossary of Statistical Terms – Foreign Direct Investment, https://www.oecd-ilibrary.org/finance-and-investment/foreign-direct-investment-fdi/indicator-group/english_9a523b18-en (accessed January 7, 2024).

The Danish Institute for Human Rights. "A Human Rights based Approach to the Means of Implementation of the Sustainable Development Goals." https://www.humanrights.dk/files/media/document/Rapport_HRBA_MOI_SDG_2020.pdf (accessed May 6, 2024).

The UN Working Group on Business and Human Rights. "The UN Guiding Principles on Business and Human Rights: An Introduction." https://www.ohchr.org/sites/default/files/Documents/Issues/Business/Intro_Guiding_PrinciplesBusinessHR.pdf (accessed May 6, 2024).

United Nations Human Rights Office of the High Commissioner. "Guiding Principles on Business and Human Rights: Implementing the United Nations "Protect, Respect and Remedy" Framework." New York and Geneva: 2011. https://www.ohchr.org/sites/default/files/documents/publications/guidingprinciplesbusinesshr_en.pdf (accessed May 6, 2024).

Wijesinghe, Prasadi. "Human Rights Violations by Multinational Corporations: Nestle as the culprit." March, 2018. https://papers.ssrn.com/sol3/papers.cfm?abstract_id=3136321 (accessed January 8, 2024).

Legal Instrument

Abolition of Forced Labour Convention, 1957 (No. 105).

Alien Tort Claims Act (ATCA), 1789.

Code of Conduct on Transnational Corporations, 1978.

Code of Conduct on Transnational Corporations, 1983.

Code of Conduct on Transnational Corporations, 1988.

Code of Conduct on Transnational Corporations, 1990.

Discrimination (Employment and Occupation) Convention, 1958 (No. 111).

Equal Remuneration Convention, 1951 (No. 100).

Forced Labour Convention, 1930 (No. 29).

Freedom of Association and Protection of the Right to Organise Convention, 1948 (No. 87).

Global Compact Principles, 2005.

Guiding Principles on Business and Human Rights: Implementing the United Nations "Protect, Respect and Remedy" Framework (Guiding Principles), 2011.

International Covenant on Civil and Political Rights (ICCPR), 1966.

International Covenant on Economic, Social and Cultural Rights (ICESCR), 1966.

Minimum Age Convention, 1973 (No. 138).

Norms on the Responsibilities of Transnational Corporations and Other Business Enterprises with regard to Human Rights, 2003.

OECD Guidelines for Multinationals Enterprise, 1976.

Racketeer Influenced and Corrupt Organisation (RICO) Act, 1970.

Right to Organise and Collective Bargaining Convention, 1949 (No. 98).

Tripartite Declaration of Principles concerning Multinational Enterprises and Social Policy, adopted by the Governing Body of the International Labour Office at its 204th session (Geneva, November 1977) and amended at its 279th (November 2000), 295th (March 2006), 329th (March 2017) and 346th Session (October-November 2022).

Universal Declaration of Human Rights (UDHR), 1948.

Worst Forms of Child Labour Convention, 1999 (No. 182).

CHAPTER 9

Bilateral Development Finance Institutions, Business and Extraterritorial Human Rights Obligations

Gamze Erdem Türkelli

1 Introduction

Development finance in its broadest sense refers to financing from both public and private sources channelled towards development-linked actions. The term acquired a more specific meaning following the Monterrey Consensus that came out of the first United Nations (UN) Conference on Financing for Development (2002) with a formal development role accorded to private sector investors[1] and currently means:

> [T]he use of public sector resources to facilitate private sector investment in low- and middle-income countries where the commercial or political risks are too high to attract purely private capital, and where the investment is expected to have a positive developmental impact on the host country.[2]

Development finance lies at the intersection of sustainable development and business, while its planning, delivery and implementation have important consequences for human rights, particularly across developing countries. The Addis Ababa Action Agenda of the Third Conference on Financing for Development and the 2030 Agenda for Sustainable Development both acknowledge the role of the private sector in achieving sustainable development and call for collaboration between the public and private sectors to fulfil sustainable development objectives.[3] In essence, this collaboration means

1 "Monterrey Consensus of the International Conference on Financing for Development," (International Conference on Financing for Development, 2002), paras 20–25.

2 George Ingram and Robert A. Mosbacher, "Development Finance: Filling Today's Funding Gap," (Brookings Blum Roundtable, Brookings, 2018), 1.

3 The Third Conference on Financing for Development, Addis Ababa Action Agenda, 2015; United Nations General Assembly (UNGA), "Transforming Our World: The 2030 Agenda for Sustainable Development," (United Nations, 2015).

 | DOI:10.1163/9789004530942_010

incentivising the private sector through the use of public financial resources utilising mechanisms such as Public-Private Partnerships (PPPs), investment guarantees, loans, and market-based instruments, such as bonds.[4]

Direct development finance to developing countries is often provided by Development Finance Institutions (DFIs). Backed by public institutional structures and public financial resources in wealthy countries, DFIs are central to the 'private turn' in development financing, which has gained momentum since the adoption of the 2030 Agenda and the Sustainable Development Goals (SDGs) in 2015. This shift is driven by arguments of a financing shortfall in public resources needed to achieve the SDGs, as estimated by different entities, including the United Nations (UN).[5] DFIs have been central to the revival of PPPs as (sustainable) development solutions and providing interlocution and intermediation roles, and allowing private actors, such as corporations to integrate into national and international development governance frameworks.[6]

The Association of European Development Finance Institutions (EDFI) defines DFIs as 'specialised development organisations that are usually majority owned by national governments' and that 'invest in private sector projects in low and middle-income countries to promote job creation and sustainable

4 The African Development Bank et al., "From Billions to Trillions: Transforming Development Finance Post-2015 Financing for Development: Multilateral Development Finance" (Development Committee (Joint Joint Ministerial Committee of the Boards of Governors of the Bank and the Fund on the Transfer of Real Resources to Developing Countries), 2015), https://thedocs.worldbank.org/en/doc/622841485963735448-0270022017/original/DC20150002EFinancingforDevelopment.pdf.

5 The narrative around the financial shortfall in the public resources needed to finance sustainable development and its various components such as transport and energy infrastructure, health, education among others, is a central theme in justifying the need to turn to private financing for development and the roll-out of various private financing instruments. Estimates focus on the numerical values of how much investment is needed to achieve various SDGs and range from 5 to 7 trillion USD per year between 2015 and 2030 to achieve the SDGs globally: Dana Vorisek and Shu Yu, *Understanding the Cost of Achieving the Sustainable Development Goals* (Washington, DC: World Bank, 2020), https://doi.org/10.1596/1813-9450-9164.] to 1.3 trillion USD per year for the 2019–2030 period to make meaningful progress on infrastructure investments (Massimiliano Riva and Marcos Neto, "Discussion Paper: Mobilizing Private Finance for Sustainable Development," (United Nations Development Programme (UNDP), 30 November 2016), https://www.undp.org/publications/mobilizing-private-finance-sustainable-development).

6 Emma Mawdsley, "DFID, the Private Sector and the Re-Centring of an Economic Growth Agenda in International Development," *Global Society* 29, no. 3 (2015): 339–58. Philip Mader, "Card Crusaders, Cash Infidels and the Holy Grails of Digital Financial Inclusion," 2016, https://doi.org/10.6094/BEHEMOTH.2016.9.2.916.

economic growth'.[7] DFIs differ from development banks[8] as they focus exclusively on providing financing for private sector investment in developing countries. Similarly to MDBs, DFIs utilise public resources from donor states to achieve development objectives. DFIs can be multilateral such as the World Bank Group's International Finance Corporation (IFC) arm, where multiple shareholding states pool resources to provide development financing in a multilateral setting. Alternatively, DFIs can be termed 'bilateral', focusing on financing the private sector in developing countries through bilateral relationships based on a specific donor government's external development assistance and cooperation policies. This chapter focuses on bilateral DFIs, which link to business, human rights, and sustainable development in three keyways. First, bilateral DFIs are often themselves set up as private sector companies in their states of origin, meaning that international and national business and human rights norms and frameworks directly apply to them. Secondly, DFIs may be fully or partially state-owned in their shareholding structure and often operate within policy frameworks determined by their state of origin. This raises questions regarding the ETOs of their states of origin concerning business conduct. It is worth noting that these home countries are often also where the headquarters of many transnational corporations are located. Finally, because bilateral DFIs provide financing to business enterprises directly, their self-regulatory and safeguard standards serve as benchmarks against which the activities of business enterprises are measured. DFIs that provide grievance or complaints mechanisms for failures to meet these standards serve as avenues for addressing business-related human rights violations.

In what follows, the chapter deals with questions of accountability to human rights holders when DFIs providing financing to private sector companies in developing countries in five sections. In Section 1, the chapter starts out by inspecting the state of affairs regarding the ETOs of the home states of DFIs and the human rights duties of the DFIs themselves. In Section 2, DFIs and their legal status are used as an entry point to the question of DFI accountability to rights-holders by applying existing business and human rights frameworks to DFIs. The chapter then inspects in Section 3 how bilateral DFIs, through their self-regulatory standards and safeguards, shape the operationalisation of business and human rights norms in relation to the business enterprises they finance. This section also tackles the question of access

7 EDFI Website, "About DFIs: European DFIs", https://www.edfi.eu/about-dfis/what-is-a-dfi/, (accessed April 4, 2023).

8 Development banks may provide private financing but also work to provide public financing to developing country governments in the form of policy or project finance.

to remedy for business-related human rights violations through DFI grievance and complaints mechanisms. In Section 4, the chapter addresses the ETOs of the home states of bilateral DFIs. Finally, the concluding section identifies future challenges in relation to DFIs within the context of business, human rights, and sustainable development, drawing attention particularly to new developments around sustainable finance and the increasing prominence of various Environmental, Social, and Governance (ESG) standards.

2 Bilateral DFIs as Businesses: Legal Status and Applicability of 'Business and Human Rights' Norms to DFIs

Many of the largest bilateral DFIs hail from member states of the OECD Development Assistance Committee (DAC) that are considered traditional 'donor' states. Some of these DFIs were founded much earlier in previous iterations, mostly to promote investments of private companies from their jurisdictions abroad (for instance, in colonised territories, newly independent formerly colonised countries or 'developing' countries more broadly. These include the first DFI British International Investment (BII), which was founded as the Colonial Development Corporation in 1948, Germany's Deutsche Investitions und Entwicklungsgesellschaft (DEG) founded in 1962, the Netherlands' Nederlandse Financierings-Maatschappij voor Ontwikkelingslanden N.V. (FMO) founded in 1970, the US International Development Corporation founded as the Overseas Private Investment Corporation (OPIC) in 1971 and France's Société de Promotion et de Participation pour la Coopération Economique (PROPARCO) founded in 1977. Newer bilateral DFIs date from 2000s following the adoption of the Millennium Development Goals in 2000 and the Monterrey Consensus in 2002.[9] In addition to Global North-led DFIs, Southern-led DFIs are also becoming important players in South-South and

9 Today, the main bilateral DFIs from OECD DAC donors include, in addition to the BII (UK), FMO (Netherlands), DFC (US), DEG (Germany), PROPARCO (France), Austria's Oesterreichische Entwicklungsbank AG – OeEB, Belgium's BIO, Denmark's Investment Fund for Developing Countries (IFU), Finland's Finnfund, Italy's Cassa Depositi E Prestiti (CDP) Development Finance Division and Società Italiana per le Imprese All'estero (SIMEST), Norway's Norwegian Investment Fund for Developing Countries (Norfund), Portugal's Sociedade Para o Financiamento do Desenvolvimento (SOFID), Spain's Compañía Española de Financiación del Desarrollo (COFIDES), Sweden's Swedfund International and Switzerland's Swiss Investment Fund for Emerging Markets (SIFEM).

Triangular Cooperation, often but not exclusively established as regional multilateral institutions.[10]

Bilateral DFIs are often set up as companies under domestic law, either as separate entities or as subsidiaries of a broader development bank or export credit agency (such as the Germany's DEG, which is a subsidiary of the KfW Development Bank or Canada's FinDev, which is a subsidiary of Export Development Canada). They may be established as public limited companies (PLC) or limited liability companies (LLC). Some bilateral DFIs such as Belgium's BIO, BII (UK), DFC (US), Norfund (Norway) among others are wholly owned by the State. Other DFIs have different shareholding structures, with their home States as majority shareholders where minority shares may be held by regional governments, private companies and commercial banks, international financial institutions, trade unions, among others. Examples include Germany's DEG, which is a fully owned subsidiary of KfW Bank, which in turn is owned 80% by the German Federal Government and 20% by regional governments (Länder).[11] 51% of the shares of Netherlands' FMO are owned by the Dutch state, of the rest of the shares 42% are reportedly held by 3 Dutch Banks (ABN Amro, ING and Rabobank) and 7% are held by employer's associations, trade unions, private companies and individual shareholders.[12] France's development cooperation agency Agence Française de Développement (AFD) owns 79.76% of the shares of the DFI PROPARCO, while 8.24% of the shares are owned by French financial institutions (BPIFRANCE, BNP Paribas, BPCE IOM, Credit Agricole SA, Société Générale), 10.03% owned by financial institutions from abroad France, and the remainder owned by private investors and funds.[13] In summary, many bilateral DFIs are, legally speaking, fully State-owned Enterprises (SOE), while others are partially but majority state-owned. This fits with the UN Working Group on Business and Human Rights (UNWG-BHR), which relies on the OECD Guidelines on Corporate Governance of SOEs and defines SOEs as entities recognised as business enterprises under national

10 United Nations Development Programme (UNDP). 'South – South Ideas: The Role of Southern-Based Development Finance Institutions in South-South Cooperation and Mobilization of the Private Sector for Sustainable Development'. United Nations Development Programme (UNDP), February 2021.

11 This is the case of the (EDFI Website, "DEG Germany," https://www.edfi.eu/member/deg/ (accessed April 4, 2023).

12 BankTrack, "FMO Netherlands," https://www.banktrack.org/bank/fmo (accessed April 4, 2023).

13 PROPARCO, *PROPARCO SA Shareholding Composition on March 8th, 2022.*

law that are under the ownership of the State and under its effective control, which may be exercised even in the cases of minority shareholding.[14]

While bilateral DFIs be under independent and professional management following a corporate model, the priority sectors and domains of their investments are determined by the external affairs and development cooperation policies of their home State governments. For instance, the UK's British International Investment has independence in day-to-day operations and financing decisions, but its investment policies are set out by the Foreign, Commonwealth & Development Office (FCDO), which also appoints its Chairperson.[15] This gives bilateral DFIs a dual and hybrid character: they are at once business enterprises, and an integral part of their home States' investment and private sector development structures both in terms of their ownership structure and in terms of their mandates. The Better Utilization of Investments Leading to Development (BUILD) Act of 2018, established the US International Development Finance Corporation (DFC) by expanding the mandate of the previous US DFI OPIC, clearly states that DFC's mandate to mobilise private capital for sustainable development as a part of the 'policy of the United States to facilitate market-based private sector development and economic growth in less developed countries through the provision of credit, capital, and other financial support' (sec. 101) with the aim of *inter alia* 'complement[ing] and be[ing] guided by overall United States foreign policy, development, and national security objectives, taking into account the priorities and needs fo countries receiving support'.[16]

2.1 *Applying Business and Human Rights Frameworks to DFIs*

Bilateral DFIs, as business enterprises under domestic law, must respect the national laws and international law obligations of their home States as well as of host States in which they operate. Because they operate in the financial sector, there is often a lack of clarity around the applicability of specific business and human rights norms to their activities and financing decisions as DFIs often only come into contact with rights-holders indirectly. Yet, existing

14 United Nations Working Group on the issue of human rights and transnational corporations and other business enterprises (UN WGBHR), "The Duty of States to Protect against Human Rights Abuses Involving Those Business Enterprises That They Own or Control," (United Nations Human Rights Council, May 4, 2016), paras 9–11.

15 British International Investment Website, "Our corporate governance," https://www.bii.co.uk/en/about/our-company-2/our-corporate-governance/ (accessed April 5, 2023).

16 "The Better Utilization of Investments Leading to Development (BUILD) Act of 2018," H.R. 5105 § (2018), sec. 101.

soft law frameworks on business and human rights such as the UN Guiding Principles on Business and Human Rights (UNGPs), the OECD Guidelines on Multinational Enterprises and the ILO Multinational Enterprises Declaration are clear that they apply across the board to all business enterprises without exempting specific sectors or business activities. In fact, the financial industry itself has recognised the importance of regulatory norms in making financing decisions, particularly as they relate to project finance. Accordingly, the Equator Principles, which set the benchmark for the financial industry in its assessment of social and environmental risks in financed projects were adopted two decades ago in 2003 in the wake of the adoption of IFC's Performance Standards in 2002.[17] Although the Equator Principles adopt a risk-based framework as opposed to a rights-based framework for addressing the impacts of financing decisions and activities on rights-holders and the environment, they are demonstrative of the broader consensus that regulatory norms seeking to prevent, mitigate and remedy business-related harms on rights-holders also extend to the financial sector. In that vein, UNGP 14 notes that the business responsibility to respect human rights applies 'fully and equally' to businesses 'regardless of their size, sector, operational context, ownership and structure'.[18]

One solution to whether a certain economic actor fits within the definition of a business enterprises and which type of business is to focus not 'on the legal character of the economic actor' but the impacts of the economic activity on rights-holders 'as a first step toward better integration of international human rights standards into the operations of states and their economic and financial instrumentalities'.[19] In that vein, *the Third revised draft legally binding instrument to regulate, in international human rights law, the activities of transnational corporations and other business enterprises*, defines business activities broadly as

> [A]ny economic or other activity … undertaken by a natural or legal person, including State-owned enterprises, financial institutions and investment funds, transnational corporations, other business enterprises, joint

17 Equator Principles Financial Institutions (EPFIs), "The Equator Principles (EP4)," (Equator Principles Financial Institutions (EPFIs), July 2020).

18 'United Nations Guiding Principles on Business and Human Rights (UNGPs)' (United Nations, 2011), Principle 14 and Commentary.

19 Larry C Backer, "The Human Rights Obligations of State-Owned Enterprises: Emerging Conceptual Structures and Principles in National and International Law and Policy," *Vanderbilt Journal of Transnational Law* 50, no. 4 (October 2017): 888.

ventures, and any other business relationship undertaken by a natural or legal person.[20]

The activities of bilateral DFIs fall squarely within this definition of business activities.

The UNGP 13 underscores the business responsibility to respect human rights, which in the first instance requires that businesses *do no harm*, meaning that they should avoid causing or contributing to human rights violations 'through their own activities' and address harms when they occur. The 'own' activities of bilateral DFIs relate to financing private sector investments in developing countries. In addition, in the context of their responsibility to respect human rights, business enterprises should also 'seek to prevent or mitigate adverse human rights impacts that are directly linked to their operations, products or services by their business relationships, even if they have not contributed to those impacts'.[21]

For bilateral DFIs, as for other business enterprises, the responsibility to respect entails a number of components, including adopting clear policies on human rights, having in place due diligence processes including by conducting ex ante, ongoing and ex post human rights impact assessments for financing activities as well as projects financed in consultation with potentially affected persons and communities, by preventing and if necessary, mitigating impacts(UNGPs 15 through 18). In addition, putting in place remedial mechanisms for business-related human rights harms in which they are involved as financiers (UNGP 22).

The legal status of bilateral DFIs as fully or majority SOEs even more directly link them to business and human rights duties. Per UNGP 11, the responsibility to respect is a duty incumbent upon all businesses, including SOEs. As Seck notes, '[h]owever, due to the close State-business nexus, SOEs that are controlled by the State or whose acts can be attributed to the State, are under a heightened responsibility to respect human rights',[22] which is also recognised

20 Open-ended intergovernmental working group on transnational corporations and other business enterprises with respect to human rights, "The Third Revised Draft Legally Binding Instrument to Regulate, in International Human Rights Law, the Activities of Transnational Corporations and Other Business Enterprises," Pub. L. No. A/HRC/52/41/Add.1 (2023), art. 1.3.

21 United Nations Guiding Principles on Business and Human Rights (UNGPs), Principle 13.

22 Sara L. Seck, "Guiding Principle 11: The Responsibility of Business Enterprises to Respect Human Rights," in *The UN Guiding Principles on Business and Human Rights: A Commentary*, ed. Barnali Choudhury (Cheltenham: Edward Elgar, 2023), 88.

by the OECD Guidelines for Multinational Enterprises.[23] In addition to a heightened responsibility to respect human rights, the direct State-business nexus created through the home State ownership of bilateral DFIs triggers human rights obligations of their home States beyond their borders, colloquially termed ETOs.

3 Extraterritorial Human Rights Obligations and Home States of DFIs

Home States of bilateral DFIs retain all their international law obligations, including their human rights obligations to respect, protect and fulfil human rights, when they engage in economic activities such as financing private sector enterprises abroad. The 2011 Maastricht Principles on Extraterritorial Obligations of States in the Area of Economic, Social and Cultural Rights (The Maastricht Principles) underscore that States have an obligation to take all necessary measures to ensure that non-State actors, including business enterprises, they are in a position to regulate do not cause human rights violations.[24] The UN Committee on Economic, Social and Cultural Rights (ESCR Committee) General Comment 24 reiterates the transboundary nature of this obligation: that a State's extraterritorial obligation to protect extends to preventing and redressing the violations of economic, social and cultural rights by businesses they control.[25]

The UN Protect, Respect and Remedy Framework notes that the home State authority over SOEs, particularly in controlling decisions around appointment of management means that States are in principle in a better position to ensure compliance with human rights from SOEs.[26] 7Principle 4 of the UN Guiding Principles on Business and Human Rights (UNGPs) deals with SOEs as well as businesses that are substantially supported by the State and requires States to 'take additional steps' to protect human rights, including by imposing human

23 OECD, "The OECD Guidelines for Multinational Enterprises," (OECD, 2011), Commentary on General Policies, para. 10.

24 Olivier De Schutter et al., "Commentary to the Maastricht Principles on Extraterritorial Obligations of States in the Area of Economic, Social and Cultural Rights," *Human Rights Quarterly* 34, no. 4 (2012): 1084–1169, https://doi.org/10.1353/hrq.2012.0063.

25 Committee on Economic, Social and Cultural Rights (CESCR), "General Comment No. 24 (2017) on State Obligations under the International Covenant on Economic, Social and Cultural Rights in the Context of Business Activities," August 10, 2017, para. 30.

26 United Nations Human Rights Council (UNHRC), "Protect, Respect and Remedy: A Framework for Business and Human Rights," April 7, 2008, para. 32.

rights due diligence. The Commentary clearly states that where the business-State nexus is closer, for instance, where the business activity is financed by the public, home States have a greater capacity to regulate through policy, legislation, and regulation. In this nexus, the home State plays a double role: both as an owner/controller of the SOE and the regulator that is supposed to foster compliance with human rights.[27]

The UN Working Group on Business and Human Rights (UNWGBHR) provides further context on the UNGPs in relation to SOEs in its 2016 report to the Human Rights Council.[28] Recognising that SOEs may be present in all sectors in the economy, including finance and others,[29] the UNWGBHR reads the home State obligations of SOEs as extending to 'all government entities and departments in charge of exercising ownership rights for either all or some State-owned enterprises'.[30] Home States of SOEs should take all steps necessary to ensure that their SOEs respect human rights, which, according to the UNWGBHR would require 'at a minimum, requir[ing] that SOEs adopt – explicit human rights targets, and monitor their achievement'.[31] The General Comment 16 of the UN Committee on Children's Rights (CRC Committee) is explicit that home States should not only require their SOEs to carry out children's rights due diligence and public reporting but also 'make public support and services, such as those provided by an export credit agency, development finance and investment insurance conditional on businesses carrying out child-rights due diligence'.[32]

The intertwined nature of bilateral DFI activities and the economic policy priorities of their home States abroad, including in relation to developing countries, also evoke UNGP 8 on policy coherence. Martin notes, accordingly, that States should ensure their business and human rights policies and regulations

27 Larry Catá Backer, "Guiding Principle 4: The Obligations of States in Markets with Respect to Enterprises Owned, Controlled, or Supported by the State," in *The UN Guiding Principles on Business and Human Rights: A Commentary*, ed. Barnali Choudhury (Cheltenham: Edward Elgar, 2023), 38.

28 Although the UNWGBHR distinguished development finance institutions from SOEs in that report, bilateral DFIs straddle these two types of economic actors, rendering the report and its content relevant to bilateral DFIs.

29 United Nations Working Group on the issue of human rights and transnational corporations and other business enterprises (UN WGBHR), "The Duty of States to Protect against Human Rights Abuses Involving Those Business Enterprises That They Own or Control," para. 13.

30 Ibid, para. 58.

31 Ibid, para. 67.

32 CRC Committee, "General Comment No. 16 (2013) on State Obligations Regarding the Impact of the Business Sector on Children's Rights," April 17, 2013, para. 64.

are coherent across different state institutions and processes, including SOEs, public procurement and economic and trade agencies (horizontal policy coherence).[33] The State – whether it is a financier of investments or a procurer of goods and services – is required to 'embody human rights through all of these different roles' through vertical policy coherence.[34] Accordingly, policy coherence entails that home States of bilateral DFIs should ensure the full application of human rights standards to the policy frameworks and strategic plans governing bilateral DFIs as well as the investments financed by these DFIs.

Bilateral DFIs also routinely work with multilateral development banks and the private sector, often jointly on specific projects through co-financing. The UNGP 10 speaks to the obligations of States as members of multilateral institutions and to international policy coherence. Home States of bilateral DFIs continue to be bound by the full range of their human rights obligations as members of multilateral institutions and should protect human rights from infringement by these institutions. Experiences with development projects show that when bilateral DFIs collaborate with multilateral/international financial institutions (IFIs) such as multilateral development banks (MDBs), they may defer to the safeguard policies of these institutions.[35] Yet, these safeguard policies are known to fall short of the human rights protections required by international law and international legal obligations of home and host States.[36] Consequently, the lack of harmonisation in the safeguards implemented by various multilateral and bilateral development finance institutions as well as the gaps in their normative content are important roadblocks to the collaboration and international policy coherence envisaged in UNGP 10.[37] Of course, the UNGPs and other soft law governance frameworks on business and human rights do not draw distinctions between different States with respect

33 Jena Martin, "Guiding Principle 8: Ensuring Policy Coherence," in *The UN Guiding Principles on Business and Human Rights: A Commentary*, ed. Barnali Choudhury (Cheltenham: Edward Elgar, 2023), 69.

34 Martin, 69.

35 Gamze Erdem Türkelli, *Children's Rights and Business: Governing Obligations and Responsibility* (Cambridge: Cambridge University Press, 2020).

36 Stéphanie De Moerloose, Gamze Erdem Türkelli, and Joshua Curtis, "Extraterritorial Human Rights Obligations and International Financial Institutions," in *The Routledge Handbook on Extraterritorial Human Rights Obligations*, ed. Mark Gibney et al., 1st ed. (London: Routledge, 2021), 271–83, https://doi.org/10.4324/9781003090014.

37 Gamze Erdem Türkelli, "Guiding Principle 10: States as Members of Multilateral Institutions," in *The UN Guiding Principles on Business and Human Rights: A Commentary*, ed. Barnali Choudhury (Cheltenham: Edward Elgar, 2023), 80.

to their relative economic and political power and the historical determinants of that current power. This shortcoming can be remedied by placing differentiated and heightened duties on today's wealthy States in the realisation of sustainable development, including through financial assistance. Accordingly, home States of bilateral DFIs should ensure that they not only abide by their human rights obligations as owners of bilateral DFIs and as members (shareholders) of MDBs and other IFIs but also that they take all appropriate measures and use their greater leverage and influence to ensure that these institutions themselves also respect human rights.[38]

When business related human rights violations do occur, the closer business-State nexus of SOEs means a more direct trigger for State responsibility. With respect to responsibility for wrongdoings related to SOEs that happen beyond a State's borders, the UN Protect, Respect, Remedy Framework reiterates Article 8 of the Articles of State Responsibility for Internationally Wrongful Acts (ARSIWA), concluding that the home States of SOEs may be attributed international legal responsibility for the wrongful acts of their SOEs if the latter can be considered State organs, acting on their behalf or under their orders.[39] The Maastricht Principles on ETOs also hold that "acts and omissions of non-State actors acting on the instructions or under the direction or control of the State" as well as of other actors such as 'corporations and other business enterprises, where they are empowered by the State to exercise elements of governmental authority' are attributable to the State, including in extraterritorial settings (Principle 12).

4 Bilateral DFIs as Intermediaries of Business and Human Rights Norms and Access to Remedy in Sustainable Development

The steadily growing investment portfolios of bilateral DFIs cement their importance in the business and human rights domain, particularly in relation to business activities linked to sustainable development. In fact, development finance through DFIs has grown at a rate much higher than overall amounts dedicated to Official Development Assistance (ODA) during the same period.[40] Besides being addressees of business and human rights norms

38 The twofold duty of States is also noted by the CRC Committee in its General Comment 16. (CRC Committee, "General Comment No. 16 (2013) on State Obligations Regarding the Impact of the Business Sector on Children's Rights," paras 47–48).

39 Erdem Türkelli, *Children's Rights and Business*, 283.

40 Roman Herre and Stephan Backes, "Financialization of Development Cooperation: ETO Responses," in *The Routledge Handbook on Extraterritorial Human Rights Obligations*, ed.

themselves, DFIs intermediate the application of business and human rights norms to the activities and decisions business enterprises in which they invest (their so-called 'investees'). United Nations Working Group on Business and Human Rights (UN WGBHR) has also drawn attention to this intermediary role and, at the time of writing, is working on a report on Development Finance Institutions and Human Rights, to address the UNGPs in the context of DFI activities:

> Financial actors – such as private sector commercial banks, institutional investors, development finance institutions, and other sources of financial capital – have an unparalleled ability to influence companies and scale up progress on implementation of the [UNGPs]. Many are increasingly recognizing their own responsibility under the [UNGPs] and are probing the companies that they finance or invest in about how their business models and decision-making processes integrate respect for human rights – a development supported in part by the increased use of ESG criteria in investment processes.[41]

DFIs intermediate the application of business and human rights frameworks in sustainable development in three ways: Firstly, most bilateral DFIs provide a framework of environmental and social standards and/or safeguard policies applicable to their investments, which is largely based on a single framework – that of the International Finance Corporation (IFC) Performance Standards (PS). Secondly, they utilise various international frameworks on business and human rights and sustainability and thus intermediate the practical interpretation of these frameworks. Thirdly, the complaints and grievance mechanisms provided by DFIs shape the conditions of access to remedy for rights-holders adversely affected by DFI-financed development projects.

4.1 *DFI Environmental and Social Standards and/or Safeguard Policies*

The social and environmental safeguards and standards of many bilateral DFIs are versions of the IFC PS adopted in 2002 and revised 2012. The IFC, as the private sector financing arm of the World Bank Group, has set the development finance sector's overall tone in relation to human rights impacts of

---

Mark Gibney et al., 1st ed. (London: Routledge, 2021), 228, https://doi.org/10.4324/9781003090014.

41 United Nations Working Group on the issue of human rights and transnational corporations and other business enterprises (UN WGBHR), "Guiding Principles on Business and Human Rights at 10: Taking Stock of the First Decade," April 22, 2021, para. 77.

private sector promotion in developing countries. The IFC PS cover environmental and social sustainability issues, including a general standard on the assessment and management of environmental and social risks and impacts (PS 1) as well as specific standards on labour and working conditions (PS 2), resource efficiency and the pollution prevention (PS 3), community health, safety and security (PS 4), land acquisition and involuntary resettlement (PS 5), biodiversity conservation and management of living natural resources (PS 6), indigenous peoples (PS 7) and cultural heritage (PS 8). Many bilateral DFIs, such as BIO (Belgium), DEG (Germany), FMO (Netherlands) and PROPARCO (France) directly use IFC's PS as their ESG benchmark to assess their clients' performance.[42] The IFC's PS also act as benchmarks for the EDFI harmonised environmental and social standards framework that define and set standards for ESG at the member European bilateral DFIs.[43]

The 2007 IFC Exclusion list, which lists the various sectors in which the IFC will not invest, has also been adopted by various DFIs.[44] This list includes production or trade in products deemed illegal in host countries or under international law, in weapons and munitions, in alcoholic beverages, in tobacco, in radioactive chemicals, in unbonded asbestos fibres, gambling, drift net fishing. Further exclusions are applied to financial intermediaries and microfinance investments, which excluded production or activities that involve harmful/exploitative child labour and forced labour among others.[45]

Besides ESG frameworks of the IFC PS, various external frameworks utilised by bilateral DFIs range from business and human rights linked frameworks such as the UNGPs, the OECD Guidelines for Multinational Enterprises, and the Equator Principles to sustainability and impact linked frameworks such as IFC Impact Principles, Principles for Responsible Investment, UN Environmental Programme (UNEP) Finance Initiative and UN Principles for Investors in Inclusive Finance. Not all DFIs apply all aforementioned frameworks to their

42 FMO, "The implementation of our human rights commitment," https://www.fmo.nl/the-implementation-of-our-human-rights-commitment (accessed April 8, 2023).

43 EDFI, "Policy," https://www.edfi.eu/policy/ (accessed April 8, 2023).

44 One example is the Association of European Development Finance Institutions (EDFI) Harmonised Exclusion List that is used by all of its members and is based on the IFC Exclusion List. (https://edfi-website-v1.s3.fr-par.scw.cloud/uploads/2021/02/EDFI-Exclusion-List_-September-2011.pdf).

45 IFC, Exclusion List 2007, https://www.ifc.org/wps/wcm/connect/topics_ext_content/ifc_external_corporate_site/sustainability-at-ifc/company-resources/ifcexclusionlist#2007.

work and many limit their engagement to only a limited selection of these frameworks.[46]

There is a wide margin of variation among bilateral DFIs as regards direct engagement with human rights and recognition of human rights duties. IFC PS 1 explicitly mentions human rights in its Introduction (para 3) in a generalised manner that applies a 'do no harm' standard to businesses it finances in the context of a given project and with an accent on due diligence.[47] While this statement notes the relevance of human rights to all IFC PS, it does not directly invoke direct duties for the IFC itself. Similarly, many bilateral DFI ESG frameworks focus on expectations from clients and not the duties of the bilateral DFIs themselves. For instance, the EDFI Principles for Responsible Financing of Sustainable Development used by fifteen European bilateral DFIs '[r]equire that all [EDFI] investee companies, including financial intermediaries, comply with the legal and regulatory requirements in the jurisdictions where they operate'[48] but does not pronounce the same duty for EDFI members themselves. Yet, as the 2022 OHCHR Report *Remedy in Development Finance: Guidance and Practice* (February 2022) notes,

> DFIs are not themselves involved in the establishment and operation of projects and are usually at least one step removed from human rights impacts. However, DFIs may contribute to harms, by action or omission, and may have significant leverage over client behaviour and project outcomes in particular cases[.][49]

FinDev Canada, one of the more recently established bilateral DFIs and its parent company EDC have in this vein adopted a Human Rights Policy, which underscores and recognises the agency's own responsibility to respect human

46 The Dutch FMO, for instance, has one of the broadest scopes and explicitly mentions all of these frameworks.

47 Business should respect human rights, which means to avoid infringing on the human rights of others and address adverse human rights impacts business may cause or contribute to. Each of the Performance Standards has elements related to human rights dimensions that a project may face in the course of its operations. Due diligence against these Performance Standards will enable the client to address many relevant human rights issues in its project. (IFC, Performance Standards, 2012).

48 EDFI, EDFI Principles for Responsible Financing of Sustainable Development, 2019, https://www.finnfund.fi/wp-content/uploads/2019/10/EDFI-Responsible-Financing-SDG_Principles-May-2019.pdf (accessed April 8, 2023).

49 *Remedy in Development Finance Guidance and Practice* (New York: United Nations, 2022), 10.

rights, in addition to its responsibility to assess, identify, prevent and mitigate the potential adverse human rights impacts of its customer relationships.[50]

Bilateral DFIs often take human rights to mean rights in the International Bill of Rights and the International Labor Organization (ILO) Declaration on Fundamental Principles and Rights at Work, in line with the UNGPs.[51] Unfortunately, this effectively means that persons and groups that are often most disadvantaged and marginalised such as children, indigenous peoples, persons with disabilities and women do not benefit from the specific human rights provisions that are enshrined in international law to protect their rights. In addition, each bilateral DFI is free to intermediate the application of business and human rights in frameworks in sustainable development in more specific ways, for instance by deciding on a particular interpretation of the substantive content of human rights norms they deem applicable to their operations. For instance, the FMO has a list of five substantive human rights that it considers 'salient human rights issues' for its work: right to life, right to just and favourable conditions of work, rights of vulnerable people, right to an adequate standard of living and right to not be subject to cruel and inhumane or degrading treatment.[52] This type of differentiation may create the impression that beyond such 'salient' human rights issues, a bilateral DFI's work does not routinely or consequentially generate equally relevant impacts on other human rights. Of course, real life examples of human rights violations linked to development finance demonstrate that development projects can impact all human rights, ranging from the right to life to the right to education or health both in terms of procedural and substantive guarantees.[53] In addition, using aggregated concepts such as 'vulnerable people' instead of referring to specific groups of rights-holders such as children, persons with disabilities, indigenous peoples and others whose rights are enumerated under international law in

50 Export Development Canada (EDC), Human Rights Policy, November 2019, https://www.findevcanada.ca/sites/default/files/2020-04/FinDev%20Canada%20ES%20Policy%20-%20%2002Mar%202020.pdf (accessed April 8, 2023).

51 United Nations Guiding Principles on Business and Human Rights (UNGPs), Principle 12. This definition is also adopted in the EDFI Principles for Responsible Financing of Sustainable Development revised in 2019 (ibid).

52 FMO, "Salient Human Rights", https://www.fmo.nl/salient-human-rights (accessed April 8, 2023).

53 For examples, see: Kinnari I. Bhatt, *Concessionaires, Financiers and Communities: Implementing Indigenous Peoples' Rights to Land in Transnational Development Projects* (Cambridge: Cambridge University Press, 2020); Erdem Türkelli, *Children's Rights and Business: Governing Obligations and Responsibility*; Jennifer Lander, *Transnational Law and State Transformation: The Case of Extractive Development in Mongolia* (Oxon: Routledge, 2020).

specific human rights instruments, obscures the specific rights and entitlements of each of these groups of rights-holders.

The intermediation of business and human rights norms by DFIs ultimately creates three consequences. First, the template chosen by bilateral DFIs (namely, the IFC PS) in engaging with the social and environmental impacts of their activities perpetuates a risk-based due diligence model as opposed to a rights-based due diligence model. This risk-based model in turn results in a 'pick and choose' approach to human rights and to human rights holders in determining what rights are entitled to respect and protection and which rights-holders are entitled to a voice, through consultation and consent. The risk-based models may delimit the scope of what is considered social risk and thus 'unjustifiably exclude project-affected people from safeguard consultation and protection and exclude higher-risk components from the project's scope'.[54] For example, when impacts on more marginalised or disadvantaged persons are seen as a business risk, they are often considered 'vulnerable groups' and the rights of specific rights-holders within those groups may be side-lined. But when due diligence processes focus on potential impacts on rights and rights-holders, these processes disaggregate 'vulnerable groups' into specific rights holders (such as children, women, persons with disabilities, indigenous peoples) and impacts on their rights need to be assessed by using the legal instruments for those specific rights-holders as benchmarks. Second, DFIs may 'ring-fence' their duties by shifting the burden of project components considered riskier on to other partners in the project to reduce their risk and potential to be subject to complaints through IAMs.[55] Third, when bilateral DFIs intermediate the use and interpretation of business and human rights frameworks such as the UNGPs and the OECD Guidelines, they imbue norms contained in these frameworks such as due diligence or access to remedy with their own, often narrow, interpretations. This may create further fragmentation in the implementation of the frameworks even within one country, for instance, if the said country's National Action Plan (NAP) and the policies of the bilateral DFI it fully or majority owns are not aligned. To avoid this fragmentation, OHCHR's *Benchmarking Study of Development Finance Institutions' Safeguard Policies* notes that '[t]ighter alignment between DFI Safeguards and the UN Guiding Principles on Business and Human Rights (UNGPs) can help DFIs and

54 *Remedy in Development Finance Guidance and Practice*, 27.

55 Ibid, 28.

their clients to satisfy Safeguard policy requirements and other evolving due diligence regulatory requirements simultaneously'.[56]

4.2 *Access to Remedy*

Access to remedy, the third pillar of the UN Protect, Respect, Remedy Framework and the UNGPs, is an important site of bilateral DFI intermediation. DFI grievance mechanisms, whether provided by a multilateral DFI like the IFC's Compliance Advisor Ombudsman (CAO) or by bilateral DFIs, constitute a significant part of non-judicial remedy mechanisms available to rightsholders for business-related human rights violations. Many of the largest bilateral DFIs have started providing Independent Accountability Mechanisms (IAMs), a development that has accelerated over the last years. In addition, three of the largest European bilateral DFIs, Germany's DEG, Netherlands' FMO and France's PROPARCO have decided to work through a joint Independent Complaints Mechanism (ICM), which works through an Independent Expert Panel (IEP). Set up in 2014 by the DEG and FMO and joined by PROPARCO in 2018, the ICM is modelled after the IFC's Compliance Advisor Ombudsman (CAO).[57] The ICM has a three-person Independent Expert Panel (IEP). The joint ICM is governed separately by the policies of each member DFI: the DEG-ICM policy, the FMO-ICM policy and the PROPARCO-ICM policy. The ICM policies are based on the IFC CAO Policy, providing similar services such as compliance review, dispute resolution and monitoring. Each bilateral DFI provides its own complaint secretariat for the ICM and its own website for the ICM.[58] This means that while the IAM mechanism is harmonised, the norms that it applies in complaints against different DFIs are not.

Normatively speaking, the access to remedy provided by bilateral DFIs is risk-based because it remains in line with the risk-based nature of DFI environmental and social standards and safeguards. When project-affected persons bring their grievances to DFI accountability and remedy mechanisms, they are often only able to invoke non-compliance with that specific DFI's own ESG regulatory frameworks. Thus, there is often a mismatch between the content

56 "Benchmarking Study of Development Finance Institutions' Safeguard Policies," (Office of the United Nations High Commissioner for Human Rights (OHCHR), February 2023), ix.

57 The Independent Complaints Mechanism (ICM), "The Independent Complaint Mechanism (ICM) Serving Several European Development Finance Institutions," Presentation at GRAM WebinarApril 27, 2021, https://irm.greenclimate.fund/sites/default/files/page/1st-gram-webinar-fit-purpose-grms-overview-different-models.pdf.

58 Ibid.

of the rights violations that rights-holder seek to have redressed and how DFIs themselves approach norms around safeguards and what triggers remedy.

Remedy encompasses both the process and the outcome, with various components, including providing redress for those harmed, prevention of future instances of harm and deterrence of such future instances.[59] In the context of business and human rights, the UNWGBHR has called on duty-bearers to provide 'a bouquet of remedies' to rights-holders, including restitution, compensation, guarantees of non-repetition among others.[60] The processes by which remedy is made available also bears on its content and the outcomes. For instance, one discontent of complainants who have used DFI IAMs is that there are no formal appeals procedures when DFIs in question do not comply with the recommendations issued by the IAMs.[61] In this respect, he effectiveness criteria for non-judicial business and human rights grievance mechanisms that UNGP 31 lists can serve as an important procedural benchmark for complaints and grievance mechanisms of (bilateral) DFIs.[62] With respect to the substantive contentive of remedy,

> DFIs should take into account not only their involvement and that of clients in the given harms, but also (a) the development mandate of DFIs; (b) other factors that can significantly impede access to remedy; (c) the complexity of the investment structure and operating context; and (d) any legacy issues.[63]

5 Future Challenges

Backed by public architectures in wealthy countries, bilateral DFIs play central roles in the 'private turn' in development financing, particularly by incentivising

59 *Remedy in Development Finance Guidance and Practice*, 12.

60 "Statement by Mr. Surya Deva, Chairperson of the Working Group on the Issue of Human Rights and Transnational Corporations and Other Business Enterprises 3rd Session of the Open-Ended Intergovernmental Working Group on Transnational Corporations and Other Business Enterprises with Respect to Human Rights," https:// www.ohchr.org/EN /NewsEvents/Pages/DisplayNews.aspx?NewsID=22303&LangID=E.

61 *Remedy in Development Finance Guidance and Practice*, 31.

62 These effectiveness criteria require non-judicial grievance mechanisms to be 'legitimate', 'accessible', 'predictable', 'equitable', 'transparent', 'rights-compatible' and 'a source of continuous learning' (United Nations Guiding Principles on Business and Human Rights (UNGPs), art. 31.).

63 *Remedy in Development Finance Guidance and Practice*, 82.

public-private partnerships (PPPs) and so-called 'innovative' forms of development finance.[64] Since 2015, the SDGs framework that accompanies the 2030 Agenda has also buttressed 'the institutional interfaces for deepening state–private capital hybrid formations'[65] of which bilateral DFIs are an important reflection. Bilateral DFIs take the form of SOEs that enmesh state authority with private market-based operational structures. Their financial operations mainly concern private sector promotion and investments in developing countries. Taking the legal form of SOEs, bilateral DFIs invoke important debates around ETOs of their home states, which often happen to be the politically and economically powerful states of the world. As has been reiterated in the Maastricht Principles, in line with their obligation to cooperate internationally for development and specifically for the realisation of economic, social, and cultural rights under Art. 2 ICESCR, states incur direct duties to ensure that they respect and protect human rights, including in relation to the activities of bilateral DFIs that they own. If we go a step further, to remedy structural power imbalances in the global economic order, the obligations of different states to rights-holders beyond their borders should be 'differentiated by the measure of power accorded to each of those states in the globalised market economy as well as the historical underpinnings of these power structures'.[66]

Bilateral DFIs themselves are a part of the broader power structures of the global economy. I have argued elsewhere that norms around the human rights obligations of businesses and financial institutions are being constructed through a legal process of contestation between different norm entrepreneurs supporting non-binding voluntary standards on the one hand and binding obligations on the other.[67] In this ongoing process of norm formation and contestation, bilateral DFIs are able to keep direct human rights scrutiny at bay by relying on the non-binding nature of most business and human rights frameworks, by highlighting they are at least one step removed from rights-holders and by placing the burden of 'risk' on businesses they finance. To ensure that the rights of individuals and communities affected by development projects financed or facilitated by DFIs are respected and protected, the risk-based governance models for environmental and social impact should be replaced

64 Romero, "Development Finance Takes "Private Turn"".

65 Emma Mawdsley, '"From Billions to Trillions": Financing the SDGs in a World "beyond Aid,"' *Dialogues in Human Geography* 8, no. 2 (July 2018): 193, https://doi.org/10.1177/2043820618780789.

66 De Moerloose, Erdem Türkelli, and Curtis, 'Extraterritorial Human Rights Obligations and International Financial Institutions', 278.

67 Erdem Türkelli, *Children's Rights and Business*, 86.

by rights-based governance of impacts backed up by procedurally and substantively effective mechanisms of access to remedy. Ultimately, development finance should work to deliver for the individual or community rights-holders who should be the real beneficiaries of sustainable development projects and policies, whether they are implemented through the public or the private sector.

Bibliography

Books

Bhatt, Kinnari I. *Concessionaires, Financiers and Communities: Implementing Indigenous Peoples' Rights to Land in Transnational Development Projects*. Cambridge: Cambridge University Press, 2020.

Erdem Türkelli, Gamze. *Children's Rights and Business: Governing Obligations and Responsibility*. Cambridge: Cambridge University Press, 2020.

Lander, Jennifer. *Transnational Law and State Transformation: The Case of Extractive Development in Mongolia*. Oxon: Routledge, 2020.

Vorisek, Dana, and Shu Yu. *Understanding the Cost of Achieving the Sustainable Development Goals*. World Bank, Washington, DC, 2020. https://doi.org/10.1596/1813-9450-9164.

Chapters in Edited Books

Catá Backer, Larry. 'Guiding Principle 4: The Obligations of States in Markets with Respect to Enterprises Owned, Controlled, or Supported by the State'. In *The UN Guiding Principles on Business and Human Rights: A Commentary*, edited by Barnali Choudhury, 35–41. Cheltenham: Edward Elgar, 2023.

De Moerloose, Stéphanie, Gamze Erdem Türkelli, and Joshua Curtis. 'Extraterritorial Human Rights Obligations and International Financial Institutions'. In *The Routledge Handbook on Extraterritorial Human Rights Obligations*, edited by Mark Gibney, Gamze Erdem Türkelli, Markus Krajewski, and Wouter Vandenhole, 1st ed., 271–83. London: Routledge, 2021.

Erdem Türkelli, Gamze. 'Guiding Principle 10: States as Members of Multilateral Institutions'. In *The UN Guiding Principles on Business and Human Rights: A Commentary*, edited by Barnali Choudhury, 77–84. Cheltenham: Edward Elgar, 2023.

Herre, Roman, and Stephan Backes. 'Financialization of Development Cooperation: ETO Responses'. In *The Routledge Handbook on Extraterritorial Human Rights Obligations*, edited by Mark Gibney, Gamze Erdem Türkelli, Markus Krajewski, and Wouter Vandenhole, 1st ed., 226–41. London: Routledge, 2021.

Martin, Jena. 'Guiding Principle 8: Ensuring Policy Coherence'. In *The UN Guiding Principles on Business and Human Rights: A Commentary*, edited by Barnali Choudhury, 63–69. Cheltenham: Edward Elgar, 2023.

Seck, Sara L. 'Guiding Principle 11: The Responsibility of Business Enterprises to Respect Human Rights'. In *The UN Guiding Principles on Business and Human Rights: A Commentary*, edited by Barnali Choudhury, 85–91. Cheltenham: Edward Elgar, 2023.

Articles

Catá Backer, Larry. 'The Human Rights Obligations of State-Owned Enterprises: Emerging Conceptual Structures and Principles in National and International Law and Policy'. *Vanderbilt Journal of Transnational Law* 50, no. 4 (October 2017): 827–88.

De Schutter, Olivier, Asbjørn Eide, Ashfaq Khalfan, Marcos Orellana, Margot Salomon, and Ian Seiderman. 'Commentary to the Maastricht Principles on Extraterritorial Obligations of States in the Area of Economic, Social and Cultural Rights'. *Human Rights Quarterly* 34, no. 4 (2012): 1084–1169.

Mawdsley, Emma. 'DFID, the Private Sector and the Re-Centring of an Economic Growth Agenda in International Development'. *Global Society* 29, no. 3 (2015): 339–58.

Mawdsley, Emma. '"From Billions to Trillions": Financing the SDGs in a World "beyond Aid"'. *Dialogues in Human Geography* 8, no. 2 (July 2018): 191–95.

Romero, María José. 'Development Finance Takes "Private Turn": Implications and Challenges Ahead'. *Development* 59, no. 1–2 (June 2016): 59–65.

Official Documents

Deva, Surya. 'Statement by Mr. Surya Deva, Chairperson of the Working Group on the Issue of Human Rights and Transnational Corporations and Other Business Enterprises 3rd Session of the Open-Ended Intergovernmental Working Group on Transnational Corporations and Other Business Enterprises with Respect to Human Rights'. 25 October 2017. https:// www.ohchr.org/EN/NewsEvents/Pages/DisplayNews.aspx?NewsID=22303&LangID=E.

International Conference on Financing for Development. 'Monterrey Consensus of the International Conference on Financing for Development'. International Conference on Financing for Development, 2002.

Open-ended intergovernmental working group on transnational corporations and other business enterprises with respect to human rights. The Third revised draft legally binding instrument to regulate, in international human rights law, the activities of transnational corporations and other business enterprises, Pub. L. No. A/HRC/52/41/Add.1 (2023).

The African Development Bank et al. "From Billions to Trillions: Transforming Development Finance Post-2015 Financing for Development: Multilateral Development Finance" (Development Committee (Joint Joint Ministerial

Committee of the Boards of Governors of the Bank and the Fund on the Transfer of Real Resources to Developing Countries), 2015).
The Better Utilization of Investments Leading to Development (BUILD) Act of 2018, H.R. 5105 § (2018).
UN Committee on Economic, Social and Cultural Rights (CESCR). 'General Comment No. 24 (2017) on State Obligations under the International Covenant on Economic, Social and Cultural Rights in the Context of Business Activities', 10 August 2017.
UN Committee on the Rights of the Child (CRC Committee). 'General Comment No. 16 (2013) on State Obligations Regarding the Impact of the Business Sector on Children's Rights', 17 April 2013.
United Nations General Assembly (UNGA). 'Transforming Our World: The 2030 Agenda for Sustainable Development'. United Nations, 2015.
United Nations Human Rights Council (UNHRC). 'Protect, Respect and Remedy: A Framework for Business and Human Rights', 7 April 2008.
United Nations Human Rights Council. 'United Nations Guiding Principles on Business and Human Rights (UNGPs)'. United Nations, 2011.
United Nations Working Group on the issue of human rights and transnational corporations and other business enterprises (UN WGBHR). 'Guiding Principles on Business and Human Rights at 10: Taking Stock of the First Decade', 22 April 2021.
United Nations Working Group on the issue of human rights and transnational corporations and other business enterprises (UN WGBHR). 'The Duty of States to Protect against Human Rights Abuses Involving Those Business Enterprises That They Own or Control'. United Nations Human Rights Council, 4 May 2016.

Miscellaneous

Equator Principles Financial Institutions (EPFIs). 'The Equator Principles (EP4)'. Equator Principles Financial Institutions (EPFIs), July 2020.
Gaspar, Vitor, David Amaglobeli, Mercedes Garcia, Delphine Prady, and Mauricio Soto. 'Fiscal Policy and Development: Human, Social, and Physical Investment for the SDGs'. IMF Staff Discussion Note, January 2019.
Ingram, George, and Robert A Mosbacher. 'Development Finance: Filling Today's Funding Gap'. Brookings, 2018.
Mader, Philip. 'Card Crusaders, Cash Infidels and the Holy Grails of Digital Financial Inclusion', 2016. https://doi.org/10.6094/BEHEMOTH.2016.9.2.916.
Riva, Massimiliano, and Marcos Neto. 'Discussion Paper: Mobilizing Private Finance for Sustainable Development'. United Nations Development Programme (UNDP), 30 November 2016. https://www.undp.org/publications/mobilizing-private-finance-sustainable-development.
UN Office of the High Commissioner for Human Rights (OHCHR). *Remedy in Development Finance Guidance and Practice*. New York: United Nations, 2022.

UN Office of the United Nations High Commissioner for Human Rights (OHCHR), 'Benchmarking Study of Development Finance Institutions' Safeguard Policies'. February 2023.

United Nations Development Programme (UNDP). 'South – South Ideas: The Role of Southern-Based Development Finance Institutions in South-South Cooperation and Mobilization of the Private Sector for Sustainable Development'. United Nations Development Programme (UNDP), February 2021.

PART 3

Business and Human Rights: Challenges for Implementation

CHAPTER 10

Human Rights Violations in Global Supply Chains: Acknowledging and Addressing Systemic Abuses

Olga Martin-Ortega

1 Introduction

Human and labour rights violations are not merely incidents in global supply chains. The complex structures through which the global production of goods is organised seek the minimisation of costs through highly fragmented and geographically dispersed networks. Through several tiers of production across several jurisdictions, the lower tiers of manufacture are often located in low and middle income countries. In this way, production in global supply chains minimises not just labour costs, but legal responsibility for most of the corporate actors involved.[1] Global supply chains are not only characterised by their transnational dimension and complexity, but also by the asymmetric power relations between brands and suppliers, contractor and subcontractors and ultimately corporate actors and workers.[2] In this context, workers at the lower tiers of the chain become vulnerable to abuse, from the moment they get recruited to how they are paid and made to work and when they are dismissed.

Classifying the violations of human and labour rights in the context of global supply chain is not an easy exercise. As Klara Skrivankova has argued, violations of human rights in supply chains compound a continuum of exploitation, ranging from low wages and abusive working conditions to forced labour and human trafficking.[3] As Genevieve LeBaron puts it: 'more often than not,

1 Radu Mares, "The Limits of Supply Chain Responsibility: A Critical Analysis of Corporate Responsibility Instruments," *Nordic Journal of International Law* 79 (2010): 194.

2 Opi Outhwaite and Olga Martin-Ortega, "Worker-driven monitoring – Redefining supply chain monitoring to improve labour rights in global supply chains," *Competition and Change* 23, no. 4 (2019): 378–396; Karin Lukas, "Human Rights in the Supply Chain: Influence and Accountability," in *The UN Guiding Principles on Business and Human Rights: Foundations and Implementation*, ed. Radu Mares (Leiden: Koninklijke Brill, 2012), 163.

3 Klara Skrivankova, "Between Decent Work and Forced Labour: Examining the Continuum of Exploitation," *Programme Paper 17* (Joseph Rowntree Foundation 2010), https://www.jrf.org.uk/report/between-decent-work-and-forced-labour-examining-continuum-exploitation.

 | DOI:10.1163/9789004530942_011

the forms of labour exploitation and abuse that workers confront in global supply chains are messy rather than clear-cut instances of forced labour, difficult to demarcate, and change over time'.[4]

The condition of vulnerability is not only linked to inherent personal characteristics, but also context specific. In other words, it is caused by diverse situational, and often temporary, elements which evolve into situations in which a person does not have any alternative but to submit to exploitation and other forms of abuse.[5] The ways in which the inequality of power, dependency, capacity or need make people vulnerable to harm or exploitation of others is what Mackenzie, Rogers and Dodds, refer to as 'situational vulnerability.'[6] By this concept they highlight how vulnerability is fostered by diverse factors, which include personal, social, political, economic and environmental situations, including abusive interpersonal and social relationships, socio-political oppression and injustice.[7] Therefore, abuses do not arise spontaneously in supply chains; rather, as LeBaron demonstrates in her work, patterns which result in vulnerability are part of the business models and commercial dynamics.[8] As the author asserts, 'working in an industry where low wages and minor forms of exploitation are endemic is a key factor that renders workers vulnerable to more severe forms of exploitation, including forced labour'.[9]

The international human rights and labour rights regimes have so far failed to provide an adequate response to this reality. Global supply chains dynamics

She articulated workers' experiences as been able to be placed somewhere on the continuum between "free", decent work, and "un-free" labour, ranging from minor harms to major and extreme ones, such as forced labour.

4 Genevieve LeBaron, "Wages: An Overlooked Dimension of Business and Human Rights in Global Supply Chains," *Business and Human Rights Journal* 6, no. 1 (2021): 5. See as well, Stephanie Barrientos, Uma Kothari and Nicola Phillips, "Dynamics of Unfree Labour in the Contemporary Global Economy," *The Journal of Development Studies* 49 (2013): 8.

5 Letizia Palumbo and Alessandra Sciurba, "The vulnerability to exploitation of women migrant workers in agriculture in the EU: the need for a Human Rights and Gender based approach". Study for the FEMM Committee, European Parliament, PE 604.966. May 2018.

6 Catriona Mackenzie, Wendy Rogers and Susan Dodds. "Introduction: What Is Vulnerability and Why Does It Matter for Moral Theory?," in *Vulnerability. New Essays in Ethics and Feminists Philosophy*, eds. Catriona Mackenzie, Wendy Rogers and Susan Dodds (Oxford: Oxford University Press, 2015), 6.

7 LeBaron, "Wages", 5.

8 Ibid, 16, on her study in the cocoa and tea industries which workers reporting that together with wage violations they experience violent treatment, threats, coercion and gender-based violence by employers, LeBaron, "Wages," 16. Also, on debt as a marker for vulnerability, even in non-migrant workers see: also Genevieve LeBaron, "Reconceptualizing Debt Bondage: Debt as a Class-Based Form of Labour Discipline," *Critical Sociology* 40, no. 5 (2014).

9 LeBaron, "Wages", 5.

demand regulatory frameworks which devise how to extend human and labour rights protection beyond individual states' borders, and how to remedy violations which take place away from where the decision maker sits. Human Rights Due Diligence (HRDD) is being suggested as a response to address human rights in global supply chains. The question that arises, however, is it enough to address systemic issues which perpetuate violations of workers' rights? This chapter looks at two specific issues: abusive labour recruitment – which subject workers to debt and bondage even before starting their employment relationship- and low wages – this is, wages that cannot be considered living wages, therefore, not enough to have a dignified life. Further, this chapter reflects on the nature of these as systemic issues in supply chains and whether HRDD can provide an answer to addressing them.

2 Systemic Human Rights Abuses in Global Supply Chains: Labour Recruitment and Wages

Low wages, wage underpayment, wage deductions, unfair and abusive labour recruitment are systemic problems in global supply chains as companies try to minimise costs. The need to minimise labour costs has resulted in the development of labour recruitment practices which rely on the outsourcing of this element of the employment relationship. When the recruitment of workers is undertaken in abusive ways and lack of living wages lead to indebtedness workers become vulnerable to subsequent abuses. Structures which expose workers to exploitation before they join the work force, and which do not allow them to cover their basic needs once they are in employment, serve to prevent their capacity to enjoy human rights, and therefore a dignified life.

2.1 *Unfair and Abusive Labour Recruitment*

Outsourcing labour recruitment is a common practice in the labour market, and, given the complexity of current supply chains, it takes place at a multiplicity of levels, both in the provision of services and the manufacturing of products. In global supply chains, labour is a commodity being sourced through recruitment. Most companies turn to recruitment agencies to fulfil this part of the business. Recruitment agencies play a key role in connecting the employer with the employee and address the supply and demand for labour across geographies and sectors and are an important aspect of the economy.[10]

10 UNODC, 'The Role of Recruitment Fees and Abusive and Fraudulent Recruitment Practices of Recruitment Agencies in Trafficking in Persons' 2015, 1.

Recruitment agencies can be responsible for making travel arrangements, organising visas, medical check-ups, orientation, training, and contract negotiation.[11] Significant risks of human rights abuse arise with the intervention of unscrupulous employment agencies, individual recruiters and intermediaries – where workers are recruited by illegal agencies or individual labour brokers, or even by genuine agencies that are complicit in the exploitation that follows, or negligently exacerbate it. Unscrupulous employment agencies and recruiters may demand illegal recruitment fees, practice retention of identification and travel documents, provide misleading information about the job offer and working and living conditions. Some resort to methods of control, which can include debt bondage, isolation, surveillance, withholding money, withholding identification documents, threats of and actual violence, and threats of denunciation to authorities for irregular migrant workers.

The charging of illegal recruitment fees is a prevalent issue in global production systems and leads to further exploitation. The indebtedness that often follows abusive recruitment processes and the need to repay the debt incurred during them often drives workers to accept exploitative working conditions.[12] These forms of recruitment may lead to "unfree labour".[13] These are forms of labour which do not fall within the definitions of slavery, forced labour or trafficking for the purposes of labour exploitation, but still defy the definition of free wage labour. Unfree labour is devised as a wider concept than forced labour by Breznik, resulting from practices that are directly related to abusive recruitment and akin to 'purchasing' the labour power of workers,[14] most frequently migrant workers. Abuses are therefore facilitated by debt, and as the author puts it:"an employment relationship entered voluntarily can easily turn into unfree labour because of the debt trap which prevents the worker to terminate the exploitative relations."[15]

A great number of those most affected by unfair and abusive labour recruitment are migrant workers, who are more likely to become bonded and trapped in an inescapable situation due to recruitment agencies taking advantage of their vulnerability and dependent status. The Special Rapporteur on Human Rights of Migrants specifically identified a series of factors which place migrants at a heightened risk of exploitation and abuse in the workplace.[16]

11 Ibid, 5.

12 Ibid, 1.

13 Maja Breznik, "Unfree wage labour", *Critical Sociology,* 49, nos 7–8 (February 2023): 1; 3.

14 Breznik, "Unfree", 11.

15 Ibid.

16 Report of the Special Rapporteur on the human rights of migrants, Labour exploitation of migrants, A/HRC/26/35, 3 April 2014, para 18.

These include deceptive recruitment practices, both by employers and intermediaries; lack of social support systems; lack of familiarity with the local culture, language, and lack of awareness regarding their rights at work and national labour and migration laws in the country of employment; limited or denied access to legal and administrative systems; dependence on the job and employer due to migration-related debt, legal status, or practices including employers restricting their freedom to leave the workplace; and the pressure which derives from reliance by family members on remittances sent back home by the migrant worker.

The international legal framework relating to labour recruitment is relatively recent. Recruitment as such appears as one of the activities which constitutes human trafficking, when its done by means of threat or use of force or other forms of coercion, of abduction, of fraud, of deception, of the abuse of power or of a position of vulnerability or of the giving or receiving of payments or benefits to achieve the consent of a person having control over another person and with the purpose of exploitation (Article 3 of the Protocol to Prevent, Suppress and Punish Trafficking in Persons Especially Women and Children 2003). Nevertheless, the global understanding of 'recruitment' in relation to forced labour has remained limited. In 2009, the ILO published the 'Operational Indicators of Trafficking in Human Beings'[17] in which it categorised trafficking indicators according to different types of exploitation. Three of the six categories refer to recruitment: deceptive recruitment, coercive recruitment, and recruitment by abuse of vulnerability. The indicators within those categories include: violence, confiscation of documents, debt bondage, isolation, threat of denunciation to authorities, withholding money, excessive working hours, no salary, wage manipulation, bad living conditions, deception about the conditions of work, deception about migration status, and deception about travel conditions, among others. That same year the ILO published it Global Report 'Cost of Coercion' which made a thematic link between labour exploitation and recruitment, or more specifically, recruitment agencies.[18] The report expresses serious concerns regarding the substantial profits made by a range of recruiting intermediaries, from informal labour brokers to registered agencies, at the expense of workers, including migrant workers.[19]

17 ILO, Operational indicators of trafficking in human beings (March 2009, revised September 2009). https://www.ilo.org/wcmsp5/groups/public/---ed_norm/---declaration/documents/publication/wcms_105023.pdf, accessed December 18, 2023.

18 ILO, The Cost of Coercion. Global Report on Forced Labour 2009. https://www.ilo.org/wcmsp5/groups/public/---ed_norm/---declaration/documents/publication/wcms_106268.pdf, accessed December 18, 2023.

19 Ibid, 2.

The concept of 'fair recruitment' has only recently entered international discourse. It was first developed in the context of the ILO project "Towards stronger measures to combat abusive labour recruitment and to prevent human trafficking, "[20] launched in 2013 and followed by its 'Fair Recruitment Initiative' (FAIR), two years later.[21] Significantly, in 2016, the ILO published the General Principles and Operational Guidelines for Fair Recruitment (GPOG). and expanded them in 2019 to include the 'Definition of recruitment fees and related costs'.[22]

Parallel to this development, civil society and multistakeholder initiatives have attempted to address unfair labour recruitment practices through principles and frameworks of action. In 2012, the Dhaka Principles for Migration with Dignity were finalised by the Institute for Human Rights and Business (IHRB),[23] which include the principles: "No fees are charged to migrant workers", known as the "employer pays" principle (Principle 1); "all migrant worker contracts are clear and transparent" (Principle 2) and "no migrant workers" passports or identity documents are retained' (Principle 4).[24] Many other civil society organisations, international organisations and academics have

---

20 ILO, Towards stronger measures to combat abusive labour recruitment and to prevent human trafficking (2013–2015), https://www.ilo.org/global/topics/forced-labour/projects/WCMS_320238/lang--en/index.htm, accessed December 18, 2023. The project culminated in the publication of a report titled 'Regulating labour recruitment to prevent human trafficking and to foster fair migration: Models, challenges and opportunities' in 2015, https://www.ilo.org/wcmsp5/groups/public/---ed_norm/---declaration/documents/publication/wcms_377813.pdf, accessed December 18, 2023.

21 ILO, https://www.ilo.org/global/topics/fair-recruitment/fri/lang--en/index.htm. FAIR has now been extended until 2025 IOLO Fair Recruitment Initiative Strategy 2021–2025- Taking stock, moving forward, https://www.ilo.org/global/topics/fair-recruitment/WCMS_817166/lang--en/index.htm, August 2021). In 2014, the ILO and the IOM, founded by the EU convened with "Asian recruitment agencies in Manila on 1–2 April to discuss ways to improve migration governance systems, ethical recruitment and the professionalization of the industry" (ILO 2014a and 2014b). Between 2017 and 2020, the ILO implemented a Global Action to Improve the Recruitment Framework of Labour Migration (REFRAME) project, founded by the European Union.

22 ILO, General principles and operational guidelines for fair recruitment and definition of recruitment fees and related costs, 2019, https://www.ilo.org/global/topics/labour-migration/publications/WCMS_536755/lang--en/index.htm.

23 Dhaka Principles for Migration with Dignity, https://dhakaprinciples.org/, accessed December 18, 2023.

24 In 2013, the IHBR published a report on 'Fees and IDs: Tackling recruitment fees and confiscation of workers' passports' which also contributed to the understanding of recruitment in international discourse. And, since 2017, runs an annual 'Global Forum on Responsible Recruitment', see https://www.ihrb.org/employerpays/global-forum-for-responsible-recruitment, accessed December 18, 2023.

addressed the issue of fair recruitment since then.[25] In 2019, Electronics Watch published the 'Guidance for Remediation and prevention of Migrant Worker Recruitment Fees and Related Costs in Public Procurement'[26] making it the first, and so far only, guidance directed at the public sector.

The most authoritative definition of abusive labour recruitment practices is the one found in the ILO GPOG. The GPOG refer to recruitment which does not take place in a way that respects, protects and fulfils internationally recognised international labour standards, and in particular the right to freedom of association and collective bargaining, and prevention and elimination of forced labour, child labour and discrimination in respect of employment and occupation.[27] Unfair labour recruitment is thus directly related to risks of forced labour, as practices such as the collection of recruitment fees increase workers' risks of experiencing debt bondage, a key indicator for this type of abuse.[28] These risks, in turn, are significantly higher in migration corridors to labour-intensive, low-skilled labour and poorly paid industries. According to the ILO's own figures from 2022, the share of migrants among those in forced labour is much higher than the share of migrants in the overall labour force.[29]

The GPOG establish a clear responsibility for governments to protect workers from recruitment abuses and to address them were they to happen, both when acting as employers and through their procurement activities.[30] They also explicitly refer to the use of human rights due diligence assessments to identify abusive labour recruitment.[31] However, as will be discussed in the next section, human rights due diligence could prove insufficient to address violations related to abusive recruitment.

---

25 Including, but by no means limited to, the ETI, ICCR, NYU STERN, Polaris, Verité, and the UNODC.

26 Electronics Watch, "Guidance for Remediation and prevention of Migrant Worker Recruitment Fees and Related Costs in Public Procurement" (2019), https://electronicswatch.org/guidance-for-remediation-and-prevention-of-migrant-worker-recruitment-fees-and-related-costs-in-public-procurement-april-2019_2557767.pdf, accessed December 18, 2023.

27 GPOG, III.1.

28 ILO, Walk Free and the International Organization for Migration., *Global Estimates of Modern Slavery: Forced Labour and Forced Marriage* (12 September 2022), 4.

29 Ibid, 3. See as well ILO Global Estimates on International Migrant Workers, Results and Methodology (Labour Migration Branch Conditions of Work, Equality Department and Department of Statistics (2021), https://www.ilo.org/global/topics/labour-migration/publications/WCMS_808935/lang--en/index.htm, accessed December 18 2023).

30 GPOG Principles 14 and 15.

31 GPOG Principle 15.

Abusive labour recruitment intersects with all International Core Labour Standards, as workers subjected to unfair recruitment practices tend to also be the victims of other labour rights abuses. Therefore, it can be argued that preventing and addressing such practices also fall within the scope of the state obligations established in the Declaration of Fundamental Rights and Principles as Work (1998).

Furthermore, ILO member states have a series of legal obligations directly related to the prevention of forced labour and the remediation and redress for victims, which are directly linked to the prevention of abusive labour recruitment, and these include the public sector. Protocol 029 (2014) to the Forced Labour Convention, 1930 (P029), which requires members to take "effective measures" to address forced labour, suggests that the latter may include a specific focus on preventing abusive recruitment practices, and on supporting due diligence efforts also by the public sector aimed to address forced labour risks.[32] The Forced Labour Supplementary Measures Recommendation (No. 203), 2014, adds to this by stating that members should eliminate abusive labour recruitment practices by recruiters and employment agencies, including the charging of recruitment fees to workers.[33] Lastly, some ILO normative instruments relating to recruitment also refer to public employment, but are mostly focused on private recruitment and abuse in the private sector.[34]

2.2 *Low Wages and the Lack of Living Wages*

The role of low wages in enabling workers' vulnerability to exploitation, as well as deepening and accelerating it, has received little attention in the literature and practice.[35] LeBaron refers to both low wages and wage violations. She uses this term to encompass sub-minimum wages, unlawful deductions from wages and rendering wage payment conditional on involuntary work.[36] Importantly, the author links low wages to the patterns of vulnerability to forced labour. Low wages also play a key role in unfree labour, defined above. Debt spirals brought by low income facilitate dependability of the worker from the employer and makes them vulnerable to exploitation.[37] The relationship between wages and

32 Protocol 029 (2014) to the Forced Labour Convention, 1930 (P029) Arts 1 and 2.

33 R203 – Forced Labour (Supplementary Measures) Recommendation, 2014 (No. 203).

34 E.g. ILO C094 – Labour Clauses (Public Contracts) Convention, 1949 (No. 94); ILO Private Employment Agencies Convention No. 181 (1997), Art 7; ILO Migration for Employment Convention No. 97 (1949) Art 4.

35 LeBaron, "Wages".

36 Ibid.

37 Sabine Damir-Geilsdorf, "Contract labour and debt bondage in the Arab Gulf States: Policies and practices within the kafala system" in *Bonded Labour: Global and*

vulnerability to forced labour in global supply chains has important implications for efforts to understand and promote responsible business conduct, and as LeBaron argues, attention should be paid to "business models and supply chain dynamics, traceable to stable patterns including those surrounding workers earning and wage violations perpetrated by employers."[38] This is explored further in the next section when considering the coverage of the supply chain and purchasing dynamics in the context of human rights due diligence.

The debate on low wages is directly related to the efforts to advocate for a minimumliving wage or living income. Being paid less than a living wage means that workers are unable to cover their basic needs and in turn this has significant repercussions towards adequate nutrition, access to health services, decent housing, social security and education for them and their families.[39] Also, in order to supplement their income – and therefore have a living income – workers need to work overtime and excessive hours, potentially not being able to reject hazardous and dangerous work and working conditions.

Living wages cannot be equated to minimum wages, as the former do not necessarily guarantee an adequate standard of living for workers and their families.[40] Minimum wages are protected by International law and most countries have regulatory frameworks establishing them. According to ILO Minimum Wage Fixing Convention, 1970 (No. 131) two factors should be taken into consideration when establishing minimum wages: the needs of workers and their families and economic factors, which relate to levels of development of the country, productivity, and desirability of attaining and maintaining high levels of employment (art. 3). Therefore, minimum wages are set as part of a political process and as such they reflect the relative power of both employers and workers,[41] which in global supply chains is not equal, as argued above. Living wages are estimated based on the cost of basic acceptable living standards. The fact that minimum wages are not solely determined by the needs of workers and their families is consistent with the significant gap in many

---

Comparative Perspectives 18th–21st Century ed. Sabine Damir-Geilsdorf, Ulrike Lindner, Geise Muller, Oliver Tappe and Michael Zeuske (Transcript, Global Studies, 2016), 163–90.

38 LeBaron, "Wages", 3.

39 Valerie Nelson, Olga Martin-Ortega and Michael Flint, *Making Human Rights Due Diligence Work: An Analysis of Impact and Legal Options*, Fair Trade Advocacy Office and Brot für die Welt, 2020.

40 See for example, Clean Clothes Campaign, *Tailored Wages 20219. The state of pay in the global garment industry* (lead study author Anna Bryher), June 2019, arguing that in most garment producing countries minimum wages are not enough to live on.

41 Richard Anker and Marth Anker, *Living Wages around the World. Manual for Measurements* (Cheltenham, Edward Elgar, 2017), 11.

countries between most definitions of a living wage and the legal minimum wage. In contrast, as Anker and Anker argue, living wages are only concerned with worker needs and therefore their estimation should be insulated from political considerations and the relative power of workers.[42] In practice, minimum wages are generally significantly below any research-determined living wage level. Legal enforcement of national or sub-national minimum wages will not, in general, therefore achieve a living wage.

There is no internationally agreed definition of living wages, which have led to differing definitions of what they encompass and how they should be calculated. A comprehensive one is the definition offered by the Global Living Wage Coalition:

> The remuneration received for a standard workweek by a worker in a particular place sufficient to afford a decent standard of living for the worker and her or his family. Elements of a decent standard of living include food, water, housing, education, health care, transportation, clothing and other essential needs including provision for unexpected events.[43]

Whilst international legal instruments do not define living wages as a right, there is a good case for considering the right to a living wage as an internationally recognised human right. Article 23 of the Universal Declaration of Human Rights (UDHR) states that everyone who works has the right to: 'just and favourable remuneration ensuring for himself and his family an existence worthy of human dignity, and supplemented, if necessary, by other means of social protection'. The International Covenant on Economic, Social and Cultural Rights (ICECSR) guarantees the right of everyone to: 'just and favourable conditions of work which ensure in particular (a) remuneration which provides all workers, as a minimum, with [...] (ii) a decent living for themselves and their families in accordance with the provisions of the present Covenant' (Article 7). ILO Declarations and Conventions provide further, but not complete, support for living wages as a right. The preamble of the Constitution of the ILO (1919) mentions the provision of an 'adequate living wage', as do a number of other ILO Declarations adopted since, including the 1994 Philadelphia Declaration on the aims and purpuses of the ILO, which refers to 'a minimum

42 Ibid.

43 Global Living Wage Coalition website (n.d.), https://www.globallivingwage.org/, accessed December 18, 2023.

living wage.'[44] However, a living wage is not mentioned in the ILO Declaration on Fundamental Principles and Rights at Work (1988) nor in the ILO Centenary Declaration (2019); it is not covered by the eight 'fundamental' Conventions; and it is not guaranteed by Conventions 131 and 135 on minimum wages, as argued above.

The case for considering a right to a living wage is endorsed by major human rights bodies in charge of the interpretation of human rights instruments,[45] all of which state that a right to work includes a right to remuneration that must provide for a decent living.[46] In General Comment No. 23 on the right to just and favourable conditions of work (Article 7 ICESCR) – in which agricultural workers are granted special consideration due to their vulnerable labour conditions – [47] the Committee on Economic, Social and Cultural Rights (CESCR) states that the remuneration must guarantee a decent living. Meaning by this: a remuneration 'sufficient to enable the worker and his or her family to enjoy other rights in the Covenant, such as social security, health care, education and an adequate standard of living, including food, water and sanitation, housing, clothing and additional expenses such as commuting costs.'[48] A similar approach is taken by the European Committee of Social Rights (ECSR). While arguing that a minimum wage must satisfy a decent standard of living, the ECSR states that such a standard 'goes beyond merely material basic

44 See ILO, *The International Labour Organisation and the Living Wage: a Historical Perspective.* Conditions of Work and Employment Series No. 90 (2017).

45 The right to fair remuneration and minimum wage is contained within core human rights instruments UDHR, ICESCR and European Social Charter, the American Declaration and the San Salvador Protocol. See Annex 1 for complete international human rights instruments references to this topic. See also the report The Circle 'Fashion Focus: The Fundamental Right to a Living Wage' 2017 27–30.

46 See Annex 1 UDHR Article 23 'existence worthy of human dignity' ICESCR Article 7 'decent living'; American Declaration on the Rights and Duties of Men Article 7 'standard of living'; Salvador Protocol Article 7 'decent living conditions' European Social Charter Article 4.1 'decent standard of living'.

47 CESCR, General Comment No. 23 on the right to just and favourable conditions of work (Article 7 ICESCR) E/C.12/GC/23 para. 47(h); See also Annex 1(g).

48 ibid. para. 18. In its *Greek General Confederation of Labour* (GSEE) *v. Greece* (2017) case the ESCRC considered that Greece had violated its obligations regarding the right to a minimun wage by reducing its threashold in such a way that it would not meet the conditions of a decent standard of living: cover basic necessities and provide resources for participating in cultural, educational and social activities for the worker and their families. 'Digest of the Case Law of the European Committee of Social Rights' (2018) 85. See also the case *General Federation of Employees of the National Electric Power Corporation* (*GENOP-DEI*) *and Confederation of Greek Civil Servants' Trade Unions* (*ADEDY*) *v. Greece* (2011) 23-05-2012. paras. 57–65.

necessities such as food, clothing and housing, and includes resources necessary to participate in cultural, educational and social activities.'[49]

However, linking decent living conditions to wages excludes people whose income does not depend on formal payment through wages, for example small farm holders. To address this gap the concept of living income has been proposed. A living income revolves around households having the ability to afford a decent standard of living and is defined as 'the net annual income required for a household in a particular place to afford a decent standard of living for all members of that household'.[50] The concept of living income recognises that a household earns can come from multiple sources. The Living Income Community of Practice definition of Living Income:

> The net annual income required for a household in a particular place to afford a decent standard of living for all members of that household. Elements of a decent standard of living include: food, water, housing, education, healthcare, transport, clotting and other essential needs including provisions for unexpected events.[51]

Nonetheless, there is no internationally recognised definition of living income, nor is it protected as a right by international human rights law. Similar arguments to those used for living wages, analysed above, have been used to argue that a living income is an internationally recognised as a human right.[52] However, whilst the right to a living wage has been further developed in international treaties and jurisprudence, the same cannot be said for the right to a living income.[53]

In the absence of a human right to a living income, human rights bodies, specifically successive Special Rapporteurs on the Right to Adequate Food,

---

49 European Committee of Social Rights 'Digest of the Case Law of the European Committee Of Social Rights' (2018) 85.

50 IDH, What is a living income? Website (n.d.), https://www.idhsustainabletrade.com/roadmap-on-living-income/, accessed December 18, 2023.

51 The Living Income Community of Practice website (n.d.), https://www.living-income.com/, accessed December 18, 2023.

52 Fountain, A.C, and Hütz-Adams, F. "Defining a Decent Living. Living Income for Smallholder Cocoa Farmers in West Africa. On calculations of living wages in the cocoa sector see too Duncan Brack, Towards sustainable cocoa supply chains: Regulatory options for the EU" (Fern, Tropenbos International and Fair Trade Advocacy Office, 2020), https://www.fern.org/fileadmin/uploads/fern/Documents/2019/Fern-sustainable-cocoa-supply-chains-report.pdf, accessed December 18 2023.

53 Nelson, Martin-Ortega and Flint, "Making."

have addressed the situation of poverty and sustainability of small holders from a right to food's approach.[54] This approach argues for state obligations arising from the right to food (respect, protect and fulfil) to be accomplished. Therefore, states should implement policies that include legislation towards guaranteeing fair prices, competition law and prevent abusive practices.[55] As a result, such policies contribute to move towards a decent price for the products elaborated by small-holders and the realisation of the right to an adequate standard of living.[56]

This section demonstrates that the lack of living wages, and living incomes, do not only enhance human rights risks in supply chains but are risks in themselves, which as will be discussed below are not specifically considered in the context of efforts to identify, prevent, mitigate, and remedy human rights violations through due diligence.

3 Addressing Systemic Abuses in Global Supply Chains: Is Human Rights Due Diligence Enough?

In recent years, states and regional organisations have developed the normative framework of corporate responsibility to respect human rights through the passing of laws and regulations obliging companies to undertake HRDD in their supply chain. These regulations focus on the most severe violations, which to some extent means that some of the comparatively less severe systemic issues such as the lack of living wages and risks associated with unfair labour recruitment, remain unaddressed.

The existence of these systemic issues and their impact on the vulnerability of workers in the supply chain are acknowledged by the Organisation for Economic Co-operation and Development (OECD) as problems which are prevalent in business operations contexts. The OECD Due Diligence Guidance for Responsible Business Conduct (2018) acknowledges that they may be driven by root causes outside of the enterprise's immediate control, but that nonetheless increase the risk of adverse impacts within the enterprise's own operations or supply chain.[57] According to the OECD Guidance, systemic risks may arise

54 ibid. para. 26.

55 'Report of the Special Rapporteur on the right to food' (2009) A/HRC/13/33 Add2. paras. 30, 34.

56 'The right to food' 4 August 2011A/66/262 para. 12. See Annex 2.

57 OECD Due Diligence Guidance for Responsible Business Conduct (2019), https://www.oecd.org/investment/due-diligence-guidance-for-responsible-business-conduct.htm, accessed December 18, 2023.

from governance failures and the failure of governments to fulfil their duty to enforce the laws and protect human rights. To some extent, the OECD Guidance relieves companies of their responsibility, expressing that enterprises are not responsible for the failure of governments, even though it acknowledges that "the decision to conduct activities in contexts where systemic risks exist will increase the nature and extent of due diligence."[58] This definition of systemic issues fails to recognise the role of companies in perpetuating and enhancing risks by specifically placing them outside of companies' control. Relying upon a labour force recruited through abusive practices which make workers vulnerable to abuse and resorting to purchasing practices which push down the cost of labour to suppliers, resulting in low wages and lack of a living income, together with other issues such as short lead times and constant need for overtime to undertake production, should fall within the scope of what companies are required to address to fulfil their human rights responsibilities.

This section, after introducing the concept of HRDD and how it is developing in current normative frameworks, considers the deficiencies of HRDD in addressing abusive labour recruitment and lack of living wages.

3.1 *Definition and Normative Development of HRDD*

The UN Framework on Business and Human Rights (2008) proposed a three pillars approach to addressing corporate impact on human rights: states duty to protect, corporate responsibility to respect and victims' right to remedy. In their development of the framework, the UN Guiding Principle on Business and Human Rights (UNGPs) (2011) developed the corporate responsibility to respect around the standard of HRDD.[59] The concept has taken shape through state practice and business commitments and has been further developed by other soft law instruments, most prominently, by its insertion in the OECD Guidelines for Multinational Enterprises and the OECD Due Diligence Guidance for Responsible Business Conduct, referred to above.[60] These

58 Ibid, 76.

59 UN Human Rights Council, 'Guiding Principles on Business and Human Rights: Implementing the United Nations "Protect, Respect and Remedy" Framework', *Report of the Special Representative of the Secretary-General on the issue of human rights and transnational corporations and other business enterprises – Guiding Principles on Business and Human Rights: Implementing the United Nations "Protect, Respect and Remedy" Framework* (UN Doc A/HRC/17/31, (21 March 2011), Annex 2011) 16–20.

60 Guidelines for Multinational Enterprises 2011, Chapter IV. Human Rights, para 5, Commentary (paras 45–46); OECD Due Diligence Guidance.

embody a shift from a process to identify material risks for the company to a mechanism to address the salient impact of corporate activities on people.[61]

HRDD consists of embedding responsible business conduct into policy and management systems; identifying and assessing actual and potential adverse impacts associated with the enterprise's operations, products or services; ceasing, preventing and mitigating adverse impacts; tracking implementation and results; communicating how impacts are addressed and providing for or cooperating in remediation when appropriate. HRDD should cover adverse human rights impacts that business enterprises may cause or contribute to through their own activities, or which may be directly linked to their operations, products or services by its business relations. It will vary in complexity with the size of the specific business enterprise undertaking it, the severity of human rights impacts of its practices and commercial relationships, and the nature and context of its operations. It is an ongoing process; recognising that the human rights risks may change over time as the business enterprise's operations and operating context evolve. The UNGPs and the OECD Due Diligence Guidance focus on a process-oriented approach.

The standard continues to be developed through international soft law frameworks and guidance for states and companies, including sectoral guidance (for example, agri-food -and directly related, land tenure-,[62] garment and footwear sector,[63] financial sector).[64] Furthermore, HRDD has continued to evolve as a standard through the development of national and regional (EU) legislation which has further elaborated on the scope of companies' legal obligations within the context of their broader corporate responsibility to respect. The first national instruments to create obligations for companies regarding their human rights impact in their supply chains focused on the transparency aspect of HRDD, more precisely, establishing obligations to

61 Olga Martin-Ortega, "Human Rights Due Diligence for Corporations: From Voluntary Standards to Hard Law at Last?," *Netherlands Quarterly of Human Rights* 32, no.1, 2014: 44–74. See as well, Jonathan Bonnitcha and, Robert McCorquodale, "The Concept of 'Due Diligence' in the UN Guiding Principles on Business and Human Rights," *European Journal of International Law* 28, no.3 (2017): 899–919; Justine Nolan, "Hardening Soft Law: Are the Emerging Corporate Social Disclosure Laws Capable of Generating Substantive Compliance with Human Rights?," *Brazilian Journal of International Law* 15 (2018): 65.

62 OECD-FAO Guidance for Responsible Agricultural Supply Chains 2016; Voluntary Guidelines on the Responsible Governance of Tenure of Land, Fisheries and Forests in the Context of National Food Security 2022.

63 OECD Due Diligence Guidance for Responsible Supply Chains in the Garment and Footwear Sector 2018.

64 IFC Performance Standards on Environmental and Social Sustainability 2012.

report on their efforts to exercise HRDD. Mandatory reporting instruments include the EU Non-Financial Reporting Directive, UK Modern Slavery Act, California Transparency in the Supply Chain Act, and the Australia Modern Slavery Act. These frameworks prescribe what should be reported and how, including suggestions on what HRDD measures companies ought to take, but do not demand further corporate action, nor do they seek a specific outcome regarding the prevention of human rights abuses. These frameworks have been lauded in responsible business discourse, but widely critiqued by civil society and the scholarly literature for their limited scope and impact, because they do not formally require the implementation of a HRDD process, and in some cases, HRDD reporting is only a suggestion.[65]

Mandatory HRDD instruments go a step further, requiring substantive HRDD action from companies to assess, prevent and mitigate critical human rights risks, and as necessary, to remedy actual harm, in addition to requiring them to publicly report on their HRDD. Examples of existing mandatory due diligence frameworks include the US Dodd-Frank Act Section 1502 on conflict minerals, the French Duty of Vigilance Law, Australian Illegal Logging, the Dutch Child Labour Due Diligence Law, the German Act on Corporate Due Diligence in Supply Chains and the Norwegian Transparency Law.[66] At regional level, the EU is leading the development of regulation with its EU Conflict Minerals Regulation, EU Timber Regulation and most significantly the Directive on Corporate Sustainability Due Diligence (CSDDD), adopted in June 2024.[67]

Enforcement provisions and sanctions for non-compliance vary in current regulatory models.[68] Sanctions range from fines impossed at administrative

65 See for example, Olga Martin-Ortega, "Transparency and human rights in global supply chains: from corporate-led disclosure to a right to know" in *Research Handbook on Global Governance, Business and Human Rights* eds. Axel Marx, Geert Van Calster, Jean Monnet, Jan Wouters, Kari Otteburn, Diana Lica (Cheltenham: Edward Elgar, 2022), 99–119; Radu Mares, "Corporate transparency laws: A hollow victory?," *Netherlands Quarterly of Human Rights* 36, no. 3 (2018): 189–213; Robert McCorquodale and Justine Nolan, "The Effectiveness of Human Rights Due Diligence for Preventing Business Human Rights Abuses," *Netherlands International Law Review* 68 (2021): 455–478.

66 For several years Switzerland debated the passing of a due diligence law, which was finally rejected, See for example Nicolas Bueno and Christine Kaufmann, "The Swiss Human Rights Due Diligence Legislation: Between Law and Politics," *Business and Human Rights Journal* 6, no. 3 (2021): 542–549.

67 Directive (EU) 2024/1760 of the European Parliament and of the Council of 13 June 2024 on Corporate Sustainability Due Diligence and amending Directive (EU) 2019/1937 and Regulation (EU) 2023/2859. OJ L, 2024/1760, 5.7.2024.

68 Claire Methven O'Brien and Olga Martin-Ortega, "EU Human Rights Due Diligence Legislation: Monitoring, Enforcement and Access to Justice for Victims' Study for the

level to civil and criminal liability.[69] The EU CSDDD establishes competences to supervisory authorities in Member States to impose administrative sanctions when infringements of the national provisions adopted pursuant the Directive have occurred (arts. 24 and 25).

The extent and type of legal liability for the human rights violations derived from lack of exercise of HRDD is a key issue, which is yet to be tested in most legislative frameworks. This includes the extent of the liability of parent companies for the actions of their suppliers. Important open questions remain regarding the need to prove causality links between corporate action, or that of their subsidiaries and suppliers and the harm suffered, as well as where the burden of proof that actions were not enough to prevent harm were undertaken. The EU CSDDD Directive establishes civil liability for companies which fail to comply with their due diligence obligations and if as result of this failure an adverse impact on human rights should have been identified, prevented, mitigated, brought to an end or its extent minimised through the appropriate measures which should have been established as part of the due diligence obligations and have led to damage (art. 29).

Finally, provisions for remediation within HRDD frameworks are closely related to enforcement and legal liability. In voluntary frameworks, particularly those that focus narrowly on the due diligence process, remediation measures are often ignored. In the UNGPs, adverse impacts that are only linked to a company's operation (i.e. it has not 'caused' or 'contributed' to them) do not trigger a requirement that the enterprise itself should provide remediation, although they may choose to be involved.[70] Remediation is also a grey area in some of the mandatory HRDD frameworks.[71] The EU CSDDD provides a siginificant advancement in the consideration of remediation as a key element of due diligence. Article 5 includes the establishment of complaint procedures and remediation of actual adverse impacts as part of the actions which form part of the due diligence obligation. Companies which have caused or jointly cased an actual adversy impact have to provide remediation whilst they may

---

DROI Subcommittee, European Parliament, PE 603.505 (2020), https://www.europarl.europa.eu/thinktank/en/document/EXPO_BRI(2020)603505, accessed December 18, 2023.

69 Criminal sanctions were removed from the French law by the Constitutional Court, see Elsa Savourey and Stéphane Brabant, "The French Law on the Duty of Vigilance: Theoretical and Practical Challenges Since Its Adoption," *Business and Human Rights Journal* 6, no. 1 (2021): 141–52.

70 UNGP, 2011, Principle 22, Commentary.

71 Claire Methven O'Brien and Olga Martin-Ortega, "EU Human Rights Due Diligence Legislation.

choose to do it voluntarily when the actual adverse impact is cased only by their business partners (Article 12). Companies should enable complaints procedures for persons affected by adverse impacts, trade unions and other workers' representatives and civil society organisations (Art. 14). These provisions were strengthened in the process of negotiation between the Council and the Parliament, by reinforcing the civil liability provisions and the access to justice of persons affected and limiting disclosure of evidence, injunctive measures and cost of the proceedings for claimants.[72]

3.2 *The Scope of Human Rights Protection and the Deficiencies of Focusing on Severity*

Major differences exist in the sectoral scope of the differing frameworks and instruments, with some not focusing specifically on human rights.[73] Whilst some laws focus on specific violations, such as forced labour, human trafficking and child labour, most of the mandatory HRDD norms aligning with the UNGPs, defining human rights as 'internationally recognised human rights', which is understood as a minimum as those expressed in the International Bill of Human Rights (Universal Declaration of Human Rights and the International Covenants of Civil and Political Rights and Economic, Social and Cultural Rights), and the fundamental rights as set out in the ILO Declaration on Fundamental Principles and Rights at Work. The definition of risks in the supply chain through their inclusion in international human rights instruments can have unintended consequences when considering whether HRDD extends to systemic issues, including the exposure to debt and the lack of living wages. The first one regards the nature and legal force living wages, and living income, as international human rights recognised by international human rights law and implemented as such; this is, establishing an obligation for states to enforce the rights and resulting on violation of such obligations when individuals are denied the enjoyment of such rights for failing to respect and protect them, including from corporations.

72 See Council of the EU, Press Release, Corporate sustainability due diligence: Council and Parliament strike deal to protect environment and human rights (14 December 2023), https://www.consilium.europa.eu/en/press/press-releases/2023/12/14/corporate-sustainability-due-diligence-council-and-parliament-strike-deal-to-protect-environment-and-human-rights/, accessed December 18, 2023.

73 Eg. The EU Conflict Minerals Regulation and EU Timber Regulation focus on breaking the nexus between illegal exploitation of minerals and illegal lodging and armed conflict and environmental damage and social conflict respectively.

The second main challenge regards the operationalisation of HRDD, in particular, the way in which risks are identified and prioritised. As demonstrated by McCorquodale, Smit, Neely and Brooks in their empirical study of human rights due diligence practices, business tend to use risk-based methodologies to identify human rights impacts.[74] Fasterling states that the human rights due diligence requirement, as defined by the UNGPs, is hardly compatible with management of social risk as conventional risk management methods are generally inadequate to identify human rights risks.[75]

The concept of salience of risk also presents an obstacle for the practical implementation when it comes to systemic issues such as abusive labour recruitment and low wages, which are difficult to assess though social risks assessment methodologies. Furthermore, an assessment of the risks of negative human rights impacts and the design of procedures to address them cannot be established in isolation of the context – and its systemic risks –, but also of the dynamics that the commercial relations establish and how they impact on the workers, as analysed below when considering coverage of the supply chain and purchasing practices. Whilst in principle the definition of HRDD explicitly acknowledges this, in practice, not all human rights, even if internationally recognised as such, will be addressed in HRDD processes. Both the UNGPs and the OECD Guidelines recognise that it may not always be possible to do so immediately. In these circumstances, businesses are expected to prioritise adverse impacts according to the likely *severity* of impacts or salience which is judged by the *scale* (gravity), *scope* (number of individuals), and *irremediable character* (the extent to which any harms can be remediated or need to be remediated without delay).[76]

The focus on the severity of the risk, and the prioritisation of severe risk when developing and implementing HRDD strategies, presents an important problem to address systemic issues such as abusive recruitment and low wages. A risk-based approach may lead to excluding adverse impacts which are not immediately visible. This means certain adverse impacts may be excluded, notably failure to pay a living wage, because the risk is not judged

74 Robert McCorquodale, Lise Smith, Stuart Neely and Robin Brooks, "Human Rights Due Diligence in Law and Practice: Good Practices and Challenges for Business Enterprises", *Business and Human Rights Journal*, 2 (2017), pp. 195–224.

75 Bjorn Fasterling, Human Rights Due Diligence as Risk Management: Social Risk versus Human Rights Risk. *Business and Human Rights Journal*, 2 (2017): 229.

76 Shift, *Salient Human Rights Issues*, Website (n.d.), https://www.ungpreporting.org/resources/salient-human-rights-issues, accessed December 18, 2023; UNGPs, Principle 14 and Commentary.

severe enough relative to other adverse impacts[77] or abusive labour recruitment because it is hidden and rarely visible. Specifically, in the case of living wages, even if the right to living wages is accepted as a human right, and even if it is reasonably rather than restrictively defined, there is no guarantee that it will be identified and acted upon within HRDD.[78] First, low living wages may not be judged to be 'salient', in the sense of being prominent, important and conspicuous. Other adverse human rights issues may be judged to be more salient. Second, it is not clear – in fact not likely – that violations concerning the payment of wages below a decent standard of living will be considered 'severe' when implementing these frameworks.[79]

3.3 *Coverage of the Supply Chain and Purchasing Practices*

The scope of the existing HRDD instruments varies, but they mainly apply to the largest companies registered in the jurisdiction. Likewise, the reach of a HRDD framework downstream the supply chain and requirements for a company to assess and address their suppliers beyond Tier 1 varies. The UNGPs define the corporate responsibility to respect human rights as extending to actual or potential adverse human rights impacts with which they may be involved either through their own activities or due to their business relationships.[80] Therefore, HRDD should cover adverse impacts of a business enterprise when it *causes* or *contributes to* an adverse impact, as well as when it is involved solely because the impact is 'directly linked ... by a business relationship'.[81] Appropriate action would therefore vary according to the level of involvement, as well as the extent of its *leverage* over its business relationships.[82] The extent to which enterprises linked to the parent company as subsidiaries, subcontractors or suppliers are covered by binding national and regional legislation differs, ranging from coverage of the whole supply chain[83] to more limited established commercial relationships.[84]

77 Nelson, Martin-Ortega and Flint, "Making."

78 Ibid.

79 Ibid.

80 UNGP, 2011, Principle 13.b.

81 UNGP, 2011, Principle 17.a. Causation relates to the impacts of a company's own activities, and where it causes harm, it must take steps to avoid doing so and provide remedy if harms do occur. Contribution occurs when a company contribute to adverse impacts on human rights, such as through their purchasing practices.

82 UNGP, Principle 19.b.

83 Eg. The Dutch Child Labour Law. The EU CSDDD establishes obligations for companies relating to the impact of their own operations those of their subsidiearies and those of their business partners where they are related to their chain of activities.

84 Eg French Duty of Vigilance.

The way these relationships are defined should be able to include the harm brought by abusive recruitment practices and low wages. However, the reality is that many occasions it is the behaviour of the main company or the brand the one which has a significant impact on the actions of the entities at the lower tiers of the supply chain. Whilst the OECD Due Diligence Guidance does address the business model of the corporation to some extent, by expressing that "enterprises retain responsibility to address adverse impacts that they cause or contribute to, even when operating in contexts where systemic issues are prevalent" it states clearly that "it is not the responsibility of enterprises to resolve systemic issues at a societal level," although they "may find that addressing such challenges may be effective in preventing or mitigating adverse impacts."[85]

The pressure to reduce cost is passed down to suppliers and in turn leads to them reducing labour costs. Therefore, as discussed throughout the chapter, human rights violations are a consequence of the nature and structure of the supply chain and directly related to the purchasing practices of business enterprises in the chain. These practices include constraints on price, reduced time leads for delivery, delayed payments, or refusal to accept products that have been ordered. However, the relationship between purchasing practices and human rights abuses in the supply chain hardly features in HRDD frameworks and practice.[86]

There are no specific regulatory frameworks which address the link between purchasing practices and abusive labour conditions, let alone systemic issues such as abusive recruitment practices and low wages. However, the OECD Due Diligence Guidance specifically acknowledges the responsibility of the leading companies in the supply chain to address practices which prevent their suppliers from developing their own due diligence to respect human rights. As part of their responsibilities companies need to embed responsible business conduct into policies and management systems, and this includes incorporating responsible business conduct expectations and policies into engagement with suppliers and other business relationships. Among its proposed practical actions to implement this responsibility, the Guidance encourages companies to seek to understand and address barriers arising from the way they do business that may impede the ability of suppliers and other business relationships to implement their own responsible business conduct. It is in this context that it includes a reference to enterprises' purchasing practices and commercial

85 OECD Due Diligence Guidance, 75.

86 Nelson, Martin-Ortega and Flint, "Making."

incentives.[87] Whilst this is a call for awareness, there is no specific prohibition of these practices. The only regional initiative, and sectoral specific relevant instrument which addresses purchasing practices is the EU Directive on Unfair Trading Practices adopted in 2019.[88] The Directive contains new rules that ban for the first time certain unfair trading practices imposed unilaterally by one trading partner on another. The aim of the Directive is to improve the position of businesses and farmers in the food supply chain. It recognises that due to the major imbalances in the bargaining power between suppliers and buyers of the agricultural products, several unfair trading practices take place and that this situation negatively impact living standard of the agricultural community.[89] Therefore it prohibits dynamics such as late payments, short notice cancellation or orders, changes to agreed contract terms unilaterally, unjustified charges to the supplier and the refusal to sign written contracts.[90] The Directive states that such practices affect the enjoyment of the decent living of the agriculture community in question.

However, there is no specific reference to the need to pay living wages and the impact that abusive trading practices has on the income of those in the supply chain and their capacity to have an adequate standard of living with such income. Although a decent living entails several rights, at a minimum, violation of the human right to an adequate standard of living (ICESCR Article 11) could be linked to such practices. The Directive prohibits 16 specific unfair trading practices. In doing so, it distinguishes between black practices –which are prohibited whatever the circumstances- and grey practices- which are allowed if the supplier and the buyer agree on them before hand in a clear an unambiguous manner. The obligation to agree clearly and unambiguously aims to provide transparency and predictability: both parties know what they signed up to and what their rights and obligations are.[91] The Directive does not directly cover pricing however, it has been argued that a case against excessive low prices could be based on the same unjust conditions.[92]

87 Guidance 1.3.

88 Directive 2019/633 on unfair trading practices in business-to-business relationships in the agricultural and food supply chain, 17 April 2019.

89 Ibid., para 7.

90 Ibid., paras. 17, 21, 22 and 23.

91 European Commission, Directorate General for Agriculture and Rural Development, The Directive on Unfair Trading Practices in the Agricultural and Food Supply Chain Brochure (2019), https://agriculture.ec.europa.eu/common-agricultural-policy/agri-food-supply-chain/unfair-trading-practices_en, accessed December 18, 2023.

92 Nelson, Martin-Ortega and Flint, "Making."

Therefore, either because violations at the lower tiers, or those that occur before the relationship of employment starts, as is the case with abusive recruitment practices, or because pressures through purchasing practices are disregarded, human rights due diligence does not seem a silver bullet to address them. Current definitions of the standard are not sufficient to place systemic issues at the heart of due diligence, addressing the underlying conditions of work in the supply chain which enhances vulnerability to human rights abuses.

4 Conclusions

This chapter has argued that human and labour rights violations do not occur by accident in global supply chains. Asymmetric power relations between brands and suppliers, contractors and subcontractors and ultimately corporate actors and workers provides the context in which workers at the lower tiers of the chain become vulnerable to abuse. Violations commence from the moment they are recruited through abusive recruitment practices and vulnerability to further abuse is exacerbated by low wages, which are not sufficient to cover workers and their families' basic needs. This can lead to debt or increased debt if they already acquired it during the recruitment process, in turn further enhancing vulnerability to exploitation. This cycle continues when workers leave employment in debt, and the likelihood of further violations is high. This chapter has characterised unfair labour recruitment and low wages as two systemic issues which lead to human rights violations in the supply chain. The lack of acknowledgment of these systemic abuses prevents them from being addressed. This chapter has also argued that deficiencies exist in current models of human rights due diligence in addressing these systemic issues, mainly because they focus on the severity of risks and ignore the role of purchasing practices in perpetuating abusive dynamics.

It is therefore important that systemic abuses of human rights in supply chains and their link to purchasing practices are explicitly included in the definition of the standard of HRDD and the design of specific HRDD frameworks as a core element, rather than waiting for the implementation phase. We cannot rely on systemic issues, including abusive recruitment practices and low wages, to be addressed by human rights due diligence if we are not explicitly establishing obligations to address purchasing practices –and therefore overlooking the link between them and the vulnerability to human rights abuses- in the design of HRDD norms.

Bibliography

Books

Anker, Richard and Marth Anker. *Living Wages around the World. Manual for Measurements*. Cheltenham: Edward Elgar, 2017.

Chapters in Edited Books

Damir-Geilsdorf, Sabine. "Contract labour and debt bondage in the Arab Gulf States: Policies and practices within the kafala system." In *Bonded Labour: Global and Comparative Perspectives 18th–21st Century*, eds. Sabine Damir-Geilsdorf, Ulrike Lindner, Geise Muller, Oliver Tappe and Michael Zeuske, 163–90. Transcript, Global Studies, 2016.

Lukas, Karin. "Human Rights in the Supply Chain: Influence and Accountability." In *The UN Guiding Principles on Business and Human Rights: Foundations and Implementation*, ed. Radu Mares. Leiden: Koninklijke Brill, 2012.

Mackenzie, Catriona, Wendy Rogers and Susan Dodd. "Introduction: What Is Vulnerability and Why Does It Matter for Moral Theory?." In *Vulnerability. New Essays in Ethics and Feminists Philosophy*, eds. Catriona Mackenzie, Wendy Rogers and Susan Dodds. Oxford: Oxford University Press, 2015.

Martin-Ortega, Olga. "Transparency and human rights in global supply chains: from corporate-led disclosure to a right to know." In *Research Handbook on Global Governance, Business and Human Rights*, eds. Axel Marx, Geert Van Calster, Jean Monnet, Jan Wouters, Kari Otteburn, Diana Lica, 99–119. Cheltenham: Edward Elgar, 2022.

Journal Articles

Barrientos, Stephanie, Uma Kothari and Nicola Phillips. "Dynamics of Unfree Labour in the Contemporary Global Economy." *The Journal of Development Studies* 49 (2013): 8.

Bonnitcha, Johnathan and, Robert McCorquodale. "The Concept of 'Due Diligence' in the UN Guiding Principles on Business and Human Rights." *European Journal of International Law* 28, no.3 (2017): 899–919.

Bueno, Nicolas and Christine Kaufmann. "The Swiss Human Rights Due Diligence Legislation: Between Law and Politics." *Business and Human Rights Journal* 6, no. 3 (2021): 542–549.

Fasterling, Bjorn. "Human Rights Due Diligence as Risk Management: Social Risk versus Human Rights Risk." *Business and Human Rights Journal*, 2 (2017): 229.

LeBaron, Genevieve. "Reconceptualizing Debt Bondage: Debt as a Class-Based Form of Labour Discipline." *Critical Sociology* 40, no. 5 (2014).

LeBaron, Genevieve. "Wages: An Overlooked Dimension of Business and Human Rights in Global Supply Chains." *Business and Human Rights Journal* 6, no. 1 (2021): 5.

Mares, Radu. "The Limits of Supply Chain Responsibility: A Critical Analysis of Corporate Responsibility Instruments." *Nordic Journal of International Law* 79 (2010): 194.

Mares, Radu. "Corporate transparency laws: A hollow victory?." *Netherlands Quarterly of Human Rights* 36, no. 3 (2018): 189–213.

McCorquodale, Robert, Lise Smith, Stuart Neely and Robin Brooks. "Human Rights Due Diligence in Law and Practice: Good Practices and Challenges for Business Enterprises." *Business and Human Rights Journal*, 2 (2017), pp. 195–224.

McCorquodale, Robert and Justine Nolan. "The Effectiveness of Human Rights Due Diligence for Preventing Business Human Rights Abuses." *Netherlands International Law Review* 68 (2021): 455–478.

Martin-Ortega, Olga. "Human Rights Due Diligence for Corporations: From Voluntary Standards to Hard Law at Last?." *Netherlands Quarterly of Human Rights* 32, no.1, 2014: 44–74.

Nolan, Justine. "Hardening Soft Law: Are the Emerging Corporate Social Disclosure Laws Capable of Generating Substantive Compliance with Human Rights?." *Brazilian Journal of International Law* 15 (2018): 65.

Outhwaite, Opi and Olga Martin-Ortega. "Worker-driven monitoring – Redefining supply chain monitoring to improve labour rights in global supply chains." *Competition and Change* 23, no. 4 (2019): 378–396.

Savourey, Elsa and Stéphane Brabant. "The French Law on the Duty of Vigilance: Theoretical and Practical Challenges Since Its Adoption." *Business and Human Rights Journal* 6, no. 1 (2021): 141–52.

Reports

Electronics Watch. "Guidance for Remediation and prevention of Migrant Worker Recruitment Fees and Related Costs in Public Procurement" (2019). Accessed December 18, 2023 https://electronicswatch.org/guidance-for-remediation-and-prevention-of-migrant-worker-recruitment-fees-and-related-costs-in-public-procurement-april-2019_2557767.pdf,.

Fountain, A.C, and Hütz-Adams, F. "Defining a Decent Living. Living Income for Smallholder Cocoa Farmers in West Africa. On calculations of living wages in the cocoa sector see too Duncan Brack, Towards sustainable cocoa supply chains: Regulatory options for the EU" (Fern, Tropenbos International and Fair Trade Advocacy Office, 2020). Accessed December 18, 2023. https://www.fern.org/fileadmin/uploads/fern/Documents/2019/Fern-sustainable-cocoa-supply-chains-report.pdf.

ILO. Operational indicators of trafficking in human beings (March 2009, revised September 2009). Accessed December 18, 2023. https://www.ilo.org/wcmsp5/groups/public/---ed_norm/---declaration/documents/publication/wcms_105023.pdf.

ILO. The Cost of Coercion. Global Report on Forced Labour 2009. Accessed December 18, 2023. https://www.ilo.org/wcmsp5/groups/public/---ed_norm/---declaration/documents/publication/wcms_106268.pdf.

ILO. Towards stronger measures to combat abusive labour recruitment and to prevent human trafficking (2013–2015). Accessed December 18, 2023. https://www.ilo.org/global/topics/forced-labour/projects/WCMS_320238/lang--en/index.htm.

ILO. Regulating labour recruitment to prevent human trafficking and to foster fair migration: Models, challenges and opportunities (2015). Accessed December 18, 2023. https://www.ilo.org/wcmsp5/groups/public/---ed_norm/---declaration/documents/publication/wcms_377813.pdf.

ILO. Global Estimates on International Migrant Workers, Results and Methodology (Labour Migration Branch Conditions of Work. Equality Department and Department of Statistics 2021. Accessed December 18, 2023. https://www.ilo.org/global/topics/labour-migration/publications/WCMS_808935/lang--en/index.htm.

Methven O'Brien, Claire and Olga Martin-Ortega. "EU Human Rights Due Diligence Legislation: Monitoring, Enforcement and Access to Justice for Victims' Study for the DROI Subcommittee, European Parliament, PE 603.505 (2020). Accessed December 18, 2023. https://www.europarl.europa.eu/thinktank/en/document/EXPO_BRI(2020)603505.

Nelson, Valerie, Olga Martin-Ortega and Michael Flint. *Making Human Rights Due Diligence Work: An Analysis of Impact and Legal Options*. Fair Trade Advocacy Office and Brot für die Welt, 2020.

Palumbo, Letizia and Alessandra Sciurba. "The vulnerability to exploitation of women migrant workers in agriculture in the EU: the need for a Human Rights and Gender based approach". Study for the FEMM Committee, European Parliament, PE 604.966, May 2018.

Skrivankova, Klara. "Between Decent Work and Forced Labour: Examining the Continuum of Exploitation". *Programme Paper 17* Joseph Rowntree Foundation 2010. https://www.jrf.org.uk/report/between-decent-work-and-forced-labour-examining-continuum-exploitation.

Special Rapporteur on the human rights of migrants, labour exploitation of migrants. Report, A/HRC/26/35, April 3, 2014.

Special Rapporteur on the right to food. Report, A/HRC/13/33 Add2, 2019.

UNODC, 'The Role of Recruitment Fees and Abusive and Fraudulent Recruitment Practices of Recruitment Agencies in Trafficking in Persons' 2015.

International Instruments

Dhaka Principles for Migration with Dignity. Accessed December 18, 2023. https://dhakaprinciples.org/.

European Commission, Directive 2019/633 on unfair trading practices in business-to-business relationships in the agricultural and food supply chain, April 17, 2019.

European Commission, Directive (EU) 2024/1760 of the European Parliament and of the Council of 13 June 2024 on Corporate Sustainability Due Diligence and amending Directive (EU) 2019/1937 and Regulation (EU) 2023/2859. OJ L, 2024/1760, 5.7.2024.

ILO. General principles and operational guidelines for fair recruitment and definition of recruitment fees and related costs, 2019. https://www.ilo.org/global/topics/labour-migration/publications/WCMS_536755/lang--en/index.htm.

OECD Due Diligence Guidance for Responsible Supply Chains in the Garment and Footwear Sector, 2018.

OECD. Due Diligence Guidance for Responsible Business Conduct (2019). Accessed December 18, 2023. https://www.oecd.org/investment/due-diligence-guidance-for-responsible-business-conduct.htm.

OECD. Guidelines for Multinational Enterprises, 2011.

OECD-FAO. Guidance for Responsible Agricultural Supply Chains, 2016.

UN Human Rights Council. Guiding Principles on Business and Human Rights: Implementing the United Nations "Protect, Respect and Remedy" Framework'. *Report of the Special Representative of the Secretary-General on the issue of human rights and transnational corporations and other business enterprises – Guiding Principles on Business and Human Rights: Implementing the United Nations "Protect, Respect and Remedy" Framework*. UN Doc A/HRC/17/31, March 21, 2011), Annex 2011, 16–20.

Websites

Council of the EU. Press Release, Corporate sustainability due diligence: Council and Parliament strike deal to protect environment and human rights, 14 December 2023. Accessed December 18, 2023. https://www.consilium.europa.eu/en/press/press-releases/2023/12/14/corporate-sustainability-due-diligence-council-and-parliament-strike-deal-to-protect-environment-and-human-rights/.

European Commission, Directorate General for Agriculture and Rural Development, The Directive on Unfair Trading Practices in the Agricultural and Food Supply Chain Brochure, 2019. Accessed December 18, 2023. https://agriculture.ec.europa.eu/common-agricultural-policy/agri-food-supply-chain/unfair-trading-practices_en.

Global Living Wage Coalition. Accessed December 18, 2023. https://www.globallivingwage.org/.

IDH> What is a living income?. Accessed December 18, 2023. https://www.idhsustainabletrade.com/roadmap-on-living-income/,.

Shift, *Salient Human Rights Issues*. Accessed December 18, 2023. https://www.ungpreporting.org/resources/salient-human-rights-issues..

The Living Income Community of Practice. Accessed December 18, 2023. https://www.living-income.com/.

Cases

Economic, Social and Cultural Rights Committee. *Greek General Confederation of Labour* (GSEE) *v. Greece* 2017.

European Committee of Social Rights. *General Federation of employees of the national electric power corporation* (GENOP-DEI) *and Confederation of Greek Civil Servants' Trade Unions* (ADEDY) *v. Greece* 2011, 23-05-2012. Digest of the Case Law of the European Committee of Social Rights' 2018, 85.

CHAPTER 11

Transparency: See and Be Seen

Robert Stumberg

1 Introduction

Depending on whom you ask, supply-chain transparency is –

- a business tool for reputation management.
- the key to accountability for human rights of workers.
- a corporate trap to forestall effective regulation.
- commonly used but rarely successful.
- all the above.

The Oxford definition of *transparent* is to be 'visible *through something*, … [e]asily seen through, recognised, understood, or detected.'[1] So, what is to be seen? A business and human rights (BHR) manager wants customers to see the process, policy, and statistics a brand uses to manage its chain. A worker wants purchasers to see him or herself and the place, conditions, and chain in which he/she toils. A purchaser wants to see both: the manager's process and the worker.[2]

And what is that *something* to see through? For BHR, *transparent* means visible through the supply chain itself, the chain links that separate suppliers from users, the co-mingling of materials, and locations of production that are hidden behind borders. The *UN Guiding Principles for Business and Human Rights* (UNGPs) say this: businesses need to 'know' their supply chains and to 'show' their diligence to protect the lives and rights of workers.[3]

You cannot protect what you do not know. For example, Tazreen Fashions was not transparent in 2012 when its factory in Bangladesh caught fire. When the smoke cleared, 177 workers were dead, 200 injured, and 200 traumatised.

1 'Transparent,' *Oxford English Dictionary*, adjective (and noun) 1.d., 2.b (online ed: Oxford: Oxford University Press, 2023).

2 *See* Electronics Watch, *Worker-Driven Transparency* (2018), 2–3.

3 Special Representative of the Secretary-General, Guiding Principles on Business and Human Rights: Implementing the United Nations 'Protect, Respect and Remedy' Framework, UN Doc. A/HRC/17/31 (New York: 2011), 16 (UNGP 15 Commentary).

 | DOI:10.1163/9789004530942_012

Walmart and the U.S. Marines were surprised to learn that Tazreen was hidden in their supply chains, a link beyond their known distributors.[4]

Stories like Tazreen propelled interest in the UNGPs and transparency. More than 20 initiatives provide some type of transparency.[5] They include voluntary brand disclosures, modern slavery laws, general reporting frameworks, human rights benchmarks, procurement by governments and institutions, and border controls.

The prevailing mode shows corporate process measures, a kind of tell-us-what-you-do transparency (e.g., codes of conduct, audit protocols, and supplier screening).[6] But full transparency includes three elements: (1) process measures, (2) performance measures (e.g., risk assessment, audit results, and remedies),[7] and (3) actual supply-chain data (e.g., supplier names, factory addresses, number of workers, and output of factories).[8]

Supply-chain data enables traceability, 'a critical first step of due diligence' to see the workers and investigate a company's performance.[9] Very few companies show actual supply chains and fewer still achieve full transparency.[10] Some show audits but not locations; some show locations but not audits.[11]

With all their diversity, transparency initiatives are a natural experiment. The literature tends to focus on one or two initiatives at a time, thus not showing the whole field. This chapter surveys the field from a higher altitude to compare initiatives in a common frame: their theory of change (TOC), accountability gaps, and transferrable reforms. The chapter proceeds in three stages.

4 Steven Greenhouse, "Documents Reveal New Details About Walmart's Connection to Tazreen Factory Fire," *New York Times* (December 10, 2012); Matthew Mosk, "Marines Move to Dump Clothes Company After Deadly Factory Fire," *ABC News* (December 11, 2012).

5 Casey O'Connor and Sara Labovitz, *Putting the "S" in ESG: Measuring Human Rights Performance for Investors* (New York: NYU Stern Center for Business and Human Rights, 2017), 18.

6 David Hess, "The Transparency Trap: Non-Financial Disclosure and the Responsibility of Business to Respect Human Rights," *American Business Law Journal* 56 no. 1 (2019): 16, 27–29; Global Reporting Initiative (GRI), G4 Sustainability Reporting Guidelines (2015), G4-LA14 (Percent of suppliers screened).

7 *E.g.*, GRI, G4-LA6 (Rates of injury, days missed, deaths).

8 *See* Hess, "Transparency Trap," 16.

9 US Dept. of Homeland Security, Strategy to Prevent the Importation of Goods Mined, Produced, or Manufactured with Forced Labor in the People's Republic of China (June 17, 2022), 44–45, accessed March 3, 2023 https://www.dhs.gov/sites/default/files/2022-06/22_0617_fletf_uflpa-strategy.pdf.

10 *See* ibid; O'Connor, *Putting the "S" in ESG*, 18.

11 *See Fashion Transparency Index 2022* (London: Fashion Revolution, 2022), 60, 70, 72.

- *Critics and accountability* – Part 2 summarises critics of transparency and distills a framework of accountability gaps. The gaps include (1) the disconnect from users, (2) vagueness of disclosures, and (3) incomparability – any of which diminish transparency into a mere tool to manage brand reputations.
- *Initiatives* – Part 3 profiles six types of initiatives using the framework from part 2 to describe their theories of change and assess their accountability gaps.
- *Agenda for progress* – Part 4 gathers transferable reforms. When combined, they create a mosaic of transparency from multiple sources, a systematic approach that connects transparency with workers, monitoring networks, purchasers, and regulators.

2 Critics and Accountability

2.1 *General Critics*

Omri Ben-Shahar and Carl Schneider see transparency mandates as ubiquitous – health, consumer protection, securities, climate change, nutrition, and more.[12] 'Orthodox thinking,' they observe, presumes transparency to be a public good, when in fact, it is barely understood and rarely used by consumers. There is no consensus on its purpose.[13] They provide abundant evidence that corporate actors use transparency to project a misleading appearance of efficacy and forestall more effective regulation. It is 'the most common and least successful regulatory technique in American Law.'[14]

Aarti Gupta and Michael Mason study carbon markets and greenhouse gas disclosures. They report how corporate actors promote transparency as a 'market-based solution' to avoid more stringent regulation. Disclosures flood the market with data without connection to standards for users to reduce their GHG emissions. Transparency policies 'decenter' regulation and 'open up space' for accounting firms to seek commercial gains.[15]

---

12 Omri Ben-Shahar and Carl E. Schneider, "The Failure of Mandated Disclosure," *University of Pennsylvania. Law Review* 159 (2011): 649.

13 Ibid, 649; *see also* Margaret Kwoka and Bridget DuPey, "Targeted Transparency as Regulation," 48 *Florida State University Law Review* 48 (2021): 388.

14 Omri Ben-Shahar and Carl E. Schneider, *More than You Wanted to Know: The Failure of Mandated Disclosure* (Princeton, NJ: Princeton University Press, 2014), 3.

15 Aarti Gupta and Michael Mason, "Transparency Turn in Global Environmental Governance," in *Transparency in Global Environmental Governance,* eds. Aarti Gupta and Michael Mason (Cambridge, MA: MIT Press, 2014), 14–17.

The same decentering happens in the human rights HR context where consultants market themselves as an *alternative* to regulation. Companies lobbied *against* enforceable standards in the UK Modern Slavery Act (MSA) and *for* 'generic and promotional' reports that fail to reveal supply chains or abuse of workers. The resulting MSA disconnected disclosure from accountability.[16]

Archon Fung, Mary Graham, and David Weil completed 18 case studies to understand when transparency succeeds and fails.[17] It fails, they concluded, when there is no penalty for not disclosing, when users do not act on disclosure (e.g., to make a purchasing decision), and when users' goals conflict with policy goals. In contrast, transparency works when disclosure is 'doubly imbedded' to create a 'transparency action cycle.' Someone uses the disclosed information to make a purchasing, investment, or regulatory decision. Knowing this, the discloser changes its behavior and discloses that change to influence the next user.[18]

2.2 *Accountability Framework*

The critiques above support the need for an accountability framework to make sense of transparency.[19] They can be organised under three themes: (1) disconnect from user decisions, (2) vagueness and gaming, and (3) lack of comparability.

2.2.1 Disconnect from User Decisions

The critics agree that users of transparency drive accountability. Transparency fails if disclosure is not connected to a user's decision to reward or penalize a discloser's performance. Without a direct consequence, disclosers will remain inert. On one level, the disconnect is physical; the actual supply chain or HR performance is not disclosed.

On another level, the disconnect results from artful manipulation; the discloser presents 'a factually accurate but misleading picture'.[20] When this

16 Genevieve LeBaron & Andreas Ruhmkorff, "The Domestic Politics of Corporate Accountability Legislation: Struggles over the 2015 UK Modern Slavey Act," *Socio-Economic Review* 1 (2017): 3.

17 Archon Fung, Mary Graham & David Weil, *Full Disclosure – The Perils and Promise of Transparency* (Cambridge: Cambridge University Press, 2007), 54–68.

18 Ibid.

19 *See* literature reviews in Hess, "Transparency Trap"; and Kevin Kolben, "The Consumer Imaginary: Labor Rights, Human Rights, and Citizen-Consumers in the Global Supply Chain," *Vanderbilt Law Review* 52 (2021): 839.

20 Hess, "Transparency Trap," 32, 9–10, 26, 52; Kwoka and DuPey, "Targeted Transparency," 432, 435; Nolan, "Hardening Soft Law," 8; FLEX, *Seeing Through Supply Chain Transparency*, (Focus on Labor Exploitation [FLEX], 2018), 8, 34; Galit A. Sarfaty, "Shining Light on

happens, the discloser deceives without lying by omission or comission. Psychologists call it 'paltering'.[21] Reputation risk prompts companies to engage in selective disclosure about process rather than report working conditions, disclose actual supply chains, or reinvent their supply chains to avoid HR harms.[22]

2.2.2 Vagueness and Gaming

When disclosure mandates are vague, disclosers can game the system to 'beautify' their reputation and avoid accountability. The risk of fraud is high due to the following.[23]

- Non-disclosure: Many transparency laws have low compliance because there is no penalty for failure to disclose.[24]
- Selective disclosure without supply-chain data: Companies disclose positive reports of their internal process while ignoring supply-chain locations and negative HR performance data.[25] These narratives of internal activity are 'powerful fictions; fairy tales to help the children sleep at night.'[26]
- Too much information: Multiple disclosures can overwhelm user capacity,[27] and companies 'have every incentive to bury the proverbial needle in the haystack while resisting meaningful disclosure

Global Supply Chains," *Harvard International Law Journal* 56 (2015): 419–63; Fung, *Full Disclosure*, 45.

21 See Todd Rogers, Richard Zeckhauser, Francesca Gino, Schweitzer, and Michael Norton, "Artful Paltering: The Risks and Rewards of Using Truthful Statements to Mislead Others," 112 *Personality and Social Psychology*, no. 3 (2016): 456–457.

22 *See* Hannah Harris and Justine Nolan, "Learning from Experience: Comparing Legal Approaches to Foreign Bribery and Modern Slavery," *Cardozo International & Comparative Law Review* 4 (2021): 625–627; Kolben, "Consumer Imaginary,' 891–895; Hess, "Transparency Trap," 52.

23 *See* Gupta and Mason, "Transparency," 2; Fung, *Full Disclosure*, 90; Ben-Shahar and Schneider, "Failure of Disclosure," 692, 700.

24 *See* David Hess, "The Challenge of Modern Slavery in Global Supply Chains," 23 *Geogetown Journal of International Affairs* (2022): 35, 37; Kolben, "Consumer Imaginary," 894; Harris & Nolan, "Comparing," 603, 628, 633.

25 *See* Olivier Boiral, "Sustainability Reports as Simulacra? A Counter-Account of A and A+ GRI Reports," *Accounting, Auditing & Accountability Journal* 26 (2013): 1036, 1051–1052; Hess, "Transparency Trap," 26, 32–38.

26 Rob Gray, "Is Accounting for Sustainability Actually Accounting for Sustainability ... and How Would We Know?" *Accounting, Organization s & Society* 35 (2010): 47, 50.

27 Hess, "Transparency Trap," 35; Ben-Shahar and Schneider, "Failure of Disclosure," 690; at 16; Fung, *Full Disclosure*, 59.

of any damaging information.'[28] Since disclosure 'can obfuscate as much as it can clarify,' most users need an intermediary to monitor and verify information before they can use it.[29]

- Misleading information: Quantitative data creates an appearance of objectivity, but most HR data disclosures are subjective. For example, aggregate statistics of company performance – like the number of suppliers screened – are generated by the discloser based on subjective and self-serving selection criteria.[30] Reports that HR harms are few often reflect workers' fear of reporting, or they do not count harms that occur upstream from the facility being audited.[31]

2.2.3 Incomparability

Without comparable disclosures at the company level, purchasers cannot choose between weak and strong HR performance by suppliers. Comparing information from transparency frameworks requires an effort 'approaching academic research'.[32]

David Hess explains how transparency fails when disclosures are vague, selective, incomparable, and decoupled from an accountability mechanism. The result is a 'transparency trap', the deception that transparency alone will produce change. It becomes an end unto itself, a tool that supports reputation management, with little effect on human rights performance.[33]

3 Initiatives

Do transparency initiatives fall into the trap? This part profiles six types of initiatives using the framework above to compare their theories of change (TOC) and accountability gaps.

---

28 Alfred C. Aman, Jr. and Landyn Wm. Rookard, "Private Government and the Transparency Deficit," *Administrative Law Review* 71 (2019): 437, 456.

29 Kwoka and DePey, "Targeted Transparency," 432, 433.

30 *See* O'Conner and Labovitz 25; Hess, "Transparency Trap," 28–29.

31 Brian Finnegangan, Responsibility Outsourced: Social Audits, Workplace Certification and Twenty Years of Failure to Protect Worker Rights, (Washington: AFL-CIO, 2013), 26.

32 Hess, "Transparency Trap," 35–36; Olivier Boiral and Jean-Francois Henri, "Is Sustainability Performance Comparable? A Study of GRI Reports of Mining Organizations," *Business & Society* 56, no. 2 (2017): 283, 294–96, 303.

33 Hess, "Transparency Trap," 26, 32–42.

3.1 *Voluntary Brand Disclosures*

Leading apparel brands first disclosed a code of conduct in 1995. Since then, selective disclosure of company policies has become the norm for apparel, electronics, and other global brands.[34] As a Nike manager explained in 1999, selective disclosure without locations is 'a way to pre-empt [NGOs] and the media from playing *gotcha*.'[35] The transparency debate flared when universities required brands (in apparel-licensing agreements) to disclose factories, which the Worker Rights Consortium began publishing in 2001 (2,000–4,000 brands for most schools).[36] Students insisted that only factory disclosure would hold companies accountable.[37] Two decades later, 100 apparel brands (48 percent) published their tier-one suppliers.[38] Scott Nova observed that disclosing suppliers 'has gone from a supposed competitive risk for apparel brands to a recognised competitive advantage.'[39] However, other sectors lag by comparison.[40]

The theory of change assumes that a brand's ultimate asset is its reputation. Most surveyed consumers, up to 80 percent, prefer ethically produced products.[41] It follows that transparency promotes HR accountability *if* multiple stakeholders can leverage a brand's reputation in five-stages of cause and effect:[42]

1. Corporate disclosures reveal the supply chain and working conditions.
2. Unions, monitors, or governments investigate abuses.
3. The media reports labor abuses and brand complicity to the public.

---

34 David Doorey, "The Transparent Supply Chain: from Resistance to Implementation at Nike and Levi-Strauss." *Journal of Business Ethics* 102 (April 2016): 592, 594–595; see "Overview of HP supply chain responsibility program," Hewlett Packard, accessed March 3, 2023, https://sustainability.ext.hp.com/en/support/solutions/articles/35000146371-overview-of-hp-supply-chain-responsibility-program; "History," Responsible Business Alliance, accessed March 3, 2023, https://www.responsiblebusiness.org/about/history/.

35 Vada Manager, Nike's Director of Global Issues, quoted in Steven van Yoder, "Beware the Coming Backlash," *Industry Week* (April, 2, 2001).

36 *See* "Factory Database," WRC, accessed June 11, 2023, https://search.workersrights.org/.

37 Liza Featherstone, *Students Against Sweatshops* (Verso, 2002) 20–22.

38 "'Who's Aligned," Transparency Pledge, accessed March 22, 2023, https://transparencypledge.org/aligned/; *Fashion Index 2022*, 3.

39 WRC, Memo to Affiliates, "The Impact of Universities on Supply-Chain Transparency," (April 21, 2017).

40 *See,* Responsible Business Alliance, *Practical Guide to Transparency in Procurement* (2019), 7 (indicators).

41 *See* studies reviewed by Kolben, "Consumer Imaginary," 870–873; Monica Prasad, Howard Kimeldorf, Rachel Meyer, and Ian Robinson, "Consumers of the World Unite: A Market-based Response to Sweatshops," *Labor Studies Journal* 29 (2004): 63.

42 *See* Kolben, "Consumer Imaginary," 858; *Fashion Index 2022*, 7; Doorey, "Transparent Supply Chain," 588; FLEX, *Seeing Through Transparency*, 13.

4. Some consumers react and shift consumption to other brands.
5. A brand mitigates reputation risk by promoting a remedy and preventing future abuses.

Industry resistance to factory disclosure softened after thousands of workers died in Bangladesh fires (2012) and the collapse of Rana Plaza (2013).[43] Among other initiatives, the Accord on Fire and Building Safety in Bangladesh emerged from the ruins. In 2021, the Accord's partners – unions, brands, and retailers – evolved into two entities: a national tripartite organisation, the RMG Sustainability Council (RSC) and an ongoing *International Accord* that promotes the model in other countries,[44] starting with the Pakistan Accord in 2023.[45]

Accord/RSC factories commit to inspections that are reinforced with worker training, a complaint mechanism, and a commitment of financial support from brands.[46] Their transparency is public; a web page reveals the factory name, location, number of workers, remediation status, inspection reports, corrective action plans, and progress rates.[47]

From this progress, a more neutral TOC has emerged. It uses a voluntary transparency platform to connect users with supply-chain data. To collaborate and create economies of scale, users need (a) geographic mapping of factories and (b) the ability to sort them by their customers, the brands, and retailers. On a practical level, users need data in a standard form that is machine-readable.[48] Two other initiatives are evolving with this TOC.

– BRAC University started in 2017 to organise Mapped in Bangladesh (MiB). MiB completed a census of 3,752 apparel export factories in 2022. It has surpassed 95,000 users from 188 countries.[49]

43 Jason Burke, "Rana Plaza: one year on from the Bangladesh factory disaster," *The Guardian*, April 19, 2014.

44 "A decade of progress in workplace safety in Bangladesh," International Accord, accessed June 11, 2023, https://internationalaccord.org/countries/bangladesh/; "RSC – RMG Sustainability Council," accessed June 11, 2023, https://www.rsc-bd.org/en.

45 "New workplace safety program in Pakistan," International Accord, accessed June 11, 2023, https://internationalaccord.org/countries/pakistan/.

46 "Promoting health and safety in Accord-covered factories," International Accord, accessed June 11, 2023, https://internationalaccord.org/factories/.

47 Ibid; "Factories," RSC, accessed June 14, 2023, https://www.rsc-bd.org/en/factories#.

48 "The Apparel Sector – A Case Study in Transparency," OSH, accessed June 19, 2023, https://info.opensupplyhub.org/resources/apparel-case-study-transparency.

49 MiB News Letter, vol. 23 (2023), accessed June 12, 2023, https://mailchi.mp/bracu/mib-news-letter-vol-23.

- The Open Apparel Registry started mapping factories in 2019 and expanded to become the Open Supply Hub (OSH, accepting 126 industry categories). OSH has surpassed 712 contributors for 189,000 facilities in 162 countries.[50] The Clean Clothes Campaign used OSH to link 20 brands with 30 factories that had workers arrested after they protested violation of the minimum wage law.[51]

Each of these initiatives could strengthen accountability by learning from the other. OSH identifies parent companies and data contributors, but not all customers of a facility.[52] MiB identifies all customers plus their export countries, certifications, and worker participation.[53]

Yet accountability gaps remain—beyond these two initiatives—with voluntary brand disclosures.

- Vagueness and selective disclosure: The mapping initiatives show progress using data that expands accountability. However, most brands still disclose no supply-chain data, and those that do flood the market with additional selective disclosures. Surveys indicate that brand managers view such disclosures as a tool for 'reputation management' to mitigate bad publicity rather than improve factory conditions.[54] Research indicates that disclosing company policies, *alone*, will 'shield companies from consumers' negative perceptions' after news that workers have been abused.[55]
- Connection to users: Monitoring organisations selectively use the mapping initiatives, but they do not connect to retail purchasers. Experiments indicate that up to 30 percent of consumers will pay more for ethical goods.[56] But connecting with those consumers requires monitoring, access to supply-chain data, a system to compare

50 "Open Supply HUB in Numbers," OSH, accessed June 14, 2023, https://info.opensupplyhub.org/.

51 "Civil Society Case Study – Clean Clothes Campaign," OSH, accessed June 13, 2023, https://info.opensupplyhub.org/resources/clean-clothes-campaign-case-study.

52 "How to Search Open Supply Hub," OSH, accessed June 12, 2023, https://info.opensupplyhub.org/resources/how-to-search.

53 MiB, Mapped in Bangladesh, Project Overview (Dhaka: MiB, 2020), 7.

54 *See* studies reviewed by Hess, "Transparency Trap," 12, 873–874.

55 Diane A. Mollenkopf, Simone T. Peinkofer, Yu (Jade) Chu, "Supply chain transparency: Consumer reactions to incongruent signals," *Journal of Operations Management* 68, no. 1 (2022): 306.

56 Prasad, "Consumers Unite," 69.

HR performance, and a label or app to compare for choosing at the point of sale – none of which exists.[57]

3.2 *Modern Slavery Laws*

Modern slavery laws (MSAs) require large corporations to report their risks of modern slavery and their policies to address those risks. California's 2011 Transparency in Supply Chains Act (TSCA) was the first, followed by the UK Modern Slavery Act in 2015[58] and the Australia Modern Slavery Act (AMSA) in 2018.[59] The laws vary somewhat in the size of companies they cover, the definition of 'modern slavery', and the disclosure categories.[60]

Australia's MSA improves upon its predecessors. It requires companies with gross revenue of 100 million AUD and government agencies to file an annual Modern Slavery Statement with a public registry.[61] 'Modern slavery' is defined in terms of domestic criminal prohibitions of slavery, servitude, forced labor, deceptive recruiting, trafficking in persons, debt bondage, forced marriage, and the worst forms of child labor.[62] The focus on modern slavery is narrower than most corporate codes of conduct, which include the ILO's core labor standards (freedom of association/right to organise, prohibitions of forced labor, child labor, and discrimination), prohibition of harassment, and compliance with wage and health laws in the country of production.[63]

A company's AMSA statement must describe a) corporate structure, b) operations, and supply chains; c) risks of modern slavery in its supply chains; d) actions of due diligence and remediation to address those risks; e) how the company assesses its effectiveness; and f) its process of consultation.[64]

The theory of change, in the Australian view, is to create a process that is 'led by business', to make it comfortable to disclose risks and then act on preventive measures. The law assumes that companies will use their annual statements to compete for customers and investors, which will drive a 'race to the top'.[65]

57 Charity Ryerson and Emma Cusumano, *Is the California Transparency in Supply Chains Act Doing More Harm than Good?* (Corporate Accountability Lab, 2017), 6.

58 UK Modern Slavery Act 2015, Ch. 30, §54.

59 Australia Modern Slavery Act 2018, No. 153, 2018.

60 For a detailed comparison, see Sunil Rao, Modern Slavery Legislation: Drafting History and Comparisons between Australia, UK and the USA (London: Routledge, 2020), 93.

61 Australia Modern Slavery Act, §5, §15.

62 Ibid, §4.

63 *See* "Code of Conduct," Responsible Business Alliance, accessed March 3, 2023, https://www.responsiblebusiness.org/code-of-conduct/.

64 Ibid, §16.

65 Australia Modern Slavery Bill 2018 (Cth) 45, Explanatory Memorandum.

The accountability gaps of Australia and the other MSAs hew close to those of voluntary brand disclosures:

- Connection to users: The is no connection to retail consumers at a point of sale.[66] That said, these laws have connected with corporate boards and managers who had not previously engaged with supply chains except to reduce costs.[67]
- No disclosure: There is no penalty for failure to disclose in the AMSA, CTSCA, or UKMSA.[68] The CTSCA rate of nondisclosure was reported at 57 percent.[69] For the UKMSA, 56 percent of annual statements were fragmented, unclear, or not filed at all.[70]
- Vagueness and selective disclosure: Hannah Harris and Justine Nolan summarise the MSA disclosures as 'a paucity of information' that is mostly symbolic, difficult to verify, and not comparable.[71] They do not enable consumers to relate to workers.[72] Nor do they enable workers to know who buys the goods they make and under what terms of trade.[73]

With their focus on process and non-disclosure of actual supply chains, MSAs actually enable a corporate *counter* TOC. It creates the *impression* of diligence without investing in the real thing.

Responding to this critique, four countries have coupled MSA-style disclosure with mandatory due diligence. France was the first (2017, 5,000 employees in France, civil liability, and punitive damages),[74] followed by the Netherlands (2019 for child labor, doing business in the Netherlands, fines up to €870,000

66 Adam S. Chilton & Galit A. Sarfaty, "The Limitations of Supply Chain Disclosure Regimes," *Stanford Journal of International Law* 53 (2017): 1.

67 Electronics Watch, *Transparency*, 1.

68 Australia Modern Slavery Act 2018, No. 153, 2018 §16A; CTSCA, California Civil Code §1714.43(d); UK MSA, 2015 Ch. 30 §54(11).

69 Chris N. Bayer and Jesse H. Hudson, Corporate Compliance with the California Transparency in Supply Chains Act: Anti-Slavery Performance in 2016, (Development International, 2017), 6.

70 Steven Young and Mahmoud Gad, Modern Slavery Reporting Practices in the UK – Evidence from Modern Slavery Statements and Annual Reports (Financial Reporting Council, 2022), 3.

71 *See* literature reviewed by Harris and Nolan, "Comparing," 625–627.

72 Kolben, "Consumer Imaginary," 891–892.

73 Electronics Watch, *Transparency*, 3.

74 France, LOI n° 2017–399 du 27 mars 2017 relative au devoir de vigilance des sociétés mères et des entreprises donneuses d'ordre (1); L. 225-102-4 du code de commerce, art. 1.I, art 2.

or 10% of world-wide revenue),[75] Norway (2021, 50 employees, fines to deny profitability),[76] and Germany (2021, 3,000 employees, fines up to €50,000 or 2% of annual turnover).[77]

The German, Norwegian, and Dutch laws enforce transparency, which the MSAs do not. On the other hand, these laws and MSAs have other accountability gaps in common. They allow selective disclosure of diligence measures; they do not disclose supply-chains; and they do not connect with purchasers. The German law does empower workers to authorise a union or NGO to initiate enforcement, but it sets no objective standards of disclosure.[78]

The laws vary in scope of disclosure and diligence. For example, Germany covers ILO core conventions and several environmental treaties,[79] while Norway covers ILO-core standards and decent working conditions but not environmental treaties.[80] The result is an uneven playing field across Europe, which is driving EU reforms of disclosure and due diligence.

3.3 *General Reporting Frameworks*

In December 2022, the EU adopted the Corporate Sustainability Reporting Directive (CSRD).[81] The CSRD revises several pillars of EU transparency including the Non-Financial Reporting Directive (NFRD 2014).[82] The NFRD was based on the UN's Global Reporting Initiative (GRI), the leading platform for voluntary corporate disclosures, which has similar accountability gaps as the modern slavery laws.[83] The GRI includes performance disclosures, but they are not verifiable in the absence of actual supply-chain locations.[84]

---

75 Netherlands, Act of 24 October 2019 introducing a duty of care to prevent the supply of goods and services created using child labor (Child Labor Due Diligence Act), §2(a), §4(1), §7.

76 Norway, Act relating to enterprises' transparency and work on fundamental human rights and decent working conditions, LOV-2021-06-18-99, §3(a), §11–13.

77 Germany, Act on Corporate Due Diligence Obligations in Supply Chains, BGBl I 2021, 2959; §1; §23; §24(3).

78 Germany, §11.

79 Germany, §2(2) and (3).

80 Norway, §3(c).

81 EU CSRD, Directive (EU) 2022/2464 of the European Parliament and of the Council of 14 December 2022 amending Regulation (EU) No 537/2014, Directive 2004/109/EC, Directive 2006/43/EC and Directive 2013/34/EU, as regards corporate sustainability reporting.

82 EU NFRD, Directive 2014/95/EU of the European Parliament and of the Council of 22 October 2014 amending Directive 2013/34/EU as regards disclosure of non-financial and diversity information by certain large undertakings and groups (OJ. L 330/1), art. 1(1) (inserting art. 19a(1) in the Accounting Directive 2013/34/EU).

83 *See* John McCalla-Leacy, Global Survey of Sustainability Reporting (KMPG, 2022), 24.

84 Hess, "Transparency Trap," 27–29.

The TOC depends on investors, shareholders, and advocates to press corporations into being more diligent. The CSRD mandates an annual report that combines financial with environmental-social-governance (ESG) disclosures – a 'double materiality' report – to reinforce sustainable investment. The CSRD mitigates some of the shortcomings in voluntary platforms with reforms that push companies to improve.[85] It will:

- Expand covered companies in the EU from 12,000 large EU companies listed in an EU market (2024) to over 50,000 smaller and non-EU companies by 2026.[86]
- Expand annual disclosure beyond 'modern slavery' risks to all internationally recognised labor and human rights.[87]
- Standardise disclosure by setting European Sustainability Reporting Standards for common reporting, supplemented with standards for high-risk industries.[88] CSRD requires independent auditors to assure compliance with EU reporting standards,[89] starting with *limited* assurances in 2026 and *reasonable* assurances in 2028.[90]

Several accountability gaps of the MSAs are addressed by the CSRD, except for the first and most important one:

- Connection to users: The CSRD does not directly connect to accountability through a market (like procurement) or regulation (like border measures against forced labor). However, the EU is moving to 'complement' the CSRD with the mandatory Corporate Sustainability Due Diligence Directive (CSDD), which entered into force in July 2024.[91]

---

85 CSRD, recitals 9–16, 45, 49; see Félix E. Mezzanotte, "Recent Law Reforms in EU Sustainable Finance: Regulating Sustainability Risk and Sustainable Investments," forthcoming Am. U. Bus. L. Rev. (draft March 2022), 36, 39–41, available at SSRN: http://dx.doi.org/10.2139/ssrn.4098053.

86 CSRD, recitals 17–21, art. 1(1)-(3) (public interest entities), art. 3(14) (audits), art 5(2) (Transposition); Crowell & Moring, "The Corporate Sustainability Reporting Directive," ESG Resource Center (December 1, 2022), §2, §5.

87 CSRD, recitals 31, 49; art. 1(1) [art. 1 Accounting], (2) (art. 2, Accounting), (4) (art. 19a, Accounting, (8) [art. 29b, Accounting].

88 CSRD, (8) [art. 29b, Accounting].

89 CSRD, recital 61; art. (13) [art. 34, Statutory Audits].

90 CSRD, art. 5(2) (Transposition); Musonda Kapotwe et al., "EU Corporate Sustainability Reporting Directive," Mayer Brown posting, Harvard Law School Forum on Corporate Governance (December 11, 2022).

91 EU CSDD, Directive (Eu) 2024/1760 of the European Parliament and of the Council of 13 June 2024 on corporate sustainability due diligence and amending Directive (EU) 2019/1937 and Regulation (EU) 2023/2859.

The CSDD includes civil liability for failure to be diligent. CSRD disclosures will provide evidence of diligence (or lack thereof).[92]

- Vagueness and audits: The CSRD's audits (or assurances of compliance) will police non-disclosure. Adding to penalites for noncompliance already in the Accounting Directive, the CSRD requires member states to set sanctions on *auditors* who do not comply with sustainability reporting standards.[93] Yet the audits are subjective. The CSRD asks auditors to judge whether a disclosure is 'about' an HR factor (e.g., respect for the right to organise), while avoiding a 'disproportionate administrative burden', and 'taking account, to the greatest extent possible, of the work of global standard-setting initiatives'.[94] The EU hopes that a 'diversified audit market', with auditors competing for corporate business, will somehow overcome the accountability gaps of social audits.[95]
- No supply-chain or performance data: The CSRD stops short of requiring disclosure of supply-chain locations.[96] It is likely to retain GRI indicators for self-generated process data – e.g., suppliers screened for abuses – and indicators of HR compliance that often reflect workers' fear of complaining.[97] The first round of CSRD standards does not address this gap. It organises disclosures of policy and process into categories.[98]
- Comparability: By requiring future standards for selected high-risk industries, the CSRD might make some disclosures comparable. The system will generate too much information for retail consumers to compare, but it may help HR monitors to investigate companies.

---

92 CSDD, recitals 15, 21, 79, 81, 90; arts. 1(b), 27, 29.

93 CSRD, art. 16 [art. 30g, Statutory Audits]; Directive 2013/34/EU of the European Parliament and of the Council of 26 June 2013 on the annual financial statements, consolidated financial statements and related reports of certain types of undertakings (2013) OJ L182/13, art. 51; Regulation (EU) 2020/852 of the European Parliament and of the Council of 18 June 2020 on the establishment of a framework to facilitate sustainable investment (2020), OJ L198/13, art. 22.

94 CSRD, art. 8 [art. 29b(2), Statutory Audits]; recital 45.

95 CSRD, recital 61.

96 GRI, *G4 Reporting,* G4-LA14 (suppliers screened).

97 GRI, *G4 Reporting,* G4-LA6 (Rates of injury); see literature reviewed by Hess, *Transparency Trap,* 26–31.

98 EC, European sustainability reporting standards – first set, Draft Act 9 June 2023, Annex I, S2 – Workers in the Value Chain, pages 196–211, accessed July 11, 2023, https://ec.europa.eu/info/law/better-regulation/have-your-say/initiatives/13765-European-sustainability-reporting-standards-first-set_en.

3.4 *Human Rights Benchmarks*

Human-rights benchmarks have emerged to compare brands based on their process claims, and crucially, to show where they avoid disclosure – including actual supply-chain locations, workers, and HR performance. The Corporate Human Rights Benchmark 2022 (CHRB) ranks companies in three industries: agriculture/food (57), ITC (43, information-technology-communications), and automotive (29).[99] To mitigate selective disclosures, the CHRB 'pulls the data from the companies through engagement' and publishes public rankings.[100] KnowTheChain (KTC) publishes benchmarks on ITC, apparel/footwear, and food/beverage.[101]

The benchmarks compare brand performance using a taxonomy of due diligence. For example, the *Fashion Transparency Index* applies 246 indicators within five rating sets: (1) policies/commitments, (2) governance, (3) supply-chain traceability, (4) know/show/fix, and (5) spotlight issues (which include purchasing practices).[102] Unfortunately, these three benchmarks use different categories, so their indicators are not easily aligned.

The theory of change seeks to 'normalise' transparency within otherwise opaque industries.[103] Benchmarks compare self-disclosure of corporate performance, which aspires to 'drive a 'race to the top' with reputation rewards for leaders and risk for laggards.[104] Benchmarks aim to support activists, the media, investors, governments, consumers, and producers.[105]

Accountability gaps of companies, as revealed and compared by the benchmarks, confirm the gaps reported above:

- Connection to users: Recognising a 'glacial rate of change,'[106] KTC concludes that connecting disclosers to mandatory accountability mechanisms is necessary, and the CHRB concurs.[107]

---

99 World Benchmarking Alliance, *Corporate Human Rights Benchmark* (November 2022), 7.

100 Hess, "Transparency Trap," 51; CHRB 2022, 6–7.

101 KnowTheChain, *2022 Benchmark*, accessed March 3, 2023, https://knowthechain.org/benchmark/.

102 Fashion Index 2022, 3.

103 Ibid, 23.

104 "Benchmark Methodology," KnowTheChain, accessed March 3, 2023, https://knowthechain.org/benchmark-methodology/.

105 "Theory of Change," World Benchmarking Alliance, accessed March 3, 2023, https://www.worldbenchmarkingalliance.org/theory-of-change/.

106 KtC, 2022 Information and Communications Technology Benchmark Findings Report, (New York: KnowTheChain, 2022), 8.

107 KtC, *ITC Benchmark 2022*, 42; CHRB 2022, 30.

- Supply-chain data: While most apparel companies disclose human rights policies, the *Fashion Index* reports that 46% disclose the location of first-tier suppliers, and only 30% do so for lower-tiers.[108] KTC reports that only 8% of ITC companies disclose first-tier addresses.[109]

Accountability gaps of benchmarks reflect their low utility in a mass-market compared to potentially high utility in a procurement market.

- Connect to users: The benchmarks depend on sophisticated users, which could include institutional purchasers for some industries (e.g., ICT, extractives). In the absence of a label at the point of sale, consumers are not aware of a benchmark's comparison.
- Comparability: The benchmarks' analysis and graphs in a lengthy report are not easily comprehended by a retail consumer. They demonstrate, however, that consumer-friendly labeling schemes are attainable.

Expert procurement purchasers could use benchmark comparisons as a criterion for HR capacity in a bidding process for food, ITC, manufacturing, or extractives.

3.5 *Procurement*

Governments are leading buyers of goods, services, and infrastructure – ranging from 13-to-20 percent of GDP in most countries. They have the market power to lead by example, to innovate, and achieve economies of scale for monitoring contractors and setting standards for transparency.[110]

The theory of change recognises the 'state duty to protect human rights' within the 'state-business nexus' to supply essential goods and services.[111] In contrast to private purchasers, governments have the regulatory and market power to make transparency happen and to use it to enforce HR performance in a contract. Their levers include award incentives, contract remedies, and limits on future competition.[112]

108 Fashion Index 2022, 60.

109 KtC, ITC Benchmark 2022, 21.

110 "Global Public Procurement Database," World Bank, accessed March 13, 2023, https://www.worldbank.org/en/news/feature/2020/03/23/global-public-procurement-database-share-compare-improve#; "Public Procurement and Responsible Business Conduct," OECD, accessed March 13, 2023, https://www.oecd.org/gov/public-procurement/procurement-and-rbc/.

111 UNGPS 1, 5, 6, 25.

112 Stumberg et al., *Turning a Blind Eye*, 52–54; *see* Robert Stumberg and Nicole Vander Meulen, "Supply-Chain Transparency in Public Procurement: Lessons from the Apparel Sector," in

A survey of 20 jurisdictions shows that most governments have some authority to make HR progress, with or without additional reform legislation.[113] Smaller governments have been the most flexible and innovative. For example, since 2012, Swedish counties have developed a code of conduct, appointed an HR coordinator, monitored high-risk products (e.g., ICT, textiles, surgical implements, PPE), and published occasional factory reports.[114] The power of connecting transparency with procurement was tested when Dell Computers refused to disclose remedy plans for overtime conditions in Chinese factories. The counties dropped Dell from their purchase list, and within months, Dell disclosed and implemented a remedy plan.[115]

In a similar vein, seven US cities align their codes for apparel contracts through the Sweatfree Purchasing Consortium, which developed a model policy and contract documents.[116] Madison, Wisconsin, an SPC member, showed that a small city could attract national competitors for a contract that requires annual progress on supply-chain transparency.[117]

Germany recently applied its HR diligence law to procurement. If an enterprise receives a final judgment and substantial fine (€175,000 or higher), it is excluded from procurement competition for up to three years.[118]

On a macro scale, the EU's 2014 procurement directive requires member states to ensure that procurement contractors comply with EU law, national law, and the ILO Core Conventions.[119] This would include compliance with CSRD disclosures.

In the US, The Federal Funding Accountability and Transparency Act of 2006 (FFATA) mandates supply-chain transparency of suppliers and sub-suppliers down to contracts of $25,000. However, the Office of Management and Budget

---

Public Procurement and Human Rights: Opportunities, Risks and Dilemmas for the State as Buyer, eds. Claire Methven O'Brien and Olga Martin-Ortega (Cambridge: Cambridge University Press, 2019), 206–224.

113 Claire Methven O'Brien et al., Public Procurement and Human Rights: A Survey of Twenty Jurisdictions (Washington: ICAR, 2016).

114 Pauline Göthberg, "Public Procurement and Human Rights in the Healthcare Sector: The Swedish County Councils' Collaborative Model," (London: Edward Elgar 2019), 165–179; O'Brien, *Survey of Jurisdictions,* 38.

115 Electronics Watch, Public Procurement and Human Rights Due Diligence to Achieve Respect for Labour Rights Standards in Electronics Factories: A Case Study of the Swedish County Councils and the Dell Computer Corporation (2016).

116 Sweatfree Purchasing Consortium, accessed on March 13, 2023, http://buysweatfree.org.

117 Stumberg and Vander Meulen, "Apparel Sector" 206–224.

118 Germany, §22 and §24.

119 Directive 2014/24/EU of the European Parliament and of the Council of 26 February 2014 on public procurement and repealing Directive 2004/18/EC, Annex X.

used rulemaking to exclude most supplier subcontracts.[120] The Walsh-Healy Act of 1936 prohibits procurement of Sweatshop goods, but the Secretary of Labor used rulemaking to suspend the law for imported products.[121]

As it stands, US federal procurement law prohibits purchase of goods made with forced labor, forced child labor, and human trafficking (coercive or fraudulent recruitment, worst forms of child labor, sex trafficking).[122] The law requires contract managers to require greater transparency on high-risk contracts with a prevention plan and reports of investigations. Unfortunately, an audit found that agencies were unaware of their duties under this law.[123]

3.6 *The Accountability Gaps*

- Connection to users: A few governments have authority to require transparency and use it to award and monitor contracts and subcontractors.[124] But most do not, and those that do rarely monitor suppliers or provide a remedy mechanism.[125]
- Vagueness and limited supply-chain data: The U.S. Transparency Act (USAspending.gov)[126] and the EU's TED database[127] disclose national contract amounts, volume, public purchasers, product/service codes, and identity of prime contractors. TED covers national and local procurement but does not aggregate transactions for a contractor or product code. Neither database discloses locations of production, number of workers, or HR performance.

These accountability gaps result in part from contractors' opposition.[128] Resources to manage procurement have been shrinking for decades, and

120 Federal Funding Accountability and Transparency Act of 2006, Pub. L. No. 109–282, §2(b)(1)(D), 120 Stat. 1186, 1187 (2006); Reporting Executive Compensation and First-Tier Subcontract Awards, 77 Fed. Reg. at 44052–53.

121 Walsh-Healey Public Contract Act, 41 USC. §6501–6511; Federal Acquisition Regulation (FAR), 41 C.F.R. 50–201.603(b).

122 FAR, 48 CFR 22.1503, 52.222–50.

123 US Government Accountability Office, DOD Should Address Weaknesses in Oversight of Contractors and Reporting of Investigations Related to Contracts (Washington: GAO-21-546, 2021), 1, 19.

124 *See* Directive 2014/24/EU, recital 105, art. 18, art. 57(4)(a), art. 71.1; 41 U.S.C. §4706(b)(1); FAR, 48 CFR 52.244–2 et seq.

125 O'Brien, Survey of Jurisdictions, 53–54.

126 USAspending.gov, accessed March 30, 2023, www.usaspending.gov.

127 TED, Tenders Electronic Daily, accessed March 30, 2023, http://ted.europa.eu/TED/main/HomePage.do.

128 Stumberg et al., *Turning a Blind Eye*, 30–33.

agencies have little capacity to absorb more work.[129] Procurement officers are risk-averse to litigation by contractors, which delays government orders. They are not likely to require HR disclosures without a mandate and resources.[130]

The local governments cited above address the resource gap and lack of political will by acting through a consortium that shares costs, builds political cohesion, and reduces audit burdens on suppliers. The most successful is Electronics Watch (EW).

EW sustains itself on dues from 49 direct affiliates (governments and universities) and 994 indirect affiliates (in purchasing consortia).[131] EW progressively updates a purchasing code, provides guidance to contractors, and helps workers to voice complaints and contribute to solutions through 'worker-driven monitoring'.[132] EW has a central staff that coordinates 18 monitoring partners in Southeast Asia, Central Europe, Mexico, and South Africa.[133]

EW contract clauses require supply-chain transparency to the purchaser including suppliers of component parts. EW retains the option to publish its monitoring report and disclose locations if that advances the goal of ensuring a remedy to workers.[134]

3.7 *Border Controls*

In 2016 the US Congress responded to growing forced labor by repealing the 'consumptive demand' exemption, which had suspended the U.S. ban on forced-labor imports.[135] US Customs and Border Protection (CBP) implemented its powers to exclude or seize goods at the border (withhold release orders, WROs).[136] The trigger is *reasonable but not conclusive* evidence that goods are produced with forced labor.[137] This standard sets up a rebuttable presumption, shifting the burden of proof to importers. CPB has issued WROs on products from 14 countries including apparel, auto parts, computer parts, disposable gloves, polysilicon, palm oil, sugar, tobacco, and tomatoes.[138]

---

129 Steve Kelman, "Is the performance of the procurement system improving?" *FCW*, May 30, 2017.

130 O'Brien, Survey of Jurisdictions, 53.

131 Electronics Watch, Affiliates, accessed June 6, 2023, https://electronicswatch.org/en.

132 Ibid, What We Do.

133 Ibid, Monitoring Partners.

134 Electronics Watch Contract Conditions with Guidance for Contractors (EW, June 2020), §§7–12.

135 Tariff Act of 1930, 19 U.S.C. §1307.

136 Ibid, 19 U.S.C. §1499, §1595a.

137 19 C.F.R. §12.42.

138 CBP, Withhold Release Orders and Findings, accessed March 20, 2023, https://www.cbp.gov/trade/forced-labor/withhold-release-orders-and-findings.

The theory of change is to use the WRO presumption as a transparency-forcing event. CPB provides a canvas for other agencies, disadvantaged competitors, and NGOs to build a mosaic of transparency to reveal complex supply chains and hidden abuses.

Through 2019–20, the WROs mounted on goods from Xinjiang, China. Investigators confirmed policies directed against Uyghur and other minority groups including internment camps with onsite manufacturing, subsidies for 'mutual pairing' for factories to use detained workers, constant surveillance, and threat of detention.[139]

Factories in Xinjiang export 4,800 finished products and materials, often comingled, to 177 countries. This supply-chain complexity obscures forced labor for those who source from Xinjiang.[140] To evade U.S. trade exclusions, the Xinjiang Production and Construction Corps (XPCC) uses 2,900 subsidiaries to export to partners in third countries, who re-export to the United States.[141]

Adapting to these tactics, the U.S. Congress enacted the Uyghur Forced Labor Prevention Act (UFLPA) in 2021.[142] It applies the WRO presumption to *all* goods from Xinjiang.[143] The Department of Homeland Security developed a strategy to coordinate multiple agencies, recruit NGO investigators, and deploy cutting-edge technologies to trace products and map supply-chains on a global scale.[144]

Accountability gaps are substantially closed by the UFPLA.

– Connection to users: The direct user of transparency is the CPB itself. The UFLPA converts importers into disclosers (to rebut the presumption) and recruits third-party investigators (to support or dispel the presumption). It the first two years of implementation, CPB detained

139 Amy K. Lehr, *Addressing Forced Labor in the Xinjiang Uyghur Autonomous Region: Towards a Shared Agenda* (Washinton: Cntr. for Strategic Int'l Studies, 2020); "Risks and Considerations for Businesses and Individuals with Exposure of Entities Engaged in Forced Labor and other Human Rights Abuses Linked to Xinjiang, China," US Dept. of State (July 13, 2021).

140 China Chamber of International Commerce, "Comment to the Forced Labor Enforcement Task Force," Regulations.gov (Mar. 11, 2022), 21–22.

141 Irina Bukhrin, Long Shadows: How the Global Economy supports Oppression in Xinjiang, C4ADS (2021), 5, 16–17.

142 US Pub. L. 117–78, 135 Stat. 1525, Uyghur Forced Labor Prevention Act (December 23, 2021).

143 Ibid, §3(a).

144 US Department of Homeland Security, Strategy to Prevent the Importation of Goods Mined, Produced, or Manufactured with Forced Labor in the People's Republic of China (June 17, 2022) 31–33, 35–39; 2024 Updates to the Strategy to Prevent the Importation of Goods Mined, Produced, or Manufactured with Forced Labor in the People's Republic of China (July 19, 2024).

$3.56 billion in shipments led by electronics, apparel, and industrial materials.[145]
- Supply-chain data: The UFPLA flips the narrative from selective disclosure to full transparency for each stage of due diligence, starting with supply-chain mapping. Any transparency gap works against the importer.[146]
- Comparability: Side-by-side comparison is not relevant for the UFPLA, which uses transparency-forcing regulation.[147]

The UFPLA's first objective is to close the U.S. market to forced labor, and it also calls for outreach to other governments.[148] Canada and Mexico have banned forced-labor imports, but enforcement is not visible.[149] The EU has proposed a regulation to implement WRO-style enforcement which would require governments to establish a 'substantiated concern' to exclude Xinjiang trade.[150]

China pushed back with a policy to punish 'unreliable' companies that comply with the UFPLA by limiting investment, imports, or exports.[151] This stresses companies with business in China. For example, Intel sent a letter to chip suppliers warning of forced labor risks in 2021, and one day later, apologised to Chinese suppliers for doing so.[152]

Another affected industry is solar manufacturing, which sources polysilicon products from Xinjiang. In the third quarter of 2022, 80 percent of US solar

145 US Customs & Border Protection, "Uyghur Forced Labor Prevention Act Statistics," accessed October 18, 2024, https://www.cbp.gov/newsroom/stats/trade/uyghur-forced-labor-prevention-act-statistics.

146 Jasmin Malik Chua, "'Every Supplier,' 'Every Tier': What Uniqlo's Xinjiang Links and Lapses Mean for Your Brand," *Sourcing Journal* (May 27, 2021).; 19 CFR §12.42–44.

147 *See* Glen Taylor, "Will This New Software Solve Xinjiang Traceability Challenges?" *Sourcing Journal* (December 3, 2020).

148 US Public Law 117–78, §1, §4.

149 Global Affairs Canada, Advisory on doing business with Xinjiang-related entities, accessed March 19, 2023, https://www.international.gc.ca/global-affairs-affaires-mondiales/news-nouvelles/2021/2021-01-12-xinjiang-advisory-avis.aspx?lang=eng; Ropes & Gray "Mexico Bans Imports Made with Forced Labor in Alignment with the USMCA," Alert (March 6, 2023).

150 EC Forced Labour. Proposal for a Regulation of the European Parliament and of the Council on prohibiting products made with forced labour on the Union market (September 14, 2022), arts. 4.5 and 5.1; EU Parliament News, Products made with forced labour to be banned from EU single market (April 23, 2024).

151 China MOFCOM Order No. 4 of 2020 on Provisions on the Unreliable Entity List, Ministry of Commerce, People's Republic of China (September 19, 2020), art. 10.

152 Cai Kaiming and Ruan Donghui, "The Impact of the US Forced Uyghur Labor Prevention Act and Companies' Compliance Response," CCPIT (2022), accessed March 2, 2023, https://www.ctils.com/articles/4195.

imports came from third-country suppliers using Chinese components.[153] The disruptions for US solar companies were severe as the CPB seized solar panels worth $806 million in late 2022.[154]

Nonetheless, the *Solar Industry Supply Chain Tracing Protocol 1.0* tracks closely with the UFPLA implementation strategy. The US Congress rewarded the industry with subsidies to overcome supply-chain disruptions by 2027–32.[155] The European Commission is pursuing similar legislative proposals.[156]

4 Agenda for Progress

The border control strategy creates accountability for forced labor. Its direct connection to a regulator disrupts complicit supply chains, and its risk-based presumption forces full supply-chain-transparency to happen. This approach stands in contrast …

- to voluntary brand disclosures that manage reputation risk but do not reveal supply chains or workers, and
- to MSAs and general frameworks like CSRD that mandate disclosure that is still vague and selective, without revealing supply chains.

As Electronics Watch reflected, managing reputation risk 'is not the same as reducing workers' risk of being exploited and abused. … Indeed, disclosing information is not the same as being transparent. Information can obfuscate as much as it can clarify. Information does not automatically have social value because it is released'.[157]

The initiatives that work seek full transparency, as opposed to disclosure for its own sake. These include the mapping initiatives that enable monitors to link factories with downstream brands and leverage collaboration when brands share a factory. Organisations like Electronics Watch aggregate the purchasing

153 Garrett Hering and Molly Christian, "US finds solar imports from Southeast Asia skirting tariffs; industry alarmed," S&P Global Market Intelligence (December 2, 2022).

154 Alan Newhauser, "US crackdown on Chinese forced labor hits solar industry," *Axios* (January 13, 2023).

155 Inflation Reduction Act, P.L. 117–169 (August 16, 2022), §13502(b)(1); Becca Jones-Albertus et al., "Webinar: Reaching for the Solar Future: How the Inflation Reduction Act Impacts Solar Deployment and Expands Manufacturing," US Dept. of Energy (September 2022), accessed March 19, 2023, https://www.energy.gov/sites/default/files/2022-10/SETO_IRA_Webinar_Presentation_Sept_2022.pdf.

156 *E.g.*, EC, Net-Zero Industry Act, Press release (March 16, 2023); EC, Critical Raw Materials, Press release (March 16 2023).

157 Electronics Watch, *Transparency*, 3.

power of governments and institutions to achieve upstream transparency of suppliers and engage workers in monitoring and negotiating a remedy.

This chapter concludes with an outline of proven reforms that address accountability gaps in transparency initiatives. The lessons from one are transferable to another.

4.1 *Connect to Users with Accountability Mechanisms*

- *Customs:* The strategy of targeting the highest-risk goods with an evidence-based presumption is transferable to other areas, e.g., seafood from the South China Sea.[158] Focusing on high-risk products from a region would be less disruptive than a broader ban on all products and thus more politically viable. The EU's pending customs measure will test this idea.
- *Procurement:* The Electronics Watch model is transferable to institutions outside of government and to other high-risk industries like apparel and food. For example, the Robert Wood Johnson Foundation awarded a grant to US universities (Georgetown, Michigan, and California) to explore a 'Just Purchasing Consortium' that could monitor the arduous conditions of food workers, starting with poultry plants that supply university cafeterias.[159]
- *Civil liability to workers:* The laws in France, Germany, Norway, and the Netherlands that mandate due diligence could connect transparency to workers. But they take different approaches to civil liability for failure to implement a prevention plan.[160] The result is an uneven playing field for EU businesses. The EU's CSDD aims to set a floor to level due diligence across the Union, including sanctions and civil liability for harm to workers.[161] The CSDD's mandatory diligence 'will complement' the CSRD because reporting is a step of diligence, and the CSRD is the standard for reporting.[162]
- *Domestic aid:* Brazil's Ministry of Labor investigates and reports a 'dirty list' of companies with forced labor in their supply chains.

---

158 Ian Urbina, "The Uyghur Workers Forced to Process the World's Fish," *The New Yorker* (October 9, 2023).

159 Sapna E Thottathil, "Sustainable food procurement by the University of California's health systems," *Journal of Agriculture, Food Systems & Community Development* (2022), 90.

160 CSDD, recitals 15, 21, 79, 81, 90; arts. 1(b), 27, 29.

161 Ibid, arts. 27 (Penalites), 29 (Civil Liability).

162 Ibid, Explanatory Memorandum, 4–5, arts. 4(f) (Due Diligence) and 11 (Communicating).

Agencies are advised not to provide state aid to these companies for a two-year period.[163]

- *Preferential tariffs:* US law provides tariff preferences to developing countries, but a country is only eligible if it protects 'internationally recognised workers' rights.'[164] Investigations of nine countries included forced labor in agriculture, manufacturing, and seafood industries.[165] The EU has a similar scheme.[166]

4.2 *Cure Vagueness and Selective Disclosure*

- *Supply-chain disclosure:* The most common accountability gaps include non-disclosure of supply-chain locations and flawed audits.[167] These gaps could be overcome by adopting the following measures in MSAs, the CSRD, purchasing codes, and corporate codes of conduct:
  - Disclose suppliers, locations, and workers following the examples set by the Accord/RSC, OSH, MiB, and the WRC.
  - Reform audits that use coercive surveys and subjective statistics. The Global Electronics Council proposed more objective standards for audits (e.g., corrective action plan, worker input, protection from retaliation),[168] and Electronics Watch uses worker-centered investigations.[169]
- *Default penalties or remedies:* New South Wales (Australia) reformed the MSA model by adding a penalty for non-compliance (up to 1.1 million AUD).[170] But accountability measures are easier said than done

163 Brazil Ministry of Labor and Employment Decree No. 540/2004; *see* Harris and Nolan, "Comparing," 640.

164 19 U.S.C. §2462 (b)(2)(G), 19 U.S.C. §2467(4).

165 "Products to be removed from GSP eligibility for Thailand," US Trade Representative (April 25, 2020); "Active and Recently Closed GSP Country Practices Reviews," USTR, accessed March 25, 2023, https://ustr.gov/issue-areas/preference-programs/generalized-system-preferences-gsp/current-reviews.

166 EC, DG Trade, Access2Markets, Generalized Scheme of Preferences Plus (GSP+), accessed March 25, 2023, https://trade.ec.europa.eu/access-to-markets/en/content/generalised-scheme-preferences-plus-gsp; *see* Kolben, "Consumer Imaginary," 890.

167 Finnegan, Responsibility Outsourced, 25–31.

168 Global Electronics Council, *Sustainability Assessment Criteria for Corporate ESG Performance – Draft,* (November 10, 2022), 7.1.3 Required (Part B. Supplier social audits), 7.1.4 Optional – Improving quality and transparency of supplier social audits), 7.1.5 Optional – Suppliers details for worker engagement.

169 EW, Strategic Plan 2021–2023 (2022), 5.

170 NSW Modern Slavery Act 2018 No. 30, Part 3, s.24.

in the face of corporate opposition. Recognising the challenge, Harris and Nolan propose a contract-law approach of default penalties.[171] *Default* means that a company can mitigate the penalty by committing to change its practices, potentially with deferred investigation or prosecution.[172] The default penalty could lead to a remedy plan with monitoring. Examples of default penalties include:

- *Retail brands* – publish a 'dirty list' of brands.
- *Procurement* – suspend from future contracts.
- *Licensing* – suspend license or exclude suppliers.

4.3 *Compare Suppliers*

Conventional transparency theory assumes that most consumers prefer ethically produced products, if only they can compare brands. But there is no brand comparison of working conditions at the point of sale. For retail industries, Kolben, Thottathil and others point to the success of fair trade and sustainability labels that use targeted standards and certifications.[173] Labels simplify comparison to whether products have earned a badge of HR performance. This path is leading to progress on specific products and stages of supply (e.g., farm workers).[174]

The benchmarks that compare retail brands, as the *Fashion Index* explains, are 'not … a shopping guide'.[175] They compare elements of transparency, not actual treatment of workers. So, a label/standard on brand transparency alone would be a steppingstone in the path. It could serve to distinguish brands that disclose the chain of suppliers-locations-workers, reach below tier-one suppliers, and eventually achieve full transparency.

---

171 Harris and Nolan, "Comparing," 639–642.

172 Ibid.

173 Thottathil, "Sustainable food," 89–90; Kolben, "Consumer Imaginary," 897; Harris and Nolan, "Comparing," 646–647.

174 *Eg.,* Fair Trade International, Fairtrade Trader Standard, v1.7, (2015), 3.1 Labor Rights; Center for Good Food Purchasing, Valued Workforce, accessed March 30, 2023, https://goodfoodpurchasing.org/program-overview/; Fair World Project, *International Guide to Fair Trade Labels* (2020).

175 "Brand Communication Guidelines on the Fashion Transparency Index," Fashion Revolution, linked in *Fashion Index 2022*, accessed March 25, 2025, https://docs.google.com/document/d/1ZsdKgsn-rETvhQveu23w1lzIx2aWNblv/edit.

5 Conclusion

Transparency is the key to accountability for the human rights of workers. You cannot fix what you do not know or validate what you do not show. Most suppliers claim to be transparent when, in fact, they reveal little of their supply chain. Research confirms that self-disclosure is commonly used to game the system, manage reputation risk, and forestall effective regulation.

Full transparency sees *through* the chain – through tiers of supply, comingling of materials, and distant locations behind borders – to reveal the workers and conditions in which they toil. The work of transparency critics supports a framework of accountability that: (1) connects with user decisions, (2) cures vagueness and gaming, and (3) compares suppliers. This framework makes it possible to compare six transparency initiatives: voluntary brand disclosures, modern slavery laws, general reporting frameworks, human rights benchmarks, procurement by governments and institutions, and border controls. The leading procurement and border measures close many of the accountability gaps and test reforms that are transferable to the other transparency initiatives.

Purchasers and regulators are moving beyond selective corporate disclosures. They show how stakeholders can build a mosaic of full transparency to see the supply chain and be seen by others. In their hands, the transparency key to accountability is beginning to turn.

Bibliography

Books

Ben-Shahar, Omri, and Carl E. Schneider. *More than You Wanted to Know: The Failure of Mandated Disclosure.* Princeton: Princeton University Press, 2014.

Featherstone, Liza. *Students Against Sweatshops.* London: Verso, 2002.

Frankfurt, Harry. *On Bullshit.* Princeton: Princeton University Press, 2005.

Fung, Archon, Mary Graham and David Weil. *Full Disclosure: The Perils and Promise of Transparency.* Cambridge: Cambridge University Press, 2007.

Rao, Sunil. *Modern Slavery Legislation: Drafting History and Comparisons between Australia, UK and the USA*. Abington-on-Thames: Routledge, 2020.

Book Chapters

Göthberg, Pauline. "Public Procurement and Human Rights in the Healthcare Sector: The Swedish County Councils' Collaborative Model." In *Public Procurement and Human Rights*, edited by Olga Martin-Ortega and Claire Methven O'Brien, 165–179. Cheltenham: Edward Elgar, 2019.

Gupta, Arti, and Michael Mason. "Transparency Turn in Global Environmental Governance." In *Transparency in Global Environmental Governance*, edited by Arti Gupta and Michael Mason, 3–38. Boston: MIT Press, 2014.

Stumberg, Robert, and Nicole Vander Meulen. "Supply-Chain Transparency in Public Procurement: Lessons from the Apparel Sector." In *Public Procurement and Human Rights: Opportunities, Risks and Dilemmas for the State as Buyer*, edited by Claire Methven O'Brien and Olga Martin-Ortega, 206–223. Cheltenham: Edward Elgar, 2019.

Journal Articles

Aman, Alfred C. Aman, Jr., and Landyn Wm. Rookard. "Private Government and the Transparency Deficit." *Administrative Law Review* 71 (2019): 437–489.

Boiral, Olivier, and Jean-Francois Henri. "Is Sustainability Performance Comparable? A Study of GRI Reports of Mining Organizations." *Business & Society* 56 (2017): 283–317.

Boiral, Olivier. "Sustainability Reports as Simulacra? A Counter-Account of A and A+ GRI Reports." *Accounting, Auditing & Accountability Journal* 26 (2013): 1036–1071.

Doorey, David. "The Transparent Supply Chain: from Resistance to Implementation at Nike and Levi-Strauss." *Journal of Business Ethics* 102 (April 2016): 587–603.

Gray, Rob. "Is Accounting for Sustainability Actually Accounting for Sustainability … and How Would We Know? An exploration of narratives of organisations and the planet." *Accounting, Organizations & Society* 35 (2010): 47–62.

Harris, Hannah, and Justine Nolan. "Learning from Experience: Comparing Legal Approaches to Foreign Bribery and Modern Slavery." *Cardozo International & Comparative Law Review* 4 (2021): 603–652.

Hess, David Hess. "The Transparency Trap: Non-Financial Disclosure and the Responsibility of Business to Respect Human Rights." *American Business Law Journal* 56 (2019): 5–53.

Kaiming, Cai, and Ruan Donghui. "The Impact of the U.S. Forced Uyghur Labor Prevention Act and Companies' Compliance Response." *CCPIT* (2022): 37.

Kolben, Kevin. "The Consumer Imaginary: Labor Rights, Human Rights, and Citizen-Consumers in the Global Supply Chain." *Vanderbilt Law Review* 52 (2021): 839–898.

Kwoka, Margaret, and Bridget DuPey. "Targeted Transparency as Regulation." *Florida State University Law Review* 48 (2021): 385–441.

LeBaron, Genevieve, and Andreas Ruhmkorff. "The Domestic Politics of Corporate Accountability Legislation: Struggles over the 2015 UK Modern Slavey Act." *Socio-Economic Review*, 0 (2017): 1–35.

Mezzanotte, Félix E. "Recent Law Reforms in EU Sustainable Finance: Regulating Sustainability Risk and Sustainable Investments." Forthcoming *American University*

Business Law Review (draft March 2022), available at SSRN: http://dx.doi.org/10.2139/ssrn.4098053.

Mollenkopf, Diane A., Simone T. Peinkofer, and Yu (Jade) Chu. "Supply chain transparency: Consumer reactions to incongruent signals." *Journal of Operations Management* 68 (2022): 306–327.

Prasad, Monica, Howard Kimeldorf, Rachel Meyer, and Ian Robinson. "Consumers of the World Unite: A Market-based Response to Sweatshops." *Labor Studies Journal,* 29 (2004): 57–79.

Rogers, Todd, Richard Zeckhauser, Francesca Gino, Schweitzer, and Michael Norton,."Artful Paltering: The Risks and Rewards of Using Truthful Statements to Mislead Others." *Personality and Social Psychology,* 112, no. 3 (2016): 456–473.

Sarfaty, Galit A. "Shining Light on Global Supply Chains." *Harvard International Law Journal* 56, no. 2 (2015): 419–463.

Thottathil, Sapna E. "Sustainable food procurement by the University of California's health systems." *Journal of Agriculture, Food Systems & Community Development* (2022): 79–93.

Legal Instruments

Australia Modern Slavery Act (2018). No. 153, 2018. Australia Modern Slavery Bill 2018 (Cth) 45, Explanatory Memorandum.

Brazil Ministry of Labor and Employment Decree No. 540/2004.

California Civil Code.

China MOFCOM Order No. 4 of 2020 on Provisions on the Unreliable Entity List, Ministry of Commerce, People's Republic of China (September 19, 2020).

EC CSDD. Proposal for a Regulation of the European Parliament and of the Council on prohibiting products made with forced labour on the Union market (September 14, 2022).

EC CSRD. Proposal for a Directive of the Parliament and of the Council on Corporate Sustainability Due Diligence and amending Directive (EU) 2019/1937, Explanatory Memorandum (February 23, 2022).

EC, DG Trade, Access to Markets. Generalized Scheme of Preferences Plus (GSP+). Viewed June 19, 2023.

EC. European sustainability reporting standards – first set, Draft Act. (June 9, 2023).

EC. Net-Zero Industry Act, Press release (March 16, 2023); EC, Critical Raw Materials, Press release (March 16 2023).

EC. Proposal for a Regulation of the European Parliament and of the Council on prohibiting products made with forced labour on the Union market (September 14, 2022).

EU CSDD. EU CSDD, Directive (EU) 2024/1760 of the European Parliament and of the Council of 13 June 2024 on corporate sustainability due diligence and amending Directive (EU) 2019/1937 and Regulation (EU) 2023/2859.

EU CSRD. Directive (EU) 2022/2464 of the European Parliament and of the Council of 14 December 2022 amending Regulation (EU) No 537/2014, Directive 2004/109/EC, Directive 2006/43/EC and Directive 2013/34/EU, as regards corporate sustainability reporting.

EU NFRD. Directive 2014/95/EU of the European Parliament and of the Council of 22 October 2014 amending Directive 2013/34/EU as regards disclosure of non-financial and diversity information by certain large undertakings and groups (OJ. L 330/1), art 1(1) (inserting art 19a(1) in the Accounting Directive 2013/34/EU).

EU. Directive 2013/34/EU of the European Parliament and of the Council of 26 June 2013 on the annual financial statements, consolidated financial statements and related reports of certain types of undertakings (2013) OJ L182/13 (June 26, 2013).

EU. Regulation (EU) 2020/852 of the European Parliament and of the Council of 18 June 2020 on the establishment of a framework to facilitate sustainable investment (2020), OJ L198/13 (June 18, 2020).

France, LOI n° 2017–399 du 27 mars 2017 relative au devoir de vigilance des sociétés mères et des entreprises donneuses d'ordre (1); L. 225-102-4 du code de commerce.

Germany, Act on Corporate Due Diligence Obligations in Supply Chains, BGBl I 2021, 2959.

Netherlands, Act of 24 October 2019 introducing a duty of care to prevent the supply of goods and services created using child labor (Child Labor Due Diligence Act).

Norway, Act relating to enterprises' transparency and work on fundamental human rights and decent working conditions, LOV-2021-06-18-99.

NSW Modern Slavery Act 2018 No. 30, Part 3.

UK Modern Slavery Act, 2015 Ch. 30.

US Code, 19 U.S.C. §2462, 19 U.S.C. §2467 (regarding trade preferences).

US Federal Funding Accountability and Transparency Act of 2006, Pub. L. No. 109–282, 120 Stat. 1186, (Sept. 26, 2006). Reporting Executive Compensation and First-Tier Subcontract Awards, 77 Fed. Reg. 44,047, 44,049, 44,052, 44,055, 44,056 (final rule published July 26, 2012) (codified at 48 C.F.R. Parts 1, 12, 42, and 52).

US Public Law 117–78, Uyghur Forced Labor Prevention Act.

News Articles

Burghardt-Kaufmann, Anna, Clare Connellan, Sabine Kueper, Julia Sitter and Norbert Wimmer. "Due Diligence in Supply Chains – Update on corporate human rights and environmental due diligence requirements in the EU and Germany." *White & Case Insight Alert*, January 11, 2023.

Chua, Jasmin Malik. "'Every Supplier,' 'Every Tier': What Uniqlo's Xinjiang Links and Lapses Mean for Your Brand." *Sourcing Journal*, May 27, 2021.

Greenhouse, Steven. "Documents Reveal New Details About Walmart's Connection to Tazreen Factory Fire." *New York Times*, December 10, 2012.

Kapotwe, Musonda, Peter Pears, and Marcel Hörauf. "EU Corporate Sustainability Reporting Directive." *Harvard Law School Forum on Corporate Governance*, Mayer Brown LLP posting, December 11, 2022.

Kelman, Steve. "Is the performance of the procurement system improving?" *FCW*, May 30, 2017.

Mosk, Matthew. "Marines Move to Dump Clothes Company After Deadly Factory Fire." *ABC News*, December 11, 2012.

Ropes & Gray. "Mexico Bans Imports Made with Forced Labor in Alignment with the USMCA." *Ropes & Gray Alert*, March 6, 2023.

Taylor, Glen. "Will This New Software Solve Xinjiang Traceability Challenges?" *Sourcing Journal*, December 3, 2020.

Urbina, Ian. "The Uyghur Workers Forced to Process the World's Fish." *The New Yorker*, October 9, 2023.

van Thuyne, Gauthier, et al. "The EU Commission's proposal for a directive on corporate sustainability due diligence." *Allen & Overy Alerts*, February 25, 2022.

van Yoder, Steven. "Beware the Coming Backlash." *Industry Week*, April 2, 2001.

Reports

Bayer, Chris N., and Jesse H. Hudson. *Corporate Compliance with the California Transparency in Supply Chains Act: Anti-Slavery Performance in 2016*. Development International, 2017.

Bukhrin, Irina. *Long Shadows: How the Global Economy supports Oppression in Xinjiang*. Washington: C4ADS, 2021.

Electronics Watch. *Worker-driven transparency*. Amsterdam: Electronics Watch, 2018.

Electronics Watch. *Public Procurement and Human Rights Due Diligence to Achieve Respect for Labour Rights Standards in Electronics Factories: A Case Study of the Swedish County Councils and the Dell Computer Corporation*. Amsterdam: Electronics Watch, 2016.

Fair World Project. *International Guide to Fair Trade Labels*. Portland: Fair World Project, 2020.

Fashion Revolution. *Fashion Transparency Index 2022*. London: Fashion Revolution, July 14, 2022.

Finnegan, Brian. *Responsibility Outsourced: Social Audits, Workplace Certification and Twenty Years of Failure to Protect Worker Rights*. Washington: AFL-CIO, 2013.

Fair Trade International. *Fairtrade Trader Standard*, v1.7, 2015, 3.1 Labor Rights.

FLEX, *Seeing Through Supply Chain Transparency*. London: Focus on Labor Exploitation, 2018.

Global Electronics Council. *Sustainability Assessment Criteria for Corporate ESG Performance – Draft*. Portland: Global Electronics Council, November 10, 2022.

Global Reporting Initiative. *G4 Sustainability Reporting Guidelines*. Respect International, 2015. Accessed March 30, 2023. https://respect.international/wp-content/uploads/2017/10/G4-Sustainability-Reporting-Guidelines-Implementation-Manual-GRI-2013.pdf.

Hering, Garrett, and Molly Christian. "US finds solar imports from Southeast Asia skirting tariffs; industry alarmed." *S&P Global Market Intelligence*, December 2, 2022.

KnowTheChain. *2022 Information and Communications Technology Benchmark Findings Report.* New York: KnowTheChain, 2022.

Lehr, Amy K. *Addressing Forced Labor in the Xinjiang Uyghur Autonomous Region: Towards a Shared Agenda*. Washington: Center for Strategic International Studies, 2020.

Mapped in Bangladesh. *Mapped in Bangladesh, Project Overview.* Dhaka: MiB, 2020.

McCalla-Leacy, John. *Global Survey of Sustainability Reporting.* London: KMPG, 2022.

O'Brien, Claire Methven, Amol Mehra, and Nicole Vander Meulen. *Public procurement and human rights: A survey of 20 jurisdictions*. Washington: International Learning Lab on Public Procurement and Human Rights, 2016.

O'Connor, Casey, and Sara Labovitz. *Putting the "S" in ESG: Measuring Human Rights Performance for Investors.* New York: NYU Stern Center for Business and Human Rights, March 2017.

Responsible Business Alliance. *Practical Guide to Transparency in Procurement.* Alexandria, VA: RBA, 2019.

Ryerson, Charity, and Emma Cusumano. *Is the California Transparency in Supply Chains Act Doing More Harm than Good?* Chicago: Corporate Accountability Lab, 2017.

Special Representative of the Secretary-General. *Guiding Principles on Business and Human Rights: Implementing the United Nations "Protect, Respect and Remedy" Framework.* New York: United Nations, UN Doc. A/HRC/17/31, 2011.

Stumberg, Robert, and Anita Ramasastry and Meg Roggensack (2014) *Turning a Blind Eye – Respecting Human Rights in Government Purchasing.* International Corporate Accountability Roundtable (ICAR), Washington, DC, USA.

US Department of Homeland Security. *Strategy to Prevent the Importation of Goods Mined, Produced, or Manufactured with Forced Labor in the People's Republic of China.* Washington: DHS, June 17, 2022; *2024 Updates to the Strategy to Prevent the Importation of Goods Mined, Produced, or Manufactured with Forced Labor in the People's Republic of China.* Washington: DHS, July 19, 2024

World Benchmarking Alliance. *Corporate Human Rights Benchmark.* Amsterdam: WBA, November 2022.

Worker Rights Consortium. "The Impact of Universities on Supply-Chain Transparency," Memo to Affiliates. Washington: WRC, April 21, 2017.

Young, Steven, and Mahmoud Gad. *Modern Slavery Reporting Practices in the UK – Evidence from Modern Slavery Statements and Annual Reports.* London: Financial Reporting Council, 2022.

Web Page Content

Center for Good Food Purchasing, Valued Workforce. Accessed March 30, 2023, https://goodfoodpurchasing.org/program-overview/.

China Chamber of International Commerce. "Comment to the Forced Labor Enforcement Task Force." Mar. 11, 2022. Accessed March 30, 2023. https://www.regulations.gov/comment/DHS-2022-0001-0157.

EC DG Trade. "Access2Markets, Generalized Scheme of Preferences Plus (GSP+)." Accessed March 25, 2023. https://trade.ec.europa.eu/access-to-markets/en/content/generalised-scheme-preferences-plus-gsp.

European Parliament. "MEPs push companies to mitigate their negative social and environmental impact." Accessed June 1, 2023. https://www.business-humanrights.org/en/latest-news/eu-meps-push-companies-to-mitigate-their-negative-social-and-environmental-impact/#timeline.

Fashion Revolution. "Brand Communication Guidelines on the Fashion Transparency Index," linked in *Fashion Index 2022*. Accessed March 25, 2025. https://docs.google.com/document/d/1ZsdKgsn-rETvhQveu23w1lzIx2aWNblv/edit.

Global Affairs Canada. "Advisory on doing business with Xinjiang-related entities." Accessed March 19, 2023. https://www.international.gc.ca/global-affairs-affaires-mondiales/news-nouvelles/2021/2021-01-12-xinjiang-advisory-avis.aspx-?lang=eng.

International Accord. "A decade of progress in workplace safety in Bangladesh." Accessed June 11, 2023. https://internationalaccord.org/countries/bangladesh/;.

International Accord. "New workplace safety program in Pakistan." Accessed June 11, 2023, https://internationalaccord.org/countries/pakistan/.

International Accord. "Promoting health and safety in Accord covered factories." Accessed June 11, 2023. https://internationalaccord.org/factories/.

KnowTheChain. "Benchmark Methodology." Accessed March 3, 2023. https://knowthechain.org/benchmark-methodology/.

OECD. "Public Procurement and Responsible Business Conduct." Accessed March 13, 2023. https://www.oecd.org/gov/public-procurement/procurement-and-rbc/.

Open Supply Hub. Accessed March 26, 2023. https://opensupplyhub.org/.u.

Open Supply Hub. "The Apparel Sector – A Case Study in Transparency." Accessed July 12, 2023. https://info.opensupplyhub.org/resources/apparel-case-study-transparency.

Open Supply Hub. "How to Search Open Supply Hub." Accessed June 12, 2023 https://info.opensupplyhub.org/resources/how-to-search.

Responsible Business Alliance. "Code of Conduct." Accessed March 3, 2023. https://www.responsiblebusiness.org/code-of-conduct/.

Responsible Business Alliance. "History." Accessed March 3, 2023. https://www.responsiblebusiness.org/about/history/.

RMG Sustainability Council. "RSC – RMG Sustainability Council." Accessed June 11, 2023. https://www.rsc-bd.org/en.

RMG Sustainability Council. "Factories." Accessed June 14, 2023. https://www.rsc-bd.org/en/factories#.

Sweatfree Purchasing Consortium. Accessed on March 13, 2023. http://buysweatfree.org.

TED, Tenders Electronic Daily. Accessed March 30, 2023. https://ted.europa.eu/TED/main/HomePage.do.

Transparency Pledge. "Who's Aligned." Accessed March 22, 2023. https://transparencypledge.org/aligned/.

US Trade Representative. "Products to be removed from GSP eligibility for Thailand." April 25, 2020. "Active and Recently Closed GSP Country Practices Reviews." Accessed March 25, 2023. https://ustr.gov/issue-areas/preference-programs/generalized-system-preferences-gsp/current-reviews.

US Customs & Border Protection. "Uyghur Forced Labor Prevention Act Statistics." Accessed October 18, 2024. https://www.cbp.gov/newsroom/stats/trade/uyghur-forced-labor-prevention-act-statistics.

USAspending.gov. Accessed March 30, 2023. www.usaspending.gov.

World Benchmarking Alliance. "Theory of Change." Accessed March 3, 2023. https://www.worldbenchmarkingalliance.org/theory-of-change/.

Worker Rights Consortium. "Factory Database." Accessed June 11, 2023. https://search.workersrights.org/.

World Bank. "Global Public Procurement Database." Accessed March 30, 2023. https://www.worldbank.org/en/news/feature/2020/03/23/global-public-procurement-database-share-compare-improve#.

CHAPTER 12

Transitional Justice Responses to Corporate Abuse

Nelson Camilo Sanchez

1 Introduction

Crosspollination between the transitional justice (TJ)[1] and business and human rights (B&H) fields has led to a growing scholarly focus on the role of corporations during political transition. Recent studies have highlighted examples of corporate responsibility, such as the prosecution of Nazi industrialists in Germany,[2] the South African Truth Commission's efforts to underscore corporate accountability in apartheid politics,[3] and initiatives in Argentina and Brazil to expose the conspiracy of automobile companies, such as Ford and Volkswagen, with military dictatorships.[4] These experiences – where communities, victims, trade unions, and even governments have endeavoured to confront corporate impunity in politically transitional contexts – have prompted a group of scholars with a primary interest in the TJ paradigm to broaden the field's traditional state-centric perspective to encompass the extent of the liability of private and predominantly economic actors.[5]

1 The concept of transitional justice has been the subject of intense academic debate. For the purposes of this chapter, I will make use of the United Nations model definition of Transitional Justice, which defines it as 'processes and mechanisms associated with a society's attempt to come to terms with a legacy of large-scale past abuses, in order to ensure accountability, serve justice, and achieve reconciliation.' U.N. Secretary General, Guidance Note of the Secretary-General: United Nations Approach to Transitional Justice, (March 2010).

2 Leora Bilsky, *The Holocaust, Corporations and the Law: Unfinished Business* (Michigan: University of Michigan Press, 2017).

3 Goran Koska, "Corporate Accountability in Times of Transition: The Role of Restorative Justice in the South African Truth and Reconciliation Commission," *Restorative Justice* 4, no. 1 (2016): 41–67.

4 See Fábio C. de Amorim, Valeria Sion, and Renan Machado, "Accountability for Volkswagen's Role in the Brazilian Dictatorship," in *Economic Actors and the Limits of Transitional Justice: Truth and Justice for Business Complicity in Human Rights Violations*, ed. Leigh A. Payne, Laura Bernal-Bermúdez, and Gabriel Pereira (London: British Academy Scholarship Online, 2022), 74–95; Victoria Basualdo, Tomás Ojea Quintana, and Carolina Varsky, "The Cases of Ford and Mercedes Benz," in *The Economic Accomplices to the Argentine Dictatorship: Outstanding Debts*, ed. Horacio Verbitsky and Juan P. Bohoslavsky (Cambridge: Cambridge University Press, 2015), 159–163.

5 Irene Pietropaoli, *Business, Human Rights and Transitional Justice* (Abingdon: Routledge, 2020).

 | DOI:10.1163/9789004530942_013

Contemporary scholarship acknowledges that these studies collectively form a distinct sub-discipline known today as Transitional Justice and Corporate Accountability (TJCA). However, situated at the crossroads of established disciplines, attempts to theorise the relationship between TJ and B&H face two significant justificatory challenges.[6] First, the emerging TJCA movement must convincingly distinguish itself from existing efforts to pursue corporate accountability for human rights abuses, gross violations of human rights, and breaches of international humanitarian law. A substantial portion of the current literature in the B&H field has addressed situations that could be considered part of transitional environments. Consequently, the pivotal question for this nascent TJCA field is the extent of its novelty and contributions to both academic discourse and real-world endeavours to attain greater justice for victims of corporate abuse.

Second, the emergence of the TJCA field coincides with a contentious period in TJ discourse. Some scholars express concern that TJCA might place undue pressure on the already delicate framework of political transition. They argue that imposing additional demands on TJ processes could potentially destabilize fragile post-conflict situations, rather than fostering reconciliation and healing. Hence, they question the practical and theoretical feasibility of expanding the objectives, mechanisms, and strategies that aim to deepen justice in contexts as delicate and exigent as those of political transition, particularly when addressing the reconstruction of societies that have endured protracted and devastating armed conflicts.[7]

This chapter makes the case that the emergent TJCA subfield has achieved significant strides, both theoretically and practically, in meeting associated challenges. First, the TJCA field has broadened the factual and analytical scope of B&H. Second, the penetration of B&H legal and theoretical tools into the discourses of TJ advocates has opened up fresh avenues for the development of accountability strategies and policies for non-state actors. These characteristics of corporate accountability initiatives augur well for the future trajectory of this research area, underscoring the significance of interdisciplinary

6 Hugo van der Merwe and M. Brinton Lykes, "Transitional Justice and Corporate Accountability: Introducing New Players and New Theoretical Challenges," *International Journal of Transitional Justice* 16, no. 3 (2022): 291–297.

7 Reservations on field expansions can be consulted at: Lars Waldorf, "Afterwords in Aftermaths," in *Transitional and Transformative Justice: Critical and International Perspectives*, ed. Michael Evans (Abingdon: Routledge, 2019), 161–165; Lars Waldorf, "Between Transition and Transformation: Legal Empowerment as Collective Reparations," in *From Transitional to Transformative Justice*, ed. Paul Gready and Simon Robins (Cambridge: Cambridge University Press, 2019), 131–149.

cooperation. Thus, this chapter acts as a clarion call, urging scholars in the fields of peacebuilding, sustainability studies, and accountability to ambitiously expand their research. The aim is to foster a more comprehensive understanding and generate all-encompassing solutions that address the complex issues inherent in TJCA.

The remainder of this chapter will unfold in four distinct sections. First, I will delineate the progression of the corporate responsibility subfield within the context of TJ, offering a brief overview. Subsequently, I engage with the contextual elements that a TJ perspective introduces to the narrower views founded exclusively on the legal liability of corporations in accordance with normative B&H standards. In the third section, I will explore a series of legal debates from which TJ frameworks have derived benefits thanks to legal-theoretical formulations emerging from discussions around B&H. The chapter concludes with a succinct summary of the key findings and implications.

2 Corporate Accountability and Political Transition as a Distinctive Field

Despite the foundational legal precedents established by the Nuremberg and Tokyo tribunals for the prosecution of corporate complicity in systemic crimes, the early stages of the TJ doctrine did not place an emphasis on corporate liability.[8] This was due in part to the fact that TJ was initially focused on addressing human rights abuses committed by state actors, and corporate accountability was not seen as a priority. Additionally, international discussions about corporate responsibility were in their early stages, and there was no clear consensus on the legal obligations of corporations.

It was not until several decades later that TJ began to solidify as a distinct discipline and that international discussions about corporate responsibility made significant progress.[9] Once these developments had matured, scholarly interest in the intersection between TJ and corporate misconduct began to

8 Leigh A. Payne, Maxine N. Beall, and Alexander Hutchinson, "The Roots of Corporate Accountability: From the Holocaust and Beyond," in *Economic Actors and the Limits of Transitional Justice: Truth and Justice for Business Complicity in Human Rights Violations*, ed. Leigh A. Payne, Laura Bernal-Bermúdez, and Gabriel Pereira (London: British Academy Scholarship Online, 2022), 27–55.

9 As recently as 2020, Irene Pietropaoli noted the scarcity of literature linking business and human rights with transitional justice ('While there are large number of sources on business and human rights, as well as on transitional justice in general there is little literature that links the two areas. There is only one book, edited by Sabine Michalowski and titled

emerge around the mid-2000s.[10] These epistemic communities, responding to existing activist networks within the field, stood out for their diverse composition. They included academics from both Global North and South, full-time academics and activists, and individuals with strong backgrounds in human rights and criminal accountability, alongside those with a deeper understanding of corporate dynamics.[11] In subsequent years, these networks expanded and deepened their exchange and collective work.[12]

Building upon those preliminary reflections, the focus then shifted to more systematic studies of domestic transitional justice experiences addressing corporate misconduct.[13] These studies demonstrate that impunity remains the norm, and all attempts to establish corporate accountability have encountered obstacles and unfavourable circumstances. The resistance to accountability from economic actors has proven to be proactively aggressive, even when confronting actions committed decades prior.[14]

Despite these challenging conditions, local stakeholders have continually strived to incorporate economic actors into accountability and justice proceedings. According to data collected by Payne, Pereira, and Bernal-Bermúdez, transitional justice initiatives aiming to unveil corporate accountability are

Corporate Accountability in the Context of Transitional Justice, that compiles different cases') Pietropaoli, *Business, Human Rights and Transitional Justice*, viii.

10 Sabine Michalowski, *Corporate Accountability in the Context of Transitional Justice* (Abingdon: Routledge, 2013); Gabriel Pereira and Leigh Payne, "Corporate Complicity in International Human Rights Violations," *Annual Review of Law and Social Science* 12 (2016): 63–84.

11 An analysis of two of the initial networks can be found in: Raluca Grosescu, "Transnational Advocacy Networks and Corporate Accountability for Gross Human Rights Violations in Argentina and Colombia," *Global Society* 33, no. 3 (2019): 400–418.

12 An exemplary illustration of these networks is the Corporate Liability and Sustainable Peace (CLASP) Lab, which serves as a "social lab" dedicated to promoting corporate accountability in post-conflict and transitional justice contexts worldwide. Established in February 2021, the CLASP Lab operates as a virtual platform, facilitating collaboration among over 40 lawyers and community activists from 25 countries across Latin America, Africa, and the Middle East. Its objective is to foster the exchange of experiences and the development of strategies for holding corporations accountable for human rights violations within transitional justice processes.

13 See Leigh Payne, Gabriel Pereira, and Laura Bernal-Bermúdez, *Transitional Justice from Below: Deploying Archimedes's Lever* (Cambridge: Cambridge University Press, 2020); Payne, Pereira, and Bernal-Bermúdez, eds., *Economic Actors and the Limits of Transitional Justice: Truth and Justice for Business Complicity in Human Rights Violations* (London: British Academy Scholarship Online, 2022), 27–55.

14 Payne, Pereira, and Bernal-Bermúdez, *Transitional Justice from Below*.

more prevalent and impactful than often perceived.[15] For instance, their data indicate that charges for crimes against humanity have been levied against 349 companies and their employees across 35 cases spanning three waves of accountability proceedings targeting Nazi criminals.[16]

Additionally, the authors found that a minimum of 23 truth commissions across 20 countries have addressed issues related to corporate complicity. The final reports from these commissions have disclosed the identities of 329 economic actors implicated as accomplices. Furthermore, the authors collated 104 cases of legal action in which 149 economic actors from 18 countries have been prosecuted for involvement in core international crimes.[17]

An additional insight from this literature reveals that accountability processes, particularly judicial ones, have been more prevalent in the Global South than in the North. Among these, South American countries have not only been at the forefront of these initiatives, but they have also been the most active globally in exposing complicity networks and pursuing both criminal and civil liabilities of economic actors. Indeed, as will be discussed subsequently, the region is contributing to the establishment of an international norm of corporate responsibility and specific standards on a range of issues, such as criminal prosecution and the application of civil and labour trials. This Latin American legal activism remains vibrant, even though the initial crimes in several of these countries, including Brazil, Chile, and Argentina, were committed decades ago. Nonetheless, the ongoing efforts of victims and legal activists continue to highlight the lingering impact of the violations and the enduring structures that perpetuate impunity.[18]

These findings address key criticisms of the TJCA's theoretical approach. Some scholars argue that TJCA unnecessarily expands an already broad discipline. Additionally, critics contend that it raises unrealistic expectations for victims, particularly given the prevalence of impunity. However, a thorough analysis of these experiences reveals that the call for addressing corporate involvement in crimes is a pervasive demand within local communities. The data, in fact, indicate that field proponents have been slow in recognizing these demands and in crafting theoretical reflections and public policy proposals to address them. Therefore, rather than unnecessarily expanding the field, TJCA is actually addressing a critical and sensitive gap within the TJ discipline.

15 Payne, Pereira, and Bernal-Bermúdez, *Economic Actors and the Limits of Transitional Justice*, 5.
16 Ibid., 6.
17 Ibid.
18 Ibid.

3 Transitional Justice's Holistic Approach and the Quest for Curbing Corporate Impunity

This section delves into how TJ enriches the context of corporate responsibility, expands the toolbox for accountability, encourages victims' co-creation and participation, probes the networks behind economic actors, and reshapes the role of businesses in peacebuilding and sustainable development. A TJ framework provides a robust opportunity to grapple with the multidimensional challenge of corporate impunity in conflict-ridden environments and opens avenues for a comprehensive approach to corporate accountability. TJ not only identifies and acknowledges the diverse dimensions of corporate abuse but also ensures a more inclusive, nuanced, and victim-centric pursuit of justice.

3.1 *Broadening the Context*

The TJ framework has revolutionised the pursuit of justice in contexts marked by extreme poverty, weak rule of law, unchecked impunity, and corporate dominance. By expanding its scope to encompass victims of corporate abuse, litigants, and social movements, it has broadened the avenues through which justice can be sought in conflict-related situations. This comprehensive approach allows for a thorough examination of the shortcomings in the delivery of justice while fostering a deeper understanding of the interconnected processes that fuel the escalation, proliferation, and instrumentalisation of violence as an ongoing strategy for exploiting resources. Additionally, it forms the basis for developing strategies to challenge and dismantle the justifications and impunity associated with various forms of corporate misconduct.

To illustrate the expansive contextual approach of the TJ framework, consider efforts to uncover the political economy of violence behind the integration of corporate interests into economic models of conflict and repression. The quest for accountability in the Southern Cone countries of South America, particularly Argentina, Brazil, and Chile, provides profound insights into this context.[19] The prevailing narrative surrounding the oppressive violence exerted by Argentina's most recent dictatorship originally painted a picture

19 *See*, Victoria Basualdo, Harmut Berghoff, and Marcelo Bucheli, eds., *Big Business and Dictatorships in Latin America: A Transnational History of Profits and Repression* (London: Palgrave Macmillan, 2021); Juan P. Bohoslavsky, Karina Fernández, and Sarnata Reynolds, eds., *Pinochet's Economic Accomplices: An Unequal Country by Force* (Lanham: Lexington Books, 2020); Horacio Verbitsky and Juan P. Bohoslavsky, eds., *The Economic Accomplices to the Argentine Dictatorship* (Cambridge: Cambridge University Press, 2013).

of a military regime that exploited state power to wage a 'dirty war' against guerrilla group members and political adversaries. This view is still reflected today in academic literature from the Global North, which frequently characterises the era as a military dictatorship. Nevertheless, TJ's meticulous investigations have unveiled the intricacies of this period, demonstrating that the ties between armed aggression and economic interests were not merely incidental, but fundamentally entrenched.[20]

Historic memory works in Argentina have demonstrated that the 'national reorganization process' initiated by the military regime sought to quash opposition and impose a neoliberal economic model. This process drastically restructured Argentina's economy, transitioning from an industrial to a finance-focused one.[21] The highly organised and politically active industrial working class became a primary target of the regime, with thousands of workers and union leaders abducted, tortured, or killed, leading to a major regression in labour rights and conditions. Industrialised areas with organised workforces experienced significant repression, and remaining workers faced increased exploitation due to rescinded workers' rights. The regime also prohibited collective labour activity and took control of major trade unions, resulting in a weakened labour movement. Different reports available today show how companies played an active role in this militarisation and repression of workers, benefitting significantly from the curtailed labour rights. Top executives from leading companies often held official positions within the regime and provided assistance in suppressing 'subversive' union leaders and workers. As a result, businesses gained increased control over the workplace and an enhanced ability to exploit workers, leading to increased profits. Additionally, they received benefits like debt relief, subsidies, tax exemptions, and corrupt business deals from the regime in return for their support. In line with these findings, Argentine activists refer to this period as a civic-military-business dictatorship.[22] This terminology acknowledges the varied sectors involved in implementing the oppressive plan, including the military. This widened perspective not only brings to light where vested interests were concentrated but

20 Mario Schorr, "Industrial Economic Power as Promoter and Beneficiary of Argentina's Re-Founding Project (1976–1983)," in *The Economic Accomplices to the Argentine Dictatorship: Outstanding Debts*, ed. Horacio Verbitsky and Juan P. Bohoslavsky (Cambridge: Cambridge University Press, 2015), 235–256.

21 Horacio Verbitsky and Juan P. Bohoslavsky, "State Terrorism and the Economy: From Nuremberg to Buenos Aires," in *The Economic Accomplices to the Argentine Dictatorship: Outstanding Debts* (Cambridge: Cambridge University Press, 2015), 1–7.

22 Laura García Martín, *Transitional Justice, Corporate Accountability and Socio-Economic Rights: Lessons from Argentina*, 1st ed. (Abingdon: Routledge, 2019).

also elucidates the origins of violence with greater clarity. It further highlights the lingering effects of that model of violence and expropriation, which persist to this day. An effective accountability strategy must comprehend these intricate relationships to dismantle the persistent system and formulate strategies to prevent similar situations in the future.

In conclusion, the TJ framework's merit lies in its tripartite contribution: it extends the sphere of responsibility, enabling a deeper understanding of roles within violence and expropriation; it enhances the comprehension of the roots of blood crimes; and it advocates for forward-thinking strategies that ensure such events do not recur. In this way, the TJ framework effectively broadens the context in which we understand and address corporate accountability.

3.2 *Expanding the Toolbox*

B&H accountability efforts have traditionally concentrated on three types of strategies: litigation against transnational corporations, international standard-setting to impose obligations on companies analogous to those of states in the international sphere, and the encouragement of market mechanisms that promote business adherence to legal standards and ethical business practices. However, TJ's experience extends the scope of intervention beyond these traditional approaches. TJ devised several mechanisms, such as truth commissions, that transcend judicial courts and official public policies. These mechanisms strive to construct narratives that offer a more comprehensive understanding of the various social, political, and economic processes underpinning certain business practices that violate corporate responsibility's ethical and legal principles.[23]

Although the potential of these TJ mechanisms has not been fully exploited, several instances underscore their potential. These mechanisms not only foster a conducive environment for other strategies to operate effectively but can also yield economies of scale in handling practical issues that practitioners must address for their other legal and political strategies to succeed, such as evidence gathering. Recent instances of commissions striving to uncover the connections between economic entities and severe human rights abuses can be seen in Brazil and Colombia. Although the Argentine truth commission of the 1980s did not consistently probe these relationships, recent endeavours aim to fill these voids. Several of these attempts are notable for their ingenuity and the range of public and private participants incorporated in these initiatives.

---

23 Priscilla B. Hayner, *Unspeakable Truths: Transitional Justice and the Challenge of Truth Commissions*, 2nd ed. (New York: Routledge, 2011).

These truth and memory projects include a report furnished by the Ministry of Justice and the human rights non-profit Centro de Estudios Sociales y Legales -CELS, a Congressional-approved proposition for a dedicated first of its kind truth commission on corporate complicity, and a report commissioned by the National Stock Exchange to scrutinise the role various member businesses played in the dictatorship's repressive machinery.[24]

3.3 *Giving Victims a Greater Voice in Co-creation and Participation*

The TJ framework places a significant emphasis on victims' needs, rights, and narratives. This victim-centric focus ensures that those directly impacted by corporate abuses remain at the forefront of the pursuit of justice and accountability. Such emphasis becomes particularly pivotal when it comes to devising reparations. Many litigations, particularly those presented before international courts or in jurisdictions distinct from the location of the corporate abuse, have often imposed limitations on victim involvement. These constraints affect both their participation in the judicial process and their contribution in shaping reparative measures. Such restrictions have often led to considerable dissatisfaction among victims' groups.

Consequently, the appeal of broader reparations-building processes, such as those facilitated by transitional justice measures, is heightened. Advocates of comprehensive and large-scale reparations models find particular interest in these processes. Thus, by emphasising a victim-centric approach, the TJ framework significantly broadens the context in which corporate accountability is pursued and justice is sought, making it more inclusive and representative of those directly affected.[25]

3.4 *Interrogating Networks behind Economic Actors*

The TJ framework delves into a comprehensive interrogation of terms like ‘business,’ ‘private sector,’ ‘accomplice,’ and ‘economic actor’ The interaction between economic accomplices and human rights violations has traditionally been explored within the ‘business and human rights’ discourse, primarily

24 Gabriel Pereira, Leigh A. Payne, and Laura Bernal-Bermúdez, “Justice from Below: Corporate Accountability in Argentina,” *The International Journal of Human Rights* 26, no. 8 (2022): 1418–1454.

25 As acknowledged by the United Nations Working Group on Business and Human Rights, “Reparations programmes have been considered the most victim-centred measure of transitional justice policies.” United Nations Human Rights Council, Implementing the Third Pillar: Lessons from Transitional Justice Guidance by the Working Group – Report of the Working Group on the Issue of Human Rights and Transnational Corporations and Other Business Enterprises, Report No. A/HRC/50/40/Add.4 (2022), § 52.

focusing on transnational corporations. The UN Guiding Principles on the matter affirm that their standards apply to 'all business enterprises, transnational and otherwise, regardless of size, sector, location, ownership, and structure'.[26] However, defining 'enterprise' can be ambiguous and lead to uncertainties about its applicability – specifically, whether it refers only to the legal liability of an economic unit, includes actions by individuals associated with a particular legal entity, or even extends to those conducting economic activities without a distinctive legal entity.

Moreover, academic discussions often employ the term 'private sector' to denote economically motivated activities not directly controlled by the state. However, such a stark division between 'private' and 'state' might neglect state-owned or hybrid companies from the analysis. Colombia's long-standing conflict exemplifies such contexts. Multiple actors have played varying roles, complicating their categorisation as armed actors, state agents, or business actors.[27] Certain family clans establish power structures, with some members seeking political power while others engage in economic activities or even join official or unofficial armed groups. In such situations, the 'business' category may be inadequate to elucidate the economic organisation benefiting from the crimes. Furthermore, several highly profitable activities exist outside the commercial or business registers, including agricultural production and cattle rearing.[28] Such activities complicate the task of tracing business relationships and criminal activities, as well as establishing responsibility in the market. In addition, the entanglement of public and private sectors in criminal structures using sophisticated strategies to conceal economic benefits of crimes adds another layer of complexity, as seen in the case of the Córdoba cattle fund.[29]

To address these situations, specialised literature on TJ and corporate responsibility has introduced 'corporate responsibility' as a broad concept.[30]

26 United Nations Human Rights Office of the High Commissioner, Guiding Principles on Business and Human Rights: Implementing the United Nations "Protect, Respect and Remedy" Framework (2011).

27 Laura Bernal-Bermúdez and Nelson C Sanchez, "Innovation from the Bench: Judges, Prosecutors, and Analysts Advancing Truth and Accountability for Conflict-Related Corporate Complicity in Colombia," in *Economic Actors and the Limits of Transitional Justice: Truth and Justice for Business Complicity in Human Rights Violations*, ed. Leigh A. Payne, Laura Bernal-Bermúdez, and Gabriel Pereira (Oxford: Oxford University Press, 2022), 96–121.

28 Ibid.

29 Ibid.

30 Leigh A. Payne and Gabriel Pereira, Corporate Complicity in International Human Rights Violations.

This approach accommodates the hybrid nature of economic actors' involvement with violence and repression, distinct from traditional state-based responsibility. Simultaneously, these rigorous processes of reconstructing responsibilities and victimisations enhance our understanding that the private, business, or economic sector is diverse and multifaceted in contexts of widespread violence. It's crucial to note that not all companies act similarly. Economic actors may also fall victim to violence and repression, deserving recognition and protection of their rights.[31]

3.5 *Roles of Businesses in Peace Building and Sustainable Development*

The TJ approach also allows confronting traditional visions of peacebuilding that critically establish an ideal role for economic actors in peace negotiation and democracy-building processes. According to this classical vision, to the extent that economic factors are agents that generate economic growth, they are interested in peace and will be functional to the construction of economic development and therefore of the necessary conditions for peace and democracy. This vision is not necessarily true, but as demonstrated by those who have worked on this issue, it is still given as an incontrovertible truth.[32] Hence, the discussions on TJ and specifically the discussions on civil and criminal liability of companies that contributed to the human rights violations, as well as the historical legal tax liability of companies that seek to benefit from peace processes, is a welcome and necessary contribution to the discussion of peace building. In practical terms, the accountability movement has reshaped the narrative regarding the role of business in political transition processes. Rather than solely focusing on voluntary business contributions, as seen in the corporate social responsibility model, it introduces the critical concept of accountability. This shift includes the discussion of implementing

31 Mavluda Sattorova, "Greed and Grievance: Corporations, States and International Investment Law in Times of Conflict," *European Journal of International Law* 34, no. 1 (2023): 181–212.

32 See, Brian Ganson, "Business and Peace: A Need for New Questions and Systems Perspectives," in *Business, Peacebuilding and Sustainable Development*, ed. Jason Miklian, Rina M. Alluri, and John E. Katsos (Abingdon: Routledge, 2019), 3–26. (Noting that mostly, the existing literature suggests (at times overtly, but frequently in a more subdued manner) that various business endeavours – including investment, conflict awareness, and corporate social responsibility (CSR) – contribute towards peace. However, a significant amount of the analysis assumes links between specific business activities and positive peace impacts. These links are often based not on tangible evidence of peace results (or their absence) but on a series of suppositions derived from associated yet distinct viewpoints).

coercive, albeit negotiated or mitigated, state measures. These measures aim to ensure that the rights of victims of serious human rights violations are met and any potential harm caused by economic actors to communities and territories is addressed.

4 Unlocking New Legal Tools and Strategies

The aforementioned advancements within the TJ movement, particularly in its legal activism, owe much to the legacy and support of academics and jurists who, over the last two decades, have fortified the B&H field. TJ advocates have drawn upon the theoretical and practical resources developed by the B&H movement, utilising them as a wellspring of pertinent examples, legal theories, and replicable strategies. Additionally, the dynamic network within the B&H movement has been instrumental in amplifying TJ arguments for litigation and public policy proposals, thus contributing substantially to the momentum and efficacy of TJ initiatives. In this section, I will showcase three instances illustrating the productive synergy between practitioners and activists from both the TJ and B&H fields. This fruitful exchange has given rise to innovative tools specifically designed for corporate abuse accountability. Although these tools are currently nascent, they exemplify the promising potential that lies in the further integration of these two fields in the future.

4.1 *The UN 'Heightened Human Rights Due Diligence' Doctrine*

As Sabine Michalowski has put it, a notable complexity in corporate liability for human rights abuses lies in distinguishing lawful commercial operations from those that lead to accusations of complicity.[33] Frequently, corporations implicated in these abuses maintain they were merely conducting routine business transactions, such as financing a government or supplying goods and infrastructure. Corporations argue that their mere interaction with controversial parties does not automatically make them responsible for the latter's human rights infractions. Indeed, the B&H community has long grappled with the question of corporate accountability for the misuse of their goods and services by business partners. The debate centers around the extent of this responsibility, the conditions under which it applies, and the underlying reasons for it. These questions gain heightened significance within conflict and

33 Sabine Michalowski, "Doing Business with a Bad Actor: How to Draw the Line between Legitimate Commercial Activities and Those that Trigger Corporate Complicity Liability," *Texas International Law Journal* 50, no. 3 (2015): 403–464.

post-conflict environments – settings where the TJ principles are most commonly implemented.

In recent years, the United Nations Working Group on Business and Human Rights (WG) has made substantial strides towards resolving these questions.[34] The WG has concentrated its efforts on elucidating the concept of Heightened Human Rights Due Diligence (HRDD). The WG views HRDD as a process that enables businesses to recognise, assess, and alleviate the risk of human rights abuses in conflict-prone environments. This process is envisioned as a more stringent and comprehensive form of human rights due diligence, designed to tackle the unique challenges and risks associated with conflict.[35]

In the WG's view, in situations of conflict, businesses invariably impact human rights, whether directly or indirectly. Any engagement in a conflict situation cannot be neutral, as even impartial businesses can influence the dynamics of the conflict. For instance, hiring security forces, even when they behave impeccably, can alter the local context and potentially escalate violence. Likewise, employing practices that are human rights compliant, or providing certain products or services, could still incite resentment if perceived to favour one group over another. Similarly, a simple act like land acquisition, if based on prior dispossession or forced eviction of communities, can fuel conflict. Therefore, to demonstrate respect for human rights in conflict contexts, businesses must continually identify and assess both actual and potential adverse impacts on human rights and conflict dynamics linked to their operations, products, or services. Imposed sanctions could serve as useful indicators, but they are not substitutes for rigorous due diligence. Given the volatile nature of armed conflicts and situations of widespread violence, businesses should carry out heightened due diligence on an ongoing basis, regularly updating their assessments. Thus, businesses' implementation of robust stakeholder engagement and grievance management systems is vital to achieving this goal.

Hence, HRDD requires responsible businesses to adhere to a sequence of steps to help prevent human rights abuses in conflict-affected contexts. Firstly, businesses must undertake a context analysis, delving into a comprehensive

34 See, United Nations Human Rights Council, Business, Human Rights and Conflict-Affected Regions: Towards Heightened Action – Report of the Working Group on the Issue of Human Rights and Transnational Corporations and Other Business Enterprises, Report No. A/75/212; and Implementing the Third Pillar: Lessons from Transitional Justice Guidance by the Working Group – Report of the Working Group on the Issue of Human Rights and Transnational Corporations and Other Business Enterprises, Report No. A/HRC/50/40/Add.4 (2022).

35 United Nations Development Programme, *Heightened Human Rights Due Diligence for Business in Conflict-Affected Contexts; A Guide* (New York, NY, 2022).

understanding of the local environment, encompassing the history of the conflict, the political landscape, the state of human rights, and the role businesses have played in the conflict. Secondly, they should engage in a risk assessment, pinpointing the human rights risks associated with their operations. This includes the risks of direct and indirect impacts, as well as the likelihood of contributing to or escalating the conflict. Thirdly, businesses need to design and execute mitigation measures that address the identified risks. These measures must be tailored to align with the specific risks and the context of the business. And lastly, they must ensure consistent monitoring and reporting of the effectiveness of their mitigation measures, sharing their progress transparently with stakeholders.

This standard not only offers significant insights for resolving numerous global legal disputes about corporate behavior in armed conflicts, but it also serves as a foundation for more meaningful insights from the WG. These contributions include additional reports and documents that deal with the application of this standard to specific issues. Notable examples include the 2022 report on reparations and a practical guide that allows businesses to evaluate whether they are operating in contexts that require enhanced accountability measures.[36] These advancements provide vital tools for policymakers in transitional and post-conflict situations, greatly assisting in the development of effective TJ strategies.

4.2 *The Expansion of the Imprescriptibility Doctrine*

The innovative combination of labour law and international human rights law in Argentina offers a unique and potentially effective approach to addressing corporate responsibility in human rights violations. Notable examples of this strategy are the cases brought against the steel companies SIDERCA in 2007 and Techint SA in 2012. Argentine activists have increasingly turned to civil litigation against corporations as an alternative to criminal prosecution, given that legal entities can be held liable as accomplices in civil cases. These cases also tend to be simpler to litigate and provide victims with monetary compensation.

In the SIDERCA case, an employee was forced disappeared shortly after he left work in 1977.[37] After the Supreme Court struck down the amnesty laws, the

36 United Nations Human Rights Council, Implementing the Third Pillar; United Nations Development Programme, Heightened Human Rights Due Diligence.

37 For an in-depth explanation of the case see: Laura Garcia Martin, "Overcoming Corporate-Related Human Rights Abuses in Transitional Justice: Lights and Shadows from the Case of Argentina," *Journal of Human Rights* 20, no. 5 (2021): 547–563.

worker's wife sought compensation from the company, arguing that Argentine workplace safety laws required the company to ensure the worker's safety upon entering and exiting the workplace. SIDERCA contested this claim, arguing that the statute of limitations had long expired. However, the Supreme Court of Buenos Aires ruled that the statute of limitations was not applicable in cases of enforced disappearance and ordered the company to compensate for the worker's widow.

In the case of Techint SA, an employee was abducted by state forces from his workplace in May 1977.[38] The worker's daughter brought a case to the company, seeking financial compensation for her father's disappearance. The plaintiff claimed Techint SA was complicit in her father's disappearance, which occurred on the company's premises. She combined Argentine labour law on worker safety with international human rights law on enforced disappearances, arguing that the statute of limitations should be rendered inapplicable. However, the company denied its involvement and asserted that the two-year statute of limitations for workplace safety laws barred the claim.

The Fifth Chamber of the National Court of Appeals for Labor Matters rejected the company's argument. It ruled that the statute of limitations did not apply to compensation claims associated with crimes against humanity and saw no reason to distinguish between such crimes' punitive and compensatory consequences. The Court found that the company's failure to protect its workers was a critical factor in the events leading to the worker's disappearance and awarded compensation to his daughter under domestic labour law.

The notion that the non-applicability of the statute of limitations for crimes against humanity extends beyond criminal liability to civil damage has since been a cornerstone of Argentine victims' claims. Such activism even led to a reform in 2015 of Article 2561 of the Civil Code, paragraph 3, which now expressly stipulates that 'civil actions arising from crimes against humanity are imprescriptible'.[39]

38 Ibid.

39 However, it is worth noting that in 2019, Argentina's Supreme Court overturned the appellate Court's decision in the Techint case, ruling that the two-year statute of limitations applied to labour cases, even those linked to crimes against humanity committed in the 1970s. The Court held that as civil and labour law applied prospectively, the 2015 reform could not retroactively affect events from the 1970s. Argentine activists believe that this Supreme Court doctrine infringes upon human rights obligations. As a result, they have submitted a series of cases to the Inter-American Commission on Human Rights, which is currently under review by this international body.

4.3 *Bringing Home Extraterritorial Litigation*

Historically, litigation against economic actors implicated in serious human rights violations has primarily occurred in courts in the Global North, including US Federal jurisdiction through the Alien Tort Claims Statute.[40] This trend emerged for two significant reasons. First, the countries where the violations took place often lacked independent justice systems capable of hearing these cases. In several instances, the groups that perpetrated the crimes in complicity with the companies controlled the judiciary. And second, the headquarters of these implicated companies were typically located in countries of the Global North. Consequently, for cases involving multinational companies, the courts of these home countries were deemed the most appropriate forum.[41]

However, recent restrictions have been placed on litigation against economic allies of war crime units in these Global North jurisdictions. The most notable limitation is the narrowing of the US jurisdiction to hear cases on the civil liability of companies for violations committed overseas.[42] This development necessitates the exploration of other jurisdictions, including those in the countries where the violations occurred.

Countries that adopted comprehensive TJ policies offer ideal forums for revisiting these litigations. Latin American countries, such as Argentina, Chile, and Brazil, serve as examples; their justice systems have formulated theories to reopen corporate abuse investigations, drawing upon doctrines like the aforementioned imprescriptibility of crimes against humanity-related tort action. In other instances, as seen in Colombia, specialised transitional justice courts have included the examination of cases involving corporate complicity within their mandate.[43]

Thus, a significant shift in litigation flow is underway, one that is redirecting towards courts in the Global South. Latin American activists have devised innovative strategies to overcome these obstacles despite facing evidentiary material scarcity and lack of prosecutorial momentum.

---

40 Amy Howe, "An Introduction to the Alien Tort Statute and Corporate Liability: In Plain English," SCOTUSblog, July 24, 2017, https://www.scotusblog.com/2017/07/introduction-alien-tort-statute-corporate-liability-plain-english/.

41 Beth Stephens, "The Rise and Fall of the Alien Tort Statute," in *Research Handbook on Human Rights and Business*, ed. Surya Deva and David Birchall (Cheltenham: Edward Elgar Publishing, 2020).

42 Tyler R. Giannini, "Living with History: Will the Alien Tort Statute Become a Badge of Shame or Badge of Honor?," *Yale Law Journal Forum* 132 (2022): 814.

43 Sabine Michalowski, "Addressing Criminal Responsibility of Economic Actors through Criminal Transitional Justice Mechanisms – First Lessons from Colombia," *Columbia Human Rights Law Review* 55 (2024): 444–508.

One such strategy involves Global South courts utilising evidentiary material from cases closed in US civil courts under the Alien Tort Statute. In Colombia, this strategy has been employed in two cases involving US-based companies accused of complicity with armed groups: Drummond and Chiquita Brands.[44] Despite neither of these cases ending in a judgment favouring victims at American courts, they have generated a wealth of evidentiary material. Moreover, as most of these cases have been dismissed without trial, a thorough analysis of the evidence and potential liability has not been conducted. Thus, victims are seeking to transfer this evidentiary material to transitional criminal judges in Colombia, paving the way for a more comprehensive examination of corporate responsibility. This strategy holds significant potential for application in other countries and contexts.

To address the second challenge, the lack of prosecutorial momentum, Latin American litigants have extensively utilised the role of private attorneys. Through this approach, victims and their lawyers can drive case momentum, assist in litigation investigation, present arguments on criminal charges, and foster conditions for cases to reach the trial stage. In addition, this strategy ensures that the victims' voices are heard, and their rights are advocated for in the pursuit of justice.

5 Implications and Future Research

In the span of a few years, the intersection of TJCA has made significant strides. As explored throughout this chapter, specialised literature and the tangible experiences of activists and litigators have successfully confronted two key challenges. First, TJ has proven to bring a fresh perspective to combating impunity, expanding upon the foundation laid by the B&H discourse. And second, there is growing assurance that integrating the accountability of private economic actors into TJ policy discussions need not be a cumbersome burden; rather, it is a necessary step to fulfill promises made to victims.

The UN' 'Heightened Human Rights Due Diligence' (HRDD) doctrine, the expansion of the imprescriptibility doctrine in Argentina, and the shift towards bringing home extraterritorial litigation, exemplify the substantial progress

44 Corporate Accountability Lab, "Corporate Accountability Lab Submits Report on Role of Economic Actors in the Armed Conflict to the Special Jurisdiction for Peace in Colombia," November 9, 2022, https://corpaccountabilitylab.org/calblog/2022/11/9/cal-provides-more-evidence-of-corporate-complicity-in-armed-conflict-to-colombian-peace-tribunal.

made in the field. However, both practical efforts and theoretical explorations in Transitional Justice and Corporate Accountability (TJCA) still face major challenges. In closing this chapter, I would like to spotlight three pivotal areas of focus.

The first challenge concerns the geographical expansion of our scope – specifically, addressing the overrepresentation of Latin American experiences within the field. It is crucial to balance these narratives with studies and initiatives from diverse contexts. While efforts are already underway in various regions, more work is needed. This is due to the fact that conditions enabling progress and setbacks in Latin America may not apply universally or present unique conditions for combating corporate abuses.

A second challenge involves elevating the importance of corporate accountability within broader TJ discussions. Institutions and power centres that promote reconstruction, peacebuilding, and accountability agendas must incorporate advancements in this field. The conversation surrounding business and economic actors needs to shift from being a mere backdrop to becoming a crucial factor in decision-making. For instance, it is imperative that discourses on corporate responsibility scrutinise the socio-economic conditions that enable mass violence and its enduring impunity.

Third, we must continue to refine and create policy and legal instruments that empower communities, victims, and activists to bridge the profound gap between corporate accountability and impunity. As it stands, most cases in the literature indicate that accountability is more the exception than the rule. Any approach integrating human rights into business must employ innovative legal theories and strategies, ensuring these values become tangible realities.

Bibliography

Books

Basualdo, Victoria, Harmut Berghoff, and Marcelo Bucheli, eds. *Big Business and Dictatorships in Latin America: A Transnational History of Profits and Repression.* London: Palgrave Macmillan, 2021.

Bilsky, Leora. *The Holocaust, Corporations and the Law: Unfinished Business.* Michigan: University of Michigan Press, 2017.

Bohoslavsky, Juan P., Karina Fernández, and Sarnata Reynolds, eds. *Pinochet's Economic Accomplices: An Unequal Country by Force.* Lanham: Lexington Books, 2020.

García Martín, Laura. *Transitional Justice, Corporate Accountability and Socio-Economic Rights: Lessons from Argentina.* 1st ed. Abingdon: Routledge, 2019.

Verbitsky, Horacio and Juan P. Bohoslavsky, eds. *The Economic Accomplices to the Argentine Dictatorship*. Cambridge: Cambridge University Press, 2013.

Chapters in Edited Books

Amorim, Fábio C. de, Valeria Sion, and Renan Machado. "Accountability for Volkswagen's Role in the Brazilian Dictatorship." In *Economic Actors and the Limits of Transitional Justice: Truth and Justice for Business Complicity in Human Rights Violations*, edited by Leigh A. Payne, Laura Bernal-Bermúdez, and Gabriel Pereira, 74–95. London: British Academy Scholarship Online, 2022.

Basualdo, Victoria, Tomás Ojea Quintana, and Carolina Varsky. "The Cases of Ford and Mercedes Benz." In *The Economic Accomplices to the Argentine Dictatorship: Outstanding Debts*, edited by Horacio Verbitsky and Juan P. Bohoslavsky, 159–163. Cambridge: Cambridge University Press, 2015.

Ganson, Brian. "Business and Peace: A Need for New Questions and Systems Perspectives." In *Business, Peacebuilding and Sustainable Development*, edited by Jason Miklian, Rina M. Alluri, and John E. Katsos, 3–26. Abingdon: Routledge, 2019.

Ganson, Brian. "Business and Peace: A Need for New Questions and Systems Perspectives." In *Business, Peacebuilding and Sustainable Development*, edited by Jason Miklian, Rina M. Alluri, and John E. Katsos, 3–26. Abingdon: Routledge, 2019.

Payne, Leigh A., Maxine N. Beall, and Alexander Hutchinson. "The Roots of Corporate Accountability: From the Holocaust and Beyond." In *Economic Actors and the Limits of Transitional Justice: Truth and Justice for Business Complicity in Human Rights Violations*, edited by Leigh A. Payne, Laura Bernal-Bermúdez, and Gabriel Pereira, 27–55. London: British Academy Scholarship Online, 2022.

Stephens, Beth. "The Rise and Fall of the Alien Tort Statute." In *Research Handbook on Human Rights and Business*, edited by Surya Deva and David Birchall. Cheltenham: Edward Elgar Publishing, 2020.

Verbitsky, Horacio and Juan P. Bohoslavsky. "State Terrorism and the Economy: From Nuremberg to Buenos Aires." In *The Economic Accomplices to the Argentine Dictatorship: Outstanding Debts*, 1–7. Cambridge: Cambridge University Press, 2015.

Waldorf, Lars. "Afterwords in Aftermaths." In *Transitional and Transformative Justice: Critical and International Perspectives*, edited by Michael Evans, 161–165. Abingdon: Routledge, 2019.

Waldorf, Lars. "Between Transition and Transformation: Legal Empowerment as Collective Reparations." In *From Transitional to Transformative Justice*, edited by Paul Gready and Simon Robins, 131–149. Cambridge: Cambridge University Press, 2019.

Articles

Giannini, Tyler R. "Living with History: Will the Alien Tort Statute Become a Badge of Shame or Badge of Honor?" *Yale Law Journal Forum* 132 (2022): 814.

Grosescu, Raluca. "Transnational Advocacy Networks and Corporate Accountability for Gross Human Rights Violations in Argentina and Colombia." *Global Society* 33, no. 3 (2019): 400–418.

Koska, Goran. "Corporate Accountability in Times of Transition: The Role of Restorative Justice in the South African Truth and Reconciliation Commission." *Restorative Justice* 4, no. 1 (2016): 41–67.

Martin, Laura Garcia. "Overcoming Corporate-Related Human Rights Abuses in Transitional Justice: Lights and Shadows from the Case of Argentina." *Journal of Human Rights* 20, no. 5 (2021): 547–563.

Michalowski, Sabine. "Doing Business with a Bad Actor: How to Draw the Line between Legitimate Commercial Activities and Those that Trigger Corporate Complicity Liability." *Texas International Law Journal* 50, no. 3 (2015): 403–464.

Michalowski, Sabine. "Addressing Criminal Responsibility of Economic Actors through Criminal Transitional Justice Mechanisms – First Lessons from Colombia." *Columbia Human Rights Law Review* 55 (2024): 444–508.

Pereira, Gabriel and Leigh Payne. "Corporate Complicity in International Human Rights Violations." *Annual Review of Law and Social Science* 12 (2016): 63–84.

Pereira, Gabriel, Leigh A. Payne, and Laura Bernal-Bermúdez. "Justice from Below: Corporate Accountability in Argentina." *The International Journal of Human Rights* 26, no. 8 (2022): 1418–1454.

Sattorova, Mavluda. "Greed and Grievance: Corporations, States and International Investment Law in Times of Conflict." *European Journal of International Law* 34, no. 1 (2023): 181–212.

Official Documents

U.N. Secretary General. *Guidance Note of the Secretary-General: United Nations Approach to Transitional Justice.* March 2010.

United Nations Development Programme. *Heightened Human Rights Due Diligence for Business in Conflict-Affected Contexts: A Guide.* New York, NY, 2022.

United Nations Human Rights Council. *Implementing the Third Pillar: Lessons from Transitional Justice Guidance by the Working Group – Report of the Working Group on the Issue of Human Rights and Transnational Corporations and Other Business Enterprises*, Report No. A/HRC/50/40/Add.4, 2022.

United Nations Human Rights Council. *Business, Human Rights and Conflict-Affected Regions: Towards Heightened Action – Report of the Working Group on the Issue of Human Rights and Transnational Corporations and Other Business Enterprises*, Report No. A/75/212.

United Nations Human Rights Office of the High Commissioner. *Guiding Principles on Business and Human Rights: Implementing the United Nations "Protect, Respect and Remedy" Framework*, 2011.

Online/Internet Sources

Corporate Accountability Lab. "Corporate Accountability Lab Submits Report on Role of Economic Actors in the Armed Conflict to the Special Jurisdiction for Peace in Colombia." November 9, 2022. https://corpaccountabilitylab.org/calblog/2022/11/9/cal-provides-more-evidence-of-corporate-complicity-in-armed-conflict-to-colombian-peace-tribunal.

Howe, Amy. "An Introduction to the Alien Tort Statute and Corporate Liability: In Plain English." *SCOTUSblog*, July 24, 2017. https://www.scotusblog.com/2017/07/introduction-alien-tort-statute-corporate-liability-plain-english/.

CHAPTER 13

Effective and Meaningful Dialogue through Company Grievance Mechanisms: Promoting Community Engagement, Sustainable Development and Conflict Prevention

Lisa J. Laplante

1 Introduction

Those working in the field of development have long recognised the need for companies to engage meaningfully with local populations to ensure successful projects while also preventing social conflicts that can interrupt operations. Within these settings, operational-level grievance mechanisms (OGMs) can play a pivotal role in supporting the type of community dialogue already called for in the field of sustainable development, although this connection has yet to be fully theorised or implemented in practice.

Indeed OGMs are typically viewed in the Business and Human Rights (BHR) field as serving the role of redressing human rights harms, it is important to acknowledge that the architects of the United Nations Guiding Principles on Business and Human Rights (UNGPs) also intended OGMs to provide ongoing feedback within a human rights due diligence process. Recognising this purpose helps highlight how OGMs align with the type of general community-company engagement long envisioned in the field of development. In particular, the UNGPs create the standard that, in order to be effective, OGMs should be based on dialogue, thus striving for the same type of stakeholder engagement sought in development. However, both the development and Business and Human Rights fields have much to learn on how to ensure that community engagement is truly effective.

This chapter explores the ways in which OGMs support and enhance sustainable development through fostering community-company relations. In particular, this exploration focuses on the extractive industry as a case study given its history in seeking strategies for engaging with local communities both as part of development as well as more recently to comply with the UNGPs.

 | DOI:10.1163/9789004530942_014

2 The Extractive Industry and Sustainable Development

Businesses play a critical role in supporting development in countries across the world, such as by contributing to the national gross product of these nations.[1] In particular, companies, especially multinational companies, become central players in global development through national commercial projects funded by international lending institutions like the World Bank. Such is the case with the extractive industry, which not only provides employment to the citizens of developing countries, but whose company proceeds from mineral, oil, gas, and metals add substantially to the budget of those nations as well, ultimately catalyzing poverty reduction.[2]

However, over the years, the notion of development has evolved beyond minimalist notions of simply generating economic growth and raising a Gross National Product (GNP) to embrace the tenants of sustainability, which has helped to prioritise considerations of how development impacts local communities positively and negatively.[3] Indeed, in 2004, the World Bank Group's Extractive Industries Review process recognised that 'extractive industries can contribute to sustainable development, when projects are implemented well and preserve the rights of affected people, and if the benefits they generate are well-used.'[4] Increasingly, there is more awareness that even if extractive companies support economic development and improve the lives of local populations, they also often cause adverse impacts on these same communities. As a result, there has been a growing global trend of community grievances escalating into social conflict that, at times, can even block the production of companies involved.[5]

1 James Manyika et al., "A new look at how corporations impact the economy and households," McKinsey Global Institute, May 31, 2021, https://www.mckinsey.com/capabilities/strategy-and-corporate-finance/our-insights/a-new-look-at-how-corporations-impact-the-economy-and-households#/.

2 Holly Wise and Sokol Shtylla, "The Role of the Extractive Sector in Expanding Economic Opportunity" (Corporate Social Responsibility Initiative, Report No. 18, Harvard University Kennedy School of Government, Cambridge, MA, 2007), 7.

3 International Resource Panel, *Mineral Resource Governance in the 21st Century: Gearing Extractive Industries Towards Sustainable Development* (Nairobi: United Nations Environment Programme, 2020).

4 World Bank Group, *World Bank Management Group Response: Striking a Better Balance – The World Bank Group and Extractive Industries: The Final Report of the Extractive Industries Review* (Washington, D.C.: International Bank for Reconstruction and Development/The World Bank, 2004).

5 Anthony Bebbington, ed., *Social Conflict, Economic Development and Extractive Industry: Evidence from South America* (New York: Routledge, 2012); Judith Shapiro and

Practitioners and scholars have documented this burgeoning community strife between extractive companies and communities across the world, particularly in Asia, Africa, and Latin America.[6] For example, following a twenty-year internal war (1980–2000), Peru experienced notable economic growth thanks to the extractive industries. Yet, this growth also led to a dramatic rise in social conflicts, prompting the government to establish a special office in the Ombudsman to handle the violence. In 2013, *The Economist* reported that in the previous five years, Peru had experienced a 300% increase in social conflicts, with the tracking of 149 disputes involving extractive industries.[7] The highest-profile community conflict arose in Cajamarca where the Yanacocha gold mine (operated by the US firm Newmont and Peru's Buenaventura) planned a $4.8 billion expansion that faced such fierce opposition that the project was suspended, and the government had to declare a state of emergency.[8]

John-Andrew McNeish, eds., *Our Extractive Age: Expressions of Violence and Resistance* (New York: Routledge, 2021).

6 See, e.g., Lisa Calvano, "Multinational Corporations and Local Communities: A Critical Analysis of Conflict," *Journal of Business Ethics* 82 (2008); Lisa J. Laplante and Suzanne A. Spears, "Out of the Conflict Zone: The Case for Community Consent Processes in the Extractive Sector," *Yale Human Rights and Development Law Journal* 11, no. 1 (2008); Leanne A. Farrell, Ralph Hamann, and Eric Mackres, "A Clash of Cultures (and lawyers): Anglo Platinum and Mine-affected Communities in Limpopo Province, South Africa," *Resources Policy* 37, no. 2 (2012); Fiorella Triscritti, "Mining, Development and Corporate–community Conflicts in Peru," *Community Development Journal* 48, no. 3 (2013); Maritza Paredes, "The Glocalization of Mining Conflict: Cases from Peru," *The Extractive Industries and Society* 3, no. 4 (2016); M. Omar Faruque, "The Politics of Extractive Industry Corporate Practices: An Anatomy of a Company-community Conflict in Bangladesh," *The Extractive Industries and Society* 5, no. 1 (2018); John Andrew McNeish, "Resource Extraction and Conflict in Latin America," *Colombia Internacional* 93 (2018); Troy Sternberg, "Conflict and Contestation in Kyrgyz Mining Infrastructure," *The Extractive Industries and Society* 7, no. 4 (2020); Jocelyn Fraser, "Mining Companies and Communities: Collaborative Approaches to Reduce Social Risk and Advance Sustainable Development," *Resources Policy* 74 (2021); Saenz Cesar and Ostos Jhony, "Making or Breaking Social License to Operate in the Mining Industry: Factors of the Main Drivers of Social Conflict," *Journal of Cleaner Production* 278 (2021); Chang Hoon Oh, Jiyoung Shin, and Shuna Shu Ham Ho, "Conflicts between Mining Companies and Communities: Institutional Environments and Conflict Resolution Approaches," *Business Ethics, the Environment & Responsibility* 32, no. 2 (2023); Yanina Kowszyk, Frank Vanclay, and Rajiv Maher, "Conflict Management in the Extractive Industries: A Comparison of Four Mining Projects in Latin America," *The Extractive Industries and Society* 13 (2023).

7 "Social Conflict in Peru's Mining Sector," The Economist Impact, January 3, 2013, https://impact.economist.com/sustainability/ecosystems-resources/social-conflict-in-perus-mining-sector.

8 Cindy S. Woods, "'It isn't a State Problem': The Minas Conga Mine Controversy and the Need for Binding International Obligations of Corporate Actors," *Georgetown Journal of*

The situation in Yanacocha closely resembles that in other communities where local inhabitants rise up against extractive companies due to a range of issues related to displacement, control of land, pollution of land and water, and even violent confrontations with local communities.[9] Often Indigenous Peoples reside in these communities, which adds additional complexities to how a company must operate on their land to extract natural resources.[10] Ultimately, this disruption of the economic and social ecosystem arises out of the very nature of the extractive industry which depends on the land where it operates and the many years of commitment. Since it enjoys minimal mobility once it invests in a project, this industry has experienced some of the most acute problems with local populations and thus has drawn considerable attention in both the fields of development and BHR. Certainly, the types of issues arising out of these extractive projects are typically the kind that demand the creation of channels for responding to and resolving local grievances.

3 Operational Level Grievance Mechanisms: Managing Conflict in the Extractive Industry

Given the tense history described above, companies within the extractive industry were well poised to work closely with Professor John Ruggie as he began to study the issue of accessing remedy during his mandate as UN Special Representative. Certainly, extractive companies were already in the trenches with local communities, often struggling to manage highly visible and challenging conflicts that threatened their business viability.

Ruggie sought to study the way that local, private grievance channels could manage these situations. With his team, he initiated pilot studies involving

International Law 46 (2015); Jorge Millones, "Conga Mines: Development as Conflict in Peru," *South Atlantic Quarterly* 115, no. 3 (2016).

9 See, e.g., Laplante and Spears, "Out of the Conflict Zone"; Farrell, Hamann, and Mackres, "A Clash of Cultures"; Faruque, "An Anatomy of a Company-community Conflict in Bangladesh"; Sternberg, "Conflict and Contestation in Kyrgyz Mining Infrastructure"; Fraser, "Mining Companies and Communities"; Cesar and Jhony, "Making or Breaking Social License"; Oh, Shin, and Ho, "Conflicts between Mining Companies and Communities."

10 Fraser, "Mining Companies and Communities"; Marcela Torres-Wong & Adrian Jimenez-Sandoval, "Indigenous Resource Governance as an Alternative to Mining: Redefining the Boundaries of Indigenous Participation," *The Extractive Industries and Society* 9 (2022); Julian Burger, *Indigenous Peoples, Extractive Industries and Human Rights* (Belgium: European Parliament, 2014); U.N. Human Rights Council, Report of the Special Rapporteur on the Rights of Indigenous Peoples, James Anaya, A/HRC/21/47 (July 6, 2012).

mining companies to help better understand the role of non-judicial mechanisms in providing remedies to local populations.[11] This work led Ruggie to conceptualise the OGMs and generate some basic guidelines on ensuring the effectiveness of non-judicial remedies.[12] Notably, this collaboration inspired the extractive industry itself to produce some of the earliest reports and guidelines related to OGMs.[13]

Ruggie developed OGMs as an important decentralised response to what was viewed as a 'remedy gap' since victims encountered many obstacles and

11 For example, his team elaborated principles through multi-stakeholder consultations conducted by the Corporate Responsibility Initiative in 2007, eventually setting them out in a guidance tool. Caroline Rees, "Corporations and Human Rights: Accountability Mechanisms for Resolving Complaints and Disputes" (Corporate Social Responsibility Initiative, Report No. 15, Harvard University Kennedy School of Government, Cambridge, MA, 2007), 24–25. In March 2009, the International Organisation of Employers, International Chamber of Commerce, and Business and Industry Advisory Committee to the OECD began to collaborate on this project, and four companies volunteered to take part in a pilot OGM project. These companies were: (1) Carbones del Cerrejón Ltd. in Colombia, a coal mining joint venture of Anglo American, BHP Billiton, and Xstrata Coal; (2) Esquel Group in Hong Kong, piloting a mechanism at its apparel facility in Viet Nam; (3) Sakhalin Energy Investment Corporation in the Russian Federation, an oil and gas joint venture of Gazprom, Royal Dutch Shell, Mitsui & Co. Ltd., and Mitsubishi Corporation; (4) Tesco Stores Ltd., a major United Kingdom supermarket working with a group of its fruit suppliers in South Africa. Caroline Rees, "Piloting Principles for Effective Company-Stakeholder Grievance Mechanisms: A Report of Lessons Learned" (Corporate Social Responsibility Initiative, Harvard University Kennedy School of Government, Cambridge, MA, 2011), 8.

12 See Caroline Rees, "Grievance Mechanisms for Business and Human Rights: Strengths, Weaknesses and Gaps," (Corporate Social Responsibility Initiative, Working Paper No. 40, Harvard University Kennedy School of Government, Cambridge, MA, 2008), 31; Corporate Social Responsibility Initiative, "Rights-Compatible Grievance Mechanisms: A Guidance Tool for Companies and their Stakeholders" (Corporate Social Responsibility Initiative, Working Paper No. 41, Harvard University Kennedy School of Government, Cambridge, MA, 2008), 15–40; Caroline Rees, "Access to Remedies for Corporate Human Rights Impacts: Improving Non-Judicial Mechanisms" (Corporate Social Responsibility Initiative, Report No. 32, Harvard University Kennedy School of Government, Cambridge, MA, 2008), 7–13. See also Caroline Rees and David Vermijs, "Mapping Grievance Mechanisms in the Business and Human Rights Arena" (Corporate Social Responsibility Initiative, Report No. 28, Harvard University Kennedy School of Government, Cambridge, MA, 2008), 7–22.

13 For example, the International Council on Mining and Minerals, which represents these industries, made several submissions to the Special Representatives, strongly endorsing corporate level grievance mechanisms. Deanna Kemp et al., "Just Relations and Company–Community Conflict in Mining," *Journal of Business Ethics* 101 (2011): 11–12. To learn more about the unique situation of mines, see Laplante and Spears, "Out of the Conflict Zone," 69.

challenges to accessing more formal, state-based remedies, such as courts.[14] Towards the start of his first mandate in 2008, Ruggie presented the concept of OGMs in his first report to the UN, suggesting that companies provide 'a means for those who believe they have been harmed to bring this to the attention of the company and seek remediation, without prejudice to legal channels available.'[15]

Eventually, OGMs became squarely positioned within the UNGP's 'Third Pillar on Access to Remedy.' Specifically, principle 29 states: 'To make it possible for grievances to be addressed early and remediated directly, business enterprises should establish or participate in effective operational-level grievance mechanisms for individuals and communities who may be adversely impacted.'[16] OGMs fall within the broader category of non-state-based, non-judicial grievance mechanisms ('NSGMs'),[17] whether set up by the company alone[18] or in collaboration with other stakeholders.[19]

14 Jennifer A. Zerk, "Extraterritorial Jurisdiction: Lessons for the Business and Human Rights Sphere from Six Regulatory Areas" (Corporate Social Responsibility Initiative, Working Paper No. 59, Harvard University Kennedy School of Government, Cambridge, MA, 2010).

15 U.N. Human Rights Council, Protect, Respect and Remedy: A Framework for Business and Human Rights: Report of the Special Representative of the Secretary-General on the Issue of Human Rights and Transnational Corporations and Other Business Enterprises, John Ruggie, A/HRC/8/5, ¶ 82 (April 7, 2008).

16 U.N. Office of the High Commissioner for Human Rights, Guiding Principles on Business and Human Rights: Implementing the United Nations "Protect, Respect and Remedy" Framework, HR/PUB/11/04, principle 29 (2011).

17 The commentary to the UNGPs explains that '[o]ne category of non-State-based grievance mechanisms encompasses those administered by a business enterprise alone or with stakeholders, by an industry association or a multi-stakeholder group.' U.N., Guiding Principles, principle 28. For discussion, see Mark Wielga and James Harrison, "Assessing the Effectiveness of Non-State-Based Grievance Mechanisms in Providing Access to Remedy for Rightsholders: A Case Study of the Roundtable on Sustainable Palm Oil," *Business and Human Rights Journal* 6, no. 1 (2021): 67–68.

18 For instance, even United Nations bodies engaged in the promotion of the UNGPs have approached OGMs as pertaining to company grievance mechanisms. For an early example, see U.N. Human Rights Council, Report of the Working Group on the Issue of Human Rights and Transnational Corporations and Other Business Enterprises: Addendum: Report from an Expert Workshop Entitled "Business Impacts and Non-judicial Access to Remedy: Emerging Global Experience" Held in Toronto in 2013, A/HRC/26/25/Add.3, ¶ 9 (April 28, 2014).

19 U.N. Human Rights Council, Report of the Special Representative of the Secretary-General on the Issue of Human Rights and Transnational Corporations and Other Business Enterprises, John Ruggie: Addendum: Piloting Principles for Effective Company/Stakeholder Grievance Mechanisms: A Report of Lessons Learned, A/HRC/17/31/Add.1, ¶ 1 (May 24, 2011) ('Effective judicial systems must be at the core of any such system of remedy, yet they are not always available, accessible, appropriate, or the desired avenue

The UNGPs recognise an 'ecosystem' of remedies consisting of both formal, state judicial remedies as well as state and non-state, non-judicial remedies to handle the grievances that arise from company operations, such as those occurring in situations in which sustainable development frameworks would also be applicable. Thus, it is often the case that OGMs play an ever-increasing role in managing the issues that may arise when companies operate within local communities as a part of a nation's development policy.

Although a rarely referenced term before the approval of the UNGPs by the Human Rights Council in 2011, the OGMs have become a central and mainstream feature of the BHR landscape.[20] In its current incarnation, the OGM model represents a novel expansion of traditional approaches to company grievance mechanisms intended mostly for employees and consumers. At its simplest level, these channels may have consisted of a comment box on the wall in order to help companies learn about operational problems.[21] Rarely were these processes intended for external stakeholders such as surrounding communities.[22]

---

of those impacted. Non-judicial grievance mechanisms therefore provide an important complement and supplement for such situations').

20 Benjamin Grama, "Company-Administered Grievance Processes for External Stakeholders: A Means for Effective Remedy, Community Relations, or Private Power?," *Wisconsin International Law Journal* 39, no. 1 (2022): 71. In 2013, the UN Working Group on Business and Human Rights convened an 'expert workshop' to discuss grievance mechanisms. At that meeting, a 'general impression' among participants was that OGMs were still 'not yet part of the mainstream' and that '[b]uy-in for establishing operational-level grievance mechanisms [was] still often lacking.' U.N., Report of the Working Group, ¶ 17. The Human Rights Council established 'a Working Group on the issue of human rights and transnational corporations and other business enterprises' to 'continue to explore options and make recommendations at the national, regional and international levels for enhancing access to effective remedies available to those whose human rights are affected by corporate activities, including those in conflict areas.' U.N. Human Rights Council, Resolution 17/4: Human Rights and Transnational Corporations and Other Business Enterprises, A/HRC/RES/17/4, ¶ 6(e) (July 6, 2011).

21 Lisa J. Laplante, "The Wild West of Company-Level Grievance Mechanisms: Drawing Normative Borders to Patrol the Privatization of Human Rights Remedies," *Harvard International Law Journal* 64, no. 2 (2023): 326.

22 Grama, "Company-Administered Grievance Processes," 74. See also Katharina Häusler, Karin Lukas, and Julia Planitzer, "Non-Judicial Remedies: Company-based Grievance Mechanisms and International Arbitration" in *Human Rights in Business: Removal of Barriers to Access to Justice in the European Union*, eds., Juan José Álvarez Rubio and Katerina Yiannibas (London: Routledge, 2017), 78, 81–82 (noting that companies only started to develop these mechanisms in the last decade in the course of trying to implement the UNGPs).

Yet, today there is a notable trend pointing towards a steady increase in companies adopting OGMs as part of their general effort to come into compliance with the UNGPs.[23] This development has been tracked by the Operational-Level Grievance Mechanism Research Project (hereafter the 'OGM Research Project'), founded in 2016 by the author, which conducts desktop research to track the development of company-level grievance mechanisms to study if and how companies use these mechanisms to resolve human rights related issues.[24]

The OGM Research Project focuses on companies that have adopted human rights policy statements, as required by principle 16 of the UNGPs, to capture a global view of private company-level grievance mechanisms. The aim, then, is to determine if they have created a grievance mechanism to handle complaints arising out of breaches of those policies. Indeed, companies are called upon to take responsibility for negative human rights impacts possibly resulting from their business operations, services, or goods.[25] The UNGPs direct companies to provide for or cooperate in the remediation of adverse human rights impacts[26] and includes OGMs as valid for meeting that expectation.[27]

---

23 Lisa J. Laplante, Olivia Belanger and Brianna Tsui, "Periodic Project Report: 2021 Trends and General Practices of Company Operational-Level Grievance Mechanisms" (The Center for International Law & Policy, New England Law | Boston, 2022).

24 The OGM project uses desktop research to provide information regarding a company's ability and willingness to respond to human rights-based claims through private remedies. The project operates through the Center for International Law and Policy, which the Author directs. See generally Olivia Belanger and Lisa J. Laplante, "Periodic Project Report: Trends and General Practices of Company Operational-Level Grievance Mechanisms" (The Center for International Law & Policy, New England Law | Boston, 2021).

25 U.N., Guiding Principles, principle 15(c) calls for 'processes to enable the remediation of any adverse human rights impacts they cause or to which they contribute.' U.N., Guiding Principles, principle 22 indicates: 'Where business enterprises identify that they have caused or contributed to adverse impacts, they should provide for or cooperate in their remediation through legitimate processes.'

26 U.N., Guiding Principles, principle 22 directs that '[w]here business enterprises identify that they have caused or contributed to adverse impacts, they should provide for or cooperate in their remediation through legitimate processes.'

27 Commentary to U.N., Guiding Principles, principle 22 then names OGMs as 'one effective means of enabling remediation when they meet certain core criteria, as set out in principle 31.' OGMs can be understood as a mechanism involving a process (and thus serving the function of being a procedural remedy) that leads to some substantive, remedial outcome (such as reparations). In practice, the term 'remedy' is often used interchangeably to refer to both a procedural as well as substantive aspect. For more discussion, see Erika R. George and Lisa J. Laplante, "Access to Remedy: Treaty Talks and the Terms of a New Accountability Accord," in *Building a Treaty on Business and Human Rights: Context and Contours*, eds. Surya Deva and David Bilchitz (New York: Cambridge University Press, 2018), 394–97.

As of December 2023, the OGM Research Project reviewed 667 companies across 24 industries, with 93% (618) having an identifiable grievance mechanism poised to handle human rights claims.[28] Of these mechanisms, 31% were open to complaints from anyone although only 4% explicitly reference members of the community; whereas 22% were limited to only employees, as had traditionally been the focus of company complaint channels. The data reveals that certain industries are more likely to profile their OGMs, such as manufacturing and distribution, banking and finance, mining, gas, oil, and energy, with 88.2% representing multinational corporations.[29]

Notable, the extractive industry continues to be one of the more proactive sectors to integrate OGMs into their risk management approaches. As a matter of fact, it is 'now expected practice for mining companies to have in place site-level processes … for systematically receiving, tracking, resolving and communicating with local communities and stakeholders, including workers, about their complaints or grievances.'[30] In response, the Organisation for Economic Co-operation and Development ('OECD') issued guidance on stakeholder engagement for the extractive industry specifically, noting:

> Stakeholders themselves can contribute important knowledge to help identify potential or actual impacts on themselves or their surroundings. The values and priorities of impacted stakeholders are vital considerations in evaluating impacts and identifying appropriate avoidance or mitigation steps. However, if stakeholder engagement activities are not properly supported, developed or executed, their due diligence function may not be realised, and adverse impacts may not be avoided or addressed. Furthermore, poor stakeholder engagement can in and of

28 Lisa J. Laplante, Nicole Symond and Anthony Ardizzone, "Periodic Project Report: 2023 Trends and General Practices of Company Operational-Level Grievance Mechanisms" (The Center for International Law & Policy, New England Law | Boston, 2024). The most common industries include manufacturing and distribution, banking and finance, mining, and gas, oil, and energy, most of which operate on a multinational scale.

29 "Operational Level Grievance Mechanism Research Project," New England Law | Boston, accessed September 5, 2023, https://www.nesl.edu/practical-experiences/centers/center-for-international-law-and-policy/projects/operational-grievance-mechanisms-project; Laplante, Tsui, and Symonds, "2022 Trends and General Practices."

30 Initiative for Responsible Mining Assurance (IRMA), *IRMA Standard for Responsible Mining IRMA-STD-001*, June 2018, https://responsiblemining.net/wp-content/uploads/2018/07/IRMA_STANDARD_v.1.0_FINAL_2018-1.pdf; See also "Handling and Resolving Local-level Concerns and Grievances: Human Rights in the Mining and Metals Sector," ICMM, Dec. 10, 2019, https://www.icmm.com/en-gb/guidance/social-performance/2019/grievance-mechanism.

> itself give rise to actual or perceived adverse impacts and jeopardise potential benefits to stakeholders.[31]

Of relevance here, the International Finance Corporation ('IFC'), which provides substantial funding to private companies in the name of development, especially those representing the extractive industry, has historically required these companies to establish OGMs.[32] In its 2009 guide, the IFC explains,

> The concepts of social risk management and social license to operate have become an integral part of doing business in emerging markets. These dimensions of a company's social and environmental strategy can be achieved with effective stakeholder engagement, based on active participation of and feedback from groups affected by the company's operations. A mechanism to address affected communities' concerns and complaints – a grievance mechanism – is an important pillar of the stakeholder engagement process, since it creates opportunities for companies and communities to identify problems and discover solutions together.[33]

Notably, Ruggie gleaned much from the IFC's approach to localised remedies and stakeholder engagement while developing the OGM model.[34] However, the UNGPs do not fully capture the way in which these grievance mechanisms fit within the larger sustainable development strategy, although a close analysis helps to reveal the synergy.

4 OGMs as Channels for Stakeholder Engagement and Sustainable Development

Since the approval of the UNGPs, the BHR field has tended to focus on OGMs primarily as mechanisms for resolving grievances.[35] However, it is equally

31 OECD, *Due Diligence Guidance for Meaningful Stakeholder Engagement in the Extractive Sector* (Paris: OECD Publishing, 2017), 18.

32 International Finance Corporation (IFC), *Good Practice Note: Addressing Grievances from Project-Affected Communities* (Washington DC: International Finance Corporation, 2009).

33 IFC, *Addressing Grievances from Project-Affected Communities.*

34 Laplante, "Wild West," 337.

35 For discussion, see Lisa J. Laplante, "Making the Connection: Operational-Level Grievance Mechanisms and Human Rights Due Diligence," in *A Guide to Human Rights Due Diligence for Lawyers*, eds. Corinne E. Lewis and Constance Z. Wagner (Chicago: American Bar Association Publishing, 2023), 195.

important to consider how they generally support stakeholder engagement programming designed to support sustainable development.

In particular, and above all else, OGMs may receive a wide range of complaints that do not necessarily rise to the level of human rights issues.[36] Indeed, the UNGPs explain that a 'grievance' can be understood as a 'perceived injustice evoking an individual's or a group's sense of entitlement, which may be based on law, contract, explicit or implicit promises, customary practice, or general notions of fairness of aggrieved communities.'[37] Understanding OGMs as a channel for local communities to engage generally with companies and to provide feedback on their operations and how they impact them allows for more linkage with the same type of community engagement channels called for in the development field.

In fact, as I argue elsewhere, a close reading of the UNGPs in combination with the UNGPs' drafting history shows that OGMs were *never* meant to handle the most serious human rights violations.[38] Instead, OGMs better serve the function of a low-level dispute resolution mechanism to handle smaller grievances *early* before they escalate into more serious problems.[39] On this point, Ruggie shared in his memoir:

> [M]y own research indicated that serious human-rights-related confrontations between companies and individuals or communities frequently began as lesser grievances that companies ignored or dismissed, and which then escalated. ... To make it possible for such grievances to be addressed early and remediated directly, the Framework recommends that company establish or participate in operational-level grievance mechanisms.[40]

36 U.N., Guiding Principles, principle 29 (indicating that OGMs 'need not require that a complaint or grievance amount to an alleged human rights abuse before it can be raised').

37 UN, Guiding Principles, principle 25.

38 Laplante, "Wild West," 380.

39 See U.N., Guiding Principles, principle 28 (stating that OGMs should 'make it possible for grievances to be addressed *early* and remediated directly, business enterprises should establish or participate in effective operational-level grievance mechanisms for individuals and communities who may be adversely impacted'). The UNGP Commentary views this early intervention as 'preventing harms from compounding and grievances from escalating.' U.N., Guiding Principles, principle 29.

40 John Gerard Ruggie, *Just Business: Multinational Corporations and Human Rights* (New York: w.w. Norton & Company, Inc., 2013), 104.

Thus, not surprisingly, commentary to principle 29 further indicates that once these grievances are identified, they should be 'addressed and for adverse impacts to be remediated early and directly by the business enterprise, thereby *preventing* harms from compounding and grievances from *escalating*.'[41]

Just as importantly, the commentary to principle 29 explains that a key function of OGMs is to identify 'adverse human rights impacts as a part of an enterprise's ongoing human rights due diligence' and provide 'a channel for those directly impacted by the enterprise's operations to raise concerns when they believe they are being or will be adversely impacted.'[42] For example, commentary to principle 22 instructs that OGMs help companies meet the requirement of ongoing due diligence to prevent and mitigate human rights abuses associated with their operations, services and goods.[43]

Understanding OGMs as more than simply a remedial mechanism for the worst-case scenario, in which issues have reached a level of liability for the company, helps make the important connection between OGMs and local stakeholder engagement in the field of development. Indeed, OGMs can potentially serve a company's efforts to support sustainable development by providing a mechanism that is specifically designed for stakeholder engagement and that allows for continuous monitoring so that companies can adjust operations when needed.

Again, Ruggie's own reflections on the development of OGMs emphasize this interpretation as to the two key functions of company remedies:

> [The first is] early-stage recourse which would serve as an early warning system making it possible for grievances against the company to be addressed and remediated before they escalate, thereby preventing them from compounding. The second is as a feedback loop, providing the company with information about its current or potential adverse human rights impacts. By analyzing trends and patterns in complaints, companies can identify systematic problems and adapt their practices accordingly.[44]

41 U.N., Guiding Principles, principle 29.

42 U.N., Guiding Principles, principle 29.

43 U.N., Guiding Principles, principle 22. For discussion, see Laplante, "Making the Connection," 195.

44 Ruggie, *Just Business*, 153–54. Ruggie also stated this rationale in official reports. See U.N. Human Rights Council, Report of the Special Representative of the Secretary-General on the Issue of Human Rights and Transnational Corporations and other Business Enterprises, John Ruggie: Business and Human Rights: Further Steps toward the Operationalization of

This approach, now incorporated into the UNGPs, explicitly views OGMs as instruments that support Human Rights Due Diligence which also calls for stakeholder engagement.[45] The commentary to principle 29 further elaborates on this connection to ongoing risk assessment as a key function of OGMs which:

> support the identification of adverse human rights impacts *as a part of an enterprise's ongoing human rights due diligence*. They do so by providing a channel for those directly impacted by the enterprise's operations to raise concerns when they believe they are being or will be adversely impacted. By analysing trends and patterns in complaints, business enterprises can also identify systemic problems and adapt their practices accordingly.[46]

The OGM-HRDD feedback loop which depends on local stakeholder engagement supports the type of community engagement also promoted in the field of sustainable development, although this relationship has yet to be fully explored. Indeed, as will be discussed next, the focus on stakeholder engagement in sustainable development predates the Business and Human Rights focus on the same topic and arguably is more embedded not only in practice but also in national and international legal frameworks.

5 Community Engagement in the Field of Development

Although not always the case, the theme of broad stakeholder participation, especially of local communities, now consistently figures as a central component in the fields of sustainable development.[47] As observed by Ford,

---

the "Protect, Respect and Remedy" Framework, A/HRC/14/27 (April 9, 2010) ('[G]rievance mechanisms perform two key functions regarding the corporate responsibility to respect. First, they serve as early warning systems, providing companies with ongoing information about their current or potential human rights impacts from those impacted. By analyzing trends and patterns in complaints, companies can identify systemic problems and adapt their practices accordingly. Second, these mechanisms make it possible for grievances to be addressed and remediated directly, thereby preventing harm from being compounded and grievances from escalating').

45 U.N., Guiding Principles, principle 20.

46 U.N., Guiding Principles, principle 29.

47 Yasutaka Ozaki and Rajib Shaw, "Citizens' Social Participation to Implement Sustainable Development Goals (SDGs): A Literature Review," *Sustainability* 14, no. 21 (2022). For the purpose of this chapter, the author adopts the broad understanding of development that pertains to more than economic growth and income, but also includes programmes and

> Once marginalized in the decision-making over business activities with high environmental and social impacts, local communities around the world are increasingly playing a more assertive role.' It is now common in many countries for municipalities, citizen coalitions, indigenous peoples, and other local groups to wield significant influence over the development process.[48]

Certainly, this increase in community engagement arose out of necessity as communities rose up to protest the historical marginalization in decision-making which led not only to them being excluded from the benefits of company operations, but also to often being left vulnerable to adverse impacts caused by companies.

International law has helped to reinforce the need to ensure local populations are integrated into the planning and implementation of development projects. Likewise, international donors, the United Nations, and scholars advocate for the decentralisation of decision-making to involve those most impacted to ensure sustainable development as well as responsible business practice.[49] A focus on community engagement helps to shift the paradigm from viewing communities not just as passive beneficiaries of development but instead as *active participants* in the process of development.

Companies offer a range of motivations for why it is important to meaningfully engage with local communities, especially those that are indigenous peoples and tribes. For example, studies reveal that this approach may improve environmental management of natural resources in the extractive sector, particularly related to knowledge of local ecosystems, biodiversity, environmental monitoring, and other considerations that improve operations.[50] Similarly, the UNGPs state that developing a risk assessment process should 'involve meaningful consultation with potentially affected groups and other relevant stakeholders' who should continue to be engaged while a company tracks the effectiveness of their responses.[51]

One early and direct way of engaging local populations occurs during the initial stages of a project through government-mandated Environmental and

---

policies aimed at improving the lives of all populations, especially in terms of economic and political inclusion, health, education, and even a healthy environment.

48 George K. Foster, "Community Participation in Development," *Vanderbilt Journal of Transnational Law* 51, no.1 (2018): 41.

49 Foster, "Community Participation in Development," 41.

50 Olivier Boiral, Iñaki Heras-Saizarbitoria, and Marie-Christine Brotherton, "Improving Environmental Management through Indigenous Peoples' Involvement," *Environmental Science & Policy* 103 (2020): 10.

51 UN, Guiding Principles, principles 18, 20.

Social Impact Assessments (ESIAs), which often involve private companies seeking concessions and permission to operate.[52] While the push for this local involvement developed due to local protests demanding more input, the practice has become more mainstream, with some hundred countries requiring ESIAs.[53]

Some binding international treaties require member states to conduct Environmental Impact Assessments ('EIAs') when particular activities may cause adverse transboundary impacts and most contemplate some form of public participation.[54] A greater push to ensure EIAs also incorporate more consideration for social impacts with regard to indigenous populations. For example, the Convention (No. 169) Concerning Indigenous and Tribal Peoples in Independent Countries ('ILO Convention'), developed through the International Labour Organization, requires member states to carry out studies to assess the 'social, spiritual, cultural and environmental impact' on indigenous and traditional communities and to consider the results as 'fundamental criteria for the implementation of these activities.'[55] In 2004, the Convention on Biological Diversity ('CBD') adopted a set of guidelines, referred to as the *Akwé: Kon Guidelines* that direct state parties to include cultural and social impact assessments when activities may impact sacred sites, traditional knowledge, traditional systems of production, social cohesion, and relations

52 Neil Craik, *The International Law of Environmental Impact Assessment: Process, Substance and Integration* (Cambridge: Cambridge University Press, 2008) (describing EIA regimes around the world).

53 Foster, "Community Participation in Development," 64.

54 U.N., Convention on Environmental Impact Assessment in a Transboundary Context art. 2(3), Feb. 25, 1991, 1989 U.N.T.S. 309; U.N., Convention on the Law of the Sea, Dec. 10, 1982, 1833 U.N.T.S. 397; Protocol on Environmental Protection to the Antarctic Treaty art. 8, Oct. 4, 1991, 30 I.L.M. 1461, 2941 U.N.T.S. 5778; U.N., Convention on Biological Diversity art. 14, June 5, 1992, 31 I.L.M. 818, 1760 U.N.T.S. 79; Rio Declaration on Environment and Development principle 17, June 13, 1992, 31 I.L.M. 874. See also Neil Craik, "Principle 17: Environmental Impact Assessment," in *The Rio Declaration on Environment and Development: A Commentary*, ed. Jorge E. Viñuales (New York: Oxford University Press, 2015) ('Almost every EIA system includes some form of public participation and consultation.'); Jonas Ebbesson, "Principle 10: Public Participation," in *The Rio Declaration on Environment and Development: A Commentary*, ed. Jorge E. Viñuales (New York: Oxford University Press, 2015), 293 ('[M]ost global environmental agreements adopted since [the Rio Declaration] endorse public access to information and public participation by some means').

55 International Labour Organisation (ILO), Convention (No. 169) Concerning Indigenous and Tribal Peoples in Independent countries, June 27, 1989, 1650 U.N.T.S. 383.

between different genders, generations, and other features specific to indigenous and traditional cultures.[56]

Significantly, international monitoring bodies have helped to bring a normative framework to ensuring 'effective participation' be integrated into impact assessment consultation processes. For example, the Inter-American Court of Human Rights ruled that Suriname failed to secure the Saramakas' consent before authorising development activities.[57] Similarly, in Social and Economic Rights Action Center & the Center for Economic and Social Rights ('SERAC') v. Nigeria, the African Commission for Human Rights recognised that Nigeria violated the rights of the traditional Ogoni people under the African Charter on Human and Peoples' Rights when it authorized oil companies to carry out operations on Ogoni lands without first conducting EIAs.[58] Notably, although the African Charter does not include this right specifically, the Commission recognised the participation as essential for upholding other rights, such as that to health, a satisfactory environment, and the right to wealth and natural resources.[59]

Importantly, although many of these legal frameworks observe participation as good policy, it is critical to acknowledge how participation is

---

56 Secretariat of the Convention on Biological Diversity, *Akwé: Kon Voluntary Guidelines for the Conduct of Cultural, Environmental and Social Impact Assessment regarding Developments Proposed to Take Place on, or which are Likely to Impact on, Sacred Sites and on Lands and Waters Traditionally Occupied or Used by Indigenous and Local Communities* (Montreal: Secretariat of the Convention on Biological Diversity, 2004).

57 *Saramaka People v. Suriname*, Preliminary Objections, Merits, Reparations, and Costs, Inter-Am. Ct. H.R., (ser. C) No. 172, ¶¶ 95–96 (Nov. 28, 2007); *Id.* at ¶ 146 ('[T]he State should not have granted logging concessions within Saramaka territory unless and until the three safeguards of effective participation, benefit-sharing, and prior environmental and social impact assessments were complied with.'); *Id.* at ¶¶ 147–48 (determining that Suriname failed to fulfill the IDSs). See also Saramaka People v. Suriname, Interpretation of the Judgment on Preliminary Objections, Merits, Reparations, and Costs, Inter-Am. Ct. H.R., (ser. C) No. 185, ¶ 17 (Aug. 12, 2008) ('The Tribunal has emphasized that when large-scale development or investment projects could affect the integrity of the Saramaka people's lands and natural resources, the State has a duty not only to consult with the Saramakas, but also to obtain their free, prior, and informed consent in accordance with their customs and traditions').

58 Social and Economic Rights Action Center & the Center for Economic and Social Rights ('SERAC') v. Nigeria (Communication No. 155/96), African Commission on Human and People's Rights, ACHPR/COMM/A044/1, ¶¶ 1–10 (May 27, 2002).

59 *Id.* at ¶¶ 4, 55. See also Laura Westra, "The Conflict Between Development and the Right of the Child to Health," *Denver Journal of International Law and Policy* 42, no. 1 (2013): 4 ('[T]he Ogoni people had a comfortable traditional lifestyle, cultivating their land and fishing' before adverse impacts of oil and gas development).

moreover a human right. For example, article 12 of the International Covenant on Economic, Social, and Cultural Rights recognised the right to participate in matters related to the right to health.[60] Interpreting that provision, the UN Committee on Economic, Social, and Cultural Rights has noted that meaningful participation in decision-making and monitoring processes is a valued right in itself that serves as a means of holding the state accountable for the fulfillment of the right to health.[61] Participation increases a person's control over their own health in order to 'reach a state of complete physical, mental and social well-being.'[62]

Building on this principle that humans have a right to meaningful participation in matters that impact them directly, other international documents and instruments that contribute to the field of sustainable development incorporate participation. For example, The NECE Convention on Access to Information, Public Participation in Decision-making and Access to Justice in Environmental Matters (The Aarhus Convention) which was adopted in 1998.[63] Similarly Agenda 21, the action plan for implementing the Rio Declaration, a soft-law instrument adopted by more than 170 countries in 1992, calls on states to promote sustainable development through 'increased local control.'[64] This 'community-driven approach to sustainability' includes '[g]iving communities a large measure of participation in the sustainable management and protection of the local natural resources…'. Seventy-two international instruments

60 U.N. Comm. on Econ., Soc. and Cultural Rts, Substantive Issues Arising in the Implementation of the International Covenant on Economic, Social and Cultural Rights, E/C. 12.2000/4, ¶ 11 (Aug. 11, 2000).

61 U.N. Comm. on Econ., Soc. and Cultural Rts, Substantive Issues, ¶ 54.

62 U.N. Comm. on Econ., Soc. and Cultural Rts, Substantive Issues, ¶ 4. The right to participation also figures into development theory. Article 1 of the Declaration on the Right to Development establishes that 'The right to development is an inalienable human right by virtue of which every human person and all peoples are entitled *to participate in, contribute to, and enjoy* economic, social, cultural and political development, in which all human rights and fundamental freedoms can be fully realized.' G.A. Res. 41/128, Declaration on the Right to Development (Dec. 4, 1986).

63 Convention on Access to Information, Public Participation in Decision-Making and Access to Justice in Environmental Matters, June 25, 1998, 38 I.L.M. 517, 2161 U.N.T.S. 447.

64 U.N., United Nations Conference on Environment & Development: Agenda 21, (June 1992); Rio Declaration; Stathis N. Palassis, "Beyond the Global Summits: Reflecting on the Environmental Principles of Sustainable Development," *Colorado Journal of International Environmental Law and Policy* 22, no. 1 (2011): 47–48 (discussing the adoption of these instruments).

building on the Rio Declaration, since then, have continued to recognise an important role for local authorities in sustainable development.[65]

Similarly, the 2012 United Nations Conference on Sustainable Development, referred to as the 'Rio+20 conference,' continued to reinforce this principle. For example, in *The Future We Want* report, paragraph 13 recognises that 'opportunities for people to influence their lives and future, participate in decision-making and voice their concerns are fundamental for sustainable development.'[66] The outcome document of *The Future We Want* calls on members to 'agree to work more closely with major groups and other stakeholders and encourage their active participation, as appropriate, in processes that contribute to decision-making, planning and implementation of policies and programmes for sustainable development at all levels.'[67]

Given the ongoing and sustained recognition on the importance of local participation and decision-making in environmental and developmental matters, it is not surprising that the theme plays a central role in the 2030 Agenda for Sustainable Development which was adopted by all United Nations Member States in 2015 to provide 'a shared blueprint for peace and prosperity for people and the planet, now and into the future' through 17 Sustainable Development Goals (SDGs) related to strategies not only spurring economic growth and tackling climate change, but also improving the equality, health, and education of the world's poorest people.[68] Notably, SDG 5.5 focuses on localised decision-making that includes vulnerable groups, such as women.[69] Similarly, SDG 16.7 aims to '[e]nsure responsive, inclusive, participatory and representative decision-making at *all* levels.'[70] Chapter 8 of Agenda 21 calls on countries to ensure effective decision-making processes that include broader public participation in any projects related to socio-economic and environmental issues.[71] Chapter 40 of Agenda 21 recognises that 'everyone is a user and provider of information' in sustainable development and is not just left to

65 See, e.g., U.N. General Assembly, Resolution 66/288: The Future We Want, A/RES/66/288, ¶ 42 (July 27, 2012) ('We … recognize the important role that [local] authorities and communities can play in implementing sustainable development.'); *Id.* at 193 ('[W]e commit to improving the livelihoods of people and communities by creating the conditions needed for them to sustainably manage forests, … particularly with regard to decision-making').

66 U.N., The Future We Want, ¶ 13.

67 U.N., The Future We Want, ¶ 43.

68 U.N. General Assembly, Resolution 70/1: Transforming Our world: The 2030 Agenda for Sustainable Development, A/RES/70/1 (Oct. 21, 2015).

69 U.N., 2030 Agenda for Sustainable Development, 18.

70 U.N., 2030 Agenda for Sustainable Development, 25.

71 U.N., Agenda 21, ch. 8.

senior 'expert' decision-makers at the national and international level but also includes individuals at the grassroots level.[72]

Against this background, the field of development calls on the private sector to establish channels for meaningful community engagement. Importantly, one key aspect of the development model is to recognise that 'citizens themselves becoming the main actors in research and information generation will not only promote their participation in the SDGs but may also lead to better monitoring of SDG achievement.'[73] Inevitably, this same monitoring would be the time in which grievances may also arise, but even if development-based engagement channels receive grievances, they may not be as well prepared to manage them as would an OGM. Thus, an opportunity presents itself for a holistic approach to coordinating these complimentary efforts in engaging communities. That said, IRMA recognizes, '[g]rievance mechanisms should not be considered a substitute for community and stakeholder engagement processes that allow for the airing of concerns. The two are complementary and should be mutually reinforcing.'[74]

5.1 *Case Study: Resolute Limited Community Engagement and Grievance Mechanisms*

Resolute Mining Limited offers one example of what it looks like for a company to adopt distinct but complementary channels for both community development as well as grievance mechanisms. Remarkably, Resolute gained attention for its approach to working with local populations as part of its general engagement approaches a decade before the UNGPs were approved. Specifically, in 2000, Resolute took the step of encouraging local communities to take a more empowered approach to their own development plans when starting its gold mining in Tanzania.[75]

To accomplish this goal, Resolute worked with two experienced Tanzanian facilitators to help run a participatory planning exercise with four villages close to the Golden Pride Mine in the Nzega District, Tabora Region of western Tanzania to elaborate a Community Action Plan. The company continued

72 U.N., Agenda 21, ch. 40.

73 Ozaki and Shaw, "Citizens' Social Participation," 16.

74 IRMA, *IRMA Standard for Responsible Mining*, 31. See also, ICMM, "Handling and Resolving Local-level Concerns and Grievances."

75 Catherine Macdonald, "The Role of Participation in Sustainable Community Development Programmes in the Extractive Industries," in *Extractive Industries: The Management of Resources as a Driver of Sustainable Development*, eds. Tony Addison and Alan Roe (New York: Oxford University Press, 2018), 605.

to expand this work, eventually conducting similar processes in twenty-nine villages by the end of 2006 with mixed success. While acknowledging there is no study evaluating the outcome of Resolute's approach, McDonald still commends the company for these efforts to build the community's capacity 'to make their own choices and learn from their successes and failures.'[76]

Since that earlier experience, the company continued to emphasize its commitment to 'sharing the benefits of its operations through investment in sustainable development initiatives' such as water and sanitation, community health, education, income generation, and accountability. Significantly, this commitment includes tapping into the 'inherent strengths, skills and capacities' of all stakeholders, including local communities. As the company proclaims, 'Resolute is proud and willing to help communities to reach their development goals.'[77]

Notably, In 2019 the company publicised its 'Sustainability Performance Framework (SPF)' to advance its commitment to 'international standards of good practice in the areas of social development and human rights, environmental protection, and health and safety and labour rights.'[78] The company also recognised 'the significance of the UN Sustainable Development Goals (SDGs) adopted in 2015' and pledged to align its environmental and social activities 'to support the achievement of the SDGs.'[79]

In developing its approach to both BHR and the SDGs, Resolute presents a more holistic approach to engaging with communities that includes both ongoing proactive outreach and dialogue as well as an OGM. As explained by the company:

> Resolute understands the importance of regular and transparent communication. The Company engages with communities surrounding its mine sites through a number of permanent and ad hoc consultation structures. In addition, we meet regularly with local government representatives from local and regional centres. … We aim to develop positive relations with local communities built on trust and transparency. We

76 Macdonald, "Extractive Industries," 605.

77 Resolute, *2019 Annual Report* (Perth, Australia: Resolute Mining Limited, 2020), 23.

78 These standards include the World Gold Council's Responsible Gold Mining Principles (RGMPs), Performance standards of the International Finance Corporation, Sustainability Principles of the International Council on Metals and Mining, the UN Guiding Principles on Business and Human Rights, the Voluntary Principles on Security and Human Rights, and the International Cyanide Management Code. Resolute, *2019 Annual Report*, 7.

79 Resolute, *2019 Annual Report*, 7.

> respond to community concerns through formal grievance mechanisms. Most concerns arise from miscommunication and are quickly resolved without formal registration under our grievance mechanism process or as a community incident.[80]

The company integrated a new Human Rights Policy in 2020 with an updated 'Community Complaints & Grievance Procedure' in order to include 'a human rights flag' that would provide a pathway for complaints related to human rights to be escalated to an executive committee.[81]

6 The Common Challenge: Assuring Effective Dialogue and Meaningful Participation

Proponents of participation in both fields point to its many benefits, especially in its capacity to empower local populations.[82] For that reason, the literature point towards the 'need' for broad participation, while spending less effort to better understand the 'requirements to promote participation and the effects of citizen participation.'[83] In a recent comprehensive study of community development projects funded by the World Bank, it was confirmed that '[i]n practice, little is known about how best to foster [community] engagement.'[84] Not surprisingly, the same observation has been made in the field of BHR in which there has been some discussion, but not yet a well-seasoned understanding of how to best foster stakeholder engagement that is truly effective.[85]

Notably, the OGM Research Project also diagnosed this issue as one of the more pressing areas in need of development. Specifically, only 1% (8) of the 618 companies reviewed indicated publicly that their mechanism included some form of mediation, dialogue, facilitation, or capacity building. This finding suggests that companies are falling short of UNGP Principle 31(h), which instructs

80 Resolute, *2019 Annual Report*, 23.

81 "Modern Slavery Voluntary Statement," Resolute, June 7, 2021, https://modernslaveryregister.gov.au/statements/file/d8607ca4-266b-4331-b493-7130824e0665/.

82 Ozaki and Shaw, "Citizens' Social Participation," 2.

83 Ozaki and Shaw, "Citizens' Social Participation," 14.

84 Ghazala Mansuri and Vijayendra Rao, *Localizing Development: Does Participation Work?* (Washington DC: International Bank for Reconstruction and Development / The World Bank, 2013), 1.

85 Shuana Curphey and Jared Cole, "Stakeholder Engagement," in *A Guide to Human Rights Due Diligence for* Lawyers, eds. Corinne E. Lewis and Constance Z. Wagner (Chicago: American Bar Association Publishing, 2023), 226.

that company grievance mechanisms should be 'Based on engagement and dialogue: consulting the stakeholder groups for whose use they are intended on their design and performance and focusing on dialogue as the means to address and resolve grievances.'[86]

Thus, the proposed linkage between development stakeholder engagement and OGMs remains largely theoretical, albeit remaining a promising idea. Left pending is to gather more concrete examples to begin to grow a solid understanding of what, exactly, constitutes meaningful participation both in terms of development, but also in any grievance process that arises during these projects.

Acknowledgement

I thank Eman Elshrafi for her excellent research assistance with the development of this chapter.

Bibliography

Books

Bebbington, Anthony, ed. Social Conflict, Economic Development and Extractive Industry: Evidence from South America. New York: Routledge, 2012.

Craik, Neil. The International Law of Environmental Impact Assessment: Process, Substance and Integration. Cambridge: Cambridge University Press, 2008.

Ruggie, John Gerard. Just Business: Multinational Corporations and Human Rights. New York: W.W. Norton & Company, Inc., 2013.

Chapters in Edited Books

Craik, Neil. "Principle 17: Environmental Impact Assessment." In The Rio Declaration on Environment and Development: A Commentary, edited by Jorge E. Viñuales, 451–70. New York: Oxford University Press, 2015.

Curphey, Shuana, and Jared Cole. "Stakeholder Engagement." In A Guide to Human Rights Due Diligence for Lawyers, edited by Corinne E. Lewis and Constance Z. Wagner, 219–242. Chicago: American Bar Association Publishing, 2023.

86 U.N., Guiding Principles, principle 31(h).

Ebbesson, Jonas. "Principle 10: Public Participation." In The Rio Declaration on Environment and Development: A Commentary, edited by Jorge E. Viñuales, 287–310. New York: Oxford University Press, 2015.

George, Erika R., and Lisa J. Laplante. "Access to Remedy: Treaty Talks and the Terms of a New Accountability Accord." In Building a Treaty on Business and Human Rights: Context and Contours, edited by Surya Deva and David Bilchitz, 377–407. New York: Cambridge University Press, 2018.

Häusler, Katharina, Karin Lukas, and Julia Planitzer. "Non-Judicial Remedies: Company-based Grievance Mechanisms and International Arbitration." In Human Rights in Business: Removal of Barriers to Access to Justice in the European Union, edited by Juan José Álvarez Rubio and Katerina Yiannibas, 78–118. London: Routledge, 2017.

Laplante, Lisa J. "Making the Connection: Operational-Level Grievance Mechanisms and Human Rights Due Diligence." In A Guide to Human Rights Due Diligence for Lawyers, edited by Corinne E. Lewis and Constance Z. Wagner, 195–218. Chicago: American Bar Association Publishing, 2023.

Macdonald, Catherine. "The Role of Participation in Sustainable Community Development Programmes in the Extractive Industries." In Extractive Industries: The Management of Resources as a Driver of Sustainable Development, edited by Tony Addison and Alan Roe, 591–610. New York: Oxford University Press, 2018.

Journal Articles

Boiral, Olivier, Iñaki Heras-Saizarbitoria, and Marie-Christine Brotherton. "Improving Environmental Management through Indigenous Peoples' Involvement." Environmental Science & Policy 103 (2020): 10–20.

Calvano, Lisa. "Multinational Corporations and Local Communities: A Critical Analysis of Conflict." Journal of Business Ethics 82 (2008): 793–805.

Cesar, Saenz, and Ostos Jhony. "Making or Breaking Social License to Operate in the Mining Industry: Factors of the Main Drivers of Social Conflict." Journal of Cleaner Production 278 (2021).

Farrell, Leanne A., Ralph Hamann, and Eric Mackres. "A Clash of Cultures (and lawyers): Anglo Platinum and Mine-affected Communities in Limpopo Province, South Africa." Resources Policy 37, no. 2 (2012): 194–204.

Faruque, M. Omar. "The Politics of Extractive Industry Corporate Practices: An Anatomy of a Company-community Conflict in Bangladesh." The Extractive Industries and Society 5, no. 1 (2018): 177–189.

Foster, George K. "Community Participation in Development." Vanderbilt Journal of Transnational Law 51, no.1 (2018): 39–99.

Fraser, Jocelyn. "Mining Companies and Communities: Collaborative Approaches to Reduce Social Risk and Advance Sustainable Development," Resources Policy 74 (2021).

Grama, Benjamin. “Company-Administered Grievance Processes for External Stakeholders: A Means for Effective Remedy, Community Relations, or Private Power?” Wisconsin International Law Journal 39, no. 1 (2022): 71–143.

Kemp, Deanna, John R. Owen, Nora Gotzmann, and Carol J. Bond. “Just Relations and Company–Community Conflict in Mining.” Journal of Business Ethics 101 (2011): 93–109.

Kowszyk, Yanina, Frank Vanclay, and Rajiv Maher. “Conflict Management in the Extractive Industries: A Comparison of Four Mining Projects in Latin America.” The Extractive Industries and Society 13 (2023).

Laplante, Lisa J. “The Wild West of Company-Level Grievance Mechanisms: Drawing Normative Borders to Patrol the Privatization of Human Rights Remedies.” Harvard International Law Journal 64, no. 2 (2023): 311–384.

Laplante, Lisa J., and Suzanne Spears. “Out of the Conflict Zone: The Case for Community Consent Processes in the Extractive Sector.” Yale Human Rights & Development Law Journal 11 (2008): 69–116.

McNeish, John Andrew. “Resource Extraction and Conflict in Latin America.” Colombia Internacional 93 (2018): 3–16.

Millones, Jorge. “Conga Mines: Development as Conflict in Peru.” South Atlantic Quarterly 115, no. 3 (2016): 640–647.

Oh, Chang Hoon, Jiyoung Shin, and Shuna Shu Ham Ho. “Conflicts between Mining Companies and Communities: Institutional Environments and Conflict Resolution Approaches.” Business Ethics, the Environment & Responsibility 32, no. 2 (2023): 638–656.

Ozaki, Yasutaka, and Rajib Shaw. “Citizens’ Social Participation to Implement Sustainable Development Goals (SDGs): A Literature Review.” Sustainability 14, no. 21 (2022): 1–18.

Palassis, Stathis N. “Beyond the Global Summits: Reflecting on the Environmental Principles of Sustainable Development.” Colorado Journal of International Environmental Law and Policy 22, no. 1 (2011): 41–77.

Paredes, Maritza. “The Glocalization of Mining Conflict: Cases from Peru.” The Extractive Industries and Society 3, no. 4 (2016): 1046–1057.

Sternberg, Troy. “Conflict and Contestation in Kyrgyz Mining Infrastructure.” The Extractive Industries and Society 7, no. 4 (2020): 1392–1400.

Torres-Wong, Marcela, & Adrian Jimenez-Sandoval. “Indigenous Resource Governance as an Alternative to Mining: Redefining the Boundaries of Indigenous Participation.” The Extractive Industries and Society 9 (2022).

Triscritti, Fiorella. “Mining, Development and Corporate–community Conflicts in Peru.” Community Development Journal 48, no. 3 (2013): 437–450.

Westra, Laura. “The Conflict Between Development and the Right of the Child to Health.” Denver Journal of International Law and Policy 42, no. 1 (2013): 1–18.

Wielga, Mark, and James Harrison. "Assessing the Effectiveness of Non-State-Based Grievance Mechanisms in Providing Access to Remedy for Rightsholders: A Case Study of the Roundtable on Sustainable Palm Oil." Business and Human Rights Journal 6, no. 1 (2021): 67–92.

Woods, Cindy S. "'It isn't a State Problem': The Minas Conga Mine Controversy and the Need for Binding International Obligations of Corporate Actors." Georgetown Journal of International Law 46 (2015): 629–683.

Online/Internet Sources

Economist Impact. "Social Conflict in Peru's Mining Sector." January 3, 2013. https://impact.economist.com/sustainability/ecosystems-resources/social-conflict-in-perus-mining-sector..

ICMM. "Handling and Resolving Local-level Concerns and Grievances: Human Rights in the Mining and Metals Sector." December 10, 2019. https://www.icmm.com/en-gb/guidance/social-performance/2019/grievance-mechanism.

Manyika, James, Michael Birshan, Sven Smit, Jonathan Woetzel, Kevin Russell, and Lindsay Purcell. "A new look at how corporations impact the economy and households." McKinsey Global Institute. May 31, 2021. https://www.mckinsey.com/capabilities/strategy-and-corporate-finance/our-insights/a-new-look-at-how-corporations-impact-the-economy-and-households#/.

New England Law | Boston. "Operational Level Grievance Mechanism Research Project." Accessed September 5, 2023. https://www.nesl.edu/practical-experiences/centers/center-for-international-law-and-policy/projects/operational-grievance-mechanisms-project.

Resolute. "Modern Slavery Voluntary Statement." Resolute. June 7, 2021. https://modernslaveryregister.gov.au/statements/file/d8607ca4-266b-4331-b493-7130824e0665/.

Reports

Burger, Julian. Indigenous Peoples, Extractive Industries and Human Rights. Belgium: European Parliament, 2014.

International Finance Corporation (IFC). Good Practice Note: Addressing Grievances from Project-Affected Communities. Washington DC: International Finance Corporation, 2009.

International Resource Panel. Mineral Resource Governance in the 21st Century: Gearing Extractive Industries Towards Sustainable Development. Nairobi: United Nations Environment Programme, 2020.

Mansuri, Ghazala, and Vijayendra Rao. Localizing Development: Does Participation Work? Washington DC: International Bank for Reconstruction and Development / The World Bank, 2013.

OECD. Due Diligence Guidance for Meaningful Stakeholder Engagement in the Extractive Sector. Paris: OECD Publishing, 2017.

Resolute. 2019 Annual Report. Perth, Australia: Resolute Mining Limited, 2020.

Secretariat of the Convention on Biological Diversity. Akwé: Kon Voluntary Guidelines for the Conduct of Cultural, Environmental and Social Impact Assessment regarding Developments Proposed to Take Place on, or which are Likely to Impact on, Sacred Sites and on Lands and Waters Traditionally Occupied or Used by Indigenous and Local Communities. Montreal: Secretariat of the Convention on Biological Diversity, 2004.

World Bank Group. World Bank Management Group Response: Striking a Better Balance – The World Bank Group and Extractive Industries: The Final Report of the Extractive Industries Review. Washington, D.C.: International Bank for Reconstruction and Development/The World Bank, 2004.

Working Papers and the Like

Belanger, Olivia, and Brianna Tsui. "Periodic Project Report: 2021 Trends and General Practices of Company Operational-Level Grievance Mechanisms." The Center for International Law & Policy, New England Law | Boston, 2022.

Belanger, Olivia, and Lisa J. Laplante. "Periodic Project Report: Trends and General Practices of Company Operational-Level Grievance Mechanisms." The Center for International Law & Policy, New England Law | Boston, 2021.

Corporate Social Responsibility Initiative. "Rights-Compatible Grievance Mechanisms: A Guidance Tool for Companies and their Stakeholders." Corporate Social Responsibility Initiative, Working Paper No. 41, Harvard University Kennedy School of Government, Cambridge, MA, 2008.

Initiative for Responsible Mining Assurance (IRMA). IRMA Standard for Responsible Mining IRMA-STD-001. June 2018. https://responsiblemining.net/wp-content/uploads/2018/07/IRMA_STANDARD_v.1.0_FINAL_2018-1.pdf.

Laplante, Lisa J., Brianna Tsui, and Nicole Symonds. "Periodic Project Report: 2022 Trends and General Practices of Company Operational-Level Grievance Mechanisms." The Center for International Law & Policy, New England Law | Boston, 2023 forthcoming.

Rees, Caroline. "Corporations and Human Rights: Accountability Mechanisms for Resolving Complaints and Disputes." Corporate Social Responsibility Initiative, Report No. 15, Harvard University Kennedy School of Government, Cambridge, MA, 2007.

Rees, Caroline. "Access to Remedies for Corporate Human Rights Impacts: Improving Non-Judicial Mechanisms." Corporate Social Responsibility Initiative, Report No. 32, Harvard University Kennedy School of Government, Cambridge, MA, 2008.

Rees, Caroline. "Grievance Mechanisms for Business and Human Rights: Strengths, Weaknesses and Gaps." Corporate Social Responsibility Initiative, Working Paper No. 40, Harvard University Kennedy School of Government, Cambridge, MA, 2008.

Rees, Caroline. "Piloting Principles for Effective Company-Stakeholder Grievance Mechanisms: A Report of Lessons Learned." Corporate Social Responsibility Initiative, Harvard University Kennedy School of Government, Cambridge, MA, 2011.

Rees, Caroline, and David Vermijs. "Mapping Grievance Mechanisms in the Business and Human Rights Arena." Corporate Social Responsibility Initiative, Report No. 28, Harvard University Kennedy School of Government, Cambridge, MA, 2008.

Wise, Holly, and Sokol Shtylla. "The Role of the Extractive Sector in Expanding Economic Opportunity." Corporate Social Responsibility Initiative, Report No. 18, Harvard University Kennedy School of Government, Cambridge, MA, 2007.

Zerk, Jennifer A. "Extraterritorial Jurisdiction: Lessons for the Business and Human Rights Sphere from Six Regulatory Areas." Corporate Social Responsibility Initiative, Working Paper No. 59, Harvard University Kennedy School of Government, Cambridge, MA, 2010.

Treaties

Convention on Access to Information, Public Participation in Decision-Making and Access to Justice in Environmental Matters. June 25, 1998. 38 I.L.M. 517. 2161 U.N.T.S. 447.

International Labour Organisation (ILO). Convention (No. 169) Concerning Indigenous and Tribal Peoples in Independent countries. June 27, 1989. 1650 U.N.T.S. 383.

Protocol on Environmental Protection to the Antarctic. Oct. 4, 1991. 30 I.L.M. 1461. 2941 U.N.T.S. 5778.

Rio Declaration on Environment and Development. June 13, 1992. 31 I.L.M. 874.

U.N. Convention on the Law of the Sea. Dec. 10, 1982. 1833 U.N.T.S. 397.

U.N. Convention on Environmental Impact Assessment in a Transboundary Context. Feb. 25, 1991. 1989 U.N.T.S. 309.

U.N. Convention on Biological Diversity. June 5, 1992. 31 I.L.M. 818. 1760 U.N.T.S. 79.

UN Documents

G.A. Res. 41/128. Declaration on the Right to Development. Dec. 4, 1986.

U.N. United Nations Conference on Environment & Development: Agenda 21. June 1992.

U.N. Comm. on Econ., Soc. and Cultural Rts. Substantive Issues Arising in the Implementation of the International Covenant on Economic, Social and Cultural Rights. E/C. 12.2000/4. Aug. 11, 2000.

U.N. General Assembly. Resolution 66/288: The Future We Want. A/RES/66/288. July 27, 2012.

U.N. General Assembly. Resolution 70/1: Transforming Our world: The 2030 Agenda for Sustainable Development. A/RES/70/1. Oct. 21, 2015.

U.N. Human Rights Council. Protect, Respect and Remedy: A Framework for Business and Human Rights: Report of the Special Representative of the Secretary-General on the Issue of Human Rights and Transnational Corporations and Other Business Enterprises, John Ruggie. A/HRC/8/5. April 7, 2008.

U.N. Human Rights Council. Report of the Special Representative of the Secretary-General on the Issue of Human Rights and Transnational Corporations and other Business Enterprises, John Ruggie: Business and Human Rights: Further Steps toward the Operationalization of the "Protect, Respect and Remedy" Framework. A/HRC/14/27. April 9, 2010.

U.N. Human Rights Council. Report of the Special Representative of the Secretary-General on the Issue of Human Rights and Transnational Corporations and Other Business Enterprises, John Ruggie: Addendum: Piloting Principles for Effective Company/Stakeholder Grievance Mechanisms: A Report of Lessons Learned. A/HRC/17/31/Add.1. May 24, 2011.

U.N. Human Rights Council. Resolution 17/4: Human Rights and Transnational Corporations and Other Business Enterprises. A/HRC/RES/17/4. July 6, 2011.

U.N. Human Rights Council. Report of the Special Rapporteur on the Rights of Indigenous Peoples, James Anaya. A/HRC/21/47. July 6, 2012.

U.N. Human Rights Council. Report of the Working Group on the Issue of Human Rights and Transnational Corporations and Other Business Enterprises: Addendum: Report from an Expert Workshop Entitled "Business Impacts and Non-judicial Access to Remedy: Emerging Global Experience" Held in Toronto in 2013. A/HRC/26/25/Add.3. April 28, 2014.

U.N. Office of the High Commissioner for Human Rights. Guiding Principles on Business and Human Rights: Implementing the United Nations "Protect, Respect and Remedy" Framework. HR/PUB/11/04. 2011.

Cases

Saramaka People v. Suriname, Preliminary Objections, Merits, Reparations, and Costs, Inter-Am. Ct. H.R., (ser. C) No. 172 (Nov. 28, 2007).

Saramaka People v. Suriname, Interpretation of the Judgment on Preliminary Objections, Merits, Reparations, and Costs, Inter-Am. Ct. H.R., (ser. C) No. 185 (Aug. 12, 2008).

Social and Economic Rights Action Center & the Center for Economic and Social Rights ('SERAC') v. Nigeria (Communication No. 155/96), African Commission on Human and People's Rights, ACHPR/COMM/A044/1 (May 27, 2002).

CHAPTER 14

Tort Law and the Scope of the Corporate Duty of Care in the Context of Business and Human Rights

Jindan-Karena Mann

1 Introduction

Over the course of the past several decades, increasing attention has been paid to human rights harms that arise in connection to business conduct. Although such harms can arise in all sorts of contexts, it is undeniable that the most severe and widespread impacts have been felt by the world's most vulnerable population, often those living in the Global South.[1] Victims of business-related human rights abuses tend to participate in or reside near business operations that are upstream in the supply chain, where the most salient risks related to business activities are concentrated. However, while the human rights impacts are most acutely felt by vulnerable subjects in the Global South, the decisions that give rise to their harms often originate in the boardrooms of large transnational corporations (TNCs) situated in the Global North. These powerful companies often decide on courses of action that have enormous ripple effects throughout extended global supply chains, such as when they make decisions about health and safety standards to be followed by their subsidiaries, or even when they place demands on suppliers to meet certain price and output thresholds.

Among the various strategies that have emerged to respond to business-related human rights abuses, the concept of legal liability for companies has gained significant traction. Specifically, there is a desirability to hold to account the largest, most powerful TNCs, which possess considerable influence over their business partners. These TNCs often use this leverage to prioritize their own profits over the people labouring or living in the vicinity of business activities in their supply chains. For example, large tech companies place enormous

1 The terms 'Global South' and 'Global North' are not necessarily geographic, nor are they permanent or strict categories. Instead, I use these terms to denote a position of political and epistemological global power. See Lena Salaymeh and Ralf Michaels, "Decolonial Comparative Law: A Conceptual Beginning," *Rabel Journal of Comparative and International Private Law* (*RabelsZ*) 86, no. 1 (January 2022): 166–188.

 | DOI:10.1163/9789004530942_015

pressure on the mining industry to extract and process high quantities of minerals to meet the consumer demand for new devices, even if they cannot guarantee that these resources are extracted without human rights risks.[2] Similarly, major fast-fashion brands compel garment factories to produce large amounts of clothing at fast turnaround rates and for low prices, often disregarding environmental, safety, and labour standards.[3] Ultimately, the powerful TNC's demands are usually met, as selling to these large conglomerates (or to the middle men who deal with them) is often the only way that raw materials or cheap labour providers can access global markets. Given the sway that TNCs hold over their entire supply chains, including entities several steps removed from the final products they sell, there is a growing consensus that TNCs are an appropriate subject of legal liability for business-related human rights abuses.

Despite calls to hold TNCs to account for their adverse human rights impacts, there are significant hurdles to establishing legal liability, most notably because of the distant and remote relationship between the TNCs and the victims of business-related human rights violations. This remoteness is spatial, as the headquarters of the TNCs are often located in the Global North, while the harms tend to occur in the Global South. It can also be temporal, as decisions made in Global North boardrooms sometimes happen months or years before the ultimate effects are felt by vulnerable people in the Global South. Moreover, the causal connection between TNCs and victims is often severed by the participation of intermediary parties in the supply chain. These parties, including subsidiaries or other business partners, have more direct interactions with the victims, and arguably, the harms can be more directly attributable to them.

This chapter focuses on addressing the issue of legal accountability in light of the aforementioned remoteness challenges. Part 2 argues that tort liability, especially the tort of negligence, has the potential to be a useful tool to hold TNCs liable in the context of business and human rights violations. Part 3 describes recent developments in UK case law, in which the tort law duty of care has been reframed to better accommodate the realities of transnational business and the resulting human rights impacts. While these developments are extremely promising, there remain some accountability gaps, which are

2 See Annie Kelly, "Apple and Google Named in US Lawsuit over Congolese Child Cobalt Mining Deaths," *The Guardian*, December 16, 2019, https://www.theguardian.com/global-development/2019/dec/16/apple-and-google-named-in-us-lawsuit-over-congolese-child-cobalt-mining-deaths.

3 See Sarah Hucal, "The Hidden Human Cost of Fast Fashion," *DW News*, July 12, 2018, https://www.dw.com/en/the-hidden-human-cost-of-fast-fashion/a-46577624.

also assessed in Part 3. In particular, these UK precedents may create some perverse incentives for parent companies to distance themselves from overseeing their business partners rather than assisting them in upholding human rights standards. Furthermore, the UK precedents fall short of clarifying the corporate standard of care for companies vis à vis business partners that are not subsidiaries. Part 3 also questions whether mandatory human rights due diligence obligations are necessary to close these accountability gaps. Finally, this chapter focuses on the substantive elements of tort (negligence) liability, and does not address broader procedural barriers to accountability, such as jurisdiction, *forum non conveniens*, or evidentiary or cost hurdles.

2 Business-Related Human Rights Violations and the Promise of Tort Liability

2.1 *Negligence Liability as a Tool for Addressing Business-Related Human Rights Harms*

Liability is widely regarded as a crucial component for preventing business-related human rights violations and providing victims with redress. However, the best approach to achieving this has been the subject of debate. Initially, efforts to create a framework to address business and human rights challenges tended to focus on the human rights law dimension. Some even purported to render corporations direct subjects of public international law, akin to States, by imposing binding human rights obligation directly on them.[4] These efforts were met with harsh scrutiny, especially from the business community, which argued that because companies were not members of human rights treaties, they should not be directly bound by them.

Tort liability, wherein a wrongful defendant is held liable to and pays damages to an injured plaintiff, is emerging as a viable avenue for accountability in the context of human rights. Tort law is arguably an appropriate field of law to respond to these types of harms, for a number of reasons, including its flexibility and the applicable standards. Furthermore, it provides the advantage of being able to respond promptly before more specific legal standards

---

4 See United Nations Economic and Social Council, *Norms on the Responsibilities of Transnational Corporations and Other Business Enterprises with Regard to Human Rights*, UN Doc. E/CN.4/Sub.2/2003/12/Rev.2. Geneva, 2003; *also* Nadia Bernaz, *Business and Human Rights History, Law and Policy: Bridging the Accountability Gap* (London: Routledge, 2016), 173–75.

are codified into black-letter law.[5] Tort law, and particularly the tort of negligence, is by its very nature responsive to societal change, as its standards rely on what is generally considered to be reasonable within a given context.[6] As Lord Nicholls of Birkenhead explained in *Attorney General of the British Virgin Islands v. Hartwell*,

> The law of negligence is not an area where fixed absolutes of universal application are appropriate. In each case the governing consideration is the underlying principle. The underlying principle is that reasonable foreseeability, as an ingredient of a duty of care, is a broad and flexible objective standard which is responsive to the infinitely variable circumstances of different cases. The nature and gravity of the damage foreseeable, the likelihood of its occurrence, and the ease or difficulty of eliminating the risk are all matters to be taken into account in the round when deciding whether as a matter of legal policy a duty of care was owed by the defendant to the plaintiff in respect of the damage suffered by him.[7]

As the discourse around how we expect TNCs to conduct themselves vis á vis those affected by their business activities evolves, so should the legal standards to which we hold them. In recent decades, significant changes have occurred, especially beginning with the promulgation of the *UN Guiding Principles on Business and Human Rights* and followed by the implementation of mandatory human rights due diligence laws in several European jurisdictions. These developments have reshaped our expectations of what constitutes reasonable corporate conduct. Consequently, when assessing whether a parent or lead company in a supply chain could have reasonably foreseen human rights harm, the growing awareness and evolving norms inevitably inform the scope of foreseeability and the duty of care.

Although tort law is responsive to societal change, it also operates within the bounds of whether new applications are justified. In the words of UK Supreme Court Justice Lord Toulson:

5 Leslie Bender, "Tort Law's Role as a Tool for Social Justice Struggle," *Washburn Law Journal* 37 (Winter 1998): 252.

6 See Femke Wijdekop, *Human Rights Obligations of Transnational Corporations in Tort Law* (Amsterdam: IUCN National Committee of the Netherlands, 2018), 23; Karen Ballentine and Mark B. Taylor (eds.), *Business and International Crimes: Assessing the Liability of Business Entities for Grave Violations of International Law* (Oslo: Fafo and International Peace Academy, 2004), 27; Bender, "Tort Law's Role," 252.

7 *Attorney General of the British Virgin Islands v. Hartwell* [2004] UKPC 12, para. 25.

> The development of the law of negligence has been by an incremental process rather than giant steps. The established method of the court involves examining the decided cases to see how far the law has gone and where is has refrained from going. From that analysis it looks to see whether there is an argument by analogy for extending liability to a new situation, or whether an earlier limitations is no longer logically or socially justifiable. In doing so it pays regard to the need for overall coherence. Often there will be a mixture of policy considerations to take into account.[8]

Tort law offers several advantages in comparison to its main alternative, criminal liability. For instance, the evidentiary standard is lower, and a plaintiff need only prove their case on preponderance of the evidence, rather than beyond a reasonable doubt. This is particularly relevant in the context of business and human rights in which remoteness presents a challenge, where "it may be less difficult to establish the element of causation under tort law than to establish that a corporation is criminally liable under a theory of aiding and abetting."[9] Moreover, tort lawsuits can be brought by individual victims, who do not need to rely on a prosecutor to commence a case. If successful, these victims can directly recover damages for the harms they have suffered, something that is not typical in criminal cases.[10]

Finally, tort law presents an appropriate legal response to business-related human rights harms because, unlike with criminal charges, a defendant can be held liable even if they did not intend the harm. In many cases, TNCs involved in human rights abuses do not have the intention to cause harms. Instead, they usually act negligently and irresponsibly, prioritising their profits over the welfare of those who might be adversely affected by their business decisions. As a Fafo Institute report explains:

> In certain cases, the concept of negligence may impute to business entities a minimum duty to avoid harming others in an unreasonable fashion. As such, it can be an effective tool in dispelling companies' claims that they did not know that war crimes or human rights violations were occurring, insofar as plaintiffs can demonstrate that a company failed to put in place the requisite protective systems to prevent such an outcome.

---

8 *Michael v. Chief Constable of South Wales Police* [2015] UKSC 2, para. 102.

9 Ballentine and Taylor (eds.), *Business and International Crimes*, 25.

10 See Eric Mongelard, "Corporate Civil Liability for Violations of International Humanitarian Law," *International Review of the Red Cross* 88, no. 863 (September 2006): 666.

> For example, if a company hires members of another state's military forces for security purposes but fails to take sufficient measures to prevent them from torturing civilians in the course of providing 'security,' it is conceivable that the company's failure to implement protective measures could result in a determination of negligence, and that it would be required by a court to compensate the harmed individuals.[11]

2.2 *Barriers to Establishing Tort Liability in the Context of Remote Business and Human Rights Cases*

Despite the promises of tort liability, challenges remain. The remoteness between potential victim-plaintiffs and TNC-defendants poses a significant barrier for establishing liability in the context of business-related human rights violations. As a legal matter, two aspects stand out that contribute most to this challenge: 1) the doctrines of separate legal personality and limited liability, and 2) the question of whether liability should arise when the causal chain includes the involvement of a third party.[12]

The doctrine of separate legal personality means that business entities are considered as legally separate and autonomous, regardless of the links of ownership and/or control between them.[13] The limited liability doctrine creates a corporate veil between distinct legal entities so that a parent company is normally not liable for the debts or infractions of its subsidiaries.[14] Thus, for example, a parent/holding company could own 100% stake in its subsidiary, but because it is legally a separate entity, it will not be held liable for the wrongful acts of its subsidiary. These doctrines obviously pose a challenge when trying to hold TNCs responsible for human rights harms that occur in connection to business activities which are more directly related to the subsidiary.

---

11 Ballentine and Taylor (eds.), *Business and International Crimes*, 27.

12 Notwithstanding a provision on complicit or accessory liability, which most tort law regimes do not contain.

13 Rachel Chambers, "Parent Company Direct Liability for Overseas Human Rights Violations: Lessons from the U.K. Supreme Court," *University of Pennsylvania Journal of International Law* 42, no. 3 (2021): 530.

14 Mukarrum Ahmed, "Private International Law and Substantive Liability Issues in Tort Litigation against Multinational Companies in the English Courts: Recent UK Supreme Court Decisions and Post-Brexit Implications," *Journal of Private International Law* 18, no. 1 (2022): 57; Radu Mares, "Liability within Corporate Groups: Parent Companies' Accountability for Subsidiary Human Rights Abuses," in *Research Handbook on Business and Human Rights*, eds. Surya Deva and David Birchall (Northampton, MA: Edward Elgar Publishing, 2020), 446; Gwynne Skinner, "Rethinking Limited Liability of Parent Corporations for Foreign Subsidiaries' Violations of International Human Rights Law," *Washington and Lee Law Review* 72, no. 4 (2015): 1772.

Furthermore, while many global business conglomerates are structured as parents and subsidiaries, many others conduct their global business with contractual partners, thus creating extenuated and complex supply chains in which the different links along it are all legally entirely independent, while in practice they operate as one large global enterprise.

Limited liability was intended to stimulate arms-length investment by reducing risk, but in the modern global context, it arguably does not function the way it was intended to.[15] Indeed, many scholars argue that it was never even intended to apply to tort claims.[16] While limiting liability in the context of contract law is fair because the parties agree to interact in the first place, tort victims do not avail themselves to that relationship generally.[17] Therefore, while it might be acceptable in a context in which parties that have entered into contractual relationships with the business, for tort creditors – such as victims of human rights abuses – it presents a fundamental unfairness.[18]

Moreover, the limited liability doctrine was developed at a time when corporations were not permitted to own shares in other corporations, meaning that the parent–subsidiary relationship did not exist, and thus its application to shield parent companies presents a myriad of unforeseen consequences.[19] Sarah Joseph questions 'whether the *raison d'etre* of limited liability justifies its application to TNCs. For example, TNCs, with all of their economic wealth and power, are hardly the 'entrepreneurial upstarts' for whom the protection of limited liability was originally designed'.[20]

Even more importantly, the limited liability doctrine can actually create injustices in some circumstances, as it has the potential to generate situations in which externalities occur because the parent or lead company is not legally liable for the damages created by its subsidiary's operations, and the subsidiary is not solvent enough, or is even dissolved before damages can be adjudicated and paid.[21] As Christopher Peterson notes, '[w]hen a business entity invokes

15 See Grietje Baars, *The Corporation, Law and Capitalism: A Radical Perspective on the Role of Law in the Global Political Economy* (Leiden: Brill Nijhoff, 2019), 71.

16 Skinner, "Rethinking Limited Liability," 1792.

17 Ibid, 1792–93.

18 Christopher W. Peterson, "Piercing the Corporate Veil by Tort Creditors," *Journal of Business and Technology Law* 13, no. 1 (2017): 64.

19 Chambers, "Parent Company Direct Liability," 530, *quoting* Phillip I. Blumberg, "Accountability of Multinational Corporations: The Barriers Presented by Concepts of Corporate Juridical Entity," *Hastings International and Comparative Law Review* 24 (2001): 300–304.

20 Sarah Joseph, *Corporations and Transnational Human Rights Litigation* (Oxford: Hart Publishing, 2004), 131.

21 Mares, "Liability within Corporate Groups," 447.

the principles of limited liability, it typically means that some other party is bearing the costs'.[22] Of course, in the context at hand, the victim of business-related human rights abuses and their home State are usually the ones saddled with the cost of the harm. This results in a moral hazard problem, in which "the company will be more likely to engage in activities with social costs that exceed their social benefit."[23]

The separate legal personality and limited liability doctrines create a disconnect between law on the one hand, and the reality of the interconnectedness of global value chains on the other hand, and thus, while 'trade has been globalized – justice not yet'.[24] As John Ruggie wrote in his seminal report, *Protect, Respect and Remedy: A Framework for Business and Human Rights*,

> [T]he legal framework regulating transnational corporations operates much as it did long before the recent wave of globalization. A parent company and its subsidiaries continue to be construed as distinct legal entities. Therefore, the parent company is generally not liable for wrongs committed by a subsidiary, even where it is the sole shareholder, unless the subsidiary is under such close operational control by the parent that it can be seen as its mere agent. Furthermore, despite the transformative changes in the global economic landscape generated by offshore sourcing, purchasing goods and services even from sole suppliers remains an unrelated party transaction. Factors such as these make it exceedingly difficult to hold the extended enterprise accountable for human rights harms.[25]

The Commentary to the *UN Guiding Principles on Business and Human Rights* also notes that the way in which legal responsibility is attributed among members of a corporate group presents '[l]egal barriers that can prevent legitimate cases involving business-related human rights abuse from being addressed' and calls on States to ensure that such barriers are eliminated. Indeed, one way

22 Peterson, "Piercing the Corporate Veil," 64.

23 Ibid, 65; *also* Mares, "Liability within Corporate Groups," 462.

24 Cees van Dam, "Tort Law and Human Rights: Brothers in Arms On the Role of Tort Law in the Area of Business and Human Rights," *Journal of European Tort Law* 2, no. 3 (2001): 221; Claire Bright et al., "Toward a Corporate Duty for Lead Companies To Respect Human Rights in Their Global Value Chains?," *Business and Politics* 22, no. 4 (2020): 672.

25 John Ruggie, "Protect, Respect and Remedy: A Framework for Business and Human Rights," *Report of the Special Representative of the Secretary-General on the issue of human rights and transnational corporations and other business enterprises*, UN Doc. A/HRC/8/5, 2008, para. 13.

to circumvent this barrier is to reconceptualise the law and focus on whether parent companies might owe a duty of care directly to the victims of their foreign subsidiaries.[26]

In addition to the archaic corporate rules highlighted above, third-party involvement presents another legal challenge when conceptualising TNC liability for business-related human rights harms. Generally, a person can only be liable in tort for damage caused by their own intentional or negligent behaviour. Thus, when a corporation is not the primary perpetrator of a harmful act, liability can only be successful if its conduct directly contributed to the harm suffered in some way. This principle is derived from the general rule that a mere omission does not result in liability. In other words, while misfeasance (making something worse) justifies imposing liability, nonfeasance (merely failing to make something better) does not.

This distinction, however, can be a red herring when conceptualising liability in the context of an intervention by a third party, such as is the case with many business-related human rights violations.[27] In such cases, some might argue that, absent an affirmative duty to intervene, a corporation should not be liable for failing to prevent their subsidiary or business partner's harmful conduct. However, this approach does not take into account that often, powerful TNCs are not simply failing to uphold the human rights of victims up their supply chain. Instead, they take decisions regarding timeline, production quantity, costs, safety standards, and a host of other matters that have far-reaching effects along their entire supply chains, including on the commission of human rights violations in some instances.

Another argument against indirect liability is the reluctance to hold a person liable when there is also third-party involvement, because it makes the defendant responsible for the actions of another person who has their own agency and power to decide what they do.[28] However, the nature of the tort duty of care turns in part on whether the harm was foreseeable, even when there are several links in the causal chain. While it might be difficult for a defendant to foresee what another person will do in an isolated instance, when a pattern of harm arises, then a defendant can arguably foresee the risks regardless of whether there are intermediary third-party actors also involved. Thus, while a one-off instance of a random adverse human rights impact might not create the conditions to impose a duty of care, repeated patterns most certainly

26 See Ahmed, "Private International Law," 57.

27 See Claire MacIvor, *Third Party Liability in Tort* (Oxford: Hart Publishing, 2006).

28 Except when vicarious liability is justified, such as the liability of a parent for their child, or an employer for their employee.

should if the defendant decides to engage in risky conduct regardless of a foreseeable consequential harm.

Ultimately, tort law needs to do what tort law does best: respond to societal needs and adjust with changing times and developing expectations of reasonable conduct. This means that in today's world, when tort law is applied to contexts of transnational harm involving TNCs, it should be applied in light of the fact that the global economy is closely interconnected yet deeply asymmetrical, and in which powerful companies are able to exert enormous leverage. This requires a recognition that conceptually, although they seem to be remote, plaintiffs and defendants in business and human rights cases are indeed closely situated through their business links.

As the next Section 3 of this chapter illustrates in more detail, recent tort cases in UK courts are clarifying that the barriers raised here, the doctrines of separate legal personality and limited liability and the question of third party involvement, can be overcome. This, however, demands that courts consider business and human rights cases within the context in which they arise, taking into account the interconnectedness of global supply chains, and the asymmetrical power and leverage that TNCs hold within them. In this way, the tort duty of care can properly be understood in light of these scenarios, in which decisions by powerful companies have direct and traceable impacts on the human rights of victims far removed. Thus, when courts focus on the TNC-defendant's conduct, and how its decision to proceed despite foreseeable risks of serious harms might be a negligent decision, it becomes clear that the challenges raised in this section are nothing more than unjustifiable barriers to justice.

3 The *Vedanta* and Other UK Cases: Turning Ideals into Law

The time is ripe for courts to recognise that corporations have a duty of care that extends as wide as the due diligence obligations enshrined in the *UN Guiding Principles on Business and Human Rights*.[29] Moreover, this recognition would not be expanding liability unjustly; it would be in line with way tort liability has always been applied in response to societal needs and in light of the given context. As Douglass Cassell argues, '[b]y recognizing this duty of care, courts would not impose on business enterprises any responsibility

29 Douglass Cassell, "Outlining the Case for a Common Law Duty of Care of Business to Exercise Human Rights Due Diligence," *Business and Human Rights Journal* 1 (2016): 180.

not already assigned to them by widely adopted international human rights standard, but would simply incorporate those standards into domestic law'.[30] Indeed, emerging case law from the UK, beginning first with the *Vedanta* precedent, is already recognising this duty.

3.1 *The Vedanta Precedent*

Vedanta Resources Plc and Another v. Lungowe and Others concerned claims by 1,826 Zambian farmers and fishers whose land and waterways were polluted by repeated discharges of toxic matter from the Nchanga Copper Mine in the Chingola District of Zambia, and which resulted in damages to their health and livelihood.[31] The plaintiffs sued both the mine's immediate owner, Zambian company Konkola Copper Mines plc (KCM), as well as KCM's parent company incorporated and domiciled in the UK, Vedanta Resources plc (Vedanta), alleging that the companies' negligence and breach of statutory duties were the cause of the damages they suffered as a result of the toxic dumping in their community.[32] Cognizant of the fact that it would be difficult to obtain justice in Zambian courts,[33] the plaintiffs filed their claims in the courts of England and Wales.

The inclusion of the parent company Vedanta would guarantee that the case would be heard in English courts, as at the time an EU Regulation imposed obligatory jurisdiction over UK-domiciled defendants. However, the defendants argued that the plaintiffs only joined Vedanta to the case in order to use it as an 'illegitimate hook [...] to permit claim to be brought here which would otherwise not be heard in the United Kingdom'.[34] Thus, the issue on interlocutory appeal was whether there was a 'real issue which is reasonable for the court to try' between the Zambian plaintiffs and the UK parent company.[35] In particular, because the plaintiffs alleged that Vedanta was negligent toward them, the court needed to assess whether there was an arguable duty of care owed by Vedanta to the remote Zambian plaintiffs.

The court's consideration of the parent companies' duty of care vis á vis plaintiffs in Zambia would have an enormous impact on the future of corporate accountability for business-related human rights violations. Whereas the

30 Ibid.

31 *Vedanta Resources Plc and Another v. Lungowe and Others*, [2019] UKSC 20, para.1; *Lungowe and Others v. Vedanta Resources Plc and Another*, [2017] EWCA Civ 1528, paras.15–18.

32 Vedanta, para. 2.

33 See Lungowe, paras. 118–135.

34 Ibid, para. 93.

35 Ibid, para. 41.

doctrine of separate legal entities generally means that a parent company such as Vedanta is not liable for the wrongs of its subsidiaries unless the corporate veil could be pierced, here, the plaintiffs argued not that Vedanta was vicariously liable for KCM's wrongdoing, but instead that it had breached a duty of care that it owed directly to the victims. Opening the door to parent-company liability would arguably reflect the reality of how transnational business works in practice, in which powerful transnational corporations are able to exert enormous leverage over their subsidiaries, and in some cases even significantly influence circumstances that give rise to adverse human rights impacts.

In order to establish that Vedanta owed a direct duty of care to the Zambian farmers and fishers who were harmed by the mine's toxic waste, the plaintiffs relied on a series of UK cases that had been promulgated in the years leading up to Vedanta, most notably a 2012 case *Chandler v. Cape Plc*. In *Chandler*, an employee contracted asbestosis at work, and by the time of his diagnosis, the subsidiary company that employed him had been dissolved so he sued its parent company to recover for his damages.[36] The plaintiff argued that the parent company, Cape Plc, owed him a duty of care directly, because it had been closely involved in the health and safety policies of its subsidiary, and has thus assumed responsibility over that aspect of the subsidiary's operations.[37] The court concluded that 'in appropriate circumstances the law may impose on a parent company responsibility for the health and safety of its subsidiary's employees', including where:

1) the business of the parent and the subsidiary are in a relevant respect the same;
2) the parent has, or ought to have, superior knowledge on some relevant aspect of health and safety in the particular industry;
3) the subsidiary's system of work is unsafe and the parent company know, or ought to have known; and
4) the parent knew or ought to have foreseen that the subsidiary or its employees would rely on it using that superior knowledge for the employee's protection.[38]

The court noted that Cape Plc was aware that its subsidiary was systematically failing to prevent employees from exposure to asbestos dust, and even appointed medical and scientific officers to conduct research on

36 *Chandler v. Cape Plc* [2012] EWCA Civ 525.
37 Ibid, para. 60.
38 Ibid, para. 80.

asbestos-related diseases.[39] Because it had superior knowledge about the nature and management of the risk and held itself out to be dealing with the risk and, the court held that 'Cape assumed a duty of care either to advise [its subsidiary] on what steps it had to take ... or to ensure the steps were taken'.[40]

The *Chandler* holding has some important implications on parent company liability. First, it clarified that even without piercing the corporate veil, there are some circumstances arising from the parent company's own acts or omissions that could give rise to the existence of a duty of owed to a plaintiff who is remotely situated to the parent company, and who has more directly interacted with its subsidiary.[41] This duty of care is not contingent on the status of the defendant as a parent company or its ownership of the subsidiary; instead, it turns on the degree of intervention, control, advice or supervision that the parent company exercised over the subsidiary.[42] Furthermore, the court in *Chandler* elucidated that liability could arise even in circumstances in which the parent company merely provided 'high level advice or strategy', and there is no need to show absolute control or interference over the subsidiaries relevant operations or policies.[43]

Relying on the *Chandler* precedent, the courts[44] in *Vedanta* elaborated on parent company liability. This opened the door for cases on business-related human rights violation that arise out of the negligent conduct of transnational parent companies, which are often domiciled far away from the location of the harm. Although the plaintiffs in *Vedanta* were not employees of the subsidiary, but instead residents in a community affected by subsidiary KCM's mining operations, the court upheld the *Chandler* precedent that in certain circumstances – if it avails itself to certain responsibilities – a parent company may owe a duty of care to victims who have been more directly impacted by its subsidiary. In a unanimous decision, the UK Supreme Court held that a parent company's liability in common law negligence in relation to the activities of its subsidiaries 'depends on the extent to which, and the way in which, the parent availed itself of the opportunity to take over, intervene in, control, supervise or advise the management of the relevant operations (including land use) of the subsidiary'.[45] It also clarified that this does not present a novel or controversial

39 See ibid, paras. 72–78.

40 Ibid, para. 78.

41 Ibid, para, 66.

42 Ibid, paras. 66–69.

43 Ibid, para. 66.

44 First the Court of Appeal in 2017, and then the Supreme Court in 2019.

45 Vedanta, para. 49.

extension of the boundaries of the tort of negligence, and thus this issue could be decided on interim appeal without a 'detailed investigation of the [...] case'.[46]

In its assessment of whether Vedanta could owe a duty of care to the plaintiffs as a result of its assumption of responsibility over the maintenance of environmental control over the mine's toxic waste discharge operations, the Court of Appeal relied on a number of factors.[47] It noted that Vedanta purported to have a governance framework in place to prevent water pollution at its mines in Zambia; that KCM was contractually obligated to provide KCM with support services and feasibility studies in relation to its mining operations; that Vedanta had provided training on a range of health, safety and environmental issues; that Vedanta provided extraordinary levels of financial support to KCM; that Vedanta has issued public statements regarding its commitment to addressing environmental risks and technical shortcomings in KCM's mines; and that Vedanta exercised a high degree of control over KCM's operational affairs, especially giving high-level positions at KCM to 'people from Vedanta Group companies'.[48] Based on the way that Vedanta had intervened, controlled, supervised and managed aspects of KCM's operations, and in particular its environmental risks, the court concluded that there was an arguable case to be made that Vedanta indeed owed a duty of care to the Zambian plaintiffs.

The Supreme Court upheld the Court of Appeal's holding, and further explained that there is no single overarching test to determine parent company duty of care.[49] Instead, Lord Briggs (author of the unanimous decision) posited that there were at least four possible routes by which such a duty could arise. First, a parent company might incur a duty of care when it has 'taken over the management of the relevant activity of the subsidiary in place of or jointly with the subsidiary's own management'.[50] Second, a duty of care might arise when a parent provides defective advice, or promulgates policies or guidelines that are implemented as a matter of course by the subsidiary but that fall short of protecting against the adverse impacts they purport to prevent.[51] Third, 'even

46 Ibid.

47 Lungowe, [84]; see also Vedanta, para. 61 (deferring to the Court of Appeal's holding that the facts show an arguably sufficient level of intervention by Vedanta to present a triable issue.)

48 Lungowe, para. 84.

49 Vedanta, para. 52.

50 Ibid, para. 51.

51 Ibid, para. 52.

where group-wide policies do not of themselves give rise to such a duty of care to third parties, they may do so if the parent does not merely proclaim them, but takes active steps, by training, supervision and enforcement, to see that they are implemented by relevant subsidiaries.'[52] And finally, if a parent company holds itself out to exercise a certain degree of supervision or control over its subsidiary, it may incur liability even if it does not in fact follow through.[53]

The Vedanta holding, and in particular the Supreme Court's elaboration on the four potential routes to establishing a parent company duty of care, was an instrumental factor in a subsequent case, *Okpabi and others v Royal Dutch Shell Plc and another*. In *Okpabi*, the Court of Appeals dismissed the plaintiffs' claim against the parent company for a lack of an arguable duty of care.[54] In addition to rejecting the Court of Appeal's application of a stringent approach used to determine the existence of a novel duty of care,[55] the Supreme Court asserted that a parent company's imposition of a group-wide policy or standards on its subsidiaries can, in some cases, give rise to liability, regardless of whether the parent company actually engaged in operational activities of the subsidiary.[56]

The *Vedanta* precedent has already influenced the adjudication of a similar cases, thus demonstrating the potential the precedent has for parent-company accountability for business-related human rights abuses committed abroad. In *Four Nigerian Farmers and Stichting Milieudefensie v. Shell*, a Dutch court, applying Nigerian law, relied on *Chandler* and *Vedanta* to find a parent company owed victims of its subsidiary a duty of care.[57] However, the Dutch court's approach was narrower than the UK precedent, as it relied on the more restrictive criteria that is typically reserved for novel duties of care, and furthermore held that in order for a parent company to incur a duty of care, the subsidiary must itself have been at fault.[58]

---

52 Ibid, para. 53.

53 Ibid.

54 *Okpabi and Others v. Royal Dutch Shell plc and Another*, [2018] EWCA Civ 191.

55 *Caparo Industries Plc v. Dickman* [1990] 2 AC 605 sets out a three-part test to determine whether a duty of care exists in novel situations: (1) whether there is sufficient proximity between the parties to impose a duty; (2) whether the harm is reasonably foreseeable as a result of the defendant's conduct; and (3) whether it is fair, just and reasonable to impose liability.

56 *Okpabi and Others v. Royal Dutch Shell plc and Another*, [2021] UKSC 3 [143].

57 *Four Nigerian Farmers and Stichting Milieudefensie v. Shell*, ECLI:NL:GHDHA:2021:1825.

58 Lukas Roorda and Daniel Leader, "Okpabi v Shell and Four Nigerian Farmers v Shell: Parent Company Liability Back in Court," *Business and Human Rights Journal* 6, no 2 (2021): 373.

3.2 *Vedanta and Its (Potential) Perverse Incentives*

While the *Vedanta* case is a laudable step in the direction of holding TNCs to account for their adverse human rights impacts, it also risks creating some perverse incentives.[59] If the existence of a parent-company duty of care turns on how much the parent availed itself of the opportunity to take over, intervene in, control, supervise or advise operations that result in human rights harms, it might try to avoid liability by taking a hands-off approach to its business partners. Especially in industries in which powerful TNCs are the best equipped to develop and enforce standards for the protection of human rights and the environment, their exit from this arena could in fact have negative consequences.

Anil Yilmaz-Vastardis and Sheldon Leader suggest that there are

> [T]wo ways of fixing a duty of care on a supply chain actor: taking an action oriented approach, [in which] responsibility for damage done arises from an act that falls below a standard of reasonable care, with foreseeable damage [… or] a framework-oriented approach, [which] widens the enquiry, [and] examines the relationship between various bodies that might share in the responsibility for damage done.[60]

The language in *Vedanta* and the ensuing cases appear to focus mainly on the conduct of the parent companies; as Yilmaz-Vastardis and Leader argue '[f]ixing a duty on companies by following the action oriented approach, i.e. looking for initial steps by the businesses to regulate and mentor their supply chain partners, may create incentives for companies to take a hands-off approach to their supply chain relationships, which would result in no assumption of responsibility'.[61]

How can these perverse incentives be overcome? The framework approach may provide useful guidance. Under this approach, the focus is not on the specific actions taken by the parent company, but instead on the nature of the relationship between the defendant and the plaintiff, especially in light

---

59 See Anil Yilmaz-Vastardis and Sheldon Leader, *Improving Paths to Business Accountability for Human Rights Abuses in the Global Supply Chains: A Legal Guide* (Essex: University of Essex, December 2017), 9; Cassell, "Outlining the Case," 182.

60 Yilmaz-Vastardis and Leader, *Improving Paths*, 9; also Bright, et al., "Toward a Corporate Duty", 675 (classifying two approaches: the "classic" approach which requires the parent company to exert a high degree of control over the subsidiary's corporate decisions in order for liability to arise; and the "new approach", which turns on "the existence of a 'special relationship' between the two entities, which creates the expectations that control should be exercised by the former over the activities of the latter.").

61 Yilmaz-Vastardis and Leader, *Improving Paths*, 9.

of any special characteristics of the defendant, such as their ability to exert leverage far up the supply chain. According to Yilmaz-Vastardis and Leader a duty to act could be imposed on the defendant under these circumstances, regardless of whether the defendant had actively taken certain steps to assume responsibility.[62]

However, although tort law is by its very nature flexible and responsive to the societal needs, this approach might stretch its bounds beyond a justifiable scope.[63] As Yilmaz-Vastardis and Leader point out, 'unless such a due diligence obligation is made mandatory by legislation, it would be difficult to convince the courts that a business is under a duty to take those initial steps to identify, prevent, mitigate, and remediate abuses taking within its supply chain, as common law only recognises a duty of affirmative action in tort in exceptional circumstances'.[64]

3.3 *Assessing the Vedanta Precedent for Supply Chain Liability*

Another area where the UK precedents may fall short is that they address only parent company liability, and do not clarify the corporate standard of care for companies vis à vis business partners that are not subsidiaries. Given that the majority of global supply chains consist of separate entities that relate to each other via contractual relationships, rather than ownership links of parent and subsidiary companies, justice in the context of business and human rights demands that a duty of care is extended beyond just parent-subsidiary relationships to non-equity business relationships.

The *Vendanta* holding, which relies on the degree a company avails itself of the opportunity to take over, intervene in, control, supervise or advise operations that result in human rights harms, arguably makes its direct translation to the supply chain context difficult. Whereas parent companies can, and often do, oversee certain aspects of their subsidiary's operations, and issue enterprise-wide guidelines that apply to their subsidiaries, this is not necessarily true of supply chain relationships, especially when there are multiple intermediary 'middle-men'.

On the other hand, *Vedanta* clarifies that the existence of a duty of care hinges on whether the parent voluntarily assumes responsibility. This follows that if a TNC assumes responsibility in relation to its non-equity business partners, such as through contractual clauses, it might similarly have availed itself to responsibility. However, again the focus on specific acts of the lead

62 Ibid, 16.

63 See ibid, 25.

64 Ibid, 16.

company might create perverse incentive, as companies would omit human-rights based clauses, or even avoid publicly stipulating policies with regard to human rights violations within their supply chains, for fear of opening themselves up to liability.

Just as in the parent-company context, a framework approach, which focuses on the influence and leverage of a lead company on a supply chain over its business partners, rather than the specific acts that the lead company took, would aid in circumventing the perverse incentives. In this case, perhaps even more saliently than in the parent-subsidiary context, the existence of a mandatory human rights due diligence obligation would clarify that not only are lead companies expected to check their supply chains for risks, but they are also expected to prevent, avoid or mitigate them when they are detected.

4 Conclusion

Tort law is moving in the right direction to properly address business-related human rights harms, but further development is needed to provide a comprehensive response to all instances of business-related human rights harms. This chapter emphasises that the best way to fill the existing gaps would be to establish a mandatory human rights due diligence law, which would clarify their duty of care vis à vis those impacted by their business relations, regardless of the extent the TNC availed itself to any responsibility over the conduct that caused the harm.

Many European countries, and the European Union at large are considering and passing laws that would mandate human rights due diligence, through a Directive on corporate sustainability due diligence. However, since the UK has left the European Union, it will not be subject to the Directive, and does not appear inclined to pass a comprehensive human rights due diligence law.[65]

However, given developments worldwide, including through both hard and soft law, it can be argued that the notion of responsible corporate behaviour along supply chains is changing. For example, emerging mandatory human rights due diligence laws, which essentially codify the *UN Guiding Principles on Business and Human Rights*, crystalise the notion that there is a general expectation on companies to use their leverage and influence in ways that

65 In 2015, the UK passed the Modern Slavery Act, which addresses forced labour in supply chains. However, it only requires companies to disclose the efforts they have made to address modern slavery in their supply chains, without any obligation to prevent, avoid or mitigate.

are in line with human rights. Therefore, when a company places demand on their business partners that would likely result in human rights risks, it acts contrary to what is expected of a reasonable corporation engaging in transnational business. Consequently, the duty of care of TNCs should not only exist but also extend to remote victims who are connected in a common supply chain. These victims, although they might be spatially, temporally, and causally remote, are indeed impacted by decisions made in far-away boardrooms of the Global North.

Bibliography

Books

Baars, Grietje. *The Corporation, Law and Capitalism: A Radical Perspective on the Role of Law in the Global Political Economy*. Leiden: Brill Nijhoff, 2019.

Bernaz, Nadia. *Business and Human Rights History, Law and Policy: Bridging the Accountability Gap*. London: Routledge, 2016.

Deva, Surya, and David Birchall (eds). *Research Handbook on Business and Human Rights*. Northampton, MA: Edward Elgar Publishing, 2020.

Joseph, Sarah. *Corporations and Transnational Human Rights Litigation*. Oxford: Hart Publishing, 2004.

MacIvor, Claire. *Third Party Liability in Tort*. Oxford: Hart Publishing, 2006.

Reports

Ballentine, Karen, and Mark B. Taylor (eds.). *Business and International Crimes: Assessing the Liability of Business Entities for Grave Violations of International Law*. Oslo: Fafo and International Peace Academy, 2004.

Wijdekop, Femke. *Human Rights Obligations of Transnational Corporations in Tort Law*. Amsterdam: IUCN National Committee of the Netherlands, 2018.

Yilmaz-Vastardis, Anil, and Sheldon Leader. *Improving Paths to Business Accountability for Human Rights Abuses in the Global Supply Chains: A Legal Guide*. Essex: University of Essex, December 2017.

Journal Articles

Ahmed, Mukarrum. "Private International Law and Substantive Liability Issues in Tort Litigation against Multinational Companies in the English Courts: Recent UK Supreme Court Decisions and Post-Brexit Implications." *Journal of Private International Law* 18, no. 1 (2022): 56–82.

Bender, Leslie. "Tort Law's Role as a Tool for Social Justice Struggle." *Washburn Law Journal* 37 (Winter 1998): 249–60.

Bright, Claire, et al. "Toward a Corporate Duty for Lead Companies to Respect Human Rights in Their Global Value Chains?" *Business and Politics* 22, no. 4 (2020): 667–97.

Cassell, Douglass. "Outlining the Case for a Common Law Duty of Care of Business to Exercise Human Rights Due Diligence." *Business and Human Rights Journal* 1 (2016): 179–202.

Chambers, Rachel. "Parent Company Direct Liability for Overseas Human Rights Violations: Lessons from the U.K. Supreme Court." *University of Pennsylvania Journal of International Law* 42, no. 3 (2021): 519–79.

Mongelard, Eric. "Corporate Civil Liability for Violations of International Humanitarian Law." *International Review of the Red Cross* 88, no. 863 (September 2006): 665–691.

Peterson, Christopher W. "Piercing the Corporate Veil by Tort Creditors." *Journal of Business and Technology Law* 13, no. 1 (2017): 63–95.

Roorda, Lukas and Daniel Leader. "Okpabi v Shell and Four Nigerian Farmers v Shell: Parent Company Liability Back in Court." *Business and Human Rights Journal* 6, no 2 (2021): 368–76.

Skinner, Gwynne. "Rethinking Limited Liability of Parent Corporations for Foreign Subsidiaries' Violations of International Human Rights Law." *Washington and Lee Law Review* 72, no. 4 (2015): 1769–1864.

van Dam, Cees. "Tort Law and Human Rights: Brothers in Arms on the Role of Tort Law in the Area of Business and Human Rights." *Journal of European Tort Law* 2, no. 3 (2001): 221–54.

Cases

Attorney General of the British Virgin Islands v. Hartwell [2004] UKPC 12 (UK).

Caparo Industries Plc v. Dickman [1990] 2 AC 605 (UK).

Chandler v. Cape Plc [2012] EWCA Civ 525 (UK).

Four Nigerian Farmers and Stichting Milieudefensie v. Shell, ECLI:NL: GHDHA:2021:1825 (The Netherlands).

Lungowe and Others v. Vedanta Resources Plc and Another, [2017] EWCA Civ 1528 (UK).

Michael v. Chief Constable of South Wales Police [2015] UKSC 2 (UK).

Okpabi and Others v. Royal Dutch Shell plc and Another, [2018] EWCA Civ 191 (UK).

Okpabi and Others v. Royal Dutch Shell plc and Another, [2021] UKSC 3 (UK).

Vedanta Resources Plc and Another v. Lungowe and Others, [2019] UKSC 20 (UK).

UN Documents

Ruggie, John. "Protect, Respect and Remedy: A Framework for Business and Human Rights." *Report of the Special Representative of the Secretary-General on the issue of human rights and transnational corporations and other business enterprises*, UN Doc. A/HRC/8/5, 2008.

United Nations Economic and Social Council. *Norms on the Responsibilities of Transnational Corporations and Other Business Enterprises with Regard to Human Rights*, UN Doc. E/CN.4/Sub.2/2003/12/Rev.2., Geneva, 2003.

Newspaper

Hucal, Sarah. "The Hidden Human Cost of Fast Fashion." *DW News*, July 12, 2018. https://www.dw.com/en/the-hidden-human-cost-of-fast-fashion/a-46577624.

Kelly, Annie. "Apple and Google Named in US Lawsuit over Congolese Child Cobalt Mining Deaths." *The Guardian*, December 16, 2019. https://www.theguardian.com/global-development/2019/dec/16/apple-and-google-named-in-us-lawsuit-over-congolese-child-cobalt-mining-deaths.

CHAPTER 15

Lopsided Distribution of COVID Vaccines under Stringent Pharmaceutical Patent Law and Its Marginalising Effects on the Global South: A Reformist Human Rights Approach

Khorsed Zaman and M Rafiqul Islam

1 Setting the Context

Global health has been cataclysmically impacted by the COVID-19 pandemic, which has resulted in widespread sickness, fatalities, and substantial disruptions to healthcare systems across the world. As of December 2023, the total number of confirmed COVID cases worldwide surpassed 773 million, and the number of deaths attributed to the virus exceeded 6.9 million.[1] Despite the rapid development of several effective COVID vaccines within the first year of the pandemic, many countries struggled to accessing these vaccines partly due to restrictive patents and associated intellectual property rights (IPRS) laws. Pharmaceutical patents and related IPRS regulations result in production monopolies that raise costs and restrict availability,[2] resulting in inequitable access to vaccines between countries in the Global North and Global South, as well as between the rich and the poor within countries.

Access to COVID vaccinations, therapeutics, and pharmaceuticals continue to be a major concern globally. There is a significant disparity between access to vaccines in high, low, and middle-income countries.[3] The global distribution of COVID vaccines and allied pharmaceuticals has been asymmetric,

1 World Health Organisation, WHO Coronavirus (COVID-19) Dashboard, accessed June 5, 2022 <https://covid19.who.int/?gclid=EAIaIQobChMI7P7M6eKZ_wIVjWWLCh32ow3lEAAYASABEgIBjPD_BwE>.

2 WTO, Doha Declaration on the TRIPS Agreement and Public Health, (WTO Doc. WT/MIN(01)/DEC/2 (November 20, 2001) para. 3.

3 Gavin Yamey et al, "It Is Not Too Late to Achieve Global Covid-19 Vaccine Equity", *British Medical Journal* 376, (March 2022): o812, accessed March 15, 2023, <https://www.bmj.com/content/376/bmj.o812>.

resulting in what has been termed 'vaccine apartheid',[4] 'vaccine hoarding',[5] or 'vaccine nationalism',[6] all of which have contributed to aggravate the global public health crisis. Mostly vaccines were developed in a few rich countries, while other rich countries signed Advanced Purchase Agreements and bulk purchased vaccines in advance for their own populations.[7] In contrast, most low and middle-income countries lack the technical production capability and financial resources to reserve vaccinations in advance. Vaccine manufacturing countries and other rich countries in possession of high volume of vaccines also engaged in 'vaccine diplomacy',[8] using vaccines as a political tool to attain geopolitical objectives from low and middle-income countries.[9] As a result, some countries in the Global South, notably India, profited from this unequal system.[10] The monopolisation and politicisation of COVID vaccines and pharmaceuticals appears to herald the resurgence of neo-colonialism in global health.[11]

---

4 Simar Singh Bajaj, Lwando Maki and Fatima Cody Stanford, "Vaccine Apartheid: Global Cooperation and Equity", *The Lancet* 399, no. 10334 (2022): 1452.

5 BBC News, "Covid Vaccine: WHO Warns of 'Catastrophic Moral Failure'", *BBC News* (January 18, 2021), <https://www.bbc.com/news/world-55709428>.

6 Caitlin R. Williams, Jocelyn Getgen Kestenbaum and Benjamin Mason Meier, "Populist Nationalism Threatens Health and Human Rights in the COVID-19 Response", *American Journal of Public Health* 110, no. 12 (2020): 1766; Gavi, "COVID-19 and the Cost of Vaccine Nationalism", accessed March 15, 2023, <https://www.gavi.org/vaccineswork/covid-19-and-cost-vaccine-nationalism>.

7 Global Health Centre (Geneva), "COVID-19 Vaccine Access", accessed February 8, 2023, <https://www.knowledgeportalia.org/covid-19-vaccine-access>.

8 Peter J Hotez, "'Vaccine Diplomacy': Historical Perspectives and Future Directions", *PLOS Neglected Tropical Diseases* 8, no. 6 (2014): e2808.

9 Giulio de Felice, Nihal Tutal, and Nicolina Sciaraffa, "Geopolitical Aspects of COVID-19 Vaccines Distribution", *European Journal of Environment and Public Health* 7, no. 3 (2023): 1–10; Rosa Balfour, Lizza Bimassi, and Marta Martinelli, 'Coronavirus and the Widening Global North-South Gap' Carnegie working paper (April 2022) 1–2, 12–14; Simon F Pratt and Jamie Levin, "Vaccine will shape the new geopolitical order" *Foreign Policy* (April 29, 2021) <https://foreignpolicy.com/2021/04/29/vaccine-geopolitics-diplomacy-israel-russia-china/>.

10 Achal Prabhala and Leena Menghaney, "The World's Poorest Countries Are at India's Mercy for Vaccines. It's Unsustainable", *The Guardian* (April 2, 2021), <https://www.theguardian.com/commentisfree/2021/apr/02/india-in-charge-of-developing-world-covid-vaccine-supply-unsustainable>.

11 Eve Tuck and K Wayne Yang, "Decolonization Is Not a Metaphor", *Decolonization: Indigeneity, Education and Society* 1, no. 1 (2012): 1; Candace Fujikane, "Asian American Critique and Moana Nui 2011: Securing a Future beyond Empires, Militarized Capitalism and APEC", *Inter-Asia Cultural Studies* 13, no. 2 (2012): 189; SEKALALA Sharifah, et all, "Decolonising human rights: how intellectual property laws result in unequal access to the COVID-19 vaccine" (2021) BMJ Glob Health, Jul 6(7), doi: 10.1136/bmjgh-2021-006169.

Neo-colonialism is meant to be the notion that powerful countries or multinational corporations (MNCs) may exercise significant influence through their economic clout and political leverage over the human rights policies and practices of economically and politically weaker countries in the Global South. In this so-called decolonised era, the covert presence of colonialism in its new manifestation is ubiquitous in global public health caused by the commodification of essential, particularly lifesaving, medicines. The strict IPRS protection, as used in COVID vaccines and pharmaceuticals, is a strategy used to commodify lifesaving medicines, allowing manufacturers and manufacturing countries to place a higher value on financial gains than human lives. Despite being politically independent and legally sovereign, most countries of the Global South are still beholden to the powerful countries of the Global North and their MNCs.[12] The disregard for accepting a human rights approach to global public health, the intransigence of MNCs to transfer latest medical and lifesaving technologies to capable manufacturers in the Global South, and the stringent protection of IPRS over medicines and medical technologies are seemingly nothing short of neo-colonialism.

Against the above prelude, this chapter argues that the current regime of IPRS law amplifies existing gross international and national disparities in global public health and prohibits countries of the Global South from progressively realising the right to health for their citizens. Strict IPRS laws and regulations are one of the most domineering factors that exacerbate these structural inequalities in global public health. This neo-colonial approach to public health incapacitates poor third world countries to perform their human rights obligations for their nationals, assumed through multiple international human rights treaties and legal instruments. This chapter suggests a paradigm shift in the policy approach to IPRS laws and patent protection, one that warrants their understanding and application in compliance with human rights relevant to global public health. This approach calls for the 'liberation of minds from colonial ideology' to challenge the deeply embedded assumption that having been colonised is synonymous with being inferior.[13] The Global South battles against neo-colonisation, exploitative development goals, apartheid, and inequitable public healthcare services and access to lifesaving pharmaceuticals.[14] The demand to decolonise global health has ushered a new

12 Mark Langan, *Neo-Colonialism and the Poverty of 'Development' in Africa* (UK: Palgrave Macmillan, 2018), 149.

13 Linda Tuhiwai Smith, *Decolonizing Methodologies: Research and Indigenous Peoples* (London: Zed Books, 2012).

14 Lisa Forman, "Global health governance from below: access to AIDS medicines, International human rights law and social movements" in *Innovation in global health*

momentum as a result of the power asymmetries evidenced in the global handling of the COVID pandemic.[15]

2 The Nexus between Human Rights Law and Access to Medicine

International human rights law has transformed moral imperatives into legal entitlements. It provides a universal framework for sustainable health through advancing social justice for global health. The 1946 Constitution of the World Health Organisation (WHO) states that 'the enjoyment of the highest attainable standard of health is one of the fundamental rights of every human being without distinction of race, religion, political belief, economic or social condition' (preamble).[16] The Universal Declaration of Human Rights 1948 (UDHR) states that everyone has 'the right to a standard of living adequate for the health and well-being of himself and his family, including ... medical care' (Art. 25). The International Covenant on Economic, Social, and Cultural Rights 1966 (ICESCR) reiterates that the right to health includes 'access to health facilities, goods, and services' (Art.12(2)). The 'right to health' has been recognised as a basic human right by various international organisations and bodies, including the UN, World Trade Organization (WTO), and albeit WHO. The UN has also adopted resolutions recognising the right to health, including the right to get medical care and medicines when needed.[17] In 2015, the UN adopted 17 Sustainable Development Goals (SDGs) to be accomplished by 2030. Its Goal 3 aims to 'ensure healthy lives and promote well-being for all at all ages,' outlines a variety of objectives, including addressing non-communicable diseases, substance misuse, and environmental health.[18]

governance: critical cases, ed. Andrew F Cooper, John J Kirton (New York: Routledge, 2016), 193–207.

15 Clara Affun-Adegbulu and Opemiposi Adegbulu, "Decolonising Global (Public) Health: From Western Universalism to Global Pluriversalities", *BMJ Global Health* 5, no. 8 (2020): e002947; Sriram Shamasunder et al, "COVID-19 Reveals Weak Health Systems by Design: Why We Must Re-Make Global Health in This Historic Moment", *Global Public Health* 15, no. 7 (2020): 1083.

16 The Constitution of the WHO, accessed February 11, 2023, <https://apps.who.int/gb/bd/PDF/bd47/EN/constitution-en.pdf?ua=1>.

17 GA Resolutions No. 1230 (December 14, 2020): "The UN Decade of Healthy Ageing (2021–2030)", UN Doc. A/75/L.47 (December 8, 2020); "Global health and foreign policy – strengthening health system resilience through affordable health care for all", UN Doc. A/75/L.41 (December 3, 2020); "The Right to Health" GA Res. S-26/2 (July 27, 2021), 15.

18 UNDP, "What are the Sustainable Development Goals?", accessed March 25, 2023, <https://www.undp.org/sustainable-development-goals>.

According to the ICESCR preamble, access to essential medicine is a subset of the right to 'the highest achievable standard of health' and is firmly rooted in international human rights law. The right to health includes the right to access essential medicines and right to a functioning health care system. This means that governments have a responsibility to ensure that their citizens have access to the medicines they need to stay healthy supported by their national health-care infrastructures. While respective countries are responsible to protect their own citizens' right to access to essential medicines, other non-state actors also share this responsibility. The former UN Special Rapporteur on the Right to Health stated that pharmaceutical companies have human rights responsibilities, such as taking all reasonable steps to make new medicines 'as available as possible' to people who need them.[19] The 'UN Guiding Principles on Business and Human Rights,' which were unanimously approved by the UN Human Rights Council in 2011, require the private sector to assume responsibility for violations of human rights relating to access to medicines.[20] The international community of states has an obligation, individual and collective alike, to contribute to disaster relief and humanitarian aid by delivering medical supplies as a matter of urgency in the event of a socio-economic catastrophe like the COVID-19 situation.[21]

In practice, access to medicine is a complex inter-governmental issue, especially in low- and middle-income countries, which often lack the resources and infrastructure necessary to ensure that all citizens have access to essential medicines. The high cost of many medicines and inadequate regulation of the pharmaceutical industry can also limit access to medicine. The strict patent protection of newly innovated vaccines, medical products, and process in the context of a global pandemic like the COVID-19 crisis, the complexity of access to medicine can be intensified across all countries. The responsibility to protect the right to health for their population in low- and middle-income countries is largely qualified by the scope and extent of their accessibility to essential vaccines and pharmaceuticals in the global market. This is how the

---

19 UN General Assembly, "The Right of Everyone to the Enjoyment of the Highest Attainable Standard of Physical and Mental Health", Report of the Special Rapporteur, Paul Hunt, U.N. General Assembly, 63rd Session, Agenda Item 67(b), UN Doc. A/63/263 (August 11, 2008).

20 John Ruggie, Report of the Special Representative of the Secretary-General on the Issue of Human Rights and Transnational Corporations and Other Business Enterprises: "Protect, Respect and Remedy: A Framework for Business and Human Rights", UN Doc. A/HRC/8/5 (April 7, 2008).

21 UN Committee on Economic, Social and Cultural Rights (CESCR), General Comment No. 14, Doc. 12/2000/4 (August 11, 2000), para. 40.

human rights to health and life are inseparably linked to access to essential lifesaving medicines in the Global South.

3 Human Rights and IPRs at a Cross-Roads

No other issue epitomises the conflicts between human rights and IPRs more than restrictive access to patented medicines. Patents are granted by governments to provide inventors and creators of new medicines with IPRs on their inventions to encourage innovation and reward creativity. The contemporary global IPRs regime under TRIPS[22] encourages pharmaceutical companies to invest in research and development of new drugs, which could lead to the discovery of new treatments for diseases and access to new medicines that could not be available otherwise. New medicines and innovative medical procedures are the result of huge monetary investment and arduous research that takes years or even decades to complete, many of them with little or no therapeutic value. If allowing universal access to new pharmaceuticals were to stifle this research, there would be less medical innovation and fewer treatments for future diseases. The results of such universal access to medicines will surely be incompatible with the spirit, if not the letter of the international human rights laws.[23] Nevertheless, the rigorous enforcement of IPRs or pharmaceutical patents make the medicinal products expensive and hence beyond the reach of the poor in low-, middle-, and high- income countries. If lifesaving medicines are available yet unaffordable for those poor who need them is also incongruous to international human rights law. All common sense of morality and humanity oppose the idea of denying the right to access to lifesaving pharmaceuticals, particularly to those with deadly and life-threatening health conditions precipitating a grave public health crisis when there are palatable alternatives to ensure accessibility in a cost-efficient manner.[24]

A fortified patent-protection regime often brings desirable returns to the private actors or pharmaceutical industries to recoup the costs of their research and earn expected benefits through exercising the IPRs over their products. Besides financial gains, the IPRs-based system of medical innovation

---

22 WTO Agreement on Trade-Related Aspects of Intellectual Property Rights (TRIPS), April 15, 1995, *International Legal Materials* 33 (1994): 81.

23 Integrating IPRs and Development Policy, Commission for Intellectual Property Rights Final Report, London (September 2002), accessed February 6, 2023, <http://www.iprcommission.org/graphic/documents/final_report.htm>.

24 Thomas Pogge, "Access to Medicines", *Public Health Ethics* 1, no. 2 (2008): 73.

also provides numerous social benefits. It promotes the pursuit of new medical knowledge, enforces public disclosure of medical processes and products to drive future innovation, and allows pharmaceutical companies to manufacture and deliver generic pharmaceuticals at marginal cost after the expiry of patent protection. However, the stringent patent system or IPRs regime offer little solace to those with a life-threatening illness who cannot afford patent-protected lifesaving medications. It is a delicate balance to attain, and different countries approach this issue in different ways. Contrary to the obligations of all WTO members to strike a balance between the rights and obligations of producers and users of intellectual properties and to protect public health (TRIPS Arts. 7–8 discussed below), most rich countries prioritise pharmaceutical industries' corporate interests at the expense of the majority peoples' human rights to health and life particularly in the Global South.

4 Human Rights and IPRs: The Historical Dichotomy

The American Declaration on the Rights and Duties of Man, the first international human rights instrument of the contemporary world, undertook significant consideration for IPRs by recognising the literary, artistic, and scientific works of any author, as well as the innovations of any individual.[25] The language and structure of its Article 13 on human rights was the foundation for UDHR Article 27 with the caveat that UDHR does not explicitly acknowledge IPRs or recognise new inventions as human rights. Being a declaration of the UN General Assembly, the UDHR is not legally binding for UN members, but its provisions in Article 27 had a domino effect on the subsequent human rights instruments, such as the incorporation of equivalent measures in ICESCR,[26] regional declarations and treaties,[27] and national constitutions.[28] A notable exception is the European Convention on Human Rights, which does not specifically recognise IPRs as a standalone right. Since this Convention was adopted in 1950 primarily to protect civil and political rights in the context

25 Signed in April 1948 and came into effect on May 2, 1948, Art. 13.

26 ICESCR Art. 15 (1) (b–c).

27 The Additional Protocol to the American Convention on Human Rights in the Area of Economic, Social and Cultural Rights (San Salvador Protocol) 1988, Art. 14; African Charter of Human and People's Rights 1981; and Arab Charter on Human Rights for the Middle East 1994.

28 The Constitution of Bhutan 2008, Art. 7(13); Constitution of Burundi 2005, Art. 58; Constitution of Congo 2002, Art. 29; and Constitution of Croatia 1990, Art. 69.

of addressing the atrocities committed during the World War II, it perhaps overlooked the incorporation and recognition of IPRs. However, the European Social Charter adopted in 1961 and revised in 1996 contains the right to benefit from any measures to enjoy the highest possible standard of health attainable and medical assistance (Arts. 11 and 13).

The human rights provisions of the above instruments containing IPRs create a predicament in the interactions between these two sets of rights. They preserve creators' fundamental rights over their inventions while recognising the general public's right to benefit from cultural and scientific innovations made by the creators. More specifically, their provisions reflect the dichotomy between the inventors' incentives for the innovations and the profitless public access to the advantages of innovations.[29]

International IPRs treaties have historically neglected the impact of the protection of intangible assets on human rights. Both the Paris and Berne Conventions, the two pioneering international legal instruments on IPRs, were signed at the end of the 19th century before the inception of the international human rights framework that emerged at the aftermath of the World War II. The Paris and Berne Conventions therefore are silent on the recognition and protection of human rights while undertaking measures to protect IPRs. The I961 Rome Convention on Related Rights also adopted the similar approach like other post-World War II treaties on IPRs.[30] However, a break from the ongoing trend happened in 1994 when the Agreement on TRIPS was adopted as a 'single-undertaking' and part of the Marrakesh Agreement Establishing the WTO.

The provisions of TRIPS Articles 7 and 8 have purported to transform the relationship between human rights and IPRs from intersecting to interacting.[31] All WTO members are obligated under TRIPS to protect and enforce IPRs 'to the mutual advantage of producers and users [...] in a manner conducive to social and economic welfare, and to a balance of rights and obligations' (Art. 7). This is the very first clause in an international IPRs treaty that requires interpreters to consider the rights of the users of intellectual assets while interpreting the treaty.

29 Laurence R Helfer, "Toward a Human Rights Framework for Intellectual Property" *U.C. Davis Law Review* 40 (2007): 971.

30 Laurence R Helfer and Graeme W Austin, *Human Rights and Intellectual Property: Mapping the Global Interface* (UK: Cambridge University Press, 2011), 32.

31 UN High Commissioner for Human Rights, "The impact of the Agreement on Trade-related Aspects of Intellectual Property Rights on human rights", accessed February 23, 2023, <https://digitallibrary.un.org/record/446005>.

This legally binding obligation is followed by a specific commitment 'to adopt necessary measures to protect public health' and to prevent the abuse of IPRs by right holders (Art. 8). But neither of the Articles prescribes any criteria to be relied upon in achieving the balance sought in their texts, which allow WTO members to adopt any IP measures as they deem appropriate to protect new innovations while promoting 'public interest'. Due to the very narrow scope of the Articles, striking and maintaining the balance between IPRs and human rights seems to be an oxymoron. It is often difficult, if not impossible, to create a synchronised balance between the protection of innovations and promotion of public health interests.

Notwithstanding the above requirement for balanced measures, TRIPS has in effect prioritised IPRs over human rights. TRIPS Articles 7 and 8 compel WTO members to resolve potential conflicts by enacting specific IP dispute resolution framework. The position of human rights under TRIPS is markedly different, subservient to the innovators' interests in IPRs. WTO members can resort to permissible exceptions to the laws governing IPRs (Art. 1(1)) only when the exceptions are deemed 'necessary' to comply with their own laws and regulations and safeguard the public interest (Art.3(2), 8(1), and 63(4)). The term 'necessary' is construed as adopting a 'least restrictive approach' which obliges WTO members to undertake comparatively less harmful measures in the interests of the IP owners,[32] regardless of their effects on human rights. The 'consistency' requirement also requires WTO members to follow the higher level of measures, if necessary, to protect IPRs with no requirement for human rights consideration. For example, they could be forced to follow strict three-step tests when putting copyright and patent exceptions into place under TRIPS Articles 13 and 30. This minimum, if not face-saving, respect for human rights in TRIPS was one of the most igniting factors that led to the adoption of the 2001 Doha Declaration on TRIPS and Public Health, which reaffirmed the importance of public health in intellectual property protection laws.[33]

Being the global trading organisation, the WTO and its covered agreements have been displaying scanty regard for human rights. Upon its scrutiny, the UN Sub-Commission for the Promotion and Protection of Human Rights released a report in 2000 labelling the WTO a 'veritable nightmare' for its lack

32 Henning Grosse Ruse-Khan, "Assessing the Need for a General Public Interest Exception in the TRIPS Agreement " in *Intellectual Property Rights in a Fair World Trade System – Proposals for Reform of TRIPS*, ed. Kur Annette and Marianne Levin (UK: Edward Elgar Publishing, 2011), 167.

33 Frederick M. Abbott, "The Trips Agreement, Access to Medicines, and the WTO Doha Ministerial Conference" *Journal of World Intellectual Property* 5, no. 1 (2002): 15.

of compliance with international human rights standards particularly in third world countries.[34] Enacted along the same tune, TRIPS does not protect or recognise, but makes an oblique reference to, human rights, which may be respected if not a barrier to flourishing the protection of IPRs.[35] It articulates variations of IP standard rules as a matter of WTO members' public policy that they freely determine as 'appropriate' within their own legal system (Art. 1(1)). In so doing, TRIPS authorises WTO members to replace the inherent dignity of the human person as the main justification for the implementation of harmful IPRs. It facilitates governments to promote any IP policy and regulations outweighing inherent individual rights. Individuals deserve the recognition of their rights including access to medicines only to the extent they coincide with the governmental policies. The same situation persists in all other international instruments on IPRs like WIPO Copyright Treaty or Performances and Phonogram Treaty.[36]

5 Global Health Law and Regulations: Prioritising IPRs over Right to Health

Global health law is a set of legal rules, processes, and institutions that make it possible for people worldwide to 'attain the highest possible level of physical and mental health'.[37] The regulatory framework for global health is disintegrated, with numerous competing actors and regimes intersecting many fields including health security, border control, surveillance, trade, and IP rights.[38] This disintegration is further intensified at the intersection of global health regulations and international human rights law. This convoluted situation

34 Oloka-Onyango and Deepika Udagama, *The Realization of Economic, Social and Cultural Rights: Globalization and Its Impact on the Full Enjoyment of Human Rights*, UN Doc. E/CN.4/Sub.2/2000/13, June 15, 2000.

35 Klaus D. Beiter, "Establishing Conformity Between TRIPS and Human Rights: Hierarchy in International Law, Human Rights Obligations of the WTO and Extraterritorial State Obligations Under the International Covenant on Economic, Social and Cultural Rights" in *TRIPS plus 20*, ed. Hanns Ullrich et al, (Berlin/ Heidelberg: Springer, 2016), 445.

36 WIPO Copyright Treaty 1996, preamble; WIPO Performances and Phonograms Treaty 1996, preamble.

37 WHO Constitution, preamble; Lawrence O. Gostin and AL Taylor, "Global Health Law: A Definition and Grand Challenges", *Public Health Ethics* 1, no. 1 (2008): 53.

38 Lawrence O. Gostin et al, "The Legal Determinants of Health: Harnessing the Power of Law for Global Health and Sustainable Development", *The Lancet* 393, no. 10183 (2019): 1857.

has led an urgent call for the harmonisation of global health regulations and human rights laws.[39]

In the sphere of developing and distributing of COVID vaccines, global health law has demonstrated how it exacerbates, instead of alleviates, inequalities between the rich and the poor. Its inequitable priority to IPRs has resulted in facilitating and legitimising 'vaccine hoarding', 'vaccine nationalism', and 'vaccine apartheid'. The ongoing IP protection regime under TRIPS enables global health law to condone this inequity which breaches human rights obligations under the ICESCR, UDHR, and other international human rights instruments.[40] In the absence of a clear articulation and acknowledgement of human rights within TRIPS, global health law and international human rights law are now at loggerheads as shown below.

5.1 *IPRs Protection Favours Corporate Interest over Human Health*

The rationale for stringent IPRs protection is that it is indispensable for future investments in research and innovation. TRIPS requires that WTO members must provide pharmaceutical patent protection for at least 20 years (Arts. 33 and 70(8)) to profit from their investments in inventing, testing, and upscaling pharmaceutical products worldwide. This frequently infused rationale does not apply to COVID vaccines and pharmaceuticals. There is evidence that casts doubt on the relationship between 'investment in research and development' and 'incentives for innovation' in inventing COVID vaccines.[41]

Research projections indicate that the worldwide public sector spent at least €93 billion on the development of COVID vaccines and medicines, with €85.6 billion of that amount going to vaccines.[42] Research, development, and production of most approved COVID vaccines are substantially financed by public funds. *Operation Warp Speed* (*OWS*), a US federal government initiative, supplied approximately US$12 billion from public fund to assist pharmaceutical companies, including *Moderna* and *Pfizer*, for research and development

39 "Harmonizing Global Health Law and Human Rights Law to Develop Rights-Based Approaches to Global Health Emergencies", *Opinio Juris* (February 24, 2021) <http://opiniojuris.org/2021/02/24/harmonizing-global-health-law-and-human-rights-law-to-develop-rights-based-approaches-to-global-health-emergencies/>.

40 Supra (n 16–21).

41 Patrice Trouiller et al, "Drug Development for Neglected Diseases: A Deficient Market and a Public-Health Policy Failure", *The Lancet* 359, no. 9324 (2002): 2188.

42 Madeleine Hoecklin, "€93 billion Spent by Public Sector on COVID Vaccines and Therapeutics in 11 Months, Finds New Research", Health Policy Watch (January 12, 2021), <https://healthpolicy-watch.news/81038-2/>.

of COVID vaccines.[43] *BioNTech*, a partner of *Pfizer*, received US$445 million from the German government for the development of COVID vaccine.[44] China also directly funded *Sinovac* and *Sinopharm* pharmaceuticals.[45] *Sputnik V* was developed at the Gamaleya Research Institute, a state-run research facility in Russia.[46] Had this huge amount of public funds not been immediately available, COVID vaccines could not have been developed so fast and efficiently.

In 2021–2022, *Moderna* and *Pfizer* each made over US$34 billion in revenue, which is equivalent to a profit of US$1000 every second.[47] *Pfizer* and *Moderna* increased vaccine prices from US$22.60 to US$25.50 and from US$18.30 to US$23.00, respectively, despite the fact that 98% people in low- and middle-income countries are yet to be fully immunised.[48] Since public funding played a significant role in the research and innovation of the vaccines, all brands of COVID vaccines should have been treated as 'public good'. This could have been the most humane way of spending public funds and equitable use of life-saving innovations in a pandemic. Nevertheless, the vaccine manufacturers are not inclined to cut the price, waive IPRs over the vaccines and pharmaceuticals, or transfer the technologies to low- and middle-income countries. Both the US and EU fully support their manufactures irrespective of the disdaining effect of the stringent protection of IPRs in COVID vaccines on public health in the Global South.

5.2 *COVAX Initiative: Deviation from IPRs or Derivation of Human Right?*

The COVID Vaccines Global Access (COVAX), is a donor-funded mechanism which was co-created by the WHO, Coalition for Epidemic Preparedness Innovations (CEPI), and Gavi – the Vaccine Alliance.[49] This global initiative

43 Matthew M. Kavanagh, Lawrence O. Gostin, and Madhavi Sunder, "Sharing Technology and Vaccine Doses to Address Global Vaccine Inequity and End the COVID-19 Pandemic", *Journal of American Medical Association* 326, no. 3 (2021): 219 <https://doi.org/10.1001/jama.2021.10823>.

44 Ibid.

45 Olivier J. Wouters et al, "Challenges in Ensuring Global Access to COVID-19 Vaccines: Production, Affordability, Allocation, and Deployment", *The Lancet* 397, no. 10278 (2021): 1023.

46 Ibid.

47 'Pfizer, BioNTech and Moderna Making $1,000 Profit Every Second While World's Poorest Countries Remain Largely Unvaccinated", Oxfam/ReliefWeb (November 16, 2021) <https://reliefweb.int/report/world/pfizer-biontech-and-moderna-making-1000-profit-every-second-while-world-s-poorest>.

48 Ibid.

49 GAVI, "COVAX Facility", accessed 22 March 2023, <https://www.gavi.org/covax-facility>.

was aimed at ensuring equitable access to COVID vaccines for people in all countries, regardless of their income level. This COVAX initiative should not be confused with the relaxation of IPRs or transfer of vaccine technologies, or any other deviation of IPRs protection law. Although COVAX is a humanistic effort, it is not a derivation of any human rights law.

COVAX has suffered serious shortfall in meeting the global need and failed to achieve its objectives.[50] It experienced a variety of constraints impeding its capacity to guarantee fair access to COVID vaccines. Limited supply, funding shortfalls, lopsided distribution, delays in delivery, vaccine hesitancy, and vaccine nationalism of rich countries have been the main reasons for its failure.[51] Being a charity, COVAX resorted to charitable contribution and market purchase strategy through its facility, which failed to provide equitable access to vaccines as a human right for all people across the globe. It sought to create a flimsy moral obligation for the contributing countries without offering any legal right or entitlement in the receiving ends who needed lifesaving COVID vaccines and pharmaceuticals. This emphasis on charity rather than on rights fell far short of what was required to treat the COVID public health crisis as a human rights issue entailing precise legal obligations for all countries.

Although the UN Human Rights Council issued public consensus statement in which all countries agreed that they had the right to use the TRIPS flexibilities (examined below) and right to access vaccines, this statement failed to acknowledge any corresponding state obligations to facilitate such flexibilities.[52] This disconnection between rights and obligations made it possible for countries in the Global North, along with a small number of their allies from the Global South, to support this rhetorical statement. This group of countries also consistently opposed all requests for any IPRs/TRIPS waiver in the WTO,[53] and thus consolidated their refusal to use TRIPS flexibilities.

50 Ann Danaiya Usher, "A Beautiful Idea: How COVAX Has Fallen Short", *The Lancet* 397. no. 10292 (2021): 2322.

51 Ibid.

52 Timothy Hodgson and Rossella De Falco, "Human Rights and Universal Access to COVID-19 Vaccines: Does the Human Rights Council Resolution Go Far Enough?", *Opinio Juris* (March 23, 2021), <http://opiniojuris.org/2021/03/23/human-rights-and-universal-access-to-covid-19-vaccines-does-the-human-rights-council-resolution-go-far-enough/>.

53 Khorsed Zaman, "The Waiver of Certain Intellectual Property Rights Provisions of the TRIPS for the Prevention, Containment and Treatment of COVID-19: A Review of the Proposal under WTO Jurisprudence", *European Journal of Risk Regulation* 13, no. 2 (2022): 295.

6 TRIPS Flexibility: Is It Flexible Enough to Access Lifesaving Pharmaceuticals?

Low- and middle-income countries can invoke TRIPS flexibilities, such as compulsory licensing and parallel importing, with or without any general waiver from their WTO obligations (Arts. 31 and 31 *bis*). But the TRIPS provisions on flexibilities are by default vague and lack specificity which require frequent clarification.[54] Zimbabwe in 2001,[55] at the height of HIV-AIDS pandemic, sought a clarification of Article 31(f) which resulted in a waiver on the exportation of lifesaving generic medicines to low- and middle-income countries with limited or no manufacturing capacity. This clarification issue led to the adoption of the Doha Declaration on TRIPS and Public Health in November 2001.[56] Pursuant to this Declaration, a temporary waiver of TRIPS Article 31(f) was granted in August 2003, which became a permanent exemption under Article 31*bis* and effective from 2017.[57]

Despite the TRIPS permanent provision on exemption/waiver/TRIPS flexibility in relation to exporting lifesaving pharmaceuticals, barriers emerged in exporting COVID vaccines and pharmaceuticals to low- and middle-income countries. In October 2020, India and South Africa requested the WTO for a temporary TRIPS waiver for COVID vaccines, diagnostics, and therapeutics.[58] After almost two years of protracted debate and objections from rich countries, a temporary waiver on patent rights for COVID vaccines was granted at the 12th WTO Ministerial Conference on June 17, 2022.[59] This decision has waived obligations under TRIPS Article 31(f) with respect to only COVID vaccines to the exclusion of diagnostics and therapeutics which are essential for already infected patients. Expanding global access to diagnostics and therapeutics is

54 Ibid.

55 Minutes of the TRIPS Council meeting held on April 2–5, 2001, WTO Doc. IP/C/M/30 (June 1, 2001), paras. 229–52.

56 WTO Ministerial Conferences – Doha 4th Ministerial – TRIPS Declaration, accessed February 12, 2023, <https://www.wto.org/english/thewto_e/minist_e/min01_e/mindecl_trips_e.htm>.

57 WTO, 2017 News Items – "WTO IP Rules Amended to Ease Poor Countries Access to Affordable Medicines", accessed February 12, 2023, <https://www.wto.org/english/news_e/news17_e/trip_23jan17_e.htm>.

58 The Waiver from Certain Provisions of the TRIPS Agreement for the Prevention, Containment and Treatment of COVID-19: Communication from India and South Africa, WTO Doc. IP/C/W/669 (October 2, 2020).

59 WTO, "TRIPS Council Welcomes MC12 TRIPS Waiver Decision, Discusses Possible Extension", accessed February 4, 2023, <https://www.wto.org/english/news_e/news22_e/trip_08jul22_e.htm>.

crucial for lowering the number of COVID related hospitalisations and deaths, particularly in low- and middle-income countries where vaccination rates remain extremely low and the danger of serious medical complications for the most susceptible population is alarmingly high.

COVID vaccines produced under compulsory licences are now temporarily permitted to be exported to low- and middle-income countries. However, there is nothing unique about this second TRIPS waiver since it is a recurring immunity on Article 31(f).[60] If this single TRIPS provision requires two waivers in twenty years to address global public health crises, it demonstrates that the current IP regime pertaining to global public health is grossly erroneous. The fact that two separate waivers had to be negotiated to address the two public health crises of HIV-AIDS and COVID-19 is indicative of how unsettling the IP restriction remains. Human rights to health have been compromised through sacrificing the right to access to essential lifesaving medicines in favour of protecting IPRs. A critical legal analysis on TRIPS flexibilities and IPRs waivers has shown that these are not flexible enough for accessing essential pharmaceuticals, including COVID vaccines for the patients who need them most.[61] Vaccine producing and exporting countries are not obliged to export as a matter of duty; nor can importing countries seek and receive vaccine as a matter of right. It is this gerrymandering formulation that makes the waver intrinsically voluntary in nature. This presumably explains why it took five years since the 2003 waiver to invoke and exercise this waiver in 2008 when Canada was the first country to export the first shipment of generic drugs to Rwanda.[62] Thirty-seven rich countries, including the EU, US, UK, Canada, Japan, Australia, Belgium, and Germany, do not accept and recognise this waiver and flexibility under TRIPS Article 31*bis*.[63]

It is plausible to argue that the inherent flexibility provisions in TRIPS Articles 31 and 31*bis* are insufficient to strike an appropriate balance between IPRs and access to medicine as a human right. It worked neither for the HIV-AIDS pandemic in 2001 nor for the ongoing COVID pandemic. Although

60 Jayashree Watal, "Analysis of the 12th WTO Ministerial Conference Decision on the TRIPS Agreement", accessed March 3, 2023, <https://www.ejiltalk.org/analysis-of-the-12th-wto-ministerial-conference-decision-on-the-trips-agreement/>.

61 Zaman (n 53).

62 Ibid; ICTSD, "First Generic Drugs en Route to Africa under 5 Year Old WTO Deal", *Bridges Weekly Trade News Digest* 12, no. 31 (2008).

63 James Love, "Open Letter Asking 37 WTO Members to Declare Themselves Eligible to Import Medicines Manufactured under Compulsory License in Another Country, under 31bis of TRIPS Agreement", *Knowledge Ecology International* (7 February 2023), <https://www.keionline.org/32707>.

low- and middle-income countries now have an option to use TRIPS flexibilities, they hardly invoke it as the process of utilising the flexibilities is cumbersome and skewed against them. Regulatory burdens, political pressures, economic constraints, and lack of transparency combine to enable the global IPRS protection regime to maintain and exacerbate disparities in global health.

7 Access to COVID Vaccines and Pharmaceuticals: A Human Rights Approach

A human rights-based approach to access to medicines focuses on the right to the highest attainable standard of physical and mental health, which includes access to essential medicines.[64] This approach emphasises the need for governments, pharmaceutical companies, and other stakeholders to respect, protect, and fulfill the right to health by taking steps to make essential medicines available, accessible, and affordable for all, regardless of their socio-economic status and geographical locations. It also implies that the needs and perspectives of marginalised groups, such as people living in poverty, should be considered when developing and implementing policies and programs pertaining to access to essential medicines. This human rights approach can help ensure that access to essential medicines is not merely a matter of charity or goodwill gesture but is recognised as a fundamental human right that must be protected, promoted, and respected by all actors in the healthcare system. This may inclusively include measures to increase domestic investment in research and development of new medicines, implement fair and transparent pricing policies, and strengthen healthcare systems to ensure that all individuals have equitable access to the medicines they need. In practical terms, this human rights approach seeks (a) to realise that access to medicines is a human rights issue as well as a public health issue; (b) to ensure that the needs of marginalised groups are considered in policy and practice; and (c) to emphasise that everyone has the right to live a healthy life and access to medications, just as they do with other fundamental human rights.

The UN Committee on Economic, Social and Cultural Rights (CESCR) is responsible for interpreting the ICESCR. In the context of accessibility to COVID vaccines and pharmaceuticals, CESCR has emphasised (a) that states 'have a duty to prevent intellectual property and patent legal regimes from

64 Xavier Seuba, "Round Table: A Human Rights Approach to the WHO Model List of Essential Medicines", *Bulletin of the World Health Organization* 84 (2006), 405–11.

undermining the enjoyment of economic, social and cultural rights'; and (b) that the IP regime should be interpreted and implemented in a manner that is consistent with the obligation of states 'to protect public health'.[65] This obligation has been expanded to include the equitable global distribution of vaccines to combat the development of infectious diseases like COVID.[66] Accessibility to COVID vaccines and pharmaceuticals is not a charity venture,[67] but entails precise legal obligations for states to uphold their international human rights obligations. The inaccessibility to COVID vaccines and therapeutics stultifies the realisation of several human rights, including the right to life, equal benefit from scientific advancement, and right to health. Indeed, CESCR has concluded that the commercialisation of lifesaving COVID vaccines and pharmaceuticals has widened and perpetuated inequality and violated the internationally recognised human rights to health and life.[68] This restrictive policy dominated by pharmaceutical patent law warrants a searching reappraisal with a view to make it human rights friendly.

8 Bringing IPRS within the Ambit of Human Rights

Thinking COVID-19 as the last pandemic is a sheer naivety. The proliferation of industrial agriculture, urbanisation, and globalisation heighten the risk of a novel virus/pathogen from animals to humans and rapidly spread throughout the planet. Prior to COVID-19, the SARS, H1N1, MERS, and Ebola epidemics and pandemics transpired in the 21st century. Everything humans do and learn from the COVID crisis must be considered in the perspective of preparing for the potential next one. From the context of IPRS and access to essential medicines, the international community must be prepared not to approach the WTO for yet another TRIPS waiver should another pandemic hit in the future.

The most essential step would be the adoption of a human rights approach with respect to access to lifesaving medicines. Such an approach requires that

65 "Statement on Universal Affordable Vaccination against Coronavirus Disease Covid-19, International Cooperation and Intellectual Property: Committee on Economic, Social and Cultural Rights", *International Human Rights Law Review* 10, no. 1 (2021): 180.

66 Lawrence Gostin, Safura Abdool Karim, and Benjamin Mason Meier, "Facilitating Access to a COVID-19 Vaccine through Global Health Law", *Journal of Law, Medicine & Ethics* 48, no. 3 (2020): 622.

67 As explained in section 5.2 above, COVAX falls short on this point.

68 Koen Byttebier, "Final Conclusions" in *Covid-19 and Capitalism- Economic and Financial Law & Policy – Shifting Insights & Values*, vol. 7 (UK: Springer International Publishing, 2022), 1067.

access to key treatments such as vaccinations be prioritised through domestic, regional, and international mechanisms to guarantee that all countries have sufficient opportunities to realise the right to health.[69] This step calls for a searching reappraisal of the intersecting relationship between international trade law on IPRs and human rights law with a view to ensure that pharmaceutical patent law cannot deny human right to health and access to lifesaving medicines. This re-conceptualisation of human rights in global health crises requires ingraining internationally recognised human rights as an integral part of IPRs.

8.1 *Reconceptualising the Current Approaches of IPRs to Human Right*

Reconceptualising the current approach of IPRs to human rights warrants a shift from 'an emergent trade-related, market-friendly paradigm of human rights' to a model of human rights grounded on the experience of the people whose lives and livelihood are affected by the existing model.[70] The fundamental prerequisite of such a reconceptualised approach to human rights in public health is to guarantee universal access to lifesaving drugs for all people, irrespective of their geographical location. If someone is not receiving vaccinations or essential medicines, this humanising approach would ensure that the deprived individual gets his/her necessary treatment as a human being to be prevailing over any barriers created by IPRs or market access regulations. This approach requires dismantling IP monopolies on lifesaving vaccines and therapeutics supported by the current IPRs protection regime under TRIPS. In numerous statements, different UN treaty bodies have pledged to ensure equal access to essential medicines which is crucial to realising the right to health, and that IPRs should never take precedence over human rights obligations.[71] But these statements are neither mandatory, nor do they bear any legal effect in terms of implementing human rights in upholding IPRs.

The relationship between IPRs and human rights is dichotomous and mutually non-recognisant, which is the principal barrier to attempts at

---

69 Above (nn1–17).

70 Upendra Baxi, "Market Fundamentalisms: Business Ethics at the Altar of Human Rights", *Human Rights Law Review* 5, no. 1 (2005): 1.

71 UN Human Rights Council, "Measures Taken to Implement Human Rights Council Resolution 9/8 and Obstacles to Its Implementation, Including Recommendations for Further Improving the Effectiveness of, Harmonizing and Reforming the Treaty Body System Report of the Secretary-General", UN Doc. A/HRC/46/25 (2020); OHCHR, "COVID-19: UN Experts Urge WTO Cooperation on Vaccines to Protect Global Public Health", accessed February 4, 2023, <https://www.ohchr.org/en/press-releases/2021/03/covid-19-un-experts-urge-wto-cooperation-vaccines-protect-global-public>.

reconceptualising both rights in public health. And it may well be difficult to achieve should TRIPS and its stringent IPRS protection regime remain ambivalent about human rights to health amid public health crises like HIV-AIDS and COVID. If the right to health, as the WHO constitution, UDHR, ICESCR, or other international human rights instruments proclaim,[72] is not embodied as an indispensable requirement of enforcing IPRS under TRIPS, reconceptualising human rights in public health will continue to eclipse under the shadow of IP mercantilism. If the mutual non-recognition of IPRS and human rights persists unabated, in every single pandemic, the international community will need to engage in protracted and polarised negotiations for a new IPRS waiver to access patented vaccines, drugs, and other therapeutics. The first waiver was during the HIV-AIDS pandemic and a second waiver for COVID is underway. This IPR waiver seeking will become a recurring negotiating issue in the WTO cut-throat trade diplomacy for every global health crisis in the future.

A glimpse of light can be visible through the lenses of TRIPS Articles 7, 8, and 66(2), which may serve as a guide for reconceptualising human rights in public health. Articles 7 and 8 aim to strike a balance or create 'mutual advantage' between innovators' IPRS and human rights in the form of users' rights. WTO members may take action to address social and public objectives, such as preserving public health, while fostering technological advancement by defending the rights of inventors. The WTO Appellate Body (AB) had the opportunity to create a landmark jurisprudence on this issue in *Canada–Patent* dispute, but the AB applied 'judicial economy' and kept it to be settled in the future disputes.[73] This decision is a missed opportunity for a thorough judicial interpretation of TRIPS Article 7. The WTO Panel in the *United States – Section 211 Omnibus Appropriations Act of 1998* dispute provided an explanation of the nature of Article 7 and acknowledged it as a provision with the potential to strike an effective balance between IPRS and other social rights.[74] Subsequently this issue was further raised in *Australia Tobacco Plain Packaging* dispute, whose main focus was to examine the consistency of the Australian domestic tobacco packaging laws and regulations within the set objectives of TRIPS Articles 7 and 8.[75] The inter-relationship and connectivity of IPRS and

72 Above (n 16–21).

73 *Canada – Term of Patent Protection*, WT/DS170/AB/R, AB Report (September 18, 2000) para. 101.

74 *US – Section 211 Omnibus Appropriations Act of 1998*, WT/DS176/R, Panel report (August 6, 2001) para. 8.57.

75 *Australia – Tobacco Plain Packaging*, WT/D 467/2, Panel report (August 30, 2018) para. 7.2399.

human rights could have been established and clarified through this dispute but the WTO dispute settlement body remained silent. So far, the legal value of Articles 7 and 8 is underestimated within the WTO jurisprudence.[76]

TRIPS Article 66(2) was intended to establish a practise of transferring technology from the Global North to the Global South.[77] It obligates developed countries to 'provide incentives to enterprises and institutions in their territories for the purpose of promoting and encouraging technology transfer to LDC members in order to enable them to create a sound and viable technological base'. This mandatory provision is largely inoperative. Developed countries, which are obliged to make this provision operational, have neglected, trampled on, and all but forgotten it. The unfinished tasks of TRIPS should now be facilitated as a new beginning for the recognition of human rights within the IPRS regulatory regime. The reconceptualisation of human rights in public health could be accelerated by establishing a supportive interlinkage between IPRS and human rights as already exists in TRIPS Articles 7, 8, and 66(2) within the negotiated parameters of the WTO law.

8.2 *Making Corporations Accountable for Upholding Human Rights*

A reconceptualised approach to human rights in public health necessitates to broaden corporate obligations to avoid actions and practices that disregard principles of equity and non-discrimination in their business decisions, creates artificial crisis of short supply and inaccessibility to lifesaving vaccines and medicines, moral and legal unaccountability, and preventing countries from disclosing information regarding their interactions in relation to essential vaccines and therapeutics.[78]

Countries fall short of their international commitments to ensure the right to health when they fail to ensure access to essential vaccines, treatments, and medicines for their citizens. Besides governments' responsibilities to their

76 Grosse Ruse-Khan and Henning, "The (Non) Use of Treaty Object and Purpose in Intellectual Property Disputes in the WTO" (SSRN Scholarly Paper No 1939859, September 28, 2011), accessed January 12, 2023, <https://papers.ssrn.com/abstract=1939859>; Alison Slade, "Good Faith and the TRIPS Agreement: Putting Flesh on the Bones of the TRIPS 'Objective'", *International & Comparative Law Quarterly* 63, no. 2 (2014): 353, 354.

77 Negotiating Group on Trade-Related Aspects of Intellectual Property Rights, including Trade in Counterfeit Goods, WTO Negotiation Doc. MTN.GNG/NG11/W/32/Rev.1 (1989) para. 5.

78 Baxi (n 69); Human Rights Watch, "Universal and Equitable Access to Covid-19 Vaccines, Testing, Treatments: Companies' Human Rights Responsibilities" (February 11, 2021), <https://www.hrw.org/news/2021/02/11/universal-and-equitable-access-covid-19-vaccines-testing-treatments-companies-human>.

people, corporations must be more diligent in upholding human rights and firmly consider what positive obligations they have under international human rights law. Although protecting human rights is the primary obligation of states, pharmaceutical corporations cannot escape their obligations under international human rights law. Recently, the South African Constitutional Court has ruled that besides state obligations to protect human rights, privately-owned land corporations in South Africa should also be subjected to some human rights obligations.[79]

Due to the longstanding practice of associating human rights obligations solely with states, it has been difficult for international human rights law to attribute human rights obligations to corporations. Modern corporate social responsibility is an integral part of international human rights movement, imposing a positive duty on corporations to uphold human rights including the right to health.[80] However, this corporate responsibility is perceived as emanating from soft law entailing no legal effect. Hence, the call for making this obligation mandatory for the corporations by articulating the standards and guidelines for human rights that apply to corporations and other non-state actors.[81] Such mandatory regulatory norms, guidelines, and standards must be enforced by states through domestic, regional, and international collaboration including through multilateral frameworks of the WTO and WHO.

9 Conclusion

The historical divide between human rights and IPRs is evident. Despite several international legal instruments explicitly recognise human rights considerations in asserting and enforcing IPRs, the current WTO patent protection regime under TRIPS is unwilling to embrace human rights within its purview. This divergence delivers a clarion call for a reappraisal of the relationship

79 *Daniels v. Scribante and Another* (2017) SA (CC), (2017) BCLR (CC), [2017] ZACC 13, paras. 37–39.

80 UNHCR, "General Comment No. 24 (2017) on State Obligations under the International Covenant on Economic, Social and Cultural Rights in the Context of Business Activities", accessed February 2, 2023, <https://www.refworld.org/docid/5beaecba4.html>; "OHCHR, Guiding Principles on Business and Human Rights", accessed February 2, 2023, <https://www.ohchr.org/sites/default/files/documents/publications/guidingprinciplesbusinesshr_en.pdf>.

81 Sofia Gruskin and Zyde Raad, "Are Drug Companies Living Up to Their Human Rights Responsibilities? Moving Toward Assessment", *PLOS Medicine* 7, no. 9 (2010): e1000310.

between IPRs and human rights by integrating humanising principles within the perimeters and parameters of pharmaceutical patent law of the WTO.

The COVID-19 pandemic is not the last pandemic in human civilisation. The virus has not been entirely eradicated from the world; instead, it continues to exist with its mutated variations. The COVID-19 pandemic has left a trail of devastation in human societies, economies, and almost all aspects of lives, including in the legal domains of IPRs and human rights law. This pandemic has exposed its serious marginalising effects on the human rights to health and lives in the Global South because of the lopsided distribution of vaccines and related essential drugs. These catastrophic consequences are largely attributable to the unlimited greed of COVID vaccines and drugs manufacturers and their countries of incorporation which have a vested interest of revenue earnings from corporate profit maximisation. The selfish vaccine nationalism and hoarding by rich countries has but added to the sufferings of poor countries, particularly in the Global South.

In the COVID pandemic, the perennial conundrum of North-South conflict of interests once again has preserved the inviolability of IPRs with peripheral importance to human rights. This status quo warrants a paradigm shift in its policy orientation. Highlighting the right to access to COVID-19 vaccines and pharmaceuticals as an essential component of human rights, this chapter has demonstrated that the strict IP protection regime under TRIPS has constricted already established norms and commitments of contemporaneous international human rights law. This is analogous to neo-colonialism that must be abandoned in favour of incorporating human rights consideration in interpreting and enforcing IPRs in potential global public health crises.

Bibliography

Books

Byttebier, Koen. "Final Conclusions." In *COVID-19 and Capitalism- Economic and Financial Law & Policy – Shifting Insights & Values*. Vol. 7, Brussels: Springer International Publishing, 2022.

Helfer, Laurence R. and Graeme W Austin. *Human Rights and Intellectual Property: Mapping* Laurence *the Global Interface*. UK: Cambridge University Press, 2011.

Langan, Mark. *Neo-Colonialism and the Poverty of 'Development' in Africa*. UK, Palgrave Macmillan, 2018.

Smith, Linda Tuhiwai. *Decolonizing Methodologies: Research and Indigenous Peoples*. London: Zed Books, 2012.

Chapters in Edited Books

Beiter, Klaus D. "Establishing Conformity Between TRIPS and Human Rights: Hierarchy in International Law, Human Rights Obligations of the WTO and Extraterritorial State Obligations Under the International Covenant on Economic, Social and Cultural Rights." In *TRIPS plus 20*, edited by Hanns Ullrich et al. 445–505. Berlin/ Heidelberg: Springer, 2016.

Forman, Lisa. "Global health governance from below: access to AIDS medicines, International human rights law and social movements." In *Innovation in global health governance: critical cases*, edited by Andrew F Cooper, John J Kirton, 193–207. New York: Routledge, 2016.

Ruse-Khan, Henning Grosse. "Assessing the Need for a General Public Interest Exception in the TRIPS Agreement." In *Intellectual Property Rights in a Fair World Trade System: Proposals for Reform of TRIPS*, edited by Kur Annette, 167–207. UK: Edward Elgar Publishing, 2011)..

Articles

Abbott, Frederick. "The Trips Agreement, Access to Medicines, and the WTO Doha Ministerial Conference." *Journal of World Intellectual Property* 5, no. 1 (2002): 15–52.

Affun-Adegbulu, Clara and Opemiposi Adegbulu. "Decolonising Global (Public) Health: From Western Universalism to Global Pluriversalities." *BMJ Global Health* 5, no. 8 (2020): e002947: 1–3.

Balfour, Rosa, Lizza Bimassi, and Marta Martinelli, 'Coronavirus and the Widening Global North-South Gap' Carnegie working paper (April 2022) 1–14.

Bajaj, Simar Singh, Lwando Maki and Fatima Cody Stanford. "Vaccine Apartheid: Global Cooperation and Equity." *The Lancet* 399, no. 10334 (2022): 1452–1453.

Baxi, Upendra. "Market Fundamentalisms: Business Ethics at the Altar of Human Rights." *Human Rights Law Review* 5, no. 1 (2005): 1–26.

Felice, Giulio de, Nihal Tutal, and Nicolina Sciaraffa, "Geopolitical Aspects of COVID-19 Vaccines Distribution", *European Journal of Environment and Public Health* 7, no. 3 (2023): 1–10.

Fujikane, Candace. "Asian American Critique and Moana Nui 2011: Securing a Future beyond Empires, Militarized Capitalism and APEC." *Inter-Asia Cultural Studies* 13, no. 2 (2012): 189–210.

Gostin, Lawrence O et al. "The Legal Determinants of Health: Harnessing the Power of Law for Global Health and Sustainable Development." *The Lancet* 393, no. 10183 (2019): 1857–1910.

Gostin, Lawrence O, Safura Abdool Karim, and Benjamin Mason Meier. "Facilitating Access to a COVID-19 Vaccine through Global Health Law." *Journal of Law, Medicine & Ethics* 48, no. 3 (2020): 622–626.

Gruskin, Sofia and Zyde Raad. "Are Drug Companies Living Up to Their Human Rights Responsibilities? Moving Toward Assessment." *PLOS Medicine* 7, no. 9 (2010): e1000310: 1–3.

Helfer, Laurence R. "Toward a Human Rights Framework for Intellectual Property." *U.C. Davis Law Review* 40 (2007): 971–1020.

Hodgson, Timothy and Rossella De Falco. "Human Rights and Universal Access to COVID-19 Vaccines: Does the Human Rights Council Resolution Go Far Enough?." *Opinio Juris* (March 23, 2021), <http://opiniojuris.org/2021/03/23/human-rights-and-universal-access-to-covid-19-vaccines-does-the-human-rights-council-resolution-go-far-enough/>.

Hoecklin, Madeleine. "€93 billion Spent by Public Sector on COVID Vaccines and Therapeutics in 11 Months, Finds New Research." Health Policy Watch (January 12, 2021), <https://healthpolicy-watch.news/81038-2/>.

Hotez, Peter J. "'Vaccine Diplomacy': Historical Perspectives and Future Directions." *PLOS Neglected Tropical Diseases* 8, no. 6 (2014): e2808.

ICTSD. "First Generic Drugs en Route to Africa under 5 Years Old WTO Deal." *Bridges Weekly Trade News Digest* 12, no. 31 (2008).

Kavanagh, Matthew M, Lawrence O. Gostin, and Madhavi Sunder. "Sharing Technology and Vaccine Doses to Address Global Vaccine Inequity and End the COVID-19 Pandemic." *Journal of American Medical Association* 326, no. 3 (2021): 219 <https://doi.org/10.1001/jama.2021.10823>.

Pogge, Thomas. "Access to Medicines." *Public Health Ethics* 1, no. 2 (2008): 73.

Prabhala, Achal and Leena Menghaney. "The World's Poorest Countries Are at India's Mercy for Vaccines. It's Unsustainable." *The Guardian* (April 2, 2021), <https://www.theguardian.com/commentisfree/2021/apr/02/india-in-charge-of-developing-world-covid-vaccine-supply-unsustainable>.

Seuba, Xavier. "Round Table: A Human Rights Approach to the WHO Model List of Essential Medicines." *Bulletin of the World Health Organization* 84 (2006), 405–411.

Slade, Alison. "Good Faith and the TRIPS Agreement: Putting Flesh on the Bones of the TRIPS 'Objective'." *International & Comparative Law Quarterly* 63, no. 2 (2014): 353–383.

"Statement on Universal Affordable Vaccination against Coronavirus Disease COVID-19, International Cooperation and Intellectual Property: Committee on Economic, Social and Cultural Rights." *International Human Rights Law Review* 10, no. 1 (2021): 180–187.

Trouiller, Patrice et al. "Drug Development for Neglected Diseases: A Deficient Market and a Public-Health Policy Failure." *The Lancet* 359, no. 9324 (2002): 2188.

Tuck, Eve and K. Wayne Yang. "Decolonization Is Not a Metaphor." *Decolonization: Indigeneity, Education and Society* 1, no. 1 (2012): 1–40.

Usher, Ann Danaiya. "A Beautiful Idea: How COVAX Has Fallen Short." *The Lancet* 397. no. 10292 (2021): 2322.

Williams, Caitlin R, Jocelyn Getgen Kestenbaum and Benjamin Mason Meier. "Populist Nationalism Threatens Health and Human Rights in the COVID-19 Response." *American Journal of Public Health* 110, no. 12 (2020): 1766–1768.

Wouters, Olivier J et al. "Challenges in Ensuring Global Access to COVID-19 Vaccines: Production, Affordability, Allocation, and Deployment." *The Lancet* 397, no. 10278 (2021): 1023.

Yamey, Gavin et al. "It Is Not Too Late to Achieve Global Covid-19 Vaccine Equity." *British Medical Journal* 376, (March 2022): 0812, accessed March 15, 2023, <https://www.bmj.com/content/376/bmj.o812>.

Zaman, Khorsed. "The Waiver of Certain Intellectual Property Rights Provisions of the TRIPS for the Prevention, Containment and Treatment of COVID-19: A Review of the Proposal under WTO Jurisprudence." *European Journal of Risk Regulation* 13, no. 2 (2022): 295–310.

Documents

Additional Protocol to the American Convention on Human Rights in the Area of Economic, Social and Cultural Rights (San Salvador Protocol) 1988.

African Charter of Human and People's Rights 1981.

Arab Charter on Human Rights for the Middle East 1994.

Constitution of Bhutan 2008.

Constitution of Burundi 2005.

Constitution of Congo 2002.

Constitution of Croatia 1990.

Constitution of the WHO. Accessed February 11, 2023, <https://apps.who.int/gb/bd/PDF/bd47/EN/constitution-en.pdf?ua=1>.

Human Rights Watch. "Universal and Equitable Access to Covid-19 Vaccines, Testing, Treatments: Companies' Human Rights Responsibilities." (February 11, 2021), <https://www.hrw.org/news/2021/02/11/universal-and-equitable-access-covid-19-vaccines-testing-treatments-companies-human>.

Integrating IPRS and Development Policy. Commission for Intellectual Property Rights. Final Report, London (September 2002). Accessed February 6, 2023, <http://www.iprcommission.org/graphic/documents/final_report.htm>.

Minutes of the TRIPS Council meeting held on April 2–5, 2001. WTO Doc. IP/C/M/30 (June 1, 2001).

Negotiating Group on Trade-Related Aspects of Intellectual Property Rights, including Trade in Counterfeit Goods. WTO Negotiation Doc. MTN.GNG/NG11/W/32/Rev.1 (1989).

OHCHR. "COVID-19: UN Experts Urge WTO Cooperation on Vaccines to Protect Global Public Health." Accessed February 4, 2023, <https://www.ohchr.org/en/press-releases/2021/03/covid-19-un-experts-urge-wto-cooperation-vaccines-protect-global-public>.

OHCHR. "Guiding Principles on Business and Human Rights." Accessed February 2, 2023, <https://www.ohchr.org/sites/default/files/documents/publications/guidingprinciplesbusinesshr_en.pdf>.

Oloka-Onyango and Deepika Udagama, *The Realization of Economic, Social and Cultural Rights: Globalization and Its Impact on the Full Enjoyment of Human Rights*, UN Doc. E/CN.4/Sub.2/2000/13, June 15, 2000.

Ruggie, John. Report of the Special Representative of the Secretary-General on the Issue of Human Rights and Transnational Corporations and Other Business Enterprises: "Protect, Respect and Remedy: A Framework for Business and Human Rights." UN Doc. A/HRC/8/5 (April 7, 2008).

UN General Assembly Resolutions No. 1230 (December 14, 2020): "The UN Decade of Healthy Ageing (2021–2030)". UN Doc. A/75/L.47 (December 8, 2020).

UN General Assembly. "Global health and foreign policy – strengthening health system resilience through affordable health care for all". UN Doc. A/75/L.41, December 3, 2020.

UN General Assembly. "The Right of Everyone to the Enjoyment of the Highest Attainable Standard of Physical and Mental Health." Report of the Special Rapporteur, Paul Hunt, U.N. General Assembly, 63rd Session, Agenda Item 67(b), UN Doc. A/63/263 (August 11, 2008).

UN General Assembly. "The Right to Health" GA RES. S-26/2 (July 27, 2021).

UN High Commissioner for Human Rights. "The impact of the Agreement on Trade-related Aspects of Intellectual Property Rights on human rights." Accessed February 23, 2023, <https://digitallibrary.un.org/record/446005>.

UN Human Rights Council. "Measures Taken to Implement Human Rights Council Resolution 9/8 and Obstacles to Its Implementation, Including Recommendations for Further Improving the Effectiveness of, Harmonizing and Reforming the Treaty Body System Report of the Secretary-General." UN Doc. A/HRC/46/25 (2020).

UN. Committee on Economic, Social and Cultural Rights. General Comment No. 14. Doc. 12/2000/4 (August 11, 2000).

UNHCR. "General Comment No. 24 (2017) on State Obligations under the International Covenant on Economic, Social and Cultural Rights in the Context of Business Activities." Accessed February 2, 2023, <https://www.refworld.org/docid/5beaecba4.html>.

Waiver from Certain Provisions of the TRIPS Agreement for the Prevention, Containment and Treatment of COVID-19: Communication from India and South Africa. WTO Doc. IP/C/W/669 (October 2, 2020).

WIPO Copyright Treaty 1996.

WIPO Performances and Phonograms Treaty 1996.

WTO Ministerial Conferences. Doha 4th Ministerial – TRIPS Declaration. Accessed February 12, 2023, <https://www.wto.org/english/thewto_e/minist_e/min01_e/mindecl_trips_e.htm>.

WTO. 2017 News Items. "WTO IP Rules Amended to Ease Poor Countries Access to Affordable Medicines". Accessed February 12, 2023, <https://www.wto.org/english/news_e/news17_e/trip_23jan17_e.htm>.

WTO. "TRIPS Council Welcomes MC12 TRIPS Waiver Decision, Discusses Possible Extension." Accessed February 4, 2023, <https://www.wto.org/english/news_e/news22_e/trip_08jul22_e.htm>.

WTO. Agreement on Trade-Related Aspects of Intellectual Property Rights (TRIPS), April 15, 1995, *International Legal Materials* 33 (1994).

WTO. Doha Declaration on the TRIPS Agreement and Public Health, (WTO Doc. WT/MIN(01)/DEC/2)(November 20, 2001).

Internet Sources

BBC News. "Covid Vaccine: WHO Warns of 'Catastrophic Moral Failure'." *BBC News*, (January 18, 2021), <https://www.bbc.com/news/world-55709428>.

COVID. Coronavirus Statistics – Worldometer. Accessed March 15, 2023, <https://www.worldometers.info/coronavirus/>.

GAVI. "COVAX Facility." Accessed 22 March 2023, <https://www.gavi.org/covax-facility>.

GAVI. "COVID-19 and the Cost of Vaccine Nationalism." Accessed March 15, 2023, <https://www.gavi.org/vaccineswork/covid-19-and-cost-vaccine-nationalism>.

Global Health Centre (Geneva). "COVID-19 Vaccine Access." Accessed February 8, 2023, <https://www.knowledgeportalia.org/covid-19-vaccine-access>.

Love, James. "Open Letter Asking 37 WTO Members to Declare Themselves Eligible to Import Medicines Manufactured under Compulsory License in Another Country, under 31bis of TRIPS Agreement." Knowledge Ecology International, February 7, 2023, <https://www.keionline.org/32707>.

Opinio Juris. "Harmonizing Global Health Law and Human Rights Law to Develop Rights-Based Approaches to Global Health Emergencies"., (February 24, 2021) <http://opiniojuris.org/2021/02/24/harmonizing-global-health-law-and-human-rights-law-to-develop-rights-based-approaches-to-global-health-emergencies/>.

Oxfam. "Pfizer, BioNTech and Moderna Making $1,000 Profit Every Second While World's Poorest Countries Remain Largely Unvaccinated." Oxfam/ReliefWeb (November 16, 2021) <https://reliefweb.int/report/world/pfizer-biontech-and-moderna-making-1000-profit-every-second-while-world-s-poorest>..

Pratt, Simon F and Jamie Levin. "Vaccine will shape the new geopolitical order". *Foreign Policy* (April 29, 2021) <https://foreignpolicy.com/2021/04/29/vaccine-geopolitics-diplomacy-israel-russia-china/>.

Ruse-Khan, Grosse and Henning. "The (Non) Use of Treaty Object and Purpose in Intellectual Property Disputes in the WTO." (SSRN Scholarly Paper No 1939859, September 28, 2011), accessed January 12, 2023, <https://papers.ssrn.com/abstract=1939859>.

UNDP. "What are the Sustainable Development Goals?". Accessed March 25, 2023, <https://www.undp.org/sustainable-development-goals>.

Watal, Jayashree. "Analysis of the 12th WTO Ministerial Conference Decision on the TRIPS Agreement." Accessed March 3, 2023, <https://www.ejiltalk.org/analysis-of-the-12th-wto-ministerial-conference-decision-on-the-trips-agreement/>.

Cases

Australia – Tobacco Plain Packaging, WT/D 467/2, Panel report (August 30, 2018).

Canada – Term of Patent Protection, WT/DS170/AB/R, AB Report (September 18, 2000).

Daniels v. Scribante and Another (2017) SA (CC), (2017) BCLR (CC), [2017] ZACC 13.

US – Section 211 Omnibus Appropriations Act of 1998, WT/DS176/R, Panel report (August 6, 2001).

CHAPTER 16

Digital Indigenous Cultural Heritage – Reconciling Intellectual Property Rights, Human Rights and Indigenous Worldviews through Proactive Approaches and Engagement

Rosa Ballardini, Iiris Tuominen and Dino Girardi

1 Introduction

Cultural heritage (CH) is an important element of identity for both indigenous communities and individuals. The UNESCO Convention for the Safeguarding of the Intangible Cultural Heritage[1] defines in its Article 2(1) CH as a legacy that is inherited from the past and bestowed for the future, but also as a process that is constantly recreated by communities and groups in response to their environment, their interaction with nature and their history. Consequently, there is growing focus on issues related to the protection, access and management of indigenous peoples' CH through legal means. For decades, indigenous peoples have expressed concern about the lack of representation and respect for their own ethics and human rights in decision-making processes and laws governing their culture. In recent years, however, there has been a remarkable increase in global awareness of these issues, largely due to technological developments, especially digitalisation. These include the digitisation and management of digitised objects, the application of artificial intelligence, particularly machine learning and deep learning, blockchain applications as well as the future applications of the metaverse. These advancements have greatly enhanced possibilities for protecting, accessing, promoting, and exploiting CH through digital means. Notwithstanding the opportunities, digitisation also poses several challenges, in terms of the representation and content of exhibitions, which are particularly pressing in the context of indigenous CH. The main concern is that this reduces the effective participation and inclusion of Indigenous people, hindering equitable representations of diverse values in

1 The UNESCO Convention for the Safeguarding of the Intangible Cultural Heritage adopted by the UNESCO General Conference on 17 October 2003.

 | DOI:10.1163/9789004530942_017

digitisation. Ultimately this can lead to an increased risk of misuse digital CH and can pose challenges to fundamental rights, such as in particular the right of self-determination.

In this regard, previous research has shown that intellectual property rights (IPR) are both essential and problematic for promoting innovation and creativity in the context of indigenous (digital) CH in an ethical and human-rights respecting manner. Although they have been the subject of intense academic and political debate in the past, most discussions of IPR and indigenous digital CH have been approached from separate perspectives, with the view of indigenous peoples' and Western countries' considered in isolation or presented as an unmanageable and unsolvable conflict. This fundamental structural imbalance and narrow approach has fostered mistrust among the many stakeholders involved, leading to the a number of irresponsible actions where indigenous worldviews and fundamental rights have been overlooked. Recently, this issue has been recognised, for instance, by funding trends in the EU which increasingly highlight the fact that while much has been developed in terms of research and innovation in relation to digitisation of CH, work should now be done to develop policies and strategies to better use and manage digitisation in the context of CH.[2] By focusing on selected cases in the specific context of IPR protection and intellectual property (IP) licensing related to the digitisation and use of indigenous peoples' CH, this chapter sheds light on the existing conflicts between indigenous peoples' worldviews and their fundamental rights (especially their right of self-determination), on the one hand, and the IPR frameworks, on the other. To provide concrete examples and support our theoretical arguments, we draw primarily on cases from one indigenous community, the Sámi people. First, we highlight general points of contradiction between IPR laws, indigenous worldviews and core human rights, andthen contextualise these arguments in relation to cases related of IPR protection and IP licensing, drawing on the Sámi experience in the field of digital CH. Through this case-study analysis, we will shed light on the fact that one of the main reasons for these challenges is the lack of adequate measures to promote the inclusion and participation of indigenous people in the process. Thus, our aim is to propose solid criteria for future legislative and policy actions to construct more inclusive, participatory, and ultimately respectful of indigenous' worldviews in the context of digital CH of indigenous people in general.

2 See e.g. Horizon Europe programme 2023–2024, Cluster 5. Culture, Creativity and Inclusive Society (European Commission Decision C(2022)7550 of December 6, 2022).

2 Human Rights and IPR Challenges with Digital CH of Indigenous People

Indigenous cultural appropriation is not a new phenomenon triggered by digitalisation only. Examples date back to the 19th century, and cover areas ranging from creativities, such as handicrafts and dress heritage, to the use of indigenous traditional knowledge in medicine, biology or the like.[3] These concerns are familiar from the discussions on 'orientalism',[4] the way in which Europe constructed its common identity by defining 'the oriental' as 'the others'. This is essentially a power relationship: the conceptualisation of 'the Orient' as 'the other' includes the assumptions of the superiority of Western values and systems of thought, as well as stereotypical notions of these 'others' as exotic, primitive and irrational.[5] Because the subjects of these inappropriate activities often relate to original creativities or inventive innovations, which fall under the domain of the intellectual property right (IPR) legislation, various issues related to cultural appropriation and CH in relation to IPR have been discussed in the past – also including specificities from a Sámi perspective.[6] In this chapter, we look at the issue of where digitisation of indigenous CH and IPR legislation collide, ultimately leading to challenges in respecting indigenous worldviews as well as fundamental rights of indigenous peoples, primarily the right of self-determination. However, before going into the details of how and why the IPR system challenges the respect and promotion of indigenous worldviews in the context of digital indigenous CH, it is important to provide an overview of the concept of the right of self-determination in relation to indigenous peoples.

According to Hannum, self-determination has two aspects, internal and external. Internal self-determination is the right of the people of a state to govern themselves without outside interference, while external self-determination is the right of people to determine their own political status and to be free of alien domination, including formation of their own independent

3 Kamrul Hossain and Rosa Maria Ballardini, "Protecting Indigenous Traditional Knowledge Through a Holistic Principle-Based Approach," *Nordic Journal of Human Rights* 39, no. 1 (2021): 51–72.

4 Edward Said, *Orientalism* (New York: Pantheon Books, 1978).

5 Laura Junka-Aikio, "Can the Sámi Speak Now? Deconstructive Research Ethos and the Debate on Who Is a Sámi in Finland," *Cultural Studies* 30, no. 2 (2016): 217. See also Iiris Tuominen, Rosa Ballardini, Jukka Mähönen & Taina Pihlajarinne, "Protecting and accessing indigenous peoples' digital cultural heritage through sustainable governance and IPR structures: The case of Sámi culture," *Arctic review on law and politics* 14 (2023): 194–219.

6 Tuominen et al., "Indigenous Peoples' Digital Cultural Heritage".

state.[7] In international law, the right of self-determination became recognised in the 1960s and it was interpreted as the right of all colonial territories to become independent or to adopt any other status they freely chose. Today, the right of groups to govern themselves is increasingly intertwined with human rights norms, in particular the rights of minorities and indigenous peoples. The right of self-determination is codified in the two human rights treaties adopted in 1966, that is the International Covenant on Civil and Political Rights (ICCPR)[8] and the International Covenant on Economic, Social, and Cultural Rights (ICESCR).[9] According to these instruments, self-determination is a right that belongs to all peoples. Both treaties affirm in their first article, that 'all peoples have the right of self-determination. By virtue of this right they shall freely determine their political status and freely pursue their economic, social and cultural development'. However, the concept of 'all peoples' has traditionally been understood to refer to the population of an existing state, and not to sub-state groups, such as indigenous peoples.[10] This gap led to the drafting and adoption of the UN Declaration on the Rights of Indigenous Peoples (UNDRIP),[11] which recognises indigenous peoples as equal toother peoples in terms of the right of self-determination.

Cambou describes the meaning of the UNDRIP by stating 'that the Declaration provides the first universal instrument to recognise and elaborate the content of the right to self-determination for indigenous peoples. It is also the first instrument to recognise the right of self-determination

7 Hurst Hannum, "Legal aspects of self-determination," Encyclopedia Princetoniencies, accessed April 14, 2023, https://pesd.princeton.edu/node/511.

8 United Nations (General Assembly). 1966. "International Covenant on Civil and Political Rights." Treaty Series 999 (December): 171.

9 United Nations (General Assembly). 1966. "International Covenant on Economic, Social, and Cultural Rights." Treaty Series 999 (December): 171.

10 Aureliu Cristecu, "The right to self-determination: historical and current development on the basis of United Nations instruments: study / prepared by Aureliu Cristescu, Special Rapporteur of the Sub-Commission on Prevention of Discrimination and Protection of Minorities," (New York: UN. Subcommission on Prevention of Discrimination and Protection of Minorities, 1981), https://digitallibrary.un.org/record/25252; Rauna Kuokkanen, *Restructuring Relations: Indigenous Self-Determination, Governance and Gender* (New York: Oxford University Press, 2019), 26.; Dorothée Cambou, "The UNDRIP and the legal significance of the right of indigenous peoples to self-determination: a human rights approach with a multidimensional perspective," *The International Journal of Human Rights* 23, no. 1–2 (2019): 1–17, 3.

11 Assembly, UN General. *United Nations declaration on the rights of indigenous peoples: resolution/adopted by the General Assembly, 2 October 2007*. A/RES/61/295, 2007, accessed July 14, 2023, https://documents-dds-ny.un.org/doc/UNDOC/GEN/N06/512/07/PDF/N0651207.pdf?OpenElement.

for peoples other than those territorially organised as states and colonies.'[12] However, Kuokkanen notes that the right of self-determination enshrined in the UNDRIP is 'radically curtailed by Article 4, which limits to the exercise the right of Indigenous self-determination to internal and local affairs',[13] whereas such limitations do not apply to general right of self-determination of the peoples organised around state-structure. Nevertheless, as Heinämäki notes, "by using the human rights framework, Indigenous peoples have succeeded, at least partly, in pressuring state governments to return their lost status of legal subjectivity and self-governance."[14] Heinämäki adds that international human rights law has moved from treating indigenous peoples as objects of protection to recognizing their position as self-governing powers in the matters crucial for them.[15] Thus, while the UNDRIP can be critiqued for many reasons, it can still be considered as an important step forward for international law and rights of indigenous peoples' rights in general, and self-determination in particular.

While the right of self-determination, enshrined in Article 3 of the UNDRIP, is the backbone of cultural sovereignty for indigenous peoples, also other articles address the issue. Article 5 concerns the maintaining and strengthening of distinct political, legal, economic, social and cultural institutions and Article 11 refers to the right of indigenous peoples to practise and revitalise their cultural traditions and customs. This includes the right to preserve, protect and develop the past, present and future manifestations of their cultures. Especially, Article 31 includes a reference to CH and intellectual property, affirming the right to maintain, control, protect and develop CH, traditional knowledge, and traditional cultural expressions. These articles provide the framework for indigenous governance over their CH in accordance to the right of self-determination. However, these provisions do not create new law. Rather, as Xanthaki notes, they interpret existing binding human rights treaties, including how article 15 of the ICERC and article 27 ICCPR apply to indigenous peoples' CH.[16]

From the perspective of self-determination, the principle of free, prior and informed consent (FPIC) should also be considered. According to UN Sub-Commission on the Promotion and Protection of Human Rights, FPIC:

12 Cambou, "UNDRIP," 2.

13 Kuokkanen, *Restructuring Relations*, 27.

14 Leena Heinämäki, "The Rapidly Evolving International Status of Indigenous Peoples," in *Indigenous Rights in Scandinavia: Autonomous Sami Law*, eds. Christina Allardt and Susan Funderud Skogvang (Oxon/New York: Routledge, 2015), 191.

15 Ibid.

16 Alexandra Xanthaki, "International Instruments on Cultural Heritage: Tales of Fragmentation," in *Indigenous peoples' Cultural Heritage: Rights, Debates, Challenges*, eds. Alexandra Xanthaki et al. (Leiden: Brill/Nijhoff, 2017), 11.

> [R]ecognizes indigenous peoples' inherent and prior rights to their lands and resources and respects their legitimate authority to require that third parties enter into an equal and respectful relationship with them based on the principle of informed consent. Procedurally, free, prior and informed consent requires processes that allow and support meaningful choices by indigenous peoples about their development path.[17]

FPIC is enshrined in the UNDRIP, but also the ILO Convention 169 and the Convention on Biological Diversity. According to this principle, indigenous peoples have the right to give or withdraw their consent to projects that affect them or their territories.[18] This principle has usually been interpreted in the context of land use and research, but digitalisation is undoubtedly creating new contexts in which FPIC issues arise. While FPIC is recognised in many of the international human rights documents, its integration into national legislation varies. While it has been noted that existing laws should be interpreted from the perspective of FPIC,[19] it remains more of an ethical principle than a binding international rule.

After these preliminary remarks, let's return to where we started: the conflict between the role of IPR in the context of the digital CH of indigenous peoples, especially with regard to the respect and promotion of indigenous peoples' rights such as self-determination. Generally speaking, IPR are a set of exclusive rights designed to provide authors of original works (copyright), or inventors of non-obvious inventions (patents) or creators of distinctive signs (trademarks) with a relative temporary monopoly right to exclude others from engaging in certain activities (such as copying, reproducing, remaking or using) with the protected object (e.g. a work, an invention or a sign) unless explicit permission is granted (e.g. through a license) or otherwise maintained as permissible (e.g. through so called exceptions of limitations to the right).[20] In the context of CH, copyright is perhaps the most applicable type of IPR, as many CH artefacts that are digitised or are digitally born relate to creative works (e.g. crafts, images,

---

17 Commission on Human Rights, Sub-Commission on the Promotion and Protection of Human Rights, Working Group on Indigenous Populations, Twenty-second session, 19 -13 July 2004, 5.

18 "Free, Prior and Informed Consent – An Indigenous Peoples' Right and a Good Practice for Local Communities," (Food and Agriculture Organization of the United Nations, 2016), https://www.fao.org/3/i6190e/i6190e.pdf, 13.

19 Heinämäki, "International Status of Indigenous Peoples", 19.

20 For a general overview of IP rights see Annette Kur, Thomas Dreier and Stefan Luginbuehl, *European Intellectual Property Law – Texts, Cases and Materials*, 2nd ed. (Cheltenham: Edward Edgar, 2019).

music, stories, etc..). While applying copyright to protect indigenous CH would seem logical, it also raises challenges, as mentioned above, due to the specific element of indigeneity involved.

Tuominen et al. point out that Western IPR legislation on indigenous CH is at times at odds with the indigenous worldviews and forms of self-governance – a key reason being related to the colonial past suffered by indigenous communities.[21] Thus, (digitised) materials related to indigenous CH are owned (via IPR), maintained or managed (e.g. through licensing) by organisations such as State cultural institutions such as museums and archives, which are not representative of indigenous worldviews and practices. In other words, these materials are governed by legal structures, especially IPR, that reflect a majority culture (i.e. Western IPR systems), which might not be consistent with indigenous perspectives.

As a starting and key point, Western IPR systems are justified by theories, such as utilitarian theories, which have a strong owner-centered approach and focus heavily on economic aspects and incentives.[22] This is particularly problematic in relation to regulation of indigenous peoples' CH, where ethical values rather than the economic expectations and interests of individual rights owners should play a major role.[23] This conflict becomes particularly clear when we look at the idea of 'exclusivity' in IPR – which is a key pillar of the whole IPR system. An exclusivity approach explains both the nature of ownership (e.g. of the knowledge system) and its institutional structure. In most types of IPR systems, exclusivity refers to the fact that IP rights involve exclusive rights for the IP owner to exclude others from doing certain things (such as copying, making, using, or distributing) with a protected work of innovation. This approach differs from the indigenous approach to exclusivity. Indigenous worldviews show a particular kind of exclusivity of ownership and structure where the role of the law is to preserve the exclusivity of ownership not by excluding others, *but by reconciling their interests.*[24] This very different way of conceiving of exclusive rights is one of the key issues that has led to contracts in many aspects where IPR are applied to indigenous CH in general, ranging from how the scope of IPR protection is defined tohow enforcement measures and remedies for infringement are defined. Indeed, the digitilisation of indigenous CH has acted as driving force to exacerbate this fundamental

21 Tuominen et al., "Indigenous Peoples' Digital Cultural Heritage."

22 William Fisher, "Theories of Intellectual Property," in *New Essays in the Legal and Political Theory of Property*, ed. Stephen Munzer (Cambridge: Cambridge University Press, 2001).

23 Hossain and Ballardini, "Protecting Indigenous Traditional," 2.

24 Ibid.

contrast. All in all, this has led to difficulties and misappropriations on many occasions. In addition, another fundamental problem with IPR and indigenous CH is that the profits deriving from these types of activities remain with the majority population[25] – as the history of Sámi CH as indigenous peoples in Nordic countries shows.[26]

Notwithstanding the failures, IPR also provide an important legal incentive to protect and promote creativity, including those related to indigenous CH. Thus, to promote creativity and prosperity in this area, it is important to strike a fair balance between human rights, especially access to justice and self-determination, including benefit-sharing arrangements in the context of IPR and indigenous CH in the digital context.

3 Case Studies

This session presents two exemplary cases from Sámi digital CH. On the one hand, the cases are good examples to show that the conflict between the IPR system and the indigenous worldview has clearly emerged, causing problems in enabling the respect of fundamental rights, especially the right of self-determination. On the other hand, though, they shed light on the fact that there are feasible ways that need to be further explored to reconcile IPR, indigenous CH and digitisation in line with indigenous worldviews, promoting indigenous peoples' right to self-determination in the process through engagement and participation.

3.1 *IPR Protection – The Frozen Case*

One case that illustrates particularly well the conflict between the protection of intellectual property rights, the worldviews of the Sámi and the right of indigenous people to self-determination in the context of digital CH are illustrated especially well is the so-called *Frozen* case.

Frozen, a Disney blockbuster computer-animated movie, premiered in 2013 (*Frozen I*). It was announced in 2015 that there would be a sequel in 2015 (*Frozen*

25 Rosa Maria Ballardini, Heidi Härkönen, and Iiris Kestilä, "Intellectual property rights and indigenous dress heritage: towards more social planning types of practices via user-centric approaches," in *Legal Design: Integrating Business, Design and Legal Thinking with Technology*, eds. Marcelo Corrales Compagnucci *et al.*, (Cheltenham: Edward Elgar, 2021), 82–106.

26 Rauna Kuokkanen, "The Deatnu Agreement: A Contemporary Wall of Settler Colonialism," *Settler Colonial Studies* 10, no. 4 (2020), https://doi.org/10.1080/2201473X.2020.1794211.

II). The movie tells the story of Princess Elsa of Arendelle and her sister Anna, who were left without their parents at a young age and are divided by Elsa's fear of her increasingly unpredictable powers to turn everything she touches into snow or ice. The story sees Anna teaming up with an iceman (Kristoff), his reindeer, and a snowman to find her estranged sister Elsa. *Frozen I* had already sparked controversy, as it seemed that certain characters in the movie were heavily inspired by the Sámi culture. For example, Kristoff the iceman, one of the main characters of the movie, had a wardrobe that appeared to be based on traditional Sámi dress. In addition, the film included a theme song with part of *joik* (a traditional form of a song in Sámi music), which many saw as cultural appropriation at the time.[27]

While the original controversy was perhaps a little more complicated than the internet discourse made it out to be,[28] representatives of the Sámi culture have suggested that not everything went as it should have with *Frozen I.* For example, Christina Henriksen from the Sámi Council has stated that while *Frozen I* was inspired by the Sámi culture and Disney representatives had travelled to Sápmi, that is the traditional homeland of the Sámi people,[29] and had been inspired by the Sámi culture, no actual negotiations had taken place with the Sámi people.[30] Similarly, Áile Aikio from the Sámi museum Siida commented on the case, saying that it was problematic that Disney had made a lot of money from the film, while leaving it unclear how the Sámi could benefit from it. Aikio also pointed out that the film was not available in the Sámi languages. 'The Sámi culture is not something that you can just take and make

---

27 Radheyan Simonpillai, "Disney signed a contract with Indigenous people before making Frozen II," *Now Toronto*, November 19, 2019, https://nowtoronto.com/movies/news-features/disney-frozen-2-indigenous-culture-sami/.

28 For example, the theme song of the movie was in fact composed by a Sámi musician and composer Frode Fjellheim, therefore making it hard to accuse the song for cultural appropriation. Disney was also accused of 'whitewashing' Kristoff, even though many Sámi people may have blonde hair and blue eyes. However, what happened was more likely erasing the cultural context for the film.

29 The region stretches over four countries: Norway, Sweden, Finland, and Russia.

30 Behind the Scenes of Frozen 2: How Sámi Representatives Cooperated with Disney", *Arctic Council*, January 23, 2020, https://www.arctic-council.org/news/behind-the-scenes-of-frozen-2-how-saami-representatives-cooperated-with-disney/; Kevin McGwin, "How a collaboration with Disney shaped the way Sámi cultural details were portrayed in Frozen 2," *ArcticToday*, February 3, 2020, https://www.arctictoday.com/how-a-collaboration-with-disney-shaped-the-way-sami-cultural-details-were-portrayed-in-frozen-2/.

money out of it', Aikio stated.[31] As a solution, Aikio suggested that the sequel could, for example, include more Sámi artists.

In short, *Frozen I* was heavily inspired by the Sámi culture, without giving anything back to the communities. In addition, at least in theory, Disney could have claimed copyright protection for the works (e.g. figurines of Kristoff) containing Sámi elements, or register them as its trademarks, thus, being able to enforce these rights against Sámi people. Such a work could be, for example, the Sámi dress.[32] For many indigenous peoples, dress heritage is perhaps the most striking and visible part of their CH.[33] It is also one of the cultural elements most often misused and appropriated.[34] Another set of works could be the songs, although in this case the song was composed by a Sámi person. As Ballardini et al. note:

> Because the right to use and reproduce certain elements in clothing may be determined by customary laws that are not recognized outside of the community, it is very difficult for traditional communities to use legal means to prevent these elements from being copied and used for commercial purposes by others, if these elements are not kept secret.[35]

Indeed, for example dress heritage of indigenous peoples is often governed by customary law and rules. Also, as noted above, indigenous views often differ significantly from Western-based laws and rules regarding intellectual property. For example, indigenous notions of property may have a stronger collective element, whereas Western understanding of property is often based on individual ownership.[36]

31 Mikko-Pekka Heikkinen and Jussi Pullinen, "Disney kävi Inarissa tutkimassa saamelaista elämää Frozenin jatko-osaan – Saamelaiset haluavat korvausta," *Helsingin Sanomat*, September 23, 2016, https://www.hs.fi/kotimaa/art-2000002922271.html.

32 See e.g. Ballardini, Härkönen and Kestilä, "Indigenous Dress Heritage".

33 Ibid.

34 For example, in 2015, Finland's Miss World contestant Carola Miller was supposed to represent her country in a fake Sámi dress that was bought from a joking costume store. Similar incidents have happened in other Nordic countries as well. See Samppa Rautio, 'Suomen Miss Maailma -edustaja ei esiinny pilailupuodin lapinpuvussa – "Tapahtui suuri virhe"', *YLE*, December 11, 2015, https://yle.fi/aihe/artikkeli/2015/12/11/suomen-miss-maailma-edustaja-ei-esiinny-pilailupuodin-lapinpuvussa-tapahtui.

35 Ballardini, Härkönen and Kestilä, "Indigenous Dress Heritage", 94.

36 Mattias Åhren, "The Saami Traditional Dress & Beauty Pageants: Indigenous Peoples' Rights of Ownership and Self-determination over Their Cultures" (PhD diss., University of Tromsø, 2010), 140–141.

From the perspective of self-determination, the issues in this case relate to the ownership of CH materials but also to participation rights, both of which are highlighted in the UNDRIP. While the position of the Sámi as owners of their intellectual property should be recognised, it was also seen as problematic that almost all the elements of Sámi culture were used in *Frozen I* without the consent or participation of the Sámi communities. This is a problem with regard to the digitisation of CH in general. While bringing the CH elements into digital form might benefit the Sámi, either by compensating them or by making the cultural elements more accessible to the Sámi communities themselves, and encouraging their preservation as well, it cannot be done without the consultation and participation of the communities themselves.

After the controversy, Disney wanted to do things better with the sequel (*Frozen II*). During the making of *Frozen II*, Disney entered into an agreement with Sámi representatives that affirmed their ownership of their culture.[37] The filmmakers sought advice on how to respectfully portray the indigenous culture from an expert group named *Verddet*, brought together by the Sámi parliaments of Norway, Sweden, and Finland, along with the Sámi Council, and made up of the Sámi playwrights, artists, historians, political leaders and elders.[38] The response from the Sámi communities has been mostly positive.[39] It seems that with the sequel, Disney has redeemed itself in the eyes of the Sámi. There was a contract and negotiations that were seen by many as appropriate, although some critical voices were raised.[40] Disney also produced a dubbed version of the movie in the North Sámi language and agreed to create training opportunities for Sámi filmmakers.[41]

To summarise, Disney involved the Sámi communities and their experts in the sequel in order to avoid appropriation or misuse of the Sámi CH. Also, a

---

37 Simonpillai, "Frozen II"; Trine Kvidal-Røvik and Ashley Cordes, "Into the Unknown [Amas Mu Vuordá]? Listening to Indigenous Voices on the Meanings of Disney's Frozen 2 [Jikŋon 2]", *Journal of International and Intercultural Communication* 15, no. 1 (2022): 17–35; Tuija Huuki and Kata Kyrölä, "'Show yourself': Indigenous Ethics, Sámi Cosmologies and Decolonial Queer Pedagogies of Frozen 2", *Gender and Education* 35, no. 2 (2022): 171–185.

38 Kvidal-Røvik and Cordes, "Into the Unknown," 24.

39 John Last, "Hollywood Gets Indigenous Consultation Right in Frozen 2, Sami Experts Say," *CBC News,* November 23, 2019, https://www.cbc.ca/news/canada/north/frozen-2-consultation-sami-1.5370801?fbclid=IwAR1AUXlgyUBaph4hsg6QjVwsup-HMpkWu9xxj1BvFDoOcN7mwoz2ikIaCVQ.

40 For example, scholar and activist May-Britt Öhman commented that 'priority was given to the Swedish version of the film and Swedish viewers, while the Sámi version and Sámi representatives were set up as a "side-event."' See Kvidal-Røvik and Cordes, "Into the Unknown," 27.

41 McGwin, "A Collaboration with Disney".

formal contract was drawn up between Disney and the institutions involved to ensure that the content of *Frozen II* was 'culturally sensitive, appropriate and respectful of the Sámi and their culture'.[42] In *Frozen II* the reference to the Sámi culture is more explicit and significantly expanded in the storyline and visual representations,[43] thus avoiding the erasing of the cultural context. An especially important aspect seems to be the production of a dubbed version. While these gestures do not erase the fact that the Sámi CH elements are still largely in the public domain, they can be seen as a step in the right direction within the existing legal framework to better reconcile Western-based IPR laws with indigenous peoples' human rights, such as right of self-determination.

3.2 *IP Licensing – The Sinaida Case*

Another case from the context of Sámi digital CH that is instructive in illustrating the controversy between IPR, the right of self-determination and indigenous worldviews is the so called Sinaida case. Here the crux of the controversy lay in the terms of the licenses used to provide access to copyrighted material that originally came from the Sámi communities.

In 2021, Yleisradio Oy, the Finnish Broadcasting Company, published an article about a case that had long been a topic of controversy in the field of CH for a long time already.[44] In short, Laura Feodoroff, a Skolt Sámi,[45] had become aware that the picture of her late grandmother Sinaida was being used in commercial products in an American webshop. It had been used to make various image products, from decorative boards, to leggings, cell phone cases and pillowcases. There were dozens of different options, you could also order stickers. For this site, anyone could upload material to be used as a print in different products. On this webshop, anyone could upload their own artwork, which could then be used as a print in various products for sale. A Brazilian artist had downloaded the image of Sinaida from Flickr from the account of the Finnish Museum of Photography, added colors to it and sold it online as an art product. This was possible, because the Finnish Museum of Photography had opened its collections for free use under the Creative Commons license

42 Simonpillai, "Frozen II".

43 Kvidal-Røvik and Cordes, "Into the Unknown," 17–35.

44 Linda Tammela, "Edesmenneen isoäidin kasvot päätyivät amerikkalaisnettikaupan leggingseihin – näin voi käydä sinullekin, sillä kuvia on julkaistu laajalla lisenssillä," *YLE*, June 18, 2021, https://yle.fi/a/3-11965453.

45 Skolt Sámi are a small group of Sámi people who speak the Skolt Sámi language. In Finland, mainly three Sámi languages are spoken: Inari Sámi, Northern Sámi and Skolt Sámi.

CC0 – No Rights Reserved.[46] In fact, this particular licence offers the right to use copyrighted material without a separate agreement. As the license reads: 'In contrast to CC's licenses that allow copyright holders to choose from a range of permissions while retaining their copyright, CC0 empowers yet another choice altogether – the choice to opt out of copyright and database protection, and the exclusive rights automatically granted to creators – the "no rights reserved" alternative to our licenses.' The license also allows commercial use of the work.

In 2016, the Finnish Museum of Photography made part of its photo collection available and visible to the public under a CC0 license. According to the museum's chief curator Anni Wallenius, the idea was that the museum would intervene as little as possible in how the public can use the images within the limits of the legislation and copyright.[47] After all, one of the most important tasks of museums is to disseminate and make available to everyone a variety of CH – digital sharing and online publication is a viable way to pursue this goal. However, there is a fine line between disseminating, making available and openly sharing CH in a way that promotes the open access and open data policies that museums are expected to follow, and avoiding potential misunderstandings and misuses. Indeed, as Wallenius noted, at that time the museum did not foresee the ethical and moral dimensions of making the pictures available online under the CC0 license: 'At the time, people thought about opening the collections and making them accessible, but they clearly couldn't think carefully enough about the ethical and moral side of what some kind of commercial reuse could entail', Wallenius entailed.

As soon as the museum became aware of the incident, it removed the photos from Flickr. Moreover, Laura Feodoroff and her relatives contacted the Brazilian artist, who understood the situation and removed the picture. But as we know, once a work is openly available online, its spread becomes uncontrollable. For example, Feodoroff told YLE that it took several steps to remove the picture from the webstore, as the image ended up in the online store's products again because another person had taken the image without permission. The case was dismissed only after Feodoroff filed an official complaint with the American webshop, and the image was finally removed from sale.

After this accident, however, the Finnish Museum of Photography has decided to update its practices by contacting the Sámi Museum Siida and consulting widely with Sámi researchers and activists to ensure whether the people in the pictures have living relatives and whether the use of the image

46 "CC0," Creative Commons, accessed April 17, 2023, https://creativecommons.org/share-your-work/public-domain/cc0/.

47 Tammela, "Edesmenneen isoäidin kasvot".

is acceptable to them.[48] Wallenius also said that they intend to continue this approach also in the future.

This case study illustrates some of the crucial controversies that may emerge with regard to digital CH of indigenous peoples if the practices used only rely on state legislation. For example, strictly legally speaking, the Finnish Museum of Photography, as a copyright owner of the materials, was in a legitimate position to offer them under a CC0 license. The American webshop and the Brazilian artists acted in accordance with the terms of the license when they downloaded, modified, and made available an adaptation of the Sinaida picture. Furthermore, within the context of the EU, the General Data Protection Regulation (GDPR) from 2016 is only applicable to data pertaining to living natural persons given that data protection is a personal right that cannot be enforced on behalf of others. Indeed, the GDPR has encouraged national legislators to adopt specific measures regarding data protection of deceased persons.[49] However, at the time of the incident there was not any such provision in Finland. Furthermore, even when such laws are in place, they can only partly address the issues as not all CH material includes personal data.

The question might arise, is right of self-determination not a binding legal rule as well? The answer would be that for a long time, right of self-determination was interpreted strictly as a right of independence.[50] The concept of the right of self-determination has only recently been interpreted in a broader sense, encompassing not only a legal right but also a principle. A maximalist interpretation of the right has been suggested. This approach would permit the right of self-determination to be viewed as an evolving concept and its meaning to be adjusted according to contemporary needs in order to accommodate the needs of vulnerable groups.[51] Nevertheless, this perspective on the right of self-determination also presents serious downsides. Too broad of an interpretation may distort the content of right, leading to difficulties in understanding what the actual legal rule is. Moreover, it has also been proposed that the right to culture should be separated from the right of self-determination.[52]

48 Tammela, "Edesmenneen isoäidin kasvot".

49 Francesca Bartolini and Francesco Paolo Patti, "Digital Inheritance and Post Mortem Data Protection: The Italian Reform," *European Review of Private Law* 27, no. 5 (2019), https://doi.org/10.54648/erpl2019064.

50 Alexandra Xanthaki, *Indigenous Rights and United Nations Standards: Self-Determination, Culture and Land* (Cambridge: Cambridge University Press, 2007), 146.

51 Ibid, 153.

52 Ibid, 154.

While these concerns are valid, it is our understanding that interpreting the right of self-determination as a principle in addition to interpreting it as a right might facilitate a more comprehensive recognition of the cultural interests of vulnerable groups. For example, in the case of Sinaida, while it may be challenging to pinpoint what enforceable right in terms of human rights regime would have been violated, considering right of self-determination as a principle makes it possible to take into account the ethical and moral dimensions of the case. In addition, interpreting the right of self-determination as a principle may facilitate the interpretation of other legislation in manner that aligns with the human rights framework.

Still, from an ethical and moral standpoint, as well as in terms of the enforceability of the right of self-determination of the persons involved, it is evident that there is a significant power imbalance between the parties in question, particularly in the case of vulnerable groups such as indigenous peoples. . This unavoidably leads to reduced inclusion of these vulnerable groups (as foreseen in e.g. the SDG 10.2), hindering the equal representations of diverse values in CH digitisation, and ultimately leading to increased risks of misuse of the digital cultural heritage of these groups (as considered in e.g. SDG 16.7).

4 Respecting Self-determination by Reconciling IPR and Indigenous Worldviews through Engagement in Digital CH

4.1 *User-Centric Approaches and Their Potential for Governing Indigenous Digital CH*

In both cases that were previously discussed, the issue eventually came down to the lack of consultation and engagement with the Sámi communities. As *Frozen II* demonstrates, the Sámi are not inherently opposed to the use of their CH in digital formats, including commercial ones. Nevertheless, there is a perceived need to provide some form of compensation or benefit to the communities, whether it be monetary compensation or e.g. training opportunities for filmmakers. It is evident from the, Sinaida that often causing harm might be avoided by involving the Sámi experts and other representatives of the culture at an earlier stage of the digitisation process. Even though these cases provide with initial positive indications of the potential of using participatory and engagement methods to better reflect indigenous worldviews in IPR laws in the context of indigenous CH, they do not go as far as clearly applying such methods. In light of the aforementioned considerations, it may be beneficial to explore the potential of user-centric approaches, such as legal design and citizen science, to better negotiate the tensions between state IPR laws and indigenous worldviews and needs.

The concept of legal design has been described as 'a movement to make the legal system work better for people'.[53] Its purpose is:

> [T]o develop a human-centered, participatory approach to reforming the legal system, that recognizes the importance of new technology but that does not privilege tech-driven solutions above all others; and that recognizes the value of interdisciplinary, inclusive groups building and testing new improvements to the system.[54]

In general, this means that a wider group of experts are involved in legal processes, not just e.g. lawyers. The emphasis is on people's needs and experiences, which are researched during the design process. Based on this research, the outcomes are then tested and refined, for example, through field pilots and workshops. The outcomes are then scaled and replicated to become the new standard for how the legal system should operate.[55] As Margaret Hagan notes, design thinking allows us to 'put the focus of law on innovating, testing and building systems that serve the agency of the people involved in them'.[56] Legal design is also a creative problem-solving method, that can be used to understand what causes the issues at hand.[57] For example, a user-centric design approach could be used to map out, what in practice causes the situation where the Sámi are not involved in the decisions concerning their culture and thus better navigate the possible solutions.

The design approach could, for example, help to better integrate FPIC into national legislation, but also increase the level of knowledge about its application. In Finland, where the Sinaida case took place, FPIC is not specifically included into legislation. Workshops and pilots about the interpretation of the FPIC in the context of digital materials would be highly necessary. Also, the

53 Michael Doherty, Marcelo Corrales Compagnucci, Helena Haapio and Margaret Hagan, "A New Attitude to Law's Empire: The Potentialities of Legal Design," in *Legal Design: Integrating Business, Design and Legal Thinking with Technology*, ed. Marcelo Corrales Compagnucci *et al.* (Cheltenham and Northhampton: Edward Elgar, 2021), 1.

54 Ibid, 1–2.

55 Ibid, 2.

56 Margaret Hagan, "Law by Design," accessed April 17, 2023, https://www.lawbydesign.com/.

57 Michael G Luchs, "Intro," in *Design Thinking: New Product Development Essentials from the PDMA*, eds. Michael G Luchs, Scott Swan and Abbie Griffin (New Jersey: John Wiley & Sons, 2015), xxii.

potential tensions between FPIC, freedom of speech and IPR's would require much more in-depth discussion with all the parties involved.

Citizen science (CS) is a methodology defined as the participation of non-professional scientists in the scientific process (Hacklay et al., 2021). Citizen science is seen as a key driver to facilitate and sustainably promote a more inclusive society by innovating to address key societal challenges (Robinson et al., 2018). Engaging a specific interest group is a significant challenge, as the motivation is not necessarily shared by the participants; groups may include people with low digital literacy or even limited relevant resources to access the tools and materials provided (DESI, 2019). Moreover, very often, the tools used to engage the public do not include these groups, thus negating the expected impact and reinforcing social barriers and exclusion. CS can effectively serve policy-making initiatives and processes by providing evidence and useful insights to ensure compliance with legislation in a transparent and participatory manner. It can also serve the public by enabling them to address specific societal issues that directly affect citizens and to influence decision-making on these issues at national and EU level (Strasser et al., 2018). Ensuring citizen engagement in the digitilisation of CH in general, and in the legal issues related to this process in particular, is a complex and multi-layered problem that requires contributions from diverse cultural, sociological, psychological, and behavioural perspectives. To address this challenge, CS approaches could effectively empower citizens and co-identify and co-create solutions with key stakeholders, such as indigenous people. Following a horizontal approach and a distributed expertise model, participants can be considered as competent in-the-field experts and therefore able to produce socially robust knowledge. CS can be a powerful practice both for the inclusion of indigenous people and for the design of new evidence-based laws supported by citizen participation, thus providing concrete opportunities to concretise the right of self-determination of indigenous peoples.

Overall, user-centric approaches such as legal design and citizen science could enable considering and empowering indigenous voices at all stages of decision making in the digitisation of indigenous CH, in order to achieve a balanced inclusive framework where the interests of the various stakeholders can be considered.

4.2 *Applying User-Centricity Can Help Preventing and Navigating the Challenges*

The use of approaches such as design thinking and CS has, to some extent, already begun to emerge in some practices related to the digital CH of the Sámi people, although these projects are still at a relatively early stage. For example, the ethical guidelines developed in the context of the Nuohtti service and the Collective Benefit, Authority to Control, Responsibility, and Ethics Principles for Indigenous Data Governance (CARE Principles) represent recent relevant cases where user-centricity has been tested.

The Nuohtti service brings the Sámi archival materials under one search engine.[58] The recently launched Nuohtti service was developed as part of a multidisciplinary research project that integrated user-centric design principles throughout the development process.[59] While this digital service provides new possibilities for accessing the Sámi CH, its increased accessibility creates also potential vulnerabilities and shortcomings. As Häkkilä (the project PI) et al. note: 'digital access exposes the culturally sensitive material for a wider audience, creating the potential risk for offensive or disrespectful usage, related, for example, to commercial exploitation'.[60]

In order to address and proactively prevent or mitigate these possible challenges, the project has developed ethical guidelines[61] for the use of the Nuohtti service. One ethical challenge identified in the project has been precisely the clash between the Sámi people's understandings of IP rights and Western based IP rules.[62] The ethical guidelines presented in the project's website note that:

> The user of these archive materials should be aware that different intellectual property rights, such as copyright and related rights, may cover the materials. It should also be noted that intellectual property laws do not always cover the use of cultural heritage materials in accordance with the views of Indigenous Peoples.

And that: 'the conditions under which cultural heritage materials can be ethically and legally acquired, accessed or otherwise used change through time. Some materials may have been collected or later restricted in ways which are now seen as being in contrast with community rights and laws.'

58 "Nuohtti – Search portal for Sámi Archival Materials", accessed April 17, 2023, https://nuohtti.com/?lng=en-gb.

59 Jonna Häkkilä, Siiri Paananen, Mari Suoheimo and Maija Mäkikalli, "Pluriverse Perspectives in Designing for a Cultural Heritage Context in the Digital Age," in *Artistic Cartography and Design Explorations Towards the Pluriverse* (New York: Routledge, 2022), 137.

60 Ibid, 137.

61 "Ethical Guidelines", accessed April 17, 2023, https://nuohtti.com/Content/ethical-guidelines.

62 "Ethical Guidelines", section Consideration of intellectual property rights, use and access.

This latter point suggests similar observations as the one's made in the context of our study: namely that the collection (and subsequent digitisation) of the Sámi CH materials has been a one-sided and frequently an exploitative practice. In this process the Sámi have been perceived as passive objects rather than active participants. In the context of the Nuohtti service, an attempt has been made to draw the user's attention to these issues as well as more effectively engage the main group of users, namely the Sámi people themselves.

Häkkilä et al. explain that integrating the ethical guidelines into the user interface (UI) design of the Nuohtti service has taken place through the implementation of several multidisciplinary workshops. These workshops have brought together the expertise of graphic and user interface, technical development and law and archive professionals with both Sámi and non-Sámi backgrounds.[63] In practice, when a user enters the service, the UI guides the user to consider ethical aspects, including intellectual property rights. A pop-up window with a visualisation interrupts the first-time search activity and draws the user's attention to an ethical guidelines quiz or read the ethical guidelines in full.[64] This approach facilitates greater accessibility and comprehension of the ethical guidelines. According to Häkkilä et al., participatory design methods to design the portal and reviewing of the ethical guidelines with representatives of the Sámi community in the project steering group have played a pivotal role.[65] In this context, Nuohtti can be considered as one example of the ways in which design thinking could partly contribute to closing the gap between state legislation and indigenous views.

Another example can be provided to illustrate the application of a user-centric approach in navigating and anticipating potential conflicts between indigenous worldviews and the legislation governing digital indigenous CH. This can be seen in the so-called 'CARE principles' for indigenous data governance. Although this example is not specifically in the context of IPR, it pertains to an area of law – namely data governance – where digital indigenous CH and regulation present a significant challenge from the perspective of the right of self-determination. Moreover, it is currently one of the only existing examples where user-centricity has been applied to address clashes and resolve conflicts between Western legislation and indigenous digital CH. It is therefore, an interesting example to examine also from our own perspective. The issue arises from the fact i that the availability of digital datasets belonging to indigenous CH has posed challenges ever since the numerous digitasations projects

63 Jonna Häkkiläet *al.*, "Pluriverse Perspectives," 137–138.

64 Ibid.

65 Ibid.

developed within Galleries, Library, Museum and Archives (GLAM) sector. In the context of indigenous CH, the case of the secondary use of data by making available the indigenous CH datasets in open data format with a consequent free use, re-use and exploitation of the datasets for commercial and non-commercial purposes has been a challenge at many instances. Indeed, data sovereignty and governance of indigenous CH datasets poses many different issues from an ethical perspective. To illustrate, within the context of the European Union, the current open data policy and the related legislation in the EU (e.g., the Open Data Directive 2019/1024)[66] do not fully consider indigenous peoples' rights and interests in terms of data sovereignty and control over secondary use of data. Furthermore, the already established Findable, Accessible, Interoperable, Reusable (FAIR principle)[67] for scientific data management and stewardship are based on a data-centric approach and prioritises increased data sharing without considering power differentials and historical contexts. These approaches give rise to tensions for indigenous peoples who demand control over their data and knowledge to create economic value and fully exploit the opportunities within the knowledge economy in ways that are grounded in indigenous worldviews.

In order to address, the Global Indigenous Data Alliance Promoting Indigenous Control of Indigenous Data (GIDA)[68] has published the Collective Benefit, Authority to Control, Responsibility and Ethics Principles for Indigenous Data Governance (CARE Principles).[69] These principles are designed to complement the FAIR principles by better considering indigenous innovation and self-determination principles. The CARE principles are people and purpose-oriented principles.[70] Substantially, the CARE principles address issues such as privacy, future use, and data stewardship, thereby providing a normative foundation for setting standards, crafting policy, and developing research agendas for marginalised populations. Moreover, the principles encourage data producers, stewards, and publishers to affirm indigenous rights of self-determination and increase the value of data for re-use.

66 The text of Open Data Directive is available at: https://eur-lex.europa.eu/legal-content/EN/TXT/?uri=CELEX%3A32019L1024.

67 "FAIR Principles," accessed April 17, 2023, https://www.go-fair.org/fair-principles/.

68 "Global Indigenous Data Alliance Promoting Indigenous Control of Indigenous Data", accessed April 17, 2023, https://www.gida-global.org/.

69 "CARE Principles for Indigenous Data Governance," accessed April 17, 2023, https://www.gida-global.org/care.

70 Stephanie Russo Carroll *et al.*, "Operationalizing the CARE and FAIR Principles for Indigenous data futures," *Sci Data* 8, 108 (2021). https://doi.org/10.1038/s41597-021-00892-0.

Methodologically, the CARE principles were developed by the International Indigenous Data Sovereignty Interest Group, a network of nation-statebased indigenous data sovereignty networks and individuals operating within the Global Indigenous Data Alliance. This process involved close consultation and collaboration with indigenous people representatives, scholars, non-profit organisations, and governments worldwide. Following a year-long public discussion and building on Indigenous Data Sovereignty network activities, the CARE principles were released in September 2019. In the specific context of the Sámi datasets related to their CH, the GIDA-Sápmi network[71] (which is connected to the above-mentioned global GIDA network and which composes of the Sámi representatives, universities, memory institutions, and archives from Norway, Sweden, and Finland) have further developed the CARE principles to better adapt them to the Nordic Sámi context. The ultimate objective is to raise awareness among the Nordic research community, memory and archival institutions about the CARE principles and to "strengthen Sámi data governance and Sámi research data for the needs of contemporary Sámi society".

In sum, both examples presented in this session constitute already existing practical applications of user-centric solutions to the issue of reconciling (Western-based) law (e.g., IPR but also other relevant laws, including data governance) with indigenous worldviews to make the digitisation of indigenous CH an inclusive and participatory process. The Nuohtti and the ethical guidelines provide a good example of how design processes can be used in practice to enhance the participation of focus groups, such as the Sámi people in this case, and this way perhaps contribute also to the actualisation of right to self-determination. The CARE principles can be considered a first step forward to strike a balance towards a more ethical, accountable and responsible data governance policy for indigenous CH datasets that is in line with indigenous worldview. Both examples show how user-centricity through communities' co-creation and engagement can be an effective method for proactively prevent and/or subsequently navigate the challenges discussed in this paper.

5 Conclusion

This chapter has addressed the challenges at the intersection between indigenous peoples' CH, digitisation and IPR as their regulatory frameworks in

71 "GIDA-Sápmi – Sámi Research Data Governance," accessed April 17, 2023, https://uit.no/research/sshf-no/project?pid=788403.

relation to indigenous worldviews and key human rights such as the right to self-determination. The most important finding of this work is to have highlighted concrete ways not only for coping or navigating these potential challenges after they have arisen, but especially for how to proactively prevent them. As evidenced by the literature review and the concrete cases from the Sámi people show, the clashes between IPR law and indigenous worldviews are often due to a lack of knowledge between the parties. Relying on user-centric approaches such as legal design or citizen science methods to foster inclusiveness, participation and engagement of the communities in law and decision-making could be viable and effective ways to achieve this goal – as the few already existing examples like the Nuohtti ethical guidelines and the CARE principles seem to indicate. Notwithstanding these efforts, it should be acknowledged that shortcomings might remain – unless user-centricity is applied also to the stages of e.g. implementing, monitoring and further developing the created solutions (being it the ethical guidelines, the CARE principles, or something else). In order for these solutions to be effective and respectful of fundamental principles such as the right to self-determination but also in general all those linked to right of participation,[72] communities' engagement shall be circular, constant and mainstreamed at all stages.

Bibliography

Books

Kuokkanen, Rauna. *Restructuring Relations: Indigenous Self-Determination, Governance and Gender*. New York: Oxford University Press, 2019.

Kur, Annette, Thomas Dreier, and Stefan Luginbuehl. *European intellectual property law: text, cases and materials*. 2nd ed. Cheltenham, UK: Edward Elgar Publishing, 2019.

Luchs, Michael G., Scott Swan, and Abbie Griffin. *Design thinking: New product development essentials from the PDMA*. New Jersey: John Wiley & Sons, 2015.

Said, Edward. *Orientalism*. New York: Pantheon Books, 1978.

Xanthaki, Alexandra. *Indigenous Rights and United Nations Standards: Self-Determination, Culture and Land*. Cambridge: Cambridge University Press, 2007.

Chapter or Other Part of an Edited Book

Ballardini, Rosa, Heidi Härkönen, and Iiris Kestilä. "Intellectual property rights and indigenous dress heritage: towards more social planning types of practices

72 Article 21 of the Universal Declaration of Human Rights 1948.

via user-centric approaches." In *Legal Design: Integrating Business, Design and Legal Thinking with Technology,* edited by Marcelo Corrales Compagnucci, Helena Haapio, Margaret Hagan and Michael Doherty, 82–106. Cheltenham and Northhampton: Edward Elgar, 2021.

Doherty, Michael, Marcelo Corrales Compagnucci, Helena Haapio and Margaret Hagan. "A new attitude to law's empire: The potentialities of legal design." In *Legal Design: Integrating Business, Design and Legal Thinking with Technology,* edited by Marcelo Corrales Compagnucci, Helena Haapio, Margaret Hagan and Michael Doherty, 1–8. Cheltenham and Northhampton: Edward Elgar, 2021.

Fisher, William. "Theories of intellectual property." In *New Essays in the Legal and Political Theory of Property,* edited by Stephen Munzer. Cambridge: Cambridge University Press, 2001.

Heinämäki, Leena. "The Rapidly Evolving International Status of Indigenous Peoples." In *Indigenous Rights in Scandinavia: Autonomous Sami Law,* edited by Christina Allardt and Susan Funderud Skogvang, 189–204. Oxon/New York: Routledge, 2015.

Häkkilä, Jonna, Siiri Paananen, Mari Suoheimo and Maija Mäkikalli. "Pluriverse perspectives in designing for a cultural heritage context in the digital age." In *Artistic Cartography and Design Explorations Towards the Pluriverse,* 134–143. New York: Routledge, 2022.

Xanthaki, Alexandra. "International Instruments on Cultural Heritage: Tales of Fragmentation." In *Indigenous peoples' Cultural Heritage: Rights, Debates, Challenges,* edited by Xanthaki, Alexandra, Piia Kristiina Nuorgam, Leena Heinämäki, Sanna Valkonen, 1–19. Leiden: Brill/Nijhoff, 2017.

E-Books

Hagan, Margaret. "Law by Design." Accessed April 17, 2023. https://www.lawbydesign.com/.

Journal Articles

Bartolini, Francesca, and Francesco Paolo Patti. "Digital inheritance and post mortem data protection: The Italian reform." *European Review of Private Law* 27, no. 5 (2019): 1181–1194.

Cristecu, Aureliu. "The right to self-determination: historical and current development on the basis of United Nations instruments: study / prepared by Aureliu Cristescu, Special Rapporteur of the Sub-Commission on Prevention of Discrimination and Protection of Minorities." New York: UN. Subcommission on Prevention of Discrimination and Protection of Minorities, 1981. https://digitallibrary.un.org/record/25252.

Cambou, Dorothée. "The UNDRIP and the legal significance of the right of indigenous peoples to self-determination: a human rights approach with a multidimensional perspective." *The International Journal of Human Rights* 23, no. 1–2 (2019): 34–50.

Hossain, Kamrul, and Rosa Maria Ballardini. "Protecting indigenous traditional knowledge through a holistic principle-based approach." *Nordic Journal of Human Rights,* 39, no.1 (2021): 51–72.

Huuki, Tuija, and Kata Kyrölä. " 'Show yourself': Indigenous ethics, Sámi cosmologies and decolonial queer pedagogies of Frozen 2." *Gender and Education* 35, no. 2 (2023): 171–185.

Junka-Aikio, Laura. "Can the Sámi speak now? Deconstructive research ethos and the debate on who is a Sámi in Finland." *Cultural studies* 30, no. 2 (2016): 205–233.

Kuokkanen, Rauna. "The Deatnu Agreement: a contemporary wall of settler colonialism." *Settler Colonial Studies* 10, no. 4 (2020): 508–528.

Kvidal-Røvik, Trine, and Ashley Cordes. "Into the unknown [Amas Mu Vuordá]? Listening to Indigenous voices on the meanings of Disney's Frozen 2 [Jikŋon 2]." *Journal of international and intercultural communication* 15, no. 1 (2022): 17–35.

Newspaper/Magazine Articles

Heikkinen, Mikko-Pekka and Jussi Pullinen. "Disney kävi Inarissa tutkimassa saamelaista elämää Frozenin jatko-osaan – Saamelaiset haluavat korvausta." *Helsingin Sanomat,* September 23, 2016, https://www.hs.fi/kotimaa/art-2000002922271.html.

Last, John. "Hollywood Gets Indigenous Consultation Right in Frozen 2, Sami Experts Say." *CBC News,* November 23, 2019, https://www.cbc.ca/news/canada/north/frozen-2-consultation-sami-1.5370801?fbclid=IwAR1AUXlgyUBaph4hsg6QjVwsup-HMpkWu9xxj1BvFDoOcN7mwoz2ikIaCVQ.

McGwin, Kevin. "How a collaboration with Disney shaped the way Sámi cultural details were portrayed in Frozen 2." *ArcticToday,* February 3, 2020, https://www.arctictoday.com/how-a-collaboration-with-disney-shaped-the-way-sami-cultural-details-were-portrayed-in-frozen-2/.

Rautio, Samppa. 'Suomen Miss Maailma -edustaja ei esiinny pilailupuodin lapinpuvussa – "Tapahtui suuri virhe." *YLE,* December 11, 2015, https://yle.fi/aihe/artikkeli/2015/12/11/suomen-miss-maailma-edustaja-ei-esiinny-pilailupuodin-lapinpuvussa-tapahtui.

Simonpillai, Radheyan. "Disney signed a contract with Indigenous people before making Frozen II." *Now Toronto,* November 19, 2019, https://nowtoronto.com/movies/news-features/disney-frozen-2-indigenous-culture-sami/.

Tammela, Linda. "Edesmenneen isoäidin kasvot päätyivät amerikkalaisnettikaupan leggingseihin – näin voi käydä sinullekin, sillä kuvia on julkaistu laajalla lisenssillä." *YLE,* June 18, 2021, https://yle.fi/a/3-11965453.

Interviews

"Behind the Scenes of Frozen 2: How Sámi Representatives Cooperated with Disney". Interview by *Arctic Council*, January 23, 2020, https://www.arctic-council.org/news/behind-the-scenes-of-frozen-2-how-saami-representatives-cooperated-with-disney/.

Website Contents

Carroll, Stephanie Russo *et al.*, "Operationalizing the CARE and FAIR Principles for Indigenous data futures," *Sci Data* 8, 108 (2021). https://doi.org/10.1038/s41597-021-00892-0.

"CARE Principles for Indigenous Data Governance". Accessed April 17, 2023, https://www.gida-global.org/care.

"CC0", Creative Commons. Accessed April 17, 2023, https://creativecommons.org/share-your-work/public-domain/cc0/.

"Ethical Guidelines". Accessed April 17, 2023, https://nuohtti.com/Content/ethical-guidelines.

"FAIR Principles". Accessed April 17, 2023, https://www.go-fair.org/fair-principles/.

"GIDA-Sápmi – Sámi Research Data Governance". Accessed April 17, 2023, https://uit.no/research/sshf-no/project?pid=788403..

"Global Indigenous Data Alliance Promoting Indigenous Control of Indigenous Data". Accessed April 17, 2023, https://www.gida-global.org/.

Hannum, Hurst "Legal aspects of self-determination". Encyclopedia Princetoniencies. Accessed April 14, 2023, https://pesd.princeton.edu/node/511..

Horizon Europe work programme 2023–24. Accessed December 8, 2022, https://ec.europa.eu/info/funding-tenders/opportunities/docs/2021-2027/horizon/wp-call/2023-2024/wp-5-culture-creativity-and-inclusive-society_horizon-2023-2024_en.pdf.

"Nuohtti – Search portal for Sámi Archival Materials". Accessed April 17, 2023, https://nuohtti.com/?lng=en gb..

Legal Instruments

Assembly, UN General. *United Nations declaration on the rights of indigenous peoples: resolution/adopted by the General Assembly, 2 October 2007*. A/RES/61/295, 2007. Accessed July 14, 2023, https://documents-dds-ny.un.org/doc/UNDOC/GEN/N06/512/07/PDF/N0651207.pdf?OpenElement.

Directive (EU) 2019/1024 of the European Parliament and of the Council of 20 June 2019 on open data and the re-use of public sector information (recast). https://eur-lex.europa.eu/eli/dir/2019/1024/oj.

"Free, Prior and Informed Consent – An Indigenous Peoples' Right and a Good Practice for Local Communities" (Food and Agriculture Organization of the United Nations, 2016), https://www.fao.org/3/i6190e/i6190e.pdf, 13.

UN General Assembly. "International covenant on civil and political rights (Treaty Series, Vol. 999, p. 171)." New York, NY: United Nations (1966).

UN General Assembly. "International covenant on economic, social and cultural rights." *United Nations, Treaty Series* 993.3 (1966): 2009–2057.

Reports

Commission on Human Rights, Sub-Commission on the Promotion and Protection of Human Rights, Working Group on Indigenous Populations, Twenty-second session, held in Geneva, 19–23 July 2004. https://digitallibrary.un.org/record/527396.

Thesis

Åhren, Mattias. "The Saami Traditional Dress & Beauty Pageants: Indigenous Peoples' Rights of Ownership and Self-determination over Their Cultures." PhD diss., University of Tromsø, 2010.

CHAPTER 17

Business and Human Rights in the Data Economy

Mariam Shakil, Isabel Ebert and Florian Wettstein

1 Introduction

The global digital ecosystem, also known as the data economy, is expanding rapidly. It is being sustained by data gathered from various sources of human interaction, such as the Internet of Things (IoT), search engines, social media platforms, the gig economy, and/or payment gateways.[1] A large and growing body of literature indicates how society's digital footprint promises to offer opportunities to mitigate economic, societal, and environmental issues.[2] For example, companies are known to use Artificial Intelligence (AI) to better understand consumer patterns to deliver personalised experiences, such as targeted recommendations and advertising.[3] Government agencies, on the other hand, collect data to make informed decisions on policy development, to improve public safety, and to strengthen infrastructure planning, among other things.[4] The use of Big Data in the finance sector enables banks to assess real time stock market insights, which takes into consideration political and social trends that may have an impact on the stock market, but also to identify and

1 Matthias Koch et al., "A Matter of Definition: Criteria for Digital Ecosystems," *Digital Business* 2, no. 2 (January 1, 2022): 100027, https://doi.org/10.1016/j.digbus.2022.100027; Stefan Henningsson and Jonas Hedman, "Transformation of Digital Ecosystems: The Case of Digital Payments," in *Information and Communication Technology*, ed. Linawati et al., Lecture Notes in Computer Science (Berlin, Heidelberg: Springer, 2014), 46–55.

2 Amy Jeter Hansen, 'Solving Social Problems with Data', *Scope* (blog), April 17, 2018, https://scopeblog.stanford.edu/2018/04/17/solving-social-problems-with-data/; Massimo Russo, David Young, and Marine Gerard, "Sharing Data to Address Out Biggest Societal Challenges," *BCG*, 7 January 2021; Ohio University, "How Data Science Can Be Used for Social Good," *Ohio University* (blog), December 7, 2020, https://onlinemasters.ohio.edu/blog/data-science-for-social-good/; Bayo Olushola Omoyiola, "The Social Implications, Risks, Challenges and Opportunities of Big Data," (Emerald Open Research, June 13, 2022), https://doi.org/10.35241/emeraldopenres.14646.1.

3 Kean Birch and D. T. Cochrane, "Big Tech: Four Emerging Forms of Digital Rentiership," *Science as Culture* 31, no. 1 (January 2, 2022): 44–58.

4 OECD, *The Path to Becoming a Data-Driven Public Sector*, OECD Digital Government Studies (OECD, 2019), https://doi.org/10.1787/059814a7-en; OECD, "Data Governance in the Public Sector," in *The Path to Becoming a Data-Driven Public Sector*, by OECD, OECD Digital Government Studies (OECD, 2019), 23–57.

 | DOI:10.1163/9789004530942_018

mitigate adverse impacts emanating, e.g., from modern slavery and human trafficking.[5] Moreover, unique Machine Learning (ML) strategies can further assist financial institutions to detect fraud and thereby be better equipped to prevent corruption.[6] Health service providers, too, benefit largely from the use of data – by drawing correlations and identifying health patterns relating to a specific demography (digital epidemiology),[7] or by predicting future disease outbreaks through the use of AI.[8]

Yet, this preoccupation with positive outcomes fuels what can be called technological solutionism,[9] that is, a tendency to overemphasise any benefits and ignore potential downsides of such technological advances - an increasingly popular narrative that AI will solve every societal problem. This, in turn, ignites the desire to research and develop ever more data-driven technologies,[10] without looking at the range of impacts in a holistic manner. Interestingly, such tech-solutionism on the one hand co-exists with a lively debate among scholars and activists on the misuse of data and insights derived from it.[11] For example, infringements on privacy and consumer autonomy are inherent to targeted advertising, as it hinders consumers' ability to accurately sense when and how they are being manipulated.[12] Big Data systems employed for public

5 Enas Al-Lozi et al., "The Role of Big Data in Financial Sector: A Review Paper," *International Journal of Data and Network Science* 6, 2022, https://doi.org/10.5267/j.ijdns.2022.6.003. Maria Anne Van Dijk et al, "Banks and Human Trafficking: Rethinking Human Rights Due Diligence," Business and Human Rights Journal 3, no. 1 (2018): 105–111.

6 Kazim Hussain and Elsa Prieto, "Big Data in the Finance and Insurance Sectors," in *New Horizons for a Data-Driven Economy: A Roadmap for Usage and Exploitation of Big Data in Europe*, ed. José María Cavanillas, Edward Curry, and Wolfgang Wahlster (Cham: Springer International Publishing, 2016), 209–23, https://doi.org/10.1007/978-3-319-21569-3_12.

7 Chris Wymant et al., "The Epidemiological Impact of the NHS COVID-19 App," *Nature*, May 12, 2021, 1–8, https://doi.org/10.1038/s41586-021-03606-z.

8 Rayner Alfred and Joe Henry Obit, "The Roles of Machine Learning Methods in Limiting the Spread of Deadly Diseases: A Systematic Review," *Heliyon* 7, no. 6 (June 23, 2021): e07371, https://doi.org/10.1016/j.heliyon.2021.e07371.

9 Evgeny Morozov, *To Save Everything, Click Here*, 2017, https://www.publicaffairsbooks.com/titles/evgeny-morozov/to-save-everything-click-here/9781610393706/.

10 Ian Tucker, "Evgeny Morozov: "We Are Abandoning All the Checks and Balances,"" *The Observer*, March 9, 2013, sec. Technology, https://www.theguardian.com/technology/2013/mar/09/evgeny-morozov-technology-solutionism-interview.

11 Brent Mittelstadt, "Principles Alone Cannot Guarantee Ethical AI," *Nature Machine Intelligence* 1, no. 11 (November 2019): 501–7, https://doi.org/10.1038/s42256-019-0114-4; Anna Jobin, Marcello Ienca, and Effy Vayena, "The Global Landscape of AI Ethics Guidelines," *Nature Machine Intelligence* 1, no. 9 (September 2019): 389–99.

12 Joanna Strycharz and Bram Duivenvoorde, "The Exploitation of Vulnerability through Personalised Marketing Communication: Are Consumers Protected?," *Internet Policy*

safety may include flawed predictive AI instruments that are fed with historic data, leading to biased and discriminatory predictions about future behaviour, often negatively impacting minority groups in particular.[13] Credit scoring used in the financial sector can undermine the dignity of customers, as some data-driven analytical tools make assessments based on social, familial, and/or religious associations.[14] Additionally, predictive or diagnostic ML tools used in the health sector have faced critique over their lack of representative data across demographics,[15] which begs the question of how effective they are in mitigating health-related issues beyond the purpose of mere commercialisation.

As these examples demonstrate, the use of data-driven technologies can have substantial impacts on human rights. A solid ex-ante analysis before digital technology is designed and deployed needs to, first, understand the Rationale behind the use and whether this is the appropriate solution to close an identified gap of societal need, and, second, to ensure that potential adverse impacts on human rights connected with such use of digital technologies are identified and assessed/prevented. Furthermore, the key role of the private sector, and Big Tech companies in particular, is evident in many of these examples. This makes these developments relevant for the fast-evolving business and human rights (BHR) discussion and, more specifically, for the United Nations Guiding Principles on Business and Human Rights (UNGPs). In a nutshell, the UNGPs spell out and integrate governments' duty to protect human rights from adverse corporate impacts, the responsibility of companies to respect human rights, and the necessity to improve victims' access to effective remedies in case human rights have been violated.

The normative standard set out by the UNGPs applies to all types of companies and thus includes the technology sector.[16] On the one hand, this implies

---

Review 10, no. 4 (November 8, 2021), https://policyreview.info/articles/analysis/exploitation-vulnerability-through-personalised-marketing-communication-are.

13 Litska Strikwerda, "Predictive Policing: The Risks Associated with Risk Assessment," *The Police Journal* 94, no. 3 (1 September 2021): 422–36; Mareile Kaufmann, Simon Egbert, and Matthias Leese, "Predictive Policing and the Politics of Patterns," *The British Journal of Criminology* 59, no. 3 (April 9, 2019): 674–92.

14 M. Hurley and Julius Adebayo, "Credit Scoring in the Era of Big Date," *Yale Journal of Law and Technology*, April 2, 2017, https://www.semanticscholar.org/paper/CREDIT-SCORING-IN-THE-ERA-OF-BIG-DATA-Hurley-Adebayo/6830f672c1765867a914155d5eb7df140fe7de16.

15 Hussein Ibrahim et al., "Health Data Poverty: An Assailable Barrier to Equitable Digital Health Care," *The Lancet Digital Health* 3, no. 4 (April 1, 2021): e260–65, https://doi.org/10.1016/S2589-7500(20)30317-4.

16 OHCHR, "A/HRC/50/56: The Practical Application of the Guiding Principles on Business and Human Rights to the Activities of Technology Companies," (Geneva: United Nations,

that, by default, each technology company has a responsibility to respect human rights, which the UNGPs define as a responsibility to identify, assess, and mitigate adverse human rights impacts which they cause, contribute or are linked to. States, on the other hand, ought to protect human rights against potential abuse by technology companies.[17] Thus, the UNGPs ask States to adopt a 'smart mix' of voluntary and mandatory measures to ensure that companies respect human rights. Based on this premise, the European Union (EU), for example, has introduced the Digital Services Act (DSA), which aims at creating a safe online environment, among other aspects, requiring very large online platforms (i.e., platforms that have more than 45 million users per month in the EU) to identify, assess and mitigate impacts on fundamental rights in relation to the digital services they offer.[18]

The purpose of this chapter is to provide an analysis of the data economy from the perspective of BHR generally, and the UNGPs in particular. This is done by applying a data lifecycle approach (i.e., how data is collected, analysed, used, and erased) to structure and systematise the potential adverse human rights impacts connected to the conduct of technology companies. The linkages between individual data and its potential use and misuse make the right to privacy the centrepiece in discussions concerning digital ethics, and more generally digital human rights.[19] However, as is evidenced in the following section, privacy is not the *only* right that is at risk of being violated.[20] The analysis shows how human rights abuses may occur at various stages of the data life cycle, while involving multiple actors. It then outlines the challenge to adequately address such adverse impacts through BHR principles, guidelines, and regulations. Finally, the chapter concludes with an outlook and some recommendations on how to operationalise BHR principles in the digital realm.

April 21, 2022), https://www.ohchr.org/en/documents/thematic-reports/ahrc5056-practical-application-guiding-principles-business-and-human.

17 OHCHR B-Tech Project, "Bridging Governance Gaps in the Age of Technology – Key Characteristics of the State Duty to Protect," May 2021, https://www.ohchr.org/sites/default/files/Documents/Issues/Business/B-Tech/b-tech-foundational-paper-state-duty-to-protect.pdf.

18 Official Journal of the European Union, 'Digital Services Act', L.277/1 § (2022), https://eur-lex.europa.eu/legal-content/EN/TXT/PDF/?uri=CELEX:32022R2065&from=EN.

19 Isabel Ebert, Isabelle Wildhaber, and Jeremias Adams-Prassl, "Big Data in the Workplace: Privacy Due Diligence as a Human Rights-Based Approach to Employee Privacy Protection," *Big Data & Society* 8, no. 1 (January 1, 2021): 20539517211013052, https://doi.org/10.1177/20539517211013051, 14.

20 Paul Bernal, "Data Gathering, Surveillance and Human Rights: Recasting the Debate," *Journal of Cyber Policy* 1, no. 2 (July 2, 2016): 243–64.

2 Identifying Human Rights Impacts in the Data Economy: A Data Life Cycle Approach

Data life cycle models can help to avoid blind spots and capture potential human rights impacts of technology companies holistically. However, as many public and private institutions utilise Big Data for various purposes, Big Data analytics life cycle models range in form and complexity.[21] Irrespective of the complexities, there are four general stages that can be identified across the different models – i) data collection, ii) data analysis, iii) data usage, and iv) data erasure/archiving.[22] It is imperative to ensure human rights compliance at the onset of each stage, as harm at one stage may have a ripple effect on the subsequent stages. Hence, these generic four stages can be used as a baseline for human rights assessments and as a starting point for a more comprehensive inquiry into particularised data life cycle models. Therefore, for the purpose of this chapter, we aim to analyse these four stages by illustrating their varying significance across different sectors.

2.1 *Data Collection*

Data traces from human life can be monitored and tracked in increasingly pervasive and comprehensive ways. The respective data is collected from a wide variety of sources such as surveillance cameras, sensors, logging of browser search histories, online purchasing habits, financial records, social media posts, comments, likes and searches, as well as physical appearances and security data.[23] There are several methods used to collect data, including web scraping, which involves using AI tools such as Application Programming Interfaces (APIs) provided by websites to access data in a structured format. This process enables businesses to strengthen collaboration with other online platforms and applications in order to access and share collected data.[24] Universal logins are a prime example of the use of APIs, where a user can log

---

21 Amir Sinaeepourfard et al., "Towards a Comprehensive Data Lifecycle Model for Big Data Environments," in *Proceedings of the 3rd IEEE/ACM International Conference on Big Data Computing, Applications and Technologies*, BDCAT '16 (New York, NY, USA: Association for Computing Machinery, 2016), 100–106, https://doi.org/10.1145/3006299.3006311.

22 Kumar Rahul and Rohitash Banyal, "Data Life Cycle Management in Big Data Analytics," *Procedia Computer Science* 173 (January 1, 2020): 364–71.

23 Maddalena Favaretto et al., "What Is Your Definition of Big Data? Researchers' Understanding of the Phenomenon of the Decade," *PLoS ONE* 15, no. 2 (February 25, 2020): e0228987, https://doi.org/10.1371/journal.pone.0228987, 2.

24 Stine Lomborg and Anja Bechmann, "Using APIs for Data Collection on Social Media," *The Information Society* 30, no. 4 (August 8, 2014): 256–65.

into different websites by linking their Google, Twitter, or Meta accounts, subsequently allowing online platforms to seamlessly draw data from other existing accounts.[25]

If the data is collected without informed consent and transparency, it can have a significant impact on users' privacy. Despite the introduction of internet cookies (i.e., informed consent mechanism), a survey study conducted by Cisco in 2020 indicated that 79% of respondents (2600 adults from 12 countries) were not able to identify what companies were doing with their data.[26] This points to the lack of disclosure regarding the purposes for which companies are collecting data. Certain jurisdictions put guardrails on data collection in place, such as the EU's General Data Protection Regulations (GDPR).[27] As a consequence, companies do seek consent from users, but may at the same time provide extensive terms and privacy policies that are often agreed to by users without ever reviewing them.[28] Information overload can allow companies to bury and obfuscate the intended use and sharing of collected data by inflicting users with information overload fatigue.[29] Additionally, many online platforms require users to accept terms and privacy policies to be able to access services, ultimately reinforcing the power asymmetry between users and provider.

Non-representative data is another point of concern with regards to data collection. Inequality around access to information and communication technologies (ICTs) leads to marginalised and vulnerable groups not being represented during the data collection process, which can later lead to the development of applications and products which are ill-suited or even harmful for such groups.[30] However, it is important to note that the lack of representative

25 Maria Mollah, "APIs and Ethics: What Are the Ambiguities?," *PlektonLabs* (blog), November 25, 2020, https://www.plektonlabs.com/api-and-ethics-what-are-the-ambiguities/.

26 Cisco, "Protecting Data Privacy to Maintain Digital Trust," (U.S.: Cisco, July 2020), https://www.cisco.com/c/dam/en_us/about/doing_business/trust-center/docs/cybersecurity-series-2020-cps.pdf, 14.

27 General Data Protection Regulation, Art. 7 & recital 32.

28 Tony Gjerlufsen et al., "Digital Nudges for Privacy Awareness: From Consent to Informed Consent?," (Proceedings of the 28th European Conference on Information Systems (ECIS),: AIS, 2020), https://libra.unine.ch/handle/123456789/28886.

29 Jonathan A. Obar and Anne Oeldorf-Hirsch, "The Biggest Lie on the Internet: Ignoring the Privacy Policies and Terms of Service Policies of Social Networking Services," *Information, Communication & Society* 23, no. 1 (January 2, 2020): 128–47, 140.

30 Stephanie Kelley et al., "Removing Demographic Data Can Make AI Discrimination Worse," *Harvard Business Review*, March 6, 2023, https://hbr.org/2023/03/removing-demographic-data-can-make-ai-discrimination-worse.

data should not per se be considered a malicious endeavour, but rather one that often unintentionally contributes to discrimination.[31] Additionally, tension arises when trying to balance between individual rights and collective rights. Privacy regulations prohibit the collection of excessive amounts of data to protect individual users' sensitive information, which may hinder a company's ability to collect more detailed and representative data. The latter issue subsequently leads to potential discrimination and exclusions and thus affecting marginalised groups' collective rights.[32] The next subsection will show in more detail, how the analysis of demographically weak representative data can lead to ineffective and biased AI and ML systems.

2.2 *Data Analysis*

Once data has been collected, quantitative analysis is required to structure data and establish correlations, classifications, and predictions of respective trends on a more aggregate level. Data analysis implies the structuring of information based on data collection and the process of making sense of such data. When analyses are statistically incorrect or mis/unrepresentative, this stage of the life cycle can potentially lead to discriminatory practices and produce biased outcomes, primarily discriminating against marginalised groups. This is particularly true when datasets are used that are not representative of the actual demographics to make inferences on a larger population. For example, ML applications use algorithms and statistical models to recognise patterns to identify trends or anomalies that may not be revealed through manual analysis.[33] Most ML algorithms are trained to learn from historical datasets to make predictions about future events and behaviour, such as customers' buying decisions, stock market trends, criminal offences and delinquencies, and even health outcomes.[34] The accuracy of an ML tool's analysis therefore depends on the quality and representativeness of the datasets that the system learns from.

---

31 Brian d'Alessandro, Cathy O'Neil, and Tom LaGatta, "Conscientious Classification: A Data Scientist's Guide to Discrimination-Aware Classification," *Big Data* 5, no. 2 (June 2017): 120–34, https://doi.org/10.1089/big.2016.0048.

32 Brent Mittelstadt, "From Individual to Group Privacy in Big Data Analytics," *Philosophy & Technology* 30, no. 4 (December 1, 2017): 475–94.

33 Mark Latonero, "Big Data Analytics and Human Rights: Privacy Considerations in Context,'" in *New Technologies for Human Rights Law and Practice*, ed. Jay D. Aronson and Molly K. Land (Cambridge: Cambridge University Press, 2018), 149–61, https://doi.org/10.1017/9781316838952.007.

34 Iqbal H. Sarker, "Data Science and Analytics: An Overview from Data-Driven Smart Computing, Decision-Making and Applications Perspective," *SN Computer Science* 2, no. 5 (July 12, 2021): 377, https://doi.org/10.1007/s42979-021-00765-8, 7.

Accordingly, data analysis can be biased based on the incompleteness of such data. Hence, the data collection stage, as discussed in the previous section, is pivotal for the data analysis stage – if the collected data overrepresents a certain demographic, the outcomes of the analysis cannot be adequately reflective of the broader population.[35]

Even if the initial collected data is representative of the population or phenomenon being studied, there is still a potential for introducing biases through the data processing and cleaning phase. This step is required to remove or fix any corrupt, incorrectly formatted, or incomplete data.[36] However, at the same time, it can result in the exclusion of certain data points, or the removal of outliers based on subjective criteria.[37] The decisions made during this stage can have a tremendous impact on the results of the analysis, often leading to biases, e.g., based on race or gender, particularly within sensitive areas such as employment, education, and health. If the analysis of an ML algorithm is used to make, for instance, diagnostic or procurement decisions, it can create a so-called 'feedback loop', which perpetuates pre-existing discrimination.[38] For example, if an algorithm is used to identify suitable candidates for healthcare programmes, and the outcomes of the algorithm are used to feed back into the system, it may become biased against certain groups. For example, a study found a decision-making algorithm implemented in U.S. hospitals to disproportionately allocate healthcare to white patients, while systematically discriminating against millions of black patients, despite both demographics being equally in need of such healthcare programmes and services.[39] This tendency occurs over time as algorithms' biased recommendations and predictions are looped back into the system to provide similarly biased future outputs.

35 Maddalena Favaretto, Eva De Clercq, and Bernice Simone Elger, "Big Data and Discrimination: Perils, Promises and Solutions. A Systematic Review," *Journal of Big Data* 6, no. 1 (February 5, 2019): 12, 13.

36 Hong Liu et al., "FAIXID: A Framework for Enhancing AI Explainability of Intrusion Detection Results Using Data Cleaning Techniques," *Journal of Network and Systems Management* 29, no. 4 (May 24, 2021): 40.

37 Liu et al, 2.

38 European Union Agency for Fundamental Rights, "Bias in Algorithms: Artificial Intelligence and Discrimination," (Vienna: FRA, 2022), 8, https://fra.europa.eu/sites/default/files/fra_uploads/fra-2022-bias-in-algorithms_en.pdf.

39 Heidi Ledford, "Millions of Black People Affected by Racial Bias in Health-Care Algorithms," *Nature* 574, no. 7780 (October 24, 2019): 608–9.

2.3 *Data Use*

As briefly described earlier, ML and other more advanced algorithm-based data analyses are often used in decision-making processes in various sectors, both private and public. The use of such analyses can exacerbate power asymmetries between service providers and users.[40] Data-based monitoring of employees, for example, might not account for varying circumstances of employees. If an employer tracks their delivery staff's movements, the analytic tool they use may not consider changing weather or traffic conditions which may slow down delivery times. Consequently, 'slow' employees may be 'flagged', despite the circumstances being beyond their control.[41] A further example can be seen in digital health apps, which are being developed and introduced into the market at staggering speed, with more than 90,000 new apps being added in 2020 alone.[42] Though some of these apps can indeed empower users and support them in staying healthy, problems can arise based on how and in what contexts the analyses of data gathered by these apps is being used.

A recent study conducted by the University of New South Wales showed that 12 fertility apps used by Australian consumers failed to provide adequate safeguards against privacy infringements.[43] Sensitive health data, such as pregnancy test results, menstrual cycles, mood changes, and the like, were inadequately disassociated from the users when shared with other organisations.[44] In other words, the users were not appropriately anonymised, subsequently linking them to their sensitive data. Moreover, users were provided with confusing and misleading privacy policies, creating information overload as discussed in the section on data collection.[45] Some U.S. based fertility apps have faced similar criticism; against the background of the overruling of *Roe*

40 Jonne Maas, "Machine Learning and Power Relations," *AI & SOCIETY*, February 25, 2022, https://doi.org/10.1007/s00146-022-01400-7, 4.

41 Isabel Ebert, Isabelle Wildhaber, and Jeremias Adams-Prassl, "Big Data in the Workplace: Privacy Due Diligence as a Human Rights-Based Approach to Employee Privacy Protection," *Big Data & Society* 8, no. 1 (January 1, 2021): 3, 20539517211013052, https://doi.org/10.1177/20539517211013051.

42 Emily May, "How Digital Health Apps Are Empowering Patients," *Deloitte* (blog), October 19, 2021, https://www2.deloitte.com/us/en/blog/health-care-blog/2021/how-digital-health-apps-are-empowering-patients.html.

43 Katharine Kemp, "Your Body, Our Data: Unfair and Unsafe Privacy Practices of Popular Fertility Apps," (Sydney: University of New South Wales, March 2023), https://allenshub.unsw.edu.au/sites/default/files/2023-03/KKemp%20Your%20Body%20Our%20Data%2022.03.23.pdf.

44 Ibid, 5.

45 Ibid, 6.

v. Wade,[46] cybersecurity experts warned users that their fertility data recorded by the app could be used against them in a court of law if they choose to have an abortion.[47]

Data analysis has also been used to censor or intimidate human rights defenders. Online surveillance allows those in power to track dissidents and suppress their right to freedom of expression and association, subjecting them to threats, attacks, or incarceration.[48] Similarly, targeted advertising can over-emphasise universally protected classes such as gender, race, and religion as data analysis points, which has the potential to exacerbate social exclusion, marginalisation, and to fuel existing stigmas.[49] Meta is a classic example of how such discriminatory practices are being employed. The company allowed landlords using their advertising platform to use race as an exclusion criterion, which automatically meant that the housing advertisements were primarily shown to white audiences. Though Meta signed a legal settlement restricting it from using targeting tools within such contexts, it only applies within U.S. borders.[50] Moreover, even if online platforms and advertisers have no intention to discriminate against certain groups, the ML tools themselves can reinstate biases due to the above-mentioned 'feed-back loop', as it could be optimised to show ads primarily to users the system deems most likely to respond. On the job market, this can lead to job adverts for roles in nursing or secretarial work being suggested primarily to women, whereas men, particularly those from minority backgrounds, being shown predominantly janitorial or taxi driver job vacancies.[51]

The first two stages of the data life cycle showcase the instances of how improper collection and analysis can lead to potential human rights harms, whereas the use stage solidifies such issues by taking action based on biased

46 Josh Gerstein and Alexander Ward, "Supreme Court Has Voted to Overturn Abortion Rights, Draft Opinion Shows," *Politico*, March 5, 2022, https://www.politico.com/news/2022/05/02/supreme-court-abortion-draft-opinion-00029473.

47 Hannah Norman Knight Victoria, "Should You Worry About Data From Your Period-Tracking App Being Used Against You?," *Kaiser Health News* (blog), May 13, 2022, https://khn.org/news/article/period-tracking-apps-data-privacy/.

48 Article 19, "MENA: Stop Censoring the Voices of Women Human Rights Defenders," ARTICLE 19, November 29, 2022, https://www.article19.org/resources/mena-stop-censoring-the-voices-of-women-human-rights-defenders/.

49 Deborah Lupton, "Quantified Sex: A Critical Analysis of Sexual and Reproductive Self-Tracking Using Apps," *Culture, Health & Sexuality* 17, no. 4 (April 21, 2015): 440–53.

50 Roy L. Austin Jr, "Expanding Our Work on Ads Fairness," *Meta*, June 21, 2022, https://about.fb.com/news/2022/06/expanding-our-work-on-ads-fairness/.

51 Rory Cellan-Jones, "Facebook Accused of Allowing Sexist Job Advertising," *BBC News*, September 8, 2021, sec. Technology, https://www.bbc.com/news/technology-58487026.

results. Not only does it impact groups of society (i.e., collective rights) at scale, but can equally harm individuals when analyses are used to inform decisions about them. Even if data collection and data analysis has been conducted in a representative manner, results that are used out of context or do not adequately consider boundary conditions, may have consequences for the appropriateness and connected impacts of the use of data. These practices can unfairly restrict certain groups or individuals from having access to services (e.g., health programmes, educational or employment opportunities). Moreover, when analyses are used to create individual or group profiles based on their personal characteristics or behaviour, discrimination is an imminent causal effect.

2.4 *Data Erasure/Archiving*

Properly erasing or 'forgetting' data is perhaps a lesser thought of part of the data life cycle, but of similar importance in protecting users' right to privacy and in reappropriating power asymmetries between tech companies and users.[52] To ensure that personal information is not used or disclosed without consent, companies and governmental bodies alike must have a clear process in place for deleting or anonymising data once it is no longer needed.[53] This is of relevance not only to adults, but perhaps even more important for data on children and youth. These groups are being profiled at early ages and their data traces can follow – and sometimes haunt – them for their entire lives.[54] In the European Union, for example, according to GDPR Art. 17, all individuals have the right to request their personal data to be deleted, subsequently placing an obligation on the organisation to erase it, barring certain exceptions – data will not be erased in the interest of protecting freedom of expression (i.e., journalistic rights), legal obligation to retain the data (i.e., criminal proceedings), or for reasons of public interest (i.e., public health or scientific research purposes).[55]

Data erasure, or a lack thereof, can raise important questions regarding human rights. For example, it can cause a conflict between two competing interests – the right to privacy and the right to freedom of expression. The

52 Alexander Tsesis, "Data Subjects' Privacy Rights: Regulation of Personal Data Retention and Erasure," *University of Colorado Law Review* 90, no. 2 (2019): 593–630.

53 Evgeni Aizenberg and Jeroen van den Hoven, "Designing for Human Rights in AI," *Big Data & Society* 7, no. 2 (July 11, 2020): 3, 2053951720949566, https://doi.org/10.1177/2053951720949566.

54 Veronica Barassi, *Child Data Citizen: How Tech Companies Are Profiling Us from Before Birth* (Cambridge, Massachusetts: The MIT Press, 2020).

55 European Union's General Data Protection Regulation, Art. 17 and Recitals 65 & 66.

famous 2014 *Google Spain* judgment[56] of the European Court of Justice (CJEU) reaffirmed that the right to data erasure can lead to lopsided consideration of the merits of privacy over free expression, if not both sides of the coin are adequately considered.[57] The Court ultimately ruled that every European citizen is allowed to request removal of information granted that the data is no longer 'relevant'. However, this ruling did not extend to media and journalistic reporting, as this category falls within the protection of freedom of expression.[58] The judgment ultimately grants courts of law discretionary power to determine whether the right to privacy trumps the right to freedom of expression or vice versa. The foundational 'necessity and proportionality' test can be used to assess the facts of each individual case and thereby deduce which right to prioritise within that specific context.

Despite the fact that this CJEU judgment is recognised as a global standard and is implemented within varying cultural contexts,[59] it does not take into consideration the impact it may have in different social settings. Due to a State's power of sovereignty, it has immense discretionary powers of how precisely it interprets international law and regulations and are therefore likely to prioritise a specific right over another. This can be problematic when States use this judgment as a precedent to disproportionately target certain groups. Human rights activists, for instance, are particularly at risk because authoritarian regimes may either disproportionately censor their voices[60] (i.e., violating their freedom of expression), or deny their personal data to be erased, thereby retaining it to continue harmful surveillance techniques (i.e., violating their right to privacy).[61]

---

56 Google Spain SL and Google Inc v Agencia Española de Protección de Datos (AEPD) and Mario Costeja González, No. Case C-131/12 (ECJ May 13, 2014).

57 Joanna Connolly, "The Right to Erasure: Comparative Perspectives on an Emerging Privacy Right," *Alternative Law Journal* 46, no. 1 (March 1, 2021): 58–63.

58 Bernhard Gross, "Harvesting Social Media for Journalistic Purposes in the UK: The Balance between Privacy Rights and Freedom of Expression," in *Privacy, Data Protection and Cybersecurity in Europe*, eds. Wolf J. Schunemann and Max-Otto Baumann (Cham, Switzerland: Springer 2017), 31–42.

59 Franz Werro, ed., *The Right to Be Forgotten: A Comparative Study of the Emergent Right's Evolution and Application in Europe, the Americas, and Asia*, 1st ed. 2020 edition (Cham, Switzerland: Springer, 2020), 2.

60 Bassel El Mrawed and Liz Shelbred, "Standing Against Digital Dictatorships," *Human Rights Foundation* (blog), March 12, 2023, https://hrf.org/standing-against-digital-dictatorships/.

61 Civil Rights Defenders, "Cambodia Should Scrap Rights-Abusing National Internet Gateway," *Civil Rights Defenders* (blog), May 16, 2022, https://crd.org/2022/05/16/cambodia-should-scrap-rights-abusing-national-internet-gateway/.

Even when organisations erase or archive data when requested, users may not be aware of third parties that continue to have access to the data in question. In such cases, there remains the possibility of third parties not only using the data for their own purposes, but further monetise the data and sell it to more organisations. This closes the loop to the issues raised in the data collection stage (i.e., ambiguous privacy policies and information overload fatigue), which highlights the interconnected, albeit nuanced, characteristics of the data lifecycle. If data is not erased in appropriate ways, it might be re-used for purposes not communicated to the data subjects and in doing so, breach data protection laws, a tendency known as 'function creep'.

3 Addressing Human Rights Impacts in the Data Economy: Gaps and Ambiguities

Concerns of human rights harms along the data life cycle as discussed in the previous section have been on the rise. According to the UNGPs, both technology companies themselves as well as governments have a role to play in addressing them adequately. At the corporate level, the UNGPs recommend companies to conduct Human Rights Due Diligence (HRDD). This requirement applies to all companies, irrespective of their size, international outlook, or industry.

HRDD broadly consists of four steps, which builds on extensive stakeholder engagement:[62]

1. Identifying and assessing impacts to gauge the nature and extent of human rights risks
2. Acting to prevent and mitigate risks to people, including via integration within internal functions and processes
3. Tracking the effectiveness of risk mitigation responses over time; and
4. Appropriate communication of performance with respect to addressing human rights impacts.

Each technology company has a responsibility to respect human rights by identifying, assessing, and mitigating adverse impacts on people stemming from or being linked to its business conduct, products and services. Technology company value chains are complex yet can be dissected and analysed with regard

62 OHCHR B-Tech, Key Characteristics of Business Respect for Human Rights (2020), https://www.ohchr.org/sites/default/files/Documents/Issues/Business/B-Tech/key-characteristics-business-respect.pdf.

to their human rights impact as any other value chain. Every company that uses sophisticated digital technology needs to further assess and manage the adverse impacts emanating from the development, deployment and end-use of digital technologies in its business realm and value chains. This entails engaging with potentially affected stakeholders and carrying out ongoing due diligence practices regarding risk to people. Human Rights Impact Assessments (HRIAS), act as a key starting point for companies to determine existing and potential human rights risks of business activities. Although there are several HRIA approaches and guides available (e.g., businesses operating in conflict and high-risk zones), very few of them directly address corporate functions and services in the digital economy and their distinctive features, especially those that target data life cycles.[63] Social media platforms, for example, face immense pressure to identify and mitigate online harms through robust content moderation measures.

Given that most Big Tech companies operate across various jurisdictions and cultures, issues around duty and culpability arise, thereby making it much more difficult to operationalise existing guidance into practice. Diverse cultures may have different perspectives on rights such as free speech, referencing the argument made on the *Google Spain* CJEU judgment mentioned above. The importance of independently led HRIAS can be evidenced by a more recent example. The report published by BSR on Meta's impact on people in Israel and Palestine in May 2021 indicated that though Meta facilitated several appropriate measures in accordance with the UNGPS to combat human rights abuses in the regions, various adverse impacts on people did arise, particularly in terms of freedom of expression and related rights.[64] There were instances where over-enforcement (excessively and disproportionately removing unharmful content) and under-enforcement (failure to remove harmful content) of content moderation occurred.[65] Such assessments can thereby point

63 UNDP (United Nations Development Programme), "The Impact of Digital Technology on Human Rights in Europe and Central Asia: Trends and Challenges related to Data Protection, Artificial Intelligence and Other Digital Technology Issues," (Istanbul: United Nations Development Programme, 2023), https://www.undp.org/sites/g/files/zskgke326/files/2023-03/The%20Impact%20of%20Digital%20Technology%20on%20Human%20Rights%20in%20Europe%20and%20Central%20Asia.pdf, 19.

64 Business for Social Responsibility (BSR), "Human Rights Due Diligence of Meta's Impacts in Israel and Palestine in May 2021," (BSR, September 22, 2022), https://www.bsr.org/reports/BSR_Meta_Human_Rights_Israel_Palestine_English.pdf.

65 Business for Social Responsibility (BSR), "Human Rights Due Diligence of Meta's Impacts in Israel and Palestine in May 2021," (BSR, September 22, 2022), https://www.bsr.org/reports/BSR_Meta_Human_Rights_Israel_Palestine_English.pdf, 4.

at the particularities of harms explicitly, implicitly, and complicitly occurring within the specific data life cycle and how they affect different rights, considering the nuanced nature of cultural differences.

The corporate responsibility to conduct HRDD is closely intertwined with the State duty to protect human rights. For example, a type of regulation that is in line with the UNGPs would in most cases expect companies to carry out HRDD, in line with the expectations set out in UNGP 13. As part of implementing a 'smart mix' of measures to ensure corporate respect of human rights, States have responded by drawing up so-called National Action Plans on BHR, as well as targeted policies and, in some instances, legislation to mandate HRDD. The EU's Digital Services Act (DSA), for example, requires very large online platforms to assess and mitigate systemic risks that arise from the 'design, including algorithmic systems, functioning and use made of their services.'[66] Another example is the latest proposal by the Brazilian Federal Commission on the regulation on AI, which foresees risk management of AI companies. One of the biggest concerns surrounding existing HRDD guidance and regulations is the lack of clarity and non-alignment in terminology concerning what HRDD truly entails.[67] Articles 26 and 27 of the DSA have been criticised to be vague and to require further clarification during its enforcement to ensure alignment with the UNGPs. At present, the provisions leave ample room for corporations to apply their own discretion in deciding how systemic risks ought to be mitigated.[68] Therefore, technology companies ought to involve more seasoned experts within this field, as well as rights holders, to encourage more meaningful engagement to ensure alignment with the UNGPs when implementing laws.

When it comes to access to remedy, as laid out in Pillar 3 of the UNGPs, there are State-based judicial and non-judicial measures that can be tailored to the technology sector, as well as non-State based measures. For example, OECD National Contact Points have acted as a mediator in technology-related cases, e.g., products offered on platforms that were used to violate human rights.[69]

66 Official Journal of the European Union, Digital Services Act, § 26 and 27.

67 Isabel Ebert and Ana Bedusch, "Regulating Business Conduct in the Technology Sector: Gaps and Ways Forward in Applying the UNGPs," (Geneva: Geneva Academy and OHCHR, April 2022), https://www.geneva-academy.ch/joomlatools-files/docman-files/Regulating%20business%20conduct%20in%20the.pdf, 6.

68 Article 19, "EU: Will the Digital Services Act Hold Big Tech to Account?," (July 5, 2022), https://www.article19.org/resources/digital-services-act-big-tech-accountable/, 3.

69 See for example: OECD Watch, "Society for Threatened Peoples Switzerland vs. UBS Group," OECD Watch, June 22, 2020, https://www.oecdwatch.org/complaint/society-for-threatened-peoples-switzerland-vs-ubs-group/.

Equally, companies or a set of companies (within one sector operating in a single market) together can offer operational-level grievance mechanisms (OGMs) to rightsholders, to address concerns in an accessible and fast manner. However, for OGMs to be functional, meaningful engagement with rightsholders is crucial – corporations should involve rightsholders during the design and development of remedy mechanisms, and prioritise specific groups given the context they operate in. Furthermore, Big Tech companies, particularly those operating in various sectors and countries, should avoid creating broad blanket remedial mechanisms, as they would not adequately represent the needs of certain vulnerable groups.

While various efforts are ongoing both at the corporate as well as at the regulatory level, the overall picture resembles a piecemeal approach. More clarification is needed on what responsible business conduct looks like in the tech sector and how it can be mandated by law. This holds particularly for jurisdictions in which companies fail to uphold their corporate responsibility to respect human rights on voluntary grounds.

4 Outlook

This chapter has demonstrated that the BHR lens can inform the debate about responsible business conduct in the technology sector. However, the nature and scale of potential adverse impacts of human rights in the technology sector was not fully taken into consideration when the UNGPs were drafted. The extent of affected groups and people and the speed with which harm is spreading might require additional collective means to cope with the human rights record of this sector. At the same time, the technology sector also raises human rights concerns that are more 'conventional' and well-known from other sectors. For example, the underpaid and exploited workers labelling data for large-language models are reminiscent of issues encountered with regard to labour conditions in textile supply chains.[70]

Drawing on the experience from other sectors, the following actions could be applied to overcome gaps and shortcomings and build capacity to move towards a more rights-respecting technology sector:

- Expand financial support for rights-respecting technological solutions and research, and to ensure a strong narrative on the protection

70 Billy Perrigo, "OpenAI Used Kenyan Workers on Less Than $2 Per Hour to Make ChatGPT Less Toxic," *TIME Magazine*, January 18, 2023, https://time.com/6247678/openai-chatgpt-kenya-workers/.

of collective rights complements the narrative on the protection of individual ones;

- Require companies to meaningfully engage with stakeholders, including potentially affected rightsholders, which should ideally take into consideration cultural differences to promote a more pluralistic approach to identify and mitigate harms;
- Ensure collaborative communication channels in companies in order for executive management to be aware of and consulted upon salient human rights impact stemming from or being linked to their business;
- Foster peer-learning within different subsectors of the technology sector in order to provide mitigation measures where harms may have occurred, e.g., human rights-based data life cycle assessments and mitigation measures; and
- Where such voluntary measures fail to deliver rights-respecting results and do not establish a level-playing field, States need to introduce laws to require technology companies to respect human rights and enable the companies to involve BHR and digital rights experts to interpret the laws in a truly rights-respecting manner.

With the staggering speed of current technological innovation, the analytical lens of the UNGPs remains relevant to account for human rights risk connected with it. Scholars have an important role to play in pointing out such risks through conceptual and empirical work, and thus to see the ground for the development of effective solutions aiming at the prevention and mitigation of technology-based harm.

Bibliography

Books

Barassi, Veronica. *Child Data Citizen: How Tech Companies Are Profiling Us from Before Birth*. Cambridge, Massachusetts: The MIT Press, 2020.

Morozov, Evgeny. *To Save Everything, Click Here*, 2017. https://www.publicaffairsbooks.com/titles/evgeny-morozov/to-save-everything-click-here/9781610393706/.

Werro, Franz, ed. *The Right to Be Forgotten: A Comparative Study of the Emergent Right's Evolution and Application in Europe, the Americas, and Asia*. 1st ed. Cham, Switzerland: Springer, 2020.

Chapters in Edited Books

Gross, Bernhard. "Harvesting Social Media for Journalistic Purposes in the UK: The Balance between Privacy Rights and Freedom of Expression." In *Privacy, Data Protection and Cybersecurity in Europe*, edited by Wolf J. K. Schunemann and Max-Otto Baumann, 31–42. Cham, Switzerland, 2017.

Henningsson, Stefan, and Jonas Hedman. "Transformation of Digital Ecosystems: The Case of Digital Payments." In *Information and Communication Technology*, edited by Linawati, Made Sudiana Mahendra, Erich J. Neuhold, A. Min Tjoa, and Ilsun You, 46–55. Lecture Notes in Computer Science. Berlin, Heidelberg: Springer, 2014.

Hussain, Kazim, and Elsa Prieto. "Big Data in the Finance and Insurance Sectors." In *New Horizons for a Data-Driven Economy: A Roadmap for Usage and Exploitation of Big Data in Europe*, edited by José María Cavanillas, Edward Curry, and Wolfgang Wahlster, 209–23. Cham: Springer International Publishing, 2016.

Latonero, Mark. "Big Data Analytics and Human Rights: Privacy Considerations in Context." In *New Technologies for Human Rights Law and Practice*, edited by Jay D. Aronson and Molly K. Land, 149–61. Cambridge: Cambridge University Press, 2018.

Sinaeepourfard, Amir, Jordi Garcia, Xavier Masip-Bruin, and Eva Marín-Torder. "Towards a Comprehensive Data Lifecycle Model for Big Data Environments." In *Proceedings of the 3rd IEEE/ACM International Conference on Big Data Computing, Applications and Technologies*, 100–106. BDCAT '16. New York, NY, USA: Association for Computing Machinery, 2016.

Journal Articles

Aizenberg, Evgeni, and Jeroen van den Hoven. "Designing for Human Rights in AI." *Big Data & Society* 7, no. 2 (July 1, 2020): 2053951720949566. https://doi.org/10.1177/2053951720949566.

Al-Lozi, Enas, Amjed Alfityani, Ayman Alsmadi, Amer Al_Hazimeh, and Jassim Al-Gasawneh. "The Role of Big Data in Financial Sector: A Review Paper." *International Journal of Data and Network Science* 6, 2022. https://doi.org/10.5267/j.ijdns.2022.6.003.

Alessandro, Brian d', Cathy O'Neil, and Tom LaGatta. "Conscientious Classification: A Data Scientist's Guide to Discrimination-Aware Classification." *Big Data* 5, no. 2 (June 2017): 120–34. https://doi.org/10.1089/big.2016.0048.

Alfred, Rayner, and Joe Henry Obit. "The Roles of Machine Learning Methods in Limiting the Spread of Deadly Diseases: A Systematic Review." *Heliyon* 7, no. 6 (June 23, 2021): e07371. https://doi.org/10.1016/j.heliyon.2021.e07371.

Bernal, Paul. "Data Gathering, Surveillance and Human Rights: Recasting the Debate." *Journal of Cyber Policy* 1, no. 2 (July 2, 2016): 243–64.

Birch, Kean, and D. T. Cochrane. "Big Tech: Four Emerging Forms of Digital Rentiership." *Science as Culture* 31, no. 1 (January 2, 2022): 44–58.

Connolly, Joanna. "The Right to Erasure: Comparative Perspectives on an Emerging Privacy Right." *Alternative Law Journal* 46, no. 1 (March 1, 2021): 58–63.

Ebert, Isabel, Isabelle Wildhaber, and Jeremias Adams-Prassl. "Big Data in the Workplace: Privacy Due Diligence as a Human Rights-Based Approach to Employee Privacy Protection." *Big Data & Society* 8, no. 1 (January 1, 2021): 20539517211013052. https://doi.org/10.1177/20539517211013051.

Favaretto, Maddalena, Eva De Clercq, and Bernice Simone Elger. "Big Data and Discrimination: Perils, Promises and Solutions. A Systematic Review." *Journal of Big Data* 6, no. 1 (February 5, 2019): 12.

Favaretto, Maddalena, Eva De Clercq, Christophe Olivier Schneble, and Bernice Simone Elger. "What Is Your Definition of Big Data? Researchers' Understanding of the Phenomenon of the Decade." *PLoS ONE* 15, no. 2 (February 25, 2020): e0228987. https://doi.org/10.1371/journal.pone.0228987.

Hurley, M., and Julius Adebayo. "Credit Scoring in the Era of Big Data." *Yale Journal of Law and Technology* (April 2, 2017). https://www.semanticscholar.org/paper/CREDIT-SCORING-IN-THE-ERA-OF-BIG-DATA-Hurley-Adebayo/6830f672c1765867a914155d5eb7df140fe7de16.

Ibrahim, Hussein, Xiaoxuan Liu, Nevine Zariffa, Andrew D. Morris, and Alastair K. Denniston. "Health Data Poverty: An Assailable Barrier to Equitable Digital Health Care." *The Lancet Digital Health* 3, no. 4 (April 1, 2021): e260–65. https://doi.org/10.1016/S2589-7500(20)30317-4.

Jobin, Anna, Marcello Ienca, and Effy Vayena. "The Global Landscape of AI Ethics Guidelines." *Nature Machine Intelligence* 1, no. 9 (September 2019): 389–99.

Kaufmann, Mareile, Simon Egbert, and Matthias Leese. "Predictive Policing and the Politics of Patterns." *The British Journal of Criminology* 59, no. 3 (April 9, 2019): 674–92.

Koch, Matthias, Daniel Krohmer, Matthias Naab, Dominik Rost, and Marcus Trapp. "A Matter of Definition: Criteria for Digital Ecosystems." *Digital Business* 2, no. 2 (January 1, 2022): 100027. https://doi.org/10.1016/j.digbus.2022.100027.

Ledford, Heidi. "Millions of Black People Affected by Racial Bias in Health-Care Algorithms." *Nature* 574, no. 7780 (October 24, 2019): 608–9. https://doi.org/10.1038/d41586-019-03228-6.

Liu, Hong, Chen Zhong, Awny Alnusair, and Sheikh Rabiul Islam. "FAIXID: A Framework for Enhancing AI Explainability of Intrusion Detection Results Using Data Cleaning Techniques." *Journal of Network and Systems Management* 29, no. 4 (May 24, 2021): 40.

Lomborg, Stine, and Anja Bechmann. "Using APIs for Data Collection on Social Media." *The Information Society* 30, no. 4 (August 8, 2014): 256–65.

Lupton, Deborah. "Quantified Sex: A Critical Analysis of Sexual and Reproductive Self-Tracking Using Apps." *Culture, Health & Sexuality* 17, no. 4 (April 21, 2015): 440–53.

Maas, Jonne. "Machine Learning and Power Relations." *AI & SOCIETY*, February 25, 2022. https://doi.org/10.1007/s00146-022-01400-7.

Mittelstadt, Brent. "From Individual to Group Privacy in Big Data Analytics." *Philosophy & Technology* 30, no. 4 (December 1, 2017): 475–94.

Mittelstadt, Brent. "Principles Alone Cannot Guarantee Ethical AI." *Nature Machine Intelligence* 1, no. 11 (November 2019): 501–7.

Obar, Jonathan A., and Anne Oeldorf-Hirsch. "The Biggest Lie on the Internet: Ignoring the Privacy Policies and Terms of Service Policies of Social Networking Services." *Information, Communication & Society* 23, no. 1 (January 2, 2020): 128–47.

Rahul, Kumar, and Rohitash Banyal. "Data Life Cycle Management in Big Data Analytics." *Procedia Computer Science* 173 (January 1, 2020): 364–71.

Sarker, Iqbal H. "Data Science and Analytics: An Overview from Data-Driven Smart Computing, Decision-Making and Applications Perspective." *SN Computer Science* 2, no. 5 (July 12, 2021): 377.

Strikwerda, Litska. "Predictive Policing: The Risks Associated with Risk Assessment." *The Police Journal* 94, no. 3 (September 1, 2021): 422–36.

Strycharz, Joanna, and Bram Duivenvoorde. "The Exploitation of Vulnerability through Personalised Marketing Communication: Are Consumers Protected?" *Internet Policy Review* 10, no. 4 (November 8, 2021). https://policyreview.info/articles/analysis/exploitation-vulnerability-through-personalised-marketing-communication-are. http://doi.org/10.14763/2021.4.1585.

Tsesis, Alexander. "Data Subjects' Privacy Rights: Regulation of Personal Data Retention and Erasure." *University of Colorado Law Review* 90, no. 2 (2019): 593–630.

Wymant, Chris, Luca Ferretti, Daphne Tsallis, Marcos Charalambides, Lucie Abeler-Dörner, David Bonsall, Robert Hinch, et al. "The Epidemiological Impact of the NHS COVID-19 App." *Nature*, May 12, 2021, 1–8. https://doi.org/10.1038/s41586-021-03606-z.

Magazine Articles

Kelley, Stephanie, Anton Ovchinnikov, Adrienne Heinrich, and David R. Hardoon. "Removing Demographic Data Can Make AI Discrimiantion Worse." *Harvard Business Review* (March 6, 2023). https://hbr.org/2023/03/removing-demographic-data-can-make-ai-discrimination-worse.

Perrigo, Billy. "OpenAI Used Kenyan Workers on Less Than $2 Per Hour to Make ChatGPT Less Toxic." *TIME Magazine* (January 18, 2023). https://time.com/6247678/openai-chatgpt-kenya-workers/.

Russo, Massimo, David Young, and Marine Gerard. "Sharing Data to Address Out Biggest Societal Challenges." *BCG* (January 7, 2021).

Newspaper Article

Business for Social Responsibility (BSR). "Human Rights Due Diligence of Meta's Impacts in Israel and Palestine in May 2021." BSR (September 22, 2022). https://www.bsr.org/reports/BSR_Meta_Human_Rights_Israel_Palestine_English.pdf.

Gerstein, Josh, and Alexander Ward. "Supreme Court Has Voted to Overturn Abortion Rights, Draft Opinion Shows." *Politico* (March 5, 2022). https://www.politico.com/news/2022/05/02/supreme-court-abortion-draft-opinion-00029473.

Tucker, Ian. "Evgeny Morozov: 'We Are Abandoning All the Checks and Balances'." *The Observer*, (March 9, 2013), sec. Technology. https://www.theguardian.com/technology/2013/mar/09/evgeny-morozov-technology-solutionism-interview.

Online/Internet Resources

Article 19. "MENA: Stop Censoring the Voices of Women Human Rights Defenders." ARTICLE 19, November 29, 2022. https://www.article19.org/resources/mena-stop-censoring-the-voices-of-women-human-rights-defenders/.

OECD Watch. "Society for Threatened Peoples Switzerland vs. UBS Group." OECD Watch, June 22, 2020. https://www.oecdwatch.org/complaint/society-for-threatened-peoples-switzerland-vs-ubs-group/.

Reports

Article 19. "EU: Will the Digital Services Act Hold Big Tech to Account?". (July 5, 2022). https://www.article19.org/resources/digital-services-act-big-tech-accountable/.

Business for Social Responsibility (BSR). "Human Rights Due Diligence of Meta's Impacts in Israel and Palestine in May 2021." BSR (September 22, 2022). https://www.bsr.org/reports/BSR_Meta_Human_Rights_Israel_Palestine_English.pdf.

Cisco. "Protecting Data Privacy to Maintain Digital Trust." (U.S.: Cisco, July 2020). https://www.cisco.com/c/dam/en_us/about/doing_business/trust-center/docs/cybersecurity-series-2020-cps.pdf.

Ebert, Isabel, and Ana Bedusch. "Regulating Business Conduct in the Technology Sector: Gaps and Ways Forward in Applying the UNGPs." Geneva: Geneva Academy and OHCHR (April 2022). https://www.geneva-academy.ch/joomlatools-files/docman-files/Regulating%20business%20conduct%20in%20the.pdf.

European Union Agency for Fundamental Rights. "Bias in Algorithms: Artificial Intelligence and Discrimination." (Vienna: FRA, 2022). https://fra.europa.eu/sites/default/files/fra_uploads/fra-2022-bias-in-algorithms_en.pdf.

Kemp, Katharine. "Your Body, Our Data: Unfair and Unsafe Privacy Practices of Popular Fertility Apps." (Sydney: University of New South Wales, March 2023). https://allenshub.unsw.edu.au/sites/default/files/2023-03/KKemp%20Your%20Body%20Our%20Data%2022.03.23.pdf.

OHCHR. "A/HRC/50/56: The Practical Application of the Guiding Principles on Business and Human Rights to the Activities of Technology Companies." (Geneva: United Nations, April 21, 2022). https://www.ohchr.org/en/documents/thematic-reports/ahrc5056-practical-application-guiding-principles-business-and-human.

OHCHR B-Tech Project. "Bridging Governance Gaps in the Age of Technology – Key Characteristics of the State Duty to Protect." (May 2021). https://www.ohchr.org/sites/default/files/Documents/Issues/Business/B-Tech/b-tech-foundational-paper-state-duty-to-protect.pdf.

Omoyiola, Bayo Olushola. "The Social Implications, Risks, Challenges and Opportunities of Big Data." (Emerald Open Research, June 13, 2022). https://doi.org/10.35241/emeraldopenres.14646.1.

UNDP (United Nations Development Programme). "The Impact of Digital Technology on Human Rights in Europe and Central Asia: Trends and Challenges Related to Data Protection, Artificial Intelligence and Other Digital Technology Issues." (Istanbul: United Nations Development Programme, 2023). https://www.undp.org/sites/g/files/zskgke326/files/2023-03/The%20Impact%20of%20Digital%20Technology%20on%20Human%20Rights%20in%20Europe%20and%20Central%20Asia.pdf.

Cases

Google Spain SL and Google Inc v Agencia Española de Protección de Datos (AEPD) and Mario Costeja González, No. Case C-131/12 (ECJ May 13, 2014).

Legislation

European Union's General Data Protection Regulation, (EU) 2016/679 § (2016). https://gdpr-info.eu/.

Official Journal of the European Union. Digital Services Act, L.277/1 § (2022). https://eur-lex.europa.eu/legal-content/EN/TXT/PDF/?uri=CELEX:32022R2065&from=EN.

Miscellaneous

Austin Jr, Roy L. "Expanding Our Work on Ads Fairness." *Meta*, June 21, 2022. https://about.fb.com/news/2022/06/expanding-our-work-on-ads-fairness/.

Civil Rights Defenders. "Cambodia Should Scrap Rights-Abusing National Internet Gateway." *Civil Rights Defenders* (blog), May 16, 2022. https://crd.org/2022/05/16/cambodia-should-scrap-rights-abusing-national-internet-gateway/.

El Mrawed, Bassel, and Liz Shelbred. "Standing Against Digital Dictatorships." *Human Rights Foundation* (blog), March 12, 2023. https://hrf.org/standing-against-digital-dictatorships/.

Gjerlufsen, Tony, Paul Maingot, Valéry Bezençon, and Adrian Holzer. "Digital Nudges for Privacy Awareness: From Consent to Informed Consent?'" AIS, 2020. https://libra.unine.ch/handle/123456789/28886.

Hansen, Amy Jeter. "Solving Social Problems with Data." *Scope* (blog), April 17, 2018. https://scopeblog.stanford.edu/2018/04/17/solving-social-problems-with-data/.

Knight, Hannah, Norman, Victoria. "Should You Worry About Data from Your Period-Tracking App Being Used Against You?" *Kaiser Health News* (blog), May 13, 2022. https://khn.org/news/article/period-tracking-apps-data-privacy/.

May, Emily. "How Digital Health Apps Are Empowering Patients." *Deloitte* (blog), October 19, 2021. https://www2.deloitte.com/us/en/blog/health-care-blog/2021/how-digital-health-apps-are-empowering-patients.html.

Mollah, Maria. "APIs and Ethics: What Are the Ambiguities?" *PlektonLabs* (blog), November 25, 2020. https://www.plektonlabs.com/api-and-ethics-what-are-the-ambiguities/.

OECD. "Data Governance in the Public Sector." In *The Path to Becoming a Data-Driven Public Sector*, by OECD, 23–57. OECD Digital Government Studies. OECD, 2019. https://doi.org/10.1787/9cada708-en.

OECD. "The Path to Becoming a Data-Driven Public Sector." OECD Digital Government Studies. OECD, 2019. https://doi.org/10.1787/059814a7-en.

Ohio University. "How Data Science Can Be Used for Social Good." *Ohio University* (blog), December 7, 2020. https://onlinemasters.ohio.edu/blog/data-science-for-social-good/.

CHAPTER 18

Aligning Business Efforts to Combat Corruption and Respect Human Rights

David Hess

1 Introduction

Under frameworks such as the United Nations Global Compact (UNGC)[1] and the OECD's *Guidelines for Multinational Enterprises* (hereafter the OECD's *Guidelines*),[2] businesses have responsibilities related to both respecting human rights and combatting corruption. Regarding human rights, the leading framework on the topic – the United Nations *Guiding Principles on Business and Human Rights* (UNGPs) – sets out what it means for a business to respect human rights. This responsibility requires companies to avoid causing, contributing to, or being directly linked with an adverse human rights impact, and to provide a remedy to individuals in certain situations. To meet this responsibility, businesses must adopt a 'due diligence process to identify, prevent, mitigate and account for how they address their impacts on human rights.'[3] The human rights due diligence process involves 'assessing actual and potential human rights impacts, integrating and acting upon the findings, tracking responses, and communicating how impacts are addressed.'[4]

Likewise, to combat corruption under the OECD *Guidelines*, businesses should:

> Develop and adopt adequate internal controls, ethics and compliance programmes or measures for preventing and detecting bribery, developed on the basis of a risk assessment addressing the individual circumstances

1 United Nations Global Compact, *The Ten Principles of the UN Global Compact*, https://unglobalcompact.org/what-is-gc/mission/principles.

2 OECD, *OECD Guidelines for Multinational Enterprises* (2011), 31.

3 Special Representative of the Secretary-General on the Issue of Human Rights and Transnational Corporations and Other Business Enterprises, *Guiding Principles on Business and Human Rights: Implementing the United Nations "Protect, Respect and Remedy" Framework*, U.N. Doc. A/HRC/17/31 (Mar. 21, 2011), Principle 15.

4 Special Representative, *Guiding Principles*, Principle 17.

 | DOI:10.1163/9789004530942_019

> of an enterprise, in particular the bribery risks facing the enterprise (such as its geographical and industrial sector of operation).[5]

Looking just at these necessary policies and procedures under the UNGPs and the OECD *Guidelines*, businesses have similar actions they should undertake to respect human rights and to combat corruption. In practice, however, companies often manage these responsibilities in parallel;[6] businesses typically treat anticorruption and bribery (ABC) as a matter of criminal law and business and human rights (BHR) as a matter of soft law.

Beyond the fact that combatting corruption and respecting human rights have significant potential overlaps in policies and procedures, corruption and human rights violations are often highly correlated. A company operating in a region with a high risk of human rights abuses, either through the company's own activities or those of business partners, is also likely to face high risks of corruption in that area, and *vice versa*.[7] As stated in a recent OECD report:

> The anti-corruption and human rights agendas have much in common. Corrupt practices and human rights abuses share many of the same root causes, frequently occur in areas in which there is weak governance and pose similar risks to companies (reputational, financial, legal, operational, etc.). Moreover, there often exist interlinkages between the two areas.[8]

This connection between corruption and human rights is now well recognised by the global community. In 2013, the United Nations Office of the High Commissioner for Human Rights passed a resolution recognising 'that corruption constitutes one of the obstacles to the effective promotion and protection of human rights.'[9] Another United Nations report stated that '[i]t is difficult

5 OECD, *Guidelines*, 47.

6 David Hess, "Business, Corruption, and Human Rights: Towards a New Responsibility for Corporations to Combat Corruption," *Wisconsin Law Review* 4 (2017): 642.

7 United Nations Global Compact, *Linking Human Rights and Anti-Corruption Compliance* (Dec. 2016), 5–6.

8 Business at OECD (BIAC) & International Organisation of Employers (IOE), *Connecting the anti-corruption and human rights agendas: A guide for business and employers' organisations* (Sept. 2020), 2.

9 Human Rights Council, *The Negative Impact of Corruption on the Enjoyment of Human Rights*, UN Doc. A/HRC/Res/23/9 (June 20, 2013), 2.

to find a human right that could not be violated by corruption.'[10] For example, corruption impacts economic and social rights, such as the rights to food, work, health, education, and non-discrimination.[11] Corruption also impacts civil and political rights, including the rights to a fair trial and to participate in the political system.[12]

This chapter explores the ways in which corruption and business and human rights can be brought together, with a particular emphasis on the management of these issues by business. The last twenty years have seen significant developments in both the fight against corruption in international business and in the field of business and human rights. Due to development of a global anti-corruption norm, and the widespread acknowledgement that corporations have a responsibility to respect human rights under the UNGPs, corporations now have obligations in both areas that exist wherever they operate across the globe. These efforts can be enhanced by recognising the linkages between these two areas and having businesses coordinate the governance and implementation of these efforts. Importantly, both responsibilities are founded on the need to move beyond compliance-oriented approaches and to embed these obligations in the corporation's ethical culture.[13]

This chapter proceeds by first describing the development of a global anti-corruption norm over the last twenty-five years. The following section then explores the different ways that corruption can negatively impact human rights. Next, this chapter uses the Rana Plaza tragedy and the issue of modern slavery in supply chains as examples to illustrate the connection between corruption and business and human rights. The subsequent section discusses the ways businesses can connect combatting corruption with respecting human rights and the benefits in doing so. This section also includes a discussion of the role of the state in the effort to bring corruption and business and human rights together.

---

10 Human Rights Council, *Final Report of the Human Rights Council Advisory Committee on the Issue of the Negative Impact of Corruption on the Enjoyment of Human Rights*, UN Doc. A/HRC/28/73 (Jan. 5, 2015), 5.

11 Human Rights Council, *Final Report*, 6.

12 Human Rights Council, *Final Report*, 6.

13 UN Global Compact, *Linking Human Rights*, 7.

2 The Development of a Global Anti-corruption Norm

Corruption is a broad term that encompasses a wide range of behaviors. Because there is not a single definition of corruption, the United Nations Convention Against Corruption (UNCAC) does not even define the term. Transparency International (TI) – a leading anticorruption non-governmental organisation – has referred to corruption as 'the abuse of entrusted power for private gain.' As examples of the different forms that corruption can take, TI has described it to include, 'public servants demanding or taking money or favours in exchange for services, politicians misusing public money or granting public jobs or contracts to their sponsors, friends and families, corporations bribing officials to get lucrative deals.'[14] Overall, at a minimum, the term includes bribery, extortion, nepotism, cronyism, embezzlement, and fraud.

The first major attempt to combat corruption in international business occurred in 1977 when the United States (US) passed the Foreign Corrupt Practices Act (FCPA).[15] This law was unique in that it had extraterritorial reach. In other words, a US businessperson would be in violation of the law even if all actions related to the bribe, and any benefits directly received from the bribe, occurred outside the jurisdiction of the US. In other countries at this time, although domestic bribery may have been illegal, the home country could not prosecute a company for bribes paid in a foreign country. In fact, in many countries, the bribe payment was a tax-deductible business expense.

The FCPA prohibits individuals, and companies connected to the US, from 'corruptly' giving 'anything of value' to foreign government officials for purposes of 'obtaining or retaining business' due to some 'improper advantage' or an influence over the official.[16] The law also contains accounting provisions, which requires that all transactions – including bribe payments – be accurately reflected in the company's records. In the FCPA's first twenty-five years of operation, however, the US government rarely enforced its provisions, and the law had little impact on US businesses. However, starting in the early 2000s, the US government slowly ramped up enforcement and began regularly issuing multimillion-dollar fines and obtaining settlement agreements that required corporations that violated the law to adopt major governance and compliance program reforms.

---

14 Transparency International, *What is Corruption?* https://www.transparency.org/en/what-is-corruption.

15 Foreign Corrupt Practices Act of 1977, 15 US Code § 78dd–1.

16 Foreign Corrupt Practices Act of 1977, 15 U.S. Code § 78dd–1(a).

This increase in enforcement occurred around the same time that the UNCAC was adopted in 2003, which was preceded by a rapid change in worldwide attitudes toward corruption. An early event precipitating this change was the end of the Cold War in the 1990s, which resulted in democratic countries no longer believing that they needed to support corrupt autocracies for strategic reasons.[17] In addition to political reasons, the anticorruption norm was furthered by the growing recognition that corruption harms a country's economic development. In 1996, World Bank President John Wolfensohn publicly denounced the problem of the 'cancer of corruption' and announced that the World Bank would provide assistance to member countries to fight corruption.[18] Previously, the World Bank had been silent on the topic. Then, in 1997, the OECD adopted the *Convention on Combating Bribery of Foreign Public Officials.*[19] The Convention required signatories to criminalise the act of bribing foreign officials.

During this time when more states were criminalising bribery in international business, combatting corruption also started making an appearance in discussions of a corporation's social responsibilities. For example, in 2000, the UNGC was officially launched with nine principles, which covered human rights, labour rights, and environmental issues, but it failed to mention corruption. Not long after this launch, however, many argued that the business community would make little progress on the nine principles if corruption was not brought under control.[20] In response, in 2004, the UNGC added a 10th Principle, which states that 'Businesses should work against corruption in all its forms, including extortion and bribery'. This need to combat corruption to support progress on corporate social responsibilities matters – as opposed to treating corruption solely as a matter for criminal law – was captured by a commentator's statement that 'If ending corruption is not treated as a prerequisite

17 Susan Rose-Ackerman, "Corruption and the Global Corporation: Ethical Obligations and Workable Strategies," in *Transnational Legal Processes: Globalization and Power Disparities,* ed. Michael Likosky (Trowbridge; Cromwell Press, 2002), 151.

18 James D. Wolfensohn, *People and development: address to the Board of Governors,* Washington, DC, (October 1, 1996), http://documents.worldbank.org/curated/en/243871468141893629/People-and-development-address-to-the-Board-of-Governors-Washington-DC-October-1-1996.

19 OECD, *Convention on Combating Bribery of Foreign Public Officials in International Business Transactions* (Nov. 21, 1997).

20 Peter Eigen, "Removing a Roadblock to Development: Transparency International Mobilizes Coalitions Against Corruption," *Innovations* 3 no. 2 (2008): 29.

to all corporate efforts, CSR [Corporate Social Responsibility] practitioners will continue to work upon a foundation of quicksand.'[21]

Other CSR initiatives also started to include anticorruption in their guidelines and principles. However, these initiatives focused primarily on ensuring that the corporation was not directly involved in a bribe payment – to ensure the corporation was in compliance with the criminal law – but the initiatives did not address how corruption intersects with other aspects of a corporation's social responsibilities. For example, the Global Reporting Initiative (GRI) – which provides standards for corporate sustainability reports – did not include corruption and bribery in its original standards. It was only in subsequent versions, around the same time as the changes to the UNGC, that it was added.[22] These required disclosures on corruption focused on the company's policies and procedures, employee training, risk assessments, and any instances of employees or business partners paying bribes.[23] The GRI did state that corporations should disclose whether they participate in 'collective action [initiatives] to combat corruption'.[24] Overall, however, the GRI – and other CSR guidelines, such as the *ISO 26000: Guidance on Social Responsibility* – focus on ensuring that corporations are not paying bribes. These guidance initiatives treat anticorruption primarily as a legal compliance issue and do not encourage corporations to consider how corruption intersects with other CSR issues, including business and human rights matters.

3 Corruption and Human Rights

Prior to the development of the global anticorruption norm, there was a belief that corruption could 'grease the wheels' of a nation's economy.[25] Under this belief, corruption facilitated economic development.[26] Although there may be

21 Mohamed A. Arafa, "Battling Corruption Within a Corporate Social Responsibility Strategy," *Indiana International and Comparative Law Review* 21, no. 3 (2011): 408.

22 David Hess, and Thomas W. Dunfee. "Taking Responsibility for Bribery: The Multinational Corporation's Role in Combating Corruption," in *Business and Human Rights: Dilemmas and Solutions*, ed. Rory Sullivan (Sheffield, UK: Greenleaf, 2003), 269.

23 Global Reporting Initiative (GRI), *GRI 205: Anti-Corruption* 2016 (2016), https://www.globalreporting.org/standards.

24 Global Reporting Initiative, *GRI 205*, 6.

25 Toke S. Aidt, "Corruption, Institutions, and Economic Development," *Oxford Review of Economics* 25 no. 2 (2009): 273.

26 Elizabeth Spahn, "Nobody Gets Hurt?" *Georgetown International Law Journal* 41 (2010): 864–65.

some anecdotal evidence in support of this view, the weight of the evidence showed that corruption slows economic development.[27] For example, rather than greasing the wheels of an economy, corruption incentivises government officials to impose inefficient regulation to create opportunities for bribe extraction. Beyond its impact on economic development, corruption imposes other societal costs, including its severe negative impact on human rights. Moreover, these impacts disproportionately fall on women, children, indigenous people, migrant workers, the poor, and other disadvantaged groups.[28]

To better understand the impact of corruption on human rights, the International Council on Human Rights (ICHR) and TI issued a joint report placing these connections in the categories of direct, indirect, and remote.[29] The report's goal was not to create categorisations for determining legal liability, but to raise 'awareness among key stakeholders and the public of the links between corruption and human rights, thereby diminishing public tolerance of corruption and strengthening public support for anticorruption measures'.[30]

Corruption has a direct impact on human rights when it is used to violate a right. For example, the right to a fair trial is violated when a business pays a bribe to a judge to influence the outcome of litigation.[31] An indirect violation occurs when corruption plays a contributing factor to the human rights violation.[32] For instance, an indirect violation occurs when a business pays a bribe to evade government regulations, such as on health and safety, and someone is harmed in the manner that those regulations were designed to prevent.[33] A remote violation occurs when corruption is one of multiple factors that contribute to an adverse human rights impact.[34] If a business engages in corruption to influence the results of a political election and that corrupt elected official takes actions that violate human rights, then the business is remotely connected to the violation.[35] Overall, by expanding the focus beyond just direct connections, this categorisation helps the public to understand the numerous ways that corruption negatively impacts human rights, as opposed to seeing corruption as a victimless crime.

---

27 Aidt, "Corruption, Institutions," 275–84; Spahn, "Nobody Gets Hurt?" 866–67.

28 International Council on Human Rights (ICHR) and Transparency International (TI), *Corruption and Human Rights: Making the Connection* (2009), 1.

29 ICHR and TI, "Making the Connection," 1.

30 ICHR and TI, "Making the Connection," 1.

31 ICHR and TI, "Making the Connection," 27.

32 ICHR and TI, "Making the Connection," 27.

33 ICHR and TI, "Making the Connection," 27.

34 ICHR and TI, "Making the Connection," 28.

35 ICHR and TI, "Making the Connection," 28.

A second classification system, which focuses on who is impacted by corruption, further helps us understand corruption's connections to human rights violations. A 2015 report from United Nations Human Rights Council Advisory Committee looked at the negative impact on individuals, groups, and then society at large.[36] At the individual level, the focus is placed on those specific individuals that are suffering a negative impact. Moving up a level of analysis, at the group level ('collective negative impact'), this classification scheme recognises that corruption may systematically impact specific, identifiable groups, such as the poor, women, children, ethnic minorities, indigenous people, and other groups. Third, at the society level ("general negative impact"), the report lists two categories of impact. First, corruption can negatively impact economic development and the resources available to the state for the realisation of individuals' rights. Second, corruption can impact the rule of law and undermine people's confidence in government.

Taken together, these two classification schemes show the many ways that corruption negatively impacts human rights. A traditional criminal law perspective on corruption, on the other hand, places the focus only on the bribe payor and bribe recipient.[37] On the benefit of expanding the view of corruption's impacts, the Human Rights Council stated:

> Analysing the link between corruption and impairment of the enjoyment of human rights may contribute to a better understanding of the effects of corruption – notably, its human dimension and social implications – and can be an important step towards making corruption a public issue. In that way, the social impact of corruption is made visible; this generates awareness in society about the consequences of this scourge and creates new alliances in the fight against corruption.[38]

4 Connecting Combatting Corruption with Business and Human Rights

Under the UNGPs, corruption is mentioned with respect to the state's duty to protect human rights under Pillar I, and the state's responsibility to ensure access to effective remedy for human rights abuses under Pillar III. The commentary for Principle Three, on the state's general regularity obligations, notes

36 Human Rights Council, *Final Report*, 7–8.
37 Human Rights Council, *Final Report*, 9.
38 Human Rights Council, *Final Report*, 10.

the need for states to ensure adequate enforcement of laws that 'directly or indirectly regulate business respect for human rights', including anti-bribery laws. Under Pillar III, the commentary to Principle Twenty-Five states that '[p]rocedures for the provision of remedy should be impartial, protected from corruption and free from political or other attempts to influence the outcome'. Likewise, under the commentary to Principle Twenty-Six, states should 'ensure that the provision of justice is not prevented by corruption of the judicial process.'

This section sets out examples that further show how combatting corruption is necessary for achieving effective implementation of the UNGPs. The subsequent section explores how combating corruption and respecting human rights can be enhanced by aligning these efforts.

4.1 *Rana Plaza*

One of the major events in business and human rights was the 2013 Rana Plaza building collapse tragedy in Bangladesh that caused the deaths of over 1,100 workers.[39] This building housed multiple factories that were making garments for various, well-known multinational companies. In this tragedy, corruption played a key role early on. Due to corruption, the building was constructed with poor quality materials[40] and built on unsuitable land.[41] In addition, corruption allowed the owners to violate building codes and construct the building several stories higher than allowed.[42] Common in Bangladesh, and thus likely at the Rana Plaza factories, corruption allowed factories to remain in operation by passing building inspections they should have failed, receiving exemptions from safety regulations, and avoiding punishment for worker safety violations.[43]

Rana Plaza was not an isolated event in Bangladesh. For example, in the year prior to Rana Plaza, there was a fire at the Tazreen factory that led to the

39 Alexandra Rose Caleca, "The Effects of Globalization on Bangladesh' s Ready-Made Garment Industry: The High Cost of Cheap Clothing," *Brooklyn International Law Journal* 40 no. 1 (2010): 295.

40 Caleca, "Effects of Globalization," 295–96.

41 Kaunain Rahman, "Ten years since the Rana Plaza tragedy: Has fast fashion ironed out their deadly corruption problems?" Transparency International, April 21, 2022, https://www.transparency.org/en/blog/rana-plaza-tragedy-fast-fashion-deadly-corruption-problems.

42 Julfikar Ali Manik and Jim Yardley. "Building Collapse in Bangladesh Leaves Scores Dead." *New York Times,* April 24, 2013, http://www.nytimes.com/2013/04/25/world/asia/bangladesh-building-collapse.html.

43 Hess, "Business, Corruption, and Human Rights," 643–44.

deaths of over 100 workers. Among other safety problems blamed on corruption, the building grew from three floors to nine floors in a few years but did not comply with fire safety regulations.[44]

Although corruption was a known contributor to the Rana Plaza and Tazreen tragedies, it was not addressed in the subsequent policy reforms. For example, some reforms sought to improve the frequency of factory inspections by requiring the hiring of additional government inspectors. The failure to address the issue of corruption, however, caused many to be skeptical of this reform's effectiveness. In one study, a factory manager stated that '[t]he government inspectors come here for money. If you pay them, they are happy to sign off whatever you are asking for, and our buyers are aware of this'.[45] A factory owner stated, '[a]fter the Rana Plaza incident, government inspectors used to come and ask for money. If we refused to pay, they threatened to close down the premises'.[46] Another noted that motorcycles given to auditors to improve their efficiency simply allowed them to collect bribes from more factories each day.[47]

4.2 *Modern Slavery*

Issues of modern slavery, including forced labour and human trafficking, are a significant human rights concern for global supply chains. Corruption is an important contributor to the problem and a hurdle to potential solutions. As stated by Transparency International, '[m]any experts indicate that if it were not for corruption, human trafficking would not have expanded so rapidly in the wake of globalisation'.[48]

Corruption is involved in each step on the path to modern slavery. For migrant labourers, the paperwork necessary to cross borders creates many opportunities for government officials to extract bribes. One study stated, 'Ironically, these many procedures and requirements that are so vulnerable to corruption were often put in place to protect workers and ensure regular process in the highly complex governance of international migration'.[49] These

44 Hess, "Business, Corruption, and Human Rights," 644.

45 Javed Siddiqui, Kenneth McPhail, and Sharmin Shabnam Rahman. "Private Governance Responsibilisation in Global Supply Chains: The Case of Rana Plaza." *Accounting, Auditing & Accountability Journal* 33, no. 7 (2020): 1584.

46 Siddiqui, McPhail, and Rahman, "Private Governance," 1584.

47 Siddiqui, McPhail, and Rahman, "Private Governance," 1584.

48 Transparency International, *Working Paper: Corruption and Human Trafficking*, June 2011, https://www.transparency.org/en/publications/working-paper-corruption-and-human-trafficking.

49 Freedom Fund and Verite, *An Exploratory Study of the Role of Corruption in International Labor Migration* (Jan. 2016), 1.

corruption costs end up being passed on to the workers through fees that contribute to the likelihood of forced labour.[50] Often, workers are aware of that problem and avoid the corruption of the formal process by using the informal sector, which may cost the same but is perceived as cheaper and faster because it avoids the government paperwork.[51] This informal process is also facilitated by corruption, and, for the migrants, as undocumented workers, they are subject to further abuse and potential extortion by local authorities when they reach their destination.[52]

If human trafficking or forced labour is identified by government officials, corruption allows the perpetrator to avoid legal responsibility. And, as workers are aware of this problem, they do not attempt to seek government assistance. Overall, as stated by the International Bar Association, 'Corruption facilitates every aspect of trafficking, from recruitment to transportation and exploitation. Corruption aids impunity through the obstruction of justice. Anti-trafficking efforts need to fully incorporate a focus on anti-corruption'.[53]

As a further example, it is well-known that modern slavery is pervasive in the seafood industry, and that seafood produced under such conditions can end up on the shelves of major retailers, such as Walmart and Costco.[54] There are efforts underway to attempt to reform the industry and end forced labour. For example, in the private sector, the Seafood Task Force is a collective-action initiative of seafood buyers and Thai exporters that works to monitor the supply chain for labour abuses.[55] Likewise, the government has also implemented reforms to fight illegal, unreported, and unregulated (IUU) fishing.[56]

Although such initiatives appear to be making some progress, modern slavery is still a significant problem in this industry[57] in part due to the persistence

50 Freedom Fund and Verite, *Labor Migration*, 12.

51 Freedom Fund and Verite, *Labor Migration*, 2–3 & 17–18.

52 Freedom Fund and Verite, *Labor Migration*, 2–3.

53 International Bar Association. *Human Trafficking and Public Corruption: A report by the IBA's Presidential Task Force Against Human Trafficking* (Sept. 2016), 38.

54 Kate Hodal, Chris Kelly and Felicity Lawrence. "Revealed: Asian Slave Labour Producing Prawns for Supermarkets in US, UK," *The Guardian*, June 10, 2014, https://www.theguardian.com/global-development/2014/jun/10/supermarket-prawns-thailand-produced-slave-labour.

55 Praxis Labs, *Tracking Progress: Assessing Business Responses to Forced Labour and Human Trafficking in the Thai Seafood Industry* (2019), 36–37.

56 Human Rights Watch, *Hidden Chains: Rights Abuses and Forced Labor in Thailand's Fishing Industry* (January 23, 2018), https://www.hrw.org/report/2018/01/23/hidden-chains/rights-abuses-and-forced-labor-thailands-fishing-industry#.

57 Praxis Labs, *Tracking Progress*, 64–65; Human Rights Watch, *Hidden Chains*.

of corruption. Corruption allows the brokers to traffic the men into Thailand,[58] for example, and the risk of prosecution is limited because police and other Thai officials profit from the human trafficking.[59] Not only are there reports that corrupt police work with the fishing companies to protect boat operators from prosecution, but the police may even assist in preventing any human trafficking victims from escaping.[60]

The Rana Plaza tragedy and the issue of modern slavery in supply chains are just two examples of where corruption is linked to human rights abuses. There are many others. For example, displacement of individuals due to land acquisition can often be facilitated by corruption.[61] Agricultural or infrastructure projects are common ways that corporations can be linked to wrongful displacements.[62] Not only may corruption enable the transaction, but corruption within the police or judiciary, for example, may prevent any remedial actions.[63]

Corruption also plays a significant role in preventing social audits from being an effective mechanism for corporations to ensure that suppliers are respecting human rights. For example, a social auditor may threaten to fail a factory if a bribe is not paid. The bribe may also originate form the payor's end, with a factory manager offering a bribe in return for an auditor to ignore a discovered problem.[64] Certain matters, such as building safety, may be outside the social auditor's mandate, and, as stated above in the Rana Plaza example, corruption may impact the reliability of government officials' inspections related to those matters.

58 Human Rights Watch, *Hidden Chains*; Environmental Justice Foundation, *Thailand's Seafood Slaves: Human Trafficking, Slavery and Murder in Kantang's Fishing Industry* (2015), 12.

59 Editorial Board, "Slavery and the Shrimp on Your Plate." *New York Times*, June 21, 2014, https://www.nytimes.com/2014/06/22/opinion/sunday/thai-seafood-is-contaminated-by-human-trafficking.html.

60 Environmental Justice Foundation, *Thailand's Seafood Slaves*, 21.

61 See generally, Olivier De Schutter, The International Corporate Accountability Roundtable, and Global Witness, *Tainted Lands: Corruption in Large-Scale Land Deals* (Nov. 2016).

62 Working Group on the issue of human rights and transnational corporations and other business enterprises, *Connecting the business and human rights and the anti-corruption agendas*, UN Doc. A/HRC/44/43 (June 17, 2020), para. 14.

63 Working Group, *Connecting Agendas*, para. 14.

64 Hess, "Business, Corruption, and Human Rights," 668.

5 Aligning Business Efforts to Combat Corruption and Respect Human Rights

This section explores the benefits of business aligning its efforts to combat corruption and respect human rights. This does not mean that business should merge the two efforts into one program. Instead, business should look for those areas where they can be linked; working to reduce redundancies and share learnings between departments, 'without reducing the effectiveness of individual programmes'.[65] As stated in a UNGC report:

> Effectively managing these risks presents companies with common challenges such as detecting misconduct in the business organization and supply chains, and necessitates due diligence on business partners such as contracted agents and suppliers. ... Building on these linkages can also assist in improving corporate risk management, optimizing compliance systems, making anti-corruption compliance more robust and better preparing companies for mandatory human rights standards.[66]

An additional potential goal of aligning corruption and human rights is to improve corporations' motivation to combat corruption. Corporate actors may view the use of bribes in international business as a victimless crime and due simply to cultural differences between countries.[67] A human rights perspective, however, places the focus on those harmed by corruption. Professor Spahn stated '[a]bstract arguments about [corruption's] harm to society as a whole are generally not effective in motivating people to change profitable, entrenched behaviors'.[68] A human rights perspective, however, can force company actors to see the harms that corruption causes to individuals and specific groups of people.

Of course, anti-bribery compliance and human rights due diligence differ in many ways. A foundational difference is in the framing of the risk analysis. Anti-bribery compliance is focused on risks to the company; that is, avoiding exposure to prosecution for connection to a bribe payment. Human rights due diligence, on the other hand, is focused on the risks to the rights holder. Thus, fully integrating the two perspectives creates potential risks of 'watering

65 BIAC & IOE, *Connecting Agendas*, 10.
66 UN Global Compact, *Linking Human Rights*, 2.
67 Spahn, "Nobody Gets Hurt?," 894.
68 Spahn, "Nobody Gets Hurt?," 892.

down core commitments to respect human rights'.[69] Instead, the goal must be to expand the focus of anticorruption efforts, and not contract the focus of human rights due diligence. Expanding the focus of anticorruption efforts will encourage the company to understand when corruption is a root cause of adverse human rights impacts connected to their operations and when corruption is placing hurdles in the way of implementing mechanisms to respect human rights.

There are other differences to keep in mind. For example, a UNGC report stated that remediation should continue to be treated separately.[70] For corruption, the corporate response is focused on the legal responsibility, and often includes termination of the employee or agent directly involved. A human rights violation, on the other hand, would require stakeholder engagement to identify those impacted and the appropriate remedy.[71] In addition, if the company contributed to or was directly linked to the adverse impact, the UNGPS require the company to undertake an analysis of the human rights impacts of terminating the relationship with the party causing the harm before taking any action with respect to it.

Despite these differences, having corruption and human rights handled by different departments without at least formal communication channels between them creates a multitude of problems. The UN Working Group described this problem as follows:

> Such a division has resulted in poor communication, diligence fatigue, a lack of shared objectives and challenging auditing processes where red flags were missed; a lack of coordination, sharing of information and collaboration within different parts of a business, for example between geographic offices and headquarters and between different departments; poor information-sharing and knowledge management regarding business and human rights and anti-corruption cases and issues; insufficient training, guidance and support on how to implement business and human rights responsibilities and anti-corruption measures alongside each other; and resistance from operations, weary from dealing with multiple interlocutors.[72]

69 Working Group, *Connecting Agendas*, para. 55.
70 UN Global Compact, *Linking Human Rights*, 20.
71 UN Global Compact, *Linking Human Rights*, 20.
72 Working Group, *Connecting Agendas*, para. 54.

5.1 *Aligning Anticorruption and Human Rights Efforts*

Due to the criminalisation of bribery, businesses have a strong incentive to implement anticorruption compliance programs. With the increase in legislation on mandatory human rights due diligence, businesses are now starting to be expected to formalise their human rights efforts. This section explores ways in which it is beneficial to align anti-bribery compliance and human rights due diligence. In addition, for companies that are just starting to develop or expand their human rights due diligence efforts, they may prefer to build those processes on existing systems.[73] Anticorruption systems are a natural fit due to the linkages.

An important aspect of both anticorruption and human rights due diligence is governance and oversight. This responsibility starts with the board of directors and includes the active involvement of the CEO, as well as ensuring that a high-level officer has day-to-day responsibility for the programs. Not only does this ensure appropriate oversight and corporate commitment, but it also sends a consistent message to all employees – often referred to as the 'tone from the top'.[74]

At the board of directors level, the company should consider having a board committee with responsibility for both human rights and anticorruption.[75] This allows those board members to develop expertise in these areas, as well as ensure that there is appropriate board time devoted to oversight.[76] For day-to-day management, many companies may find that the human rights responsibilities naturally fit with their existing anticorruption compliance program.[77] However, that may not always be the case. For these latter companies, they should ensure that there are formal, direct communication channels between the two areas. In addition, both areas should be trained in the other's key responsibilities to ensure that managers share information, identify situations when coordination is beneficial, and avoid redundancies. The governance and oversight responsibilities should also include ensuring that there is a dialogue between all the different relevant functions, such as legal, compliance, supply chain, accounting, sustainability, and others.[78] This coordination will allow the

73 UN Global Compact, *Linking Human Rights*, 9.

74 UN Global Compact, *Linking Human Rights*, 10.

75 UN Global Compact, *Linking Human Rights*, 17.

76 David Hess, "The Management and Oversight of Human Rights Due Diligence," *American Business Law Journal* 58, no. 4 (2021); 795–86.

77 Hess, "Management and Oversight," 776–80.

78 BIAC & IOE, *Connecting Agendas*, 14; UN Global Compact, *Linking Human Rights*, 17.

areas to 'develop and manage corporate policies, assess progress being made, and identify shared risks and further areas of collaboration'.[79]

A key step in the process of aligning anticorruption and human rights is for the company to ensure that company policies and communications to employees and external stakeholders emphasise both the need to respect human rights and to combat corruption, and, where relevant, discuss the connections between the two.[80] Trainings should ensure that employees can identify risks in both areas and know how to report those observations to assist the organisation's coordinated efforts.[81] For example, scenarios used in training could include both issues to help employees understand the linkages, as well as be able to spot red flags in both areas.[82] Of course, certain personnel will need separate, specialised training on anticorruption or human rights, but there will be opportunities to combine both trainings. Coordinated trainings not only enhances each, but also reduces the length of training time.[83] Likewise, the development of joint grievance mechanisms can support efficiency by reducing resources and also allow the recognition of patterns and linkages between the issues. To ensure proper handling of grievances and maintaining the credibility of the mechanism, the personnel handling the issues must have adequate training on both issues.[84]

Companies can also coordinate their due diligence and risk assessment processes. When starting a new project or entering a new region, for example, a company's assessment for corruption risks and human rights risks may utilise similar processes, such as site visits, interviews, and other data collection practices. Thus, companies should determine the extent to which the assessments of suppliers and other business partners can be coordinated, or at a minimum, include questions from each agenda on the other's assessment.[85] Coordinating these efforts reduces costs for the company, but also allows for opportunities to understand how the issues are linked, including recognising that a 'red flag' in one area should alert the organisation to potential problems in the other area and the need for further investigation. For example, a UNGC report stated: 'if an anti-corruption audit shows that there is a culture of facilitation payments where government labor inspectors expect to have

79 UN Global Compact, *Linking Human Rights*, 17.
80 BIAC & IOE, *Connecting Agendas*, 13–14.
81 BIAC & IOE, *Connecting Agendas*, 15.
82 BIAC & IOE, *Connecting Agendas*, 15.
83 UN Global Compact, *Linking Human Rights*, 11.
84 UN Global Compact, *Linking Human Rights*, 17.
85 BIAC & IOE, *Connecting Agendas*, 15.

their palms greased for factories to pass compliance inspections, a human rights impact assessment included as part of the audit is likely to show that the same factories have issues relating to working conditions'.[86] This coordination of assessments means that the organisation must ensure that the teams have the requisite knowledge in both areas,[87] or that there is formalised process for sharing information between the two different teams.[88]

Non-financial reporting – also known as sustainability reporting or ESG reporting – is another area where corporations can align corruption and human rights. A key goal of non-financial reporting is not external accountability, but to support internal learning and development.[89] Reporting on indicators related to the linkages between corruption and human rights should support internal reforms on managing these issues.[90] It also demonstrates to employees the company's commitment to those matters.[91]

Externally, there are numerous potential benefits. Transparency supports the ability of stakeholders to hold corporations accountable for their performance. In addition, disclosures can support the sharing of information between companies, either directly or through the actions of intermediaries, on best practices for particular issues, industries, or regions.[92] Of course, to support those goals, NGOs, multi-stakeholder initiatives, and investors should also seek to understand the connections between corruption and human rights. In other words, they must not treat ESG factors separately, but they should expand the 'G' concerns of anti-bribery compliance to understand how corruption impacts the 'S' concerns related to human rights. This approach should also support pushing corporations, and other stakeholders, to not think of combatting corruption as simply a matter of avoiding criminal prosecution, but as a positive way of supporting human rights.[93] In other words, corporations should not think about corruption as 'just what they should not do, but

86 UN Global Compact, *Linking Human Rights*, 15.

87 BIAC & IOE, *Connecting Agendas*, 12–13.

88 UN Global Compact, *Linking Human Rights*, 15.

89 David Hess, "The Transparency Trap: Non-Financial Disclosure and the Responsibility of Business to Respect Human Rights," *American Business Law Journal* 56, no. 1 (2019): 16–17.

90 David Hess, "Combating Corruption through Corporate Transparency: Using Enforcement Discretion to Improve Disclosure," *Minnesota Journal of International Law* 21, no. 1 (2012): 69.

91 Hess, "Combating Corruption," 69.

92 David Hess, "Enhancing the Effectiveness of the Foreign Corrupt Practices Act through Corporate Social Responsibility," *Ohio State Law Journal* 73, no. 5 (2012): 1141–42.

93 Hess, "Business, Corruption, and Human Rights," 681.

also what they can do' to help reduce corruption in the areas where they have operations and business partners.[94]

5.2 *The Role of States*

There are various ways that governments can align policies related to corruption and human rights.[95] Many governments are already recognising the connection. For example, the US Department of Treasury's Financial Crimes Enforcement Network (FinCEN) issued an advisory stating:

> Corrupt senior foreign political figures, their subordinates and facilitators, through their corrupt actions, often contribute directly or indirectly to human rights abuses, which have a devastating impact on individual citizens and societies, undermining markets and economic development and creating instability in a region. The use of financial facilitators is one way that corrupt senior foreign political figures access the U.S. and international financial system to move or hide illicit proceeds, evade U.S. and global sanctions, or otherwise engage in illegal activity, including related human rights abuses.[96]

Laws such as the US's Global Magnitsky Act of 2016 – which has been followed by similar legislation in Australia, Canada, the United Kingdom, and the European Union – allows governments to target sanctions at those specific individuals engaged in human rights abuse or corruption.[97]

The above quote also shows the value of enforcing anti-money laundering laws in a manner that prevents foreign political figures connected to corruption and human rights abuses from hiding their assets overseas. Additional reforms to further the enforcement of anticorruption laws can also be justified on the grounds of furthering the human rights agenda. For example, the anticorruption community has long lobbied for beneficial ownership laws. These laws seek to combat corruption by preventing individuals from using a complex network of shell companies to hide illegally obtained funds and avoid taxes.[98] This transparency on the ownership behind shell companies also

94 Hess, "Enhancing the Effectiveness," 1122.

95 Working Group, *Connecting Agendas*, para. 24.

96 United States Department of Treasury Financial Crimes Enforcement Network (FinCEN), *Advisory on Human Rights Abuses Enabled by Corrupt Senior Foreign Political Figures and their Financial Facilitators* (*June 12, 2018*), 1.

97 US Treasury, "Financial Facilitators," 1–2.

98 Emile van der Does de Willebois et al, *Puppet Masters: How the Corrupt Use Legal Structures to hide Stolen Assets and What to Do About It* (Washington, D.C.: World Bank, 2011).

supports the human rights movement by allowing individuals or communities to identify the actors that should be held accountable and should contribute to remediation.[99]

There are other actions that states can take. For example, a state's national action plan on business and human rights should seek to emphasise the linkage between corruption and human rights risks.[100] As stated above, states must ensure that corruption is not preventing individuals from having access to an effective judicial remedy. For non-judicial remedy, National Contact Points for the OECD *Guidelines* may be an area where these linkages can be considered.[101]

States can also use their power as economic actors, such as through public procurement. Under Principle Six of the UNGPs, '[s]tates should promote respect for human rights by business enterprises with which they conduct commercial transactions'. Public procurement is estimated at between ten and fifteen percent of a country's GDP.[102] Thus, this is an area of significant potential impact. Due to the interactions with government officials, it is also an area with a high risk of corruption. Thus, in addition to the state ensuring that it does business with companies that respect human rights, they must also ensure they are doing business with companies that are committed to combatting corruption. This can be done, for example, through rules that prevent companies from bidding on government contracts if they have engaged in corruption or are connected to human rights abuses.[103]

6 Conclusion

It is important for business to align their anticorruption and human rights programs. Corruption and human rights violations are heavily interlinked; the presence of one type of harm is likely to be found with the other type of harm. In addition, there exists a significant overlap in the types of policies and procedures necessary for anti-bribery and corruption compliance and human rights due diligence. By recognising the linkages between these two areas and finding ways to coordinate their efforts, such as described in this chapter, businesses can enhance their overall response. Likewise, states, NGOs, multi-stakeholder

99 Working Group, *Connecting Agendas*, para. 33–35.
100 Working Group, *Connecting Agendas*, para. 27.
101 Working Group, *Connecting Agendas*, para. 63.
102 Working Group, *Connecting Agendas*, para. 12.
103 Working Group, *Connecting Agendas*, para. 36.

initiatives, and ESG investors, can also play a role in supporting efforts to align corruption and human rights.

Bibliography

Books

De Schutter, Olivier. The International Corporate Accountability Roundtable, and Global Witness, *Tainted Lands: Corruption in Large-Scale Land Deals* (Nov. 2016), https://www.globalwitness.org/en/campaigns/land-deals/tainted-lands-corruption-large-scale-land-deals.

van der Does de Willebois, Emile et al. *Puppet Masters: How the Corrupt Use Legal Structures to hide Stolen Assets and What to Do About It.* Washington, D.C.: World Bank, 2011, https://openknowledge.worldbank.org/server/api/core/bitstreams/e80259c9-d3ca-5d16-adef-fec02a3989dd/content.

Book Chapters

Hess, David and Thomas W. Dunfee. "Taking Responsibility for Bribery: The Multinational Corporation's Role in Combating Corruption." In *Business and Human Rights: Dilemmas and Solutions*, edited by Rory Sullivan, 260–271. Sheffield, UK: Greenleaf (2003).

Rose-Ackerman, Susan. "Corruption and the Global Corporation: Ethical Obligations and Workable Strategies." In *Transnational Legal Processes: Globalization and Power Disparities*, edited by Michael Likosky, 148–71. Towbridge: Cromwell Press, 2002.

Journal Articles

Aidt, Toke S. "Corruption, Institutions, and Economic Development." *Oxford Review of Economics* 25 no. 2 (2009): 271–91.

Arafa, Mohamed A. "Battling Corruption Within a Corporate Social Responsibility Strategy." *Indiana International and Comparative Law Review* 21, no. 3 (2011): 397–418.

Caleca, Alexandra Rose. "The Effects of Globalization on Bangladesh' s Ready-Made Garment Industry: The High Cost of Cheap Clothing." *Brooklyn International Law Journal* 40 no. 1 (2010): 279–320.

Eigen, Peter. "Removing a Roadblock to Development: Transparency International Mobilizes Coalitions Against Corruption." *Innovations* 3 no. 2 (2008): 19–33.

Hess, David. "Business, Corruption, and Human Rights: Towards a New Responsibility for Corporations to Combat Corruption." *Wisconsin Law Review* 2017, no. 4 (2017): 641–693.

Hess, David. "Combating Corruption through Corporate Transparency: Using Enforcement Discretion to Improve Disclosure." *Minnesota Journal of International Law* vol. 21, no. 1 (2012): 42–74.

Hess, David. "Enhancing the Effectiveness of the Foreign Corrupt Practices Act through Corporate Social Responsibility." *Ohio State Law Journal* 73, no. 5 (2012): 1121–1144.

Hess, David. "Modern Slavery in Global Supply Chains: Towards a Legislative Solution." *Cornell International Law Journal* 54, no. 2 (2021): 245–89.

Hess, David. "The Management and Oversight of Human Rights Due Diligence." *American Business Law Journal* 58, no. 4 (2021): 751–798.

Hess, David. "The Transparency Trap: Non-Financial Disclosure and the Responsibility of Business to Respect Human Rights." *American Business Law Journal* 56, no. 1 (2019): 5–54.

Siddiqui, Javed, Kenneth McPhail, and Sharmin Shabnam Rahman. "Private Governance Responsibilisation in Global Supply Chains: The Case of Rana Plaza." *Accounting, Auditing & Accountability Journal* 33, no. 7 (2020): 1569–94.

Spahn, Elizabeth. "Nobody Gets Hurt?" *Georgetown International Law Journal* 41 (2010): 861–905.

Legal Instruments

OECD. *Convention on Combating Bribery of Foreign Public Officials in International Business Transactions* (Nov. 21, 1997), http://www.oecd.org/daf/anti-bribery/ConvCombatBribery_ENG.pdf.

OECD. *OECD Guidelines for Multinational Enterprises* (2011), http://dx.doi.org/10.1787/9789264115415-en.

Newpaper Articles

Editorial Board. "Slavery and the Shrimp on Your Plate." *New York Times* (June 21, 2014), https://www.nytimes.com/2014/06/22/opinion/sunday/thai-seafood-is-contaminated-by-human-trafficking.html.

Hodal, Kate, Chris Kelly and Felicity Lawrence. "Revealed: Asian Slave Labour Producing Prawns for Supermarkets in US, UK." *The Guardian* (June 10, 2014), https://www.theguardian.com/global-development/2014/jun/10/supermarket-prawns-thailand-produced-slave-labour.

Manik, Julfikar Ali and Jim Yardley. "Building Collapse in Bangladesh Leaves Scores Dead." *New York Times* (April 24, 2013), http://www.nytimes.com/2013/04/25/world/asia/bangladesh-building-collapse.html.

Website Content

Global Reporting Initiative (GRI), *GRI 205: Anti-Corruption* 2016, https://www.globalreporting.org/standards.

Rahman, Kaunain. "Ten years since the Rana Plaza tragedy: Has fast fashion ironed out their deadly corruption problems?" Transparency International (April 21, 2022), https://www.transparency.org/en/blog/rana-plaza-tragedy-fast-fashion-deadly-corruption-problems.

Wolfensohn, James D. *People and development: address to the Board of Governors*, Washington, DC, (October 1, 1996), http://documents.worldbank.org/curated/en/243871468141893629/People-and-development-address-to-the-Board-of-Governors-Washington-DC-October-1-1996.

Reports

Business at OECD (BIAC) & International Organisation of Employers (IOE), *Connecting the anti-corruption and human rights agendas: A guide for business and employers' organisations* (Sept. 2020), https://www.ioe-emp.org/index.php?eID=dumpFile&t=f&f=147731&token=c0fecaf2120d7faf7e4214377a1754ab8170fd88.

Environmental Justice Foundation, *Thailand's Seafood Slaves: Human Trafficking, Slavery and Murder in Kantang's Fishing Industry* (2015), https://ejfoundation.org/resources/downloads/EJF-Thailand-Seafood-Slaves-low-res.pdf.

Freedom Fund and Verite, *An Exploratory Study of the Role of Corruption in International Labor Migration* (Jan. 2016), https://www.verite.org/sites/default/files/images/Verite-Report-Intl-Labour-Recruitment_0.pdf.

Human Rights Council, *Final Report of the Human Rights Council Advisory Committee on the Issue of the Negative Impact of Corruption on the Enjoyment of Human Rights*, U.N. Doc. A/HRC/28/73 (Jan. 5, 2015), http://www.ohchr.org/EN/HRBodies/HRC/RegularSessions/Session28/Pages/ListReports.aspx.

Human Rights Council, *The Negative Impact of Corruption on the Enjoyment of Human Rights*, U.N. Doc. A/HRC/Res/23/9 (June 20, 2013).

Human Rights Watch. *Hidden Chains: Rights Abuses and Forced Labor in Thailand's Fishing Industry* (January 23, 2018), https://www.hrw.org/report/2018/01/23/hidden-chains/rights-abuses-and-forced-labor-thailands-fishing-industry#.

International Bar Association. *Human Trafficking and Public Corruption: A report by the IBA's Presidential Task Force Against Human Trafficking* (Sept. 2016), https://www.ibanet.org/MediaHandler?id=E34FFA1D-8038-4AEC-A631-E0E2A7E0AD86.

International Council on Human Rights (ICHR) and Transparency International (TI), *Corruption and Human Rights: Making the Connection* (2009), http://www.ichrp.org/files/reports/40/131_web.pdf.

Praxis Labs. *Tracking Progress: Assessing Business Responses to Forced Labour and Human Trafficking in the Thai Seafood Industry* (2019), http://www.praxis-labs.com/uploads/2/9/7/0/29709145/09_hu_report_final.pdf.

Special Representative of the Secretary-General on the Issue of Human Rights and Transnational Corporations and Other Business Enterprises, *Guiding Principles on*

Business and Human Rights: Implementing the United Nations "Protect, Respect and Remedy" Framework, U.N. Doc. A/HRC/17/31 (Mar. 21, 2011).

Transparency International, *What is Corruption?*, https://www.transparency.org/en/what-is-corruption.

Transparency International, *Working Paper: Corruption and Human Trafficking* (June 2011), https://www.transparency.org/en/publications/working-paper-corruption-and-human-trafficking.

United Nations Global Compact, *Linking Human Rights and Anti-Corruption Compliance* (Dec. 2016), https://unglobalcompact.org/library/5011.

United States Department of Treasury Financial Crimes Enforcement Network (FinCEN), *Advisory on Human Rights Abuses Enabled by Corrupt Senior Foreign Political Figures and their Financial Facilitators* (June 12, 2018), https://www.fincen.gov/sites/default/files/advisory/2018-06-12/PEP%20Facilitator%20Advisory_FINAL%20508.pdf.

Working Group on the issue of human rights and transnational corporations and other business enterprises, *Connecting the business and human rights and the anti-corruption agendas*, U.N. Doc. A/HRC/44/43 (June 17, 2020).

Index

Printed in the United States
by Baker & Taylor Publisher Services